Tolley´s
Tax Computations
1996/97

by

Juliana M Watterston FCA, FTII
David Smailes FCA
Jon Golding ATT
Glyn Saunders MA
Robert Wareham BSc(Econ) FCA

Edited by
Juliana M Watterston FCA, FTII

Tolley Publishing Company Limited

Published by
Tolley Publishing Company Ltd
Tolley House
2, Addiscombe Road
Croydon Surrey CR9 5AF
England
0181–686 9141

Photoset by Interactive Sciences Ltd, Gloucester

Printed in Great Britain by
The Bath Press

ISBN 1 86012 307–4

About This Book

Tolley's Tax Computations is an established annual publication, having been first published in the early 1980s in response to interest shown by Tolley tax subscribers in worked examples, both to assist in understanding UK tax legislation and to provide guidance as to layout. The book is divided into five parts covering income tax, corporation tax, capital gains tax, inheritance tax and value added tax. In each part, chapters are arranged in alphabetical order by subject to assist reference. Most of the computations have explanatory notes, and statutory references are given wherever appropriate. The book also includes a table of statutes and an index.

This 1996/97 edition has been fully updated to take account of the provisions of the Finance Act 1996 and other relevant information up to 1 June 1996.

Comments on this annual publication and suggestions for improvements and additional computations are always welcome.

TOLLEY PUBLISHING CO LTD

Contents

Contents

Contents

VALUE ADDED TAX

Abbreviations and References

ABBREVIATIONS

ACT	=	Advance Corporation Tax
Art	=	Article
BDV	=	Budget Day Value
BPR	=	Business Property Relief
b/f	=	brought forward
C & E	=	Customs and Excise
C/A	=	Court of Appeal
CAA	=	Capital Allowances Act 1990
CCAB	=	Consultative Committee of Accountancy Bodies
C/D	=	Chancery Division
c/f	=	carried forward
CFC	=	Controlled Foreign Company
CGT	=	Capital Gains Tax
CGTA	=	Capitals Gains Tax Act 1979
CT	=	Corporation Tax
CTT	=	Capital Transfer Tax
CY	=	Current Year
DTR	=	Double Tax Relief
EIS	=	Enterprise Investment Scheme
ESC	=	Extra-Statutory Concession
ESP	=	Expected Selling Price
FA	=	Finance Act
F(No 2)A	=	Finance (No 2) Act
FIFO	=	First In, First Out
FII	=	Franked Investment Income
FY	=	Financial Year
FYA	=	First-Year Allowance
H/L	=	House of Lords
HMIT	=	Her Majesty's Inspector of Taxes
IBA	=	Industrial Buildings Allowance
ICTA	=	Income and Corporation Taxes Act 1988
IRPR	=	Inland Revenue Press Release
IHT	=	Inheritance Tax
IHTA	=	Inheritance Tax Act 1984
IT	=	Income Tax
LIFO	=	Last In, First Out
NBV	=	Net Book Value
NIC	=	National Insurance Contributions
para	=	paragraph
PAYE	=	Pay As You Earn
P/e	=	Period ended
PET	=	Potentially Exempt Transfer
PR	=	Personal Representative
PY	=	Previous Year
Reg	=	Regulation
s	=	section
SC/S	=	Scottish Court of Session
Sch	=	Schedule
Sec	=	Section

Abbreviations and References

SI	=	Statutory Instrument
SSAP	=	Statement of Standard Accounting Practice
TCGA	=	Taxation of Chargeable Gains Act 1992
TMA	=	Taxes Management Act 1970
VAT	=	Value Added Tax
VATA	=	Value Added Tax Act 1994
VCT	=	Venture Capital Trust
WDA	=	Writing-down Allowance
WDV	=	Written-down Value
Y/e	=	Year ended

REFERENCES

STC	=	Simon's Tax Cases, (Butterworth & Co (Publishers) Ltd, Halsbury House, 35 Chancery Lane, London, WC2A 1EL
TC	=	Official Tax Cases, (H.M. Stationery Office, P.O. Box 276, SW8 5DT)

Income Tax

1   Allowances and Tax Rates

Cross-reference. See also 11.1 MARRIED PERSONS for transfer of married couple's allowance.

1.1   TOTAL INCOME AND RATES OF TAX [*ICTA 1988, s 1; FA 1996, s 72*]

(A)   Savings income [*ICTA 1988, s 1A; FA 1996, s 73*]
Victor is a single man and for ten years has traded as a sole proprietor of a retail outlet. Throughout, his accounts have been drawn up to 30 June and HM Inspector of Taxes has agreed adjusted profits before capital allowances as follows:

Year ended 30 June   1995   £28,068
                                            1996   £19,000

Capital Allowances for 1996/97 have been agreed at £4,212.

Victor's other income is as follows:

	£
Building society interest (net)	2,000
Dividends from UK companies (net)	6,000
Interest on UK company loan stock (net)	1,200

His taxable income and tax liability are computed as follows

	£	£
Schedule D, Case I		19,290
Building society interest	2,000	
Add Tax deducted (£2,000 × ¼)	500	
		2,500
UK dividends	6,000	
Add Tax credit (£6,000 × ¼)	1,500	
		7,500
Taxed interest	1,200	
Add Tax deducted (£1,200 × ¼)	300	
		1,500
Total income		30,790
Deduct Personal allowance		3,765
Taxable income		£27,025

Tax payable:	
3,900 @ 20%	780.00
11,625 @ 24%	2,790.00
9,975 @ 20%	1,995.00
25,500	
1,525 @ 40%	610.00
£27,025	6,175.00
Deduct Tax credits and tax deducted at source	2,300.00
Tax payable by assessment	£3,875.00

Notes

(a)

		£
Schedule D, Case I		
(transitional year)		
Y/e 30 June 1995		28,068
Y/e 30 June 1996		19,000
Profits for 24 months		£47,068

$$\text{Average } £47,068 \times \frac{365}{365 + 366} \qquad 23,502$$

Less: Capital Allowances	4,212
	£19, 290

The basis period for 1996/97 being the transitional period on changeover to current year basis of assessment is the year ended 30 June 1996. This is extended by the gap between the basis periods for 1995/96 and 1996/97 to give the transitional period 1 July 1994 to 30 June 1996. The taxable profit (before capital allowances) for 1996/97 is then an average of the profits for the transitional period. [*FA 1994, 20 Sch 1, 2(1)(2)(5)*]. Profits in the transitional basis period are calculated by using '*the appropriate percentage*'. [*FA 1994, 20 Sch 5*]. The '*appropriate percentage*' is defined by reference to the number of days in the transitional basis period. But the Inland Revenue will be prepared to accept any other reasonable time-based computation using weeks, months or fractions of months. [*SAT 1 (1995) paragraph 6.8*].

(b)   With effect for 1996/97 and subsequent years of assessment, the tax charge on *all* savings income is grossed up by reference to a tax credit at the lower rate (20% for 1996/97). This applied with effect for 1993/94 and subsequent years for UK and foreign dividend income.

Savings income for this purpose includes dividends, interest from banks and building societies, interest distributions from authorised unit trusts, interest from gilts and other securities including corporate bonds, purchased life annuities and discounts.

UK savings income is taxed at the lower rate to the extent that it does not fall within the higher rate band. In determining the extent to which this income does fall within the higher rate band, the savings income is treated as the top slice of income.

(B)

The facts are the same as in (A) above except that Victor's trading results are as follows:

Y/e   30 June 1995 profit £36,023
           30 June 1996 loss   £ 4,468

and he makes a claim under *ICTA 1988, s 380* to set off the 1996/97 loss against his other income for 1996/97.

His tax liability is computed as follows

	£
Schedule D, Case I £(17,987 − 4,212)	13,775
Dividend and Savings Income	11,500
	25,275
Loss relief under *ICTA 1988, s 380(2)*	4,468
	20,807
Personal Allowance	3,765
Taxable income	£17,042

Tax payable:	
3,900 @ 20%	780.00
1,642 @ 24%	394.08
11,500 @ 20%	2,300.00
	3,474.08
Less: Tax credits and tax deducted at source	2,300.00
	£1,174.08

Notes

(a)   Workings

Schedule D, Case I (transitional year)	£
Y/e 30 June 1995	36,023
Y/3 30 June 1996	Nil
Profit for 731 days	£36,023

Average

$$£36,023 \times \frac{365}{366 + 365} = \qquad 17,987$$

(b)   Although savings income is generally regarded as the top slice of income (see (A) above), this does not mean that the loss must be set against savings income first. Deductions allowable in computing total income or to be made from total income are treated as reducing income of different descriptions in the order which will result in the greatest reduction of the tax liability. [*ICTA 1988, s 835(4)*]. Thus, the loss has been set against non-savings income; savings income is left intact and is all chargeable at 20% as taxable income does not exceed the basic rate limit of £25,500.

(C) Allowances given by way of income tax reduction
[*ICTA 1988, ss 256, 257A; FA 1994, s 77*]
Mark and Becky are a married couple in their thirties. Mark's main source of income is a trade from which self-assessment profits for 1996/97 amount to £12,965. He claims loss relief under *ICTA 1988, s 380* against income for 1996/97. Mark receives bank interest of £320 net in 1996/97. In that year, he pays mortgage interest of £2,700 on a £30,000 loan outside MIRAS which was used to purchase his main residence, and he pays £60 net under a charitable deed of covenant. Becky has no taxable income for 1996/97.

Mark's tax position for 1996/97 is as follows

	£
Schedule D, Case I	12,965
Bank interest received £320 × 100/80	400
Sec 380 relief	(6,500)
Payment under covenant £60 × 100/75	(80)
Total income	6,785
Deduct Personal allowance	3,765
Taxable income	£3,020

Tax payable:	
3,020 @ 20%	604.00
	604.00
Reduction for mortgage interest £2,700 @ 15%	405.00
	199.00
Reduction for married couple's allowance £1,790 @ 15% = £268.50 but restricted to	199.00
	Nil
Add Basic rate tax deducted from payment under covenant £60 × 24/76	18.95
Total liability	18.95
Deduct Tax paid at source on bank interest	80.00
Tax repayment due	£61.05

Notes

(*a*) For 1994/95 and subsequent years, married couple's allowance (and those allowances linked to it) is given by way of a reduction in income tax liability rather than as a deduction from total income. Relief was given at 20% for 1994/95 but is reduced to 15% for 1995/96 and subsequent years. [*ICTA 1988, ss 256, 257A; FA 1994, s 77*].

(*b*) Mortgage interest is no longer a deduction in arriving at total income for 1994/95 and subsequent years. See 8.1 INTEREST PAYABLE. Relief by way of income tax reduction is given for interest in priority to personal reliefs. [*ICTA 1988, s 353(1H)(a); FA 1994, s 81(2)*].

(*c*) In this example, the reduction for married couple's allowance (maximum £268.50) is restricted to the amount which reduces the tax liability to nil (£199). Note that the basic rate tax deducted from the payment under covenant (£18.95) has to be left in charge. [*ICTA 1988, s 256(3)(c)(ii); FA 1994, s 77(1)*]. It is thus added back *after* giving the income tax reductions. The credit for tax suffered on bank interest is not a reduction of tax liability but a method of paying tax, and it is thus given after all income tax reductions.

(d) If Mark's wife had sufficient taxable income, the loss of a small amount of married couple's allowance could have been avoided by electing to allocate the mortgage interest relief to the wife (see 8.1(E) INTEREST PAYABLE). Alternatively, the unused part of the reduction could have been transferred to the wife on a claim under *ICTA 1988, s 257BB* and given against her income tax liability (see 11.1(B) MARRIED PERSONS).

1.2 **AGE-RELATED ALLOWANCES** [*ICTA 1988, ss 256, 257(2)–(5), 257A(2)–(5); FA 1988, s 33; FA 1994, s 77; FA 1996, s 74*]

(A)
In 1996/97, a single man, whose 65th birthday fell on 1 April 1997, received earnings of £13,000, net dividends of £800 and bank deposit interest of £1,600 net. His tax position is as follows.

	£	£
Earnings		13,000
Dividends	800	
Add Tax credit 800 × $\frac{20}{80}$	200	1,000
Bank deposit interest	1,600	
Add Tax credit 1,600 × $\frac{20}{80}$	400	2,000
Total income		16,000
Deduct		
Personal allowance	4,910	
Less Reduction for excess		
$\frac{1}{2}$ (16,000 – 15,200)	400	4,510
Taxable income		£11,490
Tax on £3,900 at 20%	780.00	
Tax on £4,590 at 24%	1,101.60	
Tax on £3,000 at 20%	600.00	
	2,481.60	
Less Tax credits	600.00	£1,881.60

Notes
(a) The taxpayer is entitled to the age-related personal allowance by virtue of his being 65 or over *at any time* within the year of assessment.

(b) If total income had been £1,490 greater, the age-related personal allowance would have been reduced by a further £745 ($\frac{1}{2}$ × £1,490) to £3,765. It could not be reduced below this figure, regardless of the amount of extra income, as this is the normal personal allowance.

(B)

In 1996/97, a single woman, aged 78, receives UK income of £11,500, comprising state and occupational pension, and foreign income from property of £4,000 on which foreign tax of £800 has been paid.

	£	£
Tax on total income		
Schedule E		11,500
Schedule D, Case V (foreign tax £800)		4,000
		15,500
Deduct		
Personal allowance	5,090	
Less Reduction for excess $\frac{1}{2}$ (15,500 – 15,200)	150	
		4,940
Taxable income		£10,560
Tax on £3,900 at 20%	780.00	
Tax on £6,660 at 24%	1,598.40	£2,378.40
Tax on total income, excluding foreign income		
Schedule E		11,500
Deduct Personal allowance		5,090
Taxable income		£6,410
Tax on £3,900 at 20%	780.00	
Tax on £2,510 at 24%	602.40	£1,382.40

Note

(*a*)   The difference between the computations is £996. As the foreign tax is less than this, full credit of £800 is available against UK tax payable. If the foreign tax was £1,000, the credit would be limited to £996 and the balance of £4 would be unrelieved. [*ICTA 1988, s 796(1)*].

(C)

Mr and Mrs Brown are a married couple aged 75 and 70 respectively at 6 April 1996. Mr Brown's total income for 1996/97 before deductions amounts to £17,500 and Mrs Brown's to £15,500. Neither spouse has any dividend income or savings income. Mr Brown pays private medical insurance premiums of £374 (net), covering both himself and his wife, under an eligible contract under *FA 1989, s 55*. Mrs Brown elected under *ICTA 1988, s 257BA(1)* before 6 April 1996 to be given half the basic married couple's allowance for 1996/97 onwards.

IT 1.2   Allowances and Tax Rates

Taxable income and tax payable is calculated as follows

	Mr Brown £	Mrs Brown £
Total income before deductions	19,500	15,500
Deduct Personal allowances (see below)	3,765	4,760
Taxable income	£15,735	£10,740
Tax payable:		
3,900/3,900 @ 20%	780.00	780.00
11,835/6,840 @ 24%	2,840.40	1,641.60
	3,620.40	2,421.60
Reduction for married couple's allowance:		
1,435/895 (see below) @ 15%	215.25	134.25
Total liabilities	£3,405.15	£2,292.60

Calculation of allowances

		Mr Brown	Mrs Brown
Unrestricted personal allowances		5,090	4,910
Deduct $\frac{1}{2}$ × £4,300/300 (i.e. excess over £15,200)		2,150	150
		2,940	£4,760
Add back amount required to restore to level of normal allowance		825	
		£3,765	
Unrestricted married couple's allowance		3,155	
Deduct $\frac{1}{2}$ × £4,300 =	£2,150		
Less restriction in personal allowance (£2,150 − £825)	1,325	825	
		2,330	
Transfer from husband to wife (£1,790 × $\frac{1}{2}$)		(895)	£895
		£1,435	

Notes

(a)   The restriction in the married couple's allowance is by reference to the husband's income only (regardless of the transfer of half the basic married couple's allowance to the wife).

(b)   The restriction of the married couple's allowance is itself restricted by the reduction in the personal allowance. [*ICTA 1988, s 257A(5); FA 1988, s 33*].

(c)   If the husband were under 75 and the wife 75 or over, the husband would still qualify for the highest rate of married couple's allowance for the over 75s. The personal allowance is, however, calculated by reference to the individual claimant's age.

(d)   Relief for private medical insurance for the over 60s is restricted to the basic rate for 1994/95 and subsequent years and is *not* an allowable deduction in arriving at total income. Basic rate relief is normally given by deduction at source. [*FA 1989, s 54; FA 1994, 10 Sch*].

1.3   **ADDITIONAL RELIEF IN RESPECT OF CHILDREN, WIDOW'S
       BEREAVEMENT ALLOWANCE** [*ICTA 1988, ss 256, 259, 260, 261A, 262; FA 1988,
       s 30, 3 Sch 7; F(No 2)A 1992, 5 Sch 5–7; FA 1994, s 77(3)–(7), 8 Sch 6–9*]

(A) General

In 1996/97, Mr Hare and Mrs Rabbit, a widow whose husband died in early 1995/96,
commence to live together as man and wife. They have total income of £29,000 and
£15,000 respectively (neither figure including any savings income) and each has a
qualifying child, within *ICTA 1988, s 259(5)*. Mr Hare has a daughter aged 11 and Mrs
Rabbit a son aged 9. Both children live with the couple.

The couple's tax position for 1996/97 is as follows

	Mr Hare £	Mrs Rabbit £
Total income	30,000	15,000
Deduct Personal allowances	3,765	3,765
Taxable income	£26,235	£11,235
Tax payable:		
3,900/3,900 @ 20%	780.00	780.00
21,600/7,335 @ 24%	5,184.00	1,760.40
735/Nil @ 40%	294.00	—
	6,258.00	2,540.40
Additional personal allowance:		
895/895 (note (*b*)) @ 15%	(134.25)	(134.25)
Widow's bereavement allowance:		
1,790 @ 15%		(268.50)
Total liability	£6,123.75	£2,137.65

Notes

(*a*)   Mrs Rabbit would have been entitled to widow's bereavement allowance for
        1995/96 also. She remains so entitled for the year following her husband's death,
        having not re-married before the beginning of that year.

(*b*)   The couple are entitled to only one additional personal allowance between them,
        this being in respect of the youngest child. They may, however, divide the
        allowance between them in whatever proportions they decide. [*ICTA 1988, ss
        259(4A), 260; FA 1988, s 30*]. For 1994/95 and subsequent years, the allowance
        saves tax at a fixed rate (15% for 1995/96 onwards) so providing each partner has
        sufficient tax liability to cover the income tax reduction, there is no tax advantage
        in splitting the allowance in any particular way. It is assumed in this example that
        in the interests of fairness each will claim half the allowance.

(B) Additional relief in respect of children for year of separation [*ICTA 1988, s 261A; F(No 2)A 1992, 5 Sch 6; FA 1994, s 77(4), 8 Sch 8*]

Mr and Mrs Fox permanently separate in July 1996. They have two qualifying children, Reynard and Sam. After the separation and in 1996/97, Reynard lives with his father and Sam with Mrs Fox. Mr and Mrs Fox are aged 68 and 49 respectively. Prior to 6 April 1996, Mrs Fox made an election under *ICTA 1988, s 257BA(1)* to have half the basic married couple's allowance allocated to her with effect from 1996/97. For 1996/97, Mr and Mrs Fox have total income of £10,500 and £12,000 respectively.

The couple's tax position for 1996/97 is as follows

	Mr Fox £	Mrs Fox £
Total income	10,500	12,000
Deduct Personal allowance	4,910	3,765
Taxable income	£5,590	£8,235
Tax payable:		
3,900/3,900 @ 20%	780.00	780.00
1,690/4,335 @ 24%	405.60	1,040.40
	1,185.60	1,820.40
Deduct Additional relief re children:		
Mr Fox £1,790 − £2,220	Nil	
Mrs Fox £(1,790 − 895) @ 15%		134.25
	1,185.60	1,686.15
Deduct Married couple's allowance:		
£(3,115 − 895) = 2,220 @ 15%	333.00	
£895 @ 15%		134.25
Total liability	£852.60	£1,551.90

Note

(a) For 1993/94 and subsequent years, each spouse may claim additional relief in respect of children for the year of separation (as defined) if each has a qualifying child resident with him/her after the separation and in the year of assessment in which separation occurs. However, the additional relief due to each is reduced by the married couple's allowance due to him or her. Note that in this example, the husband loses the benefit of most of the age-related addition to the married couple's allowance.

1.4   **CHARGES ON INCOME** [*ICTA 1988, s 347A; FA 1988, s 36(1); FA 1995, 17 Sch 4*]

Z, a married man, has income and makes payments in the year to 5 April 1997 as follows

	£	£
Earnings		37,400
Dividends plus tax credits		8,000
		45,400
Mortgage interest paid (under MIRAS)	net 1,700	
Deeds of covenant to charities	net 3,040	
		4,740
		£40,660

In October 1996, Z makes a settlement of £20,000 on his parents which produced income of £325 (received gross on a National Savings Bank investment account) in 1996/97. The capital is to revert to him on the death of the last surviving parent.

On 31 March 1997, Z makes a single gift to charity of £304.

Z's income tax liability for the year 1996/97 is

	£	
Tax at lower and basic rates		
Income note (*a*)	45,725	
Deduct Personal allowance	(3,765)	
	£41,960	

		£
Tax at 20% on £3,900 (lower rate band)		780.00
Tax at 24% on £30,060 (balance)		7,214.40
Tax at 20% on dividends of £8,000		1,600.00
Deduct Tax retained at basic rate on		
covenants £4,400 at 24% note (*b*)		(1,056.00)
Tax retained at 15% on mortgage interest		(300.00)
Married couple's allowance £1,790 at 15%		(268.50)
		7,969.90

	£	
Tax at the higher rate		
Basic rate tax band	21,600	
Extension re charitable covenants note (*b*)	4,400	
	26,000	

		£
£3,900 at Nil (20% – 20%)		—
26,000 at Nil (24% – 24%)		—
4,060 at 16% (40% – 24%)		649.60
8,000 at 20% (40% – 20%)		1,600.00
£41,960		2,249.60
Total tax borne		£10,219.50

IT 1.4 Allowances and Tax Rates

The position could be more simply laid out as follows

	£
Income	45,725
Deduct Personal allowance	3,765
Taxable income	£41,960

Tax at 20% on £3,900	780.00
Tax at 24% on £26,000	6,240.00
Tax at 40% on £12,060	4,824.00
	£11,844.00
Deduct Married couple's allowance £1,790 at 15%	268.50
	£11,575.50

The figure of £11,575.50 will be reduced by tax paid under PAYE by tax credits of £1,600 on dividends, with the balance payable by self-assessment. As Z has retained tax of £1,356 (£1,056 + £300) on payments, he has effectively suffered tax of £10,219.50 (£11,575.50 – £1,356) for the year.

Notes

(*a*) Income arising from certain settlements of income only is treated as income of the settlor for both basic and higher rate taxes. [*ICTA 1988, s 660A; FA 1995, 17 Sch 1*]. Thus, £325 is added to Z's income. Z is, however, entitled to recover the tax from the trustees or the beneficiaries. [*ICTA 1988, s 660D; FA 1995, 17 Sch 1*].

(*b*) The single donation to charity, being at least £250, is treated as if it were a covenanted payment equal to the grossed-up amount (£400). [*FA 1990, s 25; FA 1993, s 67(2)*]. The gross equivalent of actual covenanted payments is £4,000 (£3,040 × 100/76).

(*c*) Z's total income for tax purposes is £41,325 (£45,725 – £4,400 charges on income, i.e. covenants and gift aid donation).

2   Capital Allowances

2.1   **BASIS PERIODS** [*CAA 1990, s 160 as originally enacted*]

(A) **Commencement of business. Overlapping periods. No election under *ICTA 1988*, *s 62***

S commenced business on 1.5.91 preparing accounts annually to 30 April. The following expenditure was incurred

	Plant	Motor Car
	£	£
Period 1.5.91 – 5.4.92	10,000	4,000 (no private use)
Period 6.4.92 – 30.4.92	2,000	
Period 1.5.92 – 31.10.92	3,500	
Period 1.11.92 – 30.4.93	4,000	
Period 1.5.93 – 31.10.93	1,500	
Period 1.11.93 – 30.4.94	4,500	

An item of plant was sold for £500 (original cost £1,000) on 27.4.92.

Profits will be assessed as follows
1991/92	Period 1.5.91 – 5.4.92 (actual)
1992/93	Year ended 30.4.92 (first 12 months)
1993/94	Year ended 30.4.92 (preceding year)
1994/95	Year ended 30.4.93 (preceding year)
1995/96	Year ended 30.4.94 (preceding year)

The capital allowances are

		Pool	Pool for cars	Total allowances
		£	£	£
1991/92	(basis period 1.5.91 – 5.4.92)			
	Plant	10,000		
	Motor car		4,000	
		10,000	4,000	
	Allowances			
	WDA $25\% \times \frac{11}{12}$	(2,292)	(917)	£3,209
	WDV at 5.4.92	7,708	3,083	
1992/93	(basis period 6.4.92 – 30.4.92)			
	Plant	2,000		
	Disposals	(500)		
		9,208	3,083	
	Allowances			
	WDA 25%	(2,302)	(771)	£3,073
	WDV at 5.4.93	6,906	2,312	
1993/94	(no basis period)			
	Allowances			
	WDA 25%	(1,727)	(578)	£2,305
	WDV at 5.4.94	c/f £5,179	c/f £1,734	

IT 2.1   Capital Allowances

	Qualifying for FYAs £	Pool £	Pool for cars £	Total allowances £
		b/f 5,179	b/f 1,734	
1994/95 (basis period 1.5.92 – 30.4.93)				
Plant	4,000	3,500		
	4,000	8,679	1,734	
Allowances				
FYA 40%	(1,600)			1,600
WDA 25%		(2,170)	(434)	2,604
	2,400	6,509	1,300	
Transfer to pool	(2,400)	2,400		
WDV at 5.4.95		8,909	1,300	
Total allowances 1994/95				£4,204
1995/96 (basis period 1.5.93 – 30.4.94)				
Plant	1,500	4,500		
	1,500	13,409	1,300	
Allowances				
FYA 40%	(600)			600
WDA 25%		(3,352)	(325)	3,677
	900	10,057	975	
Transfer to pool	(900)	900		
WDV at 5.4.96		£10,957	£975	
Total allowances 1995/96				£4,277

Notes

(a)   The period 1.5.91–5.4.92 falls into the profits basis periods for 1991/92, 1992/93 and 1993/94. It will therefore form the capital allowances basis period for the first year, 1991/92.

(b)   The period 6.4.92–30.4.92 falls into the profits basis periods for both 1992/93 and 1993/94. Again, for capital allowances, the overlap will fall into the earlier year, 1992/93.

(c)   In 1991/92, $\frac{11}{12}$ths of a full year's writing-down allowance will be given because the business was in operation for only eleven months of that period. If a first-year allowance had been available, it would not have fallen to be restricted in this way.

(B) Commencement of business. Overlapping periods. Election under *ICTA 1988, s 62*

Further analysis of S's capital expenditure (see (A) above) revealed the following

	Plant £	Motor Car £
Period 1.5.91 – 5.4.92	10,000	4,000
Period 6.4.92 – 30.4.92	2,000	
Period 1.5.92 – 31.10.92	3,500	
Period 1.11.92 – 5.4.93	2,400	
Period 6.4.93 – 30.4.93	1,600	
Period 1.5.93 – 31.10.93	1,500	
Period 1.11.93 – 5.4.94	3,000	
Period 6.4.94 – 30.4.94	1,500	

Following an election under *ICTA 1988, s 62*, profits will be assessed for the first five years as follows

1991/92	Period 1.5.91 – 5.4.92 (actual)
1992/93	Period 6.4.92 – 5.4.93 (actual)
1993/94	Period 6.4.93 – 5.4.94 (actual)
1994/95	Year ended 30.4.93 (preceding year)
1995/96	Year ended 30.4.94 (preceding year)

The capital allowances are

	Qualifying for FYAs £	Pool £	Pool for cars £	Total allowances £
1991/92 (basis period 1.5.91 – 5.4.92)				
Plant		10,000		
Motor car			4,000	
		10,000	4,000	
Allowances				
WDA 25% × $\frac{11}{12}$		(2,292)	(917)	£3,209
WDV at 5.4.92		7,708	3,083	
1992/93 (basis period 6.4.92 – 5.4.93)				
Plant	2,400	5,500		
Disposals		(500)		
	2,400	12,708	3,083	
Allowances				
FYA 40%	(960)			960
WDA 25%		(3,177)	(771)	3,948
	1,440	9,531	2,312	
Transfer to pool	(1,440)	1,440		
WDV at 5.4.93		c/f £10,971	c/f £2,312	
Total allowances 1992/93				£4,908

IT 2.1   Capital Allowances

	Qualifying for FYAs £	Pool £	Pool for cars £	Total allowances £
		b/f 10,971	b/f 2,312	
1993/94 (basis period 6.4.93 – 5.4.94)				
Plant	3,100	3,000		
	3,100	13,971	2,312	
Allowances				
FYA 40%	(1,240)			1,240
WDA 25%		(3,493)	(578)	4,071
	1,860	10,478	1,734	
Transfer to pool	(1,860)	1,860		
WDA at 5.4.94		12,338	1,734	
Total allowances 1993/94				£5,311
1994/95 (no basis period)				
Allowances				
WDA 25%		(3,085)	(434)	£3,519
WDV at 5.4.95		9,253	1,300	
1995/96 (basis period 6.4.94 – 30.4.94)				
Plant		1,500		
		10,753	1,300	
Allowances				
WDA 25%		(2,688)	(325)	£3,013
WDV at 5.4.96		£8,065	£975	

Notes

(a)   The period 1.5.92 – 5.4.93 falls into the profits basis periods for both 1992/93 and 1994/95. It will therefore fall into the capital allowances basis period for the earlier year, 1992/93.

(b)   The period 6.4.93 – 30.4.93 falls into the profits basis periods for both 1993/94 and 1994/95. It will therefore fall into the capital allowances basis period for the earlier year, 1993/94.

(c)   The period 1.5.93 – 5.4.94 falls into the profits basis periods for both 1993/94 and 1995/96. Again, for capital allowances, it will fall into the basis period of the earlier year, 1993/94.

(C) Cessation of business. Interval between basis periods. No Inland Revenue adjustment under _ICTA 1988, s 63_
T ceased trading on 30.9.95 having prepared accounts annually to 30 June. The following expenditure and disposals arose

	Expenditure (Plant) £	(Disposal Proceeds) £
Period 1.7.91 – 30.6.92	1,800	(2,000)
Period 1.7.92 – 31.10.92	3,100	—
Period 1.11.92 – 30.6.93	900	(300)
Period 1.7.93 – 31.10.93	1,100	—
Period 1.11.93 – 30.6.94	600	—
Period 1.7.94 – 5.4.95	800	(200)
Period 6.4.95 – 30.9.95	400	(250)

There was a written-down value of £2,600 in the machinery and plant pool at the end of 1992/93.

Profits of the closing years will be assessed as follows

1993/94	Period 1.7.91 – 30.6.92 (preceding year)
1994/95	Period 1.7.92 – 30.6.93 (preceding year)
1995/96	Period 6.4.95 – 30.9.95 (actual)

The capital allowances are

	Qualifying for FYAs £	Pool £	Total allowances £
WDV at 5.4.93		2,600	
1993/94 (basis period 1.7.91 – 30.6.92)			
Additions		1,800	
Disposals		(2,000)	
		2,400	
Allowances			
WDA 25%		(600)	£600
WDV at 5.4.94		1,800	
1994/95 (basis period 1.7.92 – 5.4.95)			
Additions	2,000	4,500	
Disposals		(500)	
	2,000	5,800	
Allowances			
FYA 40%	(800)		800
WDA 25%		(1,450)	1,450
	1,200	4,350	
Transfer to pool	(1,200)	1,200	
WDV at 5.4.95		5,550	
Total allowances 1994/95			£2,250

IT 2.1   Capital Allowances

1995/96   (basis period 6.4.95 – 30.9.95)

Additions	400	
Disposals	(250)	
	5,700	
Value at 30.9.95 (say) note (*b*)	(3,000)	
Balancing allowance	£2,700	£2,700

Notes

(*a*)   The interval between the profits basis periods (1.7.93–5.4.95) will fall into the capital allowances basis period for the earlier year, 1994/95, since the business is permanently discontinued in the later year, 1995/96. [*CAA 1990, s 160(3)(c)* as *originally enacted*].

(*b*)   The value of assets remaining at the date of cessation will consist of
    (i)   the proceeds on disposal of any assets sold subsequently, and
    (ii)   the market value of any assets appropriated for personal use.
    [*CAA 1990, s 26(1)(e)(f)*]

(*c*)   No writing-down allowances (or, where applicable, first-year allowances) are made in the final year of assessment. [*CAA 1990, ss 22(4)(a), 24(2)(a)*].

(D) Cessation of business. Interval between basis periods. Inland Revenue adjustment under *ICTA 1988, s 63*
Further analysis of T's capital expenditure (see (C) above) reveals

	Expenditure (Plant) £	(Disposal Proceeds) £
Period 1.7.91 – 30.6.92	1,800	(2,000)
Period 1.7.92 – 31.10.92	3,100	—
Period 1.11.92 – 30.6.93	900	(300)
Period 1.7.93 – 31.10.93	1,100	—
Period 1.11.93 – 5.4.94	400	—
Period 6.4.94 – 30.6.94	200	—
Period 1.7.94 – 5.4.95	800	(200)
Period 6.4.95 – 30.9.95	400	(250)

Profits are such that the Inland Revenue make an adjustment under *ICTA 1988, s 63* and the final three years are assessed as follows

1993/94	Period 6.4.93 – 5.4.94	(actual)
1994/95	Period 6.4.94 – 5.4.95	(actual)
1995/96	Period 6.4.95 – 30.9.95	(actual)

The capital allowances are

	Qualifying for FYAs	Pool	Total allowances
	£	£	£
WDV at 5.4.93		2,600	
1993/94 (basis period 1.7.91 – 5.4.94)			
Additions	2,000	5,300	
Disposals		(2,300)	
	2,000	5,600	
Allowances			
FYA 40%	(800)		800
WDA 25%		(1,400)	1,400
	1,200	4,200	
Transfer to pool	(1,200)	1,200	
WDV at 5.4.94		5,400	
Total allowances 1993/94			£2,200
1994/95 (basis period 6.4.94 – 5.4.95)			
Additions		1,000	
Disposals		(200)	
		6,200	
Allowances			
WDA 25%		(1,550)	£1,550
WDV at 5.4.95		4,650	
1995/96 (basis period 6.4.95 – 30.9.95)			
Additions		400	
Disposals		(250)	
		4,800	
Value at 30.9.95 (say)		(3,000)	
Balancing allowance		£1,800	£1,800

Note

(a)   Since the assessment for 1992/93 would have remained based on the year ended 30.6.91, the interval between profits basis periods is 1.7.91 – 5.4.93. Since the trade did not cease in the following year (1993/94), the interval will be deemed to be part of the basis period for that year. [*CAA 1990, s 160(3)(b) as originally enacted*].

IT 2.1 Capital Allowances

**(E) Changeover from preceding year to current year basis of assessment.
Transitional year. Interval between basis periods**
S, the trader in (A) and (B) above, continues to trade beyond the turn of the century. He
has the following expenditure on machinery and plant in the three years to 30 April
1997

	Plant £	Motor Car £
Year ended 30 April 1995	3,043	
Year ended 30 April 1996	2,300	4,800
Year ended 30 April 1997	6,400	

The new car was a replacement for the old, which was traded in at a value of £775. There
continued to be no private use of either car. An item of plant was sold for £300 in the year
to 30 April 1995.

The written-down values for capital allowances purposes at the end of 1995/96 were as in
(A) above.

The capital allowances for the years 1996/97 and 1997/98 are as follows

	Pool £	Pool for cars £	Total allowances £
1996/97 (basis period 1.5.94 – 30.4.96)			
WDV at 6.4.96	10,957	975	
Additions	5,343		
Disposals	(300)	(775)	
Balancing allowance		£200	200
	16,000		
Addition		4,800	
Allowances			
WDA 25%	(4,000)	(1,200)	5,200
WDV c/f	12,000	3,600	
Total allowances 1996/97			£5,400
Period of account 1.5.96 – 30.4.97			
Additions	6,400		
	18,400	3,600	
Allowances			
WDA 25%	(4,600)	(900)	£5,500
WDV c/f	£13,800	£2,700	

Notes
(a)   The capital allowances basis period for 1996/97 is the period on the profits of which
      income tax falls to be computed (*CAA 1990, s 160(2) as originally enacted*), which
      in this case is the two years to 30 April 1996 under the transitional rules in *FA 1994,
      20 Sch 1, 2*.

If 1995/96 had been the third year of assessment and had been taxed on an actual basis by election under *ICTA 1988, s 62*, the profits basis period, and therefore the capital allowances basis period, for 1996/97 would have been the year to 5 April 1997 (under *FA 1994, 20 Sch 2(3)*).

(*b*)   The capital allowances of £5,400 for 1996/97 are deductible from the averaged profit for that year (see 19.4 SCHEDULE D, CASES I AND II) in arriving at the taxable profit. The capital allowances are not themselves subject to averaging.

(*c*)   For 1997/98 and subsequent years (for businesses commenced before 6 April 1994), capital allowances are given by reference to periods of account (see 2.2 below). The allowances of £5,500 for the year to 30 April 1997 are deductible as a trading expense in arriving at the taxable profit for that year. The profit thus arrived at is taxable in 1997/98 on a current year basis, with overlap relief accruing for that part of the profit (*before* capital allowances) which arose before 6 April 1997 (see 19.4(A) SCHEDULE D, CASES I AND II). [*CAA 1990, s 140; FA 1994, s 211*].

2.2   **PERIODS OF ACCOUNT** [*CAA 1990, s 160; FA 1994, ss 211(2), 212(1), 218(1)*]

(A) General
James commences business on 1 October 1994 preparing accounts initially to 30 September. He changes his accounting date in 1996, preparing accounts for the 15 months to 31 December 1996. The following capital expenditure is incurred

	Plant £	Motor Car £
Year ended 30 September 1995	12,000	4,000 (no private use)
Period ended 31 December 1996	7,500	
Year ended 31 December 1997	4,000	

An item of plant is sold for £500 (original cost £1,000) on 25 September 1996.

Profits *before* capital allowances but otherwise as adjusted for tax purposes are as follows

	£
Year ended 30 September 1995	18,000
Period ended 31 December 1996	25,000
Year ended 31 December 1997	24,000

IT 2.2 Capital Allowances

The capital allowances are

	Pool	Pool for cars	Total allowances
	£	£	£
Year ended 30.9.95			
Qualifying expenditure	12,000	4,000	
WDA 25%	(3,000)	(1,000)	£4,000
WDV at 30.9.95	9,000	3,000	
15 months ended 31.12.96			
Additions	7,500		
Disposals	(500)		
	16,000		
WDA 25% × 15/12	(5,000)	(938)	£5,938
WDV at 31.12.96	11,000	2,062	
Year ended 31.12.97			
Additions	4,000		
	15,000		
WDA 25%	(3,750)	(516)	£4,266
WDV at 31.12.97	£11,250	£1,546	

Taxable profits for the accounting periods concerned are

	Before CAs	CAs	After CAs
	£	£	£
Year ended 30 September 1995	18,000	4,000	14,000
Period ended 31 December 1996	25,000	5,938	19,062
Year ended 31 December 1997	24,000	4,266	19,734

Taxable profits for the first four years of assessment of the business are

	£	£
1994/95 (1.10.94–5.4.95) (£14,000 × 6/12)		7,000
1995/96 (y/e 30.9.95)		14,000
1996/97 (1.10.95–31.12.96)	19,062	
Deduct Overlap relief £7,000 × 3/6	3,500	
		15,562
1997/98 (y/e 31.12.97)		19,734

Notes

(a) For businesses commencing after 5 April 1994 (and with effect for 1997/98 and subsequent years as regards businesses commenced before 6 April 1994), capital allowances are calculated by reference to periods of account and are treated as trading expenses. [*CAA 1990, ss 140, 160; FA 1994, ss 211, 212, 218(1)*]. For this purpose, a period of account may exceed 12 months (but cannot exceed 18 months — see (B) below). Note that in apportioning profits to years of assessment, one considers profits *after* capital allowances.

(b) Where a period of account exceeds 12 months, writing-down allowances are proportionately increased. See *CAA 1990, s 24(2)(a)(ii); FA 1994, s 213(4)* as regards machinery and plant — the same applies to capital allowances on other kinds of expenditure (see *FA 1994, ss 213, 214* generally).

(c)   In this example, the overlap profit is £7,000 being the profit taxed twice under the commencement rules. This represents 6 months' profit (1 October 1994 to 5 April 1995). As the basis period for 1996/97 is 3 months greater than one year, 3/6 of the overlap profit is relieved in that year, the balance being carried forward. For further examples on the current year basis of assessment for businesses, including commencement and cessation rules, overlap relief and changes of accounting date, see 19.1–19.4 SCHEDULE D. CASES I AND II.

(B) Period of account exceeding 18 months
Bianca commenced business on 1 October 1994 preparing accounts initially to 30 June. She changes her accounting date in 1996/97, preparing accounts for the 21 months to 31 March 1997. The following capital expenditure is incurred

	Plant	Motor Car
	£	£
Period ended 30 June 1995	24,000	16,000 (no private use)
Period ended 31 March 1997	10,000	
Year ended 31 March 1998	2,150	

Of the £10,000 of expenditure incurred in the 21-month accounting period to 31 March 1997, £3,000 was incurred in the 12 months to 30 June 1996 and £7,000 in the nine months to 31 March 1997.

An item of plant is sold for £675 (original cost £1,000) on 3 November 1996.

Profits *before* capital allowances but otherwise as adjusted for tax purposes are as follows

	£
Period ended 30 June 1995	30,000
Period ended 31 March 1997	75,000
Year ended 31 March 1998	50,000

IT 2.2 Capital Allowances

The capital allowances are

	Pool £	Car £	Total allowances £
9 months ended 30.6.95			
Qualifying expenditure	24,000	16,000	
Allowances			
WDA 25% × 9/12	(4,500)		4,500
WDA £3,000 × 9/12		(2,250)	2,250
WDV at 30.6.95	19,500	13,750	
Total allowances			£6,750
12 months ended 30.6.96			
Additions	3,000		
	22,500		
Allowances			
WDA 25%	(5,625)		5,625
WDA £3,000		(3,000)	3,000
WDV at 30.6.96	16,875	10,750	
Total allowances			£8,625
9 months ended 31.3.97			
Additions	7,000		
Disposals	(675)		
	23,200		
WDA 25% × 9/12	(4,350)	(2,016)	£6,366
WDV at 31.3.97	18,850	8,734	
Year ended 31.3.98			
Additions	2,150		
	21,000		
WDA 25%	(5,250)	(2,184)	£7,434
WDV at 31.3.98	£15,750	£6,550	

Taxable profits for the accounting periods concerned are

	Before CAs £	CAs £	After CAs £
Period ended 30 June 1995	30,000	6,750	23,250
Period ended 31 March 1997	75,000	(8,625 + 6,366)	60,009
Year ended 31 March 1998	50,000	7,434	42,566

Taxable profits for the first four years of assessment of the business are

	£	£
1994/95 (1.10.94 – 5.4.95) (£23,250 × 6/9)		15,500
1995/96 (1.10.94 – 30.9.95):		
1.10.94 – 30.6.95	23,250	
1.7.95 – 30.9.95 (£60,009 × 3/21)	8,573	
		31,823

1996/97 (1.10.95 – 31.3.97) (£60,009 × 18/21)	51,436	
Deduct Overlap relief	15,500	
		35,936
1997/98 (y/e 31.3.98)		42,566

Notes

(a)   Where a period of account for capital allowances purposes would otherwise exceed 18 months, it is broken down into shorter periods, the first beginning on the first day of the actual period and each subsequent period beginning on an anniversary of the first day of the actual period. No period can therefore exceed 12 months. [*CAA 1990, s 160(4); FA 1994, s 212(1)*].

(b)   The capital allowances computed for the notional periods of account referred to in (a) above are deductible in aggregate in arriving at the adjusted profit for the actual accounting period.

(c)   An accounting period exceeding 18 months cannot normally result in an immediate change of basis period, because of *ICTA 1988, s 62A(2)*. However, the conditions of *section 62A* do not have to be satisfied if the change of accounting period occurs in the second or third year of assessment of a new business, as in this example. [*ICTA 1988, s 62(1)(b); FA 1994, s 202*].

(d)   In this example, the overlap profit is £15,500 being the profit taxed twice under the commencement rules. This represents 6 months' profit (1 October 1994 to 5 April 1995). As the basis period for 1996/97 is 6 months greater than one year, the whole of the overlap profit is relieved in that year. For further examples on the current year basis of assessment for businesses, including commencement and cessation rules, overlap relief and changes of accounting date, see 19.1–19.4 SCHEDULE D, CASES I AND II.

2.3   **SUCCESSIONS** [*CAA 1990, ss 77, 78, 152*]

A change in the members of a partnership occurred on 1 September 1995 when A and B, who had been partners for a number of years, admitted C as a partner. Accounts had been prepared to 31 August annually and revealed the following expenditure on, and disposals of, machinery and plant.

	Expenditure	(Disposal Proceeds)
	£	£
Period 1.9.93 – 31.8.94	2,500	(1,000)
Period 1.9.94 – 5.4.95	7,200	(1,200)
Period 6.4.95 – 31.8.95	1,000	—
Period 1.9.95 – 31.8.96	5,000	(200)

All the expenditure in the period 1.9.93 to 31.8.94 was incurred after 31.10.93.

The market value of machinery and plant at 1.9.95 totalled £10,000. In no case did an item's market value exceed its cost.

The capital allowances treatment in the year of the change will depend on whether or not the partnership change was treated as (a) cessation and commencement [*ICTA 1988, s 113(1)*] or (b) continuation [*ICTA 1988, s 113(2) as originally enacted*].

IT 2.3　Capital Allowances

Cessation and commencement

(i) No election under *CAA 1990, s 77(3)*

	Pool £	Total allowances £
Old partnership		
1995/96 (basis period 6.4.95 – 31.8.95)		
WDV b/f at 6.4.95 (say)	7,500	
Additions	1,000	
Disposals (at market value)	(10,000)	
	(1,500)	
Balancing charge	1,500	£(1,500)
New partnership		
Period of account 1.9.95 – 31.8.96		
Transfer from old partnership	10,000	
Additions	5,000	
Disposals	(200)	
	14,800	
WDA 25%	(3,700)	£3,700
WDV at 31.8.96	£11,100	

Notes

(*a*)　If no election is made under *CAA 1990, s 77(3)* (see (ii) below), machinery and plant is treated as sold by the predecessor to the successor at open market value. [*CAA 1990, s 78(1)*]. Similar rules apply for other assets. [*CAA 1990, s 152(1)*].

(*b*)　As the partnership change occurs after 5 April 1994 and no continuation election is made, the new partnership will be taxed under the current year basis, with capital allowances being given as trading expenses and calculated by reference to periods of account (see 2.2 above). The allowances of £3,700 for the year ended 31 August 1996 are deductible in arriving at the taxable profit for that year, which must then be divided between the partners and apportioned to basis periods. For further examples on current year basis of assessment, see 19.1–19.4 SCHEDULE D, CASES I AND II and 14.1 PARTNERSHIPS.

(ii) Election under *CAA 1990, s 77(3)*

	Pool £	Total allowances £
Old partnership		
1995/96 (basis period 6.4.95 – 31.8.95)		
WDV b/f at 6.4.95 (say)	7,500	
Additions	1,000	
Disposals (at written-down value)	(8,500)	
Balancing allowance/charge	Nil	Nil

1–26

New partnership
Period of account 1.9.95 – 31.8.96

Transfer from old partnership	8,500	
Additions	5,000	
Disposals	(200)	
	13,300	
WDA 25%	(3,325)	£3,325
WDV at 31.8.96	£9,975	

Notes

(a) Under *CAA 1990, s 77(3)–(8)*, machinery and plant passing to the successor is deemed to have been sold by the predecessor to the successor at such a price as to leave no balancing allowance or balancing charge. An election must be made for these provisions to apply.

(b) An election under *CAA 1990, s 77(3)*, may be made only between connected persons, as defined by *section 77(5)*, must be made jointly by predecessor and successor and must be made within two years of the succession, i.e. by 1 September 1997 in this example.

(c) For certain assets other than machinery and plant, a similar election is available under *CAA 1990, s 158* as amended by *FA 1993, s 117* and by *FA 1994, s 119* for certain transfers between connected persons.

Continuation

If the partners elect under *ICTA 1988, s 113(2)*, the capital allowances for 1995/96 are calculated as follows.

	Pool	Total allowances
	£	£
1995/96 (basis period 1.9.93 – 31.8.94)		
WDV b/f (say) note (a)	1,875	
Additions	2,500	
Disposals	(1,000)	
	3,375	
WDA 25%	(844)	£844
WDV at 5.4.96	£2,531	
Allocated:		
Old partnership (6.4.95 – 31.8.95) (5/12)		352
New partnership (1.9.95 – 5.4.96) (7/12)		492
		£844

Notes

(a) The written-down value brought forward is that at the end of the basis period for 1994/95 which in this case is the period 1.9.92 – 31.8.93. In the previous calculations, all additions and disposals up to 5.4.95 would have been taken into account and thus, the written-down value was a different figure.

(b)   For partnership changes after 5 April 1997, continuation elections will no longer be relevant. Partnerships will automatically be treated as continuing, providing there is at least one continuing partner. This applies with effect for 1994/95 and subsequent years where the partnership business commences, or is deemed to commence, after 5 April 1994. [*ICTA 1988, s 113(2); FA 1994, ss 215(4)(5), 216(1)*].

2.4   VAT CAPITAL GOODS SCHEME [*CAA 1990, s 159A; FA 1991, s 59, 14 Sch*]

Cross-reference. See 402.1 CAPITAL GOODS in the VAT section.

T Ltd carries on a trade which is partially exempt for VAT purposes, and draws up accounts to 31 March each year. Its partial exemption year also runs to 31 March. On 1 April 1994, the company acquired a second-hand freehold commercial building (in an enterprise zone) for £900,000 plus VAT of £157,500, the vendor having opted to charge VAT. The previous owner claimed industrial buildings allowances and T Ltd inherits a residue of expenditure of £770,000 to be written-down over a period of 22 years. On 1 June 1994, T Ltd acquired computer equipment at a cost of £100,000 plus VAT of £17,500. The company had a written-down value of £40,000 on its machinery and plant pool at 1 April 1994 and, for the purposes of this example, it is assumed that there are no other acquisitions during the period covered, and no disposals.

T Ltd's claimable percentage of non-attributable input tax for the partial exemption years ended 31 March 1995, 1996 and 1997 is as follows

Year ended	
31.3.95	75%
31.3.96	80%
31.3.97	70%

The input tax position is as follows

	Building	Computer
Year ended 31.3.95		
Initial input tax claim:		
£157,500 × 75%	£118,125	
£17,500 × 75%		£13,125
Year ended 31.3.96		
Additional VAT rebate:		
$\dfrac{157,500}{10} \times (80-75)\%$	£788	
$\dfrac{17,500}{5} \times (80-75)\%$		£175
Year ended 31.3.97		
Additional VAT liability:		
$\dfrac{157,500}{10} \times (80-70)\%$	£1,575	
$\dfrac{17,500}{5} \times (80-70)\%$		£350

T Ltd deals with the appropriate VAT capital goods scheme adjustments in its quarterly VAT return to 30 September following each partial exemption year.

The capital allowances computations are as follows

Industrial buildings allowances

	£
Year to 31.3.95	
Residue of expenditure acquired	770,000
WDA (£770,000/22)	(35,000)
	735,000
Year to 31.3.96	
WDA (£770,000/22)	(35,000)
	700,000
Year to 31.3.97	
Additional VAT rebate (note (*b*))	(646)
	699,354
WDA (note (*b*))	(34,968)
	664,386
Year to 31.3.98	
Additional VAT liability (note (*c*))	1,291
	665,677
WDA (note (*c*))	(35,036)
WDV at 31.3.98	£630,641

Machinery and plant

	Pool 25% £
Year to 31.3.95	
WDV at 1.4.94	40,000
Addition (£100,000 + £(17,500 − 13,125))	104,375
	144,375
WDA	36,091
	108,281
Year to 31.3.96	
WDA	(27,070)
	81,211
Year to 31.3.97	
Disposal value	(175)
	81,036
WDA	(20,259)
	60,777
Year to 31.3.98	
Addition	350
	61,127
WDA	15,282
WDV at 31.3.98	£45,845

IT 2.4   Capital Allowances

Notes

(a)   The residue of expenditure for industrial buildings allowances is reduced by any additional VAT rebate and increased by any additional VAT liability, and writing-down allowances calculated accordingly by reference to that part of the original writing-down period that remains unexpired at the time the liability is incurred or the rebate made. [*CAA 1990, s 3(2A)–(2C); FA 1991, 14 Sch 3*]. For this purpose, that time is the last day of the 'relevant VAT interval'. [*CAA 1990, s 159A(1); FA 1991, 14 Sch 14*]. For the purpose of determining the chargeable period in which capital allowances are to be adjusted by reference to the rebate/liability, it is regarded in this case as made/incurred on the last day of the VAT return period in which the adjustment is made (i.e. the return for the quarter to 30 September in the chargeable period). [*CAA 1990, s 159A(3)(4); FA 1991, 14 Sch 14*].

(b)   Industrial buildings allowances for the year to 31.3.97 are calculated as follows

    (i)   Writing-down period unexpired (from 31.3.96)   20 years

    (ii)   Additional VAT rebate to be brought into account (see note (*d*)):

$$\frac{770,000}{939,375} \times £788 = £646$$

    (iii)   Residue £700,000 − £646 =   £699,354

    (iv) $\dfrac{699,354}{20}$ =   £34,968

(c)   Industrial buildings allowances for the year to 31.3.98 are calculated as follows

    (i)   From 31.3.97   19 years

    (ii) $\dfrac{770,000}{939,375} \times £1,575$ =   £1,291

    (iii)   £664,386 + £1,291 =   £665,677

    (iv) $\dfrac{665,677}{19}$ =   £35,036

(d)   If T Ltd's qualifying expenditure on the building was not restricted to the residue of £770,000, he could initially have claimed allowances by reference to expenditure of £939,375 (£900,000 + £(157,500 − 118,125)). The additional VAT rebate and liability relating to the building are therefore reduced, for capital allowances purposes, in the proportion 770,000:939,375. [*CAA 1990, s 159A(5); FA 1991, 14 Sch 14*].

(e)   If the expenditure on the computer equipment had been incurred between 1 November 1992 and 31 October 1993 inclusive, and had thus qualified for a first-year allowance, the additional VAT liability of £350 would likewise have qualified for a first-year allowance (at 40%) for the year to 31 March 1998. [*CAA 1990, s 22(3B)(b); FA 1993, s 115(2)*].

2.5   AGRICULTURAL BUILDINGS ALLOWANCES [CAA 1990, ss 122-133; FA 1993, 12 Sch]

(A) Calculation of allowances

Farmer Jones prepares accounts annually to 31 December and has incurred the following expenditure

		£
12.1.90	Extension to farmhouse	12,000
3.6.91	Construction of cattle court	15,000
26.4.93	Erection of barn	10,000
15.10.96	Replacement barn for that acquired on 26.4.93 which was destroyed by fire in September 1996. The insurance proceeds totalled £6,600	20,000

The agricultural buildings allowances are as follows

Date of expenditure	Cost	Residue brought forward	Allowances Initial 20%	WDA 4%	Residue carried forward
	£	£	£	£	£
1991/92 (basis period — year to 31.12.90)					
12.1.90	4,000	note (b)		160	3,840
1992/93 (basis period — year to 31.12.91)					
12.1.90	4,000	3,840		160	3,680
3.6.91	15,000			600	14,400
	£19,000	£3,840		£760	£18,080
1993/94 (basis period — year to 31.12.92)					
12.1.90	4,000	3,680		160	3,520
3.6.91	15,000	14,400		600	13,800
	£19,000	£18,080		£760	£17,320
1994/95 (basis period — year to 31.12.93)					
12.1.90	4,000	3,520		160	3,360
3.6.91	15,000	13,800		600	13,200
26.4.93	10,000		2,000	400	7,600
	£29,000	£17,320	£2,000	£1,160	£24,160
1995/96 (basis period — year to 31.12.94)					
12.1.90	4,000	3,360		160	3,200
3.6.91	15,000	13,200		600	12,600
26.4.93	10,000	7,600		400	7,200
	£29,000	£24,160		£1,160	£23,000

IT 2.5 Capital Allowances

Date of expenditure	Cost	Residue brought forward		WDA 4%	Residue carried forward
	£	£		£	£
(i) No election for a balancing adjustment					
1996/97 (basis period — two years to 31.12.96)					
12.1.90	4,000	3,200		160	3,040
3.6.91	15,000	12,600		600	12,000
26.4.93	10,000	7,200		400	6,800
15.10.96	20,000			800	19,200
	£49,000	£23,000		£1,960	£41,040
(ii) Election for a balancing adjustment					
1996/97 (basis period — two years to 31.12.96)					
12.1.90	4,000	3,200		160	3,040
3.6.91	15,000	12,600		600	12,000
15.10.96	20,000			800	19,200
	£39,000	£15,800		£1,560	£34,240

Balancing allowance

	£
Proceeds	6,600
Written-down value	7,200
Balancing allowance	£600

Notes

(a)   Balancing adjustments arise, under *CAA 1990, s 128*, only if an election is made under *section 129*. Thus on the destruction of the barn costing £10,000, allowances will continue to be available, in the absence of an election, until the expenditure has been exhausted. Allowances can also be claimed on the replacement asset in the normal way. If the election is made, a balancing charge or allowance is computed as shown (and see also (B) below).

(b)   Only a maximum of one-third of capital expenditure on a farmhouse qualifies for allowances. [*CAA 1990, ss 124(1)(a), 124A(4); FA 1993, 12 Sch 3*].

(c)   In order to qualify for a writing-down allowance in addition to an initial allowance in 1994/95, the original barn must be brought into use before 6 April 1995. [*CAA 1990, s 124B; FA 1993, 12 Sch 3*].

(B) Transfers of allowances on sale etc.

X is a farmer making up accounts to 30 June. Part of the land he farms as a tenant of Y. On this land the following expenditure is incurred:

			£
23.1.92	Farmhouse extension	(paid by Y)	15,000
5.2.92	Barn	(paid by X)	10,000
1.5.92	Cattle pens	(paid by X)	2,000
1.12.93	Drainage	(paid by X)	12,000

On 31.12.94, X assigns the lease to Z, a neighbouring farmer making up accounts to 30 April. Payment for the lease includes £11,750 for the drainage, £5,000 for the barn and £200 for the cattle pens. On 1.6.96, Z demolishes the cattle pens receiving £100 for scrap. X and Z agree to elect jointly for the sale of the cattle pens to be treated as a balancing event. Z elects for the demolition of the cattle pens to be treated as a balancing event.

The following allowances are due to X, Y and Z

X

Date of expenditure	Cost £	Residue brought forward £	Allowances WDA 4% £	Residue carried forward £
1993/94 (basis period — year to 30.6.92)				
5.2.92	10,000		400	9,600
1.5.92	2,000		80	1,920
	£12,000		£480	£11,520
1994/95				
5.2.92	10,000	9,600	400	9,200
1.5.92	2,000	1,920	80	1,840
	£12,000	£11,520	£480	£11,040
1995/96				
5.2.92	10,000	9,200	400	8,800
1.5.92	2,000	1,840	80	1,760
1.12.93	12,000		480	11,520
	£24,000	£11,040	£960	£22,080
1996/97 (basis period — two years to 30.6.96)				
5.2.92	10,000	8,800	$(400 \times \frac{6}{24})$ 100	8,700
1.5.92	2,000	1,760	Balancing event	
1.12.93	12,000	11,520	$(480 \times \frac{6}{24})$ 120	11,400
	£24,000	£22,080	see note (a) 220	£20,100

Balancing event

Residue of expenditure brought forward	1,760	
Proceeds of sale	200	
Balancing allowance to X		1,560
Total allowances to X (1996/97)		£1,780

IT 2.5 Capital Allowances

Y

Y's allowances (on the farmhouse extension) as landlord are given by way of discharge or repayment of tax and amount to a maximum of £200 (£15,000 × $\frac{1}{3}$ maximum × 4%) for 1991/92, being the year of assessment in which the expenditure was incurred, and each subsequent year up to and including 2015/2016.

Z

1996/97 (basis period — two years to 30.4.96)

Date of expenditure	Cost	Residue brought forward	Allowances WDA	Residue carried forward
	£	£	£	£
5.2.92 (1.1.95 – 30.4.96)	10,000	8,700	($\frac{16}{24}$ × £400) 267	8,433
1.5.92 (Acquired 1.1.95)	200	note (b)	9	191
1.12.93 (1.1.95 – 30.4.96)	12,000	11,400	($\frac{16}{24}$ × £480) 320	11,080
	£22,200	£20,100	£596	£19,704

Period of account 1.5.96 to 30.4.97

	Cost	Residue	Allowances	Residue
5.2.92	10,000	8,433	400	8,033
1.5.92	200	191	Balancing event	
1.12.93	12,000	11,080	480	10,600
	£22,200	£19,704	880	£18,633

Balancing event

Residue of expenditure	191	
Scrap proceeds	100	
Balancing allowance to Z		91
Total allowance to Z		£971

Notes

(a) X and Z may jointly elect for balancing adjustments on the cattle pens, barn and drainage. As no election is made in respect of the barn and drainage the writing-down allowances are given to X for the period 1.7.94 to 31.12.94, claimed in 1996/97. Z can claim allowances from 1.1.95 to 30.4.96 in 1996/97 and full allowances in subsequent periods of account. Apportionment of allowances consequent upon a transfer of the relevant interest is made by reference to the basis period which spans the date of transfer, which for both X and Z is a two-year basis period in this example.

(b) As an election for a balancing adjustment was made on the cattle pens, Z claims allowances on the residue of expenditure £1,760 less balancing allowance given to X of £1,560. The allowances are due to Z from 1996/97 to 5.4.2018, the last year of the original writing-down period which began on 6.4.93. As this covers approximately 23 chargeable periods, Z's allowance for each year is £200 divided by 23, which is approximately £9.

2.6   **CEMETERIES AND CREMATORIA** [*ICTA 1988, s 91*]
GE, who operates a funeral service, owns a cemetery for which accounts to 31 December are prepared. The accounts to 31.12.96 reveal the following

(i)	Cost of land representing 110 grave spaces sold in period	£3,400
(ii)	Number of grave spaces remaining	275
(iii)	Residual capital expenditure on buildings and other land unsuitable for interments	£18,250

The allowances available are

		£
(*a*)	Item (i)	3,400
(*b*)	$\dfrac{110}{110+275} \times £18,250$	5,214
		£8,614

Note
(*a*)   £8,614 will be allowed as a deduction in computing GE's Schedule D, Case I profits for the accounting period ending on 31 December 1996.

IT 2.7 Capital Allowances

2.7 **DREDGING** [*CAA 1990, ss 134, 135*]

D is the proprietor of an estuary maintenance business preparing accounts to 30 June. Expenditure qualifying for dredging allowances is incurred as follows

	£
Year ended 30.6.93	4,000
Year ended 30.6.94	5,000

On 2 January 1997, D sells the business to an unconnected third party. The Revenue do not revise the 1994/95 and 1995/96 assessments under *ICTA 1988, s 63*.

The allowances available are

Date of expenditure	Cost £	Residue brought forward £	Allowances WDA 4% £	Residue carried forward £
1994/95 (basis period — year ended 30.6.93)				
1993	4,000	—	160	3,840
1995/96 (basis period — 1.7.93 – 5.4.96)				
1993	4,000	3,840	160	3,680
1994	5,000	—	200	4,800
			£360	
1996/97 (basis period — 6.4.96 – 2.1.97, nine months)				
1993	4,000	3,680	($\frac{9}{12}$) 120	3,560
1994	5,000	4,800	($\frac{9}{12}$) 150	4,650
			270	£8,210
Balancing allowance note (*a*)			8,210	
Total allowances (1996/97)			£8,480	

Note

(*a*) On a permanent discontinuance of the trade, including a sale other than one falling within *CAA 1990, s 157(1)*, a balancing allowance is given and is equal to the residue of expenditure after deducting writing-down allowances for the final year of assessment. There are no provisions for a balancing charge or a transfer of allowances to a purchaser.

2.8 **INDUSTRIAL BUILDINGS** [*CAA 1990, ss 1–21; FA 1993, s 113*]

(A) **Initial and writing-down allowances and balancing adjustments**
Prior to commencing business on 1 June 1993, P incurred the following expenditure

	£
10.1.93 Plot of land	5,000
20.2.93 Clearing and levelling site	2,000
20.4.93 Construction of factory	50,000
	£57,000

The factory was brought into use for a qualifying purpose on commencement of trade and remained in such use until 1 May 1996, when it was sold to Y for £55,000, being £48,000 for the factory and £7,000 for the land. P drew up accounts annually to 31 May, and did not elect for the second and third years of assessment to be taxed on an actual basis. Y draws up accounts to 30 April, having commenced trading on 1 May 1996, and uses the factory for a qualifying purpose.

The allowances available to P

Year of assessment			Residue of expenditure £
1993/94	Qualifying expenditure		52,000
	Initial allowance	20% of £52,000	(10,400)
	Writing-down allowance	4% of £52,000	(2,080)
			39,520
1994/95, 1995/96	Writing-down allowance for 2 years	4% of £52,000 × 2	(4,160)
			35,360
1996/97	Writing-down allowance		—
	Sale proceeds		(48,000)
	Balancing charge		£12,640

The allowances available to Y

Date of first use	1.6.93
Date of purchase by Y	1.5.96
Number of years remaining	22 years 1 month
Residue of expenditure	£48,000

Y is therefore entitled to writing-down allowances of £2,174 p.a. until total allowances reach £48,000. His first writing-down allowance will be given for the period of account 1.5.96 to 30.4.97.

Notes

(a) Writing-down allowances are first due in 1993/94, being P's first chargeable period, but are *not* restricted to the length of the basis period (which runs from 1 June 1993 to 5 April 1994).

(b) No allowances are due on the cost of the land.

(c) Provided that the factory is used by Y for a qualifying purpose he will be entitled to writing-down allowances on the residue of expenditure after sale (being the residue immediately prior to sale, plus the balancing charge on P) over the number of years still remaining to 25 years from first use (22 years 1 month).

(*d*)   P's basis period for 1996/97 is the two years to 31 May 1996 (see 2.1(E) above) so the balancing event on 1 May 1996 falls into 1996/97.

(B) Non-qualifying purposes and balancing adjustments [*CAA 1990, s 4(5)–(9)*]
A, B and C entered into partnership in 1974 and prepare accounts annually to 31 March. The partnership incurred £40,000 of capital expenditure in 1980 on the construction of a building which was brought into use as an industrial building on 1 April 1981. After three years of use for a qualifying industrial purpose, it was used for three years, from 1 April 1984 to 31 March 1987, for non-qualifying purposes after which the original qualifying activity was resumed until the building was destroyed by fire.

The fire occurred on 1 October 1995 with an insurance recovery of (i) £50,000 (ii) £35,000. The partnership's 1996/97 industrial buildings allowance position will be as follows.

1996/97 Balancing charge

(i)   *Proceeds exceed cost*

Actual allowances given	note (*a*)	£37,600
Balancing charge		£37,600
		£

(ii)   *Proceeds less than cost*

Net cost (£40,000 − £35,000)		5,000
Reduction $\dfrac{3y}{14y\ 6m}$	note (*b*)	(1,034)
Adjusted net cost		3,966
Allowances given	note (*a*)	37,600
Excess		£33,634
Balancing charge		£33,634

Notes

(*a*)   Allowances given in previous years are

	£
Initial allowance £40,000 × 50%	20,000
Writing-down allowances £40,000 × 4% × 11	17,600
	£37,600

Writing-down allowances would not have been given for the three years 1985/86 to 1987/88 as the building was not an industrial building at the end of the basis period for each of those years.

(*b*)   In example (ii), the net cost is reduced by the proportion which the period of non-qualifying use bears to the total period from first use to date of balancing event.

(C) Disregard of non-industrial part [*CAA 1990, s 18(4)(7)*]

In 1991, H, who prepares accounts annually to 31 May, incurred expenditure of £230,000 on the construction of a new factory. Of this amount, £60,000 related to the provision of office accommodation. H brought the factory into use for his trade in August 1991. Because of the expansion of his business, H requires additional storage and office accommodation and he incurs expenditure of £56,000 on the construction of an extension in September 1993. £9,000 of this cost relates to office accommodation. The extension is brought into use in November 1993.

The allowances available to H are

Year of assessment	Qualifying expenditure £	Residue brought forward £	Initial allowance (20%) £	Writing-down allowance (4%) £	Residue carried forward £
1993/94	170,000	—	—	6,800	163,200
1994/95	170,000	163,200	—	6,800	156,400
1995/96	170,000	156,400	—	6,800	149,600
	56,000	—	11,200	2,240	42,560
	60,000	—	—	2,400	57,600

Note

(*a*)   After completion of the extension, the non-industrial proportion of the building is under 25% (£69,000 out of £286,000) so that allowances are due on the full cost of the extension. Additional allowances are available for expenditure on the original office accommodation, but only in respect of the basis period of the change and subsequent basis periods.

(D) Buildings in enterprise zones [*CAA 1990, ss 1, 6, 10A, 10B, 17A, 21; F(No 2)A 1992, 13 Sch*]

(i)

In 1994, J, a builder, incurs expenditure of £400,000 on the construction of a building in a designated enterprise zone. The whole of the expenditure was incurred (or contracted for) within ten years of the site's first being included in the zone. In January 1995, he sells the building unused to K for £600,000 (excluding land). In February 1995, K lets the building to a trader who immediately brings it into use as a supermarket. K claims a reduced initial allowance of £50,000. In March 1997, he sells the building to L for £750,000 (excluding land).

IT 2.8 Capital Allowances

K's allowances are as follows

			£	Residue of expenditure £
1994/95	Qualifying expenditure			600,000
	Initial allowance (maximum 100%)		50,000	
	Writing-down allowance	25% of £600,000	150,000	
	Total IBA due		200,000	(200,000)
1995/96	Writing-down allowance		150,000	(150,000)
				250,000
1996/97	Writing-down allowance		—	—
	Sale proceeds			(750,000)
				£500,000
	Balancing charge (restricted to allowances given)			£350,000

Notes

(*a*) Allowances for buildings in enterprise zones are given for commercial buildings as well as industrial buildings.

(*b*) K's qualifying expenditure would normally be the lesser of cost of construction and the net price paid by him for the building. [*CAA 1990, s 10A(2)(b); F(No 2)A 1992, 13 Sch 2*]. However, on purchase from a builder, whose profit on sale is taxable as a trading profit, his qualifying expenditure is equal to the net price paid for the relevant interest (excluding the land). [*CAA 1990, s 10A(9); F(No 2)A 1992, 13 Sch 2*].

(*c*) K's allowances as a non-trader will be given by way of discharge or repayment of tax primarily against letting income from buildings qualifying for IBAs. [*CAA 1990, s 9(2)(3)(5)*]. For 1995/96 onwards, for income tax purposes only, allowances and balancing charges are treated as expenses and receipts of a Schedule A business. [*CAA 1990, s 9(1)–(1B); FA 1995, 6 Sch 29*]. K could have claimed a 100% initial allowance in 1994/95 if he had so wished.

(*d*) Providing the building continues to be used for a qualifying purpose, L can claim writing-down allowances over the remainder of the 25-year writing-down period — see (A) above. His qualifying expenditure is restricted to £600,000, i.e. the residue of expenditure (£250,000) plus the balancing charge on K.

(*e*) In this example, the first sale after the building was first used took place just over two years after the date of first use. If the sale had taken place within two years after first use, the balancing charge on K would have been computed in the same manner, but L could have claimed an initial allowance and 25% writing-down allowances as if he had bought the building unused. His qualifying expenditure would again have been restricted to £600,000, being the lesser of the price paid by him for the relevant interest in the building and that paid on the original purchase by K from the builder. These provisions apply where the date of first use falls after 15 December 1991. [*CAA 1990, s 10B; F(No 2)A 1992, 13 Sch 8, 15*].

(ii)

The facts are as in (i) above, except that, of the £400,000 construction expenditure actually incurred, only £360,000 is incurred (or contracted for) within ten years of the site's first being included in an enterprise zone, and the first sale occurred after the expiry of that ten-year period.

K's qualifying expenditure of £600,000 (arrived at as in (i) above) is divided into an enterprise zone element and a non-enterprise zone element. [*CAA 1990, s 10A(3)–(6); F(No 2)A 1992, 13 Sch 2*].

The enterprise zone element is $£600,000 \times \dfrac{360,000}{400,000} = \underline{£540,000}$

The non-enterprise zone element is $£600,000 - £540,000 = \underline{£60,000}$

The non-enterprise zone element does not qualify for enterprise zone allowances. [*CAA 1990, s 10A(7); F(No 2)A 1992, 13 Sch 2*]. (It could have qualified for normal IBAs if the building had been an industrial building.)

K's allowances are as follows

		£	Residue of expenditure £
1994/95	Qualifying expenditure (enterprise zone element)		540,000
	Initial allowance (maximum 100%)	50,000	
	Writing-down allowance (25% of £540,000)	135,000	
		185,000	(185,000)
1995/96	Writing-down allowance	135,000	(135,000)
			220,000
1996/97	Writing-down allowance	—	—
	Sale proceeds $£750,000 \times \dfrac{540,000}{600,000}$		(675,000)
			£455,000
	Balancing charge (restricted to allowances given)		£320,000

L's qualifying expenditure is £540,000, i.e. the residue of £220,000 plus the balancing charge of £320,000 on K.

Notes

(*a*)   *CAA 1990, s 10A* applies where the purchase price on a sale before first use becomes payable after 15 December 1991. [*F(No 2)A 1992, 13 Sch 14*].

(*b*)   If the sale to L had taken place within two years after first use (as in note (*e*) to (i) above), L's deemed expenditure of £600,000 would also have been divided into an enterprise zone element of £540,000 and a non-enterprise zone element of £60,000. [*CAA 1990, s 10B; F(No 2)A 1992, 13 Sch 8*].

(*c*)   The apportionment of sale proceeds in 1996/97 is considered to be a 'just apportionment' as required by *CAA 1990, s 21(3)*.

2.9   MACHINERY AND PLANT [*CAA 1990, Pt II; FA 1993, s 115, 13 Sch*]

Cross-reference. See also 23.3(B) SCHEDULE E.

(A) Writing-down allowances, motor cars, partial non-business use, acquisitions from connected persons and balancing adjustments

A has for some years been in business as a builder and demolition contractor. He normally makes up his accounts to 5 April, but makes up accounts for the two years to 5 April 1997 as the basis for the 1996/97 assessment. The accounts reveal the following additions and disposals.

	£
Additions	
Plant	
Dumper Truck	5,000
Excavator	32,000
Bulldozer	20,000
	£57,000
Fittings	
Office furniture	£2,000
Motor Vehicles	
Land Rover	6,000
Van	5,000
Car 1 (used by A)	12,200
Car 2 (no private use)	2,000
	£25,200

Disposals	Cost	Proceeds
	£	£
Excavator	32,000	30,000
Digger loader	15,000	4,000
Car (Audi)	5,200	4,200
Fittings	3,500	500
	£55,700	£38,700

The dumper truck was bought second-hand from Q, brother of A, but had not been used in a trade. The truck had originally cost Q £6,000, but its market value at sale was only £2,000.

The excavator was sold without having been brought into use.

The bulldozer and car 2 were both purchased from P, father of A and had originally cost P £25,000 and £3,500 respectively. Both assets had been used for trading purposes. In both cases the price paid by A was less than the market value.

The Audi sold and the new car 1 are both used for private motoring by A. Private use has always been 30%.

The capital allowances for 1996/97 are

	Pool	Car pool	Audi	Car 1	Total allowances
	25%	25%	\[Motor vehicles\]		
	£	£	£	£	£
WDV b/f (say)	7,500		3,900		
Additions					
Plant (excavator) note (*a*)	2,000				
Plant (dumper truck) note (*b*)	2,000				
Plant (bulldozer) note (*c*)	20,000				
Fittings	2,000				
Vehicles (Land Rover, van)	11,000				
Vehicles (cars) note (*d*)		2,000		12,200	
Disposals					
Plant (digger)	(4,000)				
Fittings	(500)				
Audi			(4,200)		
	40,000	2,000	(300)	12,200	
Allowances					
WDA note (*e*)	(10,000)	(500)		(3,000)	13,500
30% private use restriction (car 1)					(900)
WDV c/f	£30,000	£1,500		£9,200	

Total allowances £12,600

Balancing charge (Audi) £300 less 30% private use £(210)

Notes

(*a*) Writing-down allowances are available even though an asset is disposed of without being brought into use, always provided that the expenditure was incurred for the purposes of the trade and the appropriate notification is made under *FA 1994, s 118* (see note (*f*) below). Where disposal takes place in the same period as acquisition, the addition to the pool is effectively the excess of cost over disposal value. [*CAA 1990, ss 24(2), 25(1)*].

(*b*) Qualifying expenditure on the dumper truck is restricted to the lowest of
   (i)   open market value;
   (ii) capital expenditure incurred by the vendor (or, if lower, by a person connected with him);
   (iii) capital expenditure incurred by the purchaser.
   [*CAA 1990, ss 75, 76(2)*].

(*c*) Qualifying expenditure on the bulldozer is the lesser of A's actual expenditure and the disposal value brought into account in the vendor's computations. [*CAA 1990, s 75(1)*]. (The vendor's disposal value would have been open market value but for the fact that the purchaser is himself entitled to claim capital allowances on the acquisition. [*CAA 1990, s 26(1)(b)*].) A's qualifying expenditure is thus equal to his actual expenditure. The same applies to the purchase of Car 2.

(*d*) Car 1, by virtue of its costing over £12,000 is not pooled. [*CAA 1990, s 34(1)(2); F(No 2)A 1992, s 71(2)*]. Car 2 is separately pooled by virtue of *CAA 1990, s 41(1)(c)(2)*. See note (*c*) above as regards the amount of qualifying expenditure to be brought into account in respect of Car 2. The Audi was not pooled as it was used partly for non-trade purposes. [*CAA 1990, ss 41(6), 79(2)-(5)*].

(*e*)   The writing-down allowance on Car 1 is restricted to £3,000 before adjustment for private use. [*CAA 1990, s 34(3); F(No 2)A 1992, s 71(3)*].

(*f*)   In order to qualify for allowances, expenditure must be notified to the Inspector within two years after the end of the chargeable period (different rules apply for chargeable periods ended before 30 November 1993). In this example, the chargeable period is the tax year 1995/96 so the expenditure must be notified by 5 April 1998. If notification was delayed beyond that date, the expenditure could still qualify for writing-down allowances (but not, where applicable, first-year allowances) in a later chargeable period providing the item of machinery or plant in question still belongs to the trader at some time in that later chargeable period or in its basis period. [*FA 1994, s 118*].

(B) Reduced claim for writing-down allowances [*CAA 1990, s 24(3); FA 1990, 17 Sch 5(2), 19 Sch Pt V*]

Q, a 36 year old bachelor, married Miss P on 10 October 1996. Q has traded as a self-employed plumber for many years. His adjusted taxable profits for 1996/97 (the transitional year) are £13,300. During the basis period Q purchases plant and machinery for £35,600 which qualifies for capital allowances. Q has no other income for 1996/97 but makes a personal pension contribution of £880.

In order to make full use of Q's personal allowances for the year it will be necessary to restrict the claim to writing-down allowance. This may be achieved as follows:

	£	£
Schedule D, Case I profits (£13,300 − Capital allowances £7,984)		5,316
Relief for pension contribution	880	
Personal allowance	3,765	4,645
Taxable income		671
Tax payable: £671 @ 20%		134.20
Deduct Reduction for married couple's allowance		
£1,790 × $\frac{6}{12}$ @ 15%		134.25
Tax liability		Nil

Notes

(a) Had Q not restricted his claim for writing-down allowances, he would have lost the benefit of his married couple's allowance (subject to note (d) below).

(b) Following the restricted claim to writing-down allowances, a higher personal pension contribution could be made, i.e. £1,063 (20% of £5,316). This would, however, result in wasted personal reliefs. Q may therefore restrict his claim to capital allowances to a greater extent in order to relieve in full the premium he wishes to pay.

The optimum position would be as follows

	£
Profits	13,300
Less	
Writing-down allowances (restricted)	7,755
	5,545
Relief for pension contributions	
maximum £5,545 × 20%	(1,109)
Personal allowance	(3,765)
Taxable income	£671

(c) A person should claim only the allowances which he requires. A revised claim will normally be allowed where circumstances change, as in this example, after an assessment has been agreed (Revenue Statement of Practice SP A26).

(d) By restricting his capital allowances, Q leaves a greater written-down value to carry forward in his machinery and plant pool. Alternatively, he could have transferred unused married couple's allowance to his wife under *ICTA 1988, s 257BB*. As a further option, he and his wife could jointly elect that the whole allowance be transferred to her under *ICTA 1988, s 257BA*. See 11 MARRIED PERSONS.

(C) Short-life assets [*CAA 1990, ss 37, 38; FA 1993, 13 Sch 4*]
A, who prepares trading accounts to 30 June each year, buys and sells machines as follows

	Cost	Date of acquisition	Disposal proceeds	Date of disposal
Machine X	£20,000	30.4.94	£10,000	1.10.96
Machine Y	£25,000	1.9.93	£4,000	1.12.99

A elects under *CAA 1990, s 37* for both machines to be treated as short-life assets. His pool of qualifying expenditure brought forward at the beginning of 1995/96 is £80,000.

IT 2.9   Capital Allowances

A's capital allowances are as follows

	Pool £	Machine X £	Machine Y £	Allowances £
1995/96 (basis period 1.7.93–30.6.94)				
WDV b/f	80,000			
Additions		20,000	25,000	
FYA 40%			(10,000)	10,000
WDA 25%	(20,000)	(5,000)	—	25,000
	60,000	15,000	15,000	£35,000
1996/97 (basis period 1.7.94–30.6.96)				
WDA	(15,000)	(3,750)	(3,750)	£22,500
	45,000	11,250	11,250	
Period of account 1.7.96–30.6.97				
Disposal		(10,000)		
Balancing allowance		£1,250		1,250
WDA	(11,250)		(2,813)	14,063
				£15,313
	33,750		8,437	
Period of account 1.7.97–30.6.98				
WDA	(8,437)		(2,109)	£10,546
	25,313		6,328	
Period of account 1.7.98–30.6.99				
WDA	(6,328)		(1,582)	£7,910
	18,985		4,746	
Period of account 1.7.99–30.6.2000				
Transfer to pool	4,746		(4,746)	
	23,731		—	
Disposal	(4,000)			
	19,731			
WDA	(4,933)			£4,933
WDV c/f	£14,798			

Notes

(a)   Only machinery and plant which is not specified in *CAA 1990, s 38* is eligible to be treated as short-life assets. Note that items qualifying for first-year allowances under *CAA 1990, s 22(3B)*, introduced by *FA 1993, 115(2)*, *are* so eligible.

(b)   Where separate identification of short-life assets is impracticable, a form of pooling may be adopted (Revenue Statement of Practice SP 1/86).

(c)   The basis period for 1996/97 is extended, this being the transitional year for the changeover to the current year basis of assessment (see 2.1(E) above). For subsequent years, capital allowances are calculated by reference to periods of account — this applies immediately for businesses starting after 5 April 1994 (see 2.2 above).

(d)   The chargeable period related to the incurring of the expenditure on both machines in this example is the tax year 1995/96. The fourth anniversary of the end of that chargeable period is 5 April 2000. The balance of expenditure on Machine Y is thus transferred to the pool in the period of account ended 30 June 2000, this being the first chargeable period ending after 5 April 2000. [*CAA 1990, s 37(5)*].

IT 2.10 Capital Allowances

2.10 **LEASING OF MACHINERY AND PLANT** [*CAA 1990, ss 22(6A), 39–50; FA 1993, s 115(3), 13 Sch 5–11*]

(A) Separate pooling [*CAA 1990, s 41*]
L has a leasing business preparing accounts annually to 31 May. In the year to 31 May 1994, his expenditure included the following

		£
(i)	Machine 1, leased to M Ltd, a UK resident company for the purposes of its trade	20,000
(ii)	Machine 2, leased to N, a UK resident individual, for private use	8,000
(iii)	Machine 3, leased to P, a non-UK resident, for his overseas trade	16,000
(iv)	Fixtures and fittings for use in L's business	2,000
(v)	Motor car used by L entirely for business	6,000

All the above expenditure was incurred before 1 November 1993. At 6 April 1995, there is a written-down value of £40,000 brought forward in L's machinery and plant pool.

The leasing in (iii) above is neither 'short-term leasing' (as defined) nor the leasing of a ship, aircraft or transport container to be used for a 'qualifying purpose' (as defined).

L's capital allowances for 1995/96, assuming no capital expenditure for the year to 31 May 1994 other than as listed above, are as follows

	Expenditure qualifying for FYAs £	Main Pool £	Car Pool £	Pool for overseas leasing £	Total allowances £
WDV b/f		40,000			
Additions					
(i) (ii) (iv)	30,000				
(iii) (v)			6,000	16,000	
FYA 40%	(12,000)				12,000
WDA 25%		(10,000)	(1,500)		11,500
WDA 10%				(1,600)	1,600
Transfer to pool	(18,000)	18,000			
WDV c/f		£48,000	£4,500	£14,400	
Total allowances					£25,100

Notes
(*a*) Machines 1 and 2 go into the general pool for machinery and plant, as do the fixtures and fittings. Machine 3 goes into a separate pool under *CAA 1990, s 41* by virtue of its falling within *Sec 42* (assets leased outside the UK). The car also goes into a separate pool by virtue of *Sec 41(1)(c)*.

(*b*) The writing-down allowance for Machine 3 is restricted to 10% under *Sec 42(2)*. A first-year allowance is not available for Machine 3, by virtue of *CAA 1990, s 22(6A)*.

(B) Recovery of excess relief [*CAA 1990, s 46; FA 1993, 13 Sch 9*]

M, who has a 30 September accounting date, incurred expenditure of £16,000 in March 1992 on a machine leased to Q Ltd, a company trading in the UK. In May 1995, Q Ltd terminated the lease and M then leased the machine, with effect from June 1995, to P Ltd, a company resident in Panama, for the purposes of its trade there. The leasing was not 'permitted leasing'.

A balancing charge arises in 1996/97 (basis period two years to 30.9.96) as follows

Actual allowances

	£	Total allowances £
Expenditure (year ended 30.9.92)	16,000	
WDA 25% for 1993/94	4,000	4,000
	12,000	
WDA 25% for 1994/95	3,000	3,000
	9,000	
WDA 25% for 1995/96	2,250	2,250
	6,750	
WDA 25% for 1996/97	1,688	1,688
Residue of expenditure	£5,062	
Total allowances claimed		£10,938

Notional allowances

		£	Total allowances £
Expenditure (year ended 30.9.92)		16,000	
WDA 10% for 1993/94	note (*a*)	1,600	1,600
		14,400	
WDA 10% for 1994/95		1,440	1,440
		12,960	
WDA 10% for 1995/96		1,296	1,296
		11,664	
WDA 10% for 1996/97		1,166	1,166
		£10,498	
Notional allowances			£5,502

Balancing charge, equal to the excess of actual allowances over notional allowances, for 1996/97   note (*b*)   £5,436

M will then be deemed to have incurred qualifying expenditure of £10,498 (equal to the residue of expenditure plus the balancing charge for the year ending 30.9.97), i.e. the chargeable period following the basis period in which the change of use arose, and will then be entitled to writing-down allowances of 10% for that and subsequent chargeable periods. The expenditure will constitute, or form part of, a separate pool for the purposes of *CAA 1990, s 41*.

IT 2.11 Capital Allowances

Notes

(a)   Notional writing-down allowances are restricted to 10% by virtue of *CAA 1990, s 42*, notwithstanding the fact that the machine was used for a qualifying purpose up to May 1995. It is used as mentioned in *Sec 42(1)* at some time in the requisite period (as defined in *Sec 40*).

(b)   In practice, the machine would originally have been included in the general pool for machinery and plant. For the purpose of calculating the balancing charge, it is assumed to have been the only item of machinery and plant qualifying for writing-down allowances. In 1996/97, a disposal value equal to the residue of expenditure (£5,062) must be deducted from the pool.

(c)   If expenditure originally qualified for a first-year allowance under *CAA 1990, s 22(3B)*, this also enters into the calculation of excess relief and is thus effectively clawed back. [*CAA 1990, s 46(8); FA 1993, 13 Sch 9*].

2.11   **MINERAL EXTRACTION** [*CAA 1990, Pt IV*]

X has for some years operated a mining business with two mineral sources, G and S. Accounts are prepared to 30 September. On 31 December 1996 the mineral deposits and mineworks at G are sold at market value to Z for £80,000 and £175,000 respectively. A new source, P, is purchased on 30 April 1997 for £170,000 (including land with an undeveloped market value of £70,000) and the following expenditure incurred before the end of the accounting period ended 30 September 1997.

	£
Machinery and plant	40,000
Construction of administration office	25,000
Construction of mining works which are likely to have little value when mining ceases	50,000
Staff hostel	35,000
Winning access to the deposits	150,000
	£300,000

During the year to 30 September 1997, X incurred expenditure of £20,000 in seeking planning permission to mine a further plot of land, Source Q. Permission was refused.

Residue of expenditure brought forward (based on accounts to 30 September 1993)		
Mineral exploration and access	– Source G	170,000
	– Source S	200,000
Mineral assets	– Source G	95,250
	– Source S	72,000

The mineral extraction allowances due for the year ending 30.9.97 are

Source G	£	£
Mineral exploration and access		
WDV b/f	170,000	
Proceeds	175,000	
Balancing charge	£5,000	(5,000)

1–50

Mineral assets		
WDV b/f	95,250	
Proceeds	80,000	
Balancing allowance	£15,250	15,250

Source S		
Mineral exploration and access		
WDV b/f	200,000	
WDA 25%	(50,000)	50,000
WDV c/f	£150,000	

Mineral assets		
WDV b/f	72,000	
WDA 10%	(7,200)	7,200
WDV c/f	£64,800	

Source P		
Mineral exploration and access		
Expenditure	150,000	
WDA 25%	(37,500)	37,500
WDA c/f	£112,500	

Mineral assets		
Expenditure	100,000	
WDV 10%	(10,000)	10,000
WDV c/f	£90,000	

Mining works		
Expenditure	50,000	
WDA 25%	(12,500)	12,500
WDV c/f	£37,500	

Source Q		
Mineral exploration and access		
Expenditure	20,000	
WDA 25%	(5,000)	5,000
WDV c/f	£15,000	
Total allowances (net of charges)		£132,450

Notes

(a)   Expenditure on the acquisition of mineral assets, which includes expenditure on the acquisition of, or of rights in or over, both the site of a source and of mineral deposits, qualifies for a 10% writing-down allowance. The other types of expenditure illustrated in this example qualify for a 25% writing-down allowance. [*CAA 1990, ss 98(5), 105(1)(7)*].

(b)   Allowances are not due on either the office or staff hostel although the hostel may qualify for industrial buildings allowances under *CAA 1990, s 18(1)(4)(5)*. Machinery and plant qualify for allowances under *CAA 1990, Pt II* rather than for mineral extraction allowances.

(c)   Abortive expenditure on seeking planning permission is qualifying expenditure by virtue of *CAA 1990, s 105(6)* as if it were expenditure on mineral exploration and access.

(d)   The undeveloped market value of land is excluded from qualifying expenditure and from disposal receipts. [*CAA 1990, ss 110, 112*].

2.12   **PATENT RIGHTS** [*ICTA 1988, ss 520–523, 528, 533(1)–(6)*]
P, who prepares accounts to 31 December, acquires three new patent rights for trading purposes

	Date	Term	Cost
Patent 1	20.2.87	20 years	£6,800
Patent 2	19.4.94	15 years	£4,500
Patent 3	5.10.95	5 years	£8,000

On 1.10.89 P sold his rights under patent 1 for £5,000 and on 1.12.96 he sold part of the rights under patent 2 for £2,000.

The allowances for each patent are

Patent 1	£
Expenditure	6,800
1988/89 (basis period — y/e 31.12.87)	
WDA $\frac{1}{17} \times$ £6,800	(400)
	6,400
1989/90	
WDA $\frac{1}{17} \times$ £6,800	(400)
	6,000
1990/91 (basis period — y/e 31.12.89)	
Disposal proceeds	(5,000)
Balancing allowance	£1,000

Patents 2 and 3	Pool	WDA
1995/96 (basis period — y/e 31.12.94)	£	£
Expenditure (patent 2)	4,500	
WDA 25%	(1,125)	£1,125
	3,375	
1996/97 (basis period — 2 years to 31.12.96)		
Expenditure (patent 3)	8,000	
Disposal proceeds (patent 2)	(2,000)	
	9,375	
WDA 25%	(2,344)	£2,344
WDV c/f	£7,031	

Note

(a)   The system of giving allowances was changed for expenditure incurred after 31 March 1986. The spreading of expenditure over a maximum of 17 years was replaced by a 25% writing-down allowance on a reducing balance basis.

2.13   **SCIENTIFIC RESEARCH** [*CAA 1990, ss 136–139*]

C is in business manufacturing and selling cosmetics, and he prepares accounts annually to 30 June. For the purposes of this trade, he built a new laboratory adjacent to his existing premises, incurring the following expenditure

		£
April 1992	Laboratory building	50,000
June 1992	Technical equipment	3,000
March 1993	Technical equipment	4,000
June 1993	Plant	2,500
	Extension to existing premises comprising 50% further labo-	
August 1995	ratory area and 50% sales offices.	30,000

In July 1993 a small fire destroyed an item of equipment originally costing £2,000 in June 1992; insurance recoveries totalled £3,000. In March 1994, the plant costing £2,500 was sold for £1,800.

The allowances due are

1993/94 (basis year ended 30.6.92)	£
Laboratory building	50,000
Technical equipment	3,000
Plant note (*a*)	700
	£53,700

1994/95 (basis year ended 30.6.93)	
Technical equipment	£4,000

1995/96 (basis year ended 30.6.94)
No allowance due, but balancing adjustment of £2,000 arises (note (*b*)).

1996/97 (transitional year)	
Extension note (*d*)	£15,000

Notes

(*a*)   As the plant was sold prior to 1994/95, the year in which an allowance would have been obtained, no allowance is due for that year. Instead, an allowance (£700) based on the excess of the cost (£2,500) over proceeds (£1,800) is made for the chargeable period, i.e. the tax year, in which the sale took place.

(*b*)   The destruction of the equipment in the year to 30 June 1994 results in a balancing adjustment limited to the allowance originally given. The deemed trading receipt is assessable in 1995/96.

(*c*)   A capital gain of £1,000 (£3,000 – £2,000) will also have arisen on the destruction of equipment and insurance recovery. However, the gain will be exempt from tax under the chattels exemption. [*TCGA 1992, s 262*].

(*d*)   Capital expenditure which is only partly for scientific research is apportioned on a just basis to arrive at the amount qualifying for allowances. [*CAA 1990, s 137(4)*].

3   Deceased Estates

[ICTA 1988, ss 695–702; FA 1993, 6 Sch 11; FA 1995, ss 75, 76, 18 Sch]

3.1   ABSOLUTE INTEREST

C died on 5 July 1994 leaving his estate of £400,000 divisible equally between his three children. The income arising and administration expenses paid in the administration period, which ends on 25 January 1997, are as follows

	Period to 5.4.95		Year to 5.4.96		Period to 25.1.97	
	£	£	£	£	£	£
Dividends received (net)		15,000		8,850		3,000
Administration expenses chargeable to income		(1,500)		(750)		(300)
		13,500		8,100		2,700
Other income (gross)	10,000		3,200		1,000	
Basic rate tax thereon payable by executors	(2,500)		(800)		(240)	
		7,500		2,400		760
Net residuary income		£21,000		£10,500		£3,460
Each child's share		£7,000		£3,500		£1,153

Dates and amounts of payments to each child are as follows

	Payment £	Allocated to tax years (see note (a))
30.4.95	5,000	1995/96
16.10.95	3,000	1995/96
21.6.96	2,000	1996/97
22.1.97	1,000	1996/97
30.7.97	653	1996/97

Each child's income for tax purposes is as follows

	1994/95	1995/96	1996/97
Share of basic rate income	Nil	3,300.00*	253.33
Basic rate tax	Nil	1,100.00	80.00
Gross basic rate income	Nil	£4,400.00	£333.33

*   £(7,500 + 2,400) × $\frac{1}{3}$ = £3,300 (which is less than £8,000 distributed up to 5.4.96).

	1994/95	1995/96	1996/97
Share of lower rate income	Nil	4,700.00**	3,400.00
Lower rate tax	Nil	1,175.00	850.00
Gross lower rate income	Nil	£5,875.00	£4,250.00

**   £8,000 (amount distributed up to 5.4.96) less £3,300 allocated to basic rate income (see note (b)).

Notes

(a)   For distributions after 5 April 1995 and to the extent that his aggregate income entitlement is not exceeded, a beneficiary is taxed on the amount distributed to him as income in each tax year spanned by the administration period. Any outstanding balance on completion of the administration period after 5 April 1995 is deemed to have been distributed immediately before completion. [*ICTA 1988, s 696; FA 1995, 18 Sch 3*]. Previously, a beneficiary's taxable income was established by reference to the tax years in which the income actually arose in the estate (see the 1994/95 and earlier editions of this book for an illustration).

(b)   Payments to a beneficiary of an estate are deemed to be made out of his share of income bearing tax at the basic rate in priority to his share of income bearing tax at the lower rate. [*ICTA 1988, s 701(3A); FA 1993, 6 Sch 11(3)*]. Therefore, administration expenses chargeable to income are effectively relieved primarily against lower rate income.

(c)   Each beneficiary would receive tax certificates (Forms R185E) showing the gross amount of his entitlement and the tax paid by the executors for each of the three tax years. Where the estate has income (i.e. savings income before 1996/97 dividend income) bearing tax at the lower rate the tax certificate should show such income separately from income which has borne tax at the basic rate.

(d)   In the hands of a beneficiary, estate income which has borne tax at the lower rate is treated as income within *ICTA 1988, s 1*. [*ICTA 1988, s 698A; FA 1993, 6 Sch 11(2)*]. Therefore, the beneficiary will have a further liability only to the extent that the income exceeds the basic rate limit but will be able to reclaim tax at only 20% to the extent that the income is covered by personal reliefs.

3.2   **LIMITED INTEREST**

Mrs D died on 5 January 1994 leaving her whole estate with a life interest to her husband and then the capital to her children on his death. The administration of the estate was completed on 7 February 1996. Mr D received payments on account of income of £1,200 on 30 September 1994, £2,500 on 31 December 1995, £1,050 on 7 February 1996 and £300 on 31 May 1996.

The actual income and deductible expenses of the estate were as follows

	1993/94 (from 6.1.94)	1994/95	1995/96 (to 7.2.96)
	£	£	£
Dividends received (net)	750	2,400	2,000
Other income (gross)	400	600	200
Basic rate tax thereon	(100)	(150)	(50)
Expenses	(150)	(450)	(400)
Net residuary income	£900	£2,400	£1,750

IT 3.2   Deceased Estates

D's income from the estate for tax purposes is calculated as follows

	1993/94	1994/95		1995/96	
		Basic rate income	*Lower rate income*	*Basic rate income*	*Lower rate income*
	£	£	£	£	£
Gross income	Nil	1,000	562	200	4,625
Basic rate tax		(250)	112	(50)	
Lower rate tax					(925)
Net income	Nil	£750*	£450*	£150**	£3,700**

*   The payments to the beneficiary in each year must be allocated between (i) income bearing tax at the basic rate and (ii) income bearing tax at the lower rate, (i) taking priority over (ii). [*ICTA 1988, s 701(3A); FA 1993, 6 Sch 11(3)*]. Total basic rate income for 1993/94 and 1994/95 is £750 (£400 + £600 − £100 − £150), so £750 of the £1,200 payment in 1994/95 is deemed to have been made out of basic rate income.

**   Total basic rate income for the three tax years is £900 (£400 + £600 + £200 − £100 − £150 − £50) of which £750 was paid out in 1994/95 leaving £150 of the 1995/96 payments to be allocated to basic rate income. The balance of the 1995/96 payments (£2,500 + £1,050 + £300 − £150 = £3,700) is deemed to have been made out of lower rate income.

Notes

(*a*)   The £300 paid to D in May 1996 is deemed for tax purposes to have been paid in 1995/96, being the tax year in which the administration period ends. This rule applies where the administration is completed after 5 April 1995. [*ICTA 1988, s 695(3); FA 1995, 18 Sch 2*]. Where the administration period ended on or before that date, the aggregate of all income payments made or due to a beneficiary was treated as having accrued evenly throughout the administration period and allocated to tax years on that basis (see the 1994/95 and earlier editions for an illustration).

(*b*)   See also notes (*b*) to (*d*) to 3.1 above.

(*c*)   For 1995/96, D is also likely to have taxable income from his life interest in his wife's settlement. This will be income covering the period 8 February 1996 to 5 April 1996. It does not enter into the above calculations, but is dealt with as in 24.3(A) SETTLEMENTS.

4 Double Tax Relief

[*ICTA 1988, ss 788–816*]

4.1 A UK resident has the following income, allowances and UK tax liability for the year 1996/97 before double tax relief

	£
Earned income	
UK directorship	16,000
USA directorship (foreign tax £1,500)	6,000
Dutch partnership (foreign tax £3,750)	7,500
	29,500
Unearned income	
UK dividends and tax credits	5,000
Foreign dividends (foreign tax £300)	2,000
Total income	36,500
Deduct	
Personal allowance	3,765
Taxable income	£32,735
Tax on £3,900 at lower rate (20%)	780.00
£21,600 at basic rate (24%)	5,184.00
£7,235 at higher rate (40%)	2,894.00
	8,858.00
Deduct Married couple's allowance £1,790 @ 15%	268.50
Tax borne before double tax relief	£8,589.50

The maximum double tax relief is obtained by progressively taking relief under *ICTA 1988, s 796(2)* for each foreign source with the source with the highest rate of foreign tax being eliminated first.

	£	£	£
Taxable income from all sources	32,735	32,735	32,735
Deduct foreign income			
Dutch partnership	(7,500)	(7,500)	(7,500)
USA directorship	—	(6,000)	(6,000)
Dividends	—	—	(2,000)
	£25,235	£19,235	£17,235
Tax thereon (see note (*a*))	5,351.90	3,911.90	3,511.90
Tax on income before eliminating foreign source under review	8,589.50	5,351.90	3,911.90
Tax attributable to that source (A)	£3,237.60	£1,440.00	£400.00
Foreign tax suffered (B)	£3,750.00	£1,500.00	£300.00
Double tax relief i.e. lesser of (A) and (B)	£3,237.60	£1,440.00	£300.00

IT 4.1 Double Tax Relief

The UK income tax borne after credit for double tax relief is

As computed before double tax relief	£8,589.50
Deduct Double tax relief	4,937.60
	£3,611.90

Notes

(a) The recalculation of tax after each element of foreign income has been deducted is as follows

	£	£	£
Non-dividend income	22,000	16,000	16,000
Deduct Personal allowance	3,765	3,765	3,765
	£18,235	£12,235	£12,235
Tax at lower rate (20%) on	3,900	3,900	3,900
Tax at basic rate (24%) on	14,335	8,335	8,335
	18,235	12,235	12,235
Tax at lower rate (20%) on	7,000	7,000	5,000
	£24,550	19,235	17,235
Tax at lower rate (20%)	780.00	780.00	780.00
Tax at basic rate (24%)	3,440.40	2,000.40	2,000.40
Tax at lower rate (20%)	1,400.00	1,400.00	1,000.00
	5,620.40	4,180.40	3,780.40
Married couple's allowance: £1,790 @ 15%	(268.50)	(268.50)	(268.50)
	£5,351.90	£3,911.90	£3,511.90

(b) The UK tax borne is partly satisfied by tax credits of £1,000 on UK dividends. This, together with any UK tax paid under PAYE will be deducted from the tax borne of £3,611.90 in arriving at the net liability/repayment.

(c) The income tax reduction (for married couple's allowance in this example) is given in priority to double tax relief. [*ICTA 1988, ss 256(3)(c)(i), 796(1); FA 1994, s 77(1), 8 Sch 12*].

5   Enterprise Investment Scheme

[*ICTA 1988, ss 289–312; TCGA 1992, ss 150A, 150B; FA 1994, s 137, 15 Sch; FA 1995, ss 66, 67, 13 Sch*]

5.1   CONDITIONS FOR AND FORM OF RELIEF

(A)

Mr Jones is a married man with a salary of £30,000 per annum and no other income. In 1995/96 he subscribes for ordinary shares in two unquoted companies issuing shares under the enterprise investment scheme (EIS).

A Ltd was formed by some people in Mr Jones' neighbourhood to publish a local newspaper. 200,000 ordinary £1 shares were issued at par in August 1995 and the company started trading in September 1995. Mr Jones subscribed for 16,000 of the shares. Mr Jones becomes a director of A Ltd in September 1995, receiving director's fees of £5,000 per annum (£2,500 in 1995/96), a level of remuneration which is considered reasonable for services rendered by him to the company in his capacity as a director.

B Ltd, which is controlled by an old friend of Mr Jones, has acquired the rights to manufacture in the UK a new type of industrial cleaning solvent and requires additional finance. Mr Jones subscribed for 8,000 ordinary £1 shares at a premium of £1.50 per share in October 1995. The issue increases the company's issued share capital to 25,000 ordinary £1 shares.

Mr Jones will obtain tax relief in 1995/96 as follows

Amount eligible for relief

	£
A Ltd notes (*a*) and (*b*)	16,000
B Ltd note (*c*)	Nil
Total (being less than the maximum of £100,000)	£16,000

Relief given   note (*d*)

	£
Salary	30,000
Director's remuneration (A Ltd)	2,500
Total income	32,500
Deduct Personal allowance	3,525
Taxable income	£28,975

Tax payable:	
3,200 @ 20%	640.00
21,100 @ 25%	5,275.00
4,675 @ 40%	1,870.00
	7,785.00
Deduct EIS relief £16,000 @ 20%	3,200.00
	4,585.00
Deduct Married couple's allowance £1,720 @ 15%	258.00
Net tax liability	£4,327.00

IT 5.1 Enterprise Investment Scheme

Notes

(a) Mr Jones is entitled to relief on the full amount of his investment in A Ltd regardless of the amount of relief claimed by other investors.

(b) The fact that Mr Jones becomes a paid director of A Ltd *after* an issue to him of eligible shares does not prevent his qualifying for relief in respect of those shares providing his remuneration as a director is reasonable and he is not otherwise connected with the company. [*ICTA 1988, ss 291(1)(2), 291A; FA 1994, 15 Sch 5*].

(c) Mr Jones is not entitled to relief against his income for his investment of £20,000 in B Ltd. As a result of the share issue he owns more than 30% of the issued ordinary share capital (8,000 out of 25,000 shares) and is therefore regarded as connected with the company and denied relief. [*ICTA 1988, ss 291(1)(2), 291B(1); FA 1994, 15 Sch 5*].

(d) EIS relief is given at the lower rate of tax only (currently 20%) and by way of an income tax reduction. The relief cannot exceed what would otherwise be the income tax liability (no restriction being necessary in this example). For this purpose, the income tax liability is before taking into account married couple's allowance (and certain other specified items). [*ICTA 1988, s 289A(1)(2)(5); FA 1994, 15 Sch 2*].

(e) It is assumed that Mr Jones makes no claim under *ICTA 1988, s 289A(3)* to carry back relief to 1994/95. See note (a) to (B) below. If he did so, an overriding limit of £40,000 applies to the amount eligible for relief in 1994/95 under the enterprise investment scheme and the old business expansion scheme. [*FA 1994, 15 Sch 3(3)(4)*].

(B)

In 1996/97 Mr Jones subscribes for shares in three more unquoted companies trading in the UK and issuing shares under the EIS.

C Ltd is a local company engaged in the manufacture of car components. It issues a further 200,000 ordinary £1 shares at £1.80 per share in June 1996 and Mr Jones subscribes for 5,000 shares costing £9,000, increasing his stake in the company to 2%. He had originally held 9,000 shares, acquired by purchase at arm's length in May 1994 for £10,800.

D Ltd has been trading as a hotel and restaurant company for several years and requires an injection of capital to finance a new restaurant. Mr Jones and three other unconnected individuals each subscribe for 12,500 ordinary £1 shares at par in November 1996. The balance of 80,000 shares are held by Mr Jones' sister and niece.

E Ltd is an electronics company controlled by two cousins of Mr Jones. The company is seeking £1 million extra capital to enable it to expand and take advantage of new computer technology. Mr Jones subscribes for 85,000 ordinary £1 shares at par in December 1996.

If he makes the optimum claims Mr Jones will obtain tax relief as follows

1995/96

C Ltd   note (*a*)   £4,500 @ 20% =   £900

1996/97
Amount eligible for relief

	£
C Ltd (£9,000 − £4,500 carried back)	4,500
D Ltd	12,500
E Ltd	85,000
Total amount subscribed	£102,000

But amount eligible for relief restricted to subscriptions of   £100,000

Relief given

	£
Salary	30,000
Director's remuneration	5,000
Total income	35,000
Deduct Personal allowance	3,765
Taxable income	£31,235

Tax payable:	
3,900 @ 20%	780.00
21,600 @ 24%	5,184.00
5,735 @ 40%	2,294.00
	8,258.00

Deduct EIS relief:
   £100,000 @ 20% = £20,000, but
   restricted to   8,258.00

Net tax liability   Nil

Attribution of relief to shares   note (*b*)

	£
C Ltd shares $\dfrac{4,500}{102,000} \times £8,258$	364
D Ltd shares $\dfrac{12,500}{102,000} \times £8,258$	1,012
E Ltd shares $\dfrac{85,000}{102,000} \times £8,258$	6,882
	£8,258

IT 5.2 Enterprise Investment Scheme

Notes

(a) Since the C Ltd shares were issued before 6 October 1996, Mr Jones may elect to carry back up to half the amount subscribed, subject to an overriding maximum of £15,000, to the preceding tax year. The relief will be given in addition to that previously claimed for 1995/96 (see (A) above). If Mr Jones had previously claimed relief on say £98,000 in 1995/96 the amount carried back would be restricted to £2,000 as relief in any one year may not be given on subscriptions of more than £100,000. [*ICTA 1988, ss 289A(3)(4), 290(2); FA 1994, 15 Sch 2, 3(1)*].

(b) Relief is restricted in this example by (i) the £100,000 maximum (see (a) above) and (ii) an insufficiency in Mr Jones' tax liability. The relief attributable to each issue of shares (which will be relevant in the event of a disposal of the shares or withdrawal of relief — see 5.2 below) is found by apportioning the income tax reduction by reference to the amounts subscribed for each issue. (For this purpose, half of the C Ltd shares are regarded as having been separately issued in the previous year.) The relief so attributed to each issue is then apportioned equally between all the shares comprised in that issue. [*ICTA 1988, s 289B; FA 1994, 15 Sch 2*].

(c) The unused married couple's allowance may be transferred to Mr Jones' wife under *ICTA 1988, s 257BB* (see 11.1(B) MARRIED PERSONS).

5.2 WITHDRAWAL OF RELIEF/GAINS AND LOSSES ON EIS SHARES

(A)

In June 1997, Mr Jones, the investor in 5.1 above, sells 12,000 ordinary £1 shares in C Ltd (see 5.1(B) above), in an arm's length transaction, for £30,000.

The position is as follows

Income Tax

1995/96	£
Relief attributable to 2,500 shares treated as issued in 1995/96: 2,500 shares at £1.80 per share = £4,500 @ 20%	900
Consideration received $\left(\dfrac{2,500}{12,000} \times £30,000 \right)$ = £6,250 @ 20%	1,250
Excess of consideration over relief	£350
Relief withdrawn — Schedule D, Case VI assessment	£900

1996/97		£
Relief attributable to 500 shares		
500/2,500 × £364		73

Consideration received

$$\left(\frac{500}{12,000} \times £30,000\right) = £1,250 \times 73/(900 @ 20\%) = £507 @ 20\% \qquad 101$$

		£
Excess of consideration over relief		£28
Relief withdrawn — Schedule D, Case VI assessment		£73

Capital Gains Tax

1996/97	£	£
Disposal proceeds (12,000 shares)		30,000
Cost: 9,000 shares acquired May 1994	10,800	
3,000 shares acquired June 1996	5,400	16,200
Unindexed gain		13,800
Indexation allowance:		
£10,800 × (say) 0.15 (May 1994 to June 1997)	1,620	
£5,400 × (say) 0.05 (June 1996 to June 1997)	270	
		1,890
Chargeable gain		£11,910

Notes

(a)   For both income tax and capital gains tax purposes, a disposal is matched with acquisitions on a first in/first out basis. [*ICTA 1988, s 299(6); TCGA 1992, s 150A(4); FA 1994, 15 Sch 12, 30*]. Thus, the 12,000 shares sold in June 1997 are matched with 9,000 shares purchased in May 1994 and with 3,000 of the 5,000 EIS shares subscribed for in June 1996. For income tax purposes, 2,500 of the 5,000 EIS shares are treated as having been issued in 1995/96 (by virtue of Mr Jones' carry-back claim — see note (a) to 5.1(B) above). [*ICTA 1988, s 289B(5); FA 1994, 15 Sch 2*]. Therefore, those shares are treated as disposed of in priority to those on which relief was given in 1996/97.

(b)   EIS relief is withdrawn if shares are disposed of before the end of the requisite five-year period. In this example, relief attributable to the shares sold is fully withdrawn as consideration received, reduced as illustrated, exceeds the relief attributable. See (B) below for where the reverse applies. The consideration is reduced where the relief attributable (X) is less than tax at the lower rate on the amount subscribed (Y), and is so reduced by applying the fraction X/Y. [*ICTA 1988, s 299; FA 1994, 15 Sch 12*].

(c)   Relief is withdrawn by means of a Schedule D, Case VI assessment for the year(s) in which relief was given. [*ICTA 1988, s 307(1); FA 1994, 15 Sch 22(a)*].

(d)   The capital gain on the disposal is fully chargeable as the shares are not held for the requisite five-year period.

IT 5.2 Enterprise Investment Scheme

(B)

In December 1997 Mr Jones disposes of his 12,500 ordinary £1 shares in D Ltd (see 5.1(B) above), in an arm's length transaction, for £10,000.

The position is as follows

Income Tax

1996/97	£
Relief attributable to shares sold	1,012

$$\text{Consideration received } £10,000 \times \frac{1,012}{£12,500 \times 20\%} = £4,048 \text{ @ } 20\% \qquad 810$$

Excess of relief over consideration	£202
Relief withdrawn — Schedule D, Case VI assessment	£810

Capital Gains Tax

1997/98

	£	£
Disposal proceeds (December 1997)		10,000
Cost (November 1996)	12,500	
Less Relief attributable to shares:		
£1,012 − £810	202	
		12,298
Allowable loss		£2,298

Notes

(a) See notes (b) and (c) to (A) above.

(b) The EIS relief withdrawn is limited to the consideration received, reduced as illustrated, at the lower rate of tax for the year for which relief was given. If the disposal had been made otherwise than by way of a bargain made at arm's length, the full relief would have been withdrawn. [*ICTA 1988, s 299; FA 1994, 15 Sch 12*].

(c) An allowable loss may arise for capital gains tax purposes on a disposal of EIS shares, whether or not the disposal occurs within the requisite five-year period. In computing such a loss, the allowable cost is reduced by EIS relief attributable to the shares (and not withdrawn). [*TCGA 1992, s 150A(1); FA 1994, 15 Sch 30*].

(d) A loss, as computed for capital gains tax purposes, may be relieved against income on a claim under *ICTA 1988, s 574* (losses on unquoted shares — see 10.5 LOSSES). [*ICTA 1988, s 305A; FA 1994, 15 Sch 20*].

(C)

(i) In September 1997, Mr Jones receives from E Ltd (one of the companies in 5.1(B) above) an asset with a market value of £3,500 but for which he pays the company only £500.

(ii) In March 2001, Mr Jones sells his 85,000 shares in E Ltd for their market value of £140,000.

Income Tax

(i) The difference of £3,000 between the market value of the asset and the consideration given for it represents value received by the investor from the company within the relevant period (within *ICTA 1988, s 312(1A)(a)*). The value received (reduced in like manner as is mentioned in note (*b*) to (A) above) is compared to the relief attributable to the shares.

1996/97

	£
Relief attributable to 85,000 E Ltd shares	6,882

$$\text{Value received } £3,000 \times \frac{6,882}{£85,000 \times 20\%} = £1,214 \text{ @ } 20\% \qquad 243$$

Excess of relief over value received	£6,639
Relief withdrawn — Schedule D, Case VI assessment	£243

[*ICTA 1988, ss 299(4), 300, 307(1); FA 1994, 15 Sch 12, 14, 22(a)*].

(ii) As Mr Jones holds the shares for the requisite five-year period, there is no withdrawal of relief on disposal.

Capital Gains Tax

(ii) As Mr Jones holds the shares for the requisite five-year period, and EIS relief has not been fully withdrawn, any gain on disposal is generally exempt from capital gains tax (although this does not prevent an allowable loss from arising). [*TCGA 1992, s 150A(2)(2A); FA 1994, 15 Sch 30; FA 1995, 13 Sch 2(2)*]. A proportion of the gain could become chargeable under *Sec 150A(3)* where the relief given was less than tax at the lower rate on the amount subscribed but this does not apply where, as in the case of Mr Jones, the relief fell to be restricted due to his having insufficient income tax liability to cover it. [*TCGA 1992, s 150A(3); FA 1994, 15 Sch 30; FA 1995, 13 Sch 2(3)*]. A proportion of the gain does, however, become chargeable where value is received after 28 November 1994 leading to a part-withdrawal of relief. [*TCGA 1992, s 150B; FA 1995, 13 Sch 3*].

2000/2001

	£
Disposal proceeds (March 2001)	140,000
Cost (December 1995)	85,000
Unindexed gain	55,000
Indexation allowance £85,000 × (say) 25%	21,250
Indexed gain	£33,750

$$\text{Chargeable gain} = \text{indexed gain} \times \frac{\text{Relief withdrawn}}{\text{Relief attributable (before reduction)}}$$

$$\textit{viz. } £33,750 \times \frac{243}{6,882} \qquad\qquad £1,192$$

Exempt gain £(33,750 − 1,192)	£32,558

5.3   RESTRICTION OF RELIEF BY REFERENCE TO PERMITTED MAXIMUM

[ICTA 1988, s 290A; FA 1988, s 51; FA 1994, 15 Sch 4]

G Ltd, an unquoted company engaged in confectionery manufacture, decides to expand, and issues, on 1 June 1996, 525,000 £1 ordinary shares at £2 per share under the EIS. There have been no previous issues in the preceding six months. 50,000 of the new shares are subscribed for other than by individuals and the remaining 475,000 by individuals qualifying for EIS relief. Mr Smith subscribes for 40,000 shares and duly claims and receives relief of £80,000 at 20% = £16,000. On 1 June 1997, G Ltd sets up a new subsidiary which enters into a joint venture with an unconnected company for the purpose of developing a proposed new brand of low calorie chocolate.

Restriction of relief

As a result of the joint venture within the relevant period of three years from date of issue, the relief available as a result of the 1 June 1997 issue is restricted as follows.

	£
Total amount raised	1,050,000
Deduct: amounts not eligible for relief	100,000
	950,000

Permitted maximum (originally £1,000,000) but now

$$\frac{£1,000,000}{1+1} \; \text{note } (c) = \qquad 500,000$$

Excess over permitted maximum	£450,000

	£
Relief originally claimed by Mr Smith £80,000 @ 20%	16,000

Revised relief available $\dfrac{500,000}{950,000} \times £80,000$ @ 20% =

$$8,421$$

Notes

(a)   Any amounts raised from eligible shares issued in the period of six months ending with the date of the current issue or, if longer, the period from the preceding 6 April to the date of the current issue would fall to be aggregated with the amount raised from the current issue in deciding if and to what extent the permitted maximum of £1 million is exceeded. *[ICTA 1988, s 290A(1)(2); FA 1994, 15 Sch 4(1)(a)].*

(b)   Shares issued other than to individuals qualifying for relief are disregarded. *[ICTA 1988, s 290A(3)(a)].*

(c)   The denominator of the fraction is 1 plus the number of companies involved in the venture apart from the company in question or any of its subsidiaries. *[ICTA 1988, s 290A(4); FA 1994, 15 Sch 4(1)(b)].*

(d)   The available relief is apportioned on a pro rata basis between qualifying individuals. *[ICTA 1988, s 290A(5)].*

6   Herd Basis

[ICTA 1988, s 97, 5 Sch; Revenue pamphlet IR9 (1984)]

6.1   A farmer acquires a dairy herd and elects for the herd basis to apply. The movements in the herd and the tax treatment are as follows

Year 1	No	Value £
Mature		
Bought @ £150	70	10,500
Bought in calf @ £180		
(Market value of calf £35)	5	900
Immature		
Bought @ £75	15	1,125

Herd Account		£
70	Friesians	10,500
5	Friesians in calf (5 × £(180 − 35))	725
75	Closing balance	£11,225

Trading Account	£
5 Calves (5 × £35)	175
15 Immature Friesians	1,125
Debit to profit and loss account	£1,300

Year 2	No	Value £
Mature		
Bought @ £185	15	2,775
Sold @ £200 note (*a*)	10	2,000
Died	3	—
Immature		
Born	52	—
Matured @ 60% of market value of £200 note (*a*)	12	1,440

Herd Account			£
75	Opening balance		11,225
	Increase in herd		
15	Purchases	2,775	
12	Transferred from trading stock	1,440	
27		4,215	
	(13) Replacement cost £4,215 × 13/27	2,029	
14	Non-replacement animals cost		2,186
89	Closing balance		£13,411

IT 6.1 Herd Basis

Trading Account   £
Sale of 10 mature cows replaced   (2,000)
Transfer to herd — 14 animals   (2,186)
Cost of 13 mature cows purchased to replace those
     sold/deceased ($\frac{13}{15} \times$ £2,775)   2,405

Net credit to profit and loss account   note (*b*)   £(1,781)

Year 3

	No	Value £
Mature		
Jerseys bought @ £250	70	17,500
Friesians slaughtered @ £175	52	9,100
Immature		
Friesians born	20	—
Matured		
Friesians @ 60% of market value of £190 note (*a*)	15	1,710

	Herd Account		£
89	Opening balance		13,411
	Increase in herd		
18	Jerseys		4,500
	52 Improvement Jerseys @	£250	
	less Market value of Friesians (say)	185	
	52 @ /	65	3,380
	Transfer from trading stock		
15	Friesians		1,710
122	Closing balance		£23,001

Trading Account	£
Compensation	(9,100)
Transfer to herd	(1,710)
Purchase of replacements note (*c*) (52 × £185)	9,620
Net credit to profit and loss account	£(1,190)

Year 4
The farmer ceases dairy farming and sells his whole herd.

	No	Value £
Mature		
Jersey sold @ £320	70	22,400
Friesians sold @ £200	52	10,400
Immature		
Friesians sold @ £100	65	6,500

Herd Account	£
Opening balance	23,001
52 Friesians	
70 Jerseys	
(122) Sales	(32,800)
– Profit on sale note (*d*)	£(9,799)

Trading Account	£
Sale of 65 immature Friesians	(6,500)
Credit to profit and loss account	£(6,500)

Notes

(*a*)   The use of 60% of market value was originally by agreement between the National Farmers' Union and the Revenue (see now Revenue Business Economic Note 19: Farming — Stock Valuation for Income Tax purposes, at paragraph 7.2). Alternatively, the actual cost of breeding or purchase and rearing could be used.

(*b*)   As the cost of rearing the 12 cows to maturity will already have been debited to the profit and loss account, no additional entry is required to reflect that cost. Due to the fact that the animals were in opening stock at valuation and will not be in closing stock, the trading account will in effect be debited with that valuation.

(*c*)   The cost of the replacements is restricted to the cost of replacing like with like.

(*d*)   Provided these animals are not replaced by a herd of the same type within five years the proceeds will be tax-free.

7   Interest on Unpaid Tax

[*TMA 1970, ss 69, 86, 88, 88A, 90, 91; FA 1989, ss 156, 158–161, 178, 179; SI 1989 No 1297*]

7.1   A received three estimated assessments dated 13.11.95

	Year of assessment	Tax charged £
Schedule A	1995/96	4,000
Taxed income (higher rates)	1994/95	12,750
Schedule D, Case I	1995/96	7,000

Each assessment was appealed against and events thereafter were as follows

Schedule A assessment
A applied to postpone £1,600 of tax which HMIT agreed to on 17.12.95.
He paid the balance of £2,400 on 23.2.96.
The appeal was determined on 12.8.96 and a revised assessment showing tax payable of £3,450 was issued on 15.8.96.
A paid the remaining balance of £1,050 on 3.10.96.

The dates of consequence are

(i)	Due date of payment had there been no appeal	1 January 1996
(ii)	Revised due date of payment of amount not postponed and date from which interest runs	16 January 1996 (30 days after HMIT's agreement)
(iii)	Due date of determined balance (£1,050)	14 Sept 1996 (30 days after date of revised assessment)
(iv)	Date from which interest will run on determined balance	1 July 1996 (the reckonable date)

The interest charge will be calculated on

£2,400 for 38 days (16.1.96 to 23.2.96)
£1,050 for 94 days (1.7.96 to 3.10.96)

Taxed income assessment
A applied to postpone £5,000 of tax which HMIT agreed to on 28.12.95.
He paid the balance of £7,750 on 23.2.96.
The appeal was determined on 11.3.96 and a revised assessment showing tax payable of £8,500 was issued on 11.3.96.
A paid the remaining balance of £750 on 26.4.96.

The dates of consequence are

(i)	Due date of payment had there been no appeal	13 December 1995 (30 days after issue of assessment)
(ii)	Revised due date of payment of amount not postponed and date from which interest runs	27 January 1996 (30 days after HMIT's agreement)

(iii)   Due date of determined balance (£750)   10 April 1996 (30 days
                                                 after date of revised
                                                 assessment)
(iv)   Date from which interest will run on determined   10 April 1996 (the
        balance   reckonable date)

The interest charge will be calculated on

£7,750 for 27 days (27.1.96 to 23.2.96)
  £750 for 16 days (10.4.96 to 26.4.96)

Schedule D assessment
A applied to postpone £1,500 of tax which HMIT agreed to on 28.12.95, leaving £5,500
payable in two instalments, the first of which was paid on 23.2.96.
The second instalment was paid on 1.7.96.
The appeal was determined on 23.8.96 and a revised assessment showing tax payable of
£7,800 was issued on 26.8.96.
A paid the remaining balance of £2,300 on 23.9.96.

The dates of consequence are
 (i)   Due dates of payment had there been no appeal   One half on 1 Jan 1996
                                                        One half on 1 July 1996
 (ii)   Revised due dates of payment of amount not   One half (£2,750) on
        postponed and dates from which interest will run   27 January 1996 (30 days
                                                        after HMIT's agreement).
                                                        One half on 1 July 1996
(iii)   Due date of determined balance (£2,300)   25 September 1996
                                                        (30 days after date of
                                                        revised assessment)
(iv)   Date from which interest will run on determined   1 July 1996
        balance

The interest charge will be calculated on

£2,750 for 27 days (27.1.96 to 23.2.96)
£2,300 for 84 days (1.7.96 to 23.9.96)

Notes
(a)   On determination of the appeal, the tax payable is £800 greater than that charged
       by the original assessment. However, interest will accrue as if the tax had been
       charged by the original assessment. [*TMA 1970, s 86(3)(3A)*; *FA 1989, s
       156(1)*].

(b)   Interest is also chargeable under *TMA 1970, s 86* on Class 4 national insurance
       contributions (not illustrated here).

IT 7.2　Interest on Unpaid Tax

7.2　C omitted to include details of untaxed interest on his income tax returns. His returns were subsequently discovered to be incomplete and the following omitted income was agreed, in May 1995, to be assessable on C with tax due as shown

	Income £	Tax £
1991/92	2,500	1,000
1992/93	4,800	1,920
1993/94	4,775	1,910

Because of C's failure to make a full return, he is liable to interest under *TMA 1970, s 88* and a penalty under *TMA 1970, s 95* (see notes (*a*)–(*d*)). Interest due from the normal due date for payment (1 January in the year of assessment) to 1.6.95, the expected date for payment, is calculated using the following rates

9.25% p.a. from 6.10.91 to 5.11.92
7.75% p.a. from 6.11.92 to 5.12.92
7% p.a. from 6.12.92 to 5.3.93
6.25% p.a. from 6.3.93 to 5.1.94
5.5% p.a. from 6.1.94 to 5.10.94
6.25% p.a. from 6.10.94 to 5.3.95
7% p.a. from 6.3.95

Interest due is thus

	£
1991/92 Interest on £1,000 from 1.1.92	238
1992/93 Interest on £1,920 from 1.1.93	285
1993/94 Interest on £1,910 from 1.1.94	162
	£685

Notes

(*a*)　Interest under *TMA 1970, s 88* arises in respect of tax lost through any error in a return or failure to make a return. The interest charge is not dependent on fraud or neglect. [*TMA 1970, s 88(1); FA 1989, s 159(2)*].

(*b*)　If the possibility of a *Sec 88* interest charge for failure to make a return is to be avoided, the Revenue should be notified of income from a new source by 31 October following the end of the tax year in which it arose. (Revenue Statement of Practice SP 6/89 and Revenue Tax Bulletin August 1992 pages 25–28).

(*c*)　For errors or omissions made fraudulently or negligently, the maximum penalty, in addition to interest, is the amount of tax lost. [*TMA 1970, s 95; FA 1989, s 163*].

(*d*)　The Inland Revenue will mitigate the penalty depending on factors such as disclosure, co-operation and the reason for the omission.

(*e*)　The Inland Revenue publish Interest Factor tables for use as ready reckoners in calculating interest on tax, and these are updated as rates change.

8   Interest Payable

[*ICTA 1988, ss 353–358, 366–379; FA 1988, ss 42–44; FA 1993, ss 55–58; FA 1994, ss 80, 81, 9 Sch; FA 1995, s 42*]

8.1   RELIEF FOR INTEREST PAID—ONLY OR MAIN RESIDENCE

(A) General
An individual pays interest on the following loans

(i) A bank mortgage of £18,000 on his main residence (R) which he acquired in 1982. He moved to house (S) on 6.9.95 (see (iii) below), eventually selling house (R) on 5.1.96 when he repaid the mortgage. Interest on the mortgage had been at 8% since 1.4.95. The loan was within the MIRAS scheme in 1995/96.

(ii) A building society mortgage of £8,000 on a bungalow which he bought in 1986 for occupation, rent-free, by his widowed mother. It was within the MIRAS scheme in 1995/96 and 1996/97. On 5.10.96 the bungalow was sold, following the mother's death shortly beforehand, and the mortgage repaid. Interest paid amounted to £408 (net), £136 (net) and £340 (net) for the periods 6.4.95 to 5.1.96, 6.1.96 to 5.4.96 and 6.4.96 to 5.10.96 respectively.

(iii) On 6.9.95 he took out a bridging loan of £44,000 for the purchase of house (S), his new main residence. The loan was repaid on 6.1.96. Interest was payable gross and amounted to £1,400 in all.

(iv) On 6.1.96 he took out a £26,000 mortgage with the same building society as in (ii) above in part repayment of the bridging loan in (iii) above. It was within the MIRAS scheme in 1995/96 and 1996/97 with net interest paid amounting to £374 in 1995/96, £748 for the period 6.4.96 to 5.10.96 and £935 for the period 6.10.96 to 5.4.97, and gross interest of £80 and £171 paid for the first two of those periods respectively.

(v) An advance from a bank of £5,000 to finance an extension to house S. This loan carried interest at 9%, payable monthly in arrears, from 1.4.96, the date it was taken out, and was not brought within the MIRAS scheme.

Relief for the interest paid will be as follows for the years 1995/96 and 1996/97

		Interest
1995/96	£	£
6.4.95 – 5.1.96		
Overall limit on property loans	30,000	
Interest paid under deduction of tax		
House (R)	(18,000)	918
Mother's home	(8,000)	408
Limit not utilised	£4,000	
		£1,326
Gross interest paid on loans within MIRAS		
(£1,326 + tax £234)		£1,560
15% relief given at source		£234

IT 8.1   Interest Payable

		Interest
	£	£
Bridging loan interest		
Overall limit as above	30,000	
Mother's home	8,000	
Amount of bridging loan qualifying for relief	£22,000	note (*d*)

Allowable interest £1,400 × $\dfrac{22,000}{44,000}$ £700

Maximum tax relief due at 15% £105

6.1.96 – 5.4.96

Overall limit on property loans	30,000	
Interest paid under deduction of tax		
Mother's home	8,000	£136
Amount of mortgage qualifying for relief	£22,000	
Interest payable on £22,000 for three months		£374
Gross interest paid on loans within MIRAS (£136 + £374 + total tax £90)		£600
15% relief given at source		£90

1995/96 summary

Interest relieved by deduction at source £1,560 + £600		£2,160
15% tax relief given at source (no further relief due) £234 + £90		£324
Bridging loan interest relieved		£700
Maximum 15% tax relief due		£105
Interest unrelieved on £4,000 for three months		£80
Bridging loan interest unrelieved (£1,400 – £700)		£700

1996/97
6.4.96 – 5.10.96

Overall limit on property loans	30,000	
Interest paid under deduction of tax		
Mother's home	8,000	£340
Amount of mortgage qualifying for relief	£22,000	
Interest payable on £22,000 for six months		£748
Gross interest paid on loans within MIRAS (£340 + £748 + total tax £192)		£1,280
15% relief given at source		£192

	£	Interest £
6.10.96 – 5.4.97		
Overall limit on property loans	30,000	
Interest paid under deduction of tax		
House (S)	26,000	£935
Limit not utilised	£4,000	
Gross interest paid on loan within MIRAS (£935 + tax £165)		£1,100
15% relief given at source		£165
1996/97 summary		
Interest relieved by deduction at source £1,280 + £1,100		£2,380
15% tax relief given at source (no further relief due) £192 + £165		£357
Interest unrelieved on £4,000 for six months		171
Interest unrelieved on £5,000 at 9%		450
Total interest unrelieved		£621

Notes

(a) MIRAS applies automatically, up to the tax relief limit, to all loans made after 5 April 1987 by the same qualifying lender. [*ICTA 1988, s 373*]. Thus, in this example, only £22,000 of the £26,000 mortgage is within the MIRAS scheme up to 5 October 1996 with interest on the remaining £4,000 payable gross.

(b) Interest paid after 5 April 1988 on home improvements loans made after that date does not qualify for tax relief (and, consequently, cannot be within the MIRAS scheme). [*ICTA 1988, s 355(2A)–(2C); FA 1988, s 43*]. Interest on such loans made before 6 April 1988 continues to be deductible but subject to the £30,000 overall maximum.

(c) Interest on the bungalow occupied by the widowed mother continues to qualify for relief after 5 April 1988 (notwithstanding the abolition of such relief by *FA 1988, s 44*) as the loan was made before 6 April 1988 *and* the loan qualified immediately before that date by reason of the property being used as the dependent relative's main residence.

(d) Interest relief continues to be available in respect of house (R) for up to twelve months (or such longer period as the Revenue may allow) after it ceases to be the borrower's main residence, providing it remains his intention to dispose of it. For the purpose of applying the £30,000 limit to other loans, including the bridging loan, the aforementioned loan is disregarded as long as it continues to qualify for relief. [*ICTA 1988, s 355(1A)(1B)(2); FA 1993, s 57(1)(2)(5)*].

(e) Relief for mortgage interest payments is restricted to 20% from 6 April 1994 and 15% from 6 April 1995. Such payments are not deductible in computing total income. Where relief is given under MIRAS no further relief is available, but nor

IT 8.1 Interest Payable

is relief clawed back if the borrower has insufficient income to cover the interest. [*ICTA 1988, s 369; FA 1994, s 81(3)(4)(6)*]. For the method of giving relief on mortgage interest paid gross, see (B) below.

(B) Method of giving relief for mortgage interest paid gross after 5 April 1994
[*ICTA 1988, s 353(1)(1A)(1F)-(1H); FA 1994, s 81(1)(2)(6)*]
Scott is a married man with the following details for 1996/97: Schedule D, Case II £15,924, bank deposit interest (net) £640, dividend income (net) £960, investment made under enterprise investment scheme (EIS) £500, interest paid gross on a £40,000 endowment mortgage taken out some years ago for purchase of main residence £3,600, payment under charitable deed of covenant (net) £45. Scott's wife has no income.

Scott's tax liability for 1995/96 is computed as follows

	£
Schedule D, Case II	15,585
Bank deposit interest (gross)	800
Dividends plus tax credits	1,200
	17,585
Deduct Charges (covenanted donation) (gross)	60
Total income	17,525
Deduct Personal allowance	3,765
Taxable income	£13,760

Tax payable;	
3,900 @ 20%	780.00
7,860 @ 24%	1,886.40
2,000 @ 20%	400.00
13,760	3,066.40
Deduct EIS relief £500 @ 20%	100.00
	2,996.40

Deduct Mortgage interest relief:

$$£3,600 \times \frac{30,000}{40,000} = 2,700 \text{ @ } 15\%$$

	405.00
	2,561.40
Deduct Married couple's allowance:	
£1,790 @ 15%	268.50
	2,292.90
Add Basic rate tax retained on covenanted donation	15.00
Total tax liability	2,307.90
Deduct Tax suffered at source on bank deposit interest	(160.00)
Tax credits on dividends	(240.00)
Net tax liability	£1,907.90

ICTA 1988, s 380 loss reief of £12,000 is available for 1996/97 which Scott claims accordingly.

His tax liabilty is revised as follows

	£
Total income as above	17,525
Deduct loss relief	12,000
Revised total income	5,525
Deduct Personal allowance	3,765
Taxable income	£1,760

Tax payable:	
1,760 @ 20%	352.00
Deduct EIS relief £500 @ 20%	100.00
	252.00
Deduct Mortgage interest relief:	
£2,700 @ 15% = 405.00 but restricted to	252.00
	Nil
Add Basic rate tax retained on covenanted donation	15.00
Total tax liability	15.00
Deduct Tax suffered at source on bank deposit interest	(160.00)
Tax credits on dividends	(240.00)
Net tax refund due	£(385.00)

Notes

(*a*)   Relief for mortgage interest paid gross on a home loan is restricted to 20% for 1994/95 and 15% for 1995/96 and subsequent years and is given by way of an income tax reduction. The reduction is restricted to the amount required to reduce the liability to nil. This example illustrates the correct order of the various deductions and additions made in arriving at the net tax liability/repayment. [*ICTA 1988, ss 289A(5), 353(1)(1A)(1F)–(1H); FA 1994, s 81(1)(2)(6), 15 Sch 2*].

(*b*)   Some types of loan interest relief continue to be given by way of deduction against total income. [*ICTA 1988, s 353(1B); FA 1994, s 81(1)(2)(6)*].

(*c*)   If his wife had been in receipt of taxable income, Scott could have transferred to her the unused married couple's allowance in the second computation above (see 11.1(B) MARRIED PERSONS). The couple could also have elected to allocate the mortgage interest relief between them in such a way as to achieve the optimum tax position (see (E) below).

IT 8.1 Interest Payable

(C) Residence basis [*ICTA 1988, ss 356A, 356C, 356D; FA 1988, s 42; FA 1994, 9 Sch 7(1), 17 Sch 3; FA 1995, s 42*]

On 1 April 1996, Mr Romeo and Miss Juliet took out a joint mortgage for £65,000 for the purchase of a London flat to be used as their main residence. Gross interest paid in 1996/97 amounts to £5,850.

Interest relief for 1996/97

Mr Romeo

Amount on which interest is payable	£32,500
Sharer's limit — £30,000 (qualifying maximum) ÷ 2 =	£15,000
Interest paid	£2,925

Relief restricted to $£2,925 \times \dfrac{15,000}{32,500} =$ £1,350

Miss Juliet

Identical calculation — relief restricted to £1,350

Notes

(*a*) In the case of a joint loan, the total amount thereof is divided by the number of parties thereto in arriving at the amount on which each pays qualifying interest. [*ICTA 1988, s 356D(8); FA 1988, s 42*].

(*b*) The residence basis, whereby the qualifying maximum (£30,000) applies to a residence rather than to a borrower, applies to payments of qualifying interest made after 31 July 1988 with the exception of interest on certain loans made, or treated as made, before 1 August 1988. [*ICTA 1988, s 356C; FA 1988, s 42*].

(D) Residence basis — adjustment of sharer's limits

Three friends, A, B and C, decide to pool their resources and buy a house to be shared as their main residence. Each contributes his own savings and obtains a mortgage to fund the balance of his one-third share of the purchase price. The mortgages are all taken out in May 1996 and the amounts thereof, and interest paid thereon for 1996/97, are as follows

	Mortgage £	Interest payable (gross) £
A	7,000	560
B	14,000	1,120
C	16,000	1,280

Each has a sharer's limit of £10,000 (£30,000 ÷ 3). As A's limit exceeds the amount on which he pays interest, the excess is divided between B and C each of whose limits falls short of the amount on which he pays interest. B and C have shortfalls of £4,000 and £6,000 respectively, a total shortfall of £10,000, so A's excess of £3,000 is divided between them as follows

$B - \frac{4}{10} \times £3,000 = £1,200$ (revised sharer's limit £11,200)
$C - \frac{6}{10} \times £3,000 = £1,800$ (revised sharer's limit £11,800)

A's sharer's limit is reduced to £7,000.

Interest relief for 1996/97 is then calculated as follows

$A - \dfrac{7,000}{7,000} \times £560 =$ £560

$$B - \frac{11,200}{14,000} \times £1,120 = \qquad\qquad £896$$

$$C - \frac{11,800}{16,000} \times £1,280 = \qquad\qquad £944$$

(E) Married couples [*ICTA 1988, s 356B; FA 1988, 3 Sch 14*]
Mr and Mrs Lloyd, a married couple living together, have a joint mortgage of £50,000 which is outside MIRAS and on which interest of £4,250 is paid in 1996/97. They have total income of £24,400 and £2,800 respectively and are entitled to no other reliefs apart from their personal allowances and married couple's allowance. Neither spouse has any dividend income.

(i) No election under *ICTA 1988, s 356B(1)*

	Mr Lloyd £	Mrs Lloyd £
Total income	24,400	2,800
Deduct Personal allowance	3,765	2,800*
Taxable income	£20,635	Nil

* Restricted

Tax payable

3,900 @ 20%	780.00
16,735 @ 24%	4,016.40
	4,796.40

Deduct Mortgage interest relief:

$$£2,125 \times \frac{15,000}{25,000} \text{ @ } 15\% \qquad\qquad 191.25$$

	4,605.15

Deduct Married couple's allowance

£1,790 @ 15%	268.50
Total tax liability	£4,336.65

(ii) Election under ICTA 1988, *s 356B(1)*

Mr and Mrs Lloyd jointly elect that the whole of the available mortgage interest relief be allocated to Mr Lloyd.

	Mr Lloyd £	Mrs Lloyd £
Total income	24,400	2,800
Deduct Personal allowance	3,765	2,800*
Taxable income	£20,635	Nil

* Restricted

IT 8.1 Interest Payable

Tax payable

3,900 @ 20%	780.00
16,735 @ 24%	4,016.40
	4,796.40

Deduct Mortgage interest relief:

$$£4,250 \times \frac{30,000}{50,000} \text{ @ } 15\%$$

	382.50
	4,413.90

Deduct Married couple's allowance
£1,790 @ 15%   268.50

Total tax liability   £4,145.40

Tax saving with election   £191.25

Notes

(a) Under *ICTA 1988, s 356B*, husband and wife may jointly elect to allocate interest (and the sharer's limits) between them in whatever proportions they choose. This applies even where the mortgage is in the name of, and the interest is paid by, only one spouse. In the absence of an election, interest on a joint loan is divided equally.

(b) As a result of the restricted rate of tax relief for mortgage interest paid after 5 April 1994, the election under *Sec 356B* is now of limited application. It will be of benefit principally where the mortgage is outside MIRAS and one spouse has insufficient tax liability to fully utilise his or her share of the relief. If, in this example, the loan had been within MIRAS, the couple would have had the benefit of £382.50 deducted at source whether or not the election were made.

(F) Interest added to capital [*ICTA 1988, s 357*]
A, B, C and D all have loans which were used to purchase their main residences. The following are the relevant figures

	Original loan outstanding throughout 1996/97 £	Interest added to capital at 31.3.96 £	Interest paid in 1996/97 £
A	30,000	1,000	2,480
B	30,000	1,010	2,481
C	29,500	1,000	2,440
D	33,000	1,000	2,720

In 1996/97 tax relief for loan interest paid will be given as follows

A $\dfrac{31,000}{31,000} \times £2,480$ £2,480

B $\dfrac{30,000}{31,010} \times £2,481$ £2,400

$$C \quad \frac{30,500}{30,500} \times £2,440 \qquad\qquad \underline{£2,440}$$

$$D \quad \frac{30,000}{34,000} \times £2,720 \qquad\qquad \underline{£2,400}$$

Notes

(a)   In determining whether the £30,000 limit has been exceeded, up to £1,000 of interest which has been added to capital is to be ignored. [*ICTA 1988, s 357(6)*].

(b)   B obtains relief for interest paid on only £30,000 of the loan because the loan, when interest is added to capital, exceeds £30,000 and the interest so added exceeds £1,000.

(c)   C obtains relief on the full interest paid (and therefore obtains greater relief than B who paid more interest).

(d)   D also only obtains relief for interest on borrowings of £30,000. Although interest added to capital was only £1,000, his original loan already exceeded £30,000 and the capitalised interest does not have to be taken into account to determine whether the £30,000 limit is exceeded.

(G) Substitution of security [*ICTA 1988, ss 357A–357C; FA 1993, s 56; FA 1995, s 42*]
James has outstanding the following loans (all with the same lender).

	£
House purchase (main residence)	80,000
Home improvement loan 1 (made before 6 April 1988)	20,000
Home improvement loan 2 (made in 1991)	3,000

In October 1996, James arranges to sell his home for £90,000 and to buy a new home for £95,000. The lender agrees to substitute the new property as security for the three existing loans and to make a further advance of £5,000 to cover the difference between the proceeds of the old property and the cost of the new. The new arrangements all take effect from 6 October 1996.

Interest rates charged by the lender throughout 1996/97 were 9% on both the original house purchase loan and the new advance and 10% on both home improvement loans.

The interest qualifying for tax relief for 1996/97 is calculated as follows

6.4.96–5.10.96 (six months)

	£
£80,000 × 9% × $\frac{6}{12}$	3,600
£20,000 × 10% × $\frac{6}{12}$	1,000
Total interest on qualifying loans	£4,600

$$\text{Allowable interest} = £4,600 \times \frac{30,000}{100,000} = \qquad \underline{£1,380}$$

IT 8.1 Interest Payable

6.10.96–5.4.97 (six months)

The existing loans, restricted as below but disregarding home improvement loan 2 which is a non-qualifying loan, are regarded as having been made on 6.10.96 for the purchase of the new property.

The existing loans qualifying for relief are restricted to the lesser of

(i) the amount of the qualifying loans outstanding (i.e. £100,000), and

(ii) the purchase price of the new property (£95,000) *less* the loan actually used in purchasing the new property (£5,000) (i.e. £90,000).

The total loans outstanding (disregarding home improvement loan 2) are £105,000. Of this amount, £90,000 qualifies as above and the new advance of £5,000 qualifies under normal principles. Therefore, £95,000 of the total loans is a qualifying loan and the balance of £10,000 is not.

Allowable interest is calculated as follows

					£
85,000	$\times$ 9% $\times \frac{6}{12}$	= 3,825 $\times$ 95/105	=		3,461
20,000	$\times$ 10% $\times \frac{6}{12}$	= 1,000 $\times$ 95/105	=		905
£105,000	total interest	£4,825	qualifying interest		£4,366

Allowable interest = £4,366 $\times \dfrac{30,000}{95,000}$ = £1,379

Total allowable interest 1996/97 £(1,380 + 1,379) £2,759

Notes

(a) *ICTA 1988, ss 357A–357C* (introduced by *FA 1993, s 56*) have effect where a security substitution takes effect after 15 March 1993 in connection with a purchase of a main residence after that date. [*Sec 357A(1)*].

(b) Where two or more qualifying loans are resecured on the new property, they are treated as made at the time of the security substitution. [*Sec 357A(5)*]. This brings into play the rules for simultaneous loans in applying the £30,000 maximum. [*ICTA 1988, s 357(3)(b)*].

(c) If a non-qualifying loan, for example a post-5 April 1988 home improvements loan, is resecured on the new property, it is disregarded for the purposes of the calculations under *Sec 357A* illustrated in this example. [*Sec 357C(4)*].

8.2   RELIEF FOR INTEREST PAID — PROPERTY LET AT A COMMERCIAL RENT

[*ICTA 1988, s 355(1)(b)(4); FA 1994, 9 Sch 4; FA 1995, s 42*]

Mr Abel purchased a cottage for letting purposes on 1 December 1992 and took out a loan of £15,000 at a fixed interest rate of 11% payable monthly in advance.

From 1.12.92 to 5.5.93	the property is redecorated.
From 6.5.93 to 30.11.93	it is let commercially.
From 1.12.93 to 5.4.94	it is vacant but available for letting.
From 6.4.94 to 5.3.95	it is occupied rent-free by friends.
From 6.3.95 to 5.10.95	it is let commercially and sold to the tenants at the end of that period.

On 5 October 1996 Mr Abel buys another cottage for which he took out a loan of £20,000 at a fixed interest rate of 7% per annum. He immediately lets the property and draws up accounts to 5 April each year in respect of the letting income.

1992/93

There is no letting income and the relief for interest paid of £687 is carried forward to the following year.

1993/94

Relief is due against letting income for the interest paid of £1,650 during the year and £812 brought forward.

1994/95

6.4.94 to 5.3.95

The property is not available for letting and no relief is due for the interest paid.

6.3.95 to 5.4.95

As for 1995/96 (see below).

1995/96

The property is not available for letting throughout a 52-week qualifying period and no relief is due for the interest paid, despite the fact that the property was let for more than 26 weeks. If the disposal date had been deferred until 6 March 1996 and the property either let, available for letting or under repair between 6 October 1995 and 6 March 1996, the interest paid would have been deductible providing there was sufficient letting income to cover it.

1996/97

6.10.96 to 5.4.97

Interest payable of £700 is treated as a deduction against Schedule A profits for the year ended 5 April 1996.

Note

(*a*)   The above rules no longer generally apply for 1995/96 and subsequent years, interest being deductible instead as an expense in arriving at the profits of a Schedule A business, providing it is incurred wholly and exclusively for the purposes of the business. The above rules do, however, apply for 1995/96 where income from the property in question continues to be taxed under the old Schedule A or Schedule D, Case VI rules due to its ceasing in that year. [*FA 1995, s 42*].

9   Life Assurance Policies

9.1   **LIFE ASSURANCE RELIEF** [*ICTA 1988, ss 266, 274*]
Life assurance premiums totalling £2,100 (net) are paid in 1996/97 by a married woman on pre-14 March 1984 qualifying life policies in respect of her own life and that of her husband. Her income amounts to £11,700 and she pays mortgage interest of £1,853 net (equivalent to £2,180 gross) on a loan to purchase her main residence.

Calculation of limit of admissible premiums

Total income	£11,700
Limit is greater of $\frac{1}{6}$ thereof (£1,950) and £1,500	£1,950
Gross premiums paid — £2,100 × $\dfrac{100}{87.5}$	£2,400
Income tax relief on payments made £2,400 × 12½%	300
Admissible premium relief £1,950 × 12½%	244
Income tax relief clawed back	£56

Note
(a)   For 1994/95 and subsequent years, home loan interest is not a deduction in arriving at total income. [*ICTA 1988, ss 353(1)(1A), 369(3); FA 1994, s 81(1)(2)(4)(6)*].

9.2   **LIFE ASSURANCE GAINS AND NON-QUALIFYING POLICIES** [*ICTA 1988, ss 539–552*]

(A) Top-slicing relief — single chargeable event
A single policyholder realises, in 1996/97, a gain of £2,600 on a non-qualifying policy which she surrenders after 2½ years. Her other income for 1996/97 comprises earned income of £25,800 and dividends plus tax credits amounting to £2,425.

The tax chargeable on the gain is calculated as follows

	Normal basis £	Top-slicing relief claim £
Policy gain	2,600	1,300
Earnings	25,800	25,800
Dividends	2,425	2,425
	30,825	29,525
Personal allowance	3,765	3,765
	£27,060	£25,760

Tax applicable to policy gain
Higher rate
£1,560 at 40%   624.00   —

£260 at 40%   —   104.00

                                                 624.00   104.00
Deduct
Basic rate
£1,560 at 24%   374.40   —
£260 at 24%   —   62.40

                                                             £41.60

Appropriate multiple 2 × £41.60   £83.20

Tax chargeable lower of   £249.60 and £83.20

Tax payable is therefore as follows

3,900 @ 20%	780.00
18,135 @ 24%	4,352.40
2,425 @ 20%	485.00
1,040 @ 24%	249.60
25,500	
1,560 @ 40%	624.00
£27,060	
	6,491.00

Deduct: Tax credits on dividends (£2,425 @ 20%)   485.00
Basic rate of tax on policy gain (£2,600 @ 24%)   624.00
Top-slicing relief (£249.60 – £83.20)   166.40   1,275.40

Tax liability (subject to PAYE deductions)   £5,215.60

Notes

(*a*)   Tax is calculated by treating the policy gain as the top slice of income (notwithstanding *ICTA 1988, s 207A* which generally requires dividend income to be treated as the top slice).

(*b*)   Under the top-slicing relief calculation, the total policy gain is divided by the number of complete years the policy has run (two) and the resulting tax multiplied by the same factor.

(*c*)   Only the difference between higher rate tax and basic rate tax enters into the top-slicing calculation.

[*ICTA 1988, ss 207A(2)(3), 550; F(No 2)A 1992, s 19(2); FA 1993, s 77*].

(*d*)   If a qualifying policy is replaced by a new qualifying policy on a different life or lives then, if certain conditions are met, no chargeable event occurs on the surrender of the earlier policy. [*ICTA 1988, 15 Sch 20*].

(*e*)   Gains on offshore policies may, in certain circumstances, be charged to basic rate tax in addition to higher rate tax. [*ICTA 1988, s 553, 15 Sch Pt III*]. Similar rules apply to gains on policies issued by friendly societies as part of their tax exempt life or endowment business. [*ICTA 1988, s 547(7)*].

IT 9.3 Life Assurance Policies

(B) Top-slicing relief — multiple chargeable events in same tax year [*ICTA 1988, s 550(6)*]

On 1 May 1996, a policyholder realises a gain of £10,000 on the maturity of a four-year non-qualifying policy. On 1 March 1997, he realises a gain of £12,000 on the surrender of a non-qualifying policy which he took out on 1 October 1990. For 1996/97, his taxable income excluding the two policy gains is £24,300.

Tax on policy gains without top-slicing relief

1,200 @ 24%	288.00
20,800 @ 40%	8,320.00
£22,000	8,608.00
Deduct Basic rate tax (£22,000 × 24%)	5,280.00
Tax payable on policy gains	£3,328.00

Tax on policy gains with top-slicing relief

£10,000 divided by 4 years =	2,500	
£12,000 divided by 6 years =	2,000	
	£4,500	

Tax on £4,500 as top slice of income:

1,200 @ 24%	288.00
3,300 @ 40%	1,320.00
£4,500	1,608.00
Deduct Basic rate tax (£4,500 × 24%)	1,080.00
	£528.00

$$£528.00 \times \frac{2,500}{4,500} = £293.00. \quad £293.00 \times 4 = \qquad 1,172.00$$

$$£528.00 \times \frac{2,000}{4,500} = £235.00. \quad £235.00 \times 6 = \qquad 1,410.00$$

Tax payable on policy gains	£2,582.00

Top-slicing relief is therefore £746 (£3,328 − £2,582).

9.3 PARTIAL SURRENDERS OF LIFE POLICIES ETC. [*ICTA 1988, s 546*]

Jade takes out a policy on 4 February 1991 for a single premium of £15,000. The contract permits periodical withdrawals.

(i) Jade draws £750 p.a. on 4 February in each subsequent year.

There is no taxable gain because at the end of each policy year the 'reckonable aggregate value' (RAV) does not exceed the 'allowable aggregate amount' (AAA).

	£
At 3.2.95 withdrawals have been	2,250 (RAV)
Deduct $4 \times \frac{1}{20}$ of the sums paid in	3,000 (AAA)
	No gain

(ii)   On 20.7.95 Jade withdraws an additional £3,500.

	£
At 3.2.96 withdrawals have been	6,500 (RAV)
Deduct 5 × $\frac{1}{20}$ of the sums paid in	3,750 (AAA)
Chargeable to higher rate tax 1995/96	£2,750

(iii)   Jade makes no annual withdrawal on 4.2.96 but on 4.2.97 makes a withdrawal of £1,000.

In the year 1997/98 the position is

	£	£
At 3.2.98 withdrawals have been		7,500
Deduct Withdrawals at last charge		6,500
		1,000 (RAV)
Deduct 7 × $\frac{1}{20}$ of the sums paid in	5,250	
less amount deducted at last charge	3,750	
		1,500 (AAA)
		No gain

(iv)   Jade surrenders the policy on 1.7.98 for £13,250, having made a further £1,000 withdrawal on 4.2.98.

In the year 1998/99, the position is

	£	£
Proceeds on surrender		13,250
Previous withdrawals		8,500
		21,750
Deduct: Premium paid	15,000	
Gains previously charged	2,750	
		17,750
Chargeable to higher rate tax 1998/99		£4,000

Notes

(a)   Reckonable aggregate value is the total of all surrenders, withdrawals etc. for each policy year since commencement *less* the total of such values which have been brought into account in earlier chargeable events.

(b)   Allowable aggregate amount is the total of annual fractions of one-twentieth (with a maximum of 20 twentieths) of the premiums, lump sums etc. paid for each policy year since commencement *less* the total of such fractions which have been brought into account in earlier chargeable events.

(c)   A policy year is a year ending 12 months from the commencement of the policy or from an anniversary thereof.

(d)   The gain on final surrender of the policy is calculated under *ICTA 1988, s 541(1)(b)*.

(e)   The gains in (ii) and (iv) above are subject to top-slicing relief (see 9.2 above).

10 Losses

Cross-references. See also 14.2, 14.3 PARTNERSHIPS.

10.1 SET-OFF OF TRADING LOSSES ETC. AGAINST OTHER INCOME [*ICTA 1988, s 380(1)(2)*]

(A) Relief under Sec 380(1)—business commenced before 6 April 1994
A married man has been carrying on a trade for some years and prepares accounts to 5 April each year. In the year 1995/96 he receives a salary of £7,000 and investment income of £2,000 and sustains a loss of £17,000 in the trade for the year to 5 April 1996. In the year ended 5 April 1995 he made a trading profit of £6,000, assessable on the preceding year basis. His wife has earned income of £7,300, and the husband makes a payment of £375 (net) to a charity under a four-year deed of covenant. He makes a claim for relief for the loss under *ICTA 1988, s 380(1)*.

The assessable income for 1995/96 is calculated as follows

	£
Salary	7,000
Trading profits (year ended 5.4.95)	6,000
Investment income	2,000
	15,000
Deduct charges (gross)	500
	14,500
Loss relief under *Sec 380(1)*	14,500

Loss memorandum	
Loss for 1995/96	17,000
Utilised as above	14,500
Unrelieved loss note (*a*)	£2,500

Notes
(*a*)   The unrelieved loss of £2,500 could be carried forward against future trading profits under *Sec 385* or relieved against other income for 1996/97 under *Sec 380(2)* (see (B) below). The *Sec 380(1)* claim could be extended under *FA 1991, s 72* to cover capital gains for 1995/96 (if any), as could a *Sec 380(2)* claim for 1996/97 (see 10.2 below).

(*b*)   A loss relieved under *Sec 380* must be relieved against all income of the year in question even if this will waste personal reliefs. In the above example, the unused married couple's allowance could be transferred to the wife (see 11.1(B) MARRIED PERSONS) but the loss-maker's personal allowance is wasted. See also 2.9(B) CAPITAL ALLOWANCES for restriction of capital allowances to leave sufficient income in charge to cover personal reliefs. Alternatively, capital allowances need not be included in the loss relief claim (see (C) below).

(*c*)   Where annual charges paid under deduction of tax exceed taxable income the tax deducted at source from the excess is assessable under *ICTA 1988, s 350*. In the above example, the husband will therefore be liable for the income tax deducted from his annual charges, i.e. £500 at 25% = £125.

(*d*)   See 1.1(B) ALLOWANCES AND TAX RATES for losses set against income which includes dividend income.

(B) Relief under Sec 380(1)(2)—business commenced before 6 April 1994

Y, a single man, has been carrying on a trade for some years and prepares accounts to 31 December each year. His results as adjusted for tax for the three years to 31 December 1995 are as follows

	Trading profit/(loss) £	Other income £	
31.12.94	10,000	5,000	(1995/96)
31.12.95	(20,000)	9,000	(1996/97)
31.12.96	(6,000)		
31.12.97	12,000	6,000	(1997/98)

Y makes all available loss relief claims against income for 1994/95 and 1995/96.

The assessments for 1995/96 and 1996/97 are as follows

1995/96

	£
Trading income — year ended 31.12.94	10,000
Other income	5,000
Total income	15,000
Deduct Loss 1995/96 *Sec 380(1)*	15,000
	—

1996/97

	£	£
Trading income — (note (a))		—
Other income		9,000
Total income		9,000
Deduct Claim under *Sec 380(2)*	5,000	
Claim under *Sec 380(1)* Loss 1995/96 (balance)		
Loss 1996/97 (a) note (*c*)	4,000	
		9,000
		—

1997/98

	£
Trading income	12,000
Deduct Loss 1996/97 (balance b/f) (*Sec 385*)	2,000
	10,000
Other income	6,000
Assessable 1997/98	£16,000

Utilisation of losses

1995/1996	£	£
Loss available	·	20,000
Deduct Utilised 1995/96	15,000	
1996/97	5,000	20,000

1996/97		£
Loss available		6,000
Deduct Utilised 1996/97	4,000	
1997/98	2,000	6,000

Alternatively L could claim relief for the 1995/96 loss only under *Sec 380(2)* (as originally enacted), and for the 1996/97 loss under *subsections* (*a*) and (*b*) of *Sec 380(1)* (as amended). The assessments for the relevant years would then be as follows.

1995/96	£
Trading income (year ended 31.12.94)	10,000
Other income	5,000
Total income	15,000
Deduct Loss 1996/97 (*Sec 380(1)(b)*)	6,000
Assessable 1995/96	£9,000

1996/97	
Trading income (note (*a*))	—
Other income	9,000
	9,000
Deduct Loss 1995/96 (*Sec 380(2)*)	9,000
	—

1997/98	
Trading income	12,000
Deduct Loss 1995/96 (balance b/f) (*Sec 385*)	11,000
	1,000
Other income	6,000
Assessable 1997/98	£7,000

Utilisation of losses

1995/96	£	£
Loss available		20,000
Deduct Utilised 1996/97	9,000	
1997/98	11,000	20,000

1996/97		
Loss available		6,000
Deduct Utilised 1995/96		6,000

This could enable L to use his personal allowances and lower rate band in both 1995/96 and 1997/98, rather than only in 1997/98.

Note

(a)   Under the current year basis transitional provisions SCHEDULE D, CASES I AND II, the 1996/97 trading income assessment is based on the profits of the two years to 31.12.96. Since a loss was incurred in both those years, the assessment is nil.

(C) Treatment of capital allowances—business commenced before 6 April 1994
[*ICTA 1988, s 383*]
A carries on a trade for which accounts are prepared to 31 December each year. The results for the two years ended 31 December 1994 are as follows

Year	Sch D, Case I profit
31.12.93	£25,000
31.12.94	£4,500

	Capital Allowances
1994/95	£10,000
1995/96	£6,100

The assessment for 1994/95 would be as follows

	£
Case I profit — year ended 31.12.93	25,000
Deduct Capital allowances	10,000
Adjusted Case I profit	15,000
Deduct Claim under *Sec 380(1)*	1,600
Taxable income	£13,400

Utilisation of losses under *Sec 380(1)*

Loss available for 1994/95

1995/96 assessment	£
Case I profit — year ended 31.12.94	4,500
Deduct Capital allowances (part)	4,500
	—
Available for claim under *Sec 380(1)*	
Capital allowances (balance)	£1,600

For the years ended 31 December 1995 and 31 December 1996, a Schedule D, Case I loss of £10,000 and profit of £15,000 arise respectively, and the capital allowance computation (all relating to plant and machinery) for 1996/97 is as follows.

	£
WDV b/f	36,000
additions (year to 31.12.95)	4,000
(year to 31.12.96)	8,000
disposals (year to 31.12.95)	(6,000)
(year to 31.12.96)	(18,000)
	24,000
Writing down allowance	6,000
WDV c/f	18,000

IT 10.1 Losses

The allowances which may be claimed in augmentation of the £10,000 loss of 1995/96 are those which would have been available if the preceding year basis had continued to apply for 1996/97, i.e. those which would have been available for a basis period year ended 31 December 1995, as follows.

	£
WDV b/f	36,000
additions	4,000
disposals	(6,000)
	34,000
Writing down allowance	8,500

The loss available for 1995/96 is thus (10,000 + £8,500 =) £18,500.

The capital allowances available for 1996/97 (£6,000 as above) are reduced by the allowance brought forward for relief in 1995/96 (£8,500), so that a balancing charge of £2,500 arises in 1996/97.

Notes

(a)   The claim under *Sec 380* is only in respect of the non-effective capital allowances, i.e. those to which effect has not been given in the taxing of the trade.

(b)   It is not obligatory to include capital allowances in a *Sec 380* claim, or, as in this example, to create a loss by taking capital allowances into account. If A's income had been lower, he might have wasted personal reliefs by claiming the loss relief of £1,600. See also 2.9(B) CAPITAL ALLOWANCES as regards restriction of capital allowances to leave sufficient income in charge to cover personal reliefs.

(c)   See also note (c) to 10.3(A) below.

(d)   With effect for 1997/98 (1994/95 for businesses starting after 5 April 1994) and subsequent years, *ICTA 1988, s 383* is repealed by *FA 1994, s 214(1)(b)*. Capital allowances will be treated as trading expenses, and allowances claimed will thus automatically be included in (and cannot be excluded from) a trading loss for income tax purposes. [*CAA 1990, s 140(2); FA 1994, s 211*].

**(D) Cessation adjustment where loss relief has been allowed on accounts basis —
business commenced before 6 April 1994** (*Revenue Extra-statutory Concession A88*)
B ceases trading on 30 September 1995 and has the following agreed results for the last few years.

		£
Year ended 30 September 1995	Loss	9,000
Year ended 30 September 1994	Loss	10,000
Year ended 30 September 1993	Loss	12,000
Year ended 30 September 1992	Loss	4,000
Year ended 30 September 1991	Profit	3,000

B has other sources of income and claims relief under *Sec 380(1)* for each year's loss (including the final year) against other income of that year. No terminal loss relief is claimed. Loss relief is given on the accounts year basis apart from that for 1995/96 which, being the final year, has to be computed on the strict fiscal year basis (see Revenue ESC A87) and is thus £4,500 (6 April 1995 to 30 September 1995). B's marginal tax rate for all years 1991/92 to 1995/96 (both before and after giving loss relief) is 25%.

Relief is available under ESC A88 as follows

(A) Relief allowed for consecutive years before year of cessation (in terms of tax)

		£
1994/95	£10,000 @ 25%	2,500
1993/94	£12,000 @ 25%	3,000
1992/93	£4,000 @ 25%	1,000
		£6,500

(B) Relief recalculated for those years on strict basis (in terms of tax)

		£
1994/95	£(5,000 + 4,500) @ 25%	2,375
1993/94	£(6,000 + 5,000) @ 25%	2,750
1992/93	£(2,000 + 6,000) @ 25%	2,000
		£7,125

The Revenue will repay the lesser of
(1) excess of (B) over (A) =   625
(2) £4,500 (1.10.94 to 5.4.95) @ 25%   1,125

They will therefore repay £625. **In addition,** they will accept a late *Sec 380* claim in respect of a loss calculated on the strict basis for 1991/92: £(2,000 − 1,500) = £500 @ 25% = £125 repayable.

Note

(*a*)   If it were not for the concession and where, as is most often the case, the accounts year basis has been used, the loss for the period 1 October 1994 to 5 April 1995 would fall into a gap and remain unrelieved under *Sec 380*. The concession is also available where terminal loss relief (see 10.4 below) is claimed but the figure at (1) is reduced by any terminal loss relief given which would not have been due if the *Sec 380* relief had, in fact, been given on the strict basis.

(E) Relief under Sec 380(1)(2) — business commenced after 5 April 1994 [*ICTA 1988, ss 380(1)(2), 382(3); FA 1994, s 209(1)(3)(7)(8); FA 1995, s 118*]

L, a single woman, commences to trade on 1 July 1994, preparing accounts to 30 June, and has the following results (as adjusted for tax purposes and after capital allowances) for the first four years.

	Profit/(loss)
	£
Year ended 30 June 1995	9,000
Year ended 30 June 1996	3,000
Year ended 30 June 1997	(1,000)
Year ended 30 June 1998	(7,000)

L has other income of £6,000 for 1997/98 and £5,800 for 1998/99, having had no other income in the earlier years.

IT 10.1   Losses

The taxable profits for the first four tax years of the business are as follows

	£
1994/95 (1.7.94–5.4.95) (£9,000 × 9/12)	6,750*
1995/96 (y/e 30.6.95)	9,000
1996/97 (y/e 30.6.96)	3,000
1997/98 (y/e 30.6.97)	Nil
1998/99 (y/e 30.6.98)	Nil

* Overlap relief accruing – £6,750.

L claims relief under *Sec 380(1)(a)* (set-off against income of the same year) for the 1997/98 loss (£1,000). She also claims relief under *Sec 380(1)(b)* (set-off against income of the preceding year) for the 1998/99 loss (£7,000), with a further claim being made under *Sec 380(1)(a)* for the balance of that loss.

The tax position for 1997/98 and 1998/99 is as follows

	£
1997/98	
Total income before loss relief	6,000
Deduct Claim under *Sec 380(1)(a)* note (*b*)	1,000
	5,000
Deduct Claim under *Sec 380(1)(b)*	5,000
Revised total income	Nil
1998/99	
Total income before loss relief	5,800
Deduct Claim under *Sec 380(1)(a)*	2,000
Revised total income	3,800
Deduct Personal allowance	(say) 3,765
Taxable income	35

Loss utilisation

	£
1997/98	
Loss available under *Sec 380(1)(a)*	1,000
Deduct Utilised in 1997/98	1,000
Loss available under *Sec 380 (1)(b)*	7,000
Deduct Utilised in 1997/98	5,000
Loss available for relief in 1998/99 under *Sec 380(1)(a)*	£2,000
1998/99	
Balance of loss available under *Sec 380(1)(a)*	2,000
Deduct Utilised in 1998/99	2,000

Notes

(*a*)   Under *Sec 380* as amended by *FA 1994, s 209*, relief is available for the tax year in which the loss arises (*Sec 380(1)(a)*) or the immediately preceding year

(*Sec 380(1)(b)*). This applies with effect for 1994/95 and subsequent years for businesses starting after 5 April 1994 and with effect for 1996/97 and subsequent years for other businesses.

(*b*) Where losses of two different years are set against the income of one tax year, then, regardless of the order of claims, relief for the current year's loss is given in priority to that for the following year's loss. [*Sec 380(2); FA 1994, s 209(1)*]. This is beneficial to the taxpayer in this example as it leaves £2,000 of the 1998/99 loss to be relieved in that year.

(*c*) For further examples on the current year basis of assessment for businesses, see 19.1–19.4 SCHEDULE D, CASES I AND II. See also (F) below for losses in the transitional period, and 10.3(B)(F) below for losses in the opening years of a business commenced after 5 April 1994.

(F) Losses in transitional period on changeover to current year basis [*ICTA 1988, s 380(1); FA 1994, s 209(1), 20 Sch 2*]
K carries on a business which commenced before 6 April 1994 and continues beyond 5 April 1999. He has no other source of income. He prepares accounts to 31 August and has the following results (as adjusted for tax purposes, but before capital allowances) for the four years to 31 August 1997.

	Profit/(loss) £
Year ended 31 August 1994	13,000
Year ended 31 August 1995	20,000
Year ended 31 August 1996	(14,000)
Year ended 31 August 1997	5,300

Capital allowances are as follows

	£
1995/96	2,000
1996/97	1,000
Year ended 31 August 1997	500

The taxable profits before taking account of loss reliefs are as follows

	£	£
1995/96 (y/e 31.8.94)	13,000	
Less capital allowances	2,000	
		11,000
1996/97 (y/e 31.8.95)	20,000	
(y/e 31.8.96)	Nil	
	£20,000	
£20,000 × 12/24	10,000	
Less capital allowances	1,000	
		9,000
1997/98 (y/e 31.8.97)		
(net of capital allowances)		4,800*

* Transitional overlap relief accrued (1.9.96–5.4.97):
£5,300 × 7/12 = £3,092.

IT 10.2 Losses

The loss of £14,000 for the year ended 31 August 1996 may be treated under normal Revenue practice as a loss for 1996/97. K wishes to obtain loss relief against the earliest possible income. **The tax position after taking into account the optimum loss relief claims is as follows**

	£
1995/96 Total income before loss relief	11,000
Deduct Claim under *Sec 380(1)(b)*	11,000
Revised total income	Nil
1996/97 Total income before loss relief	9,000
Deduct Claim under *Sec 380(1)(a)*	3,000
Revised total income	£6,000

The position for 1997/98 is not affected.

Loss utilisation

	£
Loss for 1996/97	14,000
Used in 1995/96 under *Sec 380(1)(b)*	(11,000)
Used in 1996/97 under *Sec 380(1)(a)*	(3,000)

Notes

(a)   A loss in one part of the transitional period on changeover to current year basis is treated as nil for the purpose of averaging a profit in that period to arrive at the taxable profit for 1996/97. The profit is still averaged over the full length of the transitional period.

(b)   If the results for years ended 31 August 1995 and 1996 had been reversed, so that the loss were treated as a loss for 1995/96, the tax position before loss reliefs would have been the same. Loss relief could then have been claimed under *ICTA 1988, s 380(1)(2) as originally enacted* to achieve the same position as above.

(c)   For further examples on the transitional period, see 19.4 SCHEDULE D, CASES I AND II and 2.1(E) CAPITAL ALLOWANCES.

10.2   SET-OFF OF TRADING LOSSES ETC. AGAINST CAPITAL GAINS
[*ICTA 1988, s 380; FA 1991, s 72*]

(A)
M has carried on a trade for some years, preparing accounts to 30 June each year. For the year ended 30 June 1995, he makes a trading profit of £20,000 and for the year ended 30 June 1996 he makes a trading loss of £17,000. His other income for 1996/97 amounts to £12,000. He makes a capital gain of £11,700 and a capital loss of £1,000 for 1996/97 and has no capital losses brought forward. He makes claims for loss relief, against income and gains of 1996/97, under *ICTA 1988, s 380(1)(a)* and *FA 1991, s 72* respectively.

Calculation of 'relevant amount' under *FA 1991, s 72(2)*

	£
Trading Loss — year ended 30.6.96	17,000
Relieved against income for 1996/97	12,000
Relevant amount	£5,000

Calculation of 'maximum amount' under *FA 1991, s 72(4)*

	£
Gains for 1996/97	11,700
Deduct Losses for 1996/97	1,000
Maximum amount	£10,700

Relief under *FA 1991, s 72*

	£
Net chargeable gains for the year	10,700
Deduct Relief under *FA 1991, s 72*	5,000
Gain covered by annual exemption	£5,700

Notes

(a)   A claim under *Sec 380* can be extended to cover capital gains for the year of claim. This applies in relation to trading losses sustained in 1991/92 and subsequent years of assessment.

(b)   The amount to be set against gains is restricted to so much of the 'relevant amount' as does not exceed the 'maximum amount'. The *'relevant amount'* is so much of the loss that cannot be set against income for the year and has not been otherwise relieved. The *'maximum amount'* is the amount chargeable to capital gains tax for the year, ignoring the annual exemption and the effect of *FA 1991, s 72* itself.

(c)   The effects of the loss relief claims made in this example are that M has no income tax or capital gains tax liability for 1995/96, but wastes personal reliefs and £1,000 of the annual exemption for capital gains tax (£6,300 for 1996/97).

(B)
The facts are as in (A) above except that M has £5,800 capital losses brought forward from years prior to 1996/97.

The 'relevant amount' is £5,000 as in (A) above.

Calculation of 'maximum amount'

	£
Gains for 1996/97	11,700
Deduct Losses for 1996/97	(1,000)
Deduct Unrelieved losses brought forward	(5,800)
Maximum amount	£4,900

Relief under *FA 1991, s 72*

	£	£
Gains for the year		11,700
Losses for the year	1,000	
Relief under *FA 1991, s 72*	4,900	
		5,900
Gain covered by annual exemption		£5,800
Capital losses brought forward and carried forward		£5,800

IT 10.3 Losses

Loss memorandum

	£
Trading loss	17,000
Claimed under *Sec 380(1)*	(12,000)
Claimed under *FA 1991, s 72*	(4,900)
Unutilised loss	£100

Notes

(a) Capital losses brought forward are deducted in ascertaining the 'maximum amount', and thus the relief due under *FA 1991, s 72*, but the relief itself is treated as an allowable loss for the year of claim and thus given in priority to capital losses brought forward.

(b) In this example, £500 of the annual capital gains tax exemption is wasted, but the brought forward capital losses are preserved for carry-forward against gains of future years. If M had *not* made the claim under *FA 1991, s 72*, his net gains for the year of £10,700 would have been reduced to the annual exempt amount of £6,300 by deducting £4,400 of the losses brought forward. A further £1,300 would remain available for carry-forward against future gains and a further £4,900 of trading losses would have been available for carry-forward against future trading profits or for relief under *Sec 380(1)(b)* against income (and, if claimed, against gains) for 1995/96. So the effect of the claim is to preserve capital losses at the expense of trading losses.

(c) There is further flexibility in that M need not have increased his trading loss by adding capital allowances. Capital allowances not so added would have been available for carry-forward under *CAA 1990, s 140(4)* against future trading profits. This flexibility will not be available for 1997/98 and subsequent years (and is not available at all for businesses starting after 5 April 1994) — see note (*d*) to 10.1(C) above.

10.3 LOSSES IN EARLY YEARS OF A TRADE

(A) Losses carried back three years — business commenced before 6 April 1994
[*ICTA 1988, s 381*]
E opened a health food cafe on 1 June 1993 and prepares accounts to 31 May. The first three years produce losses of £9,000, £4,000 and £1,000 and the year to 31 May 1997 a profit of £8,000 as adjusted for tax. In addition there were running costs of the premises before opening of £550. Capital allowances for the first four years of assessment are

	£
1993/94	4,000
1994/95	3,000
1995/96	2,250
1996/97	2,000

Other income is as follows

	£
1990/91	9,350
1991/92	10,050
1992/93	10,000
1993/94	2,000
1994/95	1,000

Losses are allocated as follows

	£
1993/94 ($\frac{10}{12}$ of 31.5.94)	7,500
1994/95 ($\frac{2}{12}$ of 31.5.94 + $\frac{10}{12}$ of 31.5.95)	4,833
1995/96 ($\frac{2}{12}$ of 31.5.95 + $\frac{10}{12}$ of 31.5.96)	1,500

In addition, £550 is available as a loss in 1993/94 — see note (b).

Loss relief under *ICTA 1988, s 381* is available as follows

		1993/94	1994/95	1995/96
		£	£	£
Case I loss		8,050	4,833	1,500
Capital allowances	note (c)	4,000	3,000	—
		£12,050	£7,833	£1,500
Set against total income				
1990/91		9,350	—	—
1991/92		2,700	7,350	—
1992/93		—	483	1,500
		£12,050	£7,833	£1,500

Notes

(a)   It would be possible to exclude the amount of capital allowances from the claims for loss relief. (This is not possible for businesses commenced after 5 April 1994.)

(b)   Expenditure incurred in the seven years before trading commences (five years for trades commencing before 1 April 1993) which would be deductible if incurred while trading, is treated as a loss for the first year of assessment of the trade. Different rules apply for businesses commencing after 5 April 1995. [*ICTA 1988, s 401; FA 1989, s 114; FA 1993, s 109(1)(4); FA 1995, s 120*].

(c)   Note that the 1995/96 capital allowances cannot enter into a loss relief claim in this example. The year of loss 1994/95 would be the basis year for both that year of assessment and for 1995/96, but can only be the basis year for the first of those years, by virtue of *ICTA 1988, s 383(5)(a)*. Also, the 1996/97 capital allowances cannot be added to the 1995/96 loss as the basis year for the tax year 1996/97 is 1996/97 itself (under the current year basis of assessment) and not the year of loss 1995/96.

Both the 1995/96 and 1996/97 capital allowances will be treated as trading expenses of the year to 31 May 1997 (taxable in 1997/98) under the transitional provision in *FA 1994, 20 Sch 9(2)*.

(B) Losses carried back three years — business commenced after 5 April 1994 [*ICTA 1988, ss 381, 382; FA 1994, ss 209(2)(3), 216(3)(c)*]

F, a single person, commences to trade on 1 December 1994, preparing accounts to 30 November. The first four years of trading produce losses of £12,000, £9,000, £2,000 and £1,000 respectively, these figures being as adjusted for tax purposes and after taking account of capital allowances. For each of the four years of assessment 1991/92 to 1994/95, F had other income of £8,000.

The losses for tax purposes are as follows

	£	£
1994/95 (1.12.94–5.4.95) (£12,000 × 4/12)		4,000
1995/96 (y/e 30.11.95)	12,000	
Less already allocated to 1994/95	4,000	
		8,000
1996/97 (y/e 30.11.96)		9,000
1997/98 (y/e 30.11.97)		2,000
1998/99 (y/e 30.11.98) note (*b*)		1,000

Loss relief under *ICTA 1988, s 381* is available as follows

	Losses available			
	1994/95	1995/96	1996/97	1997/98
	£	£	£	£
Losses available	4,000	8,000	9,000	2,000
Set against total income				
1991/92	4,000	—	—	—
1992/93	—	8,000	—	—
1993/94	—	—	8,000	—
1994/95	—	—	1,000	2,000
	£4,000	£8,000	£9,000	£2,000

Revised total income is thus £4,000 for 1991/92, nil for 1992/93 and 1993/94 and £5,000 for 1994/95.

Notes

(*a*) Losses are computed by reference to the same basis periods as profits. Where any part of a loss would otherwise fall to be included in the computations for two successive tax years (as is the case for 1994/95 and 1995/96 in this example), that part is excluded from the computation for the second of those years. [*ICTA 1988, s 382(3)(4); FA 1994, s 209(3)*].

(*b*) The loss for the year ended 30 November 1998 in this example is not available for relief under *Sec 381* as it does not fall into the first four *tax years* of the business (even though it is incurred in the first four years of trading). It is of course available for relief under *Sec 380* (depending on the level of other income for 1997/98 and 1998/99) or for carry-forward under *Sec 385*.

(C) Losses carried forward — business commenced before 6 April 1994 [*ICTA 1988, s 385*]
R commenced trading on 1 October 1993 and makes up accounts to 30 June. In the nine months ended 30 June 1994 he incurred a loss of £3,900 and in the years to 30 June 1995 and 1996 he made profits of £6,000 and £8,000 respectively. No election is made under *ICTA 1988, s 62*.

R's assessable profits will be as follows

	£	£
1993/94		
Period 1.10.93–5.4.94		Nil
1994/95		
Period 1.10.93–30.9.94 (first 12 months):		
Period 1.10.93–30.6.94	(3,900)	
Period 1.7.94–30.9.94 ($\frac{3}{12}$ × £6,000)	1,500	
	£(2,400)	Nil
1995/96		
Period 1.10.93–30.9.94 (as for 1994/95)		Nil
1996/97 (transitional year)		
Year ended 30.6.95	6,000	
Year ended 30.6.96	8,000	
	£14,000	
Average profit: £14,000 × 12/24	7,000	
Deduct Sec 385 loss relief (see below)	(900)	£6,100

If R makes a claim to carry losses forward under *ICTA 1988, s 385*, loss relief will be given as follows

1993/94		
Loss arising in year		
£(3,900) × $\frac{2}{3}$ = £(2,600)		
Loss carried forward	(2,600)	
1994/95		
Losses required to reduce assessment to nil	1,500	
Deduct loss arising in period	(1,300)	
	200	
Deduct loss brought forward	(200)	200
		£(2,400)
1995/96		
Losses required to reduce assessment to nil	1,500	
Deduct loss brought forward	(1,500)	1,500
Loss carried forward	—	(900)
1996/97		
Profits assessable (see above)	7,000	
Deduct loss brought forward	(900)	900
	£6,100	—

IT 10.3 Losses

Note

(a)   The loss at 6 April 1994 of £2,600 is reduced by the amount of relief given in computing the assessable profits for 1994/95 and 1995/96 and only the balance not so used is available for carry forward to 1996/97 under *ICTA 1988, s 385 (CIR v Scott Adamson, 17 TC 679* and *Westward Television Ltd v Hart, 45 TC 1).*

(D) Interaction of Sec 380 and Sec 385 in early years — business commenced before 6 April 1994

If R in (C) above had made a claim to relieve the loss of £2,600 incurred in 1993/94 against his other income for that year, the position would have been as follows

	£	£
1993/94		
Loss arising in year	(2,600)	
Loss relieved against other income under		
Sec 380	2,600	
Loss carried forward	Nil	—
1994/95		
Profit arising in period	1,500	
Deduct loss arising in period	(1,300)	
Assessable profits		£200
1995/96 (as for 1994/95)		
Assessable profits		£200
1996/97		
Assessable profits		£7,000

Notes

(a)   No *Sec 385* relief is due for 1994/95 or later years as the loss is relieved by the *Sec 380* claim in 1993/94 and by aggregation with profits in 1994/95 and 1995/96.

(b)   The overall taxable income of £4,800 (£7,400 less £2,600 loss claim) is £1,300 less than that in (B) above as relief for £1,300 has been given twice by aggregation.

(E) Calculation of Sec 380 relief in early years of a business commenced before 6 April 1994 — further example

Q commenced trading on 1 February 1994 and prepared accounts to 31 December. He made a trading loss of £20,900 in the eleven months to 31 December 1994 and profits of £18,000 and £16,000 in the years to 31 December 1995 and 1996 respectively. He has substantial other income for 1993/94 and 1994/95 and makes claims under *Sec 380(1)* for both years. He makes no election under *ICTA 1988, s 62* (actual basis for second and third years).

Q's assessable profits are as follows

	£	£
1993/94		
Period 1.2.94–5.4.94		Nil

1994/95
Period 1.2.94–31.1.95 (first 12 months):
Period 1.2.94–31.12.94	(20,900)	
Period 1.1.95–31.1.95 ($\frac{1}{12}$ × £18,000)	1,500	
	£(19,400)	Nil

1995/96
Period 1.2.94–31.1.95 (as for 1994/95)	Nil

1996/97 (transitional year)
Year ended 31.12.95	18,000	
Year ended 31.12.96	16,000	
	£34,000	
Average: £34,000 × 12/24	17,000	
Loss brought forward (see below)	(1,500)	£15,500

Loss relief computations under Sec 380

	£	£
1993/94		
Period 1.2.94–5.4.94 ($\frac{2}{11}$ × £20,900)		£3,800

1994/95
Period 6.4.94–5.4.95:		
Period 6.4.94–31.12.94 ($\frac{9}{11}$ × £20,900)	17,100	
Period 1.1.95–5.4.95 ($\frac{3}{12}$ × £18,000)	(4,500)	
		£12,600

Loss memorandum

	£	£
Period 1.2.94–5.4.94	3,800	
Relieved under Sec 380	3,800	—
Period 6.4.94–31.12.94	17,100	
Relieved under Sec 380	12,600	
	4,500	
Used in aggregation £1,500 × 2	3,000	
Available for carry-forward	1,500	1,500
Relieved in 1996/97 under Sec 385		1,500

Note

(a)   Although the *assessments* are computed in accordance with the rules in *ICTA 1988, s 61* for the early years of a trade, *losses* available under *Sec 380* must be computed on a strict April to April basis in the first three years of assessment (see Revenue ESC A87).

(F) Losses in early years — business commenced after 5 April 1994
The facts are as in (E) above except that all dates are one year later.

Taxable profits/(allowable losses) are as follows

	£	£
1994/95 (1.2.95–5.4.95) (£20,900) × 2/11		(3,800)
1995/96 (1.2.95–31.1.96)		
1.2.95–31.12.95	(20,900)	
Less already allocated to 1994/95	3,800	
	(17,100)	
1.1.96–31.1.96 £18,000 × 1/12	1,500	
		(15,600)
1996/97 (y/e 31.12.96)		18,000
(Overlap relief accruing — £1,500)		
1997/98 (y/e 31.12.97)		16,000

Notes

(a) Losses are computed by reference to the same basis periods as profits. Where any part of a loss would otherwise fall to be included in the computations for two successive tax years (as is the case for 1994/95 and 1995/96 in this example), that part is excluded from the computation for the second of those years. [*ICTA 1988, s 382(3)(4); FA 1994, s 209(3)*].

(b) Losses available for relief for 1994/95 and 1995/96 are £3,800 and £15,600 respectively. If both years' losses are carried forward under *Sec 385* instead of being set against other income (under either *Sec 380* or *Sec 381*), the aggregate loss of £19,400 will extinguish the 1996/97 profit and reduce the 1997/98 profit by £1,400. Note that although the actual loss was £20,900, there is no further amount available for carry-forward: the difference of £1,500 has been used in aggregation in 1995/96.

(c) The net profit for the first three accounting periods is £13,100 (£18,000 + £16,000 – £20,900). The net taxable profit for the first four tax years is £14,600 (£18,000 + £16,000 – £3,800 – £15,600). The difference of £1,500 represents the overlap relief accrued, which will be given on cessation or on a change of accounting date resulting in a basis period of more than one year. For further examples on the current year basis of assessment, including overlap relief and change of accounting date, see 19.1–19.4 SCHEDULE D, CASES I AND II.

10.4   TERMINAL LOSSES [*ICTA 1988, s 388*]

(A)   General

A carries on a trade and prepares accounts to 31 December each year. A ceases to trade on 30 September 1996 and the results for the four years and nine months to date of cessation are as follows

Period	Trading Profit/(loss) £
31.12.92	3,500
31.12.93	5,000
31.12.94	600
31.12.95	(1,200)
30.9.96	(1,500)

Year of assessment	Capital Allowances £	Non-Trade Annual Payments £
1993/94	1,800	300
1994/95	1,500	300
1995/96	1,800	—
1996/97	1,600	—

The terminal loss available is as follows

			£
1996/97 $\frac{6}{9}$ × £1,500			1,000
Capital allowances			1,600
1995/96 $\frac{3}{9}$ × £1,500		500	
$\frac{3}{12}$ × £1,200		300	800
Capital allowances			
$\frac{6}{12}$ × £1,800	note (*a*)		900
			£4,300

The assessments for these years are as follows

Year	Assessment		£	Sec 388 Relief £	Revised £
1993/94	Profits	3,500			
	Capital allowances	1,800			
			£1,700	800	£900
1994/95	Profits	5,000			
	Capital allowances	1,500			
			£3,500	3,200	£300
1995/96	Profits	600			
	Capital allowances	600			
			—		Nil
1996/97			Nil		Nil
				£4,000	(see below)

IT 10.4 Losses

		£
Terminal loss as above		4,300
Less: Utilised in 1994/95		3,200
		1,100
Less: Deduction for non-trade charges	note (c)	300
		800
Less: Utilised in 1993/94		800
		Nil

Notes

(a)   The capital allowances of £900 for 1995/96 which are included in the terminal loss do not have to be restricted as only £600 of the total of £1,800 is set against the 1995/96 assessment. If £1,000 had been required to offset the 1995/96 assessment the 1995/96 capital allowances included in the terminal loss would have been restricted to £800.

(b)   The years 1994/95 and 1995/96 would not be revised to actual as income is greater on a preceding year basis. One quarter of the loss for the year ended 31.12.95 is therefore included as terminal loss relief.

(c)   The profits available for set-off against Sec 388 loss relief are reduced by the annual payments which were paid out of income subject to tax. As they were non-trade charges, the terminal loss available against income of prior years is similarly reduced. [Sec 388(5)].

(d)   A could obtain more relief if he made a claim under Sec 380(1) for 1994/95 and then made a reduced claim for Sec 388 terminal loss relief as follows

	£
Sec 380 relief 1994/95	
Profit for the year ended 31.12.94	600
Capital allowances (1995/96)	1,800
	£1,200

The terminal loss available would then be

	£
As calculated above	4,300
Deduct 1995/96 Capital allowances relieved under Sec 380	900
	£3,400

The position would then be

Year	Assessments	Sec 380 relief	Sec 388 relief	Revised
	£	£	£	£
1993/94	1,700		1,100	£600
1994/95	3,500	1,200	2,000	£300
1995/96	Nil			Nil
1996/97	Nil			Nil
		£1,200	£3,100	(see below)

	£
Terminal loss as above	3,400
Less: Utilised in 1994/95	2,000
	1,400
Less: Deduction for non-trade charges	300
	1,100
Less: Utilised in 1993/94	1,100
Balance	Nil

(B) Further example of calculation of terminal loss
B, a trader with a 30 September year end, ceases to trade on 30 June 1996. Tax-adjusted results for his last two accounting periods are as follows

	Trading profit/(loss) £
Year ended 30 September 1995	28,000
Nine months to 30 June 1996	(9,000)

There are no capital allowances due. Profits have been falling and the Revenue do not revise the 1994/95 and 1995/96 assessments to actual.

The terminal loss available is as follows

	£	£
1996/97 (6.4.96 – 30.6.96)		
£9,000 × $\frac{3}{9}$		3,000
1995/96 (1.7.95 – 5.4.96)		
1.10.95 – 5.4.96 £9,000 × $\frac{6}{9}$	6,000	
1.7.95 – 30.9.95 (£28,000) × $\frac{3}{12}$	(7,000)	
	(1,000)	Nil
Terminal loss		£3,000

Note
(a) In determining the part of a terminal loss arising in a part of the final twelve months (the terminal loss period) that falls into any one year of assessment, a profit made in that period must be netted off against a loss in that period. In this example, no loss has been incurred in that part of the terminal loss period that falls within 1995/96. However, two different years of assessment are looked at separately, so that the 'net profit' of £1,000 arising in the part of the terminal loss period falling within 1995/96 does not have to be netted off against the 1996/97 loss and is instead treated as nil.

10.5 LOSSES ON SHARES IN UNQUOTED TRADING COMPANY [*ICTA 1988, ss 574–576; FA 1994, s 210; FA 1995, s 119*]

Over the years, X has acquired a number of shareholdings in unquoted companies and suffers the following losses in 1995 and 1996

(i) 500 shares in A Ltd (a qualifying trading company) which X subscribed for in 1987. The company went into liquidation in June 1995 and X made a negligible value claim. Allowable loss for CGT purposes 1995/96 — £12,000.

(ii) 500 shares in B Ltd which X subscribed for in 1989 at £10 per share. B Ltd traded as builders until 1992 when it changed its trade to that of buying and selling land. X received an arm's length offer for the shares of £3 per share in May 1995 which he accepted.

(iii) In 1984, X subscribed for 2,000 shares in C Ltd at £50 per share. In 1989, his aunt gave him a further 1,000 shares. The market value of the shares at that time was £60 per share. The company has been a qualifying trading company since 1980 but has fallen on hard times recently. X was offered £20 per share in June 1996 and accepted it to the extent of 1,500 shares.

The treatment of these losses in relation to income tax would be as follows

(i) Loss claim — *Sec 574*, 1995/96 or 1994/95 £12,000.

(ii) No loss claim possible under *Sec 574* as company is an 'excluded company' under *Sec 576(4)(5)*.

(iii) Disposals are identified for *Sec 574* purposes with acquisitions on a last in/first out basis:

Year	Qualifying shares	Other shares
1984	2,000	
1989		1,000
1996	(500)	(1,000)

Loss claim — *Sec 574*, 1996/97 or 1995/96

	£
Cost of 500 shares at £50 per share	25,000
Proceeds of 500 shares at £20 per share	10,000
Sec 574 loss	£15,000

X makes all possible claims under *Sec 574* so as to obtain relief against the earliest possible income. He is a single man and has total income, before *Sec 574* relief, of £7,000 for 1994/95, £11,500 for 1995/96 and £7,500 for 1996/97.

The *Sec 574* losses available are as follows

	1995/96 disposals £	1996/97 disposals £
A Ltd shares	12,000	
C Ltd shares		15,000

Sec 574 claims are made as follows

	£
1994/95	
Total income	7,000
Claim under *Sec 574(1)(b)*	(7,000)
Revised total income	Nil
1995/96	
Total income	11,500
Claim under *Sec 574(1)(a)* note(*b*)	(5,000)
	6,500
Claim under *Sec 574(1)(b)*	(6,500)
Revised total income	Nil
1996/97	
Total income	7,500
Claim under *Sec 574(1)(a)* (restricted)	(7,500)
Revised total income	Nil

Loss utilisation

	£
1995/96 loss	
Loss available	12,000
Relief claimed for 1994/95 (*Sec 574(1)(b)*)	(7,000)
Relief claimed for 1995/96 (*Sec 574(1)(a)*)	(5,000)
1996/97 loss	
Loss available	15,000
Relief claimed for 1995/96 (*Sec 574(1)(b)*)	(6,500)
Relief claimed for 1996/97 (*Sec 574 (1)(a)*)	(7,500)
Unused balance note (*c*)	£1,000

Notes

(*a*)   Losses on disposals in 1994/95 and subsequent years may be set against current year's income (*Sec 574(1)(a)*) or preceding year's income (*Sec 574(1)(b)*). [*ICTA 1988, s 574(1); FA 1994, s 210; FA 1995, s 119*]. In this example, losses have been set against preceding year's income first, as X wished to obtain relief against earliest possible income, but this need not be the case.

(*b*)   Where two years' losses are set against one year's income, the current year's loss is relieved in priority to that of the following year. [*ICTA 1988, s 574(2); FA 1994, s 210*].

(*c*)   The unused balance of the 1996/97 loss cannot be relieved under *Sec 574* due to insufficiency of income and therefore reverts to being a capital loss available to reduce chargeable gains.

11 Married Persons

11.1 INDEPENDENT TAXATION

(A) Election to transfer married couple's allowance [*ICTA 1988, ss 257A, 257BA; FA 1988, s 33; F(No 2)A 1992, 5 Sch 2; FA 1994, 8 Sch 2*]

Before 6 April 1996, Mr and Mrs Scarlet made a joint election under *ICTA 1988, s 257BA(2)* to transfer from husband to wife the whole of the basic married couple's allowance with effect for 1996/97 and later years. Mr Scarlet was born on 29 May 1930 and his wife on 6 January 1938. For 1996/97, their income is as follows.

	Mr Scarlet £	Mrs Scarlet £
Schedule D, Case I transitional year profits	8,500	—
Earnings from employment	—	25,000
Retirement pension	3,060	—
Dividends (net)	2,000	2,880
Building society interest (net)	—	441

The couple's tax position is as follows

	£	£
Schedule D, Case I	8,500	—
Schedule E	—	25,000
Retirement pension	3,060	
Dividends plus tax credits	2,500	3,600
Building society interest (gross)		680
Total income	14,060	29,280
Deduct Personal allowance	4,910	3,765
Taxable income	£9,150	£25,515

Tax payable:		
3,900/3,900 @ 20%	780.00	780.00
2,750/17,335 @ 24%	660.00	4,160.40
2,500/4,265 @ 20%	500.00	853.00
15 @ 40%		6.00
	1,940.00	5,799.40
Deduct Married couple's allowance (£3,115):		
£1,325 @ 15%	198.75	
£1,790 @ 15%		268.00
Total tax liabilities	174.25	5,531.40
Deduct: Tax credits	(500.00)	(720.00)
Tax on building society interest		(136.00)
Net tax liabilities (subject to wife's PAYE deductions)	£1,241.25	£4,675.40

Notes

(a)   With effect for 1993/94 and subsequent years, the wife can elect to receive half the basic married couple's allowance (i.e. excluding any age-related addition) or, as illustrated in this example, husband and wife can jointly elect for the whole of the basic allowance to be allocated to the wife. An election is not dependent on levels of income but, except for the year of marriage, must be made before the start of the first year for which it is to apply (e.g. before 6 April 1996 to have effect for 1996/97). [*ICTA 1988, s 257BA; F(No 2)A 1992, 5 Sch 2*].

(*b*)   If the wife's income is too low to fully utilise the married couple's allowance allocated to her, she may transfer the excess allowance back to the husband. [*ICTA 1988, s 257BB(3)–(5); F(No 2)A 1992, 5 Sch 2; FA 1994, 8 Sch 3*]. The transfer operates in the same way as a transfer of surplus married couple's allowance from husband to wife — see (B) below.

(*c*)   With effect for 1994/95 and subsequent years, the married couple's allowance attracts tax relief at a fixed rate (20% for 1994/95, 15% thereafter). This means that a *Sec 257BA* election does not save any tax, although the election may still have cash flow advantages where the wife pays tax under PAYE and the husband does not.

(B) Transfer of surplus married couple's allowance [*ICTA 1988, ss 257A, 257BB; FA 1988, s 33; F(No 2)A 1992, 5 Sch 2; FA 1994, 8 Sch 3*]
Mr Grey is a sole trader and made a profit of £1,000 in the tax year ended 30 April 1996. Mr Grey has been married for some years. He has building society interest of £2,752 (net) for 1996/97 and his wife has a salary of £15,000 and building society interest of £1,600 (net). Mr and Mrs Grey receive interest of £1,120 (net) in 1996/97 from a bank deposit account in their joint names. Mr Grey makes an investment of £500 on 1 November 1996 which qualifies for enterprise investment scheme relief. Mr Grey elects under *ICTA 1988, s 257BB(2)* to transfer the unused balance of his married couple's allowance for 1996/97 to his wife.

IT 11.1   Married Persons

The couple's tax position is as follows

	Mr Grey £	Mrs Grey £
Schedule D, Case I $\left(£1,000 \times \dfrac{365}{365 + 366}\right)$ say	500	—
Schedule E	—	15,000
Building society interest (gross)	3,440	2,000
Bank deposit interest (gross) note (c)	700	700
Total income	4,640	17,700
Deduct Personal allowance	3,765	3,765
Taxable income	£875	£13,935
Tax payable:		
875/3,900 @ 20%	175.00	780.00
7,335 @ 24%		1,760.40
2,700 @ 20%		540.00
	175.00	3,080.40
Deduct EIS relief £500 @ 20%	100.00	
	75.00	
Deduct Married couple's allowance £1,790 @ 15% = £268.50, but restricted to	75.00	
Deduct Surplus married couple's allowance £(268.50 − 75.00)		193.50
Total tax liabilities	Nil	2,886.90
Deduct Tax at source:		
Building society interest	(688.00)	(400.00)
Bank deposit interest	(140.00)	(140.00)
Net tax (repayment)/liability (subject to wife's PAYE deductions)	£(828.00)	£2,346.90

Notes

(a)   Where the married couple's allowance is restricted by *ICTA 1988, s 256(2)(b)* to the amount that reduces the tax liability to nil (or where no married couple's allowance can be given as there is no tax liability), the unused part of the allowance (or all of it) can be transferred to the spouse.

b)   Enterprise investment scheme (EIS) relief is given in priority to married couple's allowance. [*ICTA 1988, s 289A(5)(a); FA 1994, 15 Sch 2*]. Other allowances and reliefs given by way of income tax reduction are similarly given in priority to married couple's allowance, thus maximising surplus married couple's allowance available for transfer.

(c)   Income from property held in their joint names is normally divided equally between husband and wife. [*ICTA 1988, s 282A; FA 1988, s 34*]. Note that certain gifts and settlements between spouses of property from which income arises are not valid transfers of income. [*ICTA 1988, s 660A(6); FA 1995, s 74, 17 Sch 1*]. This applies where the donor retains an interest in the property. Outright gifts comprising both income and capital are not caught.

11.2 DEATH OF SPOUSE

Mr White died on 5 October 1996. His business had assessable profits of £16,025 for the year ended 30 June 1995 and £2,000 for the year ended 30 June 1996. He had no other income. Mrs White received wages of £3,000 from her husband's business to 5 October and continued the business thereafter. She receives a lump sum widow's payment of £1,000 and a widow's pension of £1,530 to 5 April 1997.

1996/97 £

Mr White

Earned income

Profits transitional year £(16,025 + 2,000) × $\dfrac{365}{365 + 366}$ =   £9000

$\frac{1}{2}$ of £9,000	4,500
Deduct Personal allowance	3,765
Taxable income	£735
Tax payable:	
735 @ 20%	147.00
Deduct Married couple's allowance	
£1,790 @ 15% = £268.50, but restricted to	147.00
Tax liability	Nil

Mrs White

Earned income

transitional year (as above)

$\frac{1}{2}$ of £9,000	4,500
Wages	3,000
Widow's pension (Sch E — actual)	1,530
	9,030
Deduct Personal allowance	3,765
Taxable income	£5,265
Tax payable:	
3,900 @ 20%	780.00
1,365 @ 24%	327.60
	1,107.60
Deduct Widow's bereavement allowance	
£1,790 @ 15%	268.50
	839.10
Deduct Surplus married couple's	
allowance £(268.50 − 147.00)	121.50
Tax liability	£717.60

Notes

(*a*) Under Revenue ESC A7, the continuation basis applies to a widow(er) continuing a deceased spouse's business, unless the discontinuance basis is claimed. The concession is withdrawn from 6 April 1995 for businesses commenced after 5 April 1994 and from a date to be announced (which will not be earlier than 6 April 1997) for businesses commenced on or before 5 April 1994 (Revenue Press Release 4 April 1995).

IT 11.3　Married Persons

(b)　The transfer of surplus married couple's allowance to the wife (see also 11.1(B) above) is dependent on a claim to that effect being made by the husband's executors.

(c)　Widow's bereavement allowance will also be available in 1997/98 if Mrs White does not remarry before 6 April 1997. [*ICTA 1988, s 262; FA 1988, 3 Sch 7; FA 1994, s 77(5)*].

(d)　The lump sum widow's payment is not chargeable to income tax. [*ICTA 1988, s 617(1)(2)*].

11.3　**MAINTENANCE PAYMENTS** [*ICTA 1988, ss 347A–349, 351; FA 1988, ss 36, 38–40; FA 1994, s 79*]

(A) Court Orders before 15 March 1988
Mr Smith separated from his wife on 31 October 1987. For 1996/97 he has assessable Schedule D, Case I profits of £22,000 and building society interest of £4,000 (net). He pays mortgage interest of £2,400 on a home loan of under £30,000 which is outside the MIRAS scheme. Under a Court Order dated 5 March 1988, Mr Smith paid £50 per week maintenance directly to his son, Paul, aged 17 in 1996/97, who lives with Mrs Smith, and £70 per week maintenance to Mrs Smith. On 1 June 1990, the payments to Mrs Smith were increased by the Court to £100 per week. In 1996/97, Mrs Smith has earnings of £5,500. Paul Smith has no other income.

1996/97

Mr Smith	£	£
Earned income		22,000
Building society interest	4,000	
Add Tax deducted at source	1,000	5,000
		27,000
Deduct: Maintenance payments:		
Wife £70 × 52　note (*a*)	3,640	
Son　£50 × 52	2,600	
	6,240	
Less the first £1,790　note (*c*)	1,790	
		(4,450)
Total income		22,550
Deduct Personal allowance		3,765
Taxable income		£18,785
Tax payable:		
3,900 @ 20%		780.00
9,885 @ 24%		2,372.40
5,000 @ 20%		1,000.00
		4,152.40
Deduct Mortgage interest relief £2,400 @ 15%		360.00
		3,792.40
Deduct Maintenance £1,790 @ 15%　note (*c*)		268.50
Total tax liability		3,523.90
Deduct Tax paid on building society interest		1,000.00
Net tax liability		£2,523.90

Mrs Smith	£	£
Earned income		5,500
Maintenance note (*a*)	3,640	
Deduction note (*a*)	1,790	
		1,850
Total income		7,350
Deduct Personal allowance note (*e*)		3,765
Taxable income		£3,585
Tax payable:		
3,585 @ 20%		717.00

Paul Smith	£
Maintenance	2,600
Deduct Personal allowance (restricted)	2,600
Taxable income	Nil
Tax payable/repayable	Nil

Notes

(*a*)   The tax relief and the amount chargeable on the recipient is limited to the relief obtainable and the amount forming part of the recipient's income for 1988/89. The recipient may then deduct from the amount otherwise chargeable an amount equal to the married couple's allowance for the year, providing the payments are from a divorced or separated spouse. [*FA 1988, s 38, 3 Sch 33*].

(*b*)   The payer may elect to have payments treated under the rules for post-14 March 1988 Court Orders and maintenance agreements illustrated in (B) below. [*FA 1988, s 39*]. This would normally be beneficial only where his relief would otherwise be less than £1,720.

(*c*)   For 1996/97 the first £1,790 of allowable maintenance payments attracts relief at 15%, such relief being given as an income tax reduction. [*ICTA 1988, s 347B; FA 1988, s 38(3)(3A); FA 1994, s 79(3)*].

(*d*)   Mrs Smith may also be entitled to the additional personal allowance in respect of Paul if all the conditions of *ICTA 1988, s 259* are satisfied. The allowance would be given as an income tax reduction.

(B) Court Orders after 14 March 1988

Mr Green separated from his wife in June 1995 and, under a Court Order dated 15 July 1996, pays maintenance of £300 per month to his ex-wife and £100 per month to his daughter, payments being due on the first of each calendar month commencing 1 August 1996. Mr Green has earned income of £17,000 and dividends of £4,000 for 1996/97. He re-marries on 6 October 1996.

	£	£
1996/97		
Mr Green		
Earned income		17,000
Dividends	4,000	
Add Tax credits (£4,000 × 1/4)	1,000	5,000
Total income		22,000
Deduct Personal allowance		3,765
Taxable income		£18,235
Tax payable:		
3,900 @ 20%		780.00
9,335 @ 24%		2,240.40
5,000 @ 20%		1,000.00
		4,020.40
Deduct Maintenance relief — wife:		
£2,700 paid, but restricted to £1,790 @ 15%		268.50
		3,751.90
Deduct Married couple's allowance		
£1,790 × 6/12 = £895 @ 15%		134.25
Total tax liability		3,617.65
Deduct Tax credits		1,000.00
Net tax liability (subject to PAYE deductions)		£2,617.65

Notes

(a) Relief for maintenance payments to a divorced or separated spouse is restricted to an amount equal to a percentage of the married couple's allowance for the year. No relief is due for other maintenance payments. For 1994/95 and subsequent years, relief is given by way of income tax reduction and is restricted to 20% for 1994/95 and 15% thereafter. [*ICTA 1988, ss 347A, 347B; FA 1988, s 36, 3 Sch 13; FA 1994, s 79(3)–(6)*].

(b) Maintenance payments are exempt from tax in the hands of the recipients.

(c) Tax relief for maintenance payments does not affect entitlement to the married couple's allowance either in the year of re-marriage or in later years. The allowance for the year of re-marriage is restricted in the normal way under *ICTA 1988, s 257A(6)*.

(d) These rules affect maintenance payments under Court Orders and maintenance agreements made after 14 March 1988 except for Court Orders applied for before 15 March 1988 and made by 30 June 1988 and Orders which vary previous Orders made before 15 March 1988; these fall within the rules in (A) above.

12   Mineral Royalties

Cross-reference. See also 215 MINERAL ROYALTIES.

[*ICTA 1988, s 122; TCGA 1992, ss 201–203*]

12.1   Miss Quarry owns land containing valuable gravel pits. She receives a royalty from a construction company based on the tonnage removed. She has to bear part of the cost of the weighbridge and ancillary facilities.

In the year to 5 April 1997 she receives £15,700 of royalty and her share of the weighbridge expenses amounted to £1,000. This is her only source of income or gains for that year. The royalty was received gross.

Her tax liabilities for 1996/97 are as follows

	£
Income Tax	
Royalty received £15,700	
Chargeable to income tax — one half	7,850
Management expenses £1,000	
Relief restricted to one half	500
	7,350
Deduct Personal allowance	3,765
	£3,585
Tax thereon	
£3,585 at 20%	717.00
Capital Gains Tax	
Royalty received £15,700	
Chargeable to capital gains tax — one half	7,850
Deduct annual exemption	6,300
	£1,550
Tax thereon	
£315 at 20%	63.00
£1,235 at 24%	296.40
	£359.40

13 Overseas Matters

13.1 NON-RESIDENT ENTERTAINERS AND SPORTSMEN [*ICTA 1988, ss 555–558; SI 1987 No 530*]

G, a professional golfer who is non-resident in the UK, visits the UK in July 1996 to play in a tournament from which he earns £50,000 in appearance and prize money. He directs that the money be paid to a non-resident company which he controls. During his visit, he receives £800 from a television company for a series of interviews and £2,000 from a national newspaper for a number of exclusive articles. He arranges for 20% of the latter sum to be paid direct to his agent, also non-resident and who pays tax on his income at a rate not exceeding 24%, who arranged the deal. G incurs allowable expenses of £15,000 in connection with the trip. He has no other taxable income in the UK during 1996/97. He does not qualify for UK personal reliefs.

G's UK tax position for 1996/97 is as follows

		Taxable income £	Tax withheld at source £
Prize and appearance money	note (*b*)	50,000	12,500
Fee from television company	note (*c*)	800	—
Fee for newspaper articles	note (*d*)	2,000	500
		52,800	13,000
Deduct Expenses		15,000	
		£37,800	

Tax payable	£	
3,900 at 20%	780	
21,600 at 24%	5,184	
12,300 at 40%	4,920	
£37,800		10,884
Tax repayable		£2,116

Notes

(*a*) G is considered to have carried on a trade in respect of the payments received, or deemed to have been received, by him in connection with his UK activities. The trade is distinct from any other trade carried on by him and is taxable on a current year basis. [*ICTA 1988, s 557*].

(*b*) A payment to a company under the entertainer's (or sportsman's) control (defined in accordance with *ICTA 1988, s 416(1)–(6)*) is treated as a payment to him and withholding tax at the basic rate must be deducted at source. [*ICTA 1988, s 556(2)–(5); SI 1987 No 530, Reg 7*].

(*c*) No withholding tax falls to be deducted from the television company fee as it does not exceed the de minimis limit of £1,000. [*SI 1987 No 530, Reg 4(3)*].

(*d*) Although a percentage of the fee for newspaper articles was paid not to G but to his agent, it falls to be treated as G's income and is subject to withholding tax by virtue of his agent's being non-resident in the UK and liable to tax at a rate not exceeding 25% in his country of residence. [*SI 1987 No 530, Reg 7(2)(b)*].

(e)   It is assumed in the above example that G has not agreed with the Inland Revenue a reduced rate of withholding tax, which he could have attempted to do by making application in writing, under *Reg 5*, not later than 30 days before any payment fell to be made.

13.2   **OFFSHORE FUNDS** [*ICTA 1988, ss 757–764, 27, 28 Schs; TCGA 1992, s 102*]
R, who is resident, ordinarily resident and domiciled in the UK, invests in non-qualifying offshore funds as follows

(i)   **ABC fund** £

30.11.82	1,000 shares purchased at £10 per share	10,000
1.1.84	Market value per share = £20	20,000
1.12.96	On amalgamation with XYZ fund (another non-qualifying offshore fund) the 1,000 original shares are exchanged for 2,000 new shares in XYZ which have a value of £15 per share	30,000
31.8.97	2,000 XYZ shares sold for £17.50 per share	35,000

(ii)   **DEF fund**

1.8.83	500 units purchased at £25 per unit	12,500
1.1.84	Market value per unit = £20	10,000
1.6.96	500 units sold for £40 per unit	20,000

(iii)   **GHJ fund** (an 'umbrella fund')

1.4.92	1,000 units in sub-fund K purchased at £20 per unit	20,000
1.2.97	1,000 units in sub-fund K exchanged for 500 units in sub-fund L which have a market value of £50 per unit	25,000

R has offshore income gains and capital gains/losses as follows

1996/97

Offshore income gains
Disposal on 1.6.96 of 500 DEF units

	Post-1983 gain £	Unindexed gain £
Disposal proceeds	20,000	20,000
Market value at 1.1.84	10,000	
Cost		12,500
	£10,000	£7,500

As the unindexed gain is less than the post-1983 gain, the offshore income gain chargeable under Schedule D, Case VI is £7,500.

Disposal on 1.12.96 of 1,000 ABC shares

Disposal consideration	30,000	30,000
Market value at 1.1.84	20,000	
Cost		10,000
	£10,000	£20,000

The offshore income gain chargeable under Schedule D, Case VI is the £10,000 post-1983 gain as this is less than the unindexed gain.

Disposal on 1.2.97 of 1,000 GHJ (sub-fund K) units   (see note (c))

	£
Disposal consideration	25,000
Cost (1.4.92)	20,000
Offshore income gain	£5,000

Capital gains computation
Disposal on 1.6.96 of 500 DEF units

	£
Disposal proceeds	20,000
Offshore income gain	7,500
	12,500
Cost	12,500
Chargeable gain/allowable loss	Nil

Disposal on 1.12.96 of 1,000 ABC shares
There is no capital gains tax liability as the share exchange is not treated as a disposal for capital gains tax purposes. [*TCGA 1992, s 135*].

Disposal on 1.2.97 of 1,000 GHJ (sub-fund K) units   (see note (c))

	£
Disposal consideration	25,000
Offshore income gain	5,000
	20,000
Cost	20,000
Chargeable gain/allowable loss	Nil

1997/98

Offshore income gain
Disposal on 31.8.97 of 2,000 XYZ shares

	£
Disposal proceeds	35,000
Cost (market value at 1.12.95)	30,000
Offshore income gain	£5,000

Capital gains computation
Disposal on 31.8.97 of 2,000 XYZ shares

	£	£
Disposal proceeds		35,000
Offshore income gain		5,000
		30,000
Cost	10,000	
Deemed consideration for new holding in XYZ note (b)	10,000	20,000
Unindexed gain		10,000
Indexation allowance (say)		8,500
Chargeable gain		£1,500

Notes

(a) Where a holding in a non-qualifying offshore fund was acquired before 1 January 1984, the offshore income gain on disposal is the lower of the unindexed gain (as calculated for capital gains tax) and the post-1983 gain (the gain accruing after 31 December 1983 on the assumption that the holding was sold and reacquired at market value on 1 January 1984). [*ICTA 1988, 28 Sch Pt I*].

(b) Where an offshore income gain arises on an exchange of shares within *TCGA 1992, s 135(3)*, the amount of that gain is treated as consideration for the new holding on a subsequent disposal. [*ICTA 1988, s 763(6)*].

(c) An exchange of rights in part of an 'umbrella fund' for rights in another part of that fund is a disposal both for capital gains tax and for the purposes of the offshore fund legislation, notwithstanding *TCGA 1992, ss 127, 132*. [*TCGA 1992, s 102*].

13.3 **NON-RESIDENT UK CITIZENS** [*ICTA 1988, ss 232, 278; FA 1995, s 128*]
Hugh and Elizabeth are non-resident in the UK throughout 1996/97. They are each entitled to a UK personal allowance under the provisions of *ICTA 1988, s 278; FA 1988, s 31*. Their tax liabilities on total UK income for 1996/97, disregarding the limit under *FA 1995, s 128*, are as follows

	Hugh	Elizabeth
	£	£
Net rental income (Schedule A)	2,000	5,000
Bank interest (received gross)	4,265	565
Dividends	3,600	—
Tax credits	900	—
Total UK income	10,765	5,565
Deduct Personal allowance	3,765	3,765
Taxable UK income	£7,000	£1,800

Tax on total UK income:

	Hugh	Elizabeth
£3,900/1,800 @ 20%	780.00	360.00
£3,100 @ 20% (savings income)	620.00	
	1,400.00	360.00
Deduct Tax credits	900.00	
	£500.00	£360.00

But tax is limited under *FA 1995, s 128* as follows

	£	£
Schedule A	2,000	5,000

(Bank interest and dividends are 'excluded income'.)

	Hugh	Elizabeth
£2,000/3,900 @ 20%	400.00	780.00
£1,100 @ 24%		264.00
	£400.00	£1,044.00

Notes

(*a*)   Personal allowances (if available) due to a non-resident are set against income from a trade carried on by a branch or agency or under Schedule A in priority to 'excluded income'.

'Excluded income' includes income chargeable under Schedule C, Schedule D, Case III and Schedule F together with any income from a certificate of tax deposit chargeable under Schedule D, Case VI, some social security benefits and any other income so designated by the Treasury. [*FA 1995, s 128*].

Hugh's UK income tax liability is therefore restricted to £400.00 (plus £900.00 in tax credits, which cannot be reclaimed). Elizabeth's liability is not reduced under *FA 1995, s 128* and is thus £360.00.

14   Partnerships

14.1   CHANGES IN PARTNERS ETC. *[ICTA 1988, ss 111, 113, 277(2); FA 1994, ss 215(1)(3)(c)(4)(5), 216(1)(2); FA 1995, s 117]*
P, Q and R have carried on a profession in partnership for a number of years, sharing profits in the ratio 2:2:1. Accounts are made up to 30 June. P leaves the partnership on 30 June 1994 and Q and R share profits 3:2 for the year to 30 June 1995 and equally thereafter. On 30 June 1997, Q leaves the partnership and on 1 July 1997, S becomes a partner. Profits are then shared between R and S in the ratio 2:1.

Results for relevant years up to 30 June 1999 are as follows

Year ended	Partners' salaries				Adjusted Profit
	P	Q	R	S	
	£	£	£	£	£
30.6.91	9,000	9,000	4,500	—	40,000
30.6.92	12,000	12,000	6,000	—	70,000
30.6.93	4,000	4,000	2,000	—	72,000
30.6.94	18,000	13,000	11,500	—	60,000
30.6.95	—	12,500	12,500	—	80,000
30.6.96	—	12,000	17,000	—	85,000
30.6.97	—	4,000	11,000	—	95,000
30.6.98	—	—	5,000	—	101,000
30.6.99	—	—	2,000	—	110,000

The adjusted profit figures above are after adding back partners' salaries. There are no capital allowances to be taken into account.

The tax position for the years 1992/93 to 1999/2000 is as follows

(i) if continuation election made on change in partners on 30.6.94

Assessments on partnership of P, Q & R

	£
1992/93 (y/e 30.6.91)	40,000
1993/94 (y/e 30.6.92)	70,000
1994/95 (y/e 30.6.93 × 3/12)	18,000

Assessments on partnership of Q & R

		£
1994/95 (y/e 30.6.93 × 9/12)		54,000
1995/96 (y/e 30.6.94)		60,000
1996/97	£	
Y/e 30.6.95	80,000	
Y/e 30.6.96	85,000	
	£165,000	

£165,000 × 12/24 = 82,500

IT 14.1 Partnerships

Taxable profits of Q, R & S individually from 1997/98

	Q £	R £	S £
1997/98 Y/e 30.6.97			
Profits £(95,000 − 11,000 − 4,000)	40,000	40,000	
Salaries	4,000	11,000	
	44,000	51,000	
1.7.97–5.4.98 £((101,000 − 5,000) × 1/3 × 9/12)			24,000
Less transitional overlap relief: (1.7.96–5.4.97 — £44,000 × 9/12)	33,000		
Schedule D, Case II	£11,000	£51,000*	£24,000
* Transitional overlap relief accrued: (1.7.96–5.4.97 — £51,000 × 9/12)	—	£38,250	—
1998/99 Y/e 30.6.98			
Profits £(101,000 − 5,000)		64,000	32,000
Salary		5,000	—
Schedule D, Case II		£69,000	£32,000*
* Overlap relief accrued: (1.7.97–5.4.98 as above)			£24,000
1999/2000 Y/e 30.6.99			
Profits £(110,000 − 2,000)		72,000	36,000
Salary		2,000	—
Schedule D, Case II		£74,000	£36,000

(ii) if no continuation election made on change in partners on 30.6.94

Assessments on partnership of P, Q & R

	Preceding year £	Actual		£	£
1992/93	40,000	3/12 × 30.6.92	17,500		
		9/12 × 30.6.93	54,000		
					71,500
1993/94	70,000	3/12 × 30.6.93	18,000		
		9/12 × 30.6.94	45,000		
					63,000
	£110,000				£134,500

Higher figure of the two is £134,500, so assessments on actual.

| 1994/95 | | 3/12 × 30.6.94 | | | £15,000 |

Taxable profits of Q, R & S individually from 1994/95

	Q £	R £	S £
1994/95			
1.7.94–5.4.95			
Profits £(80,000 − 25,000) × 9/12	24,750	16,500	
Salaries × 9/12	9,375	9,375	
Schedule D, Case II	£34,125	£25,875	
1995/96			
Y/e 30.6.95			
Profits £(80,000 − 25,000)	33,000	22,000	
Salaries	12,500	12,500	
Schedule D, Case II	£45,500*	£34,500*	
* Overlap relief accrued:			
(1.7.94–5.4.95 as above)	£34,125	£25,875	
1996/97			
Y/e 30.6.96			
Profits £(85,000 − 29,000)	28,000	28,000	
Salaries	12,000	17,000	
Schedule D, Case II	£40,000	£45,000	
1997/98			
Y/e 30.6.97			
Profits £(95,000 − 15,000)	40,000	40,000	
Salaries	4,000	11,000	
	44,000	51,000	
1.7.97–5.4.98			
£((101,000 − 5,000) × 1/3 × 9/12)			24,000
Less overlap relief (see 1995/96)	34,125		
Schedule D, Case II	£9,875	£51,000	£24,000
1998/99			
Y/e 30.6.98			
Profits £(101,000 − 5,000)		64,000	32,000
Salary		5,000	—
Schedule D, Case II		£69,000	£32,000*
* Overlap relief accrued:			
(1.7.97–5.4.98 as above)			£24,000
1999/2000			
Y/e 30.6.99			
Profits £(110,000 − 2,000)		72,000	36,000
Salary		2,000	—
Schedule D, Case II		£74,000	£36,000

IT 14.1 Partnerships

Partnership assessments are allocated between partners as follows

(iii) if continuation election made (see (i) above)

Partnership of P, Q & R

	P £	Q £	R £	Total £
1992/93				
Salaries 3/12 × 30.6.92	3,000	3,000	1,500	7,500
9/12 × 30.6.93	3,000	3,000	1,500	7,500
				15,000
Balance 2:2:1	10,000	10,000	5,000	25,000
Division of assessment	£16,000	£16,000	£8,000	£40,000
1993/94				
Salaries 3/12 × 30.6.93	1,000	1,000	500	2,500
9/12 × 30.6.94	13,500	9,750	8,625	31,875
				34,375
Balance 2:2:1	14,250	14,250	7,125	35,625
Division of assessment	£28,750	£25,000	£16,250	£70,000
1994/95				
Salaries 3/12 × 30.6.94	4,500	3,250	2,875	10,625
Balance 2:2:1	2,950	2,950	1,475	7,375
Division of assessment	£7,450	£6,200	£4,350	£18,000

Partnership of Q & R

	Q £	R £	Total £
1994/95			
Salaries 9/12 × 30.6.95	9,375	9,375	18,750
Balance 3:2	21,150	14,100	35,250
Division of assessment	£30,525	£23,475	£54,000
1995/96			
Salaries 3/12 × 30.6.95	3,125	3,125	6,250
Balance to 30.6.95 at 3:2	5,250	3,500	8,750
			15,000
Salaries 9/12 × 30.6.96	9,000	12,750	21,750
Balance from 1.7.95 at 1:1	11,625	11,625	23,250
Division of assessment	£29,000	£31,000	£60,000
1996/97			
Salaries 3/12 × 30.6.96	3,000	4,250	7,250
Salaries 9/12 × 30.6.97	3,000	8,250	11,250
			18,500
Balance 1:1	32,000	32,000	64,000
Division of assessment	£38,000	£44,500	£82,500

(iv) if continuation election not made (see (ii) above)

Partnership of P, Q & R

	P £	Q £	R £	Total £
1992/93				
Salaries 3/12 × 30.6.92	3,000	3,000	1,500	7,500
9/12 × 30.6.93	3,000	3,000	1,500	7,500
				15,000
Balance 2:2:1	22,600	22,600	11,300	56,500
	£28,600	£28,600	£14,300	£71,500
1993/94				
Salaries 3/12 × 30.6.93	1,000	1,000	500	2,500
9/12 × 30.6.94	13,500	9,750	8,625	31,875
				34,375
Balance 2:2:1	11,450	11,450	5,725	28,625
Division of assessment	£25,950	£22,200	£14,850	£63,000
1994/95				
Salaries 3/12 × 30.6.94	4,500	3,250	2,875	10,625
Balance 2:2:1	1,750	1,750	875	4,375
Division of assessment	£6,250	£5,000	£3,750	£15,000

A comparison can now be made of taxable profits under the two options under consideration

(v) If continuation election made in respect of 30.6.94 change

	P £	Q £	R £	S £	Total £
1992/93	16,000	16,000	8,000		40,000 (1)
1993/94	28,750	25,000	16,250		70,000 (1)
1994/95 (PQR)	7,450	6,200	4,350		18,000 (1)
1994/95 (QR)		30,525	23,475		54,000 (1)
1995/96		29,000	31,000		60,000 (1)
1996/97		38,000	44,500		82,500 (1)
1997/98		11,000	51,000	24,000	86,000 (2)
1998/99			69,000	32,000	101,000 (2)
1999/2000			74,000	36,000	110,000 (2)
	£52,200	£155,725	£321,575	£92,000	£621,500
Overlap relief c/f			£38,250	£24,000	£62,250

(1) = Partnership to be assessed in one sum.
(2) = Partners to be taxed individually on their shares.

(vi) If no continuation election made in respect of 30.6.94 change

	P £	Q £	R £	S £	Total £
1992/93	28,600	28,600	14,300		71,500 (1)
1993/94	25,950	22,200	14,850		63,000 (1)
1994/95 (PQR)	6,250	5,000	3,750		15,000 (1)
1994/95 (QR)		34,125	25,875		60,000 (2)
1995/96		45,500	34,500		80,000 (2)
1996/97		40,000	45,000		85,000 (2)
1997/98		9,875	51,000	24,000	84,875 (2)
1998/99			69,000	32,000	101,000 (2)
1999/2000			74,000	36,000	110,000 (2)
	£60,800	£185,300	£332,275	£92,000	£670,375

Overlap relief c/f			£25,875	£24,000	£49,875

(1) = Partnership to be assessed in one sum.
(2) = Partners to be taxed individually on their shares.

Summary

The difference between (v) and (vi) above, after taking overlap relief into account, is £61,250 ((£621,500 − £62,250) − (£670,375 − £49,875)).

With a continuation election, 12 months' profits escape tax, being half the profits for the two-year period to 30.6.96, £82,500. In addition, 9 months' profits (1.7.96 to 5.4.97) attract transitional overlap relief, £71,250. Total drop-out of profits is thus £153,750 (£82,500 + £71,250).

With no continuation election, 21 months' profits escape tax, being profits for the period 1.7.90 to 5.4.92, a total of £92,500.

The difference in profits escaping tax is thus proved to be £61,250 (£153,750 − £92,500).

Notes

(a)   A continuation election under *ICTA 1988, s 113(2) as originally enacted* must be made within two years of the date of change (before 1 July 1996 in this example). The time limit is strictly applied, although the Revenue may accept late elections in exceptional circumstances (see Revenue Press Release 23 November 1992).

(b)   On a partnership change after 5 April 1997, the partnership is automatically regarded as continuing, providing there is at least one continuing partner. This also applies to an earlier change (after 5 April 1994) if the partners are already on the current year basis of assessment. *[ICTA 1988, s 113(1)(2); FA 1994, ss 215(4)(5), 216(1)].*

(c)   On a partnership change before 6 April 1994 in respect of which no continuation election was made, special rules applied to determine the basis periods for the opening years of assessment of the new business. *[ICTA 1988, ss 61(4), 62(4)(5)].* See the 1993/94 and earlier editions of this book for an illustration. These rules can never apply to a change after 5 April 1994, as such a change will automatically bring the current year basis rules into operation if no continuation election is made.

(*d*)   Under the current year basis, profits are allocated between partners for tax purposes in accordance with the profit-sharing ratios in force during a period of account (not those in force during the tax year as under the preceding year basis). Each partner is taxed on his own share, the partnership no longer being treated as a separate entity for tax purposes. The rules used to determine the basis periods for the early years and the closing year of a business apply equally to individuals joining or leaving a partnership. [*ICTA 1988, s 111; FA 1994, s 215(1)(4)(5); FA 1995, s 117*]. See also 14.2 below.

(*e*)   For general examples on the current year basis of assessment, see 19.1 – 19.4 SCHEDULE D, CASES I AND II. See also 2 CAPITAL ALLOWANCES and 10 LOSSES.

14.2   **TRANSITION TO CURRENT YEAR BASIS — NEW PARTNER JOINING IN 1996/97**
A and B have traded in partnership since before 6 April 1994, preparing accounts to 30 June and sharing profits equally. C joins the firm on 1 January 1997 with a one-third profit share. The three partners make a continuation election. Profits as adjusted for tax purposes for relevant years are as follows.

	£
Year to 30.6.94	36,000
Year to 30.6.95	38,000
Year to 30.6.96	42,000
Year to 30.6.97	45,000
Year to 30.6.98	48,000

Assessment will be as follows.

	Total £	A £	B £	C £
Partnership assessments				
1995/96 (y/e 30.6.94)	36,000	18,000	18,000	N/A
1996/97 (2 yrs to 30.6.96 × $\frac{1}{2}$ = 40,000)				
6.4.96 to 31.12.96 ($\frac{3}{4}$)	30,000	15,000	15,000	N/A
1.1.97 to 5.4.97 ($\frac{1}{4}$)	10,000	3,334	3,333	3,333
	40,000	18,334	18,333	3,333

Individual self-assessments

1997/98

		A	B	C
A (y/e 30.6.97 × $\frac{1}{3}$)		15,000		
B (y/e 30.6.97 × $\frac{1}{3}$)			15,000	
C (1.1.97 to 31.12.97 × $\frac{1}{3}$) see note (*a*) below				
1.1.97 to 30.6.97 × $\frac{1}{3}$				7,500
1.7.97 to 31.12.97 × $\frac{1}{3}$				8,000
				15,500

1998/99

	A	B	C
A (y/e 30.6.98 × $\frac{1}{3}$)	16,000		
B (y/e 30.6.98 × $\frac{1}{3}$)		16,000	
C (y/e 30.6.98 × $\frac{1}{3}$)			16,000

Overlap relief
A & B (Transitional overlap relief)
1.7.96 to 5.4.97 — $\frac{9}{12}$ × £15,000 each   11,250   11,250

C
Transitional overlap relief:
1.1.97 to 5.4.97 — $\frac{3}{6}$ × £7,500   3,750
Actual overlap relief:
1.7.97 to 31.12.97   8,000

Total overlap relief
(overlap period — 9 months each)   11,250   11,250   11,750

Notes

(a)   1997/98 is only C's second tax year of trading and his basis period must be determined in accordance with the opening years rules (see IT 19.1(B)). It is thus his first twelve months of trading. This is the case even though the concept of partners' individual basis periods did not apply to C's first year, 1996/97.

(b)   C's overlap relief is partly transitional and partly the result of a genuine overlap of basis periods. The distinction would be of importance only if the anti-avoidance rules (see IT 19.4(C)).

14.3   **PARTNERSHIP TRADING AND INVESTMENT INCOME UNDER CURRENT YEAR BASIS** [*ICTA 1988, s 111(7)–(9); FA 1994, s 215(1); FA 1995, s 117*]
X and Y begin to trade in partnership on 1 July 1995 preparing first accounts to 30 September 1996 and sharing profits equally. Z joins the firm as an equal partner on 1 October 1997. Y leaves the firm on 31 March 1999. Accounts are prepared to that date to ascertain Y's entitlement but the accounting date then reverts to 30 September and the partnership does not give notice to the Revenue of a change of accounting date, so there is no change of basis period. In addition to trading profits, the partnership had a source of lettings income which ceased in September 1998 and is in receipt of both taxed and untaxed interest, the latter from a source commencing in October 1996. Taxed interest is received on 31 March each year. Relevant figures as adjusted for tax purposes are as follows.

	Schedule D, Case I	Schedule A	Schedule D, Case III	Taxed interest (gross)
	£	£	£	£
15 months to 30.9.96	30,000	4,500	—	750
Year to 30.9.97	24,000	5,000	1,000	1,500
Year to 30.9.98	39,000	3,000	600	300
6 months to 31.3.99	19,500	—	225	165
6 months to 30.9.99	14,000	—	140	—

The partners' shares of taxable income from the partnership for the years 1995/96 to 1999/2000 are as follows

Schedule D, Case I

	X £	Y £	Z £
1995/96 1.7.95–5.4.96 (£30,000 × 9/15)	9,000	9,000	
1996/97 1.10.95–30.9.96 (£30,000 × 12/15)	12,000*	12,000*	
* Overlap relief accrued 1.10.95–5.4.96 (£30,000 × 6/15)	(6,000)	(6,000)	
1997/98 Y/e 30.9.97	12,000	12,000	
1.10.97–5.4.98 (£39,000 × 6/12 ×1/3)			6,500
1998/99 Y/e 30.9.98	13,000	13,000	13,000*
1.10.98–31.3.99		6,500	
		19,500	
Less overlap relief		(6,000)	
		13,500	
* Overlap relief accrued 1.10.97–5.4.98 (as above)			(6,500)
1999/2000 Y/e 30.9.99 1.10.98–31.3.99 1.4.99–30.9.99	6,500 7,000		6,500 7,000
	13,500		13,500

Schedule A

	X £	Y £	Z £
1995/96 1.7.95–5.4.96 (£4,500 × 9/15)	1,350	1,350	
1996/97 1.10.95–30.9.96 (£4,500 × 12/15)	1,800*	1,800*	
* Overlap relief accrued 1.10.95–5.4.96 (£4,500 × 6/15)	(900)	(900)	
1997/98 Y/e 30.9.97	2,500	2,500	

IT 14.3 Partnerships

1.10.97–5.4.98 ($£3,000 \times 6/12 \times 1/3$)			500
1998/99 Y/e 30.9.98	1,000	1,000	1,000*
1.10.98–31.3.99		—	
		1,000	
Less overlap relief		(900)	
		100	
* Overlap relief accrued 1.10.97–5.4.98 (as above)			(500)

Schedule D, Case III

1997/98 Y/e 30.9.97	500	500	
1.10.97–5.4.98 ($£600 \times 6/12 \times 1/3$)			100
1998/99 Y/e 30.9.98	200	200	200*
1.10.98–31.3.99		75	
		275	
* Overlap relief accrued 1.10.97–5.4.98 (as above)			(100)
1999/2000 Y/e 30.9.99			
1.10.98–31.3.99	75		75
1.4.99—30.9.99	70		70
	145		145

Taxed interest

1995/96 (received 31.3.96)	375	375	
1996/97 (received 31.3.97)	750	750	
1997/98 (received 31.3.98)	100	100	100
1998/99 (received 31.3.99)	55	55	55
1999/2000	***	—	***

*** Each to be based on one-half of interest received 31.3.2000.

Notes

(a)   As regards trading profits, see also 14.1 above and in particular notes (*b*), (*d*) and (*e*) thereto.

(b)   Under the current year basis, untaxed investment income of a trading or professional partnership is taxed by reference to the same periods as Schedule D, Case I and II profits with the same rules as to overlap relief, changes of accounting date (not illustrated here) etc. For this purpose, all sources of such income are regarded as a single source which commences when a partner joins the partnership and ceases when he leaves (regardless of when any source actually commences or ceases). Thus, the basis of assessment for any tax year will always follow that for the Schedule D, Case I or II source.

(c)   Any excess of investment income overlap relief over untaxed investment income for the tax year in which the relief falls to be given is deductible in arriving at the partner's total income for that year (not illustrated in this example).

(d)   The above rules do not apply to taxed investment income, which is taxed on a fiscal year basis as for an individual but is apportioned between partners according to their shares for the accounting period in which the income arises. Nor do those rules apply to untaxed income receivable by a partnership not carrying on a trade or profession, such income being taxable on a fiscal year basis as for an individual.

(e)   For convenience, income for accounting periods has been apportioned to tax years on a time basis in this example. However, *ICTA 1988, s 72* strictly permits a time basis to be used only where 'it is necessary'. It may be more appropriate to apportion untaxed interest, for example, according to the dates when it was received. For instance, if the £600 interest received in the year to 30 September 1998 had been received as to, say, £100 on 31 December 1997 and £500 on 30 June 1998, Z's taxable interest for 1997/98 (and his overlap relief) could be taken as a one-third share of £100 rather than a one-third share of £600 × 6/12.

14.4 PARTNERSHIP LOSSES

(A)   No change in profit-sharing ratios
A partnership of J, K and L have traded for some years and share profits equally. The results as adjusted for tax for the five years to 30 September 1996 are as follows

	£
Year ended 30.9.92	2,000
30.9.93	(12,000)
30.9.94	3,000
30.9.95	15,000
30.9.96	21,050

The three partners have different personal circumstances. J has considerable other income and wishes to obtain the benefit of the loss as soon as possible. K inherited the residue of his mother's estate and interest from investments commenced in the year ended 5.4.95. L has no other income. To obtain the maximum benefit of the loss, the partners make loss claims under *ICTA 1988, ss 380(1), 380(2)* and *385(1)* respectively.

IT 14.4 Partnerships

The effect on the partnership assessment of the above is as follows

1994/95 — Nil assessment

1995/96	J £	K £	L £	Total £
Profit — year ended 30.9.94	1,000	1,000	1,000	3,000
Deduct loss claim				
L — Sec 385(1)			(1,000)	(1,000)
	£1,000	£1,000	Nil	£2,000

1996/97				
Profit — year ended 30.9.95				15,000
Profit — year ended 30.9.96				21,050
				36,050
£36,050 × $\frac{365}{731}$	6,000	6,000	6,000	18,000
Deduct loss claim				
L — Sec 385(1)			(3,000)	(3,000)
	£6,000	£6,000	£3,000	£15,000

The loss available to the partners arising from the accounts for the year to 30.9.93 has been utilised as follows

	£	£	£	£
Share of loss	4,000	4,000	4,000	12,000
Sec 380(1) 1993/94	(4,000)			
Sec 380(2) 1994/95		(4,000)		
Sec 385(1) 1995/96			(1,000)	
1996/97			(3,000)	

Note

(a) L would not make a claim under *ICTA 1988, s 380(1)* to set his share of the loss against the profits assessed in 1993/94 since he would thereby lose the benefit of personal reliefs.

(B) Change in profit-sharing ratios

The facts and the loss relief claims made are as in (A) above, except that as from 1 October 1993, the partners share profits in the ratio 2:2:1.

The partnership assessments are now as follows

1994/95 — Nil assessment

1995/96	J	K	L	Total
	£	£	£	£
Profit — year ended 30.9.94	1,200	1,200	600	3,000
Deduct loss claim				
L — *Sec 385(1)*			(600)	(600)
	£1,200	£1,200	Nil	£2,400

1996/97				
Profit — year ended 30.9.95				15,000
Profit — year ended 30.9.96				21,050
				36,050
£36,050 × $\frac{365}{731}$	7,200	7,200	3,600	18,000
Deduct loss claim				
L — *Sec 385(1)*			(3,400)	(3,400)
	£7,200	£7,200	£200	£14,600

The loss available to the partners arising from the accounts for the year to 30.9.93 has been utilised as follows

	£	£	£	£
Share of loss for *Sec 380*				
£12,000 × $\frac{6}{12}$ × $\frac{1}{3}$ each	2,000	2,000		4,000
£12,000 × $\frac{6}{12}$ × $\frac{2}{5}$ each	2,400	2,400		4,800
Share of loss for *Sec 385*				
£12,000 × $\frac{1}{3}$			4,000	4,000
	4,400	4,400	4,000	12,800
Sec 380(1) 1993/94	(4,400)			
Sec 380(2) 1994/95		(4,400)		
Sec 385(1) 1995/96			(600)	
1996/97			(3,400)	

Notes

(*a*) Although the loss amounted to £12,000, a total of £12,800 is available for relief. This is due to the fact that, for *Sec 380* purposes, the loss is apportioned according to sharing ratios for the year of assessment in which the accounting period of loss falls, whereas, for *Sec 385* purposes, it is apportioned in accordance with sharing ratios for the accounting period of loss.

(*b*) Where the current year basis of assessment applies (not illustrated in this example), losses are apportioned between partners according to sharing ratios of the accounting period of loss. [*ICTA 1988, s 111(3); FA 1994, s 215(1); FA 1995, s 117*]. This applies for the purposes of all loss relief provisions.

14.5 **LIMITED PARTNERSHIPS — LOSSES** [*ICTA 1988, ss 117, 118*]

R, S and T Ltd, who have been trading in partnership for several years preparing accounts to 30 June, share profits and losses equally. S and T Ltd are limited partners. T Ltd also prepares its accounts to 30 June.

For the year ended 30 June 1997, the partnership made a loss of £18,000. Other relevant details are as follows

	R £	S £	T Ltd £
Other income			
1997/98	10,000	8,000	
Year ended 30.6.97			20,000
Capital and accumulated profits			
At 5.4.98	4,000	5,000	
At 30.6.97			5,500

R and S may claim *Sec 380(1)* **loss relief for 1997/98 as follows**

	R £	S £
Other income	10,000	8,000
Share of partnership loss (restricted for S)	(6,000)	(5,000)
	£4,000	£3,000
Loss carried forward against future partnership trading profits	—	£1,000

T Ltd may claim *Sec 393A(1)(a)* **loss relief for the year ended 30.6.97 as follows**

	£
Other income	20,000
Share of partnership loss (restricted)	(5,500)
	£14,500
Loss carried forward against future partnership trading profits	£500

Note

(*a*) The amounts of partnership losses, interest, charges and allowances which a limited partner may set against income other than from the partnership trade is restricted to the amount of his capital contribution and accumulated profits at the end of the year of assessment (accounting period if a company) of loss. No such restriction applies to unlimited partners. [*ICTA 1988, ss 117, 118*].

14.6 PARTNERSHIP WITH COMPANY

See the example at 119.1 PARTNERSHIPS and also 14.4 above.

General Notes

(a)   Profits in 1996/97 the transitional basis period are calculated by using '*the appropriate percentage*'. [*FA 1994, 20 Sch 5*]. The '*appropriate percentage*' is defined by reference to the number of days in the transitional basis period. But the Inland Revenue will be prepared to accept any other reasonable time-based computation using weeks, months or fractions of months. [*SAT 1 (1995), paragraph 6.8*].

(b)   The overlap period is defined as '*the number of days in the period in which the overlap profit arose*'. [*ICTA 1988, s 63A(2)*]. Although the definition refers to 'days' the Inland Revenue will be prepared to accept any other reasonable measure, for example months or fractions of months, providing that measure is used consistently, and will ensure that, over the lifetime of the business, the total profits assessed exactly equal the profits made. [*SAT 1 (1995), paragraph 1.86*].

15 Patents

Cross-reference. See 2.12 CAPITAL ALLOWANCES for allowances for patent rights.

[*ICTA 1988, s 527*]

15.1 An inventor received £17,860 after deduction of tax at source (i.e. £23,500 gross) on 1 June 1996, for the use of his patent over a four-year period ending on that date. He is a single man and his only other income for the four years was a salary as set out below.

In the absence of spreading provisions, the assessments for the four years to 5 April 1997 are

Year of assessment	1993/94	1994/95	1995/96	1996/97
	£	£	£	£
Salary	7,500	8,500	9,200	10,500
Patent rights				23,500
	7,500	8,500	9,200	34,000
Personal allowance	3,445	3,445	3,525	3,765
Taxable income	£4,055	£5,055	£5,675	£30,235
Tax thereon	888.75	1,113.75	1,258.75	7,858.00
Less tax deducted at source				5,640.00
	£888.75	£1,113.75	£1,258.75	£2,218.00
Total tax payable				£5,479.25

The inventor may however claim under *ICTA 1988, s 527* for the assessment to be limited to the tax payable if the royalties had been spread over the four-year period to which they relate. The tax payable would then have been

	£	£	£	£
Salary	7,500	8,500	9,200	10,500
Patent rights	5,875	5,875	5,875	5,875
	13,375	14,375	15,075	16,375
Personal allowance	3,445	3,445	3,525	3,765
Taxable income	£9,930	£10,930	£11,550	£12,610
Tax thereon	2,357.50	2,582.50	2,727.50	2,870.40
Less tax deducted at source	1,468.75	1,468.75	1,468.75	1,410.00
	£888.75	£1,113.75	£1,258.75	£1,460.40
Total tax payable				£4,721.65

A claim would be beneficial in this case, saving tax of £757.60 over the four years.

16   Post-Cessation Receipts and Expenditure

[ICTA 1988, ss 103–110]

16.1   POST-CESSATION RECEIPTS

A trader retired and closed down his trade on 31 March 1997 and, in the year 1997/98, the following subsequent events occurred.

(i)   He paid a former customer £100 as compensation for defective work.

(ii)   In the accounts at the date of closure a specific provision was made against a debt for £722 and in addition there was a general bad debt provision of £2,000. All debts were recovered in full.

(iii)   Stock in trade considered valueless at the date of cessation was sold for £215.

(iv)   He eventually sold a piece of machinery six months after cessation for £136. This had been valued at nil at cessation.

(v)   At 31 March 1997, after obtaining maximum loss relief, there was a trading loss of £333 unrelieved.

The above will be subject to tax for 1997/98 as follows

Schedule D, Case VI	£	£
Sales		215
Bad debts recovered		722
		937
Deduct Compensation payment	100	
Balance of losses	197	
		297
		£640

Notes

(*a*)   The proceeds of sale of the plant are taken into the final capital allowances computation, i.e. for 1996/97 [*CAA 1990, s 26(1)(e)*] and the loss carried forward of £333 has been reduced by the balancing charge to £197.

(*b*)   An election could be made under *ICTA 1988, s 108* for the post-cessation receipts to be taxable in 1996/97, being the year in which cessation occurred.

16.2   POST-CESSATION EXPENDITURE *[ICTA 1988, s 109A; FA 1995, s 90]*

Simcock ceased trading in October 1995. In 1996/97, the following events occur in connection with his former trade.

(i)   Simcock pays a former customer £9,250 by way of damages for defective work carried out by him in the course of the trade.

(ii)   He incurs legal fees of £800 in connection with the above claim.

(iii)   He incurs debt collection fees of £200 in connection with trade debts outstanding at cessation and which were taken into account as receipts in computing profits.

(iv)   He writes off a trade debt of £500, giving the Revenue notice by 5 April 1997 of his having done so.

(v)   He incurs legal fees of £175 in relation to a debt of £1,000 owing by him to a supplier which, although disputed, was taken into account as an expense in computing his trading profits.

(vi)   He eventually agrees to pay £500 in full settlement of his liability in respect of the debt in (v) above, paying £250 in March 1997 and the remaining £250 in May 1997.

In 1997/98, Simcock receives £3,000 from his insurers in full settlement of their liability with regard to the expense incurred in (i) above.

For 1996/97, Simcock's total income before taking account of the above events is £9,000 and he also has capital gains of £7,500 (with £1,000 capital losses brought forward from 1995/96).

Simcock makes a claim under *ICTA 1988, s 109A* (relief for post-cessation expenditure) for 1996/97 and a simultaneous claim under *FA 1995, s 90(4)* to have any excess relief set against capital gains.

Simcock's tax position for 1996/97 is as follows

	£	£
Income		
Total income before *Sec 109A* claim		9,000
Deduct Post-cessation expenditure		
(i)	9,250	
(ii)	800	
(iii)	200	
(iv)	500	
(v) not allowable under *Sec 109A*	—	
(vi) *less* unpaid expenses at 5.4.97	(750)	
	10,000	
Restricted to total income	(9,000)	(9,000)
Excess relief	1,000	
Capital gains		
Gains before losses brought forward and annual exemption		7,500
Deduct Post-cessation expenditure (excess as above)		1,000
Net gains for the year		6,500
Losses brought forward	1,000	
Used in 1996/97	200	200
Carried forward	£800	
Net gains (covered by annual exemption)		£6,300

For 1997/98, Simcock will have taxable post-cessation receipts of £3,000 arising from the insurance recovery. He will be able to offset expenses of £175 under (v) above, which, whilst not within *Sec 109A*, should qualify as a deduction under *Sec 105* against post-cessation receipts. He will also have post-cessation expenditure within *Sec 109A* of £250 in respect of the further payment in 1997/98 under (vi) above, the 1996/97 *Sec 109A* expenditure having been restricted by at least that amount (see note (*b*)).

Notes

(*a*)   Under *Sec 109A*, relief is available against total income and, if required, chargeable gains for specified types of expenditure and for bad debts where the expenditure is incurred or the debt proved to be bad after 28 November 1994 and within seven years after the date of cessation of the trade, profession or vocation. A debt is 'proved to be bad' in the tax year in which notification that it is bad is given to the Revenue (see Revenue Press Release 7 March 1995). Any excess *Sec 109A* relief cannot be carried forward against total income or gains of a subsequent year but is available as a deduction against any future post-cessation receipts.

(*b*) *Sec 109A* expenditure is restricted to the extent that any expenses were taken into account in computing profits but remained unpaid at the end of the year to which the claim relates. Any subsequent payment is itself treated as a *Sec 109A* expense to the extent that the unpaid expense previously caused *Sec 109A* expenditure to be restricted.

17   Retirement Annuities and Personal Pension Schemes

[ICTA 1988, ss 618–629, 630–655; FA 1989, 7 Sch; SI 1993 No 2950; SI 1994 No 3009]

17.1   RELIEF FOR CONTRIBUTIONS

(A)   General

C is an employee whose date of birth is 30 April 1944 and who does not participate in his employer's occupational pension scheme. His earnings, as computed for Schedule E purposes, for 1995/96 and 1996/97 are £80,000 and £84,000 respectively. C pays annual retirement annuity premiums of £6,000 under long-standing contracts. For all years up to and including 1994/95, he has paid additional retirement annuity premiums and personal pension scheme contributions so as to take maximum advantage of the relief available to him; he thus has no unused relief.

In August 1995, C makes a contribution of £12,900 to a personal pension scheme. In December 1995, his employer contributes £750 to this scheme.

In the year ended 5 April 1997, C and his employer make contributions of £18,000 and £1,000 respectively to the scheme.

The maximum relief is calculated as follows

1995/96

	£	£
Maximum relief for personal pension contributions:		
25% of net relevant earnings of £78,600 — note (*c*)		19,650
Deduct retirement annuity relief claimed	6,000	
employer's contribution	750	6,750
Relief due		12,900
Amount paid		12,900
Unused relief		Nil
Maximum relief for retirement annuity premiums:		
$17\frac{1}{2}\%$ of net relevant earnings of £80,000		14,000
Amount paid		6,000
		8,000
Less relief claimed for personal pension contributions		12,900
Unused relief		Nil
Total relief due (£12,900 + £6,000)		£18,900

1996/97

	£	£
Maximum relief for personal pension contributions:		
30% of net relevant earnings of £82,200 — note (*c*)		24,660
Deduct retirement annuity relief claimed	6,000	
employer's contribution	1,000	7,000
Relief due		17,660
Amount paid (see note (*e*))		18,000
Unused relief		Nil

	£
Maximum relief for retirement annuity premiums:	
20% of net relevant earnings of £84,000	16,800
Amount paid	6,000
	10,800
Less relief claimed for personal pension contributions	17,660
Unused relief	Nil
Total relief due (£17,660 + £6,000)	£23,660

Notes

(a) Maximum relief is calculated by reference to a percentage of net relevant earnings, such percentage being dependent on C's age at the beginning of the tax year. In 1995/96, he was 50 at the beginning of the tax year. On 6 April 1996, he was aged 51. Different percentages apply for personal pension scheme contributions and retirement annuity premiums. [*ICTA 1988, ss 626, 640; FA 1989, 7 Sch 3*].

(b) Contributions made by an employer and premiums paid under a retirement annuity contract approved under *ICTA 1988, s 620* must be taken into account in arriving at the maximum deduction available for personal pension scheme contributions. [*ICTA 1988, s 655(1)(a)*].

(c) For 1996/97, any excess of net relevant earnings over £78,600 is disregarded in computing maximum relief for personal pension contributions. For 1995/96 the earnings cap was £78,600. [*ICTA 1988, s 640A; FA 1989, 7 Sch 4; SI 1993 No 2950; SI 1994 No 3009*].

(d) The employer's contribution is not assessable as a benefit-in-kind, providing that it is made to an approved scheme. [*ICTA 1988, s 643(1)*].

(e) For 1995/96, there are excess contributions of £340 which do not qualify for relief and must be repaid. Such an excess is deemed to relate primarily to contributions made by the individual rather than by his employer. [*ICTA 1988, s 638(3)–(5)*].

(f) Although not illustrated in this example, basic rate relief is given to *employees* by deduction at source from contributions, leaving higher rate relief to be given via the Notice of Coding or by deduction in a Schedule E assessment. [*ICTA 1988, s 639; SI 1988 No 1013*].

(B) Premiums related back

A, whose date of birth is 25 February 1958, is a partner in a firm of solicitors which prepares accounts to 5 April annually. His share of profits for 1996/97 is £23,800.

A's Schedule D furnished holiday lettings loss for 1996/97 is £2,600. He also has a salary from a non-pensionable part-time employment which for 1996/97 amounted to £4,800.

A's net relevant earnings for 1996/97 are

	£
Share of profits	23,800
Salary	4,800
	28,600
Deduct Furnished holiday lettings losses note (b)	2,600
	£26,000
Limit of relief for qualifying premiums 20% of £26,000	£5,200

IT 17.1   Retirement Annuities and Personal Pension Schemes

On 15 January 1998, A pays a single contribution of £6,000 to an approved personal pension scheme and elects, on 12 May 1998, under *ICTA 1988, s 641* to have £5,200 related back to 1996/97. This will maximise A's relief entitlement for 1996/97. The balance of £800 (£6,000 − £5,200) will be available for relief in 1997/98.

Notes

(a)   An election for a contribution, or part thereof, to be carried back to the preceding tax year must be made by 5 July in the year of assessment following that in which the contribution is actually paid. [*ICTA 1988, s 641(4)*].

(b)   A furnished holiday lettings profit would have been relevant earnings. [*ICTA 1988, ss 503(1), 644*]. Therefore, a loss from that source must be deducted in arriving at net relevant earnings. [*ICTA 1988, s 646(2)(d)*].

(C) Unused relief

P, who was born in 1972, entered non-pensionable employment in September 1993 and his recent personal pension scheme contribution record, assuming no unused relief before 6 April 1993, is as follows·

Year	Net relevant earnings £	Maximum relief due £	Amount paid £	Unused relief £
1993/94	15,000	2,625	2,425	200
1994/95	19,000	3,325	2,200	1,125
1995/96	22,000	3,850	3,375	475

In 1996/97, P pays a personal pension scheme contribution of £5,000. His net relevant earnings for that year are £24,000.

P has excess contributions for 1996/97 as follows

Net relevant earnings	£24,000

	£
Maximum relief (£24,000 × $17\frac{1}{2}$%)	4,200
Contributions made	5,000
Excess contributions	£800

Tax relief on the excess contributions can be obtained in the following way

In 1995/96
£475 may be related back to 1995/96 and relief obtained in that year.

In 1996/97
The remainder (£325) is matched on a first in, first out basis with the unused relief brought forward.

	£	£
Excess contributions as above		800
Deduct amount related back to 1995/96		475
		325
Unused relief 1993/94	200	
Unused relief 1994/95	125	325

Thus, full relief is obtained for the £5,000 paid in 1996/97 and P's revised relief record is as follows

Year	Net relevant earnings £	Maximum relief due £	Amount relieved £	Unused relief £	Unused relief c/f £
1993/94	15,000	2,625	2,425	200	200
1994/95	19,000	3,325	2,200	1,125	1,325
1995/96	22,000	3,850	3,850	—	1,325
1996/97	24,000	4,200	4,525	(325)	1,000

Notes

(a)   The balance of the 1994/95 unused relief, i.e. £1,000, will have to be utilised by 5 April 2002 (i.e. 6 years plus 1 year carry-back).

(b)   As an alternative to carrying back £475 to 1995/96, P could have utilised an additional £475 of his 1994/95 unused relief and obtained relief in 1996/97 for the whole of the £5,000 paid in that year. The £475 unused relief for 1995/96 would then be carried forward together with £525 of the 1994/95 relief. A further possibility is to carry back £1,800 to 1995/96, thus utilising all unused relief in that year and leaving £1,000 unused relief for 1996/97. This would be advantageous if the taxpayer's marginal tax rate were higher in the earlier year.

(D) Interaction between personal pension contributions and retirement annuity premiums
Y is self-employed and pays both retirement annuity premiums (RAPs), under a pre-1 July 1988 contract and contributions to a personal pension scheme (PPCs). He had no unused relief brought forward at 6 April 1989, on which date he was 47 years of age. His net relevant earnings (NRE), RAPs paid and PPCs paid in each of the years 1989/90 to 1996/97 are as set out below. At no time does Y elect to carry back an RAP or a PPC to a previous year.

	NRE £	Earnings cap £	PPCs paid £	RAPs paid £
1989/90	58,000	60,000	—	10,000
1990/91	67,000	64,800	6,400	10,000
1991/92	72,000	71,400	7,000	10,000
1992/93	74,000	75,000	8,000	10,000
1993/94	78,000	75,000	12,000	10,000
1994/95	90,000	76,800	16,500	10,000
1995/96	120,000	78,600	14,000	10,000
1996/97	125,000	82,200	16,510	10,000

IT 17.1   Retirement Annuities and Personal Pension Schemes

Y's records of amounts paid and tax relief given will look as follows

Personal pension contributions (PPCs)

	NRE £	Maximum PPC relief £	RAPs relieved £	PPCs paid £	Unused relief For year £	Unused relief Cumulative £
1989/90	58,000	14,500 (1)	(10,000)	—	4,500	4,500
1990/91	64,800	16,200 (1)	(10,000)	(6,400)	(200)	4,300
1991/92	71,400	17,850 (1)	(10,000)	(7,000)	850	5,150
1992/93	74,000	18,500 (1)	(10,000)	(8,000)	500	5,650
1993/94	75,000	22,500 (2)	(10,000)	(12,000)	500	6,150
1994/95	76,800	23,040 (2)	(10,000)	(16,500)	(3,460)	2,690
1995/96	78,600	23,580 (2)	(10,000)	(14,000)	(420)	1,850 (3)
1996/97	82,200	24,660 (2)	(10,000)	(16,150)	(1,850)	Nil

(1) = Relief at 25%
(2) = Relief at 30%
(3) = £2,690 b/f *less* £420 relieved in 1995/96 *less* £420 remaining for 1989/90 which cannot be carried forward beyond 1995/96 (although relief for the £420 could have been obtained by an election to treat part of the 1996/97 premiums as having been paid in 1995/96). The £1,850 consists of the aggregate unused relief for 1991/92, 1992/93 and 1993/94.

The aggregate for each year of the 'RAPS relieved' and 'PPCs paid' columns above represents the total relief given in each year.

Retirement annuity premiums (RAPs)

	NRE £	Maximum RAP relief £	RAPs relieved £	Unused relief £	PPCs paid £	Unused relief c/f £
1989/90	58,000	10,150 (4)	(10,000)	150	—	150
1990/91	67,000	11,725 (4)	(10,000)	1,725	(6,400)	(150)*_
1991/92	72,000	12,600 (4)	(10,000)	2,600	(7,000)	Nil*
1992/93	74,000	12,950 (4)	(10,000)	2,950	(8,000)	Nil*
1993/94	78,000	15,600 (5)	(10,000)	5,600	(12,000)	Nil*
1994/95	90,000	18,000 (5)	(10,000)	8,000	(16,500)	Nil*
1995/96	120,000	24,000 (5)	(10,000)	14,000	(14,000)	Nil
1996/97	125,000	25,000 (5)	(10,000)	15,000	(16,150)	Nil*

(4) = Relief at 17.5%
(5) = Relief at 20%

* Unused relief carried forward cannot be reduced to a negative figure, so is merely reduced to nil.

Notes

(a)   The maximum relief for PPCs for any year is reduced by any RAPs relieved in that year. [*ICTA 1988, s 655(1)(a)*]. See also (A) above. One effect of this is that if a combination of RAPs and PPCs is to be relieved in any year, the maximum relief available for that year (excluding unused relief brought forward) is restricted by reference to the earnings cap.

(*b*)   In computing unused retirement annuity relief for any year, any PPCs relieved in that year must be deducted. [*ICTA 1988, s 655(1)(b)*].

(*c*)   The maximum relief for the eight years illustrated (taking the higher of the two maxima for each year) is £161,590. The relief given is £160,410. Of the difference of £1,180, £420 is unused relief for 1989/90 which is lost under the six-year rule. The balance of £760 arises from the operation of the earnings cap for 1995/96 and 1996/97.

18   Schedule A — Property Income

Cross-reference. See 121 SCHEDULE A for the corporation tax rules.

[*ICTA 1988, ss 15, 21–43; FA 1995, s 39, 6 Sch 1, 3–12*]

18.1   **GENERAL** [*ICTA 1988, ss 15, 21; FA 1995, s 39*]

Mrs A inherited a furnished cottage in a picturesque coastal village and she and her husband decided to spend their own holiday there during the month of July and to make the cottage available for letting to other holidaymakers during the remainder of the year. The rent charged was £400 per month from June to September inclusive and £250 per month for the remainder of the year. Mrs A has no other letting income.

During 1996/97 the house was occupied from April until October, lay vacant during November, December and January and was let again for February and March. In March 1996, the tenant defaulted on two weeks' rent, which proved impossible to collect.

Several lettings were for periods of more than 31 days.

Expenses were as follows:
Business rates £480, Water rates £84, Electricity £420 (£400 received from tenants through coin operated meters), Advertising £100, Cleaning between lettings £180, House contents insurance £72, Repairs £120.

Mrs A is not assessed under Schedule D, Case I as the letting does not constitute a trade. The cottage does not qualify for relief as 'furnished holiday accommodation' under *ICTA 1988, ss 503, 504*, because of the length of the letting periods.

The Schedule A computation for 1996/97 is as follows

	£	£
Rent receivable (3 × £400 + 5 × £250)		2,450
Business rates note (*c*)	480	
Water rates ($\frac{11}{12}$ × £84)	77	
Electricity ($\frac{11}{12}$ × 420) − 400	(15)	
Advertising	100	
Cleaning $\frac{8}{9}$ × 180	160	
Insurance $\frac{11}{12}$ × 72	66	
Repairs $\frac{11}{12}$ × 120	110	
Bad debt written off	125	
Wear and tear 10% of (£2,450 − £557) note (*b*)	189	1,292
		£1,158

Notes

(*a*)   For 1995/96 onwards, subject to transitional provisions, and for income tax purposes only, all letting income from UK property, whether furnished or unfurnished, is taxed as income from a single Schedule A business carried on by the lessor. The profits of that business are computed according to Schedule D, Case I and II principles as if the business were a trade. Furnished lettings were previously chargeable under Schedule D, Case VI.

(*b*)   Expenses paid by the landlord which would otherwise be liabilities of the tenants, the most common examples being rates, water rates and council tax, are deducted from rents received in computing the 10% wear and tear charge.

(*c*)   As the business rates relate entirely to the letting, no apportionment is considered appropriate.

(d)   As the gross rental income is less than £15,000, it will be sufficient to submit to the Revenue only the following figures

	£
Rent received	2,450
Expenses	1,292
Net income	£1,158

The detailed accounts will, of course, still have to be prepared in order to arrive at the above summary. (Revenue Press Release 1 November 1991, and Revenue Leaflet IR 104 (1992) (Simple Tax Accounts)).

18.2   **TRANSITIONAL PROPOSALS** (*Revenue Press Release 10 February 1995*)

(A) Basis periods
Brown lets a number of furnished apartments and has in the past prepared furnished lettings accounts to 31 December. For tax years up to and including 1992/93, he has been assessed under Schedule D, Case VI on a preceding year basis. Both the choice of accounting date and the application of a preceding year basis are the result of a long-established practice agreed between Brown and his tax office. To enable the transition to the new Schedule A basis in *FA 1995, s 39* to be made, Brown's inspector invites him to submit accounts covering the whole of the period from the end of the 1993/94 basis period to 5 April 1995. Income and allowable expenditure are as follows

	Income	Expenditure
	£	£
Year ended 31 December 1992	14,000	3,000
27 months to 5 April 1995	36,000	9,450
Year ended 5 April 1996	17,000	4,000

Assessments will be as follows

1993/94	Schedule D, Case VI	£11,000
1994/95	Schedule D, Case VI (£36,000 − £9,450 = £26,550) × $\frac{12}{27}$	£11,800
1995/96	Schedule A	£13,000

Note
(a)   There are no statutory transitional provisions for moving from a non-statutory accounts year and/or preceding year basis to the current fiscal year basis that *must* apply for 1995/96 onwards. The above represents the Revenue's preferred option. See the 10 February 1995 press release for full details.

(B) Basis of computation
The facts are as above except that Brown also lets an unfurnished property, accounts having always been prepared to 5 April. Rent is receivable three months in advance on 6 December, 6 March, 6 June and 6 September, and was increased from £3,300 to £3,600 per annum with effect from 6 March 1995 and to £3,720 from 6 March 1996. Gross rental income receivable as shown by the Schedule A computation to 5 April 1995, prepared on the statutory basis then prevailing, is as follows

	£
3 × £825 (receivable 6.6.94, 6.9.94 and 6.12.94)	2,475
1 × £900 (receivable 6.3.95)	900
	£3,375

The accounts for the year to 5 April 1996, prepared on an accruals basis in accordance with commercial accounting practice as for trades and professions, show rent receivable of £3,610 calculated as follows

	£
Rent received on the four due dates ((3 × £900) + £930)	3,630
Less prepaid 6.4.96 to 5.6.96 (£930 × $\frac{2}{3}$)	620
	3,010
Add prepaid 6.4.95 to 5.6.95 (£900 × $\frac{2}{3}$)	600
	£3,610

Allowable expenses are £900 and £1,000 for the years to 5 April 1995 and 1996 respectively.

An adjustment to the *1994/95* computation may be agreed between taxpayer and inspector as follows

	£
Gross rents as above	3,375
Deduct Allowable expenditure	900
	2,475
Transitional adjustment:	
Deduct Rent for period 6.4.95 to 5.6.95 included	
in accounts to 5.4.96	600
Schedule A taxable income	£1,875

The position for 1995/96 is as follows

	£
Gross rents as above	3,610
Deduct Allowable expenditure	1,000
Net income from this property	2,610
Furnished lettings (see (A) above)	13,000
Profits of Schedule A business	£15,610

Note
(a)   Without the adjustment, the rent receivable for the two months to 5 June 1995 is taxed in both 1994/95 and 1995/96. In practice, adjustments are also likely to be necessary in respect of the allowable expenditure on the grounds that this is included on a payments basis for 1994/95 and an accruals basis for 1995/96. For

clarity, this example deals only with the gross rental income. See the Revenue Press Release of 10 February 1995, and, in particular, paragraph 10, for further details.

18.3   **FURNISHED HOLIDAY ACCOMMODATION** [*ICTA 1988, ss 503, 504; FA 1995, 6 Sch 21*]
Mr B owns and lets out furnished holiday cottages. None is ever let to the same person for more than 31 days. Three cottages have been owned for many years but Rose Cottage was acquired on 1 June 1996 (and first let on that day) while Ivy Cottage was sold on 30 June 1996 (and last let on that day).

In 1996/97 days available for letting and days let are as follows

	Days available	Days let
Honeysuckle Cottage	180	160
Primrose Cottage	130	100
Bluebell Cottage	150	60
Rose Cottage	150	60
Ivy Cottage	30	5

Additional information
Rose Cottage was let for 30 days between 6 April and 31 May 1997.
Ivy Cottage was let for 50 days in the period 1 July 1995 to 5 April 1996 but was available for letting for 110 days in that period.

Qualification as 'furnished holiday accommodation'

Honeysuckle Cottage qualifies as it meets both the 140-day availability test and the 70-day letting test.

Primrose Cottage does *not* qualify although it is let for more than 70 days as it fails to satisfy the 140-day test. Averaging (see below) is only possible where it is the 70-day test which is not satisfied.

Bluebell Cottage does not qualify by itself as it fails the 70-day test. However it may be included in an averaging claim.

Rose Cottage qualifies as furnished holiday accommodation. It was acquired on 1 June 1996 so qualification in 1996/97 is determined by reference to the period of twelve months beginning on the day it was first let, in which it was let for a total of 90 days.

Ivy Cottage was sold on 30 June 1996 so qualification is determined by reference to the period from 1 July 1995 to 30 June 1996 (the last day of letting). It does not qualify by itself as it was let for only 55 days in this period but it may be included in an averaging claim.

Averaging claim for 1996/97

	Days let
Honeysuckle Cottage	160
Bluebell Cottage	60
Rose Cottage	90
Ivy Cottage	55

$$\frac{160 + 60 + 90 + 55}{4} = 91.25 \text{ days} \quad \text{note } (b)$$

Notes

(a)   Income from the commercial letting of furnished holiday accommodation is treated as trading income for most purposes. In addition, capital gains tax rollover relief, retirement relief and relief for gifts of business assets are also available. [*TCGA 1992, s 241*]. See 209 HOLD-OVER RELIEFS, 222 RETIREMENT RELIEF, 223 ROLLOVER RELIEF for these reliefs.

(b)   All four cottages included in the averaging claim qualify as furnished holiday accommodation as each is deemed to have been let for 91.25 days in the year 1996/97. If the average had been less than 70, any three of these cottages could have been included in an averaging claim leaving the other as non-qualifying. If this still did not produce the desired result, an average of any two could be tried. More than one averaging claim is possible for a year of assessment, but no cottage may be included in more than one claim.

18.4   'RENT A ROOM' RELIEF [*F(No 2)A 1992, 10 Sch; FA 1995, 6 Sch 38*]

Frankie and Johnny are single persons sharing a house as their main residence. They have for some years taken in lodgers to supplement their income. Schedule D, Case VI assessments on the net rental income have been raised on a current year basis. As Frankie pays the greater share of the mortgage interest on the house, she and Johnny have an agreement to share the rental income in the ratio 2:1, although expenses are shared equally.

For each of the years ended 5 April 1993 and 1994, gross rents amounted to £4,200 and allowable expenses were £600. In the year ended 5 April 1995, the couple face a heavy repair bill after uninsured damage to one of the rooms. Gross rents for that year amount to £3,600 and expenses to £3,400. For the year ended 5 April 1996, gross rents are £5,400 and expenses £2,400.

For 1992/93, the position is as follows

Normal Schedule D, Case VI computation

	Frankie £	Johnny £
Gross rents (y/e 5.4.93)	2,800	1,400
Allowable expenses	300	300
Net rents	£2,500	£1,100

Johnny's share of *gross* rents is less than his one half share (£1,625) of the basic amount (£3,250) for 1992/93. It is assumed that he would not make the election under *10 Sch 10* for the exemption under *10 Sch 9* ('rent a room' relief) not to apply. His share of net rents is thus treated as nil.

Frankie's share of gross rents exceeds £1,625, so the exemption in *10 Sch 9* cannot apply. She can, however, elect under *10 Sch 12* for *10 Sch 11* to apply, the election to be made by 5 April 1994. Under *10 Sch 11*, she is taxed on the excess of *gross* rents over £1,625. It is assumed that she will make the election as she will then be taxed on £1,175 rather than £2,500.

For 1993/94, the position is as for 1992/93.

For 1994/95, the position is as follows

Normal Schedule D, Case VI computation

	Frankie	Johnny
	£	£
Gross rents (y/e 5.4.95)	2,400	1,200
Allowable expenses	1,700	1,700
Net rents/(loss)	£700	£(500)

Johnny's share of gross rents continues to be less than his one half share of the basic amount. Under *10 Sch 9*, his share of net rents will be treated as nil. However, he will obtain no relief, by carry-forward or otherwise, for his loss. In order to preserve his loss, he could elect under *10 Sch 10* for *10 Sch 9* not to apply, the election to be made by 5 April 1996 and having effect for 1994/95 only.

Frankie's share of gross rents continues to exceed her one half share of the basic amount. Therefore, her previous election under *10 Sch 12* will not automatically be deemed to be withdrawn. She will be taxed under *10 Sch 11* on £775 (£2,400 − £1,625). However, this is greater than the amount taxable on a normal Schedule D, Case VI computation (£700), so it is assumed she would withdraw the election with effect for 1994/95 and subsequent years. The notice of withdrawal must be made by 5 April 1996 but does not prejudice the making of a fresh election for 1995/96 or any subsequent year.

For 1995/96, the position is as follows

Normal Schedule A computation

	Frankie	Johnny
	£	£
Gross rents (y/e 5.4.96)	3,600	1,800
Allowable expenses	1,200	1,200
Net rents	£2,400	£600

Johnny's share of gross rents now exceeds his share of the basic amount, so the exemption will not apply. He could elect for *10 Sch 11* to apply, and his assessment will then be reduced to £175 (£1,800 − £1,625). This will be further reduced to nil by bringing forward (see note (c)) £175 of his £500 Case VI loss for 1994/95 (it is assumed that he has no other source of Case VI income in 1994/95 against which to relieve this loss). (Although a loss cannot enter into the ascertaining of the amount assessable under *10 Sch 11*, there appears to be no reason why a loss cannot be set off against the amount so ascertained.) If Johnny did not make the election, his assessment would be on £100 with the whole of his 1994/95 loss having been utilised.

Frankie can make a fresh election for *10 Sch 11* to apply, with effect from 1995/96, and her 1995/96 Case VI assessment will then be £1,975 (£3,600 − £1,625).

For 1996/97, the position is as follows

The normal Schedule A computation is as for 1995/96. Assuming Frankie and Johnny both elected under 10 Sch 11 for 1995/96, the elections will continue to apply for 1996/97, so that their respective 1996/97 Schedule A assessments are £1,975 and £175. Johnny's assessment is further reduced to nil by the brought forward balance of £325 of the 1994/95 Schedule D, Case VI loss (of which the balance of £150 is carried forward to 1997/98).

IT 18.5 Schedule A — Property Income

Notes

(a) 'Rent a room' relief applies with effect from the 1992/93 year of assessment, whatever the basis period for that or any subsequent year. [*10 Sch 13*]. It covers receipts for 'relevant goods and services' (meals, cleaning, laundry etc.) as well as sums (i.e. rents) received for the use of furnished accommodation. [*10 Sch 2(2), 8*]. It applies equally where the provision of accommodation and services is assessable under Schedule D, Case I. [*10 Sch 2(1)*].

(b) Where sums accrue to more than one person in respect of the same residence in one basis period, each of those persons who is a qualifying individual is entitled to a limit of one half of the 'basic amount' for the relevant year of assessment. The basic amount is £3,250 for 1992/93 and subsequent years, until varied by Treasury Order. [*10 Sch 5, 6*].

(c) Furnished lettings, including those covered by 'rent a room' relief, are chargeable under Schedule A for 1995/96 onwards, having previously been chargeable under Schedule D, Case VI. Under transitional provisions, an unrelieved Case VI loss arising from lettings is carried forward to 1995/96 as a Schedule A loss and is thus set off against Schedule A income for that and subsequent years until exhausted. [*ICTA 1988, s 379A; FA 1995, 6 Sch 19(1)(2)*].

18.5 **PREMIUMS ETC. ON LEASES OF UP TO 50 YEARS** [*ICTA 1988, ss 34–39; FA 1995, 6 Sch 9–12*]

Cross-reference. See also 212.3(C)(G)(H) LAND.

(A)
Mr Green grants a 30-year lease of premises to a trader in March 1997 for a premium of £35,000.

The amount to be included in the profits of Mr Green's Schedule A business is calculated as follows

	£
Premium on 30-year lease	35,000
Deduct (30 − 1) × 2% × £35,000	20,300
	£14,700

(B) Allowance to lessee carrying on trade etc. [*ICTA 1988, s 87; FA 1995, 6 Sch 14*]
Assuming the same figures as in (A) above

Premium paid *less* deduction	£14,700
Number of years of lease	30

The lessee will obtain relief as follows

$$\frac{£14,700}{30} = £490 \text{ p.a.}$$ treated as a payment of additional rent accruing from day to day for up to 30 years.

19   Schedule D, Cases I and II

19.1   OPENING YEARS OF ASSESSMENT

(A) Business commenced in 1993/94 [*ICTA 1988, ss 60–62 as originally enacted; FA 1994, 20 Sch 1, 2; FA 1995, s 122*]
Roy commenced business on 1 January 1994. His Schedule D, Case I adjusted profits (before capital allowances) are

	£
16 months to 30.4.95	16,000
Year to 30.4.96	36,000
Year to 30.4.97	30,000

Capital allowances for the year to 30.4.97 are £3,000.

His first five years' assessments will be either of (i) or (ii) below

(i) No election under *Sec 62(2)* for actual basis in second and third year

	Basis period		£	£
1993/94	1.1.94 – 5.4.94	£16,000 × $\frac{3}{16}$		3,000
1994/95	1.1.94 – 31.12.94	£16,000 × $\frac{12}{16}$		12,000
1995/96	1.1.94 – 31.12.94	£16,000 × $\frac{12}{16}$		12,000
	Transitional period			
1996/97	1.1.95 – 30.4.96 (16 months):			
	1.1.95 – 30.4.95	£16,000 × $\frac{4}{16}$	4,000	
	1.5.95 – 30.4.96		36,000	
			£40,000	
	£40,000 × $\frac{12}{16}$			30,000
	Basis period			
1997/98	Y/e 30.4.97 (net of capital allowances)			27,000*
Total assessments for first five years**				£84,000

* Transitional overlap relief accrued:
(1.5.96 – 5.4.97) £30,000 × $\frac{11}{12}$ £27,500

** Subject to capital allowances for 1993/94 to 1996/97 inclusive

(ii) With election under *Sec 62(2)* for actual basis in second and third year

	Basis period		£	£
1993/94	1.1.94 – 5.4.94	£16,000 × $\frac{3}{16}$		3,000
1994/95	6.4.94 – 5.4.95	£16,000 × $\frac{12}{16}$		12,000
1995/96	6.4.95–5.4.96:			
	6.4.95 – 30.4.95	£16,000 × $\frac{1}{16}$	1,000	
	1.5.95 – 5.4.96	£36,000 × $\frac{11}{12}$	33,000	
				34,000
				c/f £49,000

				£
				b/f 49,000

	Transitional period			
1996/97	6.4.96 – 5.4.97:			
	6.4.96 – 30.4.96	£36,000 × $\frac{1}{12}$	3,000	
	1.5.96 – 5.4.97	£30,000 × $\frac{11}{12}$	27,500	
				30,500

	Basis period		
1997/98	Y/e 30.4.97 (net of capital allowances)		27,000*

Total assessments for first five years**			£106,500

* Transitional overlap relief accrued:
(1.5.96 – 5.4.97) £30,000 × $\frac{11}{12}$ £27,500

** Subject to capital allowances for 1993/94 to 1996/97 inclusive

Notes

(a)   Roy would not make the election under *Sec 62(2) as originally enacted* (actual basis for second and third years) as taxable profits would thereby be greater. Note that where a business commenced in 1993/94, such an election affects not only 1994/95 and 1995/96 but also 1996/97 (the transitional year on the changeover to the current year basis of assessment — see also note (c) below): therefore, one needs to compare the position for all three of those years.

(b)   The assessment for 1995/96 on the normal basis ((i) above) would be the profits for the 12-month period ending in the previous fiscal year. As there is no such period, the Inland Revenue have power to decide which period of 12 months ending within 1994/95 will be taken. In practice the assessment would be based either on the 12 months to the date in the second tax year which will be the future accounts date or, if this is not possible (as in this example) the first 12 months.

(c)   Where 1995/96 is taxed on an actual basis, the transitional year 1996/97 is also taxed on an actual basis (with no averaging of profits). [*FA 1994, 20 Sch 2(3)*]. See 19.4 below for additional examples on the transition from preceding year basis to current year basis.

(B) Business commenced after 5 April 1994 [*ICTA 1988, ss 60, 61, 63A; FA 1994, ss 200, 201, 205*].
Simon commences trade on 1 September 1994 and prepares accounts to 30 April, starting with an eight-month period of account to 30 April 1995. His profits (as adjusted for tax purposes and *after* capital allowances) for the first three accounting periods are as follows

	£
Eight months to 30 April 1995	24,000
Year to 30 April 1996	39,000
Year to 30 April 1997	40,000

His taxable profits for the first four tax years are as follows

	Basis period		£	£
1994/95	1.9.94 – 5.4.95	£24,000 × $\frac{7}{8}$		21,000
1995/96	1.9.94 – 31.8.95:			
	1.9.94 – 30.4.95		24,000	
	1.5.95 – 31.8.95	£39,000 × $\frac{4}{12}$	13,000	
				37,000
1996/97	Y/e 30.4.96			39,000
1997/98	Y/e 30.4.97			40,000

Overlap relief accrued:

1.9.94 – 5.4.95 — 7 months	21,000
1.5.95 – 31.8.95 — 4 months	13,000
Total overlap relief accrued note (b)	£34,000

Notes

(a) The taxable profits for the first tax year are those from the commencement date to 5 April. [Sec 61(1); FA 1994, s 201]. In the second tax year, the period from commencement to the accounting date in that year is less than 12 months, so the basis period is the 12 months from commencement. [Sec 61(2)(a); FA 1994, s 201]. In the third tax year, there is an accounting period of 12 months to the normal accounting date, so the basis period is that accounting period. [Sec 60(3)(a); FA 1994, s 200]. Assessments then continue on the normal current year basis. [Sec 60(3)(b); FA 1994, s 200].

(b) The overlap relief accrued (by reference to an aggregate overlap period of 11 months) will be given on cessation (see 19.3 below) or on a change of accounting date resulting in a basis period exceeding 12 months (the relief given depending on the extent of the excess) (see 19.2(B) below). [Sec 63A; FA 1994, s 205].

19.2   CHANGE OF ACCOUNTING DATE

(A) Business commenced before 6 April 1994 [ICTA 1988, s 60 as originally enacted; Revenue pamphlet IR26]

Geoff, who has been trading for some years, has the following Schedule D, Case I adjusted profits

	£
Year to 30.9.92	24,000
Year to 30.9.93	15,000
15 months to 31.12.94	32,000

The assessable profit for 1995/96 is determined under Sec 60(4) and that for 1994/95 is considered for revision under Sec 60(5).

The assessments are calculated as follows

1995/96

Sec 60(4) determination

The 1995/96 assessment is based on 12 months to 31.12.94

i.e. $\frac{12}{15}$ of £32,000   £25,600

1994/95

The accounting periods to be considered are those entering in whole or in part into the *Sec 60(4)* basis period(s) or the 'corresponding period' under *Sec 60(5)*; viz

		Year of assessment
12 months to 30.9.93	15,000	1994/95
15 months to 31.12.94	32,000	1995/96
27 months	£47,000	24 months

Sec 60(5) consideration

The following tests are undertaken to see if the 1994/95 assessment should be amended

(i)   Aggregate Profit
$\frac{24}{27} \times £47,000$ £41,777

(ii)   Sum of assessments for relevant years without revision for 1994/95:
1994/95	£15,000
1995/96	25,600
	£40,600

(iii)   Sum of assessments for relevant years with revision for 1994/95:
1994/95 (revised to year to 31.12.93)

$\frac{9}{12} \times £15,000$	£11,250	
$\frac{3}{15} \times £32,000$	6,400	17,650
1995/96		25,600
Sum of assessments		£43,250

As the figure at (i) £41,777 is intermediate between (ii) £40,600 and (iii) £43,250 the revised assessment is

Figure at (i)	41,777
Assessed 1995/96	25,600
Revised assessment 1994/95	£16,177

Notes

(a)   If the difference between the figures at (i) and (ii) above was less than 10% of the average of the 1995/96 assessment and the unrevised 1994/95 assessment (i.e. £25,600 and £15,000) and, in addition, the difference was under £1,000, the 1994/95 assessment would not have been amended, i.e. it would remain at £15,000.

(b)   If the figure at (i) was not intermediate between the figures at (ii) and (iii) above, the Inland Revenue would decide what revised assessments, if any, were necessary. This would also be the case if any year showed a loss.

(c)   In this example, assuming that Geoff continues to prepare accounts to 31 December, the transitional basis period on the changeover to the current year basis of assessment will be the two years to 31 December 1996. For changes of accounting date within the transitional period, see 19.4(B) below.

(B) Business commenced after 5 April 1994 [*ICTA 1988, ss 62, 62A, 63A; FA 1994, ss 202, 203, 205*]

(i) Change to a date earlier in the tax year

Miranda commenced trade on 1 September 1994, preparing accounts to 31 August. In 1997, she changes her accounting date to 31 May, preparing accounts for the nine months to 31 May 1997. The conditions of *Sec 62A* are satisfied in relation to the change. Her profits (as adjusted for tax purposes and *after* capital allowances) are as follows

	£
Year ended 31 August 1995	18,000
Year ended 31 August 1996	21,500
Nine months to 31 May 1997	17,000
Year ended 31 May 1998	23,000

Taxable profits for the first five tax years are as follows

	Basis period		£	£
1994/95	1.9.94 – 5.4.95	£18,000 × $\frac{7}{12}$		10,500
1995/96	Y/e 31.8.95			18,000
1996/97	Y/e 31.8.96			21,500
1997/98	1.6.96 – 31.5.97:			
	1.6.96 – 31.8.96	£21,500 × $\frac{3}{12}$	5,375	
	1.9.96 – 31.5.97		17,000	
				22,375
1998/99	Y/e 31.5.98			23,000

Overlap relief accrued:	
1.9.94 – 5.4.95 — 7 months	10,500
1.6.96 – 31.8.96 — 3 months	5,375
Total overlap relief accrued note (*c*)	£15,875

Notes

(*a*) For a change of accounting date to result in a change of basis period, the conditions in *Sec 62A* must normally be satisfied. [*Secs 62(1), 62A; FA 1994, ss 202, 203*].

(*b*) In this example, the 'relevant period' is that from 1 September 1996 (the day following the end of the basis period for 1996/97) to 31 May 1997 (the new accounting date in the year 1997/98 — the year of change). As the relevant period is less than 12 months, the basis period for 1997/98 is the 12 months ending on the new accounting date. [*Sec 62(2)(5); FA 1994, s 202*].

(*c*) The overlap relief accrued (by reference to an aggregate overlap period of 10 months) will be given on cessation (see 19.3 below) or on a change of accounting date resulting in a basis period exceeding 12 months (the relief given depending on the extent of the excess) (see (ii) below). [*Sec 63A; FA 1994, s 205*].

(ii) Change to a date later in the tax year
Dennis starts a business on 1 July 1994, preparing accounts to 30 June. In 1997, he changes his accounting date to 31 December, preparing accounts for the six months to 31 December 1997. The conditions of *Sec 62A* are satisfied in relation to the change. His profits (as adjusted for tax purposes and *after* capital allowances) are as follows

	£
Year ended 30 June 1995	18,000
Year ended 30 June 1996	21,500
Year ended 30 June 1997	23,000
Six months to 31 December 1997	12,000
Year ended 31 December 1998	27,000

Taxable profits for the first five years are as follows

	Basis period		£	£
1994/95	1.7.94 – 5.4.95	£18,000 × $\frac{9}{12}$		13,500
1995/96	Y/e 30.6.95			18,000
1996/97	Y/e 30.6.96			21,500
1997/98	1.7.96 – 31.12.97:			
	1.7.96 – 30.6.97		23,000	
	1.7.97 – 31.12.97		12,000	
			35,000	
	Deduct Overlap relief		9,000	
				26,000
1998/99	Y/e 31.12.98			27,000

	£
Overlap relief accrued:	
1.7.94 – 5.4.95 — 9 months	13,500
Less utilised in 1997/98 — 6 months	9,000
Carried forward — 3 months	£4,500

Utilisation of overlap relief in 1997/98

Apply the formula: $A \times \dfrac{B-C}{D}$ *[Sec 63A(2)]*

where
A = aggregate overlap relief accrued (£13,500);
B = length of basis period for 1997/98 (18 months);
C = 12 months; and
D = the length of the overlap period(s) by reference to which the aggregate overlap profits accrued (9 months).

Thus, the deduction to be given in computing profits for 1997/98 is

$$£13,500 \times \frac{18-12}{9} = £9,000$$

Notes
(a)   For a change of accounting date to result in a change of basis period, the conditions in *Sec 62A* must normally be satisfied. [*Secs 62(1), 62A; FA 1994, ss 202, 203*].

(b) In this example, the 'relevant period' is that from 1 July 1996 (the day following the end of the basis period for 1996/97) to 31 December 1997 (the new accounting date in the year 1997/98 — the year of change). As the relevant period is more than 12 months, the basis period for 1997/98 is equal to the relevant period. [*Sec 62(2)(5); FA 1994, s 202*]. Note that a basis period of 18 months results in this case, even though accounts were prepared for a period of only 6 months to the new date.

(c) The overlap relief accrued (by reference to an overlap period of 9 months) is given on cessation (see 19.3 below) or, as in this example, on a change of accounting date resulting in a basis period exceeding 12 months (the relief given depending on the extent of the excess). The balance of overlap relief (£4,500) is carried forward for future relief on the happening of such an event. [*Sec 63A; FA 1994, s 205*]. If Dennis had changed his accounting date to 31 March or 5 April (instead of 31 December), the use of the formula in *Sec 63A(2)* would have resulted in overlap relief of £13,500 being given in full in 1997/98.

19.3 CLOSING YEARS OF ASSESSMENT

(A) Business commenced before 6 April 1994 [*ICTA 1988, s 63 as originally enacted*]

Chris ceased business on 30 June 1996. His adjusted Schedule D, Case I profits were

	£
Year to 30.4.93	24,000
30.4.94	48,000
30.4.95	96,000
30.4.96	36,000
2 months to 30.6.96	5,000

His assessments will be

	Basis periods			
1996/97	6.4.96 – 30.4.96	$\frac{1}{12} \times 36,000$	3,000	
	1.5.96 – 30.6.96		5,000	£8,000

Then, either

1995/96	Year to 30.4.94		48,000
1994/95	Year to 30.4.93		24,000
			£72,000

Or

1995/96	6.4.95 – 30.4.95	$\frac{1}{12} \times 96,000$	8,000	
	1.5.95 – 5.4.96	$\frac{11}{12} \times 36,000$	33,000	41,000
1994/95	6.4.94 – 30.4.94	$\frac{1}{12} \times 48,000$	4,000	
	1.5.94 – 5.4.95	$\frac{11}{12} \times 96,000$	88,000	92,000
				£133,000

Notes

(a) The Inland Revenue would assess A on profits of £41,000 for 1995/96 and on £92,000 for 1994/95 as these figures are greater in total than the profits originally assessed for these years.

(b)   The rules illustrated in this example apply where a pre-6 April 1994 business ceases at any time before 6 April 1997, and may also be applied to a cessation in 1997/98. [*FA 1994, 20 Sch 3*].

(B) Business commenced after 5 April 1994 [*ICTA 1988, ss 63, 63A(3)(5); FA 1994, ss 204, 205*].

Robin commenced to trade on 1 May 1994, preparing accounts to 30 April. He permanently ceases to trade on 30 June 1998, preparing accounts for the two months to that date. His profits (as adjusted for tax purposes and *after* capital allowances) are as follows

	£
Year ended 30 April 1995	24,000
Year ended 30 April 1996	48,000
Year ended 30 April 1997	96,000
Year ended 30 April 1998	36,000
Two months ended 30 June 1998	5,000
	£209,000

Taxable profits for the five tax years of trading are as follows

	Basis period		£	£
1994/95	1.5.94 – 5.4.95	£24,000 × $\frac{11}{12}$		22,000
1995/96	Y/e 30.4.95			24,000
1996/97	Y/e 30.4.96			48,000
1997/98	Y/e 30.4.97			96,000
1998/99	1.5.97 – 30.6.98:			
	1.5.97 – 30.4.98		36,000	
	1.5.98 – 30.6.98		5,000	
			41,000	
	Deduct Overlap relief		22,000	19,000
				£209,000

	£
Overlap relief accrued:	
1.5.94 – 5.4.95 — 11 months	22,000
Utilised in 1998/99	(22,000)

Notes

(a)   The basis period for the tax year of cessation is the period beginning immediately after the end of the basis period for the penultimate tax year and ending on the date of cessation. [*Sec 63; FA 1994, s 204*]. Note that profits taxed over the lifetime of the business equate to profits earned (as adjusted for tax purposes).

(b)   The overlap relief accrued as a result of the application of the opening years rules is given in full on cessation (in the absence of an earlier change of accounting date resulting in a basis period exceeding 12 months — see 19.2(B) above). [*Sec 63A(3); FA 1994, s 205*].

19.4 **TRANSITIONAL PERIOD ON CHANGEOVER TO CURRENT YEAR BASIS OF ASSESSMENT** [*FA 1994, 20 Sch 1, 2; FA 1995, ss 122, 123, 22 Sch*]

(A) No change of accounting date in transitional period

Mandy has been in practice as a physiotherapist since the 1980s, preparing accounts to 30 September. She ceases practice on 17 April 2000. Her profits (as adjusted for tax purposes) for the seven periods of account up to cessation are as follows

	£
Year to 30 September 1994	26,000
Year to 30 September 1995	27,500
Year to 30 September 1996	31,500
Year to 30 September 1997	34,000
Year to 30 September 1998	28,000
Year to 30 September 1999	19,000
Period to 17 April 2000	7,000

The figures for the year to 30 September 1997 and subsequent years are quoted net of capital allowances. Capital allowances for 1995/96 and 1996/97 are £1,800 and £1,500 respectively and those for the year ended 30 September 1997 (already taken into account above) are £2,000.

Mandy's taxable profits for the six tax years 1995/96 to 2000/2001 are as follows

	£	£
1995/96 (PY basis — y/e 30.9.94)	26,000	
Deduct Capital allowances	1,800	
		24,200
1996/97 (transitional year)		
Y/e 30.9.95	27,500	
Y/e 30.9.96	31,500	
Profits for 24 months	£59,000	
Average: £59,000 × $\frac{12}{24}$	29,500	
Deduct Capital allowances	1,500	
		28,000
1997/98 (CY basis — y/e 30.9.97)		34,000*
* Transitional overlap relief accrued:		
1.10.96 – 5.4.97 — £36,000 × $\frac{6}{12}$	18,000	
1998/99 (Y/e 30.9.98)		28,000
1999/2000 (Y/e 30.9.99)		19,000
2000/2001 (1.10.99 – 17.4.2000)	7,000	
Deduct Overlap relief	18,000	
		(11,000)**
		£122,200

** Allowable loss available for relief under *ICTA 1988, s 380* (set-off against other income) or *ICTA 1988, s 388* (terminal loss relief).

Notes

(*a*) This example illustrates the position for a business which commenced before 6 April 1994 and continues beyond 5 April 1999. Special rules apply where a business commenced before 6 April 1994 ceases in either 1997/98 or 1998/99. [*FA 1994, 20 Sch 3*]. A business commenced before 6 April 1994 and ceasing before 6 April 1997 never goes onto the current year basis of assessment.

(*b*)   The basis period for 1996/97 is the year to 30 September 1996. This is extended by the gap between basis periods for 1995/96 and 1996/97 to give the transitional period (1 October 1994 to 30 September 1996 in this example). The taxable profit (before capital allowances) for 1996/97 is then a 12-month average of the profits for the transitional period. [*FA 1994, 20 Sch 1, 2(1)(2)(5)*]. (See 19.1(A) above for the special rule applying for 1996/97 where a business commences in 1993/94 and 1995/96 is taxed on an actual basis.)

(*c*)   A transitional overlap profit accrues by reference to that part of the profits (before capital allowances) taxable in 1997/98 which arise after the end of the 1996/97 basis period and before 6 April 1997. Transitional overlap relief is given in the same way as other overlap relief (on cessation in this example) — see 19.2(B) and 19.3(B) above. [*FA 1994, 20 Sch 2(4)–(4B); FA 1995, s 122*].

(*d*)   See (C) below for anti-avoidance provisions aimed at preventing the artificial manipulation of the averaging rule for the transitional period and of transitional overlap relief.

(*e*)   See 2.1(E) CAPITAL ALLOWANCES and 10.1(E) LOSSES for further examples on the transitional period.

(B) Change of accounting date in transitional period
The facts are as in (A) above except that in 1997, Mandy changes her accounting date to 31 March, preparing accounts for the 18 months to 31 March 1997. Her final accounts are for the 12 months and 17 days to 17 April 2000. Her profits (as adjusted for tax purposes) up to cessation are as follows

	£
Year to 30 September 1994	26,000
Year to 30 September 1995	27,500
18 months to 31 March 1997	48,500
Year to 31 March 1998	31,000
Year to 31 March 1999	23,500
Period to 17 April 2000	16,500

The figures for the year to 31 March 1998 and subsequent periods are quoted net of capital allowances. Capital allowances for 1995/96 and 1996/97 are £1,800 and £1,500 respectively.

Mandy's taxable profits for the six tax years 1995/96 to 2000/2001 are as follows

	£	£
1995/96 (PY basis — y/e 30.9.94)	26,000	
Deduct Capital allowances	1,800	
		24,200
1996/97 (transitional year)		
Y/e 30.9.95	27,500	
18 mths to 31.3.97	48,500	
Profits for 30 months	£76,000	
Average: £76,000 × $\frac{12}{30}$ (40%)	30,400	
Deduct Capital allowances	1,500	
		28,900
1997/98 (CY basis — y/e 31.3.98)		31,000
1998/99 (Y/e 31.3.99)		23,500
1999/2000 (1.4.99 – 31.3.2000) £16,500 × $\frac{12}{12.5}$		15,840
2000/2001 (1.4.2000 – 17.4.2000) £16,500 × $\frac{0.5}{12.5}$		660
		£124,100

Notes

(a)   In this case, the basis period for 1996/97 is the 12 months to 31 March 1997. This is extended by the gap between basis periods to give a 30-month transitional period of which 12 months are taxed. [FA 1994, 20 Sch 1, 2(1)(2)(5)].

(b)   In this example, 18 months' profits drop out of assessment in the transitional period, whereas in (A) above 12 months' profits dropped out in the transitional period and a further 6 months' profits escaped tax by means of transitional overlap relief. No transitional overlap relief arises in (B) as the accounts year under current year basis corresponds to the tax year (ignoring the five days to 5 April). The total taxable profits for the years under review are greater in (B) (because in (A), later, higher profits escaped tax) but the profits in (B) are more evenly spread.

(c)   The basis period for the year 1999/2000 (in which no period of account ends) is the 12 months beginning immediately after the end of the basis period for 1998/99. [ICTA 1988, s 60(3)(b); FA 1994, s 200].

(d)   The change of accounting date does not bring the transitional period anti-avoidance provisions (see (C) below) into play, as it brings the end of the basis period for 1996/97 closer to 5 April 1997. [FA 1995, 22 Sch 14(2)].

(C) Anti-avoidance provisions [FA 1995, 22 Sch]

(i) Transitional basis period
The facts are as in (A) above except that the inspector discovers that there has been a change of business practice resulting in a decrease of £5,000 in the profits for the year ended 30 September 1994 (which would otherwise have been £31,000) and a corresponding increase in the combined profits of the two years to 30 September 1996 (which would otherwise have been £54,000). Mandy is unable to show that the change was made exclusively for commercial reasons or other than mainly to obtain a tax advantage and the anti-avoidance provisions in FA 1995, 22 Sch 1 are therefore applied. (Note that de minimis limits will operate but these will not be announced until shortly before 5 April 1997 and are thus ignored in this example.)

IT 19.4 Schedule D, Cases I and II

The addition to the 1996/97 taxable profits is calculated as follows

£5,000 × (1.25 × (100% − 50%)) = £3,125

Without the anti-avoidance rules the shift of profits would have saved tax on £2,500 (£5,000 × 50%). The adjustment cancels out the saving and (except where the shift is voluntarily and timeously disclosed) adds a penalty of £625, which is 25% of the amount on which the taxpayer sought to avoid tax. No change is made to the 1995/96 assessment.

Taxable profits for the six years 1995/96 to 2000/2001 are as follows

	£	£
1995/96 As in (A) above		24,200
1996/97 As in (A) above	29,500	
Anti-avoidance addition	3,125	
	32,625	
Deduct Capital allowances	1,500	
		31,125
1997/98 As in (A) above		34,000*
* Transitional overlap relief accrued:		
1.10.96 − 5.4.97 — £36,000 × $\frac{6}{12}$	18,000	
1998/99 As in (A) above		28,000
1999/2000 As in (A) above		19,000
2000/2001 As in (A) above	7,000	
Deduct Overlap relief	18,000	
		(11,000)
		£125,325

(ii) Transitional basis period (with change of accounting date)

The facts are as in (B) above except that the inspector discovers that there has been a change of accounting policy resulting in a decrease of £6,000 in the profits for the year ended 30 September 1994 (which would otherwise have been £32,000) and a corresponding increase in the combined profits of the 30 months to 31 March 1997 (which would otherwise have been £70,000). Mandy is unable to show that the change was made exclusively for commercial reasons or other than mainly to obtain a tax advantage and the anti-avoidance provisions in *FA 1995, 22 Sch 1* are therefore applied. (Note that *de minimus* limits will operate but these will not be announced until shortly before 5 April 1997 and are thus ignored in this example.)

The addition to the 1996/97 taxable profits is calculated as follows

£6,000 × (1.25 × (100% − 40%)) = £4,500

Without the anti-avoidance rules the shift of profits would have saved tax on £3,600 (£6,000 × 60%). The adjustment cancels out the saving and (except where the shift is voluntarily and timeously disclosed) adds a penalty of £900, which is 25% of the amount on which the taxpayer sought to avoid tax. No change is made to the 1995/96 assessment.

Taxable profits for the six tax years 1995/96 to 2000/2001 are as follows

	£	£
1995/96 As in (B) above		24,200
1996/97 As in (B) above	30,400	
Anti-avoidance addition	4,500	
	34,900	
Deduct Capital allowances	1,500	
		33,400
1997/98 As in (B) above		31,000
1998/99 As in (B) above		23,500
1999/2000 As in (B) above		15,840
2000/2001 As in (B) above		660
		£128,600

(iii) Transitional overlap period

The facts are as in (i) above except that the inspector then discovers that there has been a self-cancelling transaction resulting in expenditure of £4,000 being shifted from the year ended 30 September 1997 to the year ended 30 September 1998. Mandy is unable to show that the transaction was entered into exclusively for commercial reasons or other than mainly to obtain a tax advantage and the anti-avoidance provisions in *FA 1995, 22 Sch 3* are therefore applied. (Note that *de minimis* limits will operate but these will not be announced until shortly before 5 April 1997 and are thus ignored in this example.)

The transitional overlap relief is revised as follows

Increase in profit for y/e 30.9.97 as a result of shift	£4,000

Consequent increase in transitional overlap profit:
£4,000 × $\frac{6}{12}$ (1.10.96 – 5.4.97)   £2,000

	£
Original transitional overlap relief (as in (i) above)	18,000
Less £2,000 × 1.25	2,500
Revised transitional overlap relief	£15,500

The 25% penalty (£500) does not apply where the shift is voluntarily and timeously disclosed. The adjustment is to the transitional overlap relief only and not to the 1997/98 and/or 1998/99 assessment.

IT 19.4 Schedule D, Cases I and II

Taxable profits for the six tax years 1995/96 to 2000/2001 are now as follows

		£
1995/96 As in (i) above		24,200
1996/97 As in (i) above		31,125
1997/98 As in (i) above		34,000*
* Transitional overlap relief accrued (revised as above)	£15,500	
1998/99 As in (i) above		28,000
1999/2000 As in (i) above		19,000
2000/2001 As in (i) above	7,000	
Deduct Overlap relief	15,500	
		(8,500)
		£127,825

General Notes

(a) Profits in 1996/97 the transitional basis period are calculated by using '*the appropriate percentage*'. [*FA 1994, 20 Sch 5*]. The '*appropriate percentage*' is defined by reference to the number of days in the transitional basis period, but the Inland Revenue will be prepared to accept any other reasonable time-based computation using weeks, months or fractions of months. [*SAT 1 (1995), paragraph 6.8*].

(b) The overlap period is defined as '*the number of days in the period in which the overlap profit arose*'. [*ICTA 1988, s 63A(2)*]. Although the definition refers to 'days' the Inland Revenue will be prepared to accept any other reasonable measure, for example months or fractions of months, providing that measure is used consistently, and will ensure that, over the lifetime of the business, the total profits assessed exactly equal the profits made. [*SAT 1 (1995), paragraph 1.86*].

19.5   PROFIT COMPUTATIONS

A UK trader commences trading on 1 October 1995. His profit and loss account for the year to 30 September 1996 is

	£	£
Sales		110,000
Deduct Purchases	75,000	
Less Stock and work in progress at 30.9.96	15,000	
		60,000
Gross profit		50,000
Deduct		
Salaries (all paid by 30.6.97)	15,600	
Rent and rates	2,400	
Telephone	500	
Heat and light	650	
Depreciation	1,000	
Motor expenses	2,700	
Entertainment	600	
Bank interest	900	
Hire-purchase interest	250	
Repairs and renewals	1,000	
Accountant's fee	500	
Bad debts	200	
Sundries	700	
		27,000
Net profit		23,000
Gain on sale of fixed asset		300
Rent received		500
Bank interest received (net)		150
Profit		£23,950

Further Information

(i)   Rent and rates. £200 of the rates bill relates to the period from 1.6.95 to 30.9.95.

(ii)   Telephone. Telephone bills for the trader's private telephone (included in the accounts) amount to £150. It is estimated that 40% of these calls are for business purposes.

(iii)   Motor expenses. All the motor expenses are in respect of the proprietor's car. 40% of the annual mileage relates to private use and home to business use.

			£
(iv) Entertainment	Staff		100
	UK customers		450
	Overseas customers		50
			£600

(v)   Hire-purchase interest. This is in respect of the owner's car.

(vi)   Repairs and renewals. There is an improvement element of 20% included.

(vii)   Bad debts. This is a specific write-off.

(viii) Sundries. Included is £250 being the cost of obtaining a bank loan to finance business expenditure, £200 for agent's fees in obtaining a patent for trading purposes and a £50 bribe to a local official.

(ix) Other. The proprietor obtained goods for his own use from the business costing £400 (retail value £500) without payment.

(x) Capital allowances for the year to 30 September 1996 amount to £1,720.

Schedule D, Case I Computation — Year to 30.9.96

	£	£
Profit per the accounts		23,950
Add		
Repairs — improvement element		200
Hire-purchase interest (40% private)		100
Entertainment note (*e*)		500
Motor expenses (40% private)		1,080
Depreciation		1,000
Telephone (60% × £150)		90
Goods for own use		500
Illegal payment note (*h*)		50
		27,470
Deduct		
Bank interest received — Taxed income	150	
Rent received — Schedule A	500	
Gain on sale of fixed asset	300	
		950
		26,720
Less Capital allowances		1,520
Schedule D, Case I profit		£25,000

Notes

(*a*) Costs of obtaining loan finance are specifically allowable. [*ICTA 1988, s 77*].

(*b*) For businesses commenced after 5 April 1994, capital allowances are deductible as a trading expense.

(*c*) The adjusted profit of £25,000 would be subject to the commencement provisions for assessment purposes. See 19.1(B) above.

(*d*) Pre-trading expenses are treated as incurred on the day on which trade is commenced if they are incurred within seven years of the commencement and would have been allowable if incurred after commencement. For businesses which commenced before 5 April 1995, such expenses were treated as a separate loss. [*ICTA 1988, s 401; FA 1993, s 109; FA 1995, s 120*].

(*e*) All entertainment expenses, other than staff entertaining, are non-deductible. [*ICTA 1988, s 577; FA 1988, s 72, 14 Sch Pt IV*].

(*f*) See note (*a*) to CT120.1 PROFIT COMPUTATIONS as regards deductibility of wages and salaries. This applies equally to individuals and partnerships as it does to companies. [*FA 1989, s 43*].

(*g*) Expenditure incurred after 10 June 1993 in making a payment which itself constitutes the commission of a criminal offence is specifically disallowed. This covers bribes which are contrary to the Prevention of Corruption Acts (Revenue Press Release 11 June 1993). [*ICTA 1988, s 577A; FA 1993, s 123; FA 1994, s 141*].

19.6 **FARMING AND MARKET GARDENING — AVERAGING** [*ICTA 1988, s 96 as originally enacted*]

A, who has been farming for several years, earns the following profits as adjusted for Schedule D, Case I and *before* capital allowances

Year ended	Schedule D, Case I Profit/(loss) £
30.9.92	20,000
30.9.93	14,000
30.9.94	(5,000)
30.9.95	8,000
30.9.96	16,000

Averaged profits for all years would be

		No averaging claims £	Averaging claims for all years £
1993/94	note (*a*)	20,000	17,000
1994/95	notes (*b*)(*d*)	14,000	8,500
1995/96	note (*c*)	Nil	10,000
1996/97 (transitional year)	note (*e*)	12,000	10,500
		£46,000	£46,000

Notes

(*a*)	1993/94	20,000
	1994/95	14,000
		£34,000 ÷ 2 = £17,000

As £14,000 does not exceed $\frac{7}{10}$ × £20,000, the straight average applies.

(*b*)	1994/95	17,000
	1995/96	Nil
		£17,000 ÷ 2 = £8,500

(*c*)	1995/96	8,500
	1996/97	12,000
		£20,500

As £8,500 exceeds $\frac{7}{10}$ of £12,000 but does not exceed $\frac{3}{4}$, the adjustment is computed as follows

Difference £3,500 × 3		10,500	
Deduct $\frac{3}{4}$ × £12,000		9,000	
Adjustment		1,500	1,500
Existing 1995/96		8,500	
Existing 1996/97			12,000
		£10,000	£10,500

(d)   The loss for the year to 30 September 1994 is not taken into account for averaging, but would be available to reduce the averaged profits for 1994/95 on a claim under *ICTA 1988, s 380(1) as originally enacted.*

(e)   The assessment for 1996/97 before averaging is based on 12/24 of the profits for the two years to 30 September 1996 (the transitional period) (see 19.4 above).

(f)   For businesses commencing after 5 April 1994, the profits to be taken into account in an averaging claim are those *after* capital allowances. This is extended to all businesses where the first of the two years being averaged is 1996/97 or a later year. [*FA 1994, s 214(1)(a)(7)*].

19.7   ASSESSABLE PROFITS, ALLOWABLE DEDUCTIONS

(A) Stock in trade and work in progress

CD is a long-established partnership engaged in manufacturing and makes up its accounts to 30 April. Its profit and loss account for the year ended 30 April 1997 can be summarised as follows

	£	£
Turnover		1,200,000
Opening stock and work in progress	300,000	
Allowable expenditure	1,000,000	
Non-allowable expenditure	100,000	
	1,400,000	
Closing stock and work in progress	400,000	
		1,000,000
Net profit		£200,000

CD is entitled to capital allowances of £30,000 for 1997/98.

During the year ended 30 April 1997, CD decided to change its basis of valuing stock and work in progress (by excluding certain overheads previously included). In the accounts, both opening and closing stock is valued on the new basis, but in the accounts to 30 April 1996, closing stock and work in progress (valued on the old basis) was included at a figure of £350,000. Both bases of valuation are accepted by the Inland Revenue as valid bases for tax purposes.

CD's Schedule D, Case I computation for 1997/98 is as follows

	£
Net profit per accounts	200,000
Add non-allowable expenditure	100,000
	300,000
Deduct difference between closing stock figure at 30.4.97 and opening stock figure at 1.5.96	50,000
Schedule D, Case I	250,000
Less capital allowances	30,000
Taxable profit	£220,000

Note

(a)   When a change is made from one valid basis of valuation to another, the opening stock figure must for tax purposes be the same as the closing stock figure for the previous year. (Revenue Statement of Practice SP 3/90).

(B) Employers' pension contributions [*ICTA 1988, s 592(4); FA 1993, s 112*]

E is a trader preparing accounts to 30 April. In May 1989, he set up an exempt approved pension scheme for his employees. The contributions actually made (all being ordinary annual contributions) and the charge to profit and loss account for all years up to and including the year ended 30 April 1996 are as set out below. The figures differ each year as E makes provision in his accounts with a view to spreading the charges to profit and loss account over the estimated remaining service lives of current employees in accordance with Statement of Standard Accounting Practice 24. For each of the first three years of assessment listed below, the amount allowed for tax purposes was the figure charged in the profit and loss account for the relevant basis period.

Accounting year ended	*Year of assessment*	*Actual contributions made*	*Charge to P & L account*
		£	£
30.4.90	1991/92	30,000	40,000
30.4.91	1992/93	34,000	40,000
30.4.92	1993/94	35,000	33,000
		99,000	113,000
30.4.93	1994/95	36,000*	34,000
30.4.94	1995/96	32,000	36,000
30.4.95	1996/97	50,000	40,000
30.4.96	1996/97 note (c)	48,000	49,000
		£265,000	£272,000

*   Of the actual payments of £36,000 in the year to 30.4.93, £3,000 was paid after 5.4.93.

The amounts deductible for tax purposes for the years of assessment 1994/95–1996/97 are calculated as follows

1994/95 (y/e 30.4.93)

	£	£	£
Actual payments before 6.4.93			33,000
Actual payments after 5.4.93		3,000	
Deduct Excess of previously allowed deductions over relevant maximum:			
Previously allowed deductions	113,000		
Relevant maximum	99,000		
	£14,000		
Restricted to		3,000	
Amount deductible			£33,000

IT 19.7 Schedule D, Cases I and II

1995/96 (y/e 30.4.94)

	£	£
Actual payments during the year		32,000
Deduct Excess of previously allowed deductions over relevant maximum:		
Previously allowed deductions £(113,000 + 33,000)	146,000	
Relevant maximum £(99,000 + 36,000)	135,000	11,000
Amount deductible		£21,000
Total actual payments to date £(135,000 + 32,000) =		£167,000
Total of allowed deductions to date £(146,000 + 21,000) =		£167,000

1996/97

(y/e 30.4.95)

Actual payments during the year	£50,000
Amount deductible	£50,000

(y/e 30.4.96)

Actual payments during the year	£48,000
Amount deductible	£48,000

Notes

(a)   For accounting periods and basis periods ending after 5 April 1993, the deduction for tax purposes for employers' pension contributions to an exempt approved scheme is limited to the amount actually paid by way of contribution.

(b)   The deductibility of payments made after 5 April 1993 is restricted to the extent that the total amount allowed for all previous chargeable periods exceeds the total that would have been allowed (the 'relevant maximum') if the rule in note (a) above had applied to all those previous periods. No restriction is necessary for the year ended 30 April 1995 onwards in this example as the previously allowed deductions already match the relevant maximum.

(c)   The profits of the years to 30 April 1995 and 1996 will be aggregated and divided by two to arrive at the Schedule D, Case I assessment for 1996/97, the transitional year on the changeover to the current year basis. See 19.4 above. Only one-half of the aggregate pension contributions deductible in those years will therefore attract tax relief.

(C) Finance leases (*SSAP 21; Revenue Statement of Practice SP 3/91*)

Jones prepares accounts annually to 31 March. On 1 April 1995 he enters into a five-year finance lease to acquire new machinery at an annual rental of £6,600 payable quarterly in advance.

The fair value (cash price) of the machinery at the inception of the lease is £25,000, being a close approximation to the present value of the minimum lease rentals. This is capitalised in the balance sheet in accordance with Statement of Standard Accounting Practice (SSAP) 21, and depreciation is charged on a straight line basis at the rate of 20% per annum on the fair value. Rentals are treated as comprising a finance charge element and a capital repayment element.

The total lease rentals are £6,600 × 5 = £33,000, giving a finance charge of £(33,000 – 25,000) = £8,000.

The finance charge is allocated over the period of the lease using the sum of digits method, as follows

Quarter	Number of rentals not yet due	×	Finance charge / Sum of no of rentals	=	Finance charge per annum
				£	£
1	19			= 800	
2	18			= 758	
3	17			= 716	
4	16			= 674	
					2,948
5	15			= 632	
6	14			= 589	
7	13			= 547	
8	12			= 505	
					2,273
9	11			= 463	
10	10		$\times \dfrac{8,000}{190}$	= 421	
11	9			= 379	
12	8			= 337	
					1,600
13	7			= 295	
14	6			= 253	
15	5			= 211	
16	4			= 168	
					927
17	3			= 126	
18	2			= 84	
19	1			= 42	
20	–			= –	
					252
	190				£8,000

The deduction in each year's accounts, and the allowable deduction for tax purposes, for depreciation and finance charges over the period of the lease will therefore be as follows

Accounting year ended 31 March

	1996 £	1997 £	1998 £	1999 £	2000 £	Total £
Depreciation	5,000	5,000	5,000	5,000	5,000	
Finance charge	2,948	2,273	1,600	927	252	
	£7,948	£7,273	£6,600	£5,927	£5,252	£33,000
Compared to actual rentals paid of	£6,600	£6,600	£6,600	£6,600	£6,600	£33,000

Notes

(a)   As the rentals are payable in advance, the final payment in quarter 20 will have no finance charge allocated to it. If the rentals had been payable in arrears, a finance charge would have been allocated to quarter 20, and the charge allocated to quarter 1 would have been 20 units instead of 19, with consequential changes to all the other quarters.

(b)   The sum of the number of rentals may be computed by using the formula

$$\frac{n(n + 1)}{2}$$

where n is the number of quarters in question. Hence in this case n = 19 (see note (a)) and thus

$$\frac{19 \times 20}{2} = 190.$$

(c)   Under Revenue Statement of Practice SP 3/91, for leases entered into after 11 April 1991, the Revenue will normally allow tax relief to a lessee for amounts charged in the accounts in respect of finance charges if they are dealt with in accordance with SSAP 21. A finance lease exists under SSAP 21 where substantially all the risks and rewards of ownership, other than legal title, are transferred to the lessee, with generally the present value of the minimum lease payments (including initial payment) amounting to 90% or more of the fair value of the leased asset. Any other lease is an operating lease.

(d)   SSAP 21 permits three methods of calculating finance lease charges, i.e. straight line, actuarial and sum of digits (the so-called 'rule of 78'). The sum of digits method is a close approximation to an actuarial calculation where the lease period is normally less than eight years and interest rates are not too high.

(e)   SP 3/91 additionally allows a deduction in the accounts for depreciation charged in respect of assets acquired under finance leases, provided that the rate of depreciation used is calculated on normal commercial principles (SSAP 12). Depreciation should be charged either over the period of the lease or the useful life of the asset, whichever is the shorter.

(f)   In *Threlfall v Jones C/A, [1993] STC 537*, it was held that payments under finance leases had to be accounted for in accordance with accounting standards as they were the ordinary way to ascertain profits or losses for tax purposes.

20   Schedule D, Case III

20.1   BASIS OF ASSESSMENT

Transition from preceding year basis to current year basis [*ICTA 1988, ss 64, 66, 67; FA 1994, ss 206, 207(4), 218(1), 20 Sch 4, 5, 14(1)*]
Patrick has the following sources of untaxed interest, chargeable under Schedule D, Case III

	Opened/acquired	*Closed*
(1) National Savings income bonds	21.6.93	—
(2) National Savings Bank ordinary account	6.8.93	29.4.98
(3) National Savings Bank investment account	8.1.94	—

His wife, Judy, also opens a National Savings Bank ordinary account (Source (4)) on 21 June 1993, but closes it on 31 December 1997.

Interest credited/received in each of the tax years 1993/94 to 1998/99 is as follows

	Source (1) £	Source (2) £	Source (3) £	Source (4) £
1993/94	800	520	—	520
1994/95	700	470	600	470
1995/96	600	550	800	550
1996/97	650	350	825	350
1997/98	575	335	775	335
1998/99	550	100	725	—

The interest chargeable under Schedule D, Case III for each year is as follows

(NB: the first £70 of National Savings Bank ordinary account interest for each tax year is exempt. [*ICTA 1988, s 325*])

	Source (1)	Source (2)	Source (3)	Source (4)
1993/94 (1st year — CY)	£800	£450	—	£450
1994/95 (2nd year – CY)	700	400		400
(CY basis)			600	
	£700	£400	£600	£400
1995/96 (3rd year — election for CY basis)	600			
(3rd year — PY)		400		400
(CY basis)			800	
	£600	£400	£800	£400
1996/97 (CY basis)	650		825	
(transitional year)		380		
(PY basis)				480
	£650	£380	£825	£480

1997/98 (CY basis)	575	265	775
(Final year — CY)				265
	£575	£265	£775	£265
1998/99 (CY basis)	£550	£30	£725	—

Notes

(a) *Source 1*. Income first arose in 1993/94. Because an election is made under *ICTA 1988, s 66(1)(c)* (third year — actual), the averaging rule does not apply for 1996/97, to which the current year basis therefore applies. [*FA 1994, 20 Sch 4(3)*].

(b) *Source 2*. Transitional rules apply for 1996/97. The amount chargeable is 50% of the aggregate income arising in 1995/96 and 1996/97. [*FA 1994, 20 Sch 4(1)(2)*]. (As the source is a National Savings Bank ordinary account, the first £70 of the amount otherwise chargeable is exempt.)

(c) *Source 3*. Income first arises after 5 April 1994. Therefore the source goes directly onto the current year basis. [*ICTA 1988, s 64; FA 1994, s 206*].

(d) *Source 4*. Because income last arises before 6 April 1998, the current year basis and transitional provisions do not apply, the source being taxed throughout on the preceding year basis rules. [*FA 1994, 20 Sch 5*].

(e) There are anti-avoidance provisions aimed at artificial arrangements designed to manipulate the transitional rules on changeover to current year basis [*FA 1995, 22 Sch 9, 13, 18*]. The Revenue *may* also treat new deposits after 30 March 1994 to existing accounts as new sources which immediately go onto current year basis (see Revenue Press Release 31 March 1994).

20.2 DISCOUNTS ON SECURITIES [*FA 1996, s 102, 13 Sch*]

(A) Profit on Disposal. On 28 June 1996 Mr Knight subscribed for £10,000 3% loan stock issued by DDS plc at a price of £55 per £100 stock incurring costs of £60. He sold these same securities on 5 April 1997 for £80 per £100 stock and incurred costs of £80. The 3% Loan Stock in DDS plc is understood to be a relevant discounted security.

Mr Knight's tax position for 1996/97 on the disposal is

	£	£
Disposal proceeds		8,000
Less acquisition cost		5,500
		2,500
Deduct Costs of disposal	80	
Costs of acquisition	60	140
Schedule D, Case III assessment		£2,360

Note

(a) A '*relevant discounted security*' is any security, subject to exceptions where, a '*deep gain*' arises on redemption. A '*deep gain*' arises where the issue price is less than the amount payable on redemption by more than 15% of that amount or if less by $\frac{1}{2}$% per annum of that amount (counting months and part months as 1/12th of a year) to the earliest possible redemption date. Exceptions include company shares, gilts (but not strips), excluded indexed securities, life assurance policies, capital redemption policies and securities isued under the same prospectus as other securities issued previously but not themselves relevant discounted securities.

(B) Loss on disposal. On the assumption that Mr Knight sells the loan stock for £40 per £100 stock instead of £80 per £100 stock the following will apply:

Mr Knight's tax position for 1996/97 on the disposal is

	£	£
Disposal proceeds		4,000
Less acquisition cost		5,500
		1,500
Deduct Costs of disposal	80	
Costs of acquisition	60	140
Schedule D, Case III loss		£1,640

Note

(a)   Mr Knight will be able to claim loss relief of £1,640 against other 1996/97 income. The relief must be claimed within 12 months from 31 January 1998.

21   Schedule D, Cases IV and V

[ICTA 1988, ss 18(2)–(4), 65–67, 207A; FA 1993, s 77(1)(2)(5); FA 1994, ss 207, 218(1)(4), 20 Sch 6, 7, 10, 14; FA 1995, s 122(4)(5)]

21.1   BASIS OF ASSESSMENT

In July 1993 S inherited shares in X, a company resident outside the UK. S is resident, ordinarily resident and domiciled in the UK and is not liable to higher rate tax. The dividends which arise and tax deducted therefrom are as follows (the dividends arising on or after 1 October 1998 have UK tax deducted by a UK paying agent)

	Gross	Foreign tax at 15%	UK tax (at lower rate less foreign tax)
	£	£	£
1993/94	120	18.00	—
1994/95	175	26.25	—
1995/96	190	28.50	—
1996/97	180	27.00	—
1997/98	240	36.00	—
Period 6.4.98 – 30.9.98	135	20.25	—
		£156.00	
Period 1.10.98 – 5.4.99	145	21.75	7.25

S's assessments are as follows

	£	£
1993/94 (1st year — CY)	£120	
Tax thereon at 20%	24.00	
Deduct Tax credit relief	18.00	18.00
UK tax payable	£6.00	
1994/95 (2nd year — CY)	£175	
Tax thereon at 20%	35.00	
Deduct Tax credit relief	26.25	26.25
UK tax payable	£8.75	
1995/96 (3rd year — PY)	£175	
Tax thereon at 20%	35.00	
Deduct Tax credit relief	26.25	26.25
UK tax payable	£8.75	
1996/97 (transitional year)		
Income arising in 1995/96	190	
Income arising in 1996/97	180	
	£370	
£370 × 50%	£185	

	£	£
Tax thereon at 20%	37.00	
Deduct Tax credit relief:		
£(28.50 + 27.00) × 50%	27.75	27.75
UK tax payable	£9.25	
1997/98 (CY)	£240	
Tax thereon at 20%	48.00	
Deduct Tax credit relief	36.00	36.00
UK tax payable	£12.00	
1998/99 (period 6.4.98 to 30.9.98 — CY)	£135	
Tax thereon at 20%	27.00	
Deduct Tax credit relief	20.25	20.25
UK tax payable	£6.75	
Total tax credit relief		£154.50

Notes

(a)   S would choose to have the assessment for 1995/96 assessed under the preceding year basis since the income for 1994/95 is lower than that for 1995/96. [*ICTA 1988, s 66(1)(c)*].

(b)   The income of £145 for the period 1.10.98–5.4.99 is taxable in 1998/99 as foreign dividends. However, no further tax is payable as S is not liable to higher rate tax and the income has effectively suffered lower rate tax at source.

(c)   For 1993/94 onwards, dividends which are assessable under Schedule D, Case V are charged at the lower rate of 20% to the extent that the dividend income brings the recipient into the higher rate band. [*FA 1993, s 77(2)*].

(d)   If S had not been domiciled in the UK, his liability under Case V would have been based on income remitted to the UK.

(e)   *Double taxation relief.* Tax credit relief for 1996/97 (the transitional year on the changeover to the current year basis of assessment) is restricted to 50% of the aggregate foreign tax paid on income arising from the source in question in 1995/96 and 1996/97.

The total tax credit relief given (£154.50) is less than the total foreign tax paid (£156.00). No adjustment is made for the difference. If total tax credit relief had exceeded total foreign tax paid, an amount would have become chargeable under Schedule D, Case VI. Such amount is the excess of (A) tax credit relief given more than once because of the opening years rules (£26.25 in this example) (see *ICTA 1988, s 804(1) as originally enacted*) over (B) the tax credit relief foregone because of the 50% restriction in 1996/97 (£27.75 in this example). (In this example, there is clearly no such excess.) [*FA 1994, 20 Sch 11*]. Where a source is subject to the current year basis throughout (i.e. where income first arises after 5 April 1994), no such adjustment will be relevant.

22 Schedule D, Case VI

Cross-reference. See also 13.2 OVERSEAS MATTERS re gains on offshore funds.

22.1   **BONDWASHING — ACCRUED INCOME SCHEME** [*ICTA 1988, ss 710–728*]
The following transactions take place between individuals during the year ended 5 April 1997.

Settlement day	Sale by	Purchase by	Securities
15.6.96	X (cum div)	Y	£2,000 15% Exchequer 1997
8.9.96	X (ex div)	P	£3,000 15½% Treasury Loan 1998
15.3.97	S (cum div)	Y	£1,000 9% Treasury Loan 2012

Interest payment days are as follows

15% Exchequer 1997	27 April, 27 October
15½% Treasury Loan 1998	30 March, 30 September
9% Treasury Loan 2012	6 February, 6 August

Both X and Y owned chargeable securities with a nominal value in excess of £5,000 at some time in either 1995/96 or 1996/97, and both are resident and ordinarily resident in the UK. P is not resident and not ordinarily resident in the UK throughout 1996/97. The maximum value of securities held by S at any time in 1996/97 and 1997/98 is £4,000.

15.6.96 transaction
The transaction occurs in the interest period from 28.4.96 to 27.10.96 (inclusive)

Number of days in interest period	183
Number of days in interest period to 15.6.96	49
Interest payable on 27.10.96	£150

The accrued amount is

$$£150 \times \frac{49}{183} = £40$$

X is treated as receiving income (chargeable under Schedule D, Case VI) of £40 on 27.10.96.
Y is given credit for £40 against the interest of £150 he receives on 27.10.96. £110 remains taxable.

8.9.96 transaction
The transaction occurs in the interest period from 31.3.96 to 30.9.96 (inclusive).

Number of days in interest period	184
Number of days in interest period to 8.9.96	162
Interest payable on 30.9.96	£233

The rebate amount is

$$£233 \times \frac{184 - 162}{184} = £28$$

X is given credit for £28 against the interest of £233 he receives on 30.9.96. £205 remains taxable.
P is not assessed on any notional income as he is neither resident nor ordinarily resident in the UK.

15.3.97 transaction

The transaction occurs in the interest period from 7.2.97 to 6.8.97 (inclusive)

Number of days in interest period	181
Number of days in interest period to 15.3.97	37
Interest payable on 6.8.97	£45

The accrued amount is

$$£45 \times \frac{37}{181} = \underline{£9}$$

S is not assessed on any notional income. He is not within the accrued income scheme provisions as his holdings do not exceed £5,000 at any time in 1996/97 or 1997/98 (the year in which the interest period ends).

Y is given credit for £9 against the interest of £45 he receives on 6.8.97. £36 remains taxable.

Note

(a)   For 1996/97 onwards the accrued income scheme provisions do not apply on a transfer to which *FA 1996, 13 Sch* applies. See Example 20.2.

23   Schedule E — Emoluments

23.1   EARNINGS FROM WORK DONE ABROAD

(A) Calculation of 365-day qualifying period [*ICTA 1988, s 193(1), 12 Sch 3*]

F is sales director of G (UK) Ltd, a UK resident company. He is resident in the UK and made a number of business trips abroad, as follows

Departed UK	D1	30.9.95
Returned UK	R1	23.12.95
Departed UK	D2	3.1.96
Returned UK	R2	31.5.96
Departed UK	D3	30.6.96
Returned UK	R3	18.12.96
Departed UK	D4	16.1.97
Returned UK	R4	31.3.97.

F then worked in the UK for the next three months.

The following steps must be considered

(i)   The period D1-R1 consists of 84 consecutive days of absence and will therefore be a qualifying period.

(ii)   The period D1-R2 must next be considered to establish if the period R1-D2 exceeds 62 days or if that period exceeds $\frac{1}{6}$th of the number of days in the period D1-R2. Period R1-D2 comprises 11 days; it is therefore not more than 62 days and not more than $\frac{1}{6}$th of 244 days and so D1-R2 becomes a qualifying period.

(iii)   The period D1-R3 is then examined on the same basis as the previous period. Period R2-D3 comprises 30 days; it is therefore not more than 62 days and since R1-D2 (11 days) and R2-D3 (30 days), or 41 days in total, are not more than $\frac{1}{6}$th of D1-R3 (444 days), D1-R3 becomes a qualifying period (and is a qualifying period of at least 365 days).

(iv)   The final period D1-R4 (548 days) is then examined. Period R3-D4 comprises 29 days; it is therefore not more than 62 days and since the previous 41 days (see (iii) above) and the 29 days (70 days in total) are not more than $\frac{1}{6}$th of 548 days, D1-R4 becomes a qualifying period.

The position can be summarised as follows

	Total	1995/96	1996/97	Days in UK	1/6 of total
Abroad D1-R1	84	84			
In UK R1-D2	11	11		11	
Abroad D2-R2	149	94	55		
D1–R2	243			11	40
In UK R2-D3	30		30	30	
Abroad D3-R3	171		171		
D1–R3	445			41	74
In UK R3-D4	29		29	29	
Abroad D4-R4	74		74		
D1-R4	548	189	359	70	91

Notes

(a)   In determining if a qualifying period has arisen, the day of departure from and day of return to the UK are qualifying and non-qualifying days respectively.

(b)   D1–R3 is itself a 365-day qualifying period, so the 100% deduction conferred by *Sec 193(1)* becomes due at this point. However, the qualifying period can be extended by R3–R4, thus enabling further emoluments to qualify. As F then spent three months (i.e. more than 62 days) in the UK, the qualifying period D1–R4 cannot be further extended even if there are subsequent periods of working abroad.

(B)   Emoluments eligible for relief [*ICTA 1988, 12 Sch 1A, 2; F(No 2)A 1992, s 54*]

G, a UK resident, is employed by H Ltd, a UK resident company. He works abroad for the company during the period 20 January 1996 to 21 December 1996. He then takes a paid vacation abroad until 31 January 1997 when he returns to the UK to resume his UK duties with H Ltd. His UK visits during the period of absence are minimal and the period 20 January 1996 to 30 January 1997 inclusive constitutes a qualifying period for the purposes of the 100% deduction conferred by *Sec 193(1)*. His emoluments from H Ltd for 1995/96 and 1996/97, net of employee contributions (at 5% of salary) to an approved occupational pension scheme, amount to £38,000 and £41,800. The overseas duties are not performed under a separate contract.

G's taxable emoluments for 1995/96 and 1996/97 are as follows

	£
1995/96	
Gross emoluments	40,000
Deduct Pension contributions (allowable under *ICTA 1988, s 592*)	2,000
	38,000
100% deduction £38,000 × $\dfrac{77}{366}$ (20.1.96 – 5.4.96)	7,995
Taxable emoluments (subject to personal reliefs etc.)	£30,005

	£
1996/97	
Gross emoluments	44,000
Deduct Pension contributions	2,200
	41,800
100% deduction £41,800 × $\dfrac{300}{365}$ (6.4.95 – 30.1.96)	34,356
Taxable emoluments (subject to personal reliefs etc.)	£7,444

Notes

(a)   G continues to be resident in the UK throughout 1995/96 and 1996/97 as his absence in the performance of duties abroad does not span a complete tax year (see Revenue ESC A11). Any period of non-UK residence ending after 5 April 1992 would not count towards a qualifying period for the 100% deduction (Revenue Statement of Practice SP 18/91).

(b)   G's vacation abroad counts as part of his qualifying period. His pay for the vacation period counts as emoluments attributable to the qualifying period. [*ICTA 1988, 12 Sch 3(3)*].

(c)   For each year of assessment, the emoluments attributable to the qualifying period and those attributable to UK duties are apportioned in such manner as is reasonable, having regard to the nature of and time devoted to the duties performed outside and in the UK respectively and to all other relevant circumstances. [*12 Sch 2(1)(2)*]. G might contend that a larger proportion of total emoluments than that shown above should be eligible for the 100% deduction, for example on the grounds that his duties abroad carried a greater degree of responsibility. If the period spent abroad had been under a separate contract, this should have helped to convince the Revenue.

(d)   For 1992/93 and subsequent years of assessment, 'emoluments' for these purposes are net of capital allowances, certain pension contributions and various expenses. [*12 Sch 1A; F(No 2)A 1992, s 54*]. For the position for earlier years, see Revenue Press Release 8 June 1992.

(C)   Travelling expenses [*ICTA 1988, s 194*]
M, a married man resident and ordinarily resident in the UK, is employed by Bigbuild Ltd in Milnrow at a salary of £20,000 per annum and is involved in the management of the following construction projects.

29.8.96 – 30.11.96   Office block in Philippines
9.12.96 – 15.1.97   Factory in Germany
19.3.97 – 27.6.97   Housing development in Spain

Details of travel expenses incurred in 1996/97 are

		By M £	Reimbursed By Bigbuild £	By Bigbuild £
28. 8.96	Milnrow – Heathrow Airport (M)	40		
29. 8.96	Heathrow – Philippines (M)			400
20.10.96	Milnrow – Philippines (wife and children)			1,000
30.10.96	Philippines – Milnrow (wife and children)			1,000
30.11.96	Philippines – Milnrow (M)	500	500	
9.12.96	Milnrow – Manchester Airport (M)	10	10	
9.12.96	Manchester – Germany (M)			100
10.12.96	Milnrow – Germany (wife and children)			300
3. 1.97	Germany – Milnrow (wife and children)	300	300	
15. 1.97	Germany – Milnrow (M)			100
19. 3.97	Milnrow – Spain (M)	150	150	
31. 3.97	Milnrow – Spain (wife)	60		150
		£1,060	£960	£3,050

M's taxable income is as follows

	£	£
Salary		20,000
Cost of expenses incurred by Bigbuild		3,050
Reimbursed travel expenses		960
		24,010
Deduct Allowable part of expenses incurred by Bigbuild	2,750	
Allowable expenses incurred by M	700	
Personal allowance	3,765	7,215
Taxable		£16,795

Note

(a)   A deduction is allowed for travelling expenses of the employee from any place in the UK to take up the overseas employment. In addition where the employee is out of the UK for 60 days or more continuously, an allowance is available for up to two outward and two return trips per fiscal year for the employee's wife and minor children provided the expense is borne or reimbursed by the employer. As M is away for less than 60 days in Germany, he cannot deduct the cost of his family's Christmas and New Year trip. The part of the cost of his wife's trip to Spain not reimbursed cannot be deducted.

23.2   **PROFIT-RELATED PAY** [*ICTA 1988, ss 169–184, 8 Sch; FA 1989, s 61, 4 Sch; FA 1991, s 37; FA 1994, ss 98, 99; FA 1995, s 136*]

(A) Distributable pool – Method A

C Ltd operates an approved profit-related pay scheme with effect from its accounting year ending 31 March 1996. The scheme contains provisions for determining the distributable pool (i.e. the aggregate sum which may be paid to employees in respect of a profit period) using method A as defined by *ICTA 1988, 8 Sch 13*.

The distributable pool is to be 15% of profits, but profits in excess of 160% of (for the first profit period) £500,000 are to be disregarded. The latter figure is the amount of profits for the year ended 31 March 1994 which is chosen as the base year under *ICTA 1988, 8 Sch 13(6)*.

Profits, as computed for profit-related pay purposes, amount to £900,000 and £1 million for the years ended 31 March 1996 and 1997.

For the profit period 1.4.95 to 31.3.96, the distributable pool is

£800,000 (restricted to £500,000 @ 160%) × 15% =   £120,000

For the profit period 1.4.96 to 31.3.97, the distributable pool is

£1,000,000 (being less than £900,000 × 160%) × 15% =   £150,000

Notes

(a)   In the second and subsequent profit periods, the 160% restriction is by reference to profits for the preceding period rather than the base year. [*ICTA 1988, 8 Sch 13(4)*].

(*b*)   The base year can be any twelve-month period ending within two years prior to the start of the first profit period, but the base year so chosen must be specified when registering the scheme.

(*c*)   For schemes registered after 30 November 1993, a special rule applies if the total pay (excluding profit-related pay) of the employment unit for the profit period is less than that for the previous profit period (or, where applicable, the base year). In such a case, the limiting percentage of profits (160% in this example) is increased by X/Y × 100 where X is the decrease in pay and Y is the profit of the previous profit period (or base year). [*ICTA 1988, 8 Sch 13A(4)–(6); FA 1994, s 98(2)(4)*]. Thus, in this example, if pay for the year to 31 March 1996 was £1,500,000 and that for the year to 31 March 1997 is £1,200,000, the profits to be disregarded for the latter year are 193.33% of profits for the previous period, arrived at as follows

$$160\% + \left(\frac{1,500,000 - 1,200,000}{900,000} \times 100 \right) = 193.33\%$$

The maximum distributable pool for the year to 31 March 1997 is therefore 15% of £900,000 × 193.33% (although it would still be restricted in this example to £1,000,000 (the actual profits) × 15%).

(B) Distributable pool – Method B

D Ltd operates an approved profit-related pay scheme with effect from its accounting year ending 31 March 1995. The distributable pool is to be calculated using method B as defined by *ICTA 1988, 8 Sch 14*. The notional pool is specified as £300,000. The scheme provides that for every 3% increase (or decrease) in annual profits the distributable pool will increase (or decrease) by 2%. The scheme also provides that if annual profits fall below £500,000, no profit-related pay will be payable and that if profits exceed 160% of those for the preceding 12-month period, such excess will be disregarded.

Profits for the five years ending 31 March 1994, 1995, 1996, 1997 and 1998 are, respectively, £1,000,000, £1,060,000, £490,000, £769,000 and £1,300,000.

The distributable pool is calculated as follows

Year ending 31 March 1995

Increase in profits over previous year	$\dfrac{1,060,000 - 1,000,000}{1,000,000} \times 100 = 6\%$	
Increase in notional pool	£300,000 × 6% × $\frac{2}{3}$	£12,000
Distributable pool		£312,000

Year ending 31 March 1996

There will be no distribution of profit-related pay as profits are less than the specified minimum. However, the distributable pool must still be computed. See note (*a*).

Decrease in profits over previous year		54%
Decrease in distributable pool	£312,000 × 54% × $\frac{2}{3}$	£112,320
Distributable pool		£199,680

Year ending 31 March 1997

Increase in profits over previous year	57%
Increase in distributable pool £199,680 × 57% × $\frac{2}{3}$	£75,878
Distributable pool	£275,558

Year ending 31 March 1998

Increase in profits over previous year note (*b*)	60%
Increase in distributable pool £275,558 × 60% × $\frac{2}{3}$	£110,223
Distributable pool	£385,781

Notes

(*a*)   Where, in respect of any year, there is no distributable pool, the distributable pool for the following year is calculated as if such a pool *had* existed, and had been computed in the normal way, in the previous year. [*ICTA 1988, 8 Sch 14(6)*].

(*b*)   Although profits have increased by 69% in the year to 31 March 1998, the increase is restricted to 60% for the purpose of calculating the distributable pool, the company having taken advantage of *ICTA 1988, 8 Sch 14(4)*.

(*c*)   For schemes registered after 30 November 1993, provisions similar to those in note (*c*) to (A) above operate to increase the limiting percentage where pay is less than that of the previous year. [*ICTA 1988, 8 Sch 14A(5)–(7); FA 1994, s 98(3)(4)*].

(C)   Relief from tax [*ICTA 1988, s 171; FA 1989, 4 Sch 2; FA 1991, s 37*]
E is employed by C Ltd, the company in (A) above and receives, on 1 May 1996, profit-related pay of £4,200 for the year to 31 March 1996. His earnings received in the year to 31 March 1996, excluding profit-related pay, amounted to £16,600 and he was also provided with a company car on which both car and fuel benefits arise.

The amount of profit-related pay to be included in E's taxable emoluments for 1996/97 is as follows

	£	£
Amount received		4,200
Deduct tax-free amount, being the *lower* of		
(i) 20% of £20,800 note (*a*)	4,160	
(ii) Overriding maximum	4,000	
		4,000
Taxable profit-related pay		£200

Notes

(*a*)   The calculation in (i) above is 20% of the aggregate of the profit-related pay in respect of the profit period and the employee's other 'pay' received in the profit period. '*Pay*' excludes benefits-in-kind arising under *ICTA 1988, Pt V, Chapter II*. [*ICTA 1988, s 169*].

(*b*)   The taxable profit-related pay is taxed for the year of assessment *in* which it is received (under the normal receipts basis rules).

(*c*)   The exempt profit-related pay is within the charge to both employees' and employers' NIC.

23.3   ASSESSABLE INCOME, ALLOWABLE DEDUCTIONS — EMPLOYEE USING OWN CAR

(A) Fixed Profit Car Scheme (FPCS) [*ICTA 1988, ss 197B–197F; FA 1990, 4 Sch; Revenue Press Release 13 December 1994*]

D is employed as a buyer by CB Ltd and uses his own 2,200 cc car for business. CB Ltd operates the FPCS and pays its employees a standard mileage allowance (regardless of engine capacity) of 48 pence per business mile for 1996/97. The mileage allowance for 1989/90 was 37 pence per business mile, and subsequent increases have done no more than reflect increased motoring costs. D's business mileage is 18,000 in 1996/97 (compared to 15,000 in 1989/90).

The amount to be included in D's taxable emoluments for 1996/97 is as follows

	£	£
Mileage allowances received 18,000 × 48p		8,640
Tax free rates:		
First 4,000 business miles at $38\frac{1}{2}$ p	1,540	
Balance of 14,000 miles at 21p	2,940	4,480
Taxable amount before transitional relief		£4,160

A claim for transitional relief would give the following taxable amount:

$$£1,050 \text{ (see below)} \times \frac{18,000}{15,000} = £1,260 + £5,000 = \qquad £6,260$$

A claim is therefore not beneficial, and taxable mileage profit for 1996/97 is £4,160.

The tax-free rate for 1989/90 was 30p per mile. Therefore, the taxable amount would have been 15,000 × 7p = £1,050.

Notes

(a)   Tax-free rates changed with effect from 6 April 1990, with a lower rate applying after the first 4,000 business miles. The rates were further amended for each subsequent year. Transitional provisions ensured that there was no increase in taxable mileage allowances in 1990/91 other than that attributable to increased mileage, and that subsequent increases are restricted to £1,000 per year, subject to increased mileage.

(b)   The transitional provisions do not apply where the amount of the mileage allowance increases over the 1989/90 figure other than by reference to certain allowable factors (one of which is an increase in motoring costs). [*ICTA 1988, s 197E*].

(c)   Where employers pay the same rate of mileage allowances whatever size of car the employees use for business, the tax-free rate is the average of the two middle bands of the FPCS rates.

(B) Capital allowances [*CAA 1990, ss 24, 27, 79; FA 1990, s 87*]

H is employed by QP Ltd and uses his own car for business trips. He already owned the car when starting the employment on 1 July 1993. H claims allowances for 1993/94 and 1994/95, but does not claim for 1995/96, for which year his employer operates the Fixed Profit Car Scheme (see (A) above). H sells the car on 1 June 1996 for £1,325 and claims a balancing allowance for 1996/97. The open market value of the car at 1 July 1993 was £4,800. In 1993/94, H's business mileage is 25% of his total mileage and in 1994/95, it is 20%.

H's capital allowances are as follows

	Car £	Total Allowances £
1993/94		
Open market value 1.7.92	4,800	
WDA 25% × $\frac{9}{12}$ (1.7.92 – 5.4.93)	900	900
WDV at 5.4.94	£3,900	
Less 75% private use		675
Allowances claimed		£225
1994/95		
WDV b/fwd	3,900	
WDA 25%	975	975
WDV at 5.4.95	£2,925	
Less 80% private use		780
Allowances claimed		£195
1995/96 (No allowances claimed)		
1996/97		
WDV b/fwd	2,925	
Sale proceeds	1,325	
Balancing allowance before adjustment	£1,600	£1,600
		£
Appropriate fraction (see note (*d*)) $\frac{3}{4}$		1,200
Reduced by private use proportion: Say 1,455/1,875 × £1,200 note (*c*)		931
Balancing allowance claimed		£269

Notes

(*a*)   Capital allowances can be claimed from 1990/91 onwards in respect of a car provided by an employee for use in the performance of his duties. Previously, allowances could only be claimed if the car was 'necessarily' provided (and this still applies as regards other machinery and plant).

(*b*)   The car is introduced into the employment at open market value. [*CAA 1990, s 81(1)(a)*]. Writing-down allowances are restricted in the first year as the employment was carried on for part only of the year of assessment.

(*c*)   Allowances are reduced to the extent that the car is used other than for business. [*CAA 1990, s 79*]. It is reduced to 'such extent as may be just and reasonable'. For writing-down allowances, the restriction is normally calculated by reference to private usage in the year concerned. The balancing allowance in the above example has been computed by reference to the average private usage restriction for the two years for which writing-down allowances were claimed, which is considered to be one way of producing a just and reasonable result, although other methods are possible.

(*d*)   The balancing allowance is the 'appropriate fraction' of the excess of qualifying expenditure over sale proceeds. The fraction is equal to the number of years for which an allowance is claimed over the number of years for which it could have been claimed. [*CAA 1990, ss 24(2A), 27(2E); FA 1990, s 87(2)*]. It is assumed that both the numerator and denominator must include the year for which the balancing allowance is claimed, and that the appropriate fraction must be computed *before* the private use restriction in (*c*) above. There is no provision for a balancing charge to be similarly reduced.

23.4   BENEFITS — EMPLOYEES EARNING £8,500 PER ANNUM OR MORE AND DIRECTORS

(A) Cars and fuel [*ICTA 1988, ss 157, 158, 168(5)(6), 168A–168G, 6 Sch; FA 1993, 3 Sch; SI 1994 No 3010*]

(i)
A, B and C are employees of D Ltd. Each earns at least £8,500 per annum and each is provided with a company car throughout 1996/97. The company also bears at least part of the cost of petrol for private motoring.

A is provided with a 1,800 cc car first registered in October 1993 with a list price (including VAT, car tax (but not road tax), delivery charges and standard accessories) of £19,000. The car was made available to A in April 1994. An immobilisor was fitted in September 1994 at a cost of £200. A's business mileage is 20,000 for 1996/97. He is required to pay the company £250 per year as a condition of using the car for private motoring, and duly pays this amount.

B is provided with a 1,400 cc car first registered in March 1992 with a list price of £9,000. B drives 8,000 business miles in 1996/97. He was required to make a capital contribution of £1,000 on provision of the car in January 1995.

C is provided with a luxury car first registered in February 1995 with a list price of £85,000 (which includes optional accessories). He made a capital contribution of £3,000 in 1994/95. C's business mileage was 2,000 in 1996/97.

Car and fuel benefits for 1996/97 are as follows

	A £	B £	C £
List price	19,000	9,000	85,000
Later optional accessories	200	—	—
	19,200		
Capital contributions	—	(1,000)	(3,000)
			£82,000
Price cap for expensive cars			80,000
Price of car	£19,200	£8,000	£80,000

Cash equivalent — 35% of price of car	6,720	2,800	28,000
Discount for high business mileage (2/3)	(4,480)	—	—
Discount for moderate business mileage (1/3)	—	(933)	—
		1,867	
Discount for older cars (1/3)	—	(622)	—
	2,240		
Contribution for private use	(250)	—	—
Car benefit	1,990	1,245	28,000
Fuel benefit	890	710	1,320
Total car and fuel benefits	£2,880	£1,955	£29,320

Note

(a) A new system of car benefits came into operation in 1994/95. The benefit is based on 35% of the price of the car, with discounts for business mileage of at least 2,500 and 18,000 and for cars at least four years old at the end of the tax year. The price of the car is ascertained under *ICTA 1988, ss 168A–168G* and the annual car benefit is calculated under *ICTA 1988, 6 Sch* (as substituted by *FA 1993, 3 Sch 5*). There was no significant change in the method of computing car fuel benefits.

(ii)

J is Managing Director of K Ltd and during the year ended 5 April 1997 the company provided two cars for his use. Car 1 was a two-year old diesel car (2,200 cc with a list price of £18,000) and it was used by J for both business and private purposes until 31 October 1996 when it was written off as a result of an accident. J was subsequently prosecuted for dangerous driving, banned for one year and incurred legal costs of £800 which were ultimately paid for by K Ltd. In the period 6 April 1996 to 31 October 1996 Car 1 had travelled 11,000 miles on business, while J had paid the company £30 per month as a contribution towards private fuel. J was then provided with the use of a new 2-litre car (Car 2) and, since at first he had injuries which prevented him from driving and later lost his licence, a chauffeur. This replacement car was to be used for business purposes only.

J's benefits for 1996/97 relating to the cars are

	£	£
Car 1		
Car benefit £18,000 @ 35%	6,300	
Less $\frac{2}{3}$ discount for high business mileage note (b)	4,200	2,100
Fuel benefit		780
		£2,880
Proportion for period 6.4.95–31.10.95		
($\frac{209}{366}$ × £2,880)		1,645
Legal costs		800
Car 2		
Annual scale charge		—
Provision of chauffeur		—
		£2,445

Notes

(a)   The car and car fuel scale charges for Car 1 are reduced because the car was not available for use for part of the year. [*ICTA 1988, s 158(5), 6 Sch 6; FA 1993, 3 Sch 5, 6(2)*].

(b)   In determining business use for the purpose of discounting the car benefit, the annual 2,500 mile and 18,000 mile limits are reduced by reference to the period for which the car is available. [*ICTA 1988, 6 Sch 3; FA 1993, 3 Sch 5*]. In this example, the upper limit becomes 10,307 (18,000 × $\frac{209}{365}$) and J's 11,000 business miles thus qualify for the $\frac{2}{3}$ discount.

(c)   Since J makes a contribution only towards private fuel as distinct from private use, a reduction in the car scale charge under *ICTA 1988, 6 Sch 7* will not be available. As J is not *required* to make good the *whole* of the expense incurred by K Ltd in providing fuel for private use, his contributions do not reduce the fuel benefit. [*ICTA 1988, s 158(6)*].

(d)   The legal costs will be assessable as a benefit following *Rendell v Went H/L 1964, 41 TC 641*. No relief is available under *ICTA 1988, s 201AA* (introduced by FA 1995, s 91) (employee liabilities) as the expenses are incurred in connection with a criminal conviction. [*ICTA 1988, s 201AA(8)*].

(e)   Since Car 2 is not available for private use, no scale benefits will arise [*ICTA 1988, ss 157(1), 168(6)(a)*]. Although a benefit in respect of the chauffeur's wages will arise under *ICTA 1988, s 155(1)*, a claim under *ICTA 1988, s 198* (relief for necessary expenses) will eliminate the liability.

(f)   K Ltd will be liable to employers' Class 1A NIC for 1995/96 in respect of Car 1, under *Social Security Contributions and Benefits Act 1992, s 10*.

(B) Vans [*ICTA 1988, s 159AA, 6A Sch; FA 1993, s 73, 4 Sch*]

L is an employee of N Ltd, earning £18,000 per annum. From 1 October 1996 to 5 April 1997, L is provided by his employer with exclusive use of a one-year old company van (Van A) on terms which do not prohibit private use and which provide for a deduction of £4 per month to be made from his net salary at the end of each month in consideration for private use. For the period 6 April 1996 to 30 September 1996 inclusive, L had shared the van with another employee, M. Either L or a member of his family or household had made private use of the shared van for 42 days during that period, and M also made private use of the van. No payment for private use was required.

In addition to the van mentioned above, four other company vans are shared between five employees of N Ltd (excluding L and M) throughout the year ended 5 April 1997, three of which vans are aged less than four years at the end of that year. All the employees make some private use of one or more of the vans. One of the vans is off the road and incapable of use for three weeks in March 1997.

All vans mentioned have a normal laden weight not exceeding 3,500 kilograms.

The taxable benefit to L for 1996/97 of company vans is calculated as follows

Non-shared van

	£
Cash equivalent of benefit before adjustment	500

Exclude Period for which van is a shared van:

	£
$£500 \times \dfrac{178}{365}$ (6.4.96 – 30.9.96)	244
	256
Deduct Payment for private use (6 × £4 per month)	24
Cash equivalent of benefit	£232

Shared van

	£	£
Basic values:		
Van A	500	
Exclude Period for which van is not a shared van:		
$£500 \times \dfrac{187}{365}$ (1.10.96 – 5.4.97)	256	
		244
Other vans ((3 × £500) + (1 × £350))		1,850
Sum of basic values		£2,094
Divide £2,094 equally between seven participating employees		£299
Cash equivalent of benefit to L (maximum £500)		£299

Total benefits to L

	£
Non-shared van	232
Shared van	299
Total cash equivalent of benefit	£531
But restricted by *6A Sch 11* to	£500

L will thus be taxed on a van benefit of £500 for 1996/97.

In relation to the shared van, L then makes a claim for the alternative calculation under *6A Sch 8*.

Number of relevant days for Van A	42
Number of relevant days for other shared vans	Nil
Aggregate number of relevant days	42
Cash equivalent of benefit to L (42 × £5 per day)	£210

Total benefits to L (revised)

	£
Non-shared van	232
Shared van	210
Total cash equivalent of benefit	£442

L will thus be taxed on a van benefit of £442 for 1996/97.

Notes

(*a*)   See *6A Sch 4* for the definition of a 'shared van'.

(*b*)   The three weeks for which one of the shared vans is incapable of use does not reduce its basic value as it is not a period of at least 30 consecutive days. [*6A Sch 6*].

(*c*)   The overall restriction to £500 under *6A Sch 11* applies in this example as no more than one van was available for L's private use at any one time in the year.

(*d*)   The fuel scale charge does not apply to fuel provided for a company van.

(*e*)   The provision of a van does not attract Class 1A national insurance contributions.

(C) Assets given and leased [*ICTA 1988, s 156*]
During 1996/97 P Ltd transferred to R a television set which it had previously leased to him for a nominal rent of £2 per month. The company also leased a suit to R under the same arrangements. R's salary is £30,000 p.a.

Television
First leased to R in May 1995 (when its market value was £350); transferred to R in March 1997 for £50, the market value at that time being £125.

R's benefits are	£	£
1995/96		
Cost of benefit 20% × £350		70
Deduct Rent paid by R (11 months)		22
Cash equivalent of benefit		£48
1996/97		
Cost of benefit 20% × £350		70
Deduct Rent paid by R (12 months)		24
Cash equivalent of benefit		46
Greater of		
(i) Market value at transfer	125	
Deduct Price paid by R	50	
	£75	
and		
(ii) Original market value	350	
Deduct Cost of benefits note (*b*)	140	
	210	
Deduct Price paid by R	50	
	£160	
		160
Total		£206

Suit

First leased to R in November 1996 (when its market value was £200).

R's benefit for 1996/97 is		
Cost of benefit 20% × £200		40
Deduct Rent paid by R (5 months)		10
Cash equivalent of benefit		£30

Notes

(*a*)   Although each asset was either leased to R or transferred to him after the start of a fiscal year, he will be assessed on the full cost of the benefit for that year (as reduced by any rent paid). There is no time apportionment as in the case of cars made available for private use.

(*b*)   On the transfer of the television set, the cost of the benefits to date (2 × £70), not the cash equivalents, is deducted from the original market value. [*ICTA 1988, s 156(4)*].

(*c*)   It is assumed that the television set and suit have been bought by P Ltd and are not goods provided from within its own business. If the latter was the case, R would be assessed on the marginal or additional cost to P Ltd in providing the benefit (*Pepper v Hart H/L, [1992] STC 898*).

IT 23.4 Schedule E — Emoluments

(D) Beneficial loans [*ICTA 1988, ss 160, 161, 7 Sch; FA 1991, s 31; FA 1994, s 88; FA 1995, s 45*]

D, who is an employee of A Ltd earning £25,000 per annum, obtained a loan of £10,000 from the company on 10 October 1995 for the purpose of buying a car. Interest at a nominal rate is charged annually on the outstanding balance while the principal is repayable by instalments of £1,000 on 31 December and 30 June commencing 31 December 1995. The interest paid by D for 1995/96 amounted to £50 and for 1996/97 to £250. The official rates of interest were as listed below.

From 6.10.95   to 5.2.96   7.75% p.a.
From 6.2.96   7.25% p.a.

It is assumed *purely for the purposes of the example* that the rate is increased to 8% p.a. from 6 December 1996 and that there are no further changes before 6 April 1997.

D will be assessed in 1995/96 as follows

	£
Normal method (averaging)	
Average balance for period $\dfrac{£10,000 + £9,000}{2}$	£9,500
$£9,500 \times \frac{5}{12}$	£3,958
$£3,958 \times 7.75\% \times \frac{119}{179}$	204
$£3,958 \times 7.25\% \times \frac{60}{179}$	96
	300
Deduct Interest paid in year	50
Cash equivalent of loan benefit	£250

Alternative method

Period	Balance of loan in period £	Interest at official rate on balance	£
10.10.95 – 31.12.95	10,000	$£10,000 \times 7.75\% \times \frac{83}{366}$	176
1.1.96 – 5.2.96	9,000	$£9,000 \times 7.75\% \times \frac{36}{366}$	123
6.2.96 – 5.4.96	9,000	$£9,000 \times 7.25\% \times \frac{60}{366}$	107
			352
Deduct Interest paid in year			50
Cash equivalent of loan benefit			£302
Amount chargeable to tax note (*b*)			£302

D will be assessed in 1996/97 as follows

Normal method (averaging)	£
Average balance for year $\dfrac{£9,000 + £7,000}{2}$	£8,000
$£8,000 \times 7.25\% \times \frac{244}{365}$	388
$£8,000 \times 8\% \quad \times \frac{121}{365}$	212
	600
Deduct Interest paid in year	250
Cash equivalent of loan benefit	£350

Alternative method

Period	Balance of loan in period £	Interest at official rate on balance	£
6.4.96 – 30.6.96	9,000	$£9,000 \times 7.25\% \times \frac{86}{365}$	154
1.7.96 – 5.12.96	8,000	$£8,000 \times 7.25\% \times \frac{158}{365}$	251
6.12.96 – 31.12.96	8,000	$£8,000 \times 8\% \quad \times \frac{26}{365}$	46
1.1.97 – 5.4.97	7,000	$£7,000 \times 8\% \quad \times \frac{95}{365}$	146
			597
Deduct Interest paid in year			250
Cash equivalent of loan benefit			£347
Amount chargeable to tax note (*b*)			£350

Notes

(*a*)   The period 10 October 1995 to 5 April 1996 is, for the purpose of calculating the average balance, five complete months (months begin on the sixth day of each calendar month). However, for the purpose of applying the changing interest rates, the full number of days (179) during which the loan was outstanding is taken into account.

(*b*)   The inspector will probably require the alternative method to be applied for 1995/96. It is assumed that the employee will not elect for the alternative method in 1996/97 as the difference is negligible.

(*c*)   Note that a loan is exempt from the beneficial loan provisions for a tax year if it and other beneficial loans (excluding qualifying loans — see (E) below) do not exceed £5,000 in aggregate at any time in the year. [*ICTA 1988, s 161(1); FA 1994, s 88(3)(6)*].

(*d*)   In order for interest paid by the employee to be taken into account, it need not be paid *in* the tax year, only *for* the tax year. See Revenue Schedule E manual, volume II at SE3560–3564 for a useful discussion on this.

(E) Beneficial loans — qualifying loans [*ICTA 1988, ss 160, 161, 7 Sch; FA 1991, 6 Sch; FA 1994, s 88; FA 1995, s 45*]

B, another employee of A Ltd, earns £28,000 per annum and obtained a loan from the company of £50,000 in January 1996 for house purchase (B's principal private residence). At 5 April 1996, no capital had been repaid but on 1 August 1996 B repays £10,000 of the loan. The rate of interest on the loan is 2.5% per annum on the daily outstanding balance and interest paid in 1996/97 is £1,080. The official rates of interest are as in (D) above. B has no other source of taxable income for 1996/97. He is a single man.

A Ltd also gives B a season ticket loan of £2,400, interest-free and repayable in equal monthly instalments, on 10 January 1997.

The cash equivalent of the loan benefit for 1996/97 is computed as follows

(i) Normal method (averaging)

	£
Average balance for year $\dfrac{£50,000 + £40,000}{2}$	45,000
$£45,000 \times 7.25\% \times \frac{244}{365}$	2,181
$£45,000 \times 8\% \quad \times \frac{121}{365}$	1,193
	3,374
Deduct Interest paid in year	1,080
Cash equivalent of loan benefit	£2,294

(ii) Alternative method

Period	Balance of loan in period £	Interest at official rate on balance	£
6.4.96 – 1.8.96	50,000	$£50,000 \times 7.25\% \times \frac{118}{365}$	1,172
2.8.96 – 5.12.96	40,000	$£40,000 \times 7.25\% \times \frac{126}{365}$	1,001
6.12.96 – 5.4.97	40,000	$£40,000 \times 8\% \quad \times \frac{121}{365}$	1,061
			3,234
Deduct Interest paid in year			1,080
Cash equivalent of loan benefit			£2,154

	£
Amount chargeable to tax (on assumption that B elects for the alternative method)	£2,154

B is also treated as having paid notional interest on the loan of an amount equal to that chargeable to tax. Interest eligible for tax relief is as follows

(i) Interest actually paid

Interest paid	£	Interest eligible for relief	£
6.4.96 – 1.8.96 (118 days)			
$£50,000 \times 2.5\% \times \frac{118}{365}$	404	$£404 \times \dfrac{30,000}{50,000}$	243
	——		——
	c/f 404		c/f 243

	£ b/f 404			£ b/f 243
2.8.96 – 5.4.97 (247 days)				
$£40,000 \times 2.5\% \times \frac{247}{365}$	676	$£676 \times \dfrac{30,000}{40,000}$		507
	£1,080			£750

(ii) Notional interest paid

Interest paid

	£	Interest eligible for relief	£
6.4.96 – 1.8.96	1,172	$£1,172 \times \dfrac{30,000}{50,000}$	703
2.8.96 – 5.12.96	1,001	$£1,001 \times \dfrac{30,000}{40,000}$	751
6.12.96 – 5.4.97	1,061	$£1,061 \times \dfrac{30,000}{40,000}$	796
	3,234		2,250
Deduct actual interest	1,080		750
	£2,154		£1,500

B's tax liability for 1996/97 is computed as follows

	£	£
Salary		30,000
Benefit (home loan)		2,154
Schedule E income		32,154
Other income		—
Total income		32,154
Deduct Personal allowance		3,765
Taxable income		£28,389
Tax payable:		
3,900 @ 20%		780.00
21,600 @ 24%		5,184.00
2,889 @ 40%		1,155.60
		7,119.60
Deduct Interest relief:		
Actual interest	750	
Notional interest	1,500	
	£2,250	
£2,250 @ 15%		337.50
Tax liability		£6,782.10

Notes

(a)   The cash equivalent of the benefit is treated both as taxable income and as interest paid on the loan. [*ICTA 1988, s 160(1)(1A); FA 1994, s 88(1)*]. In this example, the interest so treated as paid qualifies for tax relief under general principles, i.e. as interest on a loan to purchase the borrower's main residence (subject to the £30,000 limit).

(b)   The season ticket loan does not give rise to a taxable benefit as it is not a qualifying loan and at no time in the tax year does the amount outstanding exceed £5,000. Two or more non-qualifying loans must be aggregated in applying the £5,000 limit. Qualifying loans are similarly exempt if all beneficial loans, taken together, fall within the £5,000 limit. [*ICTA 1988, s 161(1); FA 1994, s 88(3)*]. A qualifying loan is one on which interest paid qualifies for tax relief. [*ICTA 1988, s 160(1C); FA 1994, s 88(1)*].

23.5   **BENEFITS — LIVING ACCOMMODATION** [*ICTA 1988, ss 145, 146, 163*]

(A)

N is employed by the G Property Co Ltd, earning £12,000 p.a. He occupies, rent-free, the basement flat of a block of flats for which he is employed as caretaker/security officer. The annual value of the flat is determined at £250. In 1996/97, G Ltd incurred the following expenditure on the flat

	£
Heat and light	700
Decoration	330
Repairs	210
Cleaning	160
	£1,400

Conversion of large bedroom into two smaller bedrooms	£3,000

In addition, the company pays N's council tax which amounts to £500.

As the company does not have a pension scheme, N pays a personal pension premium of £200 (net) on 31 October 1996, but apart from his personal allowance, he has no other reliefs.

N's taxable income for 1996/97 is

	£
Salary	12,000
Annual value of flat	—
Heat and light, decoration, repairs, cleaning	
£1,400 restricted to (note (*c*))	1,200
	13,200
Deduct Personal allowance	3,765
Taxable	£9,435

Notes

(a)   N will not be assessed on the annual value of the flat if he can show that it is necessary for the proper performance of his duties for him to reside in the accommodation. [*ICTA 1988, s 145(4)(a)*]. He might equally well be able to claim under *ICTA 1988, s 145(4)(b)*.

(b)   The structural alterations costing £3,000 will not be regarded as a benefit. [*ICTA 1988, s 155(3)*].

(c)   The emoluments treated as having arisen in respect of the heat and light, decoration, repairs and cleaning costs will be restricted by *ICTA 1988, s 163* to the lesser of

(i) the expenses incurred	£1,400
(ii) 10% × £12,000 (net emoluments)	£1,200

The personal pension contribution is not deductible in arriving at net emoluments for this purpose, although retirement annuity premiums and occupational pension scheme contributions are so deductible. [*ICTA 1988, s 163(4)*]. (The contribution is not shown above as a deduction from taxable income as basic rate relief has been given at source and higher rate relief is not applicable.)

(d)   Where the benefit of living accommodation is exempt under *ICTA 1988, s 145(4)*, the payment by the employer of the employee's council tax is also exempt (Revenue Press Release 16 March 1993, para 6).

(B) Additional charge [*ICTA 1988, s 146*]
S, the founder and managing director of S Ltd, a successful transport company, has for four years occupied a mansion house owned by S Ltd. The house was acquired by S Ltd in August 1986 for £150,000 and, since acquisition, but before 6 April 1995, £80,000 has been spent by S Ltd on alterations and improvements to the house. The gross annual value of the house for rating purposes before 1 April 1990 (when the community charge replaced general rates) was £1,663. S pays annual rental of £2,000 to the company in respect of 1996/97 only. He pays all expenses relating to the property.

S's assessable benefits in respect of his occupation of the house for 1995/96 and 1996/97 are as follows

	£	£
1995/96		
Gross annual value		1,663
Additional charge		
Acquisition cost of house	150,000	
Cost of improvements	80,000	
	230,000	
Deduct	75,000	
Additional value	£155,000	
Additional value at 8% note (b)		12,400
		£14,063

		£	£
1996/97			
Gross annual value	note (*a*)		Nil
Additional charge			
Acquisition cost of house		150,000	
Cost of improvements		80,000	
		230,000	
Deduct		75,000	
Additional value		£155,000	
Additional value at 7.25%	note (*b*)		11,237
			11,237
Rental payable by S		2,000	
Deduct Gross annual value		1,663	
			337
			£10,900

Notes

(*a*)   No taxable gross annual value arises in 1996/97 because the rental of £2,000 payable by S exceeds the gross annual value of £1,663. The excess is deductible from the amount of the benefit arising under the additional charge.

(*b*)   The percentage to be used in determining the amount of the benefit is that used for the purposes of the beneficial loan arrangements (see 23.4(D) above) at the beginning of the year of assessment.

(*c*)   If S had moved into the house on, say, 6 April 1992 (more than six years after its acquisition by S Ltd), market value at that date would be substituted for cost plus improvements. If, however, original cost plus cost of improvements had not exceeded £75,000, the additional charge would not apply (regardless of market value at the date of first occupation by S) (Revenue Press Release 18 August 1988).

23.6   REMOVAL EXPENSES AND BENEFITS, INCLUDING BENEFICIAL LOAN ARRANGEMENTS [*ICTA 1988, ss 191A, 191B, 11A Sch; FA 1993, 5 Sch*]

Mr R E Locate lives in Chelsea and is employed as a store manager by T Ltd, a department store chain, at one of their London branches. In June 1996, he is asked by T Ltd to take up a similar position at their main Birmingham store with effect from 1 September 1996. The company agrees to pay Mr Locate's expenses, up to a ceiling of £7,000, in connection with his moving house to the Birmingham area. In the event, the expenses paid or reimbursed by the company amount to £6,500, all paid in 1996, all eligible expenses within *ICTA 1988, 11A Sch 7–14* and all reasonably incurred by the employee in connection with his change of residence. As he is unable to move into his new home until 15 September 1996, T Ltd provides Mr Locate with temporary living accommodation near his new place of employment. The accommodation is rented by the company and would give rise to a taxable benefit on the employee of £300 under *ICTA 1988, s 145*, but no charge under *ICTA 1988, s 146* (see 23.5 above).

T Ltd also provides Mr Locate with an interest-free bridging loan of £50,000 in connection with the change of residence. The loan is made on 1 September 1996 and is repaid on 5 March 1997 when the sale of the employee's former residence is completed.

The official rate of interest under *ICTA 1988, s 160 is assumed to be* 8% per annum up to 5 December 1996 and 8.5% per annum thereafter. In August 1996, Mr Locate had taken out a £30,000 building society mortgage towards the acquisition of his new home.

Mr Locate's salary for 1996/97 amounts to £40,000.

Mr Locate's taxable benefits for 1996/97 in respect of removal expenses and benefits plus beneficial loans are calculated as follows

	£
	£
Qualifying removal expenses	6,500
Qualifying removal benefits	300
	£6,800

The total is less than the qualifying limit of £8,000 under *11A Sch 24(9)* and is thus exempt from tax by virtue of *11A Sch 1(1)*.

Beneficial loan arrangements

The beneficial loan is treated by *ICTA 1988, s 191B* as having been made on a date later than that on which it was actually made, as follows.

Number of days in the 'relevant period' = $\dfrac{A \times B}{C \times D}$

A = 1,200 (unused qualifying limit — £8,000 – £6,800)

B = 365

C = 50,000 (maximum loan outstanding between the actual date of the loan, 1.9.96, and 5.4.97, the latter being the 'relevant day' — see *11A Sch 6* and note (*a*) below)

D = 8% (the official rate of interest as at the actual date of the loan, 1.9.96, disregarding subsequent changes of rate)

$$\frac{1{,}200 \times 365}{50{,}000 \times 8\%} = 109.5 \text{ which is rounded up to 110 days}$$

[*Sec 191B(10)–(12)*].

The 'relevant period' of 110 days runs from 1.9.96 to 19.12.96 inclusive. The loan is deemed to have been made on 19.12.96. [*Sec 191B(8)*].

Calculation of benefit:

(i) Averaging method

$$\frac{£50{,}000 + £50{,}000}{2} \times \tfrac{2}{12} \times 8.5\% = \qquad\qquad £708$$

(ii) Alternative method

20.12.96–5.3.97 = 75 days

$£50{,}000 \times 8.5\% \times \tfrac{75}{365} = \qquad\qquad £873$

Amount chargeable to tax (on the assumption that the alternative method is applied)   £873

Notes

(a)   Eligible expenses and benefits which are reasonably incurred or provided in connection with the change in the employee's residence are qualifying expenses or benefits only if they are incurred or provided on or before the end of the year of assessment following that in which the employment, new duties or duties at the new location commence, i.e. by 5 April 1997 in this example. [*11A Sch 3–6*].

(b)   'Subsistence' provided for the employee is an eligible benefit by virtue of *11A Sch 21(1)(d)*. For this purpose, 'subsistence' includes temporary living accommodation as well as food and drink. [*11A Sch 28*].

(c)   See also 23.4(D)(E) above as regards beneficial loans. See, in particular, note (a) to 23.4(D) above as regards the averaging method of computation.

(d)   No part of the beneficial loan is eligible for tax relief as the £30,000 qualifying maximum is taken up by the earlier building society loan.

23.7   **BENEFITS — MEDICAL INSURANCE, VOUCHERS ETC.** [*ICTA 1988, ss 141, 143, 144, 153–155, 167; FA 1989, s 53; FA 1994, s 89*]

(A)
T earns £6,000 p.a. and during the year ended 5 April 1997 his employer provided him with, or paid on his behalf, or reimbursed, the following

	£
BUPA contributions (self and family) of which 25% reimbursed by T	600
Special medical insurance for overseas business visit lasting four nights	250
Voucher exchangeable for rail season ticket	500
Gift token exchangeable for goods at local department store	75
Holiday pay scheme voucher, exchangeable for cash	350
Overnight incidental expenses (telephone, laundry etc.) relating to above-mentioned overseas trip	36

The rail ticket voucher was purchased in March 1996 but was not handed to T until after 6 Ap 1996. The holiday pay voucher was received by T in June 1995 at which time PAYE was applie The gift token was received in December 1996.

T's assessable emoluments for 1996/97 are

	£
Salary	6,000
Rail ticket voucher	500
Gift token	75
Holiday pay scheme voucher	350
	£6,925

Notes

(a)   T is not a director or employee earning £8,500 a year or more and so the BUPA contributions are not an assessable benefit.

(b)   The rail ticket voucher will be assessable in 1996/97 being the later of the year of receipt by the employee and the year of expense incurred by the employer.

(c)   The holiday pay voucher, being a 'cash voucher' is taxable under PAYE by virtue of *ICTA 1988, s 203I; FA 1994, s 130.*

(d)   The reimbursement of overnight incidental expenses is not taxable as the amount does not exceed £10 for each night of absence (£5 for absences within the UK). [*ICTA 1988, s 200A; FA 1995, s 93*].

(B)
Instead of earning £6,000 as in (A) above, T has a salary of £7,500 p.a.

T's assessable emoluments for 1996/97 are

	£
Salary	7,500
BUPA contributions (£600 less 25%)	450
Rail ticket voucher	500
Gift token	75
Holiday pay scheme voucher	350
	£8,875

Notes

(a)   All chargeable benefits and expenses payments, before relief for business expenditure, are taken into account in determining whether or not the £8,500 limit has been reached.

(b)   The special medical insurance for the overseas business trip is exempted from charge by *ICTA 1988, s 155(6).*

24   Self-Assessment

24.1   **CALCULATION OF INTERIM PAYMENTS FOR 1996/97** [*TMA 1970, s 59A; FA 1994, s 192; FA 1995, ss 108, 116, 21 Sch 2; FA 1996, s 126(1), 18 Sch 2, 17(1)*]

(A) Calculation of interim payments for 1996/97
Kylie is a single person with the following income and gains for 1995/96.

	£
Profit as freelance writer (year to 30.4.94)	9,000
Salary and benefits from employment (tax paid under PAYE £3,350)	19,001
Rental income net of expenses	3,000
Untaxed interest (year to 5 April 1995)	400
Dividends (including tax credits £200)	1,000
Taxed interest (tax deducted £375)	1,500
Capital gains	6,300

She makes payments of £150 in 1995/96 under charitable covenants.

Assessments for 1995/96 are raised and agreed showing the following amounts of tax due.

Schedule D, Case II	2,250.00
Schedule E	359.00
Schedule A	1,196.40
Schedule D, Case III	160.00
Higher rate tax on dividends and taxed interest	425.00
Capital gains tax	120.00

Assuming she makes no claim either to eliminate or reduce interim payment, Kylie's interim payments under self assessment for 1996/97 are calculated as follows.

(i)	Relevant amount £(2,250 + 1,196.40 + 160.00 — the Schedule E liability and higher rate liability on taxed income being excluded for this transitional year only, the capital gains tax liability always being excluded)	£3,606.40
(ii)	Part of relevant amount consisting of tax under Schedule A or any of Cases III to VI of Schedule D £(1,196.40 + 160.00)	£1,356.40
(iii)	Balance of relevant amount (i.e. Schedule D, Case II liability)	£2,250.00

First interim payment due 31.1.97 ((ii) + $\frac{1}{2}$ of (iii))	2,481.40
Second interim payment due 31.7.97 ($\frac{1}{2}$ of (iii))	1,125.00
	£3,606.40

A balancing payment/repayment will be due on 31.1.98 equal to the difference between the net income tax liability self-assessed for 1996/97 plus any capital gains tax liability and £3,606.40 paid on account.

Note

(*a*)   This example disregards any liability for 1995/96 to Class 4 national insurance contributions. Any such liability should be added to the figures at (i) and (iii), each interim payment for 1996/97 thus being increased by $\frac{1}{2}$ the previous year's Class 4 liability.

24.2   **INTEREST AND SURCHARGE ARISING ON LATE PAYMENT** [*TMA 1970, ss 55, 59B, 59C, 86; FA 1995, s 110; FA 1996, ss 131, 194, 18 Sch 3, 17(1)(2)*]

Mrs Worthington is a self-employed cook. Her self-assessment for 1996/97 shows a net income tax liability of £9,000. She makes the following interim payments for 1997/98:

31 January 1998	£4,500
31 July 1988	£4,500

Due to fortuitous circumstances Mrs Worthington's profits increase and her self-assessment for 1997/98 is £12,000 instead of the estimated £9,000. Mrs Worthington pays additional income tax of £3,000 on 1 September 1999.

Assuming interest on unpaid tax is at the rate of 6% throughout.

Mrs Worthington's interest will amount to:

–   from 31 January 1999 to 1 September 1999 on $£3,000 \times \dfrac{213}{365} \times 6\% =$ £105.04

In addition as the tax is paid more than 28 days late a surcharge will arise on 1 March 1999 of £3,000 × 5% = £150.

As the tax is still outstanding 6 months later a further surcharge will arise on 1 August 1999 of £3,000 × 5% = £150.

Notes

(*a*)   Interest accrues from the due date until date of payment. [*TMA 1970, s 86(1)(2); FA 1995, s 110(1)*].

(*b*)   These rules apply in general for 1996/97 and subsequent years of assessment. They also apply to tax charged by an assessment made on or after 6 April 1998 for the year 1995/96 or an earlier year of assessment. [*FA 1995, s 110(2)(3)*].

(*c*)   For 1996/97 and subsequent years a surcharge may arise in respect of unpaid tax due in respect of a final payment of income tax or capital gains tax under *TMA 1970, s 59B* or for postponed tax pending appeal now due under *TMA 1970, s 55*. [*TMA 1970, s 59(c); FA 1994, s 194*].

If the tax remains unpaid for more than 28 days after the due date, the taxpayer will be liable to a surcharge of 5% of the unpaid tax. A further 5% surcharge will be levied on any tax still unpaid more than six months after the due date. Interest will accrue on an unpaid surcharge with effect from the expiry of 30 days beginning with the date of the notice imposing the surcharge.

24.3   **INTEREST ARISING ON INSUFFICIENT INTERIM PAYMENT** [*TMA 1970, s 86(1); FA 1996, s 110*]

Mr Jones is a self-employed butcher with no other income who draws up accounts to 31 October each year. His liability under self-assessment for 1996/97 amounts to £25,000. Mr Jones forecasts that his profits for the accounting period ended 31 October 1997 will result in a liability under self-assessment of £10,000. He makes a claim to that effect under *TMA 1970, s 59A(4)* and duly pays £5,000 each on 31 January 1998 and 31 July 1998. However, actual profits are in excess of his expectations and result in a self-assessment liability of £16,000. Mr Jones pays an additional £6,000 income tax on 31 January 1999.

For each interim payment Mr Jones' interest will be calculated on the difference between £5,000 and the lesser of:

£8,000 being the sum of £5,000 (actual interim payment) and £3,000 (50% of the final tax payment); and

£12,500 being the interim payment based on the preceding year's tax liability.

Interest will be:

- 31 January 1998 to 31 January 1999 £3,000 × 6% =   £180.00

- 31 July 1998 to 31 January 1999 $£3,000 \times \dfrac{184}{365} \times 6\%$ £90.74

                                                                    _____

                                                                    £279.74

Note

(*a*)   Interest is charged on the difference between the final liability and the lesser of:

–   the aggregate of that interim payment and 50% of the final tax payment excluding CGT; and

–   the interim payment based on the previous year's liability. [*TMA 1970, s 86(4)–(6); FA 1995, s 110*].

25   Settlements

25.1   ASSESSMENTS ON TRUST INCOME

A is sole life-tenant of a settlement which has income and expenses in the year 1996/97 of

	£	£
Property income		500
Taxed investment income (tax deducted at source £300)		1,500
Dividends	800	
Add Tax credits	200	
	——	1,000
		£3,000
Expenses chargeable to revenue		£400

The tax assessable on the trustees will be £120 (£500 at 24%). The expenses are not deductible in arriving at the tax payable by the trustees. The 20% lower rate band applies only to individual taxpayers and not to trustees, although the 20% rate on dividends and interest does apply to trustees.

Notes

(*a*)   By prior arrangement, where there is a sole life-tenant in a trust, the Inland Revenue may allow the interest to be assessed directly on that beneficiary.

(*b*)   For treatment of the trust income in the hands of the beneficiary, see 25.3(A) below.

25.2   DISCRETIONARY TRUSTS [*ICTA 1988, ss 686, 832; FA 1988, s 24(4); FA 1993, s 79(3), 6 Sch 8, 15*]

An accumulation and maintenance settlement set up by W for his grandchildren in 1978 now comprises quoted investments and an industrial property. The property is let to an engineering company. Charges for rates, electricity etc. are paid by the trust and recharged yearly in arrears to the tenant. As a result of the delay in recovering the service costs, the settlement incurs overdraft interest.

The relevant figures for the year ended 5 April 1997 are as follows

	£
Property rents (Schedule A)	40,000
UK dividends (including tax credits of £1,000)	5,000
Taxed interest (tax deducted at source £700)	3,500
	£48,500
Trust administration expenses — proportion chargeable to revenue	1,350
Overdraft interest	1,050
	£2,400

Tax is payable by the trustees of a discretionary trust (including an accumulation and maintenance trust) at the rate applicable to trusts (35% for 1995/96).

IT 25.3   Settlements

The tax liability of the trust for 1996/97 is as follows

	£	£
Schedule A £40,000 at 34%		13,600
Taxed interest net	2,800	
Net dividends	4,000	
Deduct Expenses	(2,400)	
	£4,400	
£4,400 grossed at $\frac{100}{80}$ = £5,500 @ 14% (34 − 20)		770
Tax payable by assessment		14,370
Add: Tax deducted at source		700
Tax credits		1,000
Total tax borne		£16,070

Notes

(a)   Expenses (including in this example the overdraft interest) are set firstly against income falling within *ICTA 1988, s 207A* (dividend income). [*FA 1993, s 79(3)*]. The effect is that the expenses, grossed-up at 20%, save tax at 14% (the difference between the 20% rate applicable to dividends and the rate applicable to trusts).

(b)   The net revenue available for distribution to the beneficiaries, at the trustees' discretion, will be £30,030 (£48,500 − £16,070 − £2,400).

(c)   For treatment of the trust income in the hands of a beneficiary, see 25.3(B) below.

25.3   INCOME OF BENEFICIARIES

(A) Interests in possession

A, as sole life-tenant of the settlement in 25.1 above, is absolutely entitled to receive the whole settlement income.

A's income for 1996/97 will include the following

	£	£
Trust dividend and interest income (gross)	2,500	
Other trust income		500
Deduct: Lower rate tax (20%)	(500)	
Basic rate tax (24%)		(120)
	2,000	380
Deduct Expenses (note (b))	400	
Net income entitlement	£1,600	£380
Grossed-up amounts: £1,600 × $\frac{100}{80}$	£2,000	
£1,380 × $\frac{100}{76}$		£500

Notes

(a)   This income falls to be included in A's return even if it is not actually paid to him, as he is absolutely entitled to it. He will receive a tax certificate (form R185E) from the trust agents, showing two figures for gross income (£2,000 and £500), tax deducted (£400 and £120) and net income (£1,600 and £380).

(b)   The trust expenses are deducted from income falling within *ICTA 1988, s 1A* (savings income) in priority to other income.

(c)   That part of A's trust income which is represented by dividend income (£400 net) is treated in A's hands as if it were dividends, with attached tax credits, received directly by A. It is thus chargeable at the lower rate only, the liability being satisfied by the 20% tax credit, except to the extent, if any, that it exceeds his basic rate limit. Similar treatment applies to interest received from 1996/97.

(B) Accumulation or discretionary trusts

M, the 17-year old grandson of W, is one of the five beneficiaries to whom the trustees can pay the settlement income in 25.2 above. The trustees make a payment of £3,000 to M on 31 January 1997. He has no other income in the year 1996/97 and is unmarried.

M's income from the trust is

	£
Net income	3,000.00
Tax at $\frac{34}{66}$	1,545.45
Gross income	£4,545.45

He can claim a tax repayment for 1996/97 of

	£
Total income	4,545
Deduct Personal allowance	3,765
	£780

Tax thereon at 20% (within lower rate band)	156.00
Tax accounted for by trustees	1,545.45
Repayment due	£1,389.45

Notes

(a)   If no income was actually paid to M from the settlement, nothing would fall to be included in his return.

(b)   Unlike the position with interest in possession trusts (see (A) above), no distinction is made between dividend and interest income and other income in the beneficiary's hands, the full amount of the payment to him having suffered tax at a single rate of 34% in the hands of the trustees (see 25.2 above).

(c)   For treatment of trust income where the beneficiary is an infant under a parent's settlement, see 25.4 below.

25.4   **SETTLEMENT BY PARENT IN FAVOUR OF OWN CHILD** [*ICTA 1988, ss 660B, 686; FA 1995, s 74, 17 Sch 1*]

L set up an accumulation and maintenance trust for his two children, aged 6 and 4, in 1981. On 31 December 1983 and 31 December 1984, school fees of £550 were paid on behalf of each child. In January 1996 the trust was wound up and the assets transferred to the two beneficiaries, then aged 21 and 19, in equal shares. At that time there was £6,000 of undistributed income.

The income to be treated as the settlor's income will be as follows

1983/84 $£1,100 \times \dfrac{100}{55}$ £2,000

1984/85 $£1,100 \times \dfrac{100}{55}$ £2,000

1996/97   note (*b*)   Nil

Notes

(*a*)   The payments for 1983/84 and 1984/85 are grossed up in accordance with the basic and additional rates of tax for those years, i.e. 30% + 15% = 45%.

(*b*)   Income is not treated as that of the settlor if, at the time of payment, the children have either married or reached the age of eighteen.

25.5 **LOANS AND REPAYMENT OF LOANS TO SETTLOR** [*ICTA 1988, s 677; FA 1993, 6 Sch 7; FA 1995, s 74, 17 Sch 9*]
The trustees of a settlement with undistributed income of £1,375 at 5 April 1994 made a loan of £15,000 to B, the settlor, on 30 September 1994.

B repays the loan on 31 December 1996. Undistributed income of £3,500 arose in 1994/95, £6,500 in 1995/96 and £5,500 in 1996/97. B has taxable income of £30,000 in each year (excluding dividend income).

B will be treated as receiving the following income

		£
1994/95	£4,875 × $\dfrac{100}{65}$	7,500
1995/96	£6,500 × $\dfrac{100}{65}$	10,000
1996/97	£3,625 × $\dfrac{100}{66}$ note (*b*)	5,492

B will pay additional tax of

		£
1994/95	£7,500 at 5% (40% − 35%)	375
1995/96	£10,000 at 5% (40% − 35%)	500
1996/97	£5,492 at 6% (40% − 34%)	329
		£1,204

Notes

(*a*) The amount to be included as part of B's income for each year is limited to the amount of undistributed income, grossed up at the rate applicable to trusts, available within the settlement at the end of the tax year, but excluding *inter alia* any such income which has already been 'matched' under these provisions.

(*b*) The amount treated as income in 1996/97 is limited to the amount of the loan less amounts previously treated as income (£15,000 − (£4,875 + £6,500)).

(*c*) If B had repaid the loan on, say, 31 December 1995, the position as regards 1994/95 and 1995/96 would have been as above, but there would have been no charge for subsequent years.

26   Share Incentives and Options

26.1   **SHARE OPTIONS — CHARGE TO TAX** [*ICTA 1988, ss 135–137, 140*]

An employee is granted an option exercisable within 5 years to buy 1,000 shares at £5 each. The option costs 50p per share. He exercises the option in 1996/97 when the shares are worth £7.50. The option is not granted under an approved scheme.

He is chargeable to income tax under Schedule E in 1996/97 as follows

	£	£
Open market value of shares 1,000 × £7.50		7,500
Price paid 1,000 × £5 — shares	5,000	
1,000 × 50p — option	500	
		5,500
Assessable		£2,000

Notes

(*a*)   The result would be the same if, instead of exercising the option, the employee transferred his option to a third party for £2,500.

(*b*)   The capital gains tax base cost of the shares will be £7,500. [*TCGA 1992, s 120(4)*].

26.2   **'SHARE INCENTIVES' — CHARGE TO TAX** [*ICTA 1988, ss 138–140; FA 1988, ss 77–89; F(No 2)A 1992, s 37*]

(A) Charge where restrictions removed etc.

E, an employee of Perks Ltd, exercised, on 1 June 1987, an option, conferred on him by reason of his employment, to acquire 3,000 shares in that company, their open market value at that time being £10,000. He was duly charged to tax under Schedule E under the rules in 26.1 above. The shares were subject to one of the restrictions in *ICTA 1988, s 138(6)*. Market value per share at 26 October 1987 and at 1 June 1994 was £4.50 and £4.75 respectively. On 1 November 1996, a chargeable event under *FA 1988, s 78(2)* occurs by virtue of the restriction being removed. Removal of the restriction increases the value per share from £5.00 to £7.50. E has remained in the company's employment throughout the period and at no time has the company been a 'dependent subsidiary' as defined by *FA 1988, s 86*.

E will be charged to income tax under Schedule E as follows

		£
(i) *Charge under ICTA 1988, s 138(1)(a) in 1994/95*		
Market value at 26.10.87	note (*a*)	13,500
Less market value at 1.6.87		12,000
		£1,500
(ii) *Charge under FA 1988, s 78(3) in 1996/97*		
Increase in market value resulting from chargeable event (3,000 × £2.50)	note (*b*)	£7,500

Notes

(*a*)   A charge arises on the seventh anniversary of acquisition (1 June 1994), but under the transitional provisions of *FA 1988, s 88(2)* it is calculated by reference to market value at 26 October 1987, the date from which the *Finance Act 1988* provisions apply, as this is less than market value at 1 June 1994.

(*b*)   The charge under *FA 1988, s 78(3)* is on the increase in value as a result of the chargeable event. Note that the increase between 26 October 1987 and 31 October 1996 escapes any charge to income tax (and any decrease in value would not have attracted relief).

(*c*)   On a sale of the shares, the capital gains tax base cost would include the amounts chargeable under (i) and (ii) above, such amounts being regarded as consideration given for the acquisition of the shares, under *TCGA 1992, s 120(5)* and *s 120(1)* respectively.

(B) Charge for shares in dependent subsidiaries
On 1 February 1996, P acquires 1,000 shares with an open market value of £4,000 in a company of which he is a director. The shares are acquired under an unapproved share option scheme open only to the directors. The company is a 'dependent subsidiary' as defined by *FA 1988, s 86*. On 1 August 1996, P gifts his shares to his daughter, Q. On 31 March 1997, Q sells the shares at their then market value of £5,000.

P will be charged to tax under Schedule E in 1996/97 as follows

		£
Open market value at 31 March 1997	note (*a*)	5,000
Less open market value at 1 February 1996		4,000
Schedule E assessment on P		£1,000

Notes

(*a*)   A charge arises under *FA 1988, s 79* by virtue of P's ceasing to have a beneficial interest in the shares on 31 March 1997. His gift to Q is disregarded in determining who has the beneficial interest, this being a disposal other than by way of an arm's length bargain with an unconnected person. [*FA 1988, s 83(2)*].

(*b*)   If P had retained the beneficial interest until 1 February 2003, the seventh anniversary of acquisition, a charge under *Sec 79* would arise at that time, i.e. in 2002/2003.

(*c*)   The gift to Q is a disposal for capital gains tax purposes. As in (A) above, the amount of the Schedule E charge is deemed to have been expended by P on the acquisition of the shares, thus increasing their base cost to P for capital gains tax. Q will be regarded for capital gains tax purposes as having acquired the shares on 1 August 1996 at their market value at that date.

IT 26.3 Share Incentives and Options

26.3 **APPROVED SHARE OPTION SCHEMES** [*ICTA 1988, ss 185, 187, 9 Sch; FA 1991, s 39*]

The employee in 26.1 above is instead granted his option a company share option plan approved under *ICTA 1988, 9 Sch.*

Provided that the option is exercised not less than three nor more than ten years after being granted, there is no charge under *ICTA 1988, s 135* (see 26.1 above) when the option is exercised and no charge under the *Finance Act 1988* provisions (see 26.2 above) on any growth in value of the shares. The capital gains tax base cost of the shares (subject to indexation) will then be £5.50 per share. [*ICTA 1988, s 185(1)–(3)(5)*].

If, however, the market value of the shares at the date the option is granted was, say, £7.00 per share and the scheme includes provision pursuant to *ICTA 1988, 9 Sch 29(2)*, there would still be no charge under the above mentioned provisions, but there would be an income tax charge under Schedule E for the year in which the option is granted, as follows

		£	£
Market value	1,000 × £7.00		7,000
Price payable	1,000 × £5.00 — shares	5,000	
	1,000 × 50p — option	500	
			5,500
Schedule E assessment			£1,500

The capital gains tax base cost, subject to indexation, will then be £7.00 per share. [*ICTA 1988, s 185(6)–(6B)(7); FA 1991, s 39; TCGA 1992, s 120(6); FA 1993, s 105; FA 1996, s 114*].

26.4 **PROFIT SHARING SCHEMES** [*ICTA 1988, ss 186, 187, 9, 10 Schs; FA 1989, s 63; FA 1991, s 41*]

(A)

Ray and Bill are both employed by QZ plc and on 1 October 1997 the trustees of the company's approved profit sharing scheme appropriate 1000 ordinary shares valued at £1 per share to each of them. No tax charge arises at this time. The scheme's release date is thus 1 October 2000.

The following events subsequently arise:

(i)   On 1 October 1999 the trustees sell 500 of the shares appropriated to Bill for £1.20 per share.

(ii) On 1 December 1999 Ray is made redundant and the trustees sell all his shares for £1.10 per share.

(iii) On 1 December 2000 Bill's 500 remaining shares are sold for £1.30 per share.

The income tax position affecting each transaction is as follows:

(1)   On 1 October 1999 Bill is liable for tax under Schedule E on the lower of:

– 100% of the 'locked-in-value' i.e. 100% × £500   £500

   or

– 100% of the value at that time   £600

therefore in this case the amount is £500.

(2)   On 1 December 1999 a similar calculation must be performed in respect of Ray's disposal, but as he was made redundant he is entitled to a 50% reduction in the value of the shares.

i.e. £(1,000 × 50%) = £500

(3)   No liability arises in respect of Ray's disposal on 1 December 2000 as the disposal occurs more than three years after the shares were appropriated to him.

Notes

(a)   From 29 April 1996 onwards the 'release date' (after which no Schedule E liability will arise for the participant) is the third anniversary of the date of the appropriation of the shares to the participant.

(b)   Disposals or other chargeable events arising in respect of shares appropriated to an employee participant less than three years before the release date bring about a Schedule E income tax charge for the participant based on the lower of the value of the shares when they were first appropriated and the value at the time a disposal arises. A 50% reduction in the value is available if the employee leaves the company because of ill-health or redundancy etc.

(c)   Capital receipts for trustees or participants (e.g. sale of rights) are taxable under Schedule E on the participant as a part disposal but from 1997/98 onwards a reduction of £20 per annum is available for each complete year of ownership subject to a maximum of £60. Prior to this the maximum amount was £120 when the required period of ownership in order to avoid a Schedule E charge was 5 years.

(d)   The tax is withheld under PAYE.

(e)   'Locked-in value' is the initial market value when appropriated as reduced by certain capital receipts charged to income tax.

(B) Limit on initial market value of shares appropriated

In 1995/96 and 1996/97 an employee's salary (excluding benefits) subjected to tax under the PAYE system is £82,000 and £70,000 respectively. The maximum initial market value of shares which may be appropriated to him within the limit for 1995/96 is calculated as follows

Overall limit	£8,000
Year of appropriation 10% of PAYE salary	£7,000
Preceding year 10% of PAYE salary	£8,200

The maximum initial market value is restricted to £8,000. The relevant salary figure, which is the greater of 10% of the PAYE salary for the year of appropriation (£7,000) or the preceding year (£8,200), is subject to the overall limit of £8,000.

Note

(a)   The annual maximum limit is £8,000. There is also a minimum limit of £3,000.

26.5 **EMPLOYEE SHARE OWNERSHIP TRUSTS** [*FA 1989, ss 67–74, 5 Sch; F(No 2)A 1992, s 36; FA 1993, 6 Sch 20; FA 1994, 13 Sch*]

YME plc makes payments of £20,000 and £30,000 on 1 September 1994 and 1995 respectively to a qualifying employee share ownership (ESOP) trust. The company claims and receives corporation tax relief for these payments under *FA 1989, s 67*. The trustees purchase shares in the company as follows

	No of shares	Cost of shares £	Costs of acquisition £
1.10.94	24,500	19,600	400
10.9.95	23,500	28,200	600
	48,000	£47,800	£1,000

On 1 June 1996, the trustees, having previously transferred 30,000 shares to beneficiaries, make a transfer of 15,000 shares to beneficiaries on terms which are not qualifying terms under *FA 1989, s 69(4)*. The market value of the shares on the date of transfer was £1.50 per share.

The trustees of the ESOP trust will realise a chargeable gain (subject to indexation) on 1.6.96 as follows

	£
Consideration (15,000 × £1.50)	22,500
Deduct cost $\dfrac{15,000}{48,000} \times (£47,800 + £1,000)$	15,250
Unindexed gain	£7,250

The trustees will also be chargeable to income tax under Schedule D, Case VI for 1996/97 as follows

		£
Chargeable amount under *FA 1989, s 70(2)*		15,250
Previous chargeable amounts		—
		15,250
Deductible amount under *FA 1989, s 72(4)*	£50,000	
Excess of chargeable amounts over deductible amount		—
Schedule D, Case VI assessment		£15,250
Tax payable by trustees at 34%		£5,185

Notes

(*a*)   Tax is payable under Schedule D, Case VI on chargeable amounts at the rate applicable to trusts.

(*b*)   Although the tax, and any interest thereon, is payable by the trustees of the ESOP trust, the Revenue have a right of recourse to the company in the event of non-payment.

(*c*)   The chargeable amount in this case is the amount deductible for capital gains tax purposes under *TCGA 1992, s 38(1)(a)(b)* on the transfer giving rise to the chargeable event. This does not include indexation allowance. The aggregate of past and present chargeable amounts cannot exceed the total amount for which a corporation tax deduction has been claimed.

(*d*)   Regardless of whether or not a chargeable event occurs, each beneficiary will be chargeable to income tax under Schedule E on the market value of shares received less any amount paid by him as consideration. In practice, an ESOP trust is likely to be used in conjunction with an approved profit sharing scheme, so that beneficiaries incur no tax liability when shares are appropriated to them.

27 Underwriters

For a detailed guide to this specialised subject, see *Tolley's Taxation of Lloyd's Underwriters*.

[FA 1993, ss 171–184, 19, 20 Schs; FA 1994, s 228, 21 Sch; FA 1995, s 143; SI 1995 Nos 351–353]

27.1 SCHEDULE D ASSESSMENTS ON UNDERWRITING PROFITS — CESSATION

(A)

J commenced Lloyd's underwriting on 1 January 1988 and retired on 31 December 1993. His Lloyd's deposit is paid over to him in August 1996. For the calendar years 1994, 1995 and 1996, income from Lloyd's deposits and personal reserves amounted to £200, £200 and £100 respectively. He has no allowable expenses to set off in computing underwriting profits for those years. His underwriting results were

Account	Schedule D, Case I Profit £
1988	2,500
1989	7,000
1990	3,200
1991	1,700
1992	2,900
1993	1,000

The taxable profits are as follows

		£
1987/88		Nil
1988/89	(1988 Account)	2,500
1989/90	(1989 Account)	7,000
1990/91	(1990 Account)	3,200
1991/92	(1991 Account)	1,700
1992/93	(1992 Account)	2,900
1993/94	(1993 Account)	1,000
1994/95	(1994 income from ancillary funds)	200
1995/96	(1995 income from ancillary funds)	200
1996/97	(1996 income from ancillary funds)	100

Notes

(a) Since J commenced underwriting after 31 December 1971, there are no cessation or commencement adjustments (see also (B) below).

(b) From 6 April 1993, income from ancillary trust funds (Lloyd's deposits and personal reserves) is taxed under Schedule D, Case I. *[FA 1993, ss 171, 172]*.

(c) The final year of assessment is that which corresponds to the underwriting year in which the member's Lloyd's deposit is released. *[FA 1993, s 179; FA 1994, 21 Sch 6]*. Special rules apply where cessation is by reason of death occurring after 5 April 1994. *[FA 1993, s 179A; FA 1994, 21 Sch 6]*.

(B)

M, who has been a Lloyd's underwriter since the 1960s, also retired on 31 December 1993 and has the same results and Lloyd's investment income as J in (A) above. M's Lloyd's deposit is returned to him in August 1996. Income from Lloyd's deposits and personal reserves included in the 1993 Account result (i.e. that from 6 April 1993 onwards) amounted to £120. M's 1972 Lloyd's underwriting profit was £2,400.

The Schedule D, Case I profits are as follows

		£	£
1988/89	(1988 Account)		2,500
1989/90	(1989 Account)		7,000
1990/91	(1990 Account)		3,200
1991/92	(1991 Account)		1,700
1992/93	(1992 Account)	2,900	
	Deduct 1972 profit note (*b*)	2,400	500
1993/94	(1993 Account)	1,000	
	Less income from ancillary funds included therein	120	
		880	
	Period 6.4.93 – 31.12.93 (approximately $\frac{3}{4}$)	660	
	Add back income from ancillary funds	120	780
1994/95	(1994 income from ancillary funds)		200
1995/96	(1995 income from ancillary funds)		200
1996/97	(1996 income from ancillary funds)		100

Notes

(*a*)   Since M commenced before 1 January 1972, the profits of his first underwriting year would have been assessed $2\frac{1}{4}$ times under the old system. Since no profits fall out of assessment on a cessation under the current system, the cessation of a pre-1972 underwriter is treated as above. [*SI 1995 No 351, Reg 13*].

(*b*)   If the 1972 profit had exceeded £2,900, the deduction in 1992/93 would have been limited to £2,900. The deduction cannot create a loss.

(*c*)   The adjustments under *Reg 13(2)(b)* are made for the last year of assessment which includes syndicate profits or losses and/or syndicate investment income and for the preceding year, and are made in respect of those profits or income. Income from ancillary funds, although forming part of the Case I results from 6 April 1993 onwards (see (A) above), does not enter into these adjustments.

IT 27.2 Underwriters

27.2 LOSSES

(A)

J, who commenced underwriting on 1 January 1992 and is not a working name, had the following underwriting results

	Sch D, Case I Loss £
Account 1992	2,000
Account 1993	8,400

His other income and allowances, for relevant years, comprise

	Schedule D, Case I £	Schedule D Woodlands Losses £	Dividends (gross) £	Retirement Annuity Premiums £	Personal Allowance £
1990/91	12,600	(2,400)	3,350	1,785	3,295
1992/93	8,400	—	2,900	923	3,445
1993/94	4,800	—	3,100	457	3,445

J has already claimed relief under *ICTA 1988, s 380(1)* in respect of the woodlands losses and the 1992 underwriting loss. His date of birth is 25 May 1950.

His options regarding the 1993 loss are

(i) **Carry the loss forward to be set off against future underwriting profits. [*ICTA 1988, s 385(1)*].**

(ii) Relieve the loss under *ICTA 1988, s 380(1)* against other income for 1993/94.

(iii) Relieve the loss under *ICTA 1988, s 381* against other income for the three preceding years, beginning with 1990/91.

	£
Option (ii) (1993/94)	
Schedule D, Case I	4,800
Dividends	3,100
	7,900
Deduct Underwriting loss (1993) (part)	7,900
Taxable income	Nil

Notes

(*a*) There is no tax liability and £500 of underwriting losses (£8,400 – £7,900) are available either to carry forward or carry back to the immediately preceding tax year (see (B) below).

(*b*) J does not obtain relief for either his personal allowance or the retirement annuity premiums of £457 which J should have paid in a later year with an election that they be carried back. Following changes in *FA 1993* all income from membership of Lloyd's is earned income for tax purposes and is therefore included in relevant earnings for RAR and PPP purposes.

Option (iii) 1990/91

	£	£
Dividends (gross)		3,350
Deduct Underwriting loss (1993)	8,400	
Restricted to	3,350	3,350
	£5,050	—
Profits		12,600
Deduct Woodlands loss	2,400	
Balance of underwriting loss (1993)	5,050	7,450
		5,150
Deduct		
Retirement annuity relief		
$17\frac{1}{2}\%$ × (£12,600 − £2,400)	1,785	
Personal allowance	3,295	5,080
Taxable		£70

Notes

(*a*)   The retirement annuity relief is not restricted on account of the underwriting loss since any underwriting profits would not constitute relevant earnings (due to J's being a non-working name). The same would apply as regards relief for personal pension contributions. (For 1993/94 and later years, see note (*e*) below).

(*b*)   The facility to carry back losses under *ICTA 1988, s 381* is available to non-working names as well as working names.

(*c*)   The underwriting loss is set firstly against unearned income (as J is a non-working name). [*ICTA 1988, s 382(2)*]. (Note that this provision was repealed by *FA 1988, 14 Sch Part VIII* in relation to relief given for 1990/91 onwards.)

(*d*)   The normal time limits for claiming loss relief under either of options (ii) and (iii) is extended by two years. [*SI 1995 No 352 Reg 14*]. The two-year extended time limits available to Lloyd's underwriters will continue to 1993/94 but for 1994/95 the time limits will be extended by one year only and for 1995/96 and later years there will be no statutory extension with the exception of those relating to PPP and RAR elections which will continue for contributions made in 1996/97 but not thereafter.

(*e*)   Note that from 1993/94 onwards, all Lloyd's profits are treated as earned income, and the distinction between working and non-working names is thus removed. [*FA 1993, s 180*].

IT 27.2 Underwriters

(B)

K has been a Lloyd's Underwriter for many years. For the 1992 and 1993 Lloyd's accounts, he has Schedule D, Case I losses of £5,000 and £58,000 respectively. He is a single working name whose other income for 1992/93 and 1993/94 is as follows.

	1992/93 £	1993/94 £
Salary	25,000	26,500
Investment income (including Lloyd's deposit, personal reserves etc.)	3,000	3,500
	£28,000	£30,000

He makes a claim under *ICTA 1988, s 380(1)* to offset the 1992 loss against his 1992/93 income. He makes a similar claim to offset the 1993 loss against his 1993/94 income, reducing total income to nil but leaving £28,000 of the loss unrelieved.

K may make a claim under *FA 1993, s 171(3)* as follows

	1992/93 £
Income	28,000
Deduct 1992 loss relieved under *Sec 380(1)*	5,000
	23,000
Deduct 1993 loss relieved under *FA 1993, s 171(3)*	23,000
Total income	Nil

1993 loss memorandum

	£
Total loss	58,000
Relieved in 1993/94 under *Sec 380(1)*	30,000
	28,000
Relieved in 1992/93 under *FA 1993, s 171(3)*	23,000
Available for carry-forward under *Sec 385*	£5,000

Notes

(a) An underwriting loss can be carried back against total income of the year of assessment preceding the year of loss, providing the person concerned was a Lloyd's Underwriter in that preceding year. The loss must be relieved as far as possible against current year income first. Relief for current year losses is given in priority to relief for a loss brought back from a subsequent year.

(b) No relief is available for underwriting losses under *ICTA 1988, s 380(2) as originally enacted.*

[*FA 1993, s 171(3)*].

(c) The unused Lloyd's loss from Account 1993 and earlier can be brought forward and offset against Lloyd's profits for 1994/95 to 1996/97 even if those losses are set against personal fund income and non-syndicate receipts net of expenses incurred personally. [*FA 1993, s 171(2)(4)*].

28   Venture Capital Trusts

[ICTA 1988, ss 332A, 842AA, 15B, 28B Schs; TCGA 1992, ss 151A, 151B, 5C Sch; FA 1995, ss 70–73, 14–16 Schs]

28.1   INCOME TAX INVESTMENT RELIEF

(A) Form of relief

On 1 May 1996, Miss K, who is 66 and whose pension is £16,265 per annum, subscribes for 40,000 eligible £1 shares issued at par to raise money by VCT plc, an approved venture capital trust. On 1 September 1996, she purchases on the open market a further 90,000 £1 shares in VCT plc for £70,000. The company makes no distribution in 1996/97. Miss K's other income for that year consists of dividends of £14,400. She pays qualifying medical insurance premiums of £800 under deduction of basic rate tax, and £200 interest on a private mortgage (outside MIRAS) for the purchase of her home. Tax paid under PAYE amounts to £2,800.

Miss K's tax computation for 1996/97 is as follows

	£	£
Schedule E		16,265
Dividends	14,400	
Add Tax credits	3,600	18,000
Total income		34,265
Deduct Personal allowance		3,765
Taxable income		£30,500
Tax payable:		
3,900 @ 20%		780.00
8,600 @ 25%		2,064.00
13,000 @ 20%		2,600.00
5,000 @ 40%		2,000.00
29,720		7,444.00
Deduct VCT investment relief:		
£40,000 @ 20% = £8,000 but restricted to		7,444.00
Income tax liability		Nil
Deduct: Tax credits	3,600.00	
PAYE	2,800.00	6,400.00
Income tax repayable		£6,400.00

Notes

(a)   VCT investment relief is restricted to the lower rate of tax on the amount *subscribed for* up to a maximum subscription of £100,000 per year of assessment. It is further restricted to the income tax liability before taking into account certain reductions etc. *[ICTA 1988, 15B Sch 1; FA 1995, s 71, 15 Sch].*

(b)   There is no clawback of the basic rate tax deducted from the medical insurance premiums, but no relief is obtained for the mortgage interest (one of the reductions referred to in note (a) above).

(B) Withdrawal of relief
On 1 May 1999, Miss K in (A) above, who has since 1996/97 neither acquired nor disposed of any shares in VCT plc, gives 25,000 shares to her son. On 3 January 2000, she disposes of the remaining 105,000 shares on the open market for £80,000.

The relief given as in (A) above is withdrawn as follows

Disposal on 1 May 1999
The shares disposed of are identified, on a first in, first out basis, with 25,000 of the 40,000 shares subscribed for in May 1995. Since the disposal was not at arm's length, the relief given on those shares is fully withdrawn.

$$\text{Relief withdrawn } \frac{25,000}{40,000} \times £7,444 = \qquad\qquad £4,652.50$$

Disposal on 3 January 1999
The balance of £2,791.15 of the relief originally given was in respect of 15,000 of the 105,000 shares disposed of. The disposal consideration for those 15,000 shares is

$$£80,000 \times \frac{15,000}{105,000} = \qquad\qquad £11,428$$

As the disposal was at arm's length, the relief withdrawn is the lesser of the relief originally given and 20% of the consideration received, i.e. 20% of £11,428 = £2,285.60. [*ICTA 1988, 15B Sch 3(3)(4); FA 1995, s 71, 15 Sch*].

The 1996/97 Schedule D, Case VI assessment on relief
withdrawn will therefore charge tax of £(4,652.50 + 2,285.60) £6,938.10

Note
(*a*) VCT investment relief is withdrawn on a disposal (or deemed disposal) within five years following the issue of the shares. Withdrawal of relief is by Case VI assessment for the tax year for which the relief was given. [*ICTA 1988, 15B Sch 3, 4; FA 1995, s 71, 15 Sch*].

28.2 INCOME TAX DISTRIBUTION RELIEF
In 1997/98, Miss K, the investor in 28.1 above, receives a distribution from VCT plc of 4p per share. Her circumstances are otherwise unchanged from 1996/97. It is assumed that rates of tax and allowances are likewise unchanged.

Miss K's taxable distribution from VCT plc is arrived at as follows
The shares in VCT plc were acquired in 1996/97 for £110,000. Distributions in respect of shares representing the £10,000 excess over the permitted maximum are not exempt. The 40,000 shares first acquired for £40,000 are first identified, so that the shares representing the excess are one-seventh of the 90,000 shares subsequently acquired for £70,000, i.e. 12,857 of those shares. The taxable dividend is therefore 12,857 @ 4p per share = £514.28. The dividend on the balance of 117,143 shares (117,143 @ 4p = £4,685.72) is exempt.

Miss K's tax computation for 1997/98 is as follows

	£	£
Schedule E		16,265
Dividends (other than from VCT plc)	14,400	
Add Tax credits	3,600	18,000
Taxable dividends from VCT plc	514	
Add Tax credits *paid to investor*	128	642
Total income .		34,907
Deduct Personal allowance		3,765
Taxable income		£31,142
Tax payable:		
3,900 @ 20%		780.00
9,235 @ 24%		2,216.40
12,365 @ 20%		2,473.00
5,642 @ 40%		2,256.80
31,142		7,726.20
Deduct Mortgage interest relief £200 @ 15%		30.00
Income tax liability		7,696.20
Deduct: Tax credits	3,600.00	
PAYE	2,800.00	6,400.00
Net income tax liability		£1,296.20

Note

(*a*)   Distributions to an individual from a VCT are exempt from tax to the extent that they are made in respect of shares *acquired* (not necessarily suscribed for) for up to £100,000 in any tax year. [*ICTA 1988, 15B Sch 7, 8; FA 1995, s 71, 15 Sch*]. Tax credits relating to such shares will be reclaimed by the VCT manager and paid over to the investor under regulations to be issued in Summer 1995. [*FA 1995, s 73(3)*].

28.3   CAPITAL GAINS TAX RELIEFS

(A) Relief on disposals

On the disposals in 28.1(B) above, a chargeable gain or allowable loss arises only on the disposal of shares acquired in excess of the permitted maximum (£100,000) for 1996/97. As in 28.2 above, these are 12,857 of the 90,000 shares acquired for £70,000 on 1 September 1996. The disposal identified with those shares (on a first in, first out basis) is a corresponding proportion of the 105,000 shares disposed of for a consideration of £80,000 on 3 January 2000.

Miss K's capital gains tax computation for 1999/2000 (subject to (B) below) is therefore as follows

	£
Disposal consideration for 12,857 shares:	
$£80,000 \times \dfrac{12,857}{105,000} =$	9,796
Deduct Cost of 12,857 shares:	
$£70,000 \times \dfrac{12,857}{90,000}$	10,000
Allowable loss	£204

Notes

(*a*)   On disposals by an individual of VCT shares (whether or not they were subscribed for), capital gains are exempt and losses not allowable to the extent that the shares disposed of were not acquired in excess of the £100,000 maximum in any tax year. [*TCGA 1992, s 151A; FA 1995, s 72(3)*].

(*b*)   The capital gains tax share pooling provisions are disapplied as regards VCT shares within the above exemption. [*TCGA 1992, s 151B(1); FA 1995, s 72(3)*].

(B) Deferral on reinvestment of gains into VCT shares

On 1 August 1996, Miss K, the investor in 28.1 above, sold a holding of quoted shares on which she realised a capital gain (after indexation) of £36,300. She makes no other gains or losses for 1996/97. She makes a claim under *TCGA 1992, 5C Sch* to set £30,000 of her qualifying expenditure on VCT plc shares against the gain.

Miss K's capital gains tax computation for 1996/97 is as follows

	£
Original chargeable gain	36,300
Less deferred under *TCGA 1992, 5C Sch*	30,000
	6,300
Deduct Annual exemption	6,300
Taxable gains	Nil

A chargeable gain will accrue to Miss K in 1999/2000 as follows

	£
On the disposal of 25,000 VCT plc shares in May 1999 (identified on a first in, first out basis with 25,000 of the 40,000 acquired by subscription in May 1996), a chargeable event accrues equal to the lesser of the gain deferred and the qualifying expenditure (£25,000) on the shares to which the event relates. Therefore, a chargeable gain accrues on 1 May 1999 of	25,000
Similarly, a chargeable event accrues on 3 January 2000 of	5,000
Chargeable gain for 1999/2000	30,000
Deduct Allowable loss as in (A) above	204
	29,796
Deduct Annual exemption say	6,300
Taxable gains	£23,496

Notes

(a)   A gain accruing after 5 April 1995 may be deferred to the extent that expenditure is incurred on VCT shares *subscribed for* on which income tax investment relief (see 28.1(A) above) is given. The VCT shares must be issued within one year before or one year after the date on which the gain accrues. The investor can specify the amount of the gain to be deferred, for example so as to leave in charge an amount covered by the CGT annual exemption or to cover losses. [*TCGA 1992, s 151A(3), 5C Sch 1, 2; FA 1995, s 72, 16 Sch*].

(b)   A deferred gain is brought into charge on the happening of a chargeable event (as defined), for example a disposal (at any time) of the VCT shares the expenditure on which was matched with the original gain. The deferred gain is treated as having accrued at the time of the event. [*TCGA 1992, s 151A(3), 5C Sch 3–5; FA 1995, s 72, 16 Sch*].

Corporation Tax

101   Accounting Periods

101.1 EFFECT OF AN ACCOUNTING PERIOD OVERLAPPING TWO FINANCIAL YEARS HAVING DIFFERENT RATES OF CORPORATION TAX [*ICTA 1988, ss 8(3), 834(4); FA 1991, ss 23, 24*]

For the year ended 30 June 1991, the following information is relevant to A Ltd, a company with no associated companies.

	£
Schedule D, Case I	1,560,600
Schedule A	35,000
Schedule D, Case III	30,000 — received in two equal amounts on 1.1.91 and 30.6.91
Charges paid (gross)	1,000 — on 31.7.90
	9,000 — on 31.3.91

The rate of corporation tax for the financial year 1990 is 34% and the rate for the financial year 1991 is 33%.

The corporation tax computation of A Ltd for the 12-month accounting period ended on 30.6.91 will be

	£		
Schedule D, Case I	1,560,600		
Schedule A	35,000		
Schedule D, Case III	30,000		
	1,625,600		
Charges	10,000		
	£1,615,600		
Total profits apportioned			
1.7.90 — 31.3.91		$\frac{9}{12} \times$ £1,615,600	£1,211,700
1.4.91 — 30.6.91		$\frac{3}{12} \times$ £1,615,600	£403,900
Tax chargeable			
34% × £1,211,700			411,978
33% × £403,900			133,287
Total tax charge			£545,265

101.2 **PERIODS OF ACCOUNT EXCEEDING 12 MONTHS** [*ICTA 1988, ss 12(3), 72, 834(4)*]

B Ltd prepares accounts for 16 months ending on 31 March 1997. The following information is relevant

	£
Profit for 16 months	800,000
Schedule D, Case III income received on 1 March and 1 September each year	50,000
Charges paid on 1 January each year (gross)	70,000
Capital gain (after indexation) arising on 1.6.96	100,000
Tax written down value of plant pool at 1.12.95	40,000
Plant purchased 1.2.96	200,000
Plant purchased 1.2.97	246,000
Proceeds of plant sold 31.12.96 (less than cost)	6,000

B Ltd will be chargeable to corporation tax as follows

		Accounting period 12 months to 30.11.96 £	Accounting period 4 months to 31.3.97 £
Adjusted profits (apportioned 12)		600,000	200,000
Capital allowances	note (*a*)	(60,000)	(35,000)
Schedule D, Case I		540,000	165,000
Schedule D, Case III	note (*b*)	100,000	50,000
Chargeable gain	note (*c*)	100,000	—
		740,000	215,000
Charges on income	note (*d*)	(70,000)	(70,000)
Chargeable profits		£670,000	£145,000

Notes

(*a*)   Capital allowances

12 months to 30.11.96

	Pool £	Total allowances £
WDV b/f	40,000	
Additions	200,000	
	240,000	
WDA 25%	(60,000)	£60,000
WDV c/f	£180,000	

4 months to 31.3.97		Pool	Total allowances
		£	£
WDV b/f		180,000	
Additions		246,000	
Disposals		(6,000)	
		420,000	
WDA 25% x $\frac{4}{12}$		(35,000)	£35,000
WDV c/f		£385,000	

Writing-down allowances are a proportionately reduced percentage of 25% if the accounting period is only part of a year. [*CAA 1990, s 24(2)*].

(b)	Schedule D, Case III			£
	12 months to 30.11.96	1.3.96 receipt		50,000
		1.9.96 receipt		50,000
				£100,000
	4 months to 31.3.97	1.3.97 receipt		£50,000

The total amount received is not apportioned on a time basis. [*ICTA 1988, s 9(1)*].

(c)   The capital gain is not apportioned on a time basis, but is included for the period in which it arises. [*TCGA 1992, s 8(1)*].

(d)   The charges are not apportioned on a time basis, but are included for the period in which they are paid. [*ICTA 1988, s 338(1)*].

(e)   The tax for the two accounting periods ended 30.11.96 and 31.3.97 will be due for payment on 1.9.96 and 1.1.97 respectively. [*ICTA 1988, s 10(1)(a)*]. The CT return(s) for both accounting periods will be due by 31.3.98, i.e. the first anniversary of the last day of the sixteen-month period of account, or, if later, three months after the issue of the notice requiring the return. [*TMA 1970, s 11(4); F(No 2)A 1987, s 82(4)*]. See also 121 RETURNS.

102   Advance Corporation Tax

102.1 REDUCTION IN AMOUNT OF ACT PAYABLE BY REFERENCE TO FRANKED INVESTMENT INCOME (FII) RECEIVED [*ICTA 1988, s 241, 13 Sch*]

(A) No change in rate of ACT

C Ltd prepares accounts to 31 March each year. During the two years ended 31 March 1996, it paid and received the following dividends

		£
20.6.94	Paid	8,000
3.3.95	Received	11,200
25.6.95	Paid	8,000
30.11.95	Received	5,600
25.3.96	Paid	4,800

The rate of ACT was $\frac{1}{4}$ for both the years ended 31 March 1995 and 1996.

The ACT movements are summarised by the following table

Return period		Franked payment £	FII £	Cumulative franked payments less FII £	ACT paid/ (repaid) £
Year ended 31.3.95					
30.6.94		10,000		10,000	2,000
30.9.94	No return			10,000	
31.12.94	No return			10,000	
31.3.95	note (*a*)		14,000	(4,000)	(2,000)
Surplus FII carried forward note (*b*)				£(4,000)	
Year ended 31.3.96					
Surplus FII brought forward				(4,000)	
30.6.95		10,000		6,000	1,200
30.9.95	No return			6,000	
31.12.95	note (*a*)		7,000	(1,000)	(1,200)
31.3.96		6,000		5,000	1,000
Net ACT paid in year note (*c*)					£1,000

Notes

(*a*)   The ACT repayment is restricted to the ACT paid in the accounting period. [*ICTA 1988, 13 Sch 4*].

(*b*)   Surplus FII is carried forward to the next accounting period. [*ICTA 1988, s 241(3)*].

(*c*)   Net ACT paid is available for set-off against the CT liability of the year ended 31 March 1996 (subject to normal set-off limits). [*ICTA 1988, s 239(1)(2)*].

(B) Change in rate of ACT

D Ltd prepares accounts to 31 July each year. During the year ended 31 July 1994, it paid and received the following dividends.

		£
25.9.93	Paid	7,750
25.3.94	Received	5,425
5.7.94	Received	5,600

The rates of ACT were $\frac{9}{31}$ for the year ended 31 March 1994 and $\frac{1}{4}$ for the year ended 31 March 1995.

The ACT movements are summarised by the following table

Return period		Franked payment £	FII £	Cumulative franked payments less FII £	ACT paid/ (repaid) £
30.9.93		10,000		10,000	2,250
31.12.93	No return			10,000	
31.3.94			7,000	3,000	(1,575)
30.6.94	To 5.4.94 note (a)			3,000	
	To 30.6.94			—	
31.7.94	note (b)		7,000	(7,000)	
Surplus FII carried forward				£(7,000)	
Net ACT paid in year note (c)					£675

Notes

(a) Because the rate of ACT changed on 6 April 1994, the return period is deemed to consist of two separate periods, ending on 5 April and 30 June, although only one return is required. In this example, no return need be made for the quarter to 30 June 1994. [*ICTA 1988, s 246(6)(b)*].

(b) Because of the change of rate of ACT, this FII cannot be used to frank dividends paid before the change. It is carried forward to the next accounting period as surplus FII. [*ICTA 1988, s 246(6)(b)*].

(c) The net ACT paid is available for set-off against the CT liability of the relevant year (subject to normal set-off limits—see 102.2(B) below). [*ICTA 1988, s 239(1)(2)*].

(d) A change of rate of ACT when surplus FII already exists has no practical effect, the surplus FII at 5 April being available against future franked payments in the normal way.

102.2 SET-OFF OF ACT AGAINST CORPORATION TAX

(A) No change in rate of ACT

E Ltd, a company with no associated companies, has the following profits for the year ending 31 March 1997

	£
Schedule D, Case I	1,600,400
Schedule A	6,000
Building society interest	15,000
Chargeable gains	3,600

Annual charges of £75,000 (gross) are paid.

During the year, E Ltd pays a final dividend of £800,000 in respect of the year ended 31.3.95, and an interim dividend of £520,000 in respect of the year ending 31.3.97. ACT on dividends amounts to £200,000 and £130,000 respectively. The dividends were paid on 30.6.96 and 31.1.97.

The CT liability will be

	£	£
Schedule D, Case I		1,600,400
Schedule A		6,000
Schedule D, Case III		15,000
		1,621,400
Chargeable gains		3,600
		1,625,000
Annual charges		(75,000)
Chargeable profits		£1,550,000
CT at 33%		511,500
Deduct lesser of		
ACT paid	330,000	
Maximum set-off 20% × £1,550,000	310,000	310,000
Surplus ACT	£20,000	
'Mainstream' CT liability		£201,500

Notes

(a)   The ACT available for set-off is that relating to distributions made in the year ending 31.3.97. [*ICTA 1988, s 239(1)*].

(b)   The ACT set-off is restricted to 20% of the chargeable profits for FY 1994 to 1996 inclusive (25% for FY 1988 to FY 1992 inclusive, 22.5% for FY 1993). [*ICTA 1988, s 239(2)*].

(c)   Surplus ACT may be treated in one of the following ways.
  (i)   Carried back against the liabilities of accounting periods beginning in the six preceding years and applied against a more recent period before a more remote one. [*ICTA 1988, s 239(3)*].
  (ii)   Carried forward and treated as ACT paid in respect of distributions made in the following accounting period. [*ICTA 1988, s 239(4)*].

(B) Change in rate of ACT [*ICTA 1988, ss 239(2), 246(5)*]

F Ltd had chargeable profits of £760,000 for the year ended 31 December 1994. It paid a dividend on 30 April 1994 of £740,000. ACT on the dividend was £185,000. F Ltd has one associated company.

The CT liability is

	£	£
33% × £760,000		250,800
Deduct lesser of		
ACT paid	185,000	
Maximum set-off note (*a*)	156,750	156,750
Surplus ACT	£28,250	
'Mainstream' CT liability		£94,050

Note

(*a*)   Maximum ACT set-off is

	£		£
$\frac{3}{12}$ × £760,000	190,000 × 22.5%		42,750
$\frac{9}{12}$ × £760,000	570,000 × 20%		114,000
	£760,000		£156,750

(C) Effect of losses

G Ltd, a company with one associated company, commenced trading on 1 April 1993 and had the following adjusted trading profits

		£
Year ended 31.3.94		640,000
Year ended 31.3.95		800,000
Year ended 31.3.96	loss	(710,000)

The company paid on 1.11.94 a final dividend of £310,000 for the year ended 31.3.94 and on 1.3.95 an interim dividend of £387,500 for the year ended 31.3.95. It accounted for the ACT of £77,500 and £96,875 respectively.

Prior to a claim for loss relief, the CT position was as follows

Year ended		31.3.94	31.3.95	31.3.96
		£	£	£
Profit		640,000	800,000	—
Corporation tax		211,200	264,000	—
ACT set-off	note (*a*)	14,375	160,000	—
'Mainstream' liability		£196,825	£104,000	—

As a result of the loss, a claim under *ICTA 1988, s 393A(1)* will result in the following amended figures

Year ended	31.3.94	31.3.95	31.3.96
Profit (loss)	£640,000	£800,000	£(710,000)
Sec 393A(1) claim	—	(710,000)	710,000
Revised Profits	£640,000	£90,000	
Corporation tax	211,200	22,500	note (c)
ACT set-off notes (a) & (b)	144,000	18,000	
'Mainstream' liability	£67,200	£4,500	
Surplus ACT carried forward		£12,375	

Notes

(a)   The ACT is available for set-off first against the liability of the accounting period in which the dividends are paid and then against the liabilities of accounting periods beginning in the six preceding years assuming the relevant claim is made. It must be applied for a more recent period before a more remote one. [*ICTA 1988, s 239(3)*].

(b)   The ACT set-off in the years ended 31.3.94 and 31.3.95 is restricted to, respectively, 22.5% and 20% of the taxable profit.

(c)   As profits are reduced to less than £150,000 (half of £300,000 — there is one associated company) for the year to 31 March 1995, small companies rate at 25% applies.

102.3 SURPLUS ACT — HOW IT CAN BE USED [*ICTA 1988, s 239*]

H Ltd is a trading company with no associated companies. The following tables summarise the company's chargeable profits and its distributions.

	Year ended 30.9.90 £	6 months to 31.3.91 £	Year ended 31.3.92 £	Year ended 31.3.93 £
Chargeable profits	42,000	22,000	15,000	7,000
Dividends paid	—	—	—	45,000
ACT on dividends	—	—	—	15,000

The appropriate rates of ACT and CT are

ACT	$\frac{25}{75}$	$\frac{25}{75}$	$\frac{25}{75}$	$\frac{25}{75}$
CT	25%	25%	25%	25%

The following table shows how the ACT can be used

	£	£	£	£
CT liability	10,500	5,500	3,750	1,750
ACT set-off				
1993 dividend	(4,000)	(5,500)	(3,750)	(1,750)
1996 dividend (see below)	(6,500)	—	—	—
'Mainstream' liability	—	—	—	—

CT 102.4 Advance Corporation Tax

	Year ended 31.3.94 £	Year ended 31.3.95 £	Year ended 31.3.96 £	Year ended 31.3.97 £
Chargeable profits	30,000	30,000	1,000	23,000
Dividends paid	—	—	93,600	12,000
ACT on dividends	—	—	23,400	3,000

The appropriate rates of ACT and CT are

ACT	$\frac{9}{31}$	$\frac{20}{80}$	$\frac{20}{80}$	$\frac{20}{80}$
CT	25%	25%	25%	24%

The following table shows how the ACT can be used

	£	£	£	£
CT liability	7,500	7,500	250	5,520
ACT set-off				
1996 dividend	(6,750)	(6,000)	(200)	(3,950)
1997 dividend	—	—	—	(650)
'Mainstream' liability	750	1,500	£50	£920
Surplus ACT carried forward at period end	—	3,950	£2,350	£850

Notes

(a)　The ACT set-off is restricted to the amount of ACT that would have been payable on a distribution which, together with the ACT payable in respect of it, equals the chargeable profits. For years prior to FY 1993, the rate of set-off was equal to the small companies rate of CT. For FY 1993, the rate of set-off is 22.5% of chargeable profits, and for FY 1994 to FY 1996, it is 20%.

(b)　The 1993 ACT is used firstly against the liability for that year and then carried back against liabilities of accounting periods beginning in the six preceding years, taking later periods first.

(c)　The 1996 ACT is similarly offset firstly against 1996 corporation tax and the balance then carried back. The earliest period in which it may be used is the year to 30.9.90 as the year to 30.9.89 (not illustrated in this example) would have begun more than six years prior to the beginning of the year to 31.3.96. Surplus ACT of £2,450 (£23,400 − (£200 + £6,750 + £7,500 + £6,500)) can be carried forward to the year ended 31.3.97 and treated as ACT paid in respect of distributions made in that period.

102.4 GROUPS OF COMPANIES

For examples on surrender of ACT within groups of companies, see 112.1 and 112.2 GROUPS OF COMPANIES.

103   Capital Allowances

Capital allowances are dealt with in detail at 2 CAPITAL ALLOWANCES.

103.1 TRANSFER OF TRADE WITHIN GROUP: PERIOD OF ACCOUNT EXCEEDING 12 MONTHS [ICTA 1988, s 343; CAA 1990, ss 3, 24]

A Ltd owns 80% of the ordinary share capital of both B Ltd and C Ltd, the latter companies carrying on similar trades.

A Ltd and C Ltd prepare accounts annually to 31 July. B Ltd which previously prepared accounts to 30 April each year has prepared accounts for 15 months ending on 31 July 1996.

On 31 December 1995, C Ltd transferred the whole of its trade to B Ltd under circumstances covered by ICTA 1988, s 343.

The following information is relevant to B Ltd

		£
Trading profit for 15 months to 31.7.96		200,000
1.5.95	Tax written-down value of machinery and plant pool	5,800
11.6.95	Plant purchased	3,000
3.9.95	Plant purchased	2,000
4.10.95	Plant sold (original cost £9,000)	6,800
1.3.96	Plant purchased	8,000
10.5.96	Plant sold (original cost £40,000)	22,488
15.6.96	Plant purchased	30,000
1.8.95	Tax written-down value of machinery and plant pool owned by C Ltd	9,216

Original cost of four-year old building, owned by C Ltd and qualifying for industrial buildings writing-down allowances   300,000

B Ltd will have chargeable profits as follows

	Accounting period 12 months to 30.4.96 £	Accounting period 3 months to 31.7.96 £
Trading profits	160,000	40,000
Capital allowances on machinery and plant	(3,768)	(1,500)
Industrial buildings allowance	(4,000)	(3,000)
Chargeable profits	£152,232	£35,500

CT 103.1   Capital Allowances

Capital allowances

Machinery and plant

12 months to 30.4.96

	Pool £	Total allowances £
WDV b/f	5,800	
Additions	13,000	
Transfer from C Ltd note (a)	8,256	
	27,056	
Disposals	(6,800)	
	20,256	
WDA on assets transferred from C Ltd £9,216 × 25% × $\frac{4}{12}$ note (a)	(768)	768
WDA on balance of expenditure £(20,256 − 8,256) × 25%	(3,000)	3,000
WDV c/f	£16,488	
Total allowances		£3,768

3 months to 31.7.96

	Pool £	Allowances £
WDV b/f	16,488	
Additions	30,000	
	46,488	
Disposals	(22,488)	
	24,000	
WDA (25% × $\frac{3}{12}$) note (c)	1,500	£1,500
WDV c/f	£22,500	

	Allowances
Industrial building	
12 months to 30.4.96	
£300,000 × 4% × $\frac{4}{12}$	£4,000
3 months to 31.7.96	
£300,000 × 4% × $\frac{3}{12}$ note (c)	£3,000

Notes

(a) Where a trade is transferred part-way through an accounting period, the Inland Revenue take the view that writing-down allowances are calculated on the pool of expenditure held by the transferee at the end of its accounting period and those allowances are apportioned to the companies on a time basis for the period in which each company carried on the trade. (CCAB Guidance Note TR 500, 10 March 1983.)

	£
The transfer value of machinery and plant obtained from C Ltd is	9,216
Tax written-down value at 1.8.95	
WDA due to C Ltd (£9,216 × 25% × $\frac{5}{12}$)	960
	£8,256

(b)   The 'successor' company (B Ltd) is entitled to the capital allowances which the 'predecessor' company (C Ltd) would have been able to claim if it had continued to trade. [*ICTA 1988, s 343(1)(2)*].

(c)   No first-year or initial allowance is available to the successor on assets transferred to it by the predecessor. [*ICTA 1988, s 343(2)(b)(ii)*].

(d)   Writing-down allowances are reduced proportionately where the accounting period is less than one year. [*CAA 1990, ss 3(2), 24(2)*].

103.2 **NO CLAIM FOR FIRST-YEAR AND WRITING-DOWN ALLOWANCES** [*CAA 1990, ss 22(7), 24(3), 25(3); FA 1990, 17 Sch 3, 5, 6, 19 Sch Pt V*]
D Ltd is a company with one wholly-owned subsidiary, E Ltd, and no other associated companies. Both companies prepare accounts to 30 September. For the year ended 30 September 1995, D Ltd has trading profits of £100,000 before capital allowances, whilst E Ltd incurs a trading loss of £100,000. E Ltd also incurred trading losses in each of the previous three years and is unlikely to have any taxable profits in the foreseeable future. In the year to 30 September 1995, D Ltd spent £100,000 on machinery and plant, of which £10,000 was incurred before 1 November 1994. There was a written-down value of £70,000 on the machinery and plant pool at 1 October 1994 and there were no disposals during the year.

Assuming a group relief claim is made under *ICTA 1988, s 402* and that D Ltd claims the full capital allowances to which it is entitled, D Ltd's Schedule D, Case I computation for the year to 30 September 1995 will be as follows

	£
Trading profit	100,000
Less capital allowances (see below)	44,000
	56,000
Less loss surrendered by E Ltd	56,000
Taxable profit	Nil

E Ltd has unrelieved losses carried forward of £44,000 which will not be relieved in the foreseeable future.

D Ltd's capital allowances computation is as follows

	Expenditure qualifying for FYAs £	Pool £	Total allowances £
WDV b/f		70,000	
Additions	10,000	90,000	
	c/f £10,000	c/f £160,000	

CT 103.2 Capital Allowances

	£	£	£
	b/f 10,000	b/f 160,000	
FYA 40%	(4,000)		4,000
WDA 25%		(40,000)	40,000
	6,000	120,000	
Transfer to pool	(6,000)	6,000	
WDV c/f		£126,000	
Total allowances			£44,000

If D Ltd does not claim capital allowances, the position is as follows

	£
Trading profit	100,000
Less loss surrendered by E Ltd	100,000
Taxable profit	Nil

Capital allowances computation

	Expenditure qualifying for FYAs £	Pool £	Total allowances £
WDV b/f		70,000	
Additions	10,000	90,000	
		160,000	
Transfer to pool – FYA not claimed	(10,000)	10,000	—
		170,000	
WDA – not claimed		—	—
WDV c/f		£170,000	
Total allowances			Nil

Notes

(a)　For accounting periods ending after 30 September 1993, under 'pay and file', a company is on the same footing as an individual in that it may claim whatever allowances it chooses, if any, and is not required to make a formal disclaimer. [*CAA 1990, ss 22(7), 24(3); FA 1990, 17 Sch 3, 5, 19 Sch Pt V*]. If a person, including a company, does not claim a first-year allowance, where available, the expenditure qualifies for writing-down allowances in the same accounting period only if the person so elects, within two years after the end of the accounting period. [*CAA 1990, s 25(3); FA 1990, 17 Sch 6*]. Capital allowances claims may be withdrawn within the same time limits as apply to the making of claims. [*CAA 1990, A1 Sch; FA 1990, s 102, 16 Sch*].

(b)　As a result of the disclaimer, all of E Ltd's current year losses have been relieved, and D Ltd has a higher written-down value to carry forward on its machinery and plant pool.

(c)　See 112.3 – 112.7 GROUPS OF COMPANIES for group relief generally.

104   Capital Gains

Note: See the capital gains tax section generally for computations of gains.

104.1 **CAPITAL LOSSES** [*TCGA 1992, s 8(1)*]
P Ltd has the following capital gains/(losses)

Year ended		£
31.7.93	Gains	27,000
	Losses	(7,000)
31.7.94	Losses	(12,000)
31.7.95	Gains	5,000
	Losses	(13,000)
31.7.96	Gains	40,000
	Losses	(30,000)

The gains and losses would be dealt with as follows in the CT computations of P Ltd

	£	Gain assessable £
31.7.93		
Gains assessable to CT		£20,000
31.7.94		
Unrelieved losses carried forward	£(12,000)	Nil
31.7.95		
Losses (net)	8,000	Nil
Add Unrelieved losses brought forward	12,000	
Unrelieved losses carried forward	£(20,000)	
31.7.96		
Chargeable gains (net)	10,000	
Deduct Unrelieved losses brought forward	20,000	
Unrelieved losses carried forward	£(10,000)	Nil

Notes

(*a*)   Unrelieved losses cannot be set off against trading profits, but are available to relieve future gains.

(*b*)   Gains otherwise assessable to CT may be covered by trading losses for the same accounting period or trading losses carried back from a succeeding period under *ICTA 1988, s 393A(1)*—see 118 LOSSES.

104.2 CLOSE COMPANY TRANSFERRING ASSET AT UNDERVALUE [*TCGA 1992, s 125*]

(A)

G Ltd (a close company) sold a building in 1992 to an associated company Q Ltd, which is not a member of the same group as G Ltd, at a price below market value at the time. Relevant values relating to the asset were

	£
Cost 1988	45,000
Market value at date of disposal	95,000
Sale proceeds received	75,000

The issued share capital of G Ltd was held at the time of disposal as follows

	£1 ordinary shares	Value prior to sale of asset £
C	25,000	50,000
D	30,000	60,000
E	20,000	40,000
F	25,000	50,000
	100,000	£200,000

Sale proceeds on subsequent sale (at market value) in July 1997 of C's total shareholding (originally purchased at £0.80 per share in 1986) in G Ltd were £55,000.

G Ltd's chargeable gain on the sale of the building in 1992 is

	£
Market value note (*c*)	95,000
Cost	45,000
Unindexed gain	50,000
Indexation allowance at, say, 25% on £45,000	11,250
Chargeable gain	£38,750

C's gain on the disposal of the shares in 1997 will be

	£	£
Sale proceeds		55,000
Deduct Allowable cost:		
Purchase price (25,000 × £0.80)	20,000	
Less Apportioned undervalue note (*a*)	5,000	15,000
Unindexed gain		40,000
Indexation allowance at, say, 55% on £15,000		8,250
Chargeable gain		£31,750

Notes

(*a*)   The apportionment of undervalue on disposal is

		£
Market value at time of sale		95,000
Deduct Sale proceeds		75,000
		£20,000

	Proportion of shareholding	Value apportioned £
C	$\frac{25}{100} \times £20,000$	5,000
D	$\frac{30}{100} \times £20,000$	6,000
E	$\frac{20}{100} \times £20,000$	4,000
F	$\frac{25}{100} \times £20,000$	5,000
		£20,000

(*b*)   Indexation allowance is computed by reference to the allowable cost as reduced by the apportioned undervalue. [*TCGA 1992, s 53(3)*].

(*c*)   In the computation of the company's gain, market value is substituted for proceeds under *TCGA 1992, s 17*.

(*d*)   Transfers of assets on or before 31 March 1982 are disregarded in respect of disposals after 5 April 1988 to which re-basing applies (not illustrated in this example). [*TCGA 1992, s 125(1)(5)*].

(B)

Assume the same facts as in (A) above except that the building had a market value of £155,000 at the date of disposal and C subsequently sold his shares for their market value of £40,000. Assume now also that C purchased his shares at £0.70 per share before 31 March 1982 and that their value on that date was £21,000.

G Ltd's chargeable gain will be computed under the same principles as in (A) above

C's gain on the disposal of the shares will be as follows

(i) By reference to cost

	£	£
Sale proceeds		40,000
Deduct Allowable cost:		
Purchase price (25,000 × £0.70)	17,500	
Less Apportioned undervalue note (*a*)	20,000	—
Unindexed gain		40,000
Indexation allowance (see below)		850
Gain after indexation		£39,150

(ii) By reference to 31.3.82 value

	£	£
Sale proceeds		40,000
Deduct Allowable cost:		
31 March 1982 value	21,000	
Less Apportioned undervalue note (*a*)	20,000	
		1,000
Unindexed gain		39,000
Indexation at, say, 85% on £1,000		850
Gain after indexation		£38,150
Chargeable gain		£38,150

Notes

(*a*)   The apportionment of undervalue on disposal is

	£
Market value at time of sale	155,000
Deduct Sale proceeds	75,000
	£80,000

Proportion of shareholding		Value apportioned £
C	$\frac{25}{100} \times £80,000$	20,000
D	$\frac{30}{100} \times £80,000$	24,000
E	$\frac{20}{100} \times £80,000$	16,000
F	$\frac{25}{100} \times £80,000$	20,000
		£80,000

(*b*)   See also notes (*b*) and (*d*) to (A) above.

104.3 GROUPS OF COMPANIES

(A) Intra-group transfers of assets which are trading stock of one company but not of the other — transfer from a 'capital asset' company to a 'trading stock' company
[*TCGA 1992, ss 161, 173(1)*]

In June 1996, X Ltd transfers an item classed as a fixed asset to another group company Y Ltd, which treats it as trading stock.

The following information is relevant

	Case (i) £	Case (ii) £
Original cost (after 31.3.82)	100,000	100,000
Market value at date of transfer	120,000	40,000
Eventual sale proceeds	140,000	140,000
Indexation allowance due on original cost at date of transfer	17,000	17,000

The position of Y Ltd will be as follows if there is no election under *TCGA 1992, s 161(3)*

Chargeable gain/(allowable loss) on appropriation		
Market value	120,000	40,000
Deemed cost of asset note (*a*)	117,000	117,000
Gain/(loss)	3,000	(77,000)
Deduct Indexation allowance included in cost note (*b*)	—	17,000
Chargeable gain/(allowable loss)	£3,000	£(60,000)
Trading profit at date of sale		
Sale proceeds	140,000	140,000
Deemed cost of asset	120,000	40,000
Trading profit	£20,000	£100,000

With an election under *TCGA 1992, s 161(3)*

No chargeable gain or allowable loss arises on appropriation

Trading profit at date of sale				
Sale proceeds		140,000		140,000
Market value at appropriation	£120,000		£40,000	
Adjustment for (gain)/loss otherwise (chargeable)/allowable	(3,000)	117,000	60,000	100,000
Trading profit		£23,000		£40,000

Notes

(*a*)   The intra-group transfer by X Ltd to Y Ltd is treated as a disposal on which neither a gain nor a loss accrues after taking account of any indexation allowance due. X Ltd has no liability on the transfer and Y Ltd has a deemed acquisition cost of £117,000. [*TCGA 1992, ss 56(2), 171(1); FA 1994, s 93(5)(a)*].

(*b*)   The indexation allowance on a no gain/no loss transfer made after 29 November 1993 must be excluded on a subsequent disposal to the extent that it would otherwise contribute to an allowable loss. [*TCGA 1992, s 56(3); FA 1994, s 93(5)(b)*].

(c)   In Case (ii), with an election under *Sec 161(3)*, the adjustment for the loss cannot include any 'pre-entry loss'. [*TCGA 1992, 7A Sch 10; FA 1993, s 88, 8 Sch*]. It is assumed there is no pre-entry loss in this example. See (E) below for pre-entry losses generally.

(B) Intra-group transfers of assets which are trading stock of one company but not of the other — transfer from a 'trading stock' company to a 'capital asset' company [*TCGA 1992, ss 161, 173(2)*]
P Ltd acquires from another group company Q Ltd as a fixed asset an item previously treated as trading stock.

	£
Cost to Q Ltd (after 31.3.82)	100,000
Market value at date of transfer	150,000
Eventual sale proceeds	200,000
Indexation allowance due on transfer	
value from date of transfer to date of sale	10,000

The group will have the following trading profits and chargeable gains

	£	£
Q Ltd trading profit [*TCGA 1992, s 161(2)*]		
Deemed sale proceeds		150,000
Cost to Q Ltd		100,000
Trading profit		£50,000
P Ltd chargeable gain [*TCGA 1992, s 171(1)*]		
Sale proceeds		200,000
Cost of asset	150,000	
Indexation allowance	10,000	
		160,000
Chargeable gain		£40,000

(C) Rollover relief on the replacement of business assets [*TCGA 1992, ss 152, 153, 155, 175; FA 1995, s 48*]

M Ltd and N Ltd are 75% subsidiaries of H Ltd. On 1 February 1996 M Ltd sold a showroom for £200,000, realising a chargeable gain of £110,000. N Ltd purchased a factory for £150,000 within three years after the date of sale of the showroom.

Rollover relief could be claimed as follows

	£	£
Gain otherwise chargeable to corporation tax		110,000
Deduct Unrelieved gain:		
Sale proceeds	200,000	
Less Amount reinvested	150,000	
Chargeable gain	£50,000	50,000
Rollover relief		£60,000

New base cost of factory

	£
Purchase price	150,000
Deduct Rollover relief	60,000
	£90,000

Notes

(*a*)   To qualify for relief, the two companies concerned need not be members of the same group throughout the period between the transactions but each must be a member at the time of its own particular transaction.

(*b*)   N Ltd will be entitled to an indexation allowance, based on the deemed cost of £90,000, on a subsequent sale (to the extent that such sale produces an unindexed gain).

(*c*)   See also 204.2 ASSETS HELD AT 31 MARCH 1982 and 223 ROLLOVER RELIEF.

(D) A company ceasing to be a member of a group [*TCGA 1992, ss 171(1), 179(1)(3)(4); FA 1993, s 89; FA 1995, s 49*]

A Ltd had the following transactions

1.3.80   Purchased a freehold property £10,000.

31.3.82   Market value £25,000.

1.12.90   Sold the freehold to B Ltd (a wholly-owned subsidiary) for £20,000 (market value £50,000).

31.7.96   Sold its interest in B Ltd (at which time B Ltd continued to own the freehold property).

Both companies prepare accounts to 30 April.

Relevant values of the RPI are: March 1982 79.44, December 1990 129.9.

The taxation consequences are
(i) There will be no chargeable gain on A Ltd's disposal of the property to B Ltd as the disposal is one on which, after taking account of the indexation allowance, neither gain nor loss arises. [*TCGA 1992, ss 56(2), 171(1); FA 1994, s 93(5)(a)*].

Indexation factor

$$\frac{129.9 - 79.44}{79.44} = 0.635$$

	£
Cost to A Ltd	10,000
Indexation allowance £25,000 × 0.635 note (*a*)	15,875
Deemed cost to B Ltd	£25,875

(ii) Following the sale of A Ltd's shares in B Ltd on 31.7.96 (i.e. within six years after the transaction in (i) above), B Ltd will have a deemed disposal as follows.

Deemed disposal on 1.12.90

	£	£	£
Market value at 1.12.90		50,000	50,000
Cost (as above)	25,875		
Less indexation to date	15,875		
		10,000	
Market value at 31.3.82			25,000
Unindexed gain		40,000	25,000
Indexation allowance			
£25,000 × 0.635		15,875	15,875
Indexed gain		£24,125	£9,125
Chargeable gain subject to CT			£9,125
B Ltd's new base cost for future gains			£50,000

Although the deemed disposal occurs on 1 December 1990, i.e. immediately after B Ltd's acquisition, the gain is treated as accruing on 1 May 1996, i.e. the beginning of the accounting period in which B Ltd left the group, being later than the date of the deemed disposal. The gain thus forms part of B Ltd's profits for the year ended 30 April 1997.

Notes
(*a*)   The indexation allowance on the no gain/no loss transfer is calculated by reference to the market value at 31 March 1982 as this is higher than the original cost. [*TCGA 1992, s 55(1)(2)*].

(*b*)   For re-basing purposes, B Ltd is deemed to have held the asset at 31 March 1982. [*TCGA 1992, 3 Sch 1*]. *TCGA 1992, s 55(5)(6)* apply in the computation of B Ltd's chargeable gain.

(*c*)   Where the accounting period in which the company leaves the group ended before 1 October 1993, the gain was treated as accruing on the date of the deemed disposal. The provisions are in *TCGA 1992, s 178* and are otherwise broadly the same as those of *Sec 179* illustrated in this example.

(E) Restriction on set-off of pre-entry losses [*TCGA 1992, s 177A, 7A Sch; FA 1993, s 88, 8 Sch; FA 1994, ss 93(8)–(11), 94*]

C Ltd has a 100% subsidiary, D Ltd. D Ltd acquired a 100% subsidiary, E Ltd, on 1 April 1992 and a 75% subsidiary, F Ltd, on 1 April 1994. All the companies prepare their accounts to 31 March. The following information is relevant (neither E Ltd nor F Ltd having realised any gains or losses except as stated).

(i)   At 1 April 1992, E Ltd had unrelieved capital losses of £12,000 and its assets included a freehold property which it had acquired on 1 July 1988 for £70,000 and on which it had incurred enhancement expenditure of £10,000 on 1 October 1989. The property was valued at £70,000 at 1 April 1992. During the year ended 31 March 1993, E Ltd realised chargeable gains of £3,000 and it also realised an allowable loss of £1,000 on an asset purchased on 31 May 1992. On 1 October 1995, the company sold the above-mentioned freehold property for £55,000.

(ii)   F Ltd had no capital losses brought forward at 1 April 1994. At that date, it held 10,000 ordinary shares in XYZ plc, a quoted company. It had acquired 6,000 of these on 1 May 1988 for £10,000 and 4,000 on 1 June 1992 for £7,000. The shares had an indexed pool value of £20,671 at 1 April 1994, and their market value at that date was £11,000. On 1 November 1994, F Ltd acquired a further 5,000 XYZ ordinary shares for £3,000 and on 31 August 1995 it sold 12,000 such shares for £6,000.

F Ltd also made two disposals other than of XYZ shares during the year to 31 March 1996, realising chargeable gains on each. The first disposal, on which the gain was £5,500, was of an asset acquired by transfer from C Ltd (at no gain/no loss by virtue of *TCGA 1992, s 171*). The second, on which the gain was £3,500 was acquired from outside the group in December 1994 and used since that time in F Ltd's trade, which has continued unchanged since 31 March 1994.

The provisions restricting set-off of pre-entry losses have the following effects

(i) E Ltd

For the year to 31.3.93, E Ltd may elect (before 1 April 1995) for the whole of the £3,000 gain to be regarded as covered by pre-entry losses. The £10,000 losses carried forward at 31.3.93 then comprise pre-entry losses of £9,000 and other losses of £1,000. In the absence of an election, losses are set against gains on a first in/first out basis for these purposes, so the same result would accrue in this case. [*7A Sch 6(2)–(4)*].

The £9,000 pre-entry losses are carried forward and may be set only against gains on assets held by E Ltd immediately before 1.4.92 or gains on assets acquired by it on or after that date from outside the group and not used or held for any purposes other than those of the trade carried on by E Ltd immediately before that date and which continued to be carried on by it up to the date of disposal. [*7A Sch 7(1)*].

The overall loss on the disposal of the freehold property is as follows

	£	£
Proceeds (1.10.95)		55,000
Cost (1.7.88)	70,000	
Enhancement expenditure (1.10.89)	10,000	80,000
Allowable loss		£25,000

CT 104.3   Capital Gains

The pre-entry proportion of the allowable loss is calculated as follows

$$\pounds25,000 \times \frac{70,000}{80,000} \times \frac{\text{3y 9m (1.7.88–1.4.92)}}{\text{7y 3m (1.7.88–1.10.95)}} \qquad = \qquad 11,315$$

$$\pounds25,000 \times \frac{10,000}{80,000} \times \frac{\text{2y 6m (1.10.89–1.4.92)}}{\text{6y 0m (1.10.89–1.10.95)}} \qquad = \qquad 1,302$$

	£
Pre-entry proportion	£12,617
Balance of allowable loss	£12,383

[7A Sch 2; FA 1994, s 93(8)].

E Ltd may elect (before 1 April 1998) to use an alternative method of computing the pre-entry proportion of the allowable loss, as follows

	£	£
Market value (1.4.92)		70,000
Cost (1.7.88)	70,000	
Enhancement expenditure (1.10.89)	10,000	80,000
Pre-entry proportion of allowable loss		£10,000
Balance of allowable loss (£25,000 – £10,000)		£15,000

Where the actual disposal occurs after 29 November 1993 (so that an allowable loss cannot be created or enhanced by indexation allowance), the same indexation restrictions are deemed to apply to the deemed disposal at the date of the company's joining the group, even if, as in this example, that date was before 30 November 1993.

[7A Sch 5; FA 1994, s 93(10)].

The whole of the loss of £25,000 is available for carry-forward but the pre-entry proportion of the allowable loss (£10,000 on the assumption that the election under 7A Sch 5 is made) can be set only against the same types of gain against which the pre-entry losses of £9,000 can be set (see above).

(ii) F Ltd

Allowable loss on XYZ plc ordinary shares

	Number of shares	Qualifying expenditure £	Indexed pool £
Acquisition 1.5.88	6,000	10,000	
Acquisition 1.6.92	4,000	7,000	
At 1.4.94	10,000	17,000	20,671
Indexed rise to 1.11.94:			
£20,671 × 0.008			165
Acquisition 1.11.94	5,000	3,000	3,000
	c/f 15,000	c/f £20,000	c/f £23,836

	Number of shares	Qualifying expenditure £	Indexed pool £
	b/f 15,000	b/f 20,000	b/f 23,836
Indexed rise to 31.8.95:			
£23,836 × (say) 0.020			477
			24,313
Disposal 31.8.95	(12,000)	(16,000)	(19,450)
Pool carried forward	3,000	£4,000	£4,863

	£
Proceeds 31.8.95	6,000
Cost	16,000
Allowable loss	£10,000

Indexation allowance would be £3,450 (£19,450 − £16,000), but indexation allowance cannot increase an allowable loss. [*TCGA 1992, s 53(2A); FA 1994, s 93(3)(11)*].

Pre-entry proportion of allowable loss

Stage 1 [7A Sch 3]

The proportion of the pool disposed of (12,000 shares) exceeds the proportion *not* referable to pre-entry assets (5,000 shares). The excess of 7,000 shares is regarded as a separate asset made up as follows:

		Cost £
6,000 shares acquired 1.5.88		10,000
1,000 shares acquired 1.6.92	(£7,000 × $\frac{1}{4}$)	1,750
		£11,750

	£
Proceeds of 7,000 shares £6,000 × $\frac{7}{12}$	3,500
Cost as above	11,750
Notional allowable loss on pre-entry assets	£8,250

The pre-entry proportion of the allowable loss under *7A Sch 3* is calculated as follows

		£
$£8,250 \times \dfrac{10,000}{11,750} \times \dfrac{\text{5y 11m (1.5.88–1.4.94)}}{\text{7y 4m (1.5.88–31.8.95)}}$	=	5,665
$£8,250 \times \dfrac{1,750}{11,750} \times \dfrac{\text{1y 10m (1.6.92–1.4.94)}}{\text{3y 3m (1.6.92–31.8.95)}}$	=	693
Pre-entry proportion of allowable loss (subject to below)		£6,358

CT 104.3 Capital Gains

Stage 2 [7A Sch 4; FA 1994, s 93(9)]

		£
The amount deductible in computing the allowable loss is	(I)	16,000
The amount deductible which is attributable to the post-entry element of the disposal (5,000 shares acquired on 1.11.94) is	(II)	3,000

As (I) exceeds (II), an adjustment is required to the figure calculated at *Stage 1* above, as follows

	£	£
Expenditure actually allowed		16,000
Deduct Actual cost of assets disposed of:		
pre-entry element (see *Stage 1* above)	11,750	
post-entry element (see (II) above)	3,000	14,750
Excess		£1,250

The excess is added to the pre-entry proportion as calculated at *Stage 1* above. The pre-entry proportion of the allowable loss is thus

£6,358 + £1,250 =   £7,608

(Because an adjustment is required under *7A Sch 4*, the election for the alternative method under *7A Sch 5* is *not* available. [*7A Sch 4(5)*]. *If* the election *had been* available, the calculation would have been as follows

	£
Market value of 10,000 shares held at 1.4.94	11,000
Unindexed pool value at 1.4.94	17,000
Notional loss on 10,000 shares	£6,000

As only 7,000 of the 10,000 shares held at 1.4.94 are regarded as included in the disposal on 31.8.95 (see *Stage 1* above), the pre-entry proportion of the allowable loss would have been £6,000 × $\frac{7}{10}$ = £4,200. [*7A Sch 5(4)–(6)*].)

Stage 3 [7A Sch 4(6)–(8)]

As the adjustment at *Stage 2* applies, F Ltd may elect (before 1 April 1998) that the pre-entry proportion of the loss calculated at *Stage 2* (£7,608) be reduced to the amount of the 'alternative pre-entry loss', if lower. In calculating the alternative pre-entry loss, *Stage 1* is recomputed as if the disposal was primarily of pre-entry assets, as follows

	Cost
	£
6,000 shares acquired 1.5.88	10,000
4,000 shares acquired 1.6.92	7,000
	£17,000

	£
Proceeds of 10,000 shares £6,000 × $\frac{10}{12}$	5,000
Cost as above	17,000
Notional allowable loss on pre-entry assets	£12,000

The pre-entry proportion of the allowable loss is calculated as follows

		£
$£12,000 \times \dfrac{10,000}{17,000} \times \dfrac{\text{5y 11m (1.5.88–1.4.94)}}{\text{7y 4m (1.5.88–31.8.95)}}$	=	5,695
$£12,000 \times \dfrac{7,000}{17,000} \times \dfrac{\text{1y 10m (1.6.92–1.4.94)}}{\text{3y 3m (1.6.92–31.8.95)}}$	=	2,787
Alternative pre-entry loss (subject to below)		£8,482

In fact, the alternative loss is higher than the pre-entry proportion of the allowable loss calculated at *Stage 2* (£7,608), so, subject to *Stage 4*, the election would not be made.

Stage 4 [7A Sch 4(6)–(8), 5(4)–(6)]

In making an election under *Stage 3*, F Ltd may specify that the alternative method under 7A Sch 5 (as amended by *FA 1994, s 93(10)*) be used, as follows

	£
Market value of 10,000 shares held at 1.4.94	11,000
Unindexed pool value at 1.4.94	17,000
Notional loss on 10,000 shares	£6,000

As all the 10,000 shares held at 1.4.94 are regarded as included in the disposal on 31.8.95 (see *Stage 3*), the alternative pre-entry loss is £6,000. It is therefore beneficial for F Ltd to make the election mentioned at *Stage 3*, imputing an election under 7A Sch 5.

The pre-entry proportion of the allowable loss is then reduced from £7,608 (*Stage 2*) to	£6,000

Balance of allowable loss is £10,000 − £6,000 =	£4,000

CT 104.3 Capital Gains

Utilisation of losses [7A Sch 6(1), 7(1)(2)]

The pre-entry loss may be set against the gain of £3,500. It may not be set against the gain of £5,500. The balance of the allowable loss can be set against the gain of £5,500. F Ltd's chargeable gains for the year ended 31.3.96 are therefore as follows

	£	£
Total gains		9,000
Deduct Pre-entry losses	3,500	
Other allowable losses	4,000	7,500
Chargeable gains		£1,500
Losses carried forward (all pre-entry losses) £(6,000 – 3,500)		£2,500

Notes

(*a*)   Broadly, the provisions of *TCGA 1992, 7A Sch* restrict the use of losses realised by a company before it joins a group and remaining unrelieved at that time and of losses on assets held at the time the company joined the group and subsequently realised. Such pre-entry losses can be set only against gains on assets held by the company at the time it joined the group or subsequently acquired by the company from outside the group and used by it in a continuing trade.

(*b*)   The provisions apply in respect of the offset of losses against gains arising on disposals after 15 March 1993. They do not apply where the company joined the group before 1 April 1987. [*FA 1993, s 88(3)*].

(*c*)   See the 1993/94 edition for calculations of the pre-entry proportion of an allowable loss where that loss includes an amount of indexation allowance (i.e. on a disposal before 30 November 1993).

105   Close Companies

105.1 **CLOSE COMPANY — DEFINITION** [*ICTA 1988, ss 414 – 417*]

(A)

A plc is a quoted company whose ordinary share capital is owned as follows

		%
B	a director	10
C	wife of B	5
D	father of B	4
E		17
F	business partner of E	2
G	a director	10
H		8
I Ltd	a non-close company	30
J		7
100	other shareholders	7
		100

It can be shown that A plc is a close company by considering the following three steps

(i) Is A plc controlled by five or fewer participators or by its directors?

		%	%
I Ltd			30
B	own shares	10	
	C's shares	5	
	D's shares	4	
		—	19
E	own shares	17	
	F's shares	2	
		—	19
			68

As A plc is controlled by three participators, the initial conclusion is that the company is close. [*ICTA 1988, ss 414(1), 416(2)*].

(ii) Is A plc a quoted company, with at least 35% of the share capital owned by the public?

		%
I Ltd		30
J		7
100	other shareholders	7
		44

As at least 35% of the share capital is owned by the public it appears that A plc is exempt from close company status, subject to step (iii). [*ICTA 1988, s 415(1)*].

(iii) Is more than 85% of the share capital of A plc owned by its principal members?

	%
I Ltd	30
B	19
E	19
G	10
H	8
	86

Because the principal members own more than 85% of the share capital A plc is a close company. [*ICTA 1988, s 415(2)(6)(7)*].

Note

(*a*)   Although J owns more than 5% of the share capital, he is not a principal member because five other persons each hold more than J's 7% and so themselves constitute the principal members. [*ICTA 1988, s 415(6)*].

(B)

The ordinary share capital of A Ltd (an unquoted company) is owned as follows

		%
B	a director	9
C	son of B	9
D	works manager	5
E	wife of D	15
F	a director	9
G	a director	1
H	a director	1
J	a director	1
K	a director	1
49	other shareholders with 1% each	49
		100

A Ltd is a close company because it is controlled by its directors, thus

		%	%
B	own shares	9	
	C's shares	9	
			18
D	own shares	5	
	E's shares	15	
			20
F	own shares		9
G			1
H			1
J			1
K			1
			51

Note

(*a*)   A manager is deemed to be a director if he and his associates own 20% or more of the ordinary share capital. [*ICTA 1988, s 417(5)*].

(C)

The ordinary share capital of A Ltd is owned as follows

		%
B	a director	9
C	a director	9
D	a director	9
E		9
F		9
G Ltd	a close company	8
47	other shareholders with 1% each	47
		100

The ordinary share capital of G Ltd is owned as follows

		%
B	a director	50
C	a director	50
		100

A Ltd is not a close company under the control test because it is not under the control of five or fewer participators. The five largest shareholdings comprise only 45% of the share capital. [*ICTA 1988, ss 414(1), 416(2)*].

A Ltd is a close company under the distribution of assets test because B and C would each become entitled to one-half of G Ltd's share of the assets of A Ltd. [*ICTA 1988, s 414(2)–(2D); FA 1989, s 104*]. The shares of assets attributable to the five largest shareholdings become

		%	%
B	own share	9	
	50% of G Ltd's share	4	
		–	
			13
C	own share	9	
	50% of G Ltd's share	4	
		–	
			13
D			9
E			9
F			9
			53

(D)
A Ltd is an unquoted company with the following capital structure, owned as shown

	£1 ordinary shares	£1 non-participating preference shares (no votes attached)
B	6,000	—
C	15,000	25,000
D	6,000	19,000
E	5,000	10,000
F	1,600	13,000
G	2,000	—
Other shareholders owning less than 1,000 shares each	64,400	33,000
	100,000	100,000

The company is close by reference to share capital as follows

	Control by votes	Control of issued capital
B	6,000	6,000
C	15,000	40,000
D	6,000	25,000
E	5,000	15,000
F	—	14,600
G	2,000	—
	34,000	100,600

Note
(a)   Control of the company includes control of more than one-half of
   (i)   voting power; or
   (ii)   issued share capital.
   [*ICTA 1988, s 416(2)*].

105.2   **LOANS TO PARTICIPATORS** [*ICTA 1988, ss 419(1)(3)(4), 421(1), 826; FA 1993, s 77(4); FA 1996, s 173*]
P is a participator in Q Ltd, a close company which makes up accounts to 30 June. Q Ltd loaned P £75,000 on 29 August 1996. On 24 May 1998 P repaid the loan.

The effect of these transactions on Q Ltd is as follows

1 April 1998   The company is liable to pay 'notional ACT' of
   $£80,000 \times \frac{20}{80}$ £20,000

30 June 1999   Q Ltd is entitled to make a claim for repayment of the ACT
   paid.

1 April 2000   Following the claim, the company is entitled to a repayment
   of   £20,000

Notes

(*a*)   For loans and advances made in an accounting period ending on or after 31 March 1996 the tax is due on the day following the expiry of nine months after the end of the accounting period in which the loan or advance was made.

(*b*)   Where loans or advances, made in an accounting period ended on or after 31 March 1996, are repaid after the due date on which tax is charged relief by claim in respect of the repayment shall not be given at any time before the expiry of nine months from the end of the accounting period in which the repayment takes place.

105.3 **BENEFITS IN KIND FOR PARTICIPATORS** [*ICTA 1988, s 418*]

R is a participator in S Ltd, a close company, but he is neither a director nor an employee earning £8,500 a year or more. For the whole of 1996/97, S Ltd provides R with a new car of which the 'price' for tax purposes (i.e. under *ICTA 1988, ss 168A–168G*) is £11,200, and in which R makes no journeys on the company's business. R is required to pay S Ltd £500 a year for the use of the car. The cost of providing the car, charged in S Ltd's accounts for its year ending 31 March 1997, is £3,000.

Deemed distribution

If the benefit of the car were assessable under Schedule E, the cash equivalent would be:

	£
£11,200 @ 35% (no business use)	3,920
Less contribution	500
	£3,420

S Ltd is treated as making a distribution of £3,420 to R.

ACT payable £3,420 × $\frac{20}{80}$	£855
Income of R for 1996/97 £3,420 × $\frac{100}{80}$	£4,275
Tax credit for R for 1996/97 £4,275 @ 20%	£855

The income is Schedule F income and thus taxable at 20% to the extent that it does not fall within R's higher rate band.

S Ltd's taxable profits

In computing S Ltd's profits chargeable to corporation tax, the actual expenditure charged (£3,000) must be added back.

106   Controlled Foreign Companies

106.1   IDENTIFICATION AS CONTROLLED FOREIGN COMPANY

(A) Basic identification rules [ICTA 1988, ss 747, 750, 24 Sch; FA 1993, s 119]

CC Co, an unquoted company, is incorporated and resident in Blueland and carries on business there as a wholesaler. It obtains the majority of its goods from associated companies although 10% is obtained from local suppliers. The goods are exported to UK customers — the major one of which is ADE Co Ltd. CC Co has a share capital of 1,000 ordinary shares which are owned as follows:

SS Co Ltd (non-UK resident company)	50
ADE Co Ltd (UK incorporated and resident company)	150
John James (UK domiciled and resident individual)	300
Mrs James (wife of John James)	300
Caroline James (daughter of Mr & Mrs James) living in France	200
	1,000

The shareholders of SS Co are all non-UK residents. The shareholders of ADE Co Ltd are Mr & Mrs Andrew James (parents of John James).

The following figures (converted into sterling) have been obtained for CC Co for the year to 30 April 1996.

	£
Profit before tax	7,000,000
Depreciation	1,000,000
Dividend proposed for year	500,000
Blueland tax paid on profits of year	1,200,000
Market value of plant and machinery at 1.5.95	2,500,000
Additions to plant and machinery in year	1,800,000
Original cost of industrial buildings (acquired prior to 1.5.95)	1,500,000

There were no disposals of fixed assets during the year.

The Revenue have not given any direction under ICTA 1988, s 747(1) with respect to any earlier accounting period of CC Co.

CC is a controlled foreign company because

    (i)   it is resident outside the UK

    (ii) it is controlled by persons resident in the UK, as follows

	UK residents Ordinary shares	Non-UK residents Ordinary shares
ADE Co Ltd	150	
John James	300	
Mrs James	300	
SS Co Ltd		50
Caroline James		200
	750	250
Percentage holding	75%	25%

(iii)   it is subject to a lower level of taxation in the country where it is resident

Notional UK chargeable profits

Year ended 30 April 1996	£
Profit before tax	7,000,000
Add Depreciation	1,000,000
	8,000,000
Capital allowances note (*c*)	1,135,000
	£6,865,000
£6,865,000 × 33%	£2,265,450
75% thereof	£1,699,087
Overseas tax paid	£1,200,000

The overseas tax paid is less than three-quarters of the 'corresponding UK tax' so the company is regarded as being subject to a lower level of taxation (note (*b*)).

Notes

(*a*)   To be a controlled foreign company a company must be
   (i)   resident outside the UK
   (ii)   controlled by persons resident in the UK
   (iii)   subject to a 'lower level of taxation' in the territory in which it is resident.
      [*ICTA 1988, s 747*].

(*b*)   For accounting periods beginning after 15 March 1993, the condition at (*a*)(iii) above is satisfied if the tax paid in the country in which the company is resident is less than three-quarters of the 'corresponding UK tax'. [*ICTA 1988, s 750; FA 1993, s 119(1)*]. The fraction was previously one-half. See the 1993/94 edition for an example illustrating an accounting period straddling 16 March 1993.

(*c*)   **Capital allowances**

Plant and machinery	Pool	Allowances
	£	£
Market value at 1.5.94	2,500,000	
Additions	1,800,000	
	4,300,000	
WDA (25%)	(1,075,000)	1,075,000
WDV c/f	£3,225,000	

Industrial buildings allowance		
Original cost of building = £1,500,000		
WDA £1,500,000 at 4%		60,000
Total allowances		£1,135,000

[*ICTA 1988, 24 Sch 10*].

CT 106.1 Controlled Foreign Companies

(B) Effect of operation in second overseas territory [*ICTA 1988, ss 416, 747, 749, 750, 756, 24 Sch; FA 1993, s 119*]

FC Co is an unquoted company incorporated and resident in Redland where tax is levied at 16.5% and carries on business there as an importer/exporter. The majority of goods are exported to UK customers.

FC Co also has a presence in Whiteland where the tax rate is 30%. There is no double tax treaty in existence between Whiteland and Redland and the Whiteland authorities have ruled that the presence in Whiteland constitutes a permanent establishment. Redland gives unilateral double taxation relief in the same way as the UK. The following figures (converted into sterling) have been obtained for FC Co for the year to 30 September 1996.

	Whiteland £	Redland £	Total £
Profit before tax	40,000,000	50,000,000	90,000,000
Depreciation	—	6,000,000	6,000,000
Local tax paid on profits for year	12,000,000	8,250,000	20,250,000
Market value of plant and machinery at 1.10.95			24,000,000
Additions to fixed assets — plant and machinery			12,000,000

There were no disposals of fixed assets during the year.

FC Co has a share capital of 1,000 ordinary shares (registered) and 1,000 bearer shares which are owned as follows

	Ordinary shares	Bearer shares
TT Co Ltd (non-resident company)	50	
BDE Co Ltd (UK incorporated and resident company)	250	
XY Co (Blackland subsidiary of OY Co)	50	
Roger Brown (UK domiciled and resident individual)	300	
OY Co (incorporated and resident in Purpleland)	100	500
Will Rodgers (resident in Yellowland)		500
ACD Co (Orangeland incorporated and resident company)	250	
	1,000	1,000

The bearer shares have rights only to dividends (i.e. no voting rights).

The shares of BDE Co Ltd are owned by ACD Co. The shareholders of ACD Co are Orangeland residents.

OY Co purchased the shares in FC Co on 1 June 1996 from XZ Co Ltd — a UK incorporated and resident company — which had held the shares in FC Co for the previous three years. XZ Co Ltd is owned by UK residents.

The Revenue have not given any direction under *ICTA 1988, s 747(1)* with respect to any earlier accounting period of FC Co.

FC is a controlled foreign company because

(i)   it is resident outside the UK

(ii)   it is controlled by UK residents. The Revenue may ignore the bearer shares as they have no voting rights. The ordinary shares are held as follows

	UK residents Ordinary shares	Non-UK residents Ordinary shares
TT Co Ltd		50
BDE Co Ltd	250	
XY Co		50
Roger Brown	300	
OY Co		100
ACD Co		250
	550	450
Percentage holding	55%	45%

(iii)   it is subject to a lower level of taxation in the country where it is resident

Notional UK chargeable profits

Year ended 30 September 1996	£
Profit before tax	90,000,000
Add Depreciation	6,000,000
	96,000,000
Capital allowances note (*a*)	9,000,000
	£87,000,000
£87,000,000 × 33%	28,710,000
Less Double tax relief (Whiteland tax)	12,000,000
	£16,710,000
75% thereof	£12,532,500
Overseas tax paid note (*b*)	£8,250,000

£8,250,000 is less than £12,532,500 so the company is regarded as being subject to a lower level of taxation. [*ICTA 1988, s 750; FA 1993, s 119(1)*].

Notes

(*a*)   **Capital allowances** (plant and machinery)

	Pool	Total allowances
	£	£
Market value at 1.10.95	24,000,000	
Additions	12,000,000	
	36,000,000	
WDA 25%	9,000,000	9,000,000
WDV c/f	£27,000,000	

(*b*) **Overseas tax paid**
Whiteland

Profit before tax	£40,000,000
Whiteland tax at 30%	£12,000,000

Redland	Whiteland	Redland	Total
Profit before tax	£40,000,000	£50,000,000	£90,000,000
Redland tax at 16.5%	6,600,000	8,250,000	14,850,000
Less credit for Whiteland tax (restricted to 16.5%)	(6,600,000)		(6,600,000)
Tax in Redland	—	£8,250,000	£8,250,000

The overseas tax brought into the CFC calculation is that paid in the country of residence. Therefore even though the total tax paid during the year was £20,250,000 only the £8,250,000 paid in Redland is taken into account.

106.2 APPORTIONMENT OF PROFITS [*ICTA 1988, s 752*]

(A)

In 106.1(A) above CC Co's notional UK chargeable profits and creditable tax are apportioned among the persons who had an interest in the company during its accounting period.

Shareholder	% shareholding	Attributable profits £	Creditable tax £
SS Co Ltd	5	343,250	60,000
ADE Co Ltd	15	1,029,750	180,000
John James	30	2,059,500	360,000
Mrs James	30	2,059,500	360,000
Caroline James	20	1,373,000	240,000
	100%	£6,865,000	£1,200,000

ADE Co Ltd is the only UK resident company to which chargeable profits and creditable tax are apportioned. ADE Co Ltd is chargeable to corporation tax on a sum equal to the profits of CC Co which are apportioned to it, and this corporation tax charge is then reduced by the apportioned amount of creditable tax. The corporation tax rate applicable is the rate (or average rate) applicable to ADE Co Ltd's own profits for the accounting period in which CC Co's accounting period ends. ADE Co Ltd has a 30 April year end.

ADE Co Ltd

Tax computations — before apportionment

Year to 30 April	1996
	£
Schedule D, Case I	8,000,000
Losses brought forward	—
	8,000,000
Schedule D, Case III	50,000
Schedule D, Case V	1,250,000
Chargeable gains	250,000
	£9,550,000
UK tax at 33%	3,151,500
DTR on Schedule D, Case V income	(412,500)
ACT	—
Mainstream CT liability	£2,739,000

Tax computations — after apportionment

Schedule D, Case I	8,000,000
Losses brought forward	—
	8,000,000
Schedule D, Case III	50,000
Schedule D, Case V	1,250,000
Chargeable gains	250,000
CFC apportionment	1,029,750
	£10,579,750
UK tax at 33%	3,491,318
DTR on Schedule D, Case V income	(412,500)
ACT	—
CFC creditable tax	(180,000)
Mainstream CT liability	£2,898,818
Additional tax	£159,818

(B)
In 106.1(B) above both BDE Co Ltd and XZ Co Ltd will be chargeable to corporation tax on the profits of FC Co apportioned to them. XZ Co Ltd is liable because it owned shares in FC Co at some time during the year to 30 September 1996 (even though it had disposed of its shareholding before that date). It is likely that the Revenue will apportion such proportion of the profits as is attributable to the period to 31 May 1996 to XZ Co Ltd.

106.3 **ACCEPTABLE DISTRIBUTION POLICY** [*ICTA 1988, s 748, 25 Sch Pt 1; FA 1994, s 134; FA 1996, s 182, 36 Sch 4*]

DEF Co Ltd, a UK incorporated and resident company with one associated company, holds 15% of the shares of LNB Co, an unquoted controlled foreign company resident in Pinkland, where tax is levied at only 10%.

LNB Co has chargeable profits for the year ended 31 March 1996 of £500,000. No withholding tax is applicable in Pinkland.

The following information is available in respect of DEF.

Year to 31 March	1996	1997
	£	£
Schedule D, Case I profit	600,000	780,000
Schedule D, Case III income	10,000	10,000
Chargeable gains	90,000	—
Schedule D, Case V income (gross) (tax suffered £30,000)	100,000	—
ACT paid	139,500	140,000

LNB Co

Calculation of profits apportioned to DEF Co Ltd and dividend required to avoid apportionment

	£
Chargeable profits for the year ended 31 March 1996	500,000
Deduct creditable tax	50,000
Net chargeable profits	£450,000

	£
Amount of distribution required to avoid apportionment 90% × £450,000	£405,000

	Apportionment of profit	Dividend
	£	£
DEF share		
15% × £500,000: 15% × £405,000	75,000	60,750
Creditable underlying tax	7,500	6,750
	£82,500	£67,500

DEF Co Ltd

With apportionment

Year to 31 March	1996	1997
	£	£
Schedule D, Case I	600,000	780,000
Schedule D, Case III	10,000	10,000
Chargeable gains	90,000	
Schedule D, Case V income	100,000	
CFC apportionment	75,000	
	£875,000	£790,000

UK tax thereon at 33%		288,750	260,700
Less			
DTR on Case V income	(30,000)		
CFC creditable tax	(7,500)	(37,500)	
ACT		(139,500)	(140,000)
Mainstream tax payable		£111,750	£120,700

DEF Co Ltd

If dividend paid in y/e 31.3.97

	1996	1997
Year to 31 March	£	£
Schedule D, Case I	600,000	780,000
Schedule D, Case III	10,000	10,000
Chargeable gains	90,000	—
Schedule D, Case V income	100,000	67,500
	£800,000	£857,500
UK tax thereon at 33%	264,000	282,975
Less		
DTR	(30,000)	(6,750)
ACT	(139,500)	(140,000)
Mainstream tax payable	£94,500	£136,225
Tax saving (cost)	£17,250	£(15,525)

DEF Co Ltd will make a net tax saving of £1,725 in tax if LBN Co pays a dividend for the year ended 31 March 1996 by 31 March 1997 (see note (*b*)).

Notes

(*a*)   If a controlled foreign company pursues an acceptable distribution policy in respect of an accounting period, no apportionment is made.

(*b*)   The controlled foreign company has, in fact, 18 months after the end of the accounting period in which to pay the dividend, so, in this example, payment at any time before 1 October 1996 would have satisfied the 'acceptable distribution policy' test. The Board may allow longer than 18 months in any particular case. [*ICTA 1988, 25 Sch 2(1)(b); FA 1994, s 134(2)(a)*].

106.4 **SUBSEQUENT DIVIDEND** [*ICTA 1988, s 754(5), 26 Sch 4(1)–(3)*]

JF Co has been the subject of a direction in respect of the year ended 31 March 1995. In consequence an apportionment of its profit for that year (£900,000) has been made and KLM Ltd, a UK incorporated and resident company with a $\frac{1}{3}$ interest in JF Co, has been apportioned chargeable profits of £300,000 (gross). Creditable tax attributed to KLM is £30,000.

On 1 November 1996 following the direction notice JF Co paid a dividend of £528,000 in respect of the year ended 31 March 1995. There is no withholding tax and the underlying tax rate is 12%.

The corporation tax computations for KLM Ltd show that in the three years ended 31 March 1997 its Schedule D, Case I profits were £250,000, £300,000 and £450,000 respectively. Schedule D, Case III income for the three years was £10,000 per annum. For the year ended 31 March 1996 there were chargeable gains of £16,000 and charges on income of £8,000. Small companies rate does not apply, because there are several associated companies.

KLM Ltd paid dividends of £170,500 during the year ended 31 March 1995, £176,000 during the year ended 31 March 1995 and £200,000 during the year ended 31 March 1997.

KLM Ltd

Tax computations

Year to 31 March	1995	1996	1997
	£	£	£
Schedule D, Case I profits	250,000	300,000	450,000
Schedule D, Case III income	10,000	10,000	10,000
Chargeable gains	—	16,000	—
CFC apportionment	300,000	—	—
Schedule D, Case V income (gross)	—	—	200,000
	560,000	326,000	660,000
Charges on income		(8,000)	
	£560,000	£318,000	£660,000
Tax at 33%	184,800	104,940	217,800
CFC creditable tax	(30,000)		
DTR on dividend (£200,000 at 12%)			(24,000)
Credit for UK tax on apportionment　　note (*a*)			(46,000)
ACT	(49,500)	(44,000)	(50,000)
	£105,300	£60,940	£97,800

Note

		£
(*a*)	Tax on CFC apportionment — £300,000 × 33%	99,000
	CFC creditable tax	(30,000)
	Net tax suffered	£69,000

Actual dividend (gross) — £200,000

Credit for UK tax on apportionment $\frac{2}{3}\left(\dfrac{200,000}{300,000}\right) \times £69,000$ 　　　　£46,000

107   Double Tax Relief

107.1 MEASURE OF RELIEF

(A) Relief for withholding tax [*ICTA 1988, ss 790(4)–(6), 795, 797*]

A Ltd owns 5% of the share capital of B Ltd, a company resident in an overseas country which has no double taxation agreement with the UK. The following facts relate to A Ltd's accounting period for the year ended 31 March 1997.

	£
Trading profits	1,500,000
Dividend from B Ltd (i.e. £80,000 less withholding tax)	60,000
Dividend paid by A Ltd 28.2.97	540,000
ACT on above dividend	135,000
Surplus ACT brought forward	220,000

A Ltd's tax liability is

	Schedule D Case I £	Schedule D Case V £	Total £
Profits	1,500,000	80,000	1,580,000
CT at 33%	495,000	26,400	521,400
Relief for foreign tax note (*a*)	—	(20,000)	(20,000)
	495,000	6,400	501,400
ACT set-off note (*b*)	(300,000)	(6,400)	(306,400)
	£195,000	—	£195,000

Notes

(*a*)   Because the shareholding in B Ltd is less than 10%, no credit is available for the underlying foreign tax on B Ltd's profits. Credit is available for withholding tax.

(*b*)   ACT set off against foreign income is restricted, for FY 1995, to the lower of 20% of income and the CT liability after relief for foreign tax. Surplus ACT carried forward is £48,600.

	£
ACT on dividend	135,000
ACT brought forward	220,000
	355,000
ACT set-off	306,400
Surplus ACT	£48,600

CT 107.1   Double Tax Relief

(B) Relief for underlying tax [*ICTA 1988, ss 790(6), 795, 797, 799*]

H Ltd, a UK resident company, which prepares accounts to 31 March each year, owns 40% of the share capital and voting power of S Ltd, a company resident abroad. On 3 March 1997 H Ltd received a dividend of £70,000 from S Ltd which had suffered withholding tax at 30%. The dividend was paid out of the profits for the year ended 30 June 1996. The following is an extract from the profit and loss account of S Ltd for that year.

	£	£
Profit before tax		900,000
Tax on profits	250,000	
Deferred tax	150,000	400,000
Profit after tax		£500,000

H Ltd may obtain relief in its year ended 31 March 1997 as follows

	£	£
Dividend received		70,000
Add Withholding tax		30,000
		100,000
Add Underlying tax at $33\frac{1}{3}\%$ note (*a*)		50,000
		£150,000
UK Corporation tax at 33%		49,500
Overseas tax suffered		
Withholding tax	30,000	
Underlying tax	50,000	
	80,000	
Limited to UK tax	49,500	(49,500)
Overseas taxation unrelieved	£30,500	

Note

(*a*)   Rate of underlying tax = $\dfrac{\text{actual tax paid} \times 100}{\text{actual tax paid} + \text{relevant profit}}$

$$= \frac{250,000 \times 100}{250,000 + 500,000}$$

$$= 33\frac{1}{3}\%$$

107.2 **ALLOCATION OF CHARGES ETC.** [*ICTA 1988, ss 790(6), 795, 797, 799*]
The following information about A Ltd (which owns 20% of the voting power of B Ltd, a non-resident company) for the year ended 31 March 1996 is relevant.

	£
UK income	1,200,000
UK chargeable gains	300,000
Overseas income (tax rate 40%) from B Ltd (gross)	300,000
Charges paid (gross)	150,000
ACT paid	300,000

A Ltd may allocate charges and ACT as it wishes in order to obtain maximum double tax relief. The following calculation shows how this is best done

	UK income and gains £	Overseas income £	Total £
Income and gains	1,500,000	300,000	1,800,000
Deduct Charges note (c)	150,000	—	150,000
	£1,350,000	£300,000	£1,650,000
CT at 33%	445,500	99,000	544,500
Deduct Double tax relief note (d)	—	(99,000)	(99,000)
	445,500	—	445,500
Deduct ACT	(270,000)	—	(270,000)
'Mainstream' liability	£175,500	—	£175,500

Notes

(a)   Surplus ACT carried forward is £30,000 (£300,000 – £270,000).

(b)   Relief for foreign tax is given before ACT set-off. [*ICTA 1988, s 797(4)(a)*].

(c)   To obtain the best advantage, charges should be set off firstly against UK income and gains and then against overseas income. If there is more than one overseas income source, the charges should be set as far as possible against income subject to a lower rather than a higher rate of overseas tax. (See also note (e) below.)

(d)   Double tax relief is the lower of

    (i)   Overseas tax suffered, 40% × £300,000   £120,000

    and

    (ii)   CT liability on overseas income   £99,000

    Therefore, double tax relief   £99,000

(e)   If charges were set off against overseas income first, the following tax would be payable

	UK income and gains £	Overseas income £	Total £
Income and gains	1,500,000	300,000	1,800,000
Deduct Charges	—	150,000	150,000
	£1,500,000	£150,000	£1,650,000
CT at 33%	495,000	49,500	544,500
Deduct Double tax relief	—	(49,500)	(49,500)
Deduct ACT	(300,000)	—	(300,000)
'Mainstream' liability	£195,000	—	£195,000

This gives a maximum double tax relief of £49,500, with no ACT carried forward. Compared with the recommended allocation, £49,500 of double tax relief (£99,000 – £49,500) is lost, representing an increase in the mainstream liability of £19,500 (£195,000 – £175,500) and a decrease of £30,000 in the surplus ACT carried forward.

(f)   A Ltd may have been able to recover some or all of the surplus ACT in the main computation by electing for one or more of its dividends to be treated as a foreign income dividend. See 109 FOREIGN INCOME DIVIDENDS.

108   Exchange Gains and Losses

For a detailed guide to this specialised subject, see *Tolley's Taxation of Foreign Exchange Gains and Losses.*

[*FA 1993, ss 92–95, 125–170, 15–18 Schs; FA 1994, ss 114–116; FA 1995, ss 130–132, 24 Sch*]

108.1   TRADING EXCHANGE GAINS AND LOSSES — GENERAL

Tinman plc, a UK trading company prepares its annual accounts to 31 March and sells goods on 4 December 1996 to a customer in the land of Oz for Oz $540,000. The customer pays Oz $140,000 on account on 1 February and the balance of Oz $400,000 remains outstanding on 31 March 1997. The exchange rates on the relevant dates are as follows

4 December 1996	£1 = 3 Oz $
1 February 1997	£1 = 2.9 Oz $
31 March 1997	£1 = 2.75 Oz $

The account can be summarised over the accrual period (4.12.96 to 31.3.97) as follows

Date	Amount	Exchange Rate	(Decrease)	£ equivalent
	Oz $	Oz /£	Oz $	
4.12.96	540,000	3.0	—	180,000
1.2.97	400,000	2.9	(140,000)	(48,276)
31.3.97	400,000	2.75	—	145,455

The exchange gain is calculated as follows

	£	£
Sterling equivalent 31.3.97		145,455
Less sterling equivalent 4.12.96	180,000	
Adjusted for decrease	(48,276)	131,724
Exchange gain		£13,731

The exchange gain falls to be included in Tinman plc's profits chargeable to corporation tax for the year ended 31 March 1997.

Notes

(*a*)   Where a qualifying asset (as in this example), qualifying liability or currency contract is held or owed solely for the purposes of a company's trade, an exchange gain is treated as a taxable receipt of the trade for the accounting period in which the accrual period falls. An exchange loss is treated as a deductible trading expense. [*FA 1993, s 128*]. Special rules (not illustrated here) apply to non-trading exchange gains and losses.

(*b*)   The Finance Act 1993 foreign exchange gains and losses rules apply from a company's Commencement Day, being the first day of its first accounting period beginning on or after 23 March 1995. There are transitional provisions for calculating exchange differences on transactions straddling the Commencement Day. [*FA 1993, s 165, 16 Sch; SI 1994 No 3224*].

CT 108.2   Exchange Gains and Losses

108.2 **DEFERRAL OF UNREALISED EXCHANGE GAINS** [*FA 1993, ss 139–143*]

On 1 October 1995, Tinkerbell plc, a UK trading company preparing accounts to 30 September, obtains a three-year loan of NNL $750,000 from its parent in Neverneverland to buy plant. For the years ended 30 September 1997 and 1998, the following information relating to Tinkerbell plc is relevant.

	At 1.10.96	At 30.9.97	At 30.9.98
Exchange rate NNL $ to £	1.5	1.6	1.69
Loan from parent (in £)	500,000	468,750	443,787

	Y/e 30.9.96 £	Y/e 30.9.97 £
Net exchange gains on qualifying advances, borrowings and currency contracts	36,000	18,000
Profits chargeable to CT (inclusive of net exchange gains)	150,000	275,000

Apart from the parent company loan, there were no other exchange gains or losses on long-term (one year or more) capital assets and liabilities.

The exchange gains available for deferral for the years ended 30 September 1997 and 1998 are calculated as follows

Y/e 30.9.97
Lower of
— unrealised exchange gains on long-term
  capital assets and liabilities
  £(500,000 – 468,750)   £31,250

— net exchange gains   £36,000

	£
Lower is	31,250
Less £150,000 @ 10%	15,000
Maximum deferral claim possible	£16,250

Profits chargeable to CT if maximum deferral claim made
£(150,000 – 16,250)   £133,750

Y/e 30.9.98 (assuming that maximum claim made for y/e 30.9.97)
Lower of
— unrealised exchange gains on long-term
  capital assets and liabilities
  £(468,750 – 443,787 + 16,250*)   £41,123

— net exchange gains £(18,000 + 16,250*)   £34,250

	£
Lower is	34,250
Less £(275,000 + 16,250*) = £291,250 @ 10%	29,125
Maximum deferral claim possible	£5,125

Profits chargeable to CT if maximum deferral claim made
£(275,000 + 16,250* − 5,125)   £286,125

*   See note (*b*)

Notes
(*a*)   A company may claim to defer to the next accounting period all or part of an unrealised exchange gain on a long-term capital asset or liability, the maximum available to be deferred being calculated as above. Special rules (not illustrated here) apply to a member of a 75% group of companies.

(*b*)   The exchange gain of £16,250 deferred in the year to 30 September 1997 is then deemed to accrue in the year to 30 September 1998, so must be included in the calculations for that year.

109   Foreign Income Dividends

[ICTA 1988, ss 246A–246Y; FA 1994, 16 Sch 1; FA 1996, s 153, 27 Sch]

109.1 Q Ltd is a UK-resident company with an interest in LH Co, a company resident in Shangri-La. Q Ltd prepares accounts to 31 March, and the following details are relevant for the year to 31 March 1996 (all figures in this example are in thousands of pounds).

	£	£
Trading profits		2,000
Dividends from LH Co (net)		375
Foreign tax suffered thereon		125
Charges paid (gross)		200
Dividends paid (net):		
1.6.95	1,000	
1.12.95	400	
15.1.96	300	
	——	
		1,700
ACT paid		425

There was surplus ACT of £200 brought forward at 1 April 1995. Q Ltd has no capacity for recovering surplus ACT by carrying it back to previous years.

Q Ltd is *not* an international headquarters company.

Without any elections to treat dividends paid as foreign income dividends, Q Ltd's tax position is as follows

	UK income £	Overseas income £	Total £
Income	2,000	500	2,500
Deduct Charges	200	—	200
	——	——	——
Profits chargeable to CT	£1,800	£500	£2,300
	——	——	——
CT @ 33%	594	165	759
Deduct Double tax relief	—	125	125
	——	——	——
	594	40	634
Deduct ACT*	360	40	400
	——	——	——
'Mainstream' liability	£234	—	£234
	——	——	——

* ACT set-off is the lower of 20% of profit and the amount of UK corporation tax otherwise payable. *[ICTA 1988, s 797(4)].*

Surplus ACT

	£
B/f at 1.4.95	200
ACT paid — y/e 31.3.96	425
	——
	625
ACT set-off — y/e 31.3.96	400
	——
C/f at 31.3.96	£225
	——

If Q Ltd wishes to elect under *Sec 246A* for the 15.1.96 dividend of £300 to be treated as a foreign income dividend (FID), and thus obtain further set-off or repayment of ACT, the necessary steps are as follows

(1)   Elect under *Sec 246A* for the dividend to be treated as a FID. This election must be made *not later than* the time the dividend is paid (*Sec 246B*).

(2)   Elect under *Sec 246J* to match the FID of £300 with part of distributable foreign profit of £335 (£500 − £125 − £40). See *Secs 246J–246M* for detailed matching rules.

(3)   Elect under *Sec 246P(3)* for the matched FID of £300 to be a qualifying FID.

(4)   Identify available surplus ACT (see *Sec 246N*):

	£
ACT paid — y/e 31.3.96	425
Deduct Set-off against CT	400*
Available surplus ACT	£25

*   For this purpose, current year ACT is deemed to have been set off in priority to surplus ACT brought forward.

(5)   Identify notional foreign source ACT (see *Sec 246P*):

	£
Matched foreign source profit	500
Notional CT @ 33%	165
Deduct Double taxation relief	125
	40
Deduct ACT on FID (£75 maximum)	40
Notional foreign source ACT (£75 − £40)	£35

(6)   Claim repayment or further set-off under *Sec 246N* of the lower of the amounts identified at (4) and (5) above (i.e. £25).

Q Ltd's tax position is now as follows

	UK income £	Overseas income £	Total £
Income	2,000	500	2,500
Deduct Charges	200	—	200
Profits chargeable to CT	£1,800	£500	£2,300
CT @ 33%	594	165	759
Deduct Double tax relief	—	125	125
	594	40	634
Deduct ACT on non-FIDs	350	—	350
	244	40	284
Deduct ACT on FIDs	10	40	50
'Mainstream' liability	£234	—	£234

CT 109.1　Foreign Income Dividends

ACT repayable under *Sec 246N*	£25
Net CT liability	£209

Surplus ACT

	£
B/f at 1.4.95	200
ACT paid on non-FIDs	350
ACT paid on FIDs ·	75
	625
ACT set-off — y/e 31.3.96	400
	225
ACT repayable	25
C/f at 31.3.96	£200

Notes

(a) An election for treatment as a foreign income dividend (FID) may be made for any dividend paid after 30 June 1994, but must be made in advance and is irrevocable once the dividend has been paid. The FID rules have effect in relation to foreign source profits for accounting periods beginning after 30 June 1993. [*Secs 246B, 246Y*]. The rules are intended to tackle the problem of surplus ACT arising only because of insufficient CT liability (after relief for foreign tax) on foreign source income.

(b) Although not illustrated in this example, a FID may be matched with a distributable foreign profit of the immediately preceding accounting period. [*Sec 246J*].

(c) A FID does not carry a tax credit. An individual in receipt of a FID is deemed to have paid lower rate tax on its gross equivalent, but cannot obtain repayment of this tax. A FID received by a company is not franked investment income. [*Secs 246C–246F*].

(d) See *Secs 246S–246W* for special rules applicable to 'international headquarters companies'.

(e) See 107 DOUBLE TAX RELIEF for general examples involving the interaction of ACT and double tax relief.

110   Franked Investment Income

110.1 SURPLUS FII

Relief for trading losses under ICTA 1988, s 393A(1), and later year adjustments
[*ICTA 1988, ss 242, 244(2), 393A(1)(2); FA 1991, s 73, 15 Sch 5; FA 1993, s 78(8)(9)*]

(A) Relief

The following information is relevant to B Ltd, a company with two associated companies.

	12 months ended 31.3.93	12 months ended 31.3.94	6 months ended 30.9.94	12 months ended 30.9.95	12 months ended 30.9.96
	£	£	£	£	£
Trading profit/(loss)	200,000	400,000	160,000	200,000	(1,200,000)
Chargeable gains	—	40,000	—	—	100,000
Franked investment income	40,000	70,000	30,000	36,000	80,000
Franked payments	—	30,000	20,000	20,000	—

There was no surplus franked investment income carried forward at 1.4.92.

Dividends paid in the year ended 30 September 1993 were all paid prior to 31 March 1993.

The company claims relief under *ICTA 1988, s 393A(1)(a)(b)* for its loss for the year ended 30.9.96, and also makes claims under *ICTA 1988, s 242* for all the above accounting periods.

The loss is relieved as follows

			£
Loss incurred			1,200,000
Set-off against profits	—	y/e 30.9.96	(100,000)
Set-off against surplus FII	—	y/e 30.9.96	(80,000)
			1,020,000
Set-off against profits	—	y/e 30.9.95	(200,000)
Set-off against surplus FII	—	y/e 30.9.95	(16,000)
			804,000
Set-off against profits	—	p/e 30.9.94	(160,000)
Set-off against surplus FII	—	p/e 30.9.94	(9,687)
			634,000
Set-off against profits	—	y/e 31.3.94	(440,000)
Set-off against surplus FII	—	y/e 31.3.94	(38,750)
			155,250
Set-off against profits	—	y/e 31.3.93	(100,000)
Set-off against surplus FII	—	y/e 31.3.93	(20,000)
Loss unrelieved (c/f under *ICTA 1988, s 393(1)*)			£35,250

B Ltd's only remaining corporation tax liability for the five accounting periods under review is for the year ended 31.3.93, on profits of £100,000.

CT 110.1 Franked Investment Income

Following the above claims, franked receipts and payments can be summarised as follows

	Y/e 31.3.93 £	Y/e 31.3.94 £	P/e 30.9.94 £	Y/e 30.9.95 £	Y/e 30.9.96 £
Surplus FII b/f	—	20,000	20,000	20,000	20,000
FII	40,000	70,000	30,000	36,000	80,000
Franked payments	—	(30,000)	(20,000)	(20,000)	—
Sec 242 reduction	(20,000)	(40,000)	(10,000)	(16,000)	(80,000)
Surplus FII c/f	£20,000	£20,000	£20,000	£20,000	£20,000
Tax credit repayable	£5,000	£7,750	£2,000	£3,200	£16,000

The total tax credit repayable is £33,950. See note *(e)* as regards the *Sec 242* reduction for p/e 31.3.94.

Notes

(a) Claims under *ICTA 1988, s 393A(1)* against profits and, by virtue of *ICTA 1988, s 242*, surplus franked investment income of the three preceding years may be made in respect of trading losses.

(b) For the 12 months ended 30 September 1992, relief is restricted to half of the trading profit/surplus franked investment income for that year, as only six months of that year falls within the period of three years immediately preceding the accounting period in which the loss is incurred. [*Secs 242(4), 393A(2)*].

(c) A claim under *Sec 242* is in respect of the accounting period in which the surplus FII arose, not that in which the loss arose. The time limit for making the claim operates by reference to the year of loss and is the same as that under *Sec 393A*.

(d) There is no obligation to make a *Sec 242* claim for *each* accounting period to which the loss may be carried back. It could be made for only one or some of those periods. For each period for which a claim is made, the amount of the loss available to set against surplus FII is the lower of the surplus FII for the period (disregarding any surplus brought forward to that period) and the balance of the loss after relief has been given against profits for that period, i.e. losses are set against profits in priority to surplus FII in each period. [*Sec 242(3)(9)*].

(e) The FII for the period ended 31 March 1994 (£30,000) will have been calculated by reference to an ACT rate of 22.5%. For the purposes of the *Sec 242* claim, however, the FII comprised in the surplus FII for that year (£10,000) is recalculated by reference to a notional 20% ACT rate. £10,000 − (£10,000 @ 22.5%) = £7,750. £7,750 × 100/80 = £9,687. The tax credit repayable is £1,937 (£9,687 @ 20%). However, in computing the surplus FII available for carry-forward after the *Sec 242* claim, the full £10,000 is regarded as having been relieved. [*FA 1993, s 78(8)(9)*].

(B) Later year adjustments

The following further information is relevant to B Ltd, the company in (A) above.

	Y/e 30.9.97 £	Y/e 30.9.98 £
Trading profit	500,000	806,000
Chargeable gains	194,000	—
Franked investment income	10,000	10,000
Franked payments	90,000	210,000

Franked receipts and payments can be summarised as follows

	Y/e 30.9.97 £	Y/e 30.9.98 £
Surplus FII b/f	20,000	—
FII	10,000	10,000
	30,000	10,000
Franked payments	(90,000)	(210,000)
Excess franked payments	£(60,000)	£(200,000)

For each of the above periods, the loss for the year to 30.9.96 previously relieved under *Sec 242* is reinstated (and becomes available under *Sec 393(1)*) to the extent of the lower of excess franked payments and loss relief previously given under *Sec 242* and not previously reinstated.

Thus, for the year to 30.9.97

Sec 242 relief previously given	£164,750
Excess franked payments	£60,000
Loss reinstated	£60,000

For the year to 30.9.98

Sec 242 relief previously given	£165,687
Deduct loss previously reinstated	60,000
	£104,750
Excess franked payments	£200,000
Loss reinstated	£104,750

CT 110.1   Franked Investment Income

The company's corporation tax position for the two above accounting periods is as follows

		Y/e 30.9.97 £		Y/e 30.9.98 £
Schedule D, Case I		500,000		806,000
Sec 393(1) relief:				
Actual (see (A) above)		(35,250)		—
Loss reinstated		(60,000)		(104,750)
		404,750		701,250
Chargeable gains		194,000		—
		£598,750		£701,250

	£		£	
Corporation tax @ 33%		197,587		231,413
ACT paid: £60,000 @ 20%	12,000			
£200,000 @ 20%			40,000	
Less amount not available				
for set-off				
(note (a)(ii))	12,000	—	21,950	18,050
Mainstream liability		£197,587		£213,363

Note

(a)   Where loss relief has been claimed under *Sec 242* against surplus FII, there are two adjustments where in later accounting periods there is an excess of franked payments over FII.

   (i)   Losses so utilised are reinstated and made available for relief under *Sec 393(1)* against future profits of the trade. [*Sec 242(5)*].

   (ii)   The tax credits repaid as a result of the *Sec 242* claim (£34,937) are clawed back by reducing the ACT available for set-off against the corporation tax liability. [*Sec 244(2)*].

111   Gilts and Bonds

111.1 **LOAN RELATIONSHIPS (Trading Purpose)** [*FA 1996, ss 80, 81, 82, 84, 85 and 86*]

A Ltd requires additional trade finance and on 1 January 1997 enters into an agreement with XY Bank plc to borrow £100,000 for 3 years. Interest is payable every 6 months commencing 1 July 1997 at 10% per annum. Legal fees and negotiation expenses in respect of this loan paid in December 1996 amount to £2,800. The company's accounting reference date is 31 March and it adopts an authorised accruals basis for all loan relationships.

A Ltd's draft forecast management accounts for the year ended 31 March 1997 show the following:

	£	£
Turnover		1,400,000
Purchases and expenses		
(all allowable for corporation tax purposes)	900,000	
Finance Charges		
XY Bank plc		
interest to 31 March 1997	2,500	
Legal fees and negotiation expenses	2,800	
Depreciation*	120,000	
		1,025,300
Net profit per accounts		374,700

* Capital allowances for the same year are expected to be £95,000.

The company's draft corporation tax computation for the same period is as follows:

	£
Net profit per accounts	374,700
Add: Depreciation	120,000
Less: Capital allowances	(95,000)
Adjusted profit for corporation tax purposes	399,700

For corporation tax purposes the accrued interest on the loan with XY Bank plc taken out for trading purposes will be treated as a trading expense.

The projected profit and loss charge for each of the following accounting periods will be:

	Year ended 31.3.97	Year ended 31.3.98	Year ended 31.3.99	Year ended 31.3.2000
	£	£	£	£
'Debits'				
Expenses	2,800	—	—	—
Interest payable	2,500	10,000	10,000	7,500

CT 111.2   Gilts and Bonds

This conforms to the authorised accruals basis as interest will be allocated to the period to which it relates.

Notes

(a) A company has a loan relationship whenever it stands in the position of debtor or creditor in respect of a money debt. (A money debt being any debt not arising in the normal course of purchase and sale of goods and services for resale). [FA 1996, s 81].

(b) The taxation of loan relationship follows an authorised accounting method (either authorised accruals or mark to market). [FA 1996, s 85].

(c) Interest on current loans for trading purposes is treated as a trading expense. [FA 1996, s 82].

(d) Companies are to report details of loan relationships under Pay and File on form CT200.

111.2   Loan Relationships (Non-Trading Purposes)

Tradissimo Ltd, a trading company, bought 100 gilt edged securities @ £94 as a speculative venture on 1 January 1997. The gilts will be redeemed on 1 January 2000. Interest @ 6% is payable annually on 31 December each year. The company uses the authorised accruals accounting method for all its loan relationships.

As the purchase of the gilt-edged security does not relate to the company's trade, its income and expenditure will be assessed under Schedule D, Case III. In addition to the interest the company will also be taxable on the discount which will be spread over 4 years.

	Year ended 31.3.97 £	Year ended 31.3.98 £	Year ended 31.3.99 £	Year ended 31.3.2000 £
'Credits'				
Interest received	150	600	600	450
Discount	50	200	200	150
Schedule D, Case III	200	800	800	600

Notes

(a) Profits and losses from non-trading loan relationships are taxable under Schedule D, Case III. [FA 1996, s 80(3)].

(b) All profits and losses arising from the loan relationship are to be accounted for using the authorised accruals basis. [FA 1996, s 84].

111.3 **NON-TRADING DEFICIT ON A LOAN RELATIONSHIP** [*FA 1996, s 83, Sch 8*]

The Beta Trading Co Ltd, which is a single company and not part of a group, made a loan to the PQR Company Ltd. This transaction did not form part of Beta's normal trade. PQR Company Ltd defaulted on the loan on 1 October 1998 leaving a balance of £8,500 due to The Beta Trading Co Ltd.

The Beta Trading Co Ltd's current and forecast position is

	Year ended 31.3.97 £	Year ended 31.3.98 £	Year ended 31.3.99 £	Year ended 31.3.2000 £
Schedule D, Case I (trading income)	10,000	11,000	800	12,000
Schedule D, Case III (loan relationship income)	2,000	2,000	100	400

The £8,500 deficit may be relieved in whole or in part in four ways

		£
Total deficit		8,500
1.	Set off against total profits of the year ended 31 March 1999	(900)
2.	Group relief (not available)	Nil
3.	Carry back against Schedule D, Case III profits from loan relationships of other periods, £(2,000 + 2,000)	(4,000)
4.	Carry forward against non-trading profits of the company i.e. year ended 31 March 2000	(400)
	Net deficit to carry forward	£3,200

Notes

(*a*) Relief is provided by claim for a non-trading deficit on a loan relationship by one of the four following methods:

(i) by set off against any profits of the company of whatever description for the deficit period,

(ii) to be treated as eligible for group relief,

(iii) to be carried back to be set off against profits for earlier accounting periods, or

(iv) to be carried forward and set against non-trading profits for the next accounting period. [*FA 1996, s 83(2), 8 Sch*].

(b) The £3,200 deficit balance (which profits for the year ended 31 March 2000 are insufficient to relieve) may be carried forward for relief, by claim, against non-trading profits of the next accounting period. [*FA 1996, s 83(3)*].

112   Groups of Companies

112.1 **SURRENDER OF ACT** [*ICTA 1988, ss 239(1)-(4), 240(1)(4)*]

A Ltd owns 51% of the share capital of B Ltd which owns 51% of the share capital of C Ltd. An election under *ICTA 1988, s 247* is in force between A Ltd and B Ltd, and between B Ltd and C Ltd. All three companies prepare accounts to 31 March each year. The following information is relevant

	Year ended 31.3.95 £	Year ended 31.3.96 £	Year ended 31.3.97 £
A Ltd			
ACT surrendered to B Ltd	1,500	—	—
B Ltd			
Profits	4,000	10,000	5,000
Dividends paid other than to A Ltd	2,635	4,480	5,360
ACT thereon	765	1,120	1,340

C Ltd has a corporation tax liability for the year ended 31.3.96, but none for the years ended 31.3.95 and 31.3.97.

B Ltd may surrender ACT for the year ended 31.3.96 to C Ltd as follows

Year ended 31.3.95		£	£
CT on profits at 25%			1,000
Deduct ACT paid:			
Surrendered by A Ltd		1,500	
Paid by B Ltd		765	
		2,265	
Deduct Set-off (restricted)	note (*a*)	800	800
Surplus carried forward		£1,365	
'Mainstream' corporation tax liability			200

Year ended 31.3.96		£	£
CT on profits at 25%			2,500
Deduct ACT paid:			
During the year		1,120	
Brought forward from previous period	note (*a*)	1,465	
Carried back from succeeding period	note (*b*)	340	
		2,925	
Deduct Surrendered to C Ltd	note (*c*)	1,885	1,040
'Mainstream' corporation tax liability			£1,460

Year ended 31.3.97		£	£
CT on profits at 24%			1,200
Deduct ACT paid:		1,340	
Carried back to previous period	note (*b*)	340	1,000
'Mainstream' corporation tax liability			£200

Notes

(a) Maximum set-off of ACT for the year ended 31.3.95 is
£4,000 × 20%   =   £800

This leaves £1,465 (£2,265 – £800) to carry forward to future periods. (It is assumed that there is no possibility of B Ltd carrying back any of its own ACT (i.e. £765) to previous periods.) Because ACT surrendered to B Ltd is relieved in priority to B's own ACT, the ACT carried forward will be made up as follows

	£
ACT surrendered by A Ltd	600
Own ACT	765
	£1,365

(b) Maximum set-off of ACT for the year ended 31.3.97 is
£5,000 × 20%   =   £1,000

Therefore, surplus ACT is £340 (£1,340 – £1,000) which may be carried back to the previous period.

(c) Normally one would expect B Ltd to use its own ACT against its own CT liability, but it is not obliged to do so. For the year ended 31.3.96 B Ltd may surrender ACT to C Ltd as follows

		£
ACT paid by B Ltd during year ended 31.3.96		1,120
Surplus ACT brought forward from previous period which was paid by B Ltd	note (a)	765
		£1,885
The following ACT may not be surrendered to C Ltd		
ACT previously surrendered by A Ltd	note (a)	600
ACT which has been carried back from a succeeding period	note (b)	340
		£940

112.2 **SURRENDER OF ACT: EFFECT ON SUBSIDIARY** [*ICTA 1988, ss 239(4), 240(1)-(5); FA 1989, s 97*]

A Ltd owns 51% of the share capital of B Ltd and also a small shareholding in C Ltd. On 1 February 1996, A Ltd acquires the entire share capital of D Ltd (another trading company) which prepares accounts to 31 December each year. The following dividend payments have been made

A Ltd   paid interim dividend of £4,500 on 5.2.96
paid final dividend of £8,000 on 30.11.96
received dividend of £2,400 on 4.12.96 from C Ltd
B Ltd   paid dividends of £5,600 on 2.2.97

A Ltd prepares accounts to 31 December each year and B Ltd prepares accounts to 31 March each year. B Ltd had taxable profits of £20,000 for the year ended 31 March 1996 and £8,000 for the year ended 31 March 1997. A Ltd decides to surrender to B Ltd the ACT arising on its 1996 dividends.

CT 112.2   Groups of Companies

B Ltd may use ACT surrendered by A Ltd as follows

		Year ended 31.3.96	
		£	£
CT on profit of £20,000 at 25%			5,000
Deduct ACT paid			
Surrendered by A Ltd	note (*a*)	909	
Carried back from the year			
ended 31.3.96	note (*b*)	1,400	2,309
'Mainstream' corporation tax liability			£2,691

		Year ended 31.3.97	
		£	£
CT on profit of £8,000 at 24%			1,920
Deduct ACT paid			
Surrendered by A Ltd	note (*a*)	1,616	
Paid by B Ltd (£5,600 × $\frac{20}{80}$)		1,400	
		3,016	
Deduct Carried back to previous year	note (*b*)	(1,400)	
Carried forward to future years	note (*c*)	(16)	1,600
'Mainstream' corporation tax liability			£320

Notes

(*a*)   ACT surrendered by A Ltd — y/e 31.12.96

Date	Dividend paid/(received)by A Ltd	ACT paid
	£	£
5.2.96	4,500 × $\frac{20}{80}$	1,125
30.11.96	8,000 × $\frac{20}{80}$	2,000
4.12.96	(2,400) × $\frac{20}{80}$	(600)
ACT paid, all surrendered		£2,525

This ACT is apportioned as follows
(i)   Applicable to dividend paid on 5.2.96

$$\frac{\text{Dividend paid on 5.2.96}}{\text{Total dividend for the year}} \times £2,525$$

$$= \frac{4,500}{4,500 + 8,000} \times £2,525 = £909$$

Therefore, B Ltd is treated as having paid ACT of £909 on 5.2.96, i.e. during the year ended 31.3.96.

(ii)   Applicable to dividend paid on 30.11.96
Total ACT surrendered, less applicable to 5.2.96
= £2,525 − £909   = £1,616

Therefore, B Ltd is treated as having paid ACT of £1,616 on 30.11.96, i.e. during the year ended 31.3.97.

(b)   ACT surrendered by A Ltd must be used before ACT paid by B Ltd. As surrendered ACT exceeds the maximum set-off allowed for the year ended 31 March 1997 (20% × profit = 20% × £8,000 = £1,600), the whole of the ACT paid by B Ltd may be carried back in accordance with the usual rules.

(c)   ACT surrendered by A Ltd exceeds the maximum set-off allowed for the year ended 31 March 1997 (see note (b)) by £16. This may not be carried back to previous periods but may be carried forward to future periods. However, if B Ltd was to leave the group, any such surplus ACT could not be used during the period in which it left the group or afterwards. Further anti-avoidance rules prevent the use of surrendered ACT following a change of ownership preceded or followed by a major change in the nature of the surrendering company's trade. [ICTA 1988, s 245A; FA 1989, s 98].

(d)   A Ltd cannot surrender any of its 1996 ACT to D Ltd, because the latter was not a subsidiary *throughout* the year ended 31.12.96.

112.3 **GROUP RELIEF** [ICTA 1988, ss 402(1)(2), 403, 413(3)]
A Ltd has a subsidiary company, B Ltd, in which it owns 75% of the ordinary share capital. Relevant information for the year ended 31 March 1997 is as follows

		£
A Ltd	Trading profit	30,000
	Property income	10,000
	Chargeable gain	15,000
	Charges paid	2,000
B Ltd	Trading loss	48,000
	Charges paid	2,000

In addition, B Ltd has trading losses brought forward of £25,000.

Group relief is available as follows

	£	£
A Ltd		
Trading profit		30,000
Property income		10,000
Chargeable gain		15,000
		55,000
Deduct Charges paid		2,000
Profits		53,000
Deduct Loss surrendered by B Ltd		50,000
Chargeable profits		£3,000
B Ltd		
Losses brought forward		25,000
Trading loss for the year	48,000	
Charges paid	2,000	
	50,000	
Deduct Loss surrendered to A Ltd	50,000	—
Losses carried forward		£25,000

112.4 KINDS OF GROUP RELIEF [*ICTA 1988, ss 393(9), 403(3)(4)(7)(8)*]

A Ltd is an investment company which has three trading subsidiaries, B Ltd, C Ltd and D Ltd in which it owns 100% of the share capital. The companies have the following results for the two years ending 31 December 1996.

		Year ended 31.12.95 £	Year ended 31.12.96 £
A Ltd	Profits	10,000	20,000
	Management expenses	(20,000)	(50,000)
B Ltd	Trading loss	(10,000)	(20,000)
	Schedule D, Case III income		30,000
C Ltd	Trading profit/(loss)	(10,000)	30,000
	Schedule A income		1,000
	Capital allowances — trading assets		(5,000)
	— Schedule A assets (given by discharge or repayment)		(2,000)
	Charges paid wholly and exclusively for the purposes of the trade		(40,000)
D Ltd	Profits		70,000

Group relief may be claimed for trading losses, management expenses, capital allowances and charges on income, as follows

		Year ended 31.12.95 £	Year ended 31.12.96 £
A Ltd			
Profits		10,000	20,000
Management expenses		(20,000)	(50,000)
Excess management expenses		(10,000)	(30,000)
Deduct Surrendered to D Ltd		—	30,000
Management expenses carried forward to 1997	note (*a*)	£(10,000)	—
B Ltd			
Trading loss brought forward		—	(10,000)
Trading loss		(10,000)	(20,000)
Trading loss carried forward		£(10,000)	
			(30,000)
Deduct Surrendered to D Ltd	note (*b*)		20,000
Trading loss carried forward (not available for group relief or set-off against non-trading income)			£(10,000)
Profits chargeable to corporation tax			£30,000

C Ltd	£	£
Trading loss brought forward	—	(10,000)
Trading loss	(10,000)	
Trading loss carried forward	£(10,000)	
Trading profit (£30,000) *less* trade		
capital allowances (£5,000)		25,000
		15,000
Schedule A income (£1,000) less		
Schedule A capital allowances (£1,000) note (*c*)		—
		15,000
Trade charges paid (£40,000) less surrendered		
to D Ltd (£15,000) note (*d*)		(25,000)
Trading loss (i.e. excess charges) carried forward		£(10,000)

D Ltd		
Profits		70,000
Deduct Surrendered by A Ltd	30,000	
Surrendered by B Ltd	20,000	
Surrendered by C Ltd		
capital allowances	1,000	
charges	15,000	66,000
Profits chargeable to corporation tax		£4,000

Notes

(*a*)   It is not possible in 1996 to deduct the excess management expenses brought forward from 1995 before deducting 1996 management expenses to arrive at the amount available for group relief. The excess management expenses of £10,000 arising in 1995 are carried forward to 1996 but may not be surrendered and are, therefore, again carried forward. [*Sec 403(4)*].

(*b*)   Although a company might normally relieve a trading loss against other income of the year before surrendering the loss, it is not obliged to do so.

(*c*) Total capital allowances on Schedule A assets	£
(given by way of discharge or repayment)	2,000
Deduct Relieved against Schedule A income	1,000
Available for surrender to D Ltd	£1,000

[*Sec 403(3)*].

(*d*) Group relief for excess charges is restricted to	
Charges paid	40,000
Deduct Profits before *Sec 393(1)* relief	25,000
	£15,000

C Ltd's charges have been relieved as follows	
Charges paid	40,000
Deduct Charges relieved against income	(15,000)
Surrendered to D Ltd	(15,000)
Excess trade charges carried forward	£10,000

[*Sec 403(7)(8)*].

112.5 GROUP RELIEF 'CORRESPONDING ACCOUNTING PERIOD'

(A) [*ICTA 1988, ss 402, 403(1), 408*]

A Ltd has a subsidiary, B Ltd, in which it owns 85% of the ordinary shares. A Ltd prepares accounts to 31 December each year. B Ltd prepares accounts to 31 March each year and had profits of £60,000 for the year to 31 March 1996 and £20,000 for the year to 31 March 1997. During the year to 31 December 1996, A Ltd had a loss of £40,000.

Group relief is available as follows

		£	Losses £
A Ltd			
Loss for the year ended 31.12.96			40,000
Deduct Loss surrendered to B Ltd			
For the year ended 31.3.96	note (*b*)	10,000	
For the year ended 31.3.97	note (*b*)	15,000	25,000
Loss not available for group relief			£15,000

		Year ended 31.3.96 £	Year ended 31.3.97 £
B Ltd			
Profits		60,000	20,000
Deduct Loss surrendered by A Ltd	note (*b*)	10,000	15,000
Chargeable profits		£50,000	£5,000

Notes

(*a*) Corresponding periods

```
                 1995                    1996                         1997
               31.3  30.6  30.9  31.12  31.3  30.6  30.9  31.12  31.3
A Ltd                               |———£40,000 loss———|
B Ltd                  |———£60,000 profit———|  |——£20,000 profit——|
Common period                       |—3m—| |———9m———|
```

(*b*) Calculation of loss relieved

    (i) Against profits of the year ended 31.3.96

        Lower of loss in corresponding period $\frac{3}{12} \times £40,000 = £10,000$

        and

        profits in corresponding period $\frac{3}{12} \times £60,000 = £15,000$

        Therefore, the loss relieved   £10,000

    (ii) Against profits of the year ended 31.3.97

        Lower of loss in corresponding period $\frac{9}{12} \times £40,000 = £30,000$

        and

        profits in corresponding period $\frac{9}{12} \times £20,000 = £15,000$

        Therefore, the loss relieved   £15,000

(B) [*ICTA 1988, ss 408, 409, 411(3)*]
A Ltd has several wholly owned subsidiaries, including B Ltd and C Ltd. A Ltd prepares
accounts to 31 December, the other two companies to 31 March.
Their results were as follows

			£
A Ltd	year ended 31.12.96	loss	(150,000)
B Ltd	year ended 31.3.97	profit	100,000
C Ltd	year ended 31.3.97	profit	100,000

A Ltd makes a profit for the year ended 31.12.97.

**The common period is the nine months to 31.12.96 and A Ltd could surrender losses
as follows**

		9 months to 31.12.96 £	Surrender £
A Ltd's loss	$\frac{9}{12}$	(112,500)	(75,000) to B Ltd
B Ltd's profit	$\frac{9}{12}$	75,000	
A Ltd's loss	$\frac{9}{12}$	(112,500)	(75,000) to C Ltd
C Ltd's profit	$\frac{9}{12}$	75,000	
			£(150,000)

Notes

(*a*)   The surrender by A Ltd is not limited overall to $\frac{9}{12}$ of its loss for the year ended
31.12.96.

(*b*)   However, if B Ltd and C Ltd were themselves members of a group and had become
subsidiaries of A Ltd on 1.4.96 the maximum surrender by A Ltd would have been
restricted to that which could have been claimed by one company joining the group
on 1.4.96, i.e. to $\frac{9}{12}$ of A Ltd's loss. The surrender in this case would be restricted
to £112,500 in total, but the amount could be allocated at will between B Ltd and
C Ltd so long as neither company received relief of more than £75,000.

112.6 **GROUP RELIEF: COMPANIES JOINING OR LEAVING THE GROUP** [*ICTA
1988, ss 402, 403, 408–410*]
On 1 April 1996 B Ltd was held as to 90% by A Ltd and 10% by a non-resident.
On 1 September 1996 C Ltd became a 75% subsidiary of A Ltd.
On 31 December 1996 A Ltd sold 30% of the shares in B Ltd (retaining 60%). A Ltd, B
Ltd and C Ltd all prepare accounts to 31 March each year. During the year ended 31
March 1997 the results of the companies are as follows

A Ltd	Profit	£60,000
B Ltd	Loss	£(240,000)
C Ltd	Profit	£30,000

**Group relief for the loss sustained by B Ltd in the year ended 31.3.97 is available as
follows**

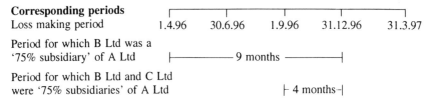

Corresponding periods

Calculation of loss relieved

Against profits of A Ltd

Lower of loss in corresponding period	$\frac{9}{12} \times £240,000 = £180,000$
and	
profits in corresponding period	$\frac{9}{12} \times £60,000 = £45,000$
Therefore, loss relieved	£45,000

Against profits of C Ltd

Lower of loss in corresponding period	$\frac{4}{12} \times £240,000 = £80,000$
and	
profits in corresponding period	$\frac{4}{12} \times £30,000 = £10,000$
Therefore, loss relieved	£10,000

Summary

	A Ltd £	B Ltd £	C Ltd £
Profit/(loss)	60,000	(240,000)	30,000
Group relief (claim)/surrender	(45,000)	55,000	(10,000)
Chargeable profit/(loss carried forward)	£15,000	£(185,000)	£20,000

Note

(a) When a company joins or leaves a group, the profit or loss is apportioned on a time basis unless this method would work unreasonably or unjustly. In the latter event a just and reasonable method of apportionment shall be used. [*ICTA 1988, s 409(2)*].

112.7 **GROUP RELIEF: RELATIONSHIP TO OTHER RELIEFS** [*ICTA 1988, ss 338(1), 393(1)(9), 393A, 402, 403, 407; FA 1991, s 73, 15 Sch 13, 14*]

B Ltd is a subsidiary of A Ltd and commenced trading on 1 April 1994. Both companies prepare accounts to 31 March each year. The results for the three years ended 31 March 1997 were as follows

				£
A Ltd	year ended 31 March	1995	Loss	(4,000)
		1996	Loss	(3,000)
		1997	Loss	(5,000)
B Ltd	year ended 31 March	1995	Loss	(5,000)
		1996	Profit	10,000
		1997	Loss	(20,000)
		1995	Schedule A income	1,000
		1996	Schedule A income	1,000
		1997	Schedule A income	1,000
		1995	Trade charges paid	(1,000)
		1996	Trade charges paid	(1,000)
		1997	Trade charges paid	(1,000)
		1997	Chargeable gains	5,000

The losses can be used as follows

	Year ended 31.3.95 £	Year ended 31.3.96 £	Year ended 31.3.97 £
B Ltd			
Trading profit/(loss)	(5,000)	10,000	(20,000)
Schedule D, Case I	—	10,000	—
Sec 393(1) loss relief	—	(5,000)	—
Schedule A	1,000	1,000	1,000
Income	1,000	6,000	1,000
Chargeable gains	—	—	5,000
Sec 393A(1)(a) loss relief	(1,000)	—	(6,000)
	—	6,000	—
Charges paid	—	(1,000)	—
Profit subject to group relief	—	5,000	—
Loss surrendered by A Ltd	—	(3,000)	—
Sec 393A(1)(b) loss relief	—	(2,000)	—
Chargeable profits	—	—	—
Losses brought forward	—	(5,000)	—
Loss of the period	(5,000)	—	(20,000)
Sec 393(1) relief	—	5,000	—
Sec 393A(1)(a) relief	1,000	—	6,000
Sec 393A(1)(b) relief	—	—	2,000
Unrelieved trade charges	(1,000)	—	(1,000)
Losses carried forward	£(5,000)	—	£(13,000)

	Year ended 31.3.95 £	Year ended 31.3.96 £	Year ended 31.3.97 £
A Ltd			
Trading loss	4,000	3,000	5,000
Deduct Surrendered to B Ltd	—	(3,000)	—
	4,000	—	5,000
Loss brought forward	—	4,000	4,000
Loss (not available for group relief) carried forward	£4,000	£4,000	£9,000

Notes

(a)   Losses brought forward from previous periods must be used before claiming group relief, as must losses incurred in the current period and available for set-off under *Sec 393A(1)(a)*. However, group relief takes priority to losses carried back from subsequent periods under *Sec 393A(1)(b)*.

(b)   Relief for charges paid in a period must be obtained before group relief is claimed but after any other relief from tax. Relief for *trade* charges is given in priority to losses carried back under *Sec 393A(1)(b)*. See also 118.3(A) LOSSES.

CT 112.8   Groups of Companies

112.8 **CONSORTIUM RELIEF**

(A) Loss by company owned by consortium [*ICTA 1988, ss 402(3)(a), 403(1)(9)*]
On 1 April 1996 the share capital of E Ltd was owned as follows:

	%
A Ltd	40
B Ltd	40
C Ltd	20
	100

All the companies were UK resident for tax purposes.

During the year ended 31 March 1997 the following events took place

On 1.7.96 D Ltd bought 20% from A Ltd
On 1.10.96 C Ltd bought 10% from B Ltd

The companies had the following results for the year ended 31 March 1997

		£
A Ltd	Profit	40,000
B Ltd	Profit	33,000
C Ltd	Profit	10,000
D Ltd	Profit	70,000
E Ltd	Loss	(100,000)

Consortium relief for the loss sustained by E Ltd would be available as follows

	A Ltd £	B Ltd £	C Ltd £	D Ltd £
Profits for the year ended 31.3.97	40,000	33,000	10,000	70,000
Deduct Loss surrendered by				
E Ltd note (*b*)	(25,000)	(33,000)	(10,000)	(15,000)
Chargeable profits	£15,000	—	—	£55,000

		£	Losses £
E Ltd			
Loss for the year ended 31.3.97			100,000
Deduct Loss surrendered to	A Ltd	(25,000)	
	B Ltd	(33,000)	
	C Ltd	(10,000)	
	D Ltd	(15,000)	(83,000)
Not available for consortium relief			£17,000

Notes
(*a*)   Loss relief for each member of the consortium is the lower of its share of the loss
and its own profit for the year. Since D Ltd was a member of the consortium for
only nine months, its claim would have been limited to $\frac{9}{12} \times$ £70,000 = £52,500 if
its share of losses had exceeded this figure.

(*b*)   The share of losses of E Ltd appropriate to each member is

		%	£
A Ltd	$40\% \times \frac{3}{12} + 20\% \times \frac{9}{12}$	25	25,000
B Ltd	$40\% \times \frac{6}{12} + 30\% \times \frac{6}{12}$	35	35,000
C Ltd	$20\% \times \frac{6}{12} + 30\% \times \frac{6}{12}$	25	25,000
D Ltd	$20\% \times \frac{9}{12}$	15	15,000
		100	£100,000

(B) Loss by company owned by consortium: claim by member of consortium company's group [*ICTA 1988, ss 405(1)–(3), 406(1)–(4), 413(2)*]
A Ltd owns 100% of the share capital of B Ltd
B Ltd owns 40% of the share capital of D Ltd
C Ltd owns 60% of the share capital of D Ltd
D Ltd owns 100% of the share capital of E Ltd
D Ltd owns 100% of the share capital of F Ltd

This can be shown as follows

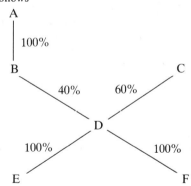

There are two groups, A and B, and D, E and F. D is owned by a consortium of B and C. This relationship has existed for a number of years with all companies having the same accounting periods. None of the companies has any losses brought forward.

The companies have the following results for year ended 31 July 1996

A Ltd	£100,000	profit
B Ltd	£(30,000)	loss
C Ltd	£Nil	
D Ltd	£(20,000)	loss
E Ltd	£10,000	profit
F Ltd	£(3,000)	loss

CT 112.8   Groups of Companies

E Ltd claims group relief as follows

			£	£
Profit				10,000
Deduct Group relief: loss surrendered by F Ltd	note (*b*)		3,000	
Group relief: loss surrendered by D Ltd	note (*b*)		7,000	(10,000)
				—

A Ltd can claim group relief and consortium relief as follows

		£	£
Profit			100,000
Deduct Group relief: loss surrendered by B Ltd	note (*c*)	30,000	
Consortium relief: loss surrendered by D Ltd	note (*d*)	5,200	(35,200)
Chargeable profit			£64,800

Notes

(*a*)   Where a company owned by a consortium is also a member of a group, its losses may be surrendered partly as group relief and partly as consortium relief.

(*b*)   Where a loss of a company owned by a consortium or of a company within its group may be used both as group relief and consortium relief, group relief claims take priority. In determining the consortium relief available, it is assumed that the maximum possible group relief is claimed after taking account of any other actual group relief claims within the consortium owned company's group. [*ICTA 1988, s 405(1)–(3)*]. As F Ltd has surrendered losses of £3,000 to E Ltd, D Ltd can only surrender £7,000 to E Ltd. Consortium relief is restricted to the balance of D Ltd's loss, i.e. £13,000. If E Ltd had not claimed £3,000 group relief for F Ltd's loss, D Ltd could have surrendered £10,000 to E Ltd by way of group relief and this would have reduced D Ltd's loss for consortium relief purposes to £10,000.

(*c*)   Group relief available to A Ltd is the lower of £100,000 and £30,000.

(*d*)   Consortium relief available to A Ltd is the lower of £70,000 (its profit as reduced by group relief) and £5,200 (40% of £13,000, see note (*b*) above). The relief available to A Ltd is the same as that which B Ltd could have claimed if it had had sufficient profits. A Ltd could also have claimed consortium relief in respect of F Ltd's loss if that had exceeded the £10,000 necessary to cover E Ltd's profit. [*ICTA 1988, s 406(1)–(4)*].

(C) Loss by subsidiary of company owned by consortium [*ICTA 1988, ss 402(3)(b), 403(1)(9), 411(9), 413(7)–(10)*]
Throughout 1996 the share capital of E Ltd was owned as follows

	%
A Ltd	35
B Ltd	30
C Ltd	25
D Ltd	10
	100

E Ltd owned 90% of the share capital of F Ltd, a trading company. The companies had the following results for the year ended 31 December 1996

		£
A Ltd	Profit	100,000
B Ltd	Loss	(40,000)
C Ltd	Profit	30,000
D Ltd	Profit	80,000
E Ltd	Profit	40,000
F Ltd	Loss	(240,000)

All the above companies were UK resident for tax purposes.

Group relief of £40,000 of the loss sustained by F Ltd is claimed by E Ltd   note (c)

Consortium relief for the loss sustained by F Ltd would be available as follows

	A Ltd £	B Ltd £	C Ltd £	D Ltd £
Profits for the year ended 31.12.96	100,000	—	30,000	80,000
Deduct Loss surrendered by				
F Ltd note (a)	(70,000)	—	(30,000)	(20,000)
Chargeable profits	£30,000	—	—	£60,000

		Losses
	£	£
F Ltd		
Loss for the year ended 31.12.96		240,000
Deduct Loss surrendered to E Ltd		(40,000)
Not available for group relief		200,000
Deduct Loss surrendered to A Ltd	(70,000)	
C Ltd	(30,000)	
D Ltd	(20,000)	(120,000)
Not available for consortium relief		£80,000

Notes

(a)   Loss relief for each consortium member is the lower of its share of the loss and its own profit for the year.

(b)   The share of the balance of losses (after group relief) of F Ltd appropriate to each member is

	%	£
A Ltd	35	70,000
B Ltd	30	60,000
C Ltd	25	50,000
D Ltd	10	20,000
	100	£200,000

(c)   Group relief claims take priority over claims for consortium relief and reduce the losses available for consortium relief. See also notes (a) and (b) to (B) above.

(D) Loss by consortium member [*ICTA 1988, ss 402(3), 403(9), 408(2)*]
A Ltd, B Ltd, C Ltd and D Ltd have for many years held 40%, 30%, 20% and 10% respectively of the ordinary share capital of E Ltd. All five companies are UK resident and have always previously had taxable profits. However, for the year ended 30 June 1996 D Ltd had a tax loss of £100,000, followed by taxable profits of £40,000 for the subsequent year. E Ltd's taxable profits were £80,000 and £140,000 for the two years ended 31 December 1995 and 31 December 1996 respectively.

With the consent of A Ltd, B Ltd and C Ltd, D Ltd can (if it wishes) surrender the following part of its loss of £100,000 to E Ltd

£

Common period 1.7.95 to 31.12.95

		£
E Ltd's profit	$\frac{6}{12} \times £80,000 \times \frac{1}{10}$	4,000
D Ltd's loss	$\frac{6}{12} \times £100,000$	(50,000)

Common period 1.1.95 to 30.6.95

E Ltd's profit	$\frac{6}{12} \times £140,000 \times \frac{1}{10}$	7,000
D Ltd's loss	$\frac{6}{12} \times £100,000$	(50,000)

The lower common figures for the two periods are £4,000 and £7,000.

Therefore, E Ltd can claim £4,000 of D Ltd's loss against its own profits for the year ended 31.12.95 and £7,000 against its profits for the year ended 31.12.96.

Note
(*a*)   The share of E Ltd's profit against which D Ltd's losses may be relieved is restricted to D Ltd's share in E Ltd, i.e. $\frac{1}{10}$ th.

113   Income Tax in relation to a Company

113.1 ACCOUNTING FOR INCOME TAX ON RECEIPTS AND PAYMENTS [*ICTA 1988, s 7(2), 16 Sch; FA 1990, s 98(2), 19 Sch Pt V*]

S Ltd, a company with one associated company, prepares accounts each year to 31 October. During the two years ended 31 October 1996 it has made several annual payments from which basic rate income tax has been deducted and has received several sums under deduction of basic rate income tax.

The following items are shown net

	Receipts £	Payments £
21.12.94		7,500
4.1.95	3,750	
9.8.95	7,500	
24.10.95	11,250	
25.3.96		7,500
14.8.96		7,600

The adjusted profits (*before* taking account of the gross equivalents of the above amounts) were

	£
Year ended 31.10.95	730,000
Year ended 31.10.96	860,000

S Ltd will use the following figures in connection with the CT61 returns rendered to the Collector of Taxes and will also be able to set off against its corporation tax liability the income tax suffered as shown

Return period	Payments £	Receipts £	Cumulative payments less receipts £	Income tax paid/ (repaid) with return £
Year ended 31.10.95				
1.11.94 to 31.12.94	7,500		7,500	2,500
1.1.95 to 31.3.95		3,750	3,750	(1,250)
1.4.95 to 30.6.95 (No return)			3,750	
1.7.95 to 30.9.95		7,500	(3,750)	(1,250)
1.10.95 to 31.10.95		11,250	(15,000)	
				—
Year ended 31.10.96				
1.11.95 to 31.12.95 (No return)				
1.1.96 to 31.3.96	7,500		7,500	2,500
1.4.96 to 30.6.96 (No return)			7,500	
1.7.96 to 30.9.96	7,600		15,100	2,400
1.10.96 to 31.10.96 (No return)			15,100	
				£4,900

CT 113.1   Income Tax in relation to a Company

Taxable profits

	Year ended 31.10.95 £	Year ended 31.10.96 £
Adjusted profits as stated	730,000	860,000
Add Cumulative receipts £15,000 × $\frac{100}{75}$	20,000	
Deduct Cumulative payments £15,100 + tax of £4,900		20,000
Taxable profits	£750,000	£840,000

Tax payable

		Year ended 31.10.95 £	Year ended 31.10.96 £
CT @ 33% on profits		247,500	277,200
Deduct Income tax suffered	note (*a*)	5,000	
Net liability		£242,500	£277,200

Notes

(*a*)   This represents tax suffered on receipts, less that which has been offset against tax deducted from payments.

	£
Tax on total receipts £(3,750 + 7,500 + 11,250) × $\frac{25}{75}$ =	7,500
Tax deducted from payments and recovered from the Revenue £7,500 × $\frac{25}{75}$ =	2,500
Cumulative receipts £15,000 × $\frac{25}{75}$ =	£5,000

(*b*)   Any change in the basic rate of income tax during an accounting period would not affect the duration of any return period or the right to set off tax borne against tax payable. This is in contrast to the position on changes in the rate of ACT — see 102.1(B) ADVANCE CORPORATION TAX.

114.1   Interest on Overpaid Tax

[ICTA 1988, ss 825, 826; FA 1989, s 178; FA 1991, 15 Sch 22, 23; SI 1989 No 1297; SI 1993 No 2212]

114.1 **(A) General: repayment of tax paid for accounting periods ended after 30 September 1993** *[ICTA 1988, s 826]*

W Ltd prepares accounts to 30 April. It makes a payment of £85,000 on 22 January 1996 on account of its CT liability for the year ended 30 April 1995. On 30 April 1996, it pays a further £2,235, having computed its total liability to be £87,235. In arriving at this amount, the company took a pessimistic view of the possibility of the Inspector allowing a particular deduction claimed in arriving at trading profits. However, after correspondence, the deduction is allowed and an assessment raised showing the company's total CT liability for the year to 30 April 1995 to be £83,750. A CT repayment of £3,485 is made to the company on 3 August 1996.

W Ltd will be entitled to interest on overpaid tax, calculated as follows

		£	£
30.4.96 to 3.8.96	£2,235 × 4% × $\frac{95}{365}$ =		23.27
1.2.96 to 3.8.96	£1,250 × 4% × $\frac{184}{366}$ =	3.67	25.14
Total interest			£48.41

Notes

(*a*)   Where a repayment is of tax paid on different dates, it is treated as far as possible as a repayment of tax paid on the later date.

(*b*)   Although in this example tax was paid on 22 January 1996, interest does not start to accrue until the normal due and payable date of 1 February 1996 (nine months and one day after the end of the accounting period).

(*c*)   An interest charge would initially be raised by the Revenue on £2,235 from 1.2.96 to 30.4.96 but the interest would be refunded in full once the final liability had been agreed and the amount of £2,235 ascertained as having never been due. See also 115.1(B) INTEREST ON UNPAID TAX.

(B) General: repayment of tax paid for accounting periods ended before 1 October 1993 [*ICTA 1988, s 825*]

X Ltd prepares accounts to 31 December. An estimated assessment showing tax payable of £15,000 in respect of the accounting period for the year ended 31 December 1993 is raised on 1 June 1994. Tax of £15,000 is paid on 1 October 1994, an appeal having been made against the estimated assessment but with no postponement application.

The appeal is not determined until 1 June 1996 and an amended assessment is issued on 15 June increasing the total tax charged to £18,935. Further tax of £3,935 is paid on 15 July 1996.

Relief is subsequently claimed under *ICTA 1988, s 393A* for the carry-back of losses from the year ended 31 December 1994 and the tax payable on the reduced assessment is £13,946, a reduction of £4,989. The repayment is made on 1 December 1996.

Repayment supplement is calculated as follows

(i)
On tax of £3,935, interest runs from the beginning of the income tax month following the next anniversary of the material date after the date of payment, i.e.

Date of payment	15 July 1996
Anniversary of material date	1 October 1996
Interest runs from	6 October 1996

Interest runs to 5 December 1996, a total of 2 months

See also note (*a*) below.

(ii)
The balance of the repayment (£1,054) is attributable to the tax paid on 1 October 1994.

Interest runs from the beginning of the income tax month following 1 October 1995, i.e. from 6 October 1995.

Interest runs to 5 December 1996, a total of 14 months.

Notes

(*a*)   Interest on overdue tax will be payable initially on additional tax of £3,935 charged by the amended assessment from the reckonable date to the date of payment, as follows

Reckonable date	1 April 1995
Date of payment	15 July 1996

This interest will eventually be repaid to X Ltd.
[*TMA 1970, ss 86, 91; FA 1989, s 156(1)*].

See also 115.2(B) INTEREST ON UNPAID TAX.

(*b*)   Repayment supplement is paid at the rate applicable under *FA 1989, s 178* for the purposes of *ICTA 1988, s 825* (7% p.a. from 6 March 1995 and 6.25% p.a. from 6 February 1996).

114.2 **REPAYMENT ARISING FROM CARRY-BACK OF LOSSES UNDER ICTA 1988, S 393A(1)**

Y Ltd prepares accounts to 31 December. It has chargeable profits of £100,000 and £60,000 for the years to 31 December 1993 and 1994 respectively and duly pays corporation tax of £25,000 and £15,000 on 1 October 1994 and 1 October 1995 respectively. For the year to 31 December 1995, the company incurs a loss of £80,000 and claims loss relief under *ICTA 1988, s 393A(1)* against profits of previous accounting periods. As a result of the claim, it receives a corporation tax repayment of £20,000 on 25 March 1997 comprising £5,000 for the year to 31 December 1993 and £15,000 for the year to 31 December 1994.

Interest on overpaid tax is calculated as follows

On tax of £15,000 for year ended 31.12.94:

Date of payment	1 October 1995
Material date	1 October 1995
Interest runs from	1 October 1995

Interest runs to 25 March 1997, a total of 540 days.

On tax of £5,000 for year ended 31.12.93:

Date of payment		1 October 1994
Material date	note (*a*)	1 October 1996
Interest runs from		1 October 1996

Interest runs to 25 March 1997, a total of 175 days.

Note

(*a*)   Where, under a *Sec 393A(1)* claim, a loss is carried back to an accounting period not falling wholly within the twelve months preceding the period of loss, the resulting corporation tax repayment is effectively treated as a repayment of tax paid for the period *in* which the loss is incurred, rather than for the period *to* which the loss is carried back. [*ICTA 1988, s 826(7A); FA 1991, 15 Sch 23; FA 1993, 14 Sch 10(2)*]. The same applies where the resulting repayment is for an accounting period ended before 1 October 1993 (i.e. a pre-pay and file period). [*ICTA 1988, s 825(4)(c); FA 1991, 15 Sch 22*].

114.3 **REPAYMENT ARISING FROM CARRY-BACK OF SURPLUS ACT**

Z Ltd prepares accounts to 31 March. Its recent chargeable profits and CT liabilities are as follows:

Year ended	Profit £	Tax paid £
31.3.95	72,000	18,000
31.3.96	32,000	—

On 1 February 1996, the company paid a dividend of £60,000, the related ACT of £15,000 being paid on 14 April 1996. £6,400 (£32,000 @ 20%) of the ACT is set against the CT liability for the year to 31 March 1996, leaving surplus ACT of £8,600. Z Ltd makes a claim under *ICTA 1988, s 239(3)* to carry back the surplus ACT to the previous year. On 1 April 1997, the company receives a CT repayment of £8,600 for the year to 31 March 1995.

It is assumed that the rate of interest under *FA 1989, s 178* for the purposes of *ICTA 1988, s 826* is 4% throughout.

Z Ltd will be entitled to interest on overpaid tax, calculated as follows

		£
2.1.97 to 1.4.97	£8,600 × 4% × $\frac{89}{365}$ =	83.88

Notes

(*a*) Where a repayment arises from the carry-back of surplus ACT, interest on overpaid tax does not begin to accrue until immediately after the date on which corporation tax becomes due and payable for the accounting period in which the surplus arises (not the accounting period to which it is carried back). [*ICTA 1988, s 826(7); FA 1993, 14 Sch 10(1)*].

(*b*) Where the surplus ACT itself arises from the carry-back of a loss for more than twelve months, and the period in which the surplus arises ends after 30 September 1993 (i.e. is a 'pay and file' period), corporation tax repayable as a result of carrying back the surplus ACT is regarded for interest purposes as a repayment for the period of loss. [*ICTA 1988, s 826(7AA); FA 1993, 14 Sch 10(3)(5)(6)*].

115   Interest on Unpaid Tax

115.1 **ACCOUNTING PERIODS ENDED AFTER 30 SEPTEMBER 1993 (PAY AND FILE)**

Cross-reference. See also 114.1(A) INTEREST ON OVERPAID TAX.

(A) General [*TMA 1970, s 87A; F(No 2)A 1987, s 85*]
S Ltd prepares accounts to 31 December. On 31 October 1996, it makes a payment of £120,000 on account of its corporation tax liability for the year to 31 December 1995, the due date being 1 October 1996. On completing its corporation tax return, the company ascertains its total CT liability for that year to be £142,500 and makes a further payment of £22,500 on 18 December 1996. Following the Inspector's examination of the accounts and tax computations, various adjustments are made and the final CT liability is agreed at £145,500. The company pays a further £3,000 on 11 May 1997.

The rate of interest under *FA 1989, s 178* for the purposes of *TMA 1970, s 87A* is assumed to be 7% throughout.

Interest on overdue tax will be payable as follows

				£
1.10.96 to 31.10.96	£120,000 × 7%	× $\frac{30}{365}$	=	690.41
1.10.96 to 18.12.96	£22,500 × 7%	× $\frac{78}{365}$	=	336.58
1.10.96 to 11.5.97	£3,000 × 7%	× $\frac{222}{365}$	=	127.73
Total interest charge				£1,154.72

(B) Refund of interest charged [*TMA 1970, s 91(1A)(2A); F(No 2)A 1987, s 86 (5)(6)*]
On 1 November 1996, T Ltd pays CT of £100,000 for its year ended 31 December 1995. The due date for payment was 1 October 1996. The liability is finally agreed at £80,000 and a repayment of £20,000 is made to T Ltd on 1 May 1997.

It is assumed that the rates of interest on overdue tax and overpaid tax are, respectively, 7% and 4% throughout.

The interest position will be as follows

(i)   T Ltd will be charged interest under *TMA 1970, s 87A* on £100,000 for the period 1.10.96 to 1.11.96 (31 days). The charge will be raised following payment of the £100,000 on 1.11.96.

$£100,000 \times 7\% \times \frac{31}{365}$ =   £594.52

(ii)   The company will be entitled, under *ICTA 1988, s 826*, to interest on overpaid tax of £20,000 for the period 1.11.96 (date of payment) to 1.5.97 (date of repayment) (181 days).

$£20,000 \times 4\% \times \frac{181}{365}$ =   £396.71

CT 115.1 Interest on Unpaid Tax

(iii)   T Ltd will also receive, under *TMA 1970, s 91(1A)*, a refund of interest charged on £20,000 for the period 1.10.96 to 1.11.96.

£20,000 × 7% × $\frac{31}{365}$ =   £118.90

Note

(*a*)   If the repayment had arisen from a carry-back of surplus ACT from a subsequent accounting period, interest on unpaid tax would have been repayable only to the extent, if any, that it covered a period beginning nine months and one day after the end of the accounting period in which the surplus arose. [*TMA 1970, ss 87A(4), 91(1B); F(No 2)A 1987, ss 85, 86(5); FA 1993, 14 Sch 4(1), 5*]. Similar rules apply where a loss is carried back more than one year under *ICTA 1988, s 393A*. [*TMA 1970, s 87A(6); F(No 2)A 1987, s 85; FA 1991, 15 Sch 2; FA 1993, 14 Sch 4(2)*]. See *TMA 1970; s 87A(7)* (inserted by *FA 1993, 14 Sch 4(2)*) for the interaction of these rules.

(C) Set-off of overpayment for one accounting period against underpayment for another

U Ltd makes CT payments of £200,000 and £120,000 for the years ended 30 November 1995 and 1996 respectively, the payments being made on the due dates of 1 September 1996 and 1997 respectively. On 25 March 1998, the liabilities are agreed at £175,000 for the year to 30 November 1995 and £180,000 for the year ended 30 November 1996. The net amount outstanding for the two years is thus £35,000, and U Ltd pays this amount on 1 April 1998.

It is assumed that the rates of interest on overdue tax and overpaid tax are, respectively, 7% and 4% throughout.

(i)   Without set-off, the interest position would be as follows

Year ended 30.11.96

Interest payable on £60,000 from 1.9.97 to 1.4.98 (212 days)

£60,000 × 7% × $\frac{212}{365}$ =   £2,439.45

Year ended 30.11.95

Interest receivable on £25,000 from 1.9.96 to 1.4.98 (577 days)

£25,000 × 4% × $\frac{577}{365}$ =   £1,580.82

Net interest payable   £858.63

(ii)   If the Inspector agrees to offset the overpayment against the underpayment, the interest position will be as follows

Year ended 30.11.96

Interest payable on £35,000 from 1.9.97 to 1.4.98 (212 days)

£35,000 × 7% × $\frac{212}{365}$ =   £1,423.01

Year ended 30.11.95

Interest receivable on £25,000 from 1.9.96 to 1.9.97 (365 days)

£25,000 × 4%	=	£1,000.00

Net interest payable	£423.01

Interest saving in (ii) above	£435.62

Notes

(*a*)   The difference of £435.62 in net interest payable between (i) and (ii) above arises from the differential in the rates of interest charged on unpaid tax and overpaid tax. The difference is £25,000 × 3% (7 − 4) for 212 days (1.9.97 to 1.4.98).

(*b*)   The position in (i) above is the statutory position. That in (ii) above has no statutory basis and could be achieved only through negotiation with the Inspector.

(D) Surrenders of tax refunds within a group of companies [*FA 1989, s 102*]

V Ltd has had, for some years, a 75% subsidiary, W Ltd, and both prepare accounts to 30 April. On 1 February 1997 (the due date), both companies make payments on account of their CT liabilities for the year ended 30 April 1996. V Ltd pays £250,000 and W Ltd pays £150,000. In January 1998, the liabilities are eventually agreed at £200,000 and £180,000 respectively. Before any tax repayment is made to V Ltd, the two companies jointly give notice under *FA 1989, s 102*(2) that £30,000 of the £50,000 tax repayment due to V Ltd is to be surrendered to W Ltd. W Ltd makes a payment of £20,000 to V Ltd in consideration for the tax refund surrendered.

It is assumed that the rates of interest on overdue tax and overpaid tax are, respectively, 7% and 4% throughout.

If no surrender had been made, and all outstanding tax payments/repayments made on, say, 1 February 1998, the interest position would have been as follows

			£
V Ltd			
Interest on CT repayment of £50,000			
for the period 1.2.97 to 1.2.98	£50,000 × 4%	=	2,000.00
W Ltd			
Interest on late paid CT of £30,000			
for the period 1.2.97 to 1.2.98	£30,000 × 7%	=	2,100.00
Net interest payable by the group			£100.00

The surrender has the following consequences

(i)   Only £20,000 of the repayment (the unsurrendered amount) is actually made, and is made to V Ltd together with interest of £800.00 (at 4% for 365 days).

(ii)   V Ltd, the surrendering company, is treated as having received a CT repayment of £30,000 (the surrendered amount) on the 'relevant date' which in this case is the normal due date of 1.2.97, V Ltd having made its CT payment on time. V Ltd is thus not entitled to any interest on this amount.

(iii)   W Ltd, the recipient company, is deemed to have paid CT of £30,000 on the 'relevant date', 1.2.97 as above. It thus incurs no interest charge.

(iv)   The group has turned a net interest charge of £100.00 into a net interest receipt of £800.00, a saving of £900.00. This arises from the differential in the rates of interest charged on unpaid and overpaid tax. (The surrendered amount £30,000 $\times$ 3% (7 − 4) $\times$ 365 days = £900.00.)

(v)   The payment of £20,000 by W Ltd to V Ltd, not being a payment in excess of the surrendered refund, has no tax effect on either company.

Note

(a)   V Ltd could have given notice to surrender its full refund of £50,000 to W Ltd, instead of just £30,000. There would, in fact, have been no point in doing so, but if W Ltd had made its original CT payment later than the due date, so as to incur an interest charge on the £150,000 originally paid, a full surrender would have produced a saving as the amount surrendered would be treated as having been paid on the due date.

115.2 ACCOUNTING PERIODS ENDED BEFORE 1 OCTOBER 1993 [*TMA 1970, s 86; FA 1989, s 156(1); FA 1991, 15 Sch 1; FA 1993, 14 Sch 3*]

(A)

A CT assessment is issued to R Ltd for its accounting year ended 31 August 1993. The relevant facts are as follows

Corporation tax charged	£60,000	
Assessment issued		25.4.94
Company appealed and claimed to postpone £20,000 of the tax charged		20.5.94
Commissioners determined that only £15,000 of the tax charged could be postponed		27.6.94
Appeal determined, total tax payable £73,000		15.11.94
Amended assessment raised by Inspector		21.11.94
Normal due date		1.6.94
Table date		1.12.94
Tax payments made £40,000		10.8.94
£33,000		19.12.94

Interest on unpaid tax will be calculated over the following periods

£40,000	27.7.94 to 10.8.94	note (*a*)
£5,000	27.7.94 to 19.12.94	note (*a*)
£15,000	1.12.94 to 19.12.94	note (*b*)
£13,000	1.12.94 to 19.12.94	note (*c*)

Notes

(*a*)   27.7.94 is 30 days after the Commissioners' determination of the amount that could be postponed.

(*b*)   The reckonable date here is the later of
  (i)   what would have been the due date had there been no appeal, i.e. 1.6.94; and
  (ii)   the table date—6 months after the normal due date, i.e. 1.12.94.

(*c*)   Interest is chargeable on the £13,000 tax due over and above the original assessment as if it had been included in the assessment issued on 25.4.94.

(*d*)   A special rule (not illustrated above) applies where, exceptionally, the notice under *TMA 1970, s 11* requiring a return of profits is served after 31 December 1993 but relates to an accounting period ended before 1 October 1993. [*TMA 1970, s 86(4A)(4B); FA 1993, 14 Sch 3*]. In the above example, it is assumed that the notice was served before 1 January 1994.

(B)

R Ltd, the company in (A) above, incurs a loss of £150,000 for the year ended 31 August 1994 which it carries back under *ICTA 1988, s 393A(1)* against profits for the year ended 31 August 1993. On 25 May 1995, it receives a CT repayment of £40,500 for the year ended 31 August 1993. (No repayment supplement is due as the tax is repaid within twelve months of the material date, i.e. 1 June 1994 — see *ICTA 1988, s 825*.)

Interest previously paid under *TMA 1970, s 86* is repayable as follows

£28,000	1.12.94 to 19.12.94
£5,000	27.7.94 to 19.12.94
£7,500	27.7.94 to 10.8.94

Notes

(*a*)   Where relief is given by way of discharge or repayment of tax, any interest paid under *TMA 1970, s 86* (or *TMA 1970, s 88*) is repayable to the extent necessary to secure that the total interest paid is what it would have been if the tax repaid or discharged had never been charged. [*TMA 1970, s 91*].

(*b*)   Where a loss is carried back under *ICTA 1988, s 393A(1)* to an accounting period *not* falling wholly within the twelve months preceding the period of loss (not illustrated above), it affects interest under *TMA 1970, s 86* for the earlier period only to the extent that such interest covers a period beginning nine months after the end of the period of loss. [*TMA 1970, s 86(2A); FA 1991, 15 Sch 1*]. Thus if in this example, the loss had been carried back from the year ended 31 August 1995 to the year ended 31 August 1993, the original charge under *TMA 1970, s 86* would still stand.

116   Investment Companies

116.1 **MANAGEMENT EXPENSES** [*ICTA 1988, ss 75, 130; CAA 1990, s 28; FA 1995, 8 Sch 24, 57*]

XYZ Ltd, an investment company, makes up accounts to 31 March.
The following details are relevant.

	31.3.96 £	31.3.97 £
Rents received	38,000	107,000
Interest received gross	10,000	5,000
Chargeable gains	18,000	48,000
Management expenses		
attributable to property	20,000	25,000
attributable to management	50,000	40,000
Capital allowances		
attributable to property	1,000	500
attributable to management	2,000	1,000
Business charges on income	30,000	30,000
Charitable charges on income	5,000	5,000

The corporation tax computations are as follows

Year ended 31.3.96

	£	£
Schedule A		
Rents		38,000
Deduct Capital allowances	1,000	
Management expenses	20,000	(21,000)
		17,000
Schedule D, Case III		10,000
Chargeable gains		18,000
		45,000
Deduct Management expenses	50,000	
Capital allowances	2,000	(52,000)
		(7,000)
Deduct Business charges	30,000	
Charitable charges	5,000	(35,000)
Unrelieved balance carried forward		£(42,000)

Year ended 31.3.97

	£	£
Schedule A		
Rents		107,000
Deduct Capital allowances	500	
Management expenses	25,000	(25,500)
		81,500
Schedule D, Case III		5,000
Chargeable gains		48,000
		c/f £134,500

	£	£
		b/f 134,500
Deduct Management expenses	40,000	
Capital allowances	1,000	
Unrelieved balance from previous accounting period	42,000	(83,000)
		51,500
Deduct Business charges	30,000	
Charitable charges	5,000	(35,000)
Profit chargeable to CT		£16,500

Notes

(*a*)   Because of the restricted use of Schedule A losses, it is necessary to distinguish expenses of a general management nature from those pertaining to properties etc.

b)   The excess management expenses (including capital allowances) in the accounting period ended 31.3.96 are carried forward to the accounting period ended 31.3.97 and are set against total profits of that period. If profits in the year ended 31.3.97 had been insufficient, the excess management expenses could have been carried forward to subsequent periods until fully used. See also note (*d*) below.

(*c*)   Non-business charges would be disallowed only where, after set-off, the amount to be carried forward exceeds the total of management expenses (other than those deducted under Schedule A) and business charges.

(*d*)   Management expenses brought forward from earlier accounting periods cannot be included in a group relief claim. [*ICTA 1988, s 403(4)*]. They may, however, be set against franked investment income under *ICTA 1988, s 242.*

(*e*)   Surplus management expenses may not be carried forward if after 28 November 1994 there is a change of ownership of an investment company and one of the following occurs
  (i)   a significant increase (as defined) in the company's capital after the change of ownership,
  (ii)   a major change in the nature or conduct of the business of the company in the period beginning three years before the change and ending three years after,
  (iii)   a considerable revival of the company's business which before the change was small or negligible.
[*ICTA 1988, ss 768B, 768C, 28A Sch; FA 1995, s 135, 26 Sch*].

117 Liquidation

117.1 **ACCOUNTING PERIODS IN A LIQUIDATION** [*ICTA 1988, ss 12(7), 342*]
On 31 August 1995 a resolution was passed to wind up X Ltd. The company's normal accounting date was 31 December.

It was later agreed between the liquidator and the Inspector that 31 January 1994 would be the assumed date of completion of winding-up. The actual date of completion was 30 April 1995.

The last accounting period of the company before liquidation is
1.1.95 to 31.8.95 — 8 months

The accounting periods during the liquidation are as follows
1.9.95 to 31.8.96 — 12 months
1.9.96 to 31.1.97 — 5 months
1.2.97 to 31.1.98 — 12 months
1.2.98 to 30.4.98 — 3 months

Notes

(*a*) The final and penultimate financial years for the above accounting periods are 1998 and 1997 respectively. Assuming the small companies rate of CT is applicable for all financial years concerned, the rate of 24% applies to the income of financial year 1997. As the rate for the financial year 1998 was proposed by Budget resolution before completion of the winding-up, that rate will apply to the income of that year.

(*b*) If the company is a close company, it may be unable, following the commencement of winding-up, to comply with *ICTA 1988, s 13A(2)*. It would then be a close investment-holding company (CIC) and liable to the full rate of corporation tax whatever the level of profits. This does not apply to the accounting period beginning on commencement of the winding-up providing the company was not a CIC for the accounting period immediately before the commencement of the winding-up; however, a company which had ceased to trade before commencement of winding-up is unlikely to be able to satisfy this condition. [*ICTA 1988, ss 13(1)(b), 13A; FA 1989, s 105*].

118   Losses

118.1 **CURRENT YEAR SET-OFF OF TRADING LOSSES** [*ICTA 1988, s 393A(1)(a); FA 1991, s 73*]

The results of A Ltd for the year ended 31 March 1997 show

	£
Trading loss	(10,000)
Schedule A	3,000
Schedule D, Case III	4,000
Chargeable gains	7,200
Trade charges	(2,000)
Non-trade charges	(1,000)

The loss may be relieved as follows

	£
Schedule A	3,000
Schedule D, Case III	4,000
Chargeable gains	7,200
	14,200
Deduct Trading loss	(10,000)
	4,200
Deduct Trade charges	(2,000)
Non-trade charges	(1,000)
Profits chargeable to CT	£1,200
CT payable at 24%	£288

Note

(a) Loss relief (other than group relief) against profits for the current year is given in priority to both trade and non-trade charges. [*ICTA 1988, s 338(1)*]. See 120.2 PROFIT COMPUTATIONS for treatment of excess charges.

118.2 **CARRY-FORWARD OF TRADING LOSSES** [*ICTA 1988, ss 338(1), 393(1)(9), 393A(1)(a); FA 1990, s 99(2)*]

B Ltd has carried on the same trade for many years. The results for the years ended 30 September 1994, 1995 and 1996 are shown below

	1994	1995	1996
	£	£	£
Trading profit/(loss)	(20,000)	10,000	5,000
Schedule A	3,000	1,000	2,000
Schedule D, Case III	2,000	2,000	3,000
Chargeable gains	5,600	4,700	4,000
Trade charges	(3,000)	(9,000)	(5,000)

CT 118.2 Losses

B Ltd may claim under *Sec 393A(1)(a)* to set off the trading loss against other profits of the same accounting period. Assuming the claim is made (and that no claim is made to carry back the balance of the loss), the loss will be set off as follows

Year ended 30 September 1994

	£	Loss memorandum £
Trading loss		(20,000)
Schedule A	3,000	
Schedule D, Case III	2,000	
Chargeable gains	5,600	
	10,600	
Deduct Trading loss	(10,600)	10,600
	—	(9,400)
Trade charges	—	(3,000)
Profits chargeable to CT	—	
		(12,400)

Year ended 30 September 1995

	£	Loss memorandum £
Schedule D, Case I	10,000	
Deduct Loss brought forward	(10,000)	10,000
	—	(2,400)
Schedule A	1,000	
Schedule D, Case III	2,000	
Chargeable gains	4,700	
	7,700	
Deduct Trade charges (restricted)	(7,700)	
Balance of trade charges carried forward		(1,300)
Profits chargeable to CT	—	
		(3,700)

Year ended 30 September 1996

	£	Loss memorandum £
Schedule D, Case I	5,000	
Deduct Loss brought forward	(3,700)	3,700
	1,300	
Schedule A	2,000	
Schedule D, Case III	3,000	
Chargeable gains	4,000	
	10,300	
Deduct Trade charges	(5,000)	
Profits chargeable to CT	£5,300	

118.3 **CARRY-BACK OF TRADING LOSSES** [*ICTA 1988, s 393A(1)(2)(8); FA 1991, s 73*]

(A) General
X Ltd has the following results for the three years ending 31 December 1994, 1995 and 1996.

	1994	1995	1996
	£	£	£
Trading profit/(loss)	30,000	14,500	(40,000)
Schedule A	1,000	1,000	3,000
Schedule D, Case III	500	500	4,000
Chargeable gains	—	1,500	2,250
Trade charges	(4,000)	(4,000)	(2,000)
Non-trade charges	—	(1,000)	—

The loss can be relieved as follows

			Loss memorandum
	£	£	£
Year ended 31 December 1996			
Trading loss			(40,000)
Schedule A		3,000	
Schedule D, Case III		4,000	
Chargeable gains		2,250	
		9,250	
Deduct Trading loss (*Sec 393A(1)(a)*)		(9,250)	9,250
Profits chargeable to CT		—	
			(30,750)
Unrelieved trade charges c/f (*Sec 393(9)*)	(2,000)		
Year ended 31 December 1995			
Schedule D, Case I		14,500	
Schedule A		1,000	
Schedule D, Case III		500	
Chargeable gains		1,500	
		17,500	
Deduct Trade charges		(4,000)	
		13,500	
Deduct Loss carried back (*Sec 393A(1)(b)*)		(13,500)	13,500
Profits chargeable to CT		—	
Unrelieved non-trade charges	(1,000)		
			c/f £(17,250)

	£	£
		b/f (17,250)

Year ended 31 December 1994

	£	£
Schedule D, Case I	30,000	
Schedule A	1,000	
Schedule D, Case III	500	
	31,500	
Deduct Trade charges	(4,000)	
	27,500	
Deduct Loss carried back	(17,250)	17,250
Profits chargeable to CT	£10,250	
Loss carried forward		—

Notes

(a) Trading losses may be carried back to accounting periods falling within the three preceding years, taking more recent periods first. Losses must be set against current year profits before being carried back. If carried back, they must be carried back to the full extent possible, i.e. if losses are not fully relieved in the immediately preceding period, any balance must then be carried back to the period before that, and so on. [*ICTA 1988, s 393A(1)(2); FA 1991, s 73*].

(b) Trade charges (but not non-trade charges) are relieved in priority to losses carried back from a later accounting period. [*ICTA 1988, s 393A(8); FA 1991, s 73*]. No relief is available for the non-trade charges for the year to 31 December 1994 in this example, as they can be carried neither forward nor back.

(B) Accounting periods of different lengths

Y Ltd, which previously made up accounts to 31 March, changed its accounting date to 31 December. Its results for the five accounting periods up to 31 December 1996 were as follows

	12 months 31.3.93 £	12 months 31.3.94 £	12 months 31.3.95 £	9 months 31.12.95 £	12 months 31.12.96 £
Trading profit/ (loss)	38,000	20,000	5,500	(9,000)	(50,000)
Schedule D, Case III	3,000	2,500	2,500	3,000	—
Chargeable gains	7,000	1,500	—	—	2,000

Y Ltd makes all available loss relief claims so as to obtain relief against the earliest possible profits.

The computations are summarised as follows

	12 months 31.3.93	12 months 31.3.94	12 months 31.3.95	9 months 31.12.95	12 months 31.12.96
	£	£	£	£	£
Schedule D, Case I	38,000	20,000	5,500	—	—
Schedule D, Case III	3,000	2,500	2,500	3,000	—
Chargeable gains	7,000	1,500	—	—	2,000
	48,000	24,000	8,000	3,000	2,000
Loss relief					
Sec 393A(1)(a)				(3,000)	(2,000)
Sec 393A(1)(b)	(12,000)	(24,000)	(8,000)		
Profits chargeable to CT	£36,000	—	—	—	—

Loss memoranda

	9 months 31.12.95	12 months 31.12.96	Total
	£	£	£
Trading loss	9,000	50,000	59,000
Relieved against current year profits	(3,000)	(2,000)	(5,000)
Relieved by carry-back:			
To y/e 31.3.95	(6,000)	(2,000)	(8,000)
To y/e 31.3.94	—	(24,000)	(24,000)
To y/e 31.3.93	—	(12,000)	(12,000)
Carried forward under *Sec 393(1)*	Nil	£10,000	£10,000

Notes

(*a*) Relief under *Sec 393A(1)(b)* (carry-back of losses) is not restricted by reference to the length of the accounting period of loss. However, where a loss is carried back to an accounting period falling partly outside the three-year period immediately preceding the accounting period of loss, relief is restricted to an appropriate proportion of profits. [*ICTA 1988, s 393A(2); FA 1991, s 73*]. In this example, the said three-year period, as regards the loss for the year to 31 December 1996, begins on 1 January 1993 and, therefore, only three-twelfths of the profit for the year to 31 March 1993 can be relieved.

(*b*) In the year to 31 March 1994, the loss carried back from the nine months to 31 December 1995 is relieved in priority to that carried back from the year to 31 December 1996, regardless of the order in which the loss relief claims are made. [*ICTA 1988, s 393A(1); FA 1991, s 73*].

118.4 **LOSSES ON UNQUOTED SHARES** [*ICTA 1988, ss 573, 575, 576*]

Z Ltd has been an investment company since its incorporation in 1971. It is not part of a trading group and has no associated companies. It makes up accounts to 31 December. On 6 February 1996, Z Ltd disposed of part of its holding of shares in T Ltd for full market value. Z Ltd makes no global re-basing election under *TCGA 1992, s 35(5)*.

CT 118.4 Losses

Details of disposal
    Contract date   6.2.96
    Shares sold   2,000 Ord
    Proceeds (after expenses)   £4,500

Z acquired its shares in T Ltd as follows

				£
6.4.79 subscribed for	1,000 shares	cost (with expenses)		5,000
6.4.89 acquired	1,500 shares	cost (with expenses)		4,000
	2,500			£9,000

T Ltd shares were valued at £3 per share at 31 March 1982. T Ltd has been a UK resident trading company since 1979. Its shares are not quoted on a recognised stock exchange.

Z Ltd may claim that part of the loss incurred be set off against its income as follows

Identification on last in, first out basis

(i) Shares acquired 6.4.89 (not subscribed for)

                                                 £

Proceeds of 1,500 shares

$$\frac{1,500}{2,000} \times £4,500 \qquad\qquad 3,375$$

Cost of 1,500 shares   (4,000)

Capital loss *not* available for set-off against income   £(625)

(ii) Shares acquired 6.4.79 (subscribed for)

	Cost basis £	31.3.82 value basis £
Proceeds of 500 shares		
$\frac{500}{2,000} \times £4,500$	1,125	1,125
Cost of 500 shares	(2,500)	
31.3.82 value		(1,500)
	£(1,375)	£(375)

Capital loss available for set-off against income   £(375)

Notes

(a) A claim under *ICTA 1988, s 573* is restricted to the loss in respect of the shares *subscribed* for.

(b) The claim must be submitted within two years of the end of the accounting period in which the loss was incurred.

(c) The loss of £375 is available primarily against income of the year ended 31 December 1996, with any balance being available against, broadly speaking, income of the 12 months ended 31 December 1995.

(d) See 10.5 LOSSES and 214.4 LOSSES for further examples on this topic.

118.5 RESTRICTION OF TRADING LOSSES ON RECONSTRUCTION WITHOUT CHANGE OF OWNERSHIP [*ICTA 1988, ss 343, 344*]

(A) Transfer of trade

A Ltd and B Ltd are two wholly-owned subsidiaries of X Ltd. All are within the charge to corporation tax, although A Ltd has accumulated trading losses brought forward and unrelieved of £200,000 and has not paid tax for several years. As part of a group reorganisation, A Ltd's trade is transferred to B Ltd on 31 October 1996.

A Ltd's balance sheet immediately before the transfer is as follows

	£		£
Share capital	100,000	Property	90,000
Debenture secured		Plant	20,000
on property	50,000	Stock	130,000
Group loan	10,000	Trade debtors	120,000
Trade creditors	300,000		
Bank overdraft	60,000		
	520,000		
Deficit on			
reserves	(160,000)		
	£360,000		£360,000

Book values represent the approximate open market values of assets. B Ltd takes over the stock and plant to continue the trade, paying £150,000 to A Ltd and taking over £15,000 of trade creditors relating to stock. A Ltd is to collect outstanding debts and pay remaining creditors.

A Ltd's 'relevant assets' are

	£
Freehold property (£90,000 − £50,000)	40,000
Trade debtors	120,000
Consideration from B Ltd	150,000
	£310,000

A Ltd's 'relevant liabilities' are

	£
Bank overdraft	60,000
Group loan	10,000
Trade creditors	285,000
	£355,000

Tax losses transferable with trade
£200,000 − £(355,000 − 310,000) = £155,000

Notes

(*a*)   Assets taken over by the successor to the trade are not included in relevant assets. Loan stock is not a relevant liability, but where the loan is secured on an asset which is not transferred, the value of the asset is reduced by the amount secured.

(*b*)   The assumption by B Ltd of liability for £15,000 of trade creditors does not constitute the giving of consideration and is not, therefore, a relevant asset of A Ltd. A Ltd's relevant liabilities are, however, reduced by the amount taken over.

(B) Transfer of part of a trade

D Ltd and E Ltd are wholly-owned subsidiaries of X Ltd. On 1 November 1996 D Ltd transfers the manufacturing part of what has been an integrated trade to E Ltd. D Ltd has accumulated trading losses brought forward and unrelieved of £150,000, of which £50,000 are attributable to the manufacturing operations.

Immediately before the transfer D Ltd's balance sheet is as follows

	£		£
Share capital	100,000	Property — shops	110,000
Share premium	18,000	factory	70,000
Loan stock	50,000	Plant	45,000
Trade creditors	290,000	Vehicles	20,000
Bank overdraft	42,000	Stock	30,000
		Trade debtors	65,000
	500,000		
Deficit on			
reserves	(160,000)		
	£340,000		£340,000

Book values represent the approximate open market value of assets. E Ltd takes over the manufacturing business together with the factory, plant and £18,000 of stock for a total consideration of £134,000.

Approximately 60% of D Ltd's turnover relates to manufacturing, and it is agreed that trade debtors and creditors are proportional to turnover.

D Ltd's 'relevant assets' apportioned to the trade transferred are

	£
Trade debtors (60%)	39,000
Consideration received from E Ltd	134,000
	£173,000

'Relevant liabilities' apportioned to the trade are

	£
Trade creditors (60%)	174,000
Overdraft (33%) note (a)	14,000
	£188,000

Tax losses transferable are restricted to
£50,000 − £(188,000 − 173,000) = £35,000

Notes

(a)   On the transfer of part of a trade, such apportionments of receipts, expenses, assets or liabilities shall be made as may be just. It is assumed that it is reasonable to apportion trade debtors and creditors in proportion to turnover and the overdraft in proportion to losses.

(b)   Loan stock, share premium and share capital are not relevant liabilities unless they have arisen in replacing relevant liabilities within the preceding year.

(c)   If the trade were transferred as a whole for market value of the assets, no restriction would apply to the losses transferable.

119   Partnerships

119.1 **ASSESSMENTS** [*ICTA 1988, ss 114, 115; FA 1994, s 215(2)–(5)*]

X Ltd and Mr Brown have been in partnership for many years and share profits in the ratio 2:1. The partnership's trading results for the years ended 30 September 1994, 1995, 1996 and 1997 are as follows

	Trading profits	Capital allowances
	£	£
1994	33,000	9,000
1995	36,000	6,000
1996	39,000	12,000
1997	51,000	15,000

X Ltd's chargeable profits in respect of the partnership are as follows

Year ended 30.9.94

	£
Trading profits	22,000
Deduct Capital allowances	6,000
Schedule D, Case I	£16,000

Year ended 30.9.95

	£
Trading profits	24,000
Deduct Capital allowances	4,000
Schedule D, Case I	£20,000

Year ended 30.9.96

	£
Trading profits	26,000
Deduct Capital allowances	8,000
Schedule D, Case I	£18,000

Year ended 30.9.97

	£
Trading profits	34,000
Deduct Capital allowances	10,000
Schedule D, Case I	£24,000

Mr Brown will have the following assessments and allowances based on the above results

		Basis of assessment	Profit £	Capital allowances £
1993/94	Capital allowances (part) $\frac{6}{12} \times £3,000$	actual		1,500
1994/95	Capital allowances $\frac{6}{12} \times £3,000 + \frac{6}{12} \times £2,000$	actual		2,500

CT 119.1 Partnerships

1995/96	Profits	y/e 30.9.94	11,000
	Capital allowances		
	$\frac{6}{12} \times £2,000 + \frac{6}{12} \times £4,000$	actual	3,000
1996/97	Profits	$\frac{1}{2} \times$ (y/e 30.9.95 + y/e 30.9.96)	12,500
	Capital allowances		
	$\frac{6}{12} \times £4,000 + \frac{6}{12} \times £5,000$	actual	4,500
1997/98	Profits	y/e 30.9.97	12,000
	(Transitional overlap relief $\frac{6}{12} \times £12,000 = £6,000$)		

Notes

(*a*)   For years up to and including 1995/96, profits apportioned to the individual partner are assessed to income tax on the normal preceding year basis. Mr Brown's profits for 1996/97 are calculated under the transitional rules on changeover to current year basis of assessment. For years up to and including 1996/97, capital allowances are given for the actual year of assessment of the accounting period with apportionment between years where necessary. [*ICTA 1988, s 114(3)(a); FA 1994, s 215(3)(a)*].

(*b*)   For businesses commencing (or deemed to commence) after 5 April 1994, and for all businesses for 1997/98 onwards, capital allowances are treated as trading expenses for income tax as well as for corporation tax, and given by reference to periods of account for income tax (see 2.2 CAPITAL ALLOWANCES).

(*c*)   Transitional overlap relief for 1997/98 is computed by reference to profits *after* capital allowances. This applies *only* where the individual is in partnership with a company and cancels out the advantage of some capital allowances being given twice on the changeover (in this case, one half of Mr Brown's share of capital allowances for the year ended 30 September 1997 is relieved in both 1996/97 and 1997/98). [*FA 1994, 20 Sch 2(4)–(4B); FA 1995, s 122(2)(3)*].

120   Profit Computations

120.1   COMPUTATIONS

Y Ltd's accounts for the 12 months to 31 December 1995 showed the following

	£		£
Wages and salaries	77,500	Gross trading profit	208,000
Rent, rates and insurance	5,000	Net rents	1,510
Motor expenses	8,000	Building society interest (gross)	
Car hire	6,000	(received 31.12.95)	1,500
Legal expenses	2,000	Dividend from UK company	
Directors' remuneration	25,000	(received 30.9.95)	4,500
Audit and accountancy	2,500	Profit on sale of investment	5,500
Miscellaneous expenses	2,600		
Debenture interest (gross)	3,375		
Ordinary dividend paid	15,000		
Depreciation	6,125		
Premium on lease written off	14,000		
Net profit	53,910		
	£221,010		£221,010

Analysis of various items gave the following additional information

(i)	Legal expenses:	£
	Re staff service agreements	250
	Re debt collecting	600
	Re new issue of debentures	1,150
		£2,000

(ii)	Miscellaneous expenses:	£
	Staff outing	400
	Subscriptions: Chamber of Commerce	250
	Political party	100
	Interest on overdue tax	250
	Contribution to training and enterprise council	350
	Charitable donation to trade benevolent fund	150
	Single charitable donations (gross) (£800 + £300)	1,100
		£2,600

The 'single charitable donations' were paid after deduction of basic rate income tax. Y Ltd is not a close company.

(iii)   On 1 July 1995, Y Ltd was granted a lease on office accommodation for a period of seven years from that date for which it paid a premium of £14,000.

(iv)   Car hire of £6,000 represents the hire, under a contract dated 1 July 1995, of a car with a retail price when new of £18,000.

(v)   All wages and salaries were paid during the period of account apart from directors' bonuses of £20,000, accrued in the accounts, voted at the AGM on 1 November 1996 and not previously paid or credited to directors' accounts with the company.

(vi)   Profit on sale of investment is the unindexed gain arising from the sale of quoted securities on 28 February 1995. The chargeable gain after indexation is £2,070.

(vii)   Capital allowances for the year to 31 December 1995 are £10,000.

(viii) The new debentures are deep discount securities [*ICTA 1988, s 57, 4 Sch*]. They were issued on 1 April 1995 at 65 (for redemption at 100) with a yield to maturity of 5% per six-monthly interest period. Total nominal value is £180,000. Interest of $2\frac{1}{2}\%$ a year is payable half yearly, the first payment being made on 30 September 1995. The charge in the accounts for debenture interest includes £1,125 accrued for the period 1 October to 31 December 1995.

The corporation tax computation is

	£	£
Net profit		53,910
Add		
Depreciation	6,125	
Directors' remuneration note (*a*)	20,000	
Subscription to political party	100	
Charitable donations notes (*d*) and (*e*)	1,100	
Interest on overdue tax	250	
Car hire note (*f*)	1,000	
Debenture interest	3,375	
Dividend paid	15,000	
Premium on lease written off	14,000	60,950
		114,860
Deduct		
Net rents	1,510	
Building society interest	1,500	
Dividend received	4,500	
Profit on sale of investment	5,500	13,010
		101,850
Deduct		
Capital allowances	10,000	
Allowance for lease premium		

$$\frac{1}{7} \times \left(£14,000 - \left(\frac{7-1}{50} \times £14,000 \right) \right) \times \frac{6}{12} \qquad 880$$

		£
		10,880
Schedule D, Case I trading profit		90,970
Schedule A		1,510
Building society interest		1,500
Chargeable gains		2,070
		96,050
Deduct Charges paid — debenture interest	2,250	
— income element of deep		
discount security	3,600	
— charitable donations		
note (*e*)	1,100	6,950
Profits chargeable to corporation tax		£89,100

Notes

(a)   Director's remuneration of £20,000 is disallowed as it remained unpaid nine months after the end of the period of account. It will, however, be allowable in the tax computation for the year to 31 December 1996, i.e. the period of account in which it is paid. [*FA 1989, s 43*]. See *ICTA 1988, s 202B* as applied by *FA 1989, s 43(12)* as to the time when emoluments are treated as paid.

(b)   Legal expenses re the new issue of debentures are allowable under *ICTA 1988, s 77*.

(c)   The contribution to a training and enterprise council is allowable under *ICTA 1988, s 79A; FA 1990, s 76*.

(d)   The charitable donation to trade benevolent fund is allowable under *ICTA 1988, s 577(9)*.

(e)   The single charitable donations are allowable under the Gift Aid provisions. If Y Ltd had been a close company, the lower donation would not have been allowable as a qualifying donation as it is less than £250 (net). [*ICTA 1988, ss 338(1)(2)(b), 339; FA 1990, ss 26, 27; FA 1993, s 67*].

(f)   The allowable proportion of the car hire expenditure is

$$\frac{£12,000 + ((£18,000 - £12,000) \times \tfrac{1}{2})}{£18,000} \times £6,000 = £5,000$$

[*CAA 1990, s 35(2); F(No 2)A 1992, s 71(5)(8)*].

(g)   The proportion of the lease premium allowable is calculated under *ICTA 1988, ss 34(1), 87*.

(h)   The income element of deep discount securities is treated as a charge on income.

$$\frac{(£180,000 \times 0.65) \times 5}{100} - 2,250 = £3,600$$

[*ICTA 1988, 4 Sch 4, 5*].

120.2 **ALLOWANCE FOR CHARGES ON INCOME** [*ICTA 1988, ss 338, 393(9)*]

X Ltd, a UK resident company made a Schedule D, Case I profit of £5,000 in the year to 31 October 1996 and had unfranked investment income of £7,000.

It paid the following charges (shown gross)

	Situation (i) £	Situation (ii) £
For business purposes (e.g. loan interest)	10,000	1,000
For non-business purposes (e.g. charitable deed of covenant)	4,000	13,000

The corporation tax position is

	£	£
Schedule D, Case I	5,000	5,000
Unfranked investment income	7,000	7,000
	12,000	12,000
Charges on income £14,000, restricted to	12,000	12,000
Chargeable profits	Nil	Nil
Excess charges carried forward	£2,000	£1,000

Notes

(*a*)   The amount available for carry-forward is always the lower of
    (i)   the excess charges; and
    (ii)   charges incurred wholly and exclusively for the purposes of the trade.

(*b*)   See 118.1, 118.2 and 118.3(A) LOSSES for interaction between charges and various loss reliefs, and 112.7 GROUPS OF COMPANIES for interaction between charges and group relief.

121   Returns

121.1 **PAY AND FILE — RETURN PERIODS** [*TMA 1970, s 11(2); F(No 2)A 1987, s 82(3); FA 1990, s 91(3)*]

(A)

Aquarius Ltd has always prepared its accounts to 31 October. In 1996, it changes its accounting date, preparing accounts for the nine months to 31 July 1996. On 31 January 1996, the Inspector issues a notice under *TMA 1970, s 11* specifying a return period of 1 November 1994 to 31 October 1995. On 31 January 1997, he issues a notice specifying a return period of 1 November 1995 to 31 October 1996.

In respect of the first-mentioned notice, Aquarius Ltd is required to make a return for the period 1.11.94 to 31.10.95 accompanied by accounts and tax computations for that period.

In respect of the second of the above-mentioned notices, the company is required to make a return for the period 1.11.95 to 31.7.96 accompanied by accounts and tax computations for that period. [*TMA 1970, s 11(2)(a); F(No 2)A 1987, s 82(3)*].

(B)

Pisces Ltd has always prepared its accounts to 31 December. In 1996, it changes its accounting date, preparing accounts for the nine months to 30 September 1996. On 15 December 1996, the Inspector issues a notice under *TMA 1970, s 11* specifying a return period of 1 October 1995 to 30 September 1996.

Pisces Ltd is required to make returns both for the period 1.1.95 to 31.12.95 and for the period 1.1.96 to 30.9.96, each return being accompanied by accounts and tax computations for the period covered by it. [*TMA 1970, s 11(2)(a); F(No 2)A 1987, s 82(3)*].

Note

(*a*)   The company will need to obtain an additional return form from the Revenue.

(C)

Aries Ltd has always prepared accounts to 31 October. After 1995, it changes its accounting date, preparing accounts for the fifteen months to 31 January 1997. On 21 August 1996, the Inspector issues a notice under *TMA 1970, s 11* specifying a return period of 1 November 1994 to 31 October 1995. On 31 January 1997, he issues a notice specifying a return period of 1 November 1995 to 31 October 1996.

In respect of the first-mentioned notice, Aries Ltd is required to make a return for the period 1.11.94 to 31.10.95 accompanied by accounts and tax computations for that period.

In respect of the second of the above-mentioned notices, the company is required to make a return for the accounting period 1.11.95 to 31.10.96, accompanied by accounts and tax computations for the period of account 1.11.95 to 31.1.97. [*TMA 1970, s 11(2)(a); F(No 2)A 1987, s 82(3)*].

(D)

Taurus Ltd has always prepared accounts to 31 October. After 1995, it changes its accounting date, preparing accounts for the fifteen months to 31 January 1997. On 31 January 1996, the Inspector issues a notice under *TMA 1970, s 11* specifying a return period of 1 November 1994 to 31 October 1995. On 1 April 1996, the Inspector issues a notice specifying a return period of 1 November 1995 to 31 January 1996.

In respect of the first-mentioned notice, the position is as in (C) above.

In respect of the second of the above-mentioned notices, Taurus Ltd is not required to make a return, but should notify the Inspector of the correct accounting dates and periods. [*TMA 1970, s 11(2)(c); F(No 2)A 1987, s 82(3)*].

(E)

Gemini Ltd was incorporated on 1 July 1994 but remains dormant until 1 April 1996 when it begins to trade. The first trading accounts are prepared for the year to 31 March 1997 and the company retains that accounting date. The Inspector issues notices under *TMA 1970, s 11* specifying return periods of 1 July 1994 to 30 June 1995, 1 July 1995 to 30 June 1996, 1 July 1996 to 30 June 1997 and 1 July 1997 to 31 March 1998.

In respect of the notice for the period 1.7.94 to 30.6.95, Gemini Ltd is required to make a return for that period.

In respect of the notice for the period 1.7.95 to 30.6.96, the company is required to make a return for the period 1.7.95 to 31.3.96.

[*TMA 1970, s11(2)(b); F(No 2)A 1987, s 82(3)*].

In respect of the notice for the period 1.7.96 to 30.6.97, the company is required to make a return for the period 1.4.96 to 31.3.97 accompanied by accounts and tax computations for that period.

In respect of the notice for the period 1.7.97 to 31.3.98, the company is required to make a return for the period 1.4.97 to 31.3.98 accompanied by accounts and tax computations for that period.

[*TMA 1970, s 11(2)(a); F(No 2)A 1987, s 82(3)*].

121.2 **PAY AND FILE — FILING DATES** [*TMA 1970, s 11(4)(5); F(No 2)A 1987, s 82(4)*]
The final dates for the filing with the Revenue of the returns in 121.1 above, and for the
payment of corporation tax, are as follows.

Return period	Filing date		Payment date note (*f*)
121.1(A) above			
1.11.94 – 31.10.95	31.10.96	note (*a*)	1.8.96
1.11.95 – 31.7.96	31.7.97		1.5.97
121.1(B) above			
1.1.95 – 31.12.95	15.3.97	note (*b*)	1.10.96
1.1.96 – 30.9.96	30.9.97		1.7.97
121.1(C) above			
1.11.94 – 31.10.95	21.11.96	note (*b*)	1.8.96
1.11.95 – 31.10.96	31.1.98	note (*c*)	1.8.97
121.1(D) above			
1.11.94 – 31.10.95	31.10.96		1.8.96
121.1(E) above			
1.7.94 – 30.6.95	1.8.98		—
1.7.95 – 31.3.96	1.8.98		—
1.4.96 – 31.3.97	1.8.98		1.1.98
1.4.97 – 31.3.98	31.3.99		1.1.99

Notes

(*a*)   The normal filing date is the first anniversary of the last day of the return
period.

(*b*)   If later than the date in (*a*) above (or, where relevant, (*c*) below), the filing date is
three months after the date on which the notice under *TMA 1970, s 11* is issued by
the Inspector.

(*c*)   Where a company's period of account extends beyond the end of the return period,
the filing date is extended to the first anniversary of the last day of that period of
account. This is subject to a limit of 30 months from the beginning of the period of
account, although this would come into play only in the exceptional case where
accounts are prepared for a period exceeding 18 months.

(*d*)   The time allowed for filing returns is effectively extended to the time allowed under
the *Companies Act 1985* if this would give a later filing date than under (*a*)–(*c*)
above. [*TMA 1970, s 94(3); F(No 2)A 1987, s 83*]. This will not be so in the
majority of cases.

(*e*)   The Inspector may grant an extension, on an application by the company, if he is
satisfied that the company has a 'reasonable excuse' for not being able to meet the
filing date under (*a*)–(*c*) above. [*TMA 1970, s 118(2); F(No 2)A 1987, s 94*].

(*f*)   Nothing in (*a*)–(*e*) above affects a company's liability to pay corporation tax within
nine months and one day following the end of an accounting period. [*ICTA 1988,
s 10(1)(a)*].

122 Schedule A — Property Income

Cross-reference. See 18 SCHEDULE A for the income tax rules.

[*ICTA 1988, ss 15, 21, 24–43*]

122.1 RENTS ETC. AND EXPENSES DEDUCTIBLE

A Ltd purchased a shop on 1 August 1996 which it lets to D Ltd (an unconnected company) for £20,000 p.a. from 1 September 1996, payable quarterly in advance on 1 September, 1 December etc. The following expenditure was incurred by A Ltd in its accounting year to 31 March 1997: insurance £600, renewing roof of shop £6,000 (paid in August/September 1996), general maintenance £500.

The company's Schedule A income for the year to 31 March 1997 is computed as follows

	£	£
Rent receivable (3 quarters)		15,000
Deduct Insurance	600	
General maintenance	500	
		1,100
		£13,900

Notes

(*a*) The rents to be included are those to which the lessor becomes entitled in the year of assessment, whether or not received in that year and with no adjustment for prepayments or accruals.

(*b*) No allowance will be given for renewing the shop roof as the deterioration will have occurred before A Ltd purchased the shop and will, in theory, have reduced the purchase price. The amount paid should, however, be an allowable deduction for the purposes of corporation tax on chargeable gains on a subsequent sale of the property.

122.2 **RENTS ETC. FROM CONNECTED PERSONS** [*ICTA 1988, s 33A; F(No 2)A 1992, s 57*]

B Ltd owns a freehold property which it lets to E Ltd (a trading company controlled by the same persons as control B Ltd) at an annual rent of £20,000, payable in arrears on 25 September each year, increasing to £22,000 with effect from 26 September 1995. On 25 September 1997, E Ltd buys the freehold from B Ltd, and the letting agreement therefore terminates. B Ltd prepares accounts to 31 March and E Ltd to 31 August.

Schedule D, Case I deductions claimed by E Ltd are as follows

Y/e 31.8.96

Paid 25.9.95	20,000
Less accrued at 31.8.95 £20,000 × $\dfrac{340}{365}$	(18,630)
Add accrued at 31.8.96 £22,000 × $\dfrac{340}{365}$	20,493
	£21,863

Y/e 31.8.97

Paid 25.9.96	22,000
Less accrued at 31.8.96	(20,493)
Add accrued at 31.8.97 £22,000 × $\dfrac{340}{365}$	20,493
	£22,000

Y/e 31.8.98

Paid 25.9.97	22,000
Less accrued at 31.8.97 £22,000 × $\dfrac{340}{365}$	(20,493)
	£1,507

The gross rents to be included in B Ltd's Schedule A computation are as follows

Y/e 31.3.96

Rent receivable 25.9.95	20,000
Less accrued at 31.3.95 £20,000 × $\dfrac{187}{365}$	(10,247)
Add accrued at 31.3.96 £22,000 × $\dfrac{187}{365}$	11,271
	£21,024

Y/e 31.3.97

Rent accruing for the year	£22,000

Y/e 31.3.98

Rent receivable 25.9.97	22,000
Less accrued at 31.3.97 £22,000 × $\dfrac{187}{365}$	(11,271)
	£10,729

CT 122.3 Schedule A — Property Income

Notes

Notes

(a) Under *Sec 33A*, certain Schedule A rents accruing after 9 March 1992 are chargeable on an accruals basis rather than a receivable basis. This applies generally to rents receivable from a connected person (within *ICTA 1988, s 839*) who can claim a deduction for them in computing taxable profits, where such rents are payable in arrears such that all or part of them accrue in a chargeable period of the recipient earlier than that in which they are receivable.

(b) Similar principles apply where, broadly, an unconnected third party, C, is interposed between the two connected persons A and B, such that A pays rent to C who in turn pays rent to B. [*ICTA 1988, s 33B; F(No 2)A 1992, s 57*].

122.3 EXPENSES AND DEFICIENCIES DEDUCTIBLE [*ICTA 1988, ss 25, 31*]

C Ltd lets out the following properties

Shop to F at full rent of £1,000 p.a., expenses £1,500 (landlord repairing lease)
Factory to G at full rent of £5,000 p.a., expenses £2,000 (landlord repairing lease)
Shop to H at full rent of £1,000 p.a., expenses £4,000 (tenant's repairing lease)
Shop to J at full rent of £6,000 p.a., expenses £500 (tenant's repairing lease)
House to K at less than full rent let at £200 p.a., expenses £500

The Schedule A position will be as follows

	Landlord repairing leases		Tenant's repairing leases		Lease at less than full rent
	£	£	£	£	£
Rents	1,000	5,000	1,000	6,000	200
Deduct Expenses	1,500	2,000	4,000	500	500
Profit/(Loss)	(500)	3,000	(3,000)	5,500	(300)
Set-off	500	(500)	—	—	—
		2,500			
Set-off		(2,500)	2,500	—	—
Assessment		—	—	£5,500	—
Losses carried forward			£(500)	—	£(300)

Notes

(a) Losses on landlord repairing leases may be set off against profits on other such leases.

(b) A loss on a tenant's repairing lease may be set off against profits on landlord repairing leases.

(c) A loss on a lease at less than full rent can be carried forward only to the end of that lease.

123   Small Companies Rate

123.1 MARGINAL RELIEF [*ICTA 1988, s 13; FA 1994, s 86; FA 1996, s 78*]

(A)

In its accounting period 1 April 1996 to 31 March 1997, X Ltd, a trading company, has chargeable profits of £300,000 including chargeable gains of £40,000, and also has franked investment income of £75,000 (representing net distributions received of £60,000). X Ltd has no associated companies.

Corporation tax payable is calculated as follows

	£
Corporation tax at full rate of 33% on £300,000	99,000
$\frac{9}{400} \times £(1,500,000 - 375,000) \times \dfrac{300,000}{375,000}$	20,250
Corporation tax payable	£78,750

Note

(*a*)   Marginal relief applies as profits, including franked investment income, fall between the lower and upper limits of £300,000 and £1,500,000 respectively.

(B)

In its accounting period 1 April 1996 to 31 March 1997, Y Ltd, a trading company, has chargeable profits of £375,000 including chargeable gains of £40,000, but has no franked investment income. Y Ltd has no associated companies.

Corporation tax payable is calculated as follows

	£
Corporation tax at full rate of 33% on £375,000	123,750.00
$\frac{9}{400} \times £(1,500,000 - 375,000)$	25,312.50
Corporation tax payable	£98,437.50

Note

(*a*)   An alternative method of calculation, where there is no franked investment income, is to apply small companies rate up to the small companies rate limit and marginal rate (35% for FY 1995) to the balance of profits. Thus

	£
£300,000 at 24%	72,000.00
75,000 at 35.25%	26,437.50
£375,000	£98,437.50

CT 123.1 Small Companies Rate

(C) Changes in relevant maximum amounts [*ICTA 1988, s 13(3)(6); FA 1994, s 86*]
In its accounting period 1 January 1994 to 31 December 1994, Z Ltd has chargeable profits of £540,000 and franked investment income of £60,000. Z Ltd has no associated companies.

Corporation tax payable is calculated as follows

Part of the accounting period falling in financial year 1993

			£	£
Profits	$\frac{3}{12} \times £600,000$	= £150,000		
Basic profits $\frac{3}{12} \times £540,000$		= £135,000		
Lower relevant maximum		= £62,500	note (*b*)	

Corporation tax at full rate
£135,000 at 33%   44,550.00

Less marginal relief   41,625.00

$\frac{1}{50} \times £(312,500 - 150,000) \times \dfrac{135,000}{150,000}$ 2,925.00

Part of the accounting period falling in financial year 1994

Profits	$\frac{9}{12} \times £600,000$	= £450,000
Basic profits $\frac{9}{12} \times £540,000$		= £405,000
Lower relevant maximum		= £225,000 note (*b*)

Corporation tax at full rate
£405,000 at 33%   133,650.00

Less marginal relief

$\frac{1}{50} \times £(1,125,000 - 450,000) \times \dfrac{405,000}{450,000}$ 12,150.00   121,500.00

Corporation tax payable   £163,125.00

Notes

(*a*)   Where the relevant maximum amounts change from one financial year to the next, an accounting period which overlaps the end of the first such year is treated as if the part before and the part after were separate accounting periods.

(*b*)   The relevant maximum and minimum amounts are proportionately reduced for an actual or notional accounting period of less than twelve months.

Upper relevant maximum amount
Financial year 1993 $\frac{3}{12} \times £1,250,000 = £312,500$
Financial year 1994 $\frac{9}{12} \times £1,500,000 = £1,125,000$

Lower relevant maximum amount
Financial year 1993 $\frac{3}{12} \times £250,000 = £62,500$
Financial year 1994 $\frac{9}{12} \times £300,000 = £225,000$

(*c*)   Note that for Financial year 1993, franked investment income is calculated, for the purposes of the marginal relief computation, as if the ACT rate for that year was one-quarter rather than nine thirty-firsts. [*FA 1993, s 78(6)*].

123.2 **A COMPANY WITH AN ASSOCIATED COMPANY OR COMPANIES** [*ICTA 1988, s 13(3)-(7); FA 1994, s 86; FA 1996, s 78*]

(A)

C Ltd has a 51% subsidiary, D Ltd. Both companies are resident in the UK. C Ltd had previously prepared accounts to 31 March but changes its accounting date and prepares accounts for the nine-month period to 31 December 1996. Its chargeable profits for that period amount to £480,000. It also receives franked investment income of £84,000 including £24,000 representing dividends from D Ltd. No group income election under *ICTA 1988, s 247* is in force. At no time in the accounting period to 31 December 1996 does C Ltd have any active associated companies other than D Ltd.

Corporation tax payable by C Ltd for the period to 31 December 1996 is calculated as follows

	£
Corporation tax at full rate of 33% on £480,000	158,400
$\frac{9}{400} \times £(562,500 - 540,000) \times \dfrac{480,000}{540,000}$	450
Corporation tax payable	£157,950

Notes

(a) The relevant maximum and minimum amounts are proportionately reduced for accounting periods of less than twelve months and further reduced where the company has associated companies (other than dormant ones) at any time during the accounting period.

Upper relevant maximum amount
$\frac{9}{12} \times \frac{1}{2} \times £1,500,000 = £562,500$

Lower relevant maximum amount
$\frac{9}{12} \times \frac{1}{2} \times £300,000 = £112,500$

(b) Profits for these purposes do not include distributions from within the group where a group income election under *ICTA 1988, s 247* (i.e. an election to pay dividends without accounting for ACT) has or could have been made. [*ICTA 1988, s 13(7)*]. Thus, the £24,000 franked investment income received from D Ltd is omitted from the calculations in this example.

(B) Changes in relevant maximum amounts

A Ltd has chargeable profits of £200,000 for the 12-month accounting period ended 30 September 1994 and has no franked investment income. It had no associated company until 1 March 1994 when all of its share capital was acquired by a company, B Ltd, with three wholly-owned subsidiaries, of which one was dormant throughout the 12-month period and another was resident overseas. B Ltd acquired a further active subsidiary on 1 May 1994.

CT 123.2 Small Companies Rate

Corporation tax payable by A Ltd is calculated as follows

Part of the accounting period falling in financial year 1993

		£	£
Profits $\frac{6}{12}$ × £200,000	= £100,000		
Lower relevant maximum	= £31,250 note (*b*)		
Upper relevant maximum	= £156,250 note (*b*)		
Corporation tax at full rate			
£100,000 at 33%		33,000.00	
Less marginal relief			
$\frac{1}{50}$ × £(156,250 − 100,000)		1,125.00	31,875.00

Part of the accounting period falling in financial year 1994

		£	£
Profits $\frac{6}{12}$ × £200,000	= £100,000		
Lower relevant maximum	= £30,000 note (*b*)		
Upper relevant maximum	= £150,000 note (*b*)		
Corporation tax at full rate			
£100,000 at 33%		33,000.00	
Less marginal relief			
$\frac{1}{50}$ × £(150,000 − 100,000)		1,000.00	32,000.00
Corporation tax payable			£63,875.00

Notes

(*a*)   Where the relevant maximum amounts change from one financial year to the next, an accounting period which overlaps the end of the first such year is treated as if the part before and the part after were separate accounting periods.

(*b*)   The relevant maximum and minimum amounts are proportionately reduced for an actual or notional accounting period of less than twelve months and also where the company has associated companies (other than dormant ones) at any time during the accounting period.

Upper relevant maximum amount
Financial year 1993 $\frac{6}{12} \times \frac{1}{4} \times$ £1,250,000 = £156,250
Financial year 1994 $\frac{6}{12} \times \frac{1}{5} \times$ £1,500,000 = £150,000

Lower relevant maximum amount
Financial year 1993 $\frac{6}{12} \times \frac{1}{4} \times$ £250,000 =   £31,250
Financial year 1994 $\frac{6}{12} \times \frac{1}{5} \times$ £300,000 =   £30,000

For FY 1993, the number of active associated companies, including A Ltd, is four (A Ltd, B Ltd and two other subsidiaries of B Ltd). For FY 1994, the figure is increased to five by B Ltd's further acquisition.

(*c*)   Small companies relief and marginal relief are not given automatically, but must be claimed. The claim must include a statement of the number of associated companies, or a statement that there were none, in the relevant accounting period. (Revenue Statement of Practice SP 1/91). The claim may be made by completing the relevant boxes of the corporation tax return CT 200.

Capital Gains Tax

201   Annual Rates and Exemptions

201.1 **GAINS CHARGEABLE AT INCOME TAX RATES** [*TCGA 1992, s 4; F(No 2)A 1992, s 23; FA 1993, 6 Sch 22*]

(A) General

M, a single person and sole trader, had trading income of £26,000 for the year ended 30 April 1995, but made a trading loss of £11,000 for the year ended 30 April 1996. He had no other source of income, but realised a capital gain of £33,300 in 1996/97 from the sale of a country cottage. He claims relief for the trading loss under *ICTA 1988, s 380(1)* against his income for 1996/97.

M's income tax position for 1996/97 is as follows

	£
Schedule D, Case I	13,000
Less: Loss relief	11,000
	2,000
Less: Personal allowance (maximum £3,765)	2,000
Taxable income	Nil

His capital gains tax computation is as follows

	£
Gain	33,300
Annual exemption	6,300
Gain chargeable to tax	£27,000

Capital gains tax payable	£
£3,900 at 20%	780.00
21,600 at 24%	5,184.00
1,500 at 40%	600.00
£27,000	£6,564.00

Note

(a)   Capital gains are charged at income tax rates as if they formed the top slice of taxable income (subject to (B) below). The unused personal allowance of £1,765 is not available to reduce the chargeable gain. If M's trading losses had exceeded his total income, he could have claimed, under *FA 1991, s 72*, to have the gain reduced by the unused losses (see 10.2 LOSSES).

(b)   **1996/97** (transitional year)

	£
Y/e 30.4.95	26.000
Y/e 30.4.96	Nil
	26,000
1996/97 assessable profits £26,000 × $\frac{12}{24}$	13,000

(B) With dividend income otherwise within the lower rate band

N, a single person, has the following income and gains for 1996/97

	£
Dividends (net)	18,080
Schedule D, Case I	4,325
Capital gains	9,800

Disregarding the capital gains, N's income tax liability is computed as follows

	£	£
Dividends	18,080	
Tax credits (£18,080 × $\frac{1}{4}$)	4,520	22,600
Schedule D, Case I		4,325
		26,925
Deduct Personal allowance		3,765
Taxable income		£23,160

Tax payable:	
£560 @ 20% (lower rate band — maximum £3,900)	112.00
22,600 @ 20% (dividend income)	4,520.00
	4,632.00
Tax credits (£22,600 × 20%)	4,520.00
Net liability	£112.00

Because part (£3,340) of the lower rate band of £3,900 is unused (other than by dividend income chargeable at 20% in any case), the income tax position is revised, and the capital gains position computed, as follows

Income tax position (basic rate limit reduced by £3,340)

Taxable income as above	£23,160

Tax payable:	
£560 @ 20% (lower rate band)	112.00
21,600 @ 20% (dividend income)	4,320.00
22,160	
1,000 @ 40% (dividend income)	400.00
	4,832.00
Tax credits as above	4,520.00
Net liability	£312.00

CGT 201.1 Annual Rates and Exemptions

Capital gains position

	£
Capital gains	9,800
Deduct Annual exemption	6,300
Taxable gains	£3,500

Tax payable:	
£3,340 @ 20% (unused part of lower rate band)	668.00
160 @ 40% (taxable income exceeds revised basic rate limit)	64.00
CGT liability	£732.00

Total net liability £(312 + 732)   £1,044.00

202 Anti-Avoidance

202.1 **VALUE SHIFTING** [*TCGA 1992, s 29*]

J owns the whole £1,000 £1 ordinary shares of K Ltd. The shares were acquired on subscription in 1968 for £1,000 and had a value of £99,000 on 31 March 1982. In December 1996, the trustees of J's family settlement subscribed at par for 3,000 £1 ordinary shares in K Ltd, thereby acquiring 75% of the voting power in the company. It is agreed that the price an unconnected party would have paid for 75% of the equity in a transaction at arm's length is £150,000. J's remaining 25% holding is valued at £15,000.

J will have a capital gain for 1996/97 as follows (subject to indexation allowance)

	£
Proceeds of deemed disposal	150,000
Allowable cost $\dfrac{150,000}{150,000 + 15,000} \times £99,000$	90,000
Unindexed gain	£60,000

202.2 **VALUE-SHIFTING TO GIVE TAX-FREE BENEFIT** [*TCGA 1992, s 30, 11 Sch 10(1)*]

M owns the whole of the issued share capital in C Ltd, an unquoted company. He is also a director of the company. M receives an offer of £100,000 from a public company for his shares. Prior to sale, C Ltd pays M £30,000 for loss of his office as director.

On the sale of M's shares, the Inland Revenue may seek to adjust the consideration in computing M's chargeable gain on the grounds that M has received a tax-free benefit and the value of his shares has been materially reduced.

202.3 **VALUE SHIFTING: DISTRIBUTION WITHIN A GROUP FOLLOWED BY A DISPOSAL OF SHARES** [*TCGA 1992, ss 30, 31, 11 Sch 10(2)*]

Topco Ltd owns 100% of A Ltd, which owns 100% of B Ltd. Both A and B were acquired for negligible amounts. A bought some land in 1984 for a relatively small sum. It is now worth £100,000. In an attempt to realise the proceeds of the land at a tax saving, Topco arranges for B to borrow £100,000. In June 1995, A sells the land to B for this amount, and A, which previously had no undistributed reserves, then pays a dividend of £100,000 to Topco. No ACT is payable as there is a group election under *ICTA 1988, s 247* in force. Topco then sells all of its shares in A Ltd to an unconnected person at their market value which is now a nominal sum.

On the sale of the A Ltd shares, the Revenue may seek to apply *TCGA 1992, ss 30, 31* to increase the consideration on the sale by Topco Ltd to £100,000.

202.4 **ASSETS DISPOSED OF IN A SERIES OF TRANSACTIONS** [*TCGA 1992, ss 19, 20*]

L purchased a set of 6 antique chairs in 1980 at a cost of £7,200. He gave 2 chairs to his daughter in February 1990, another pair to his son in November 1993, and sold the final pair to his brother for their market value in August 1996.

The market value of the chairs at the relevant dates were

	2 chairs	4 chairs	6 chairs
	£	£	£
February 1990	6,000	14,000	26,000
November 1993	7,800	18,000	34,200
August 1996	10,400	24,000	46,200

The market value of the set of 6 chairs at 31 March 1982 was £12,000. L has elected under *TCGA 1992, s 35(5)* for all his assets held at 31 March 1982 to be regarded as having been disposed of and re-acquired at market value on that date.

Indexation factors are

March 1982 – February 1990	0.513
March 1982 – November 1993	0.782
March 1982 – August 1996 (assumed)	0.890

The capital gains tax computations are as follows

February 1990
Disposal to daughter

Deemed consideration	£6,000

As the consideration does not exceed £6,000, the disposal is covered by the chattel exemption (see note (*a*)).

November 1993
(i)   *1989/90 disposal to daughter recomputed*

Original market value (deemed disposal consideration at February 1990)	£6,000
Reasonable proportion of aggregate market value as at February 1990 of all assets disposed of to date £14,000 × $\frac{2}{4}$	£7,000

	£
Deemed consideration (greater of £6,000 and £7,000)	7,000
31.3.82 value $\dfrac{6,000}{6,000 + 14,000}$ × £12,000	3,600
Unindexed gain	3,400
Indexation allowance £3,600 × 0.513	1,847
Chargeable gain 1989/90	£1,553

(ii)   *1993/94 disposal to son*

Original market value (deemed disposal consideration)	£7,800

Reasonable proportion of aggregate market value as at
November 1993 of all assets disposed of to date
£18,000 × $\frac{2}{4}$ £9,000

	£
Deemed consideration (greater of £9,000 and £7,800)	9,000

31.3.82 value $\dfrac{7,800}{7,800 + 7,800}$ × (£12,000 – £3,600)   4,200

Unindexed gain	4,800
Indexation allowance £4,200 × 0.782	3,284
Chargeable gain 1993/94	£1,516

August 1996
(i)   *Gain on 1989/90 disposal to daughter recomputed*

Original market value (deemed consideration in
recomputation at November 1993)   £7,000

Reasonable proportion of aggregate market value as at
February 1990 of all assets disposed of to date
£26,000 × $\frac{2}{6}$ £8,667

	£
Deemed consideration (greater of £8,667 and £7,000)	8,667
31.3.82 value (as before)	3,600
Unindexed gain	5,067
Indexation allowance (as before)	1,847
Revised chargeable gain 1988/89	£3,220

(ii)   *Gain on 1993/94 disposal to son recomputed*

Original market value (deemed consideration in computation at
November 1993)   £9,000

Reasonable proportion of aggregate market value as at
November 1993 of all assets disposed of to date
£34,200 × $\frac{2}{6}$ £11,400

	£
Deemed consideration (greater of £9,000 and £11,400)	11,400
31.3.82 value (as before)	4,200
Unindexed gain	7,200
Indexation allowance (as before)	3,284
Revised chargeable gain 1993/94	£3,916

(iii) *Gain on 1996/97 disposal to brother*

Original market value (actual consideration)	£10,400
Reasonable proportion of aggregate market value as at August 1996 of all assets disposed of to date £46,200 × $\frac{2}{6}$	£15,400

	£
Deemed consideration (greater of £10,400 and £15,400)	15,400
31.3.82 value (£12,000 − £3,600 − £4,200)	4,200
Unindexed gain	11,200
Indexation allowance £4,200 × 0.890	3,738
Chargeable gain 1996/97	£7,462

Notes

(a)   The disposal in February 1990 is at first covered by the chattel exemption of £6,000. As the second disposal in November 1993 is to a person connected with the recipient of the first disposal, the two must then be looked at together for the purposes of the chattel exemption, and, as the combined proceeds exceed the chattel exemption limit, the exemption is not available. [*TCGA 1992, s 262*]. See also 208.1(C) EXEMPTIONS AND RELIEFS.

(b)   The three disposals are linked transactions within *TCGA 1992, s 19* as they are made by the same transferor to persons with whom he is connected, and take place within a six-year period.

(c)   It is assumed in the above example that it is 'reasonable' to apportion the aggregate market value in proportion to the number of items. In other instances a different basis may be needed to give the 'reasonable' apportionment required by *TCGA 1992, s 20(4)*.

202.5 **DEPRECIATORY TRANSACTIONS: GROUPS OF COMPANIES** [*TCGA 1992, s 176*]

G Ltd owns 100% of the share capital of Q Ltd, which it acquired in June 1983 for £75,000. Q Ltd owns land which it purchased in 1979 for £50,000. In 1988, the land, then with a market value of £120,000, was transferred to G Ltd for £50,000. In April 1996, Q Ltd was put into liquidation, and G Ltd received liquidation distributions totalling £30,000.

The loss on the Q Ltd shares is £45,000 (£75,000 − £30,000). The Inland Revenue will be likely to disallow the whole or part of the loss on the grounds that it resulted from the depreciatory transaction involving the transfer of land at less than market value.

Note

(a)   For disposals after 5 April 1988 on which the gain or loss is computed by reference to 31 March 1982 value, depreciatory transactions before 31 March 1982 (not illustrated in this example) are not taken into account.

203   Assets held on 6 April 1965

203.1 **QUOTED SHARES AND SECURITIES** [*TCGA 1992, s 109(4)(5), 2 Sch 1–8*]

(A) Basic computation of gain

H acquired 3,000 U plc ordinary shares in 1962 for £15,000. Their market value was £10 per share on 6 April 1965 and £12 per share on 31 March 1982. In September 1996, H sells 2,000 of the shares for £25 per share. The indexation factor for March 1982 to September 1996 is assumed to be 0.895.

	£	£	£
Sale proceeds	50,000	50,000	50,000
Cost	10,000		
6 April 1965 value		20,000	
31 March 1982 value			24,000
Unindexed gain	40,000	30,000	26,000
Indexation allowance			
£24,000 × 0.895	21,480	21,480	21,480
Indexed gain	£18,520	£8,520	£4,520
Chargeable gain			£4,520

Notes

(*a*)   The comparison is firstly between the gain arrived at by deducting cost and that arrived at by deducting 6 April 1965 value. The smaller of the two gains is taken. If, however, an election had been made under either *TCGA 1992, 2 Sch 4* or *TCGA 1992, s 109(4)* for 6 April 1965 value to be used in computing all gains and losses on quoted shares held at that date, this comparison need not be made and the taxable gain, subject to (*b*) below, would be £8,520.

(*b*)   The second comparison is between the figure arrived at in (*a*) above and the gain using 31 March 1982 value. As the latter is smaller, it is substituted for the figure in (*a*) above by virtue of *TCGA 1992, s 35(2)*. If, however, an election had been made under *TCGA 1992, s 35(5)* for 31 March 1982 value to be used in computing all gains and losses on assets held at that date, neither this comparison nor that in (*a*) above need be made and the taxable gain would still be £4,520.

(*c*)   Indexation is based on 31 March 1982 value in all three calculations as this gives the greater allowance. [*TCGA 1992, s 55(1)(2)*].

(*d*)   All comparisons are between gains *after* indexation.

(B) Basic computation—no gain/no loss disposals

J acquired a holding of quoted shares in 1950 for £1,000. The market value of the holding at 6 April 1965 and 31 March 1982 respectively was £19,000 and £20,000. J sells the holding in September 1996 for £18,000. The indexation factor for the period March 1982 to September 1996 is assumed to be 0.895.

CGT 203.1 Assets held on 6 April 1965

(i) Assuming no elections made to use 1965 value or 1982 value

	£	£
Sale proceeds	18,000	18,000
Cost	1,000	
6 April 1965 value		19,000
Unindexed gain/(loss)	17,000	(1,000)
Indexation allowance		
£20,000 × 0.895 = £17,900 but restricted to	17,000	—
Indexed gain/(loss)	£Nil	£(1,000)
Chargeable gain/allowable loss		Nil

As one computation shows no gain/no loss and the other a loss, the disposal is a no gain/no loss disposal. [*TCGA 1992, 2 Sch 2(1)*]. There is no need to compute the gain or loss using 31 March 1982 value as re-basing cannot disturb a no gain/no loss position. [*TCGA 1992, s 35(3)(c)*].

(ii) Election made to use 6 April 1965 value

	£	£
Sale proceeds	18,000	18,000
6 April 1965 value	19,000	
31 March 1982 value		20,000
(Loss)	(1,000)	(2,000)
Allowable loss	£1,000	

The allowable loss is £1,000 as re-basing cannot increase a loss. [*TCGA 1992, s 35(3)(b)*].

(iii) Election made to use 31 March 1982 value

There is an allowable loss of £2,000.

(C) Parts of holding acquired at different times
L has the following transactions in shares of A plc, a quoted company

Date	Number of shares bought/(sold)	Cost/ (proceeds) £
9.1.55	1,500	1,050
10.11.62	750	600
15.7.69	1,200	3,000
12.10.80	1,400	5,000
16.12.83	850	5,950
17.9.87	1,150	9,200
19.12.96	(6,000)	(51,000)

Market value of A shares at 6 April 1965 was £1.60.
Market value of A shares at 31 March 1982 was £4.00.

Indexation factors		
	March 1982 to April 1995	0.876
	December 1983 to April 1985	0.091
	April 1985 to September 1987	0.080
	September 1987 to December 1996 (assumed)	0.455

(i) No election made to substitute 1965 market value

Identify 6,000 shares sold on a LIFO basis as follows

New holding	Shares	Qualifying Expenditure £	Indexed Pool £
16.12.83 acquisition	850	5,950	5,950
£5,950 × 0.091			541
6.4.85 pool	850	5,950	6,491
Indexed rise: April 1985 to September 1987			
£6,491 × 0.080			519
17.9.87 acquisition	1,150	9,200	9,200
	2,000	15,150	16,210
Indexed rise: September 1987 to December 1996			
£16,210 × 0.455			7,376
			23,586
19.12.96 disposal	(2,000)	(15,150)	(23,586)
Balance of pool	—	—	—

	£
Sale proceeds (2,000 × £8.50)	17,000
Cost (as above)	15,150
Unindexed gain	1,850
Indexation allowance (£23,586 − £15,150 = £8,436)	
but restricted to	(1,850)
	Nil

1982 holding	£	£
Sale proceeds (1,200 + 1,400) × £8.50	22,100	22,100
Cost (£3,000 + £5,000)	8,000	
Market value 31.3.82 (2,600 × £4)		10,400
Unindexed gain	14,100	11,700
Indexation allowance £10,400 × 0.876	9,110	9,110
Gain after indexation	£4,990	£2,590
Chargeable gain		£2,590

10.11.62 acquisition	£	£	£
Sale proceeds (750 × £8.50)	6,375	6,375	6,375
Cost	600		
Market value 6.4.65 (750 × £1.60)		1,200	
Market value 31.3.82 (750 × £4)			3,000
Unindexed gain	5,775	5,175	3,375
Indexation allowance £3,000 × 0.876	2,628	2,628	2,628
Gain after indexation	£3,147	£2,547	£747
Chargeable gain			£747

9.1.55 acquisition (part)	£	£	£
Sale proceeds (650 × £8.50)	5,525	5,525	5,525
Cost (650 × £0.70)	455		
Market value 6.4.65 (650 × £1.60)		1,040	
Market value 31.3.82 (650 × £4)			2,600
Unindexed gain	5,070	4,485	2,925
Indexation allowance £2,600 × 0.876	2,278	2,278	2,278
Gain after indexation	£2,792	£2,207	£647
Chargeable gain			£647

Summary of chargeable gains (allowable losses)	Number of shares	Chargeable gain £
New holding	2,000	—
1982 holding	2,600	2,590
10.11.62 acquisition	750	747
9.1.55 acquisition (part)	650	647
	6,000	£3,984

Remaining shares
850 acquired on 9.1.55 for £595

(ii) Election made to substitute 1965 market value

Identify 6,000 shares on a LIFO basis as follows

New holding
Disposal of 2,000 shares as in (i) above   Nil

1982 holding	Shares		Pool cost £
9.1.55	1,500 × £1.60		2,400
10.11.62	750 × £1.60		1,200
15.7.69	1,200		3,000
12.10.80	1,400		5,000
	4,850		11,600
19.12.96 Disposal	4,000	4,000/4,850 × £11,600	9,567
Remaining shares	850		£2,033

	£	£
Sale proceeds (4,000 × £8.50)	34,000	34,000
Cost (as above)	9,567	
Market value 31.3.82 (4,000 × £4)		16,000
Unindexed gain	24,433	18,000
Indexation allowance £16,000 × 0.876	14,016	14,016
Gain after indexation	£10,417	£3,984
Chargeable gain		£3,984

Summary of chargeable gains/allowable losses	Number of shares	Chargeable gain/(loss) £
New holding	2,000	—
1982 holding	4,000	3,984
	6,000	£3,984

Notes

(*a*)   Because re-basing to 31 March 1982 applies in this case, the result is the same whether or not the election to substitute 6 April 1965 value has been made, but with a lower 31 March 1982 value the computations could produce differing overall gains/losses.

(*b*)   Note that indexation is based on 31 March 1982 value whenever this gives the greater allowance, and that comparisons are between gains *after* indexation.

203.2   **LAND REFLECTING DEVELOPMENT VALUE** [*TCGA 1992, 2 Sch 9–15*]

K sells a building plot, on which planning permission has just been obtained, in November 1995 for £200,000. He acquired the plot by gift from his father in 1954 when its value was £2,000. The market value was £5,000 at 6 April 1965 and £10,000 at 31 March 1982, and the current use value in November 1996 is £15,000. The indexation factor for March 1982 to November 1996 is assumed to be 0.900.

	£	£	£
Sale proceeds	200,000	200,000	200,000
Cost	2,000		
Market value 6.4.65		5,000	
Market value 31.3.82			10,000
Unindexed gain	198,000	195,000	190,000
Indexation allowance £10,000 × 0.900	9,000	9,000	9,000
Gain after indexation	£189,000	£186,000	£181,000
Chargeable gain			£181,000

Notes

(*a*)   Time apportionment would have substantially reduced the gain of £189,000, using cost, such that re-basing to 31 March 1982 would have given a greater gain than that based on cost and would not therefore have applied. However, as the plot has been sold for a price in excess of its current use value, no time apportionment can be claimed.

(*b*)   Gains are compared after applying the indexation allowance, which is based on 31 March 1982 value, this being greater than either cost or 6 April 1965 value.

203.3 **OTHER ASSETS** [*TCGA 1992, 2 Sch 16–19*]

(A) Chattels

M inherited a painting on the death of his mother in 1943, when it was valued for probate at £5,000. On 5 October 1996 he sold the painting for £250,000 net. The painting's value was £130,000 at 6 April 1965, but only £125,000 at 31 March 1982. The indexation factor for March 1982 to October 1996 is assumed to be 0.898.

(i) Time apportionment

Period of ownership since 6 April 1945	51 years 6 months
Period of ownership since 6 April 1965	31 years 6 months

	£
Unindexed gain (£250,000 − £5,000)	245,000
Indexation allowance £125,000 × 0.898 note (*b*)	112,250
	£132,750

$$\text{Gain after indexation } £132,750 \times \frac{31y\ 6m}{51y\ 6m} \quad \text{note } (c) \qquad £81,197$$

(ii) Election for 6.4.65 value

	£
Sale proceeds	250,000
Market value 6.4.65	130,000
Unindexed gain	120,000
Indexation allowance £130,000 × 0.898 note (*b*)	116,740
Gain after indexation	£3,260

Election for 6.4.65 value is beneficial, subject to re-basing.

(iii) Re-basing to 1982

	£
Sale proceeds	250,000
Market value 31.3.82	125,000
Unindexed gain	125,000
Indexation allowance £130,000 × 0.898 note (*b*)	116,740
Gain after indexation	£8,260

Re-basing cannot increase a gain. [*TCGA 1992, s 35(3)(a)*]. **Therefore, the gain of £3,260 stands and the election for 6.4.65 value is beneficial.**

Notes

(*a*) Under time apportionment, the period of ownership is limited to that after 5 April 1945.

(*b*) In (i) above, indexation is based on 31.3.82 value, being greater than cost — it cannot be based on 6 April 1965 value as this does not enter into the calculation. In (ii), indexation is on the higher of 31.3.82 value and 6.4.65 value. This is also the case in (iii) as one is comparing the position using 6.4.65 value and 31.3.82 value. See *TCGA 1992, s 55(1)(2)*.

(*c*) The time apportionment calculation is applied to the gain *after* indexation (*Smith v Schofield H/L*, [*1993*] *STC 268*).

(B) Land and buildings

X acquired land on 5 June 1959 as a distribution in specie on liquidation of his company. The value of the land was then £8,500. He acquired access land adjoining the property for £500 on 1 January 1960 and, having obtained planning consent, on 30 July 1962 incurred expenditure of £16,000 in building houses on the land, which were let. On 6 September 1996, X sells the houses with vacant possession for £300,000, net of expenses. The value of the houses and land is £20,000 at 6 April 1965 and £210,000 at 31 March 1982. The indexation factor for March 1982 to September 1996 is assumed to be 0.895.

The gain using time apportionment is

	£	£
Net proceeds of sale		300,000
Deduct Cost of land	8,500	
Cost of addition	500	
Cost of building	16,000	25,000
Unindexed gain		275,000
Indexation allowance £210,000 × 0.895		187,950
Gain after indexation		£87,050

Apportion to allowable expenditure   note (*c*)

	£	£
(i) Land $\dfrac{8,500}{25,000} \times £87,050$	29,597	
Time apportion £29,597 × $\dfrac{31\text{y 5m}}{37\text{y 3m}}$		24,962
(ii) Addition $\dfrac{500}{25,000} \times £87,050$	1,741	
Time apportion £1,741 × $\dfrac{31\text{y 5m}}{36\text{y 8m}}$		1,492
(iii) Building $\dfrac{16,000}{25,000} \times £87,050$	55,712	
Time apportion £55,712 × $\dfrac{31\text{y 5m}}{34\text{y 1m}}$		51,353
Gain after indexation and time apportionment		£77,807

The gain using re-basing to 1982 is

	£
Net proceeds of sale	300,000
Market value at 31.3.82	210,000
Unindexed gain	90,000
Indexation allowance	
£210,000 × 0.895 = £187,950 but restricted to	90,000
Gain/loss	Nil
The chargeable gain/allowable loss is	Nil

CGT 203.3   Assets held on 6 April 1965

Notes

(a)   An election for 6 April 1965 valuation could not be favourable, even were it not for the effect of re-basing, as the value is less than historic costs.

(b)   As one calculation produces a gain and the other no gain/no loss, neither a gain nor a loss arises. Whilst it makes no difference in this example, it is the gain/loss *after* time apportionment that is compared with the gain/loss produced by re-basing. [*TCGA 1992, s 35(2)–(4), 3 Sch 6*].

(c)   The time apportionment calculation is applied to the gain *after* indexation (*Smith v Schofield H/L*, [*1993*] *STC 268*).

(C) Unquoted shares — share exchange before 6 April 1965 [*TCGA 1992, 2 Sch 19(1)(3)*]

N purchased 5,000 £1 ordinary shares in R Ltd, an unquoted company, on 1 January 1961. The purchase price was £3 per share, a total of £15,000. On 1 December 1964, R Ltd was acquired by D Ltd, an unquoted company, as a result of which N received 10,000 8% convertible preference shares in D Ltd in exchange for his holding of R shares. In November 1996, N sold the D Ltd shares for £4.25 per share. The market value of the D Ltd shares was £2.03 per share at 6 April 1965 but only £1.50 per share at 31 March 1982. The indexation factor for March 1982 to November 1996 is assumed to be 0.900.

The loss, disregarding re-basing, is

		£
Disposal consideration 10,000 at £4.25		42,500
Allowable cost	10,000 at £2.03	20,300
Unindexed gain		22,200
Indexation allowance £20,300 × 0.900		18,270
Gain after indexation		£3,930

The gain using re-basing to 1982 is

	£
Disposal consideration (as above)	42,500
Market value 31.3.82 10,000 at £1.50	15,000
Unindexed gain	27,500
Indexation allowance £20,300 × 0.900	18,270
Gain after indexation	£9,230

The overall result is

	£
Chargeable gain	£3,930

Notes

(a)   Subject to re-basing, allowable cost must be taken as 6.4.65 value.

(b)   Indexation is based on the greater of 31.3.82 value and 6.4.65 value. [*TCGA 1992, s 55(1)(2)*].

(c)   Where the effect of re-basing would be to increase a gain, re-basing does not apply. [*TCGA 1992, s 35(3)(a)*].

(D) Unquoted shares — share exchange after 5 April 1965 [*TCGA 1992, 2 Sch 19(2)(3)*]

S purchased 10,000 £1 ordinary shares in L Ltd for £5,000 on 31 May 1959. The shares are not quoted, and their value at 6 April 1965 was £6,000. On 1 September 1983, the shares were acquired by R plc, in exchange for its own ordinary shares on the basis of 1 for 2. The offer valued L ordinary shares at £2.23 per share. In February 1997, S sells his 5,000 R shares for £8.20 per share. The agreed value of the L Ltd shares at 31 March 1982 was £2.05 per share.

Indexation factors	March 1982 to September 1983 (actual)	0.083
	March 1982 to February 1997 (assumed)	0.913

The gain without re-basing to 1982 is

	£	£
Disposal consideration 5,000 at £8.20		41,000
Allowable cost		5,000
Unindexed gain		36,000
Indexation allowance 10,000 × £2.05 × 0.913		18,717
		17,283
Less gain subject to time apportionment		
Market value at 1.9.83	22,300	
Allowable cost	5,000	
	17,300	
Indexation allowance to 1.9.83 £5,000 × 0.083	415	
	£16,885	16,885
		398
Add chargeable part of time apportioned gain		
Chargeable part of gain $\dfrac{18\text{y }5\text{m}}{24\text{y }3\text{m}} \times £16,885$		12,823
Gain		£13,221

If S elected for 6.4.65 value to apply, the computation would be

	£
Disposal consideration	41,000
Allowable cost	6,000
Unindexed gain	35,000
Indexation allowance 10,000 × £2.05 × 0.913	18,717
Gain	£17,283

The election is not beneficial.

The gain using re-basing to 1982 is

	£
Disposal consideration	41,000
Market value 31.3.82 10,000 × £2.05	20,500
Unindexed gain	20,500
Indexation allowance £20,500 × 0.913	18,717
Gain after indexation	1,783

The overall result is

Chargeable gain   £1,783

Re-basing applies as it produces neither a larger gain than that using time apportionment nor a loss.

Notes

(a)   Market value at 31 March 1982 cannot be used for indexation purposes in the calculation of the gain to 1 September 1983 as a deemed disposal occurs on that date and must, it would seem, be computed by reference to legislation extant on that date.

(b)   If an election is made for 6 April 1965 value, no valuation is required at 1 September 1983.

(c)   The deemed disposal on 1 September 1983 is *only* for the purposes of *TCGA 1992, 2 Sch 16* (time apportionment). In the re-basing calculation, the shares disposed of in February 1997 are regarded as standing in the place of those held at 31 March 1982.

(E) Part disposals after 5 April 1965 [*TCGA 1992, s 42, 2 Sch 16(8)*]

H bought land for £15,000 on 31 October 1963. Its value at 6 April 1965 was £17,200. On 1 February 1987, H sold part of the land for £50,000, the balance being then worth £200,000. In May 1996, H gives the remaining land to his daughter. Its value is then £285,000. The agreed value of the total estate at 31 March 1982 was £180,000 and H made a claim on the February 1987 disposal for that value to be used for indexation purposes.

Indexation factors	March 1982 to February 1987	0.264
	March 1982 to May 1996	0.925

1987 disposal

	£
Proceeds of part disposal	50,000
Deduct allowable cost $\dfrac{50,000}{50,000 + 200,000} \times £15,000$	3,000
Unindexed gain	47,000

Indexation allowance £180,000 $\times \dfrac{50,000}{50,000 + 200,000}$ = £36,000

£36,000 $\times$ 0.264	9,504
Gain after indexation	£37,496

Time apportionment

Chargeable gain $\dfrac{21y\ 10m}{23y\ 3m} \times £37,496$	£35,211

If an election were made to substitute 6 April 1965 valuation, the computation would be

	£
Proceeds of part disposal	50,000

$Deduct$ allowable cost $\dfrac{50,000}{50,000 + 200,000} \times £17,200$ **3,440**

Unindexed gain	46,560

Indexation allowance $£180,000 \times \dfrac{50,000}{50,000 + 200,000} = £36,000$

£36,000 × 0.264	9,504
Chargeable gain	£37,056

An election would not be beneficial.

1996 disposal

The gain without re-basing to 1982 is

	£	£
Disposal proceeds		285,000
Allowable cost (£15,000 − £3,000)		12,000
Unindexed gain		273,000
Indexation allowance £180,000 − £36,000 = £144,000 × 0.925		133,200
		139,800
$Less$ gain subject to time apportionment:		
Market value at 1.2.87	200,000	
Allowable cost	12,000	
	188,000	
Indexation allowance to 1.2.87 £144,000 × 0.264	38,016	
	£149,984	149,984
		(10,184)

Add chargeable part of time apportioned gain:

$\dfrac{21y\ 10m}{23y\ 3m} \times £149,984$ note (d)   **140,845**

Gain subject to re-basing	£130,661

The gain using re-basing to 1982 is

	£
Disposal proceeds	285,000

Market value 31.3.82 $£180,000 \times \dfrac{12,000}{15,000}$ note (b)   **144,000**

Unindexed gain	141,000
Indexation allowance £144,000 × 0.925	133,200
Gain after indexation	£7,800

The overall result is

Chargeable gain £7,800

Re-basing applies as it produces neither a larger gain nor a loss.

Notes

(a) The deemed disposal on 1 February 1987 is only for the purposes of *TCGA 1992, 2 Sch 16(3)–(5)* (time apportionment). For re-basing purposes, it would appear that the asset is still regarded as having been held at 31 March 1982.

(b) Where there has been a part disposal after 31 March 1982 and before 6 April 1988 of an asset held at 31 March 1982, the proportion of 31 March 1982 value to be brought into account in the re-basing calculation is that which the cost previously unallowed bears to the total cost, giving the same effect as if re-basing had applied to the part disposal. [*TCGA 1992, 3 Sch 4(1)*].

(c) The Revenue will also accept an alternative basis of calculation on the part disposal of land. Under this method, the part disposed of is treated as a separate asset and any fair and reasonable method of apportioning part of the total cost to it will be accepted e.g. a reasonable valuation of that part at the acquisition date. (Revenue Statement of Practice SP D1).

(d) The time apportionment calculation is applied to the gain *after* indexation (*Smith v Schofield H/L, [1993] STC 268*).

204   Assets held on 31 March 1982

204.1 GENERAL COMPUTATION OF GAINS/LOSSES [*TCGA 1992, s 35, 3 Sch*]

(A)

Rodney purchased a painting on 1 October 1979 for £60,000 (including costs of acquisition) and sold it at auction for £160,000 (net of selling expenses) on 15 August 1996. Its value at 31 March 1982 was £80,000 and the indexation factor for the period March 1982 to August 1996 is assumed to be 0.890.

	£	£
Net sale proceeds	160,000	160,000
Cost	60,000	
Market value 31.3.82		80,000
Unindexed gain	100,000	80,000
Indexation allowance £80,000 × 0.890	71,200	71,200
Gain after indexation	£28,800	£8,800
Chargeable gain		£8,800

Notes

(*a*)   The asset, having been held at 31 March 1982 and disposed of after 5 April 1988, is deemed to have been sold and immediately re-acquired at its market value at 31 March 1982. [*TCGA 1992, s 35(1)(2)*].

(*b*)   Re-basing does not apply if it would produce a larger gain or larger loss than would otherwise be the case, nor if it would turn a gain into a loss or vice versa, nor if the disposal would otherwise be a no gain/no loss disposal. [*TCGA 1992, s 35(3)(4)*].

(*c*)   An *irrevocable* election may be made to treat, broadly speaking, *all* assets held on 31 March 1982 as having been sold and re-acquired at their market value on that date, in which case the restrictions in (*b*) above will not apply. [*TCGA 1992, s 35(5)*]. If the election had been made in this example, the gain would still be £8,800, but there would have been no need to compute the gain by reference to cost and make a comparison with that using re-basing.

There are some minor exclusions from the rule that the election must extend to all assets. [*TCGA 1992, 3 Sch 7*]. There are also special rules for groups of companies. [*TCGA 1992, 3 Sch 8, 9*].

(*d*)   Indexation is automatically based on 31 March 1982 value, without the need to claim such treatment, unless a greater allowance would be produced by reference to cost. [*TCGA 1992, s 55(1)(2)*]. See also 209.1(B) INDEXATION.

(*e*)   See also 203 ASSETS HELD ON 6 APRIL 1965 for the general application of the re-basing provisions to such assets. See 210.1(D)(F) INDEXATION for the position as regards an asset acquired by means of a no gain/no loss transfer from a person who held it at 31 March 1982.

CGT 204.1 Assets held on 31 March 1982

(B)
The facts are as in (A) above, except that net sale proceeds amount to £70,000.

	£	£
Net sale proceeds	70,000	70,000
Cost	60,000	
Market value 31.3.82		80,000
Unindexed gain/(loss)	10,000	(10,000)
Indexation allowance (as in (A) but restricted to)	10,000	—
Gain/(loss)	Nil	£(10,000)
Chargeable gain/(allowable loss)	Nil	

Notes
(a) Re-basing does not apply as it cannot disturb a no gain/no loss position. [*TCGA 1992, s 35(3)(c)*].

(b) An election under *Sec 35(5)* would produce an allowable loss of £10,000.

(C)
The facts are as in (A) above, except that net sale proceeds amount to £135,000.

	£	£
Net sale proceeds	135,000	135,000
Cost	60,000	
Market value 31.3.82		80,000
Unindexed gain	75,000	55,000
Indexation allowance (as in (A))	71,200	
Indexation allowance (as in (A) but restricted to)		55,000
Gain	£3,800	Nil
Chargeable gain/(allowable loss)		Nil

Note
(a) Re-basing applies as it produces the smaller gain (i.e. a nil gain).

(D)
The facts are as in (A) above, except that net sale proceeds amount to £100,000.

	£	£
Net sale proceeds	100,000	100,000
Cost	60,000	
Market value 31.3.82		80,000
Unindexed gain	40,000	20,000
Indexation allowance (as in (A) but restricted to)	40,000	20,000
Gain/loss	Nil	Nil

3–22

204.2 **DEFERRED CHARGES ON GAINS BEFORE 31 MARCH 1982** [*TCGA 1992, s 36, 4 Sch*]

Kirk purchased 3,000 unquoted ordinary shares in W Limited for £9,000 on 1 January 1980 and later gave them to his son, Michael, claiming hold-over relief under *FA 1980, s 79*. Michael sells the shares for £21,000 (net) on 10 June 1996. The shares had a value of £11,000 at 31 March 1982.

Assuming the gift to have taken place on

    (i)   1 February 1982 (market value of shares £10,500),
    (ii)   30 April 1988 (market value £19,500), and
    (iii) 1 June 1985 (market value £15,000),

the capital gains position is as set out below. The relevant indexation factors are

March 1982 to June 1985	0.202
March 1982 to April 1988	0.332
March 1982 to June 1996 (assumed)	0.885
June 1985 to June 1996 (assumed)	0.568
April 1988 to June 1996 (assumed)	0.415

(i) Gift on 1 February 1982

Kirk's chargeable gain (deferred) (£10,500 − £9,000)	£1,500

Michael's acquisition cost (£10,500 − £1,500)	£9,000

Michael's chargeable gain is

	£	£
Proceeds 10.6.95	21,000	21,000
Cost (as above)	9,000	
Market value 31.3.82		11,000
Unindexed gain	12,000	10,000
Indexation allowance £11,000 × 0.885	9,735	9,735
Gain after indexation	£2,265	£265
Chargeable gain		£265

The deferred gain of £1,500 effectively falls out of charge as Michael held the shares at 31.3.82 and thus receives the benefit of re-basing to 1982.

(ii) Gift on 30 April 1988

Kirk's chargeable gain is

	£	£
Disposal value	19,500	19,500
Cost	9,000	
Market value 31.3.82		11,000
Unindexed gain	10,500	8,500
Indexation allowance £11,000 × 0.332	3,652	3,652
Gain after indexation	£6,848	£4,848
Chargeable gain (deferred)		£4,848

Michael's chargeable gain is

	£	£
Proceeds 10.6.96		21,000
Cost	19,500	
Deduct deferred gain	4,848	
	14,652	
Indexation allowance £14,652 × 0.415	6,081	20,733
Chargeable gain		£267

Michael cannot re-base to 1982 as he did not hold the shares at 31.3.82. However, as the deferred gain was itself computed by reference to the 31.3.82 value, he has effectively received full relief for the uplift in value between 1.1.80 and 31.3.82. The small difference between his gain of £267 and that of £265 in (i) above is due to the rounding of indexation factors to three decimal places.

(iii) Gift on 1 June 1985

Kirk's chargeable gain is

	£	£
Disposal value		15,000
Cost	9,000	
Indexation allowance £11,000 × 0.202	2,222	11,222
Chargeable gain (deferred)		£3,778

It is assumed that a claim would have been made to base indexation on the 31.3.82 value, this being greater than cost.

Michael's chargeable gain is

	£	£
Proceeds 10.6.96		21,000
Cost	15,000	
Deduct one-half of deferred gain		
£3,778 × ½	1,889	
	13,111	
Indexation allowance £13,111 × 0.568	7,447	20,558
Chargeable gain		£442

Michael cannot benefit from re-basing to 1982 as he did not hold the shares at 31.3.82, nor is the deferred gain itself calculated by reference to the re-basing rules as the disposal (i.e. the gift) took place before 6.4.88. Under *TCGA 1992, s 36, 4 Sch 1(a), 2*, the deduction in respect of a deferred gain is halved where the deferral took place after 31.3.82 and before 6.4.88 and was, wholly or partly, in respect of a chargeable gain accruing on an asset held at 31.3.82, thus giving some relief, albeit on an arbitrary basis.

Notes
(a)   A claim must be made, within two years of the end of the year of assessment in which the ultimate disposal takes place, for the deduction to be halved. [*TCGA 1992, 4 Sch 9*].

(b)   These provisions apply not only to hold-over relief on gifts, under *FA 1980, s 79*, but to a number of situations in which gains are held-over or rolled over, as listed in *TCGA 1992, 4 Sch 2(5)*, of which the most common is rollover relief, on replacement of business assets, under *TCGA 1992, s 152*. [*TCGA 1992, 4 Sch 1(a), 2*].

(*c*)   There are special rules where the disposal giving rise to the deferral is preceded by a no gain/no loss disposal (as defined by *TCGA 1992, s 35(3)(d)*) and where the ultimate disposal is preceded by a no gain/no loss disposal. [*TCGA 1992, 4 Sch 5–7*].

(*d*)   See also 209 HOLD-OVER RELIEFS and 223 ROLLOVER RELIEF for the general application of these reliefs.

(*e*)   Hold-over relief under *FA 1980, s 79* is not available for gifts after 13 March 1989.

205 Companies

Cross-references. See also 104 CAPITAL GAINS.

205.1 CAPITAL LOSSES

P Ltd, which makes up accounts to 30 June annually, changes its accounting date to 31 December. It makes up 18-month accounts to 31 December 1996, and its chargeable gains and allowable losses are as follows

	Gains/(losses)
	£
31.7.95	4,600
19.10.95	11,500
1.12.95	3,500
28.3.96	(8,300)
21.7.96	8,500
1.9.96	(25,000)
20.12.96	7,000

The period of account is split into two accounting periods

1.7.95 – 30.6.96	
Net chargeable gain	£11,300
1.7.96 – 31.12.96	
Net allowable loss	£9,500

Notes

(*a*)   The loss must be carried forward and cannot be set off against the £11,300 net gain.

(*b*)   For a further example, see 104.1 CAPITAL GAINS.

205.2 SHARES — ACQUISITIONS AND DISPOSALS WITHIN SHORT PERIOD [*TCGA 1992, s 106*]

S Ltd has the following transactions in shares in Q plc, a quoted company with share capital of £1m divided into 25p ordinary shares.

	Date	Number of shares	Price £
Purchase	1.6.88	100,000	62,000
Purchase	1.8.96	50,000	49,000
Sale	15.8.96	80,000	60,000
Purchase	31.8.96	50,000	35,000

The position is as follows

The shares sold on 15.8.96 are identified with the two purchases on 1.8.96 and 31.8.96.

£

(i) Purchase on 1.8.96

Proceeds $\dfrac{50,000}{80,000} \times £60,000$ 37,500

Cost   49,000

Allowable loss   £11,500

(ii) Purchase on 31.8.96

Proceeds $\dfrac{30,000}{80,000} \times £60,000$ 22,500

Cost $\dfrac{30,000}{50,000} \times £35,000$ 21,000

Chargeable gain   note (*c*)   £1,500

Allowable loss on transaction   £10,000

Notes

(*a*) Where a company disposes of shares (including securities other than gilt-edged securities) and acquires similar shares within one month before or after the disposal through a stock exchange or within six months in other circumstances, the shares acquired and disposed of are matched. For these rules to apply, the number of shares held at some time in the one month (or six months) before the disposal must be not less than 2% of the number issued. Shares acquired within one month (or six months) before or after the disposal are called 'available shares'.

(*b*) Subject to *TCGA 1992, s 105* (matching of same day acquisitions and disposals), disposals are identified first from 'available shares', taking acquisitions before the disposal (latest first) before acquisitions after the disposal (earliest first). Once all 'available shares' have been matched with the disposal, the identification of any remaining shares disposed of follows the ordinary rules.

(*c*) Indexation allowance is not available as the disposal is in the same month as the acquisitions. [*TCGA 1992, s 54*].

206 Disposal

206.1 ALLOWABLE AND NON-ALLOWABLE EXPENDITURE

(A) Allowable expenditure [*TCGA 1992, ss 38, 39*]
In 1996/97 T sold a house which he had owned since 1984 and which was let throughout the period of ownership. The house cost £34,000, with legal costs of £900. T spent £800 on initial repairs and refurbishment, which was disallowed for income tax in computing the rental income. In 1986, he added an extension at a cost of £5,000 for which he received a local authority grant of £2,000. Legal costs of £500 were incurred on obtaining vacant possession at the end of the final tenancy, and £600 was spent on making good damage by the outgoing tenant. The sale proceeds were £70,000 before deducting legal costs of £1,200.

	£	£	£
Sale proceeds		70,000	
Deduct costs of sale		1,200	68,800
Cost of house		34,000	
Add incidental costs of purchase		900	
		34,900	
Improvement costs			
initial repairs	800		
extension, less grant	3,000	3,800	
Cost of obtaining vacant possession			
(enhancement cost)		500	39,200
Unindexed gain			£29,600

Note
(*a*) The costs of making good dilapidations at the end of the final tenancy are disallowed by virtue of *TCGA 1992, s 39*, being a deduction against income.

(B) Non-allowable expenditure — capital allowances [*TCGA 1992, s 41*]
S Ltd acquired land in March 1989 for £90,000 on which it constructed a factory for use in its manufacturing trade. The cost of construction was £45,000 incurred in June 1989. In July 1996, the company sold the freehold factory for £140,000, of which £100,000 related to the land and £40,000 to the building. Industrial buildings allowances of £10,800 had been given and there was a balancing charge of £5,800. The indexation factor for the period March 1989 to July 1996 is assumed to be 0.350.

	Land	Building	
	£	£	£
Disposal consideration	100,000		40,000
Allowable cost	90,000	45,000	
Deduct net allowances given		5,000	40,000
Unindexed gain	10,000		Nil
Indexation allowance £90,000 × 0.350			
but restricted to	10,000		
Chargeable gain/(allowable loss)	Nil		Nil

Note
(a)   For disposals on or after 30 November 1993 (subject to transitional provisions for disposals before 6 April 1995 — not available to companies), indexation allowance cannot exceed an unindexed gain or create or increase a loss. [*TCGA 1992, s 53; FA 1994, s 93(1)–(3)*].

206.2   **PART DISPOSALS** [*TCGA 1992, s 42*]

Note. See also 213.1 LAND for small part disposals of land.

(A)
T purchased a 300 acre estate in 1972 for £1m plus legal and other costs of £50,000. In 1976 he spent £87,000 on improvements to the main house on the estate (not his main residence), which he sells in September 1996 for £660,000. The costs of sale are £40,000. The value of the remaining land is £2.34m. The market value of the whole estate at 31 March 1982 was £1.35m and the indexation factor from March 1982 to September 1996 is assumed to be 0.895.

Gain without re-basing to 1982

	£	£
Sale proceeds		660,000
Deduct incidental costs		40,000
		620,000
Cost £1,050,000 × $\dfrac{660,000}{660,000 + 2,340,000}$	231,000	
Improvement costs	87,000	318,000
Unindexed gain		302,000
Indexation allowance £318,000 × 0.895		284,610
Gain after indexation		£17,390

Gain with re-basing to 1982

	£
Net proceeds as above	620,000
Market value 31.3.82	
£1,350,000 × $\dfrac{660,000}{660,000 + 2,340,000}$	297,000
Unindexed gain	323,000
Indexation allowance £318,000 × 0.895	284,610
Gain after indexation	£38,390
Chargeable gain	£17,390

Notes
(a)   Re-basing does not apply as its effect would be to increase a gain. Indexation is based on allowable cost in both calculations as this gives a greater allowance than by using market value of £297,000. [*TCGA 1992, ss 35(3), 55(1)(2)*].

(b)   The improvements expenditure is not apportioned in the first calculation as it relates entirely to the part of the estate being sold. [*TCGA 1992, s 42(4)*]. In the second calculation, this fact is irrelevant as the whole estate is deemed to have been sold and re-acquired on 31 March 1982. If this expenditure had been incurred after 31 March 1982, then, for re-basing purposes, the 31 March 1982 value of the estate would be apportioned, but the improvements expenditure would be deductible in full from the part disposal proceeds.

(B)

U inherited some land at a probate value of £500,000 in November 1981. Its market value at 31 March 1982 was £540,000. In November 1987, he sold part of the land for £240,000, the remaining land then being worth £480,000. He sells the remaining land in April 1996 for £600,000 and elects under *TCGA 1992, s 35(5)* for all his assets held at 31 March 1982 to be treated as sold and re-acquired by him at their market value on that date.

The gain, subject to indexation, on the part disposal in November 1987 is

	£
Proceeds	240,000
Cost £500,000 × $\dfrac{240,000}{240,000 + 480,000}$	166,667
Unindexed gain	£73,333

The gain, subject to indexation, on the disposal in April 1996 is

	£
Proceeds	600,000
Market value 31.3.82	
£540,000 × $\dfrac{480,000}{240,000 + 480,000}$	360,000
Unindexed gain	£240,000

Note

(a)   Where re-basing applies, whether or not the election under *Sec 35(5)* is made, and there has been a part disposal after 31 March 1982 and before 6 April 1988, the proportion of 31 March 1982 value to be brought into account on the ultimate disposal is the same as the proportion of cost unallowed on the part disposal, as if the re-basing provisions had applied to the part disposal. [*TCGA 1992, 3 Sch 4(1)*].

(C)

V bought the film rights of a novel for £50,000 in May 1983. A one-third share of the rights was sold to W Ltd in March 1984 for £20,000, when the rights retained had a value of £45,000. In December 1996, V's rights were sold to a film company for £100,000 plus a right to royalties, such right being estimated to be worth £150,000. The indexation factor for the period May 1983 to December 1996 is assumed to be 0.790.

March 1984	£
Sale proceeds	20,000
Cost £50,000 × $\dfrac{20,000}{20,000 + 45,000}$	15,385
Chargeable gain	£4,615

December 1996	£
Sale proceeds (£100,000 + £150,000)	250,000
Cost (£50,000 − £15,385)	34,615
Unindexed gain	215,385
Indexation allowance £34,615 × 0.790	27,346
Chargeable gain	£188,039

Notes

(a)   The right to royalties is itself an asset and could be the subject of a future disposal by V. See 206.3(B) below and, where applicable, 227 WASTING ASSETS.

(b)   No indexation allowance is available on the March 1984 disposal as the rights sold had not been held for the 12-month qualifying period then in force for indexation purposes.

(D)

C inherited land valued at £88,000 in May 1982. He granted rights of way over the land to a neighbouring landowner in March 1987, in consideration for a parcel of land adjacent to his, valued at £21,000. The value of the original land, subject to the right of way, was then £147,000. In March 1997, C sold the whole of the land for £170,000.

Indexation factors May 1982 to March 1987	0.233
May 1982 to March 1997 (assumed)	0.870
March 1987 to March 1997 (assumed)	0.517

Part disposal in March 1987		£
Disposal consideration		21,000
Allowable expenditure		
$\dfrac{21,000}{21,000 + 147,000} \times £88,000$		11,000
Unindexed gain		10,000
Indexation allowance £11,000 × 0.233		2,563
Chargeable gain		£7,437

Disposal in March 1997		£
Disposal consideration		170,000
Deduct Original land £(88,000 − 11,000)	77,000	
Addition	21,000	98,000
Unindexed gain		72,000
Indexation allowance		
(a) Original land £77,000 × 0.870	66,990	
(b) Addition £21,000 × 0.517	10,857	
	77,847	
Indexation allowance restricted to		72,000
Chargeable gain/(allowable loss)		Nil

3–31

Notes

(*a*) It is assumed that the additional land is merged with the existing land to give a single asset.

(*b*) A claim under what is now *TCGA 1992, s 242* (small part disposals of land—see 213.1 LAND) cannot be made in respect of the March 1987 part disposal as the consideration exceeds £20,000.

(*c*) For disposals on or after 30 November 1993 (subject to transitional provisions for disposals before 6 April 1995), indexation allowance cannot exceed the unindexed gain. [*TCGA 1992, s 53; FA 1994, s 93(1)–(3)*].

206.3 CAPITAL SUMS DERIVED FROM ASSETS [*TCGA 1992, s 22(1)*]

(A) General

A Ltd holds the remainder of a 99-year lease of land, under which it has mineral rights. The lease, which commenced in 1975, was acquired in April 1983 by assignment for £80,000. Following a proposal to extract minerals, the freeholder pays A Ltd £100,000 in June 1996 in consideration of relinquishing the mineral rights, in order to prevent such development. The value of the lease after the alteration is £150,000.

	£
Disposal proceeds	100,000
Allowable cost $\dfrac{100,000}{100,000 + 150,000} \times £80,000$	32,000
Unindexed gain	£68,000

(B) Deferred consideration

Z owns 2,000 £1 ordinary shares in B Ltd, for which he subscribed at par in August 1985. On 31 March 1990, he and the other shareholders in B Ltd sold their shares to another company for £10 per share plus a further unquantified cash amount calculated by means of a formula relating to the future profits of B Ltd. The value in March 1990 of the deferred consideration was estimated at £2 per share. On 30 April 1996, Z receives a further £4.20 per share under the sale agreement. The indexation factor for the period August 1985 to March 1990 is 0.271.

1989/90

	£	£
Disposal proceeds 2,000 at £10	20,000	
Value of rights 2,000 at £2	4,000	24,000
Cost of acquisition		2,000
Unindexed gain		22,000
Indexation allowance £2,000 × 0.271		542
Chargeable gain		£21,458

1996/97

Disposal of rights to deferred consideration

Proceeds 2,000 × £4.20	8,400
Deemed cost of acquiring rights	4,000
Unindexed gain	4,400
Indexation allowance (March 1990 to April 1996) £4,000 × 0.257	1,028
Chargeable gain	£3,372

Notes

(a)   A right to unquantified and contingent future consideration on the disposal of an asset is itself an asset, and the future consideration when received is a capital sum derived from that asset (*Marren v Ingles H/L 1980, 54 TC 76* and *Marson v Marriage C/D 1979, 54 TC 59*).

(b)   See 225.4(E) SHARES AND SECURITIES for extra-statutory concession applicable where deferred consideration is to be satisfied in shares and/or debentures in the acquiring company.

(C)

Suppose that in the previous example, the deferred consideration was valued at £4.20 per share in March 1990, but only £2 per share was received on 30 April 1996.

1989/90

	£	£
Disposal proceeds	20,000	
Value of rights	8,400	28,400
Cost of acquisition		2,000
Unindexed gain		26,400
Indexation allowance £2,000 × 0.271		542
Chargeable gain		£25,858

1996/97

Disposal of rights 2,000 × £2	4,000
Deemed acquisition cost	8,400
Allowable loss	£4,400

Notes

(a)   There is no provision for reopening the 1989/90 assessment or setting off the 1996/97 loss against the 1989/90 gain.

(b)   For disposals on or after 30 November 1993 (subject to transitional provisions for disposals before 6 April 1995), indexation allowance cannot increase an unindexed loss. [*TCGA 1992, s 53; FA 1994, s 93(1)–(3)*].

CGT 206.4 Disposal

206.4 **RECEIPT OF COMPENSATION** [*TCGA 1992, ss 22, 23*]

(A)

C owns a freehold warehouse which is badly damaged by fire as a result of inflammable goods having been inadequately packaged. The value of the warehouse after the fire is £90,000, and it cost £120,000 in 1985. The owner of the goods is held liable for the damage and pays C £60,000 compensation in October 1996.

	£
Disposal proceeds	60,000
Allowable cost $\dfrac{60,000}{60,000 + 90,000} \times £120,000$	48,000
Unindexed gain	£12,000

(B) Restoration using insurance moneys

A diamond necklace owned by D cost £100,000 in 1987. D is involved in a motor accident in which the necklace is damaged. Its value is reduced to £80,000. D receives £40,000 under an insurance policy in May 1996 and spends £45,000 on having the necklace restored.

(i) No claim under *TCGA 1992, s 23*

	£
Disposal proceeds	40,000
Allowable cost $\dfrac{40,000}{40,000 + 80,000} \times £100,000$	33,333
Unindexed gain	£6,667
Allowable cost in relation to subsequent disposal £100,000 − £33,333 + £45,000	£111,667

(ii) Claim under *TCGA 1992, s 23*

No chargeable gain arises

	£
Allowable cost originally	100,000
Deduct amount received on claim	40,000
	60,000
Add expenditure on restoration	45,000
Allowable cost in relation to subsequent disposal	£105,000

(C) Part application of capital sum received

E is the owner of a large estate consisting mainly of parkland which he acquired for £150,000 in August 1983. He grants a one-year licence in August 1996 to an exploration company to prospect for minerals, in consideration for a capital sum of £50,000. The exploration proves unsuccessful and on expiry of the licence E spends £20,000 on restoration of the drilling sites to their former state. The market value of the estate after granting the licence is £350,000, and it is £400,000 after restoration.

(i) No claim under *TCGA 1992, s 23*

	£
Disposal proceeds	50,000
Deduct allowable cost $\dfrac{50,000}{50,000 + 350,000} \times £150,000$	18,750
Unindexed gain	£31,250
Allowable expenditure remaining £150,000 − £18,750 + £20,000	£151,250

(ii) Claim made under *TCGA 1992, s 23*

	£
Deemed disposal proceeds (£50,000 − £20,000)	30,000
Deduct	
Allowable cost $\dfrac{30,000}{30,000 + 400,000} \times £(150,000 + 20,000)$	11,860
Unindexed gain	£18,140
Allowable expenditure remaining £150,000 − £20,000 − £11,860 + £20,000	£138,140

(D) Capital sum exceeding allowable expenditure

F inherited a painting in 1980 when it was valued at £2,000. Its value at 31 March 1982 was £3,000. In March 1987, by which time its value had increased considerably, the painting suffered damage whilst on loan to an art gallery and F received £10,000 compensation. The value of the painting was then £30,000. It then cost F £9,800 to have the painting restored. In June 1996, he sells the painting for £50,000.

(i) No election under *TCGA 1992, s 23(2)*

	£
Disposal proceeds March 1987	10,000
Allowable cost $\dfrac{10,000}{10,000 + 30,000} \times £2,000$	500
Unindexed gain 1986/87	£9,500
Allowable cost in relation to subsequent disposal £2,000 − £500 + £9,800	£11,300

	£	£
Disposal proceeds June 1996	50,000	50,000
Allowable cost without re-basing	11,300	
Allowable cost with re-basing		

$$£3,000 \times \frac{30,000}{10,000 + 30,000} = £2,250 + £9,800 \qquad 12,050$$

	£	£
Unindexed gain 1996/97	£38,700	£37,950

It is clear that re-basing will apply and the chargeable gain will be £37,950 less indexation allowance.

(ii) Election under *TCGA 1992, s 23(2)*

	£
Disposal proceeds March 1987	10,000
Less allowable expenditure	2,000
Unindexed gain 1986/87	£8,000
Allowable cost in relation to subsequent disposal	
£2,000 − £2,000 + £9,800	£9,800

	£	£
Disposal proceeds June 1996	50,000	50,000
Allowable cost without re-basing	9,800	
Allowable cost with re-basing note (*b*)		
£3,000 − £2,000 + £9,800		10,800
Unindexed gain 1996/97	£40,200	£39,200

Again, re-basing will clearly apply and the chargeable gain will be £39,200 less indexation allowance.

Notes

(*a*)   Although not illustrated in this example, indexation allowance must be deducted before comparing the positions with and without re-basing in order to ascertain whether or not re-basing applies.

(*b*)   Where there is a disposal after 5 April 1989 to which re-basing applies and, if re-basing had not applied, the allowable expenditure would have fallen to be reduced under *TCGA 1992, s 23(2)* by reference to a capital sum received after 31 March 1982 but before 6 April 1988, the 31 March 1982 value is reduced by the amount previously allowed against the capital sum. [*TCGA 1992, 3 Sch 4(2)*].

(E) Indexation allowance [*TCGA 1992, ss 53(3), 57*]
A Ltd owns a freehold factory which cost £100,000 in June 1985. Because of mining operations nearby, part of the factory is severely damaged by subsidence and has to be demolished and rebuilt. The value of the factory after the damage is £150,000. The risk is not covered under A's insurance policy but the mining company agrees to pay compensation of £50,000 in full settlement, received in February 1996. The cost of demolition and rebuilding is £60,000, incurred in April 1996. The factory is sold in December 1997 for £300,000.

Indexation factors	June 1985 to February 1996	0.543
	June 1985 to December 1997 (assumed)	0.648
	February 1996 to December 1997 (assumed)	0.070
	April 1996 to December 1997 (assumed)	0.050

(i) No claim under *TCGA 1992, s 23*(1)

		£
(*a*)	Part disposal February 1996	
	Disposal proceeds	50,000

$$\textit{Deduct} \text{ allowable cost } \frac{50,000}{50,000 + 150,000} \times £100,000 \qquad 25,000$$

	£
Unindexed gain	25,000
Indexation allowance £25,000 × 0.543	13,575
Chargeable gain	£11,425

		£
(*b*)	Disposal December 1997	
	Disposal proceeds	300,000
	Deduct allowable cost	
	£(100,000 − 25,000) + £60,000	135,000
	Unindexed gain	165,000

Indexation allowance		
Original cost £(100,000 − 25,000) × 0.648	48,600	
Rebuilding cost £60,000 × 0.050	3,000	51,600
Chargeable gain		£113,400

(ii) Claim under *TCGA 1992, s 23*(1)

		£
(*a*)	No chargeable gain in February 1996	
	Allowable cost	100,000
	Rebuilding cost	60,000
		160,000
	Deduct receipt rolled over	50,000
	Revised allowable cost	£110,000
(*b*)	Disposal December 1997	
	Disposal proceeds	300,000
	Deduct allowable cost	110,000
	Unindexed gain	190,000

Indexation allowance		
Original cost £100,000 × 0.648	64,800	
Rebuilding cost £60,000 × 0.050	3,000	
	67,800	
Deduct		
Receipt rolled over £50,000 × 0.070	(3,500)	64,300
Chargeable gain		£125,700

Note

(*a*) The effect of indexation in this example is to *increase* the total chargeable gains if a claim is made under *Sec 23*(*1*) (£125,700 − £(11,500 + 113,400) = £800), but the claim has the advantage of deferring part of the gain, and thus the tax payable, to a later date. The availability or otherwise of the 1996/97 annual exemption, and the rate of tax applicable, would also need to be taken into account.

206.5 OPTIONS [*TCGA 1992, ss 44, 46, 144*]

Cross-reference. See also 227.2 WASTING ASSETS.

(A)

On 1 February 1992 F granted an option to G for £10,000 to acquire freehold land bought by F for £50,000 in September 1988. The option is for a period of 5 years, and the option price is £100,000 plus 1% thereof for each month since the option was granted. On 1 February 1994, G sold the option to H for £20,000. On 30 June 1996, H exercises the option and pays F £141,000 for the land. Neither G nor H intended to use the land for the purposes of a trade.

| Indexation factors | September 1988 to June 1996 (assumed) | 0.380 |
| | February 1992 to February 1994 | 0.043 |

1992 Grant of option by F

	£
Disposal proceeds	10,000
Allowable cost	—
Chargeable gain	£10,000

1994 Disposal of option by G

	£
Disposal proceeds	20,000
Allowable cost $\dfrac{5-2}{5} \times £10,000$	6,000
Unindexed gain	14,000
Indexation allowance £6,000 × 0.043	258
Chargeable gain	£13,742

1996 Exercise of option

		£
(i)	Earlier assessment on F vacated	
(ii)	Aggregate disposal proceeds	
	(£10,000 + £141,000)	151,000
	Allowable cost of land	50,000
	Unindexed gain	101,000
	Indexation allowance £50,000 × 0.380	19,000
	Chargeable gain (on F)	£82,000

H's allowable expenditure is

	£	£
Cost of option	20,000	
Deduct Wasted up to date exercised $\left(\dfrac{1y\ 5m}{3y} \right)$	9,444	
		10,556
Cost of land		141,000
		£151,556

(B)

In February 1992, P granted T Ltd an option to purchase 100,000 £1 ordinary shares (unquoted) in R Ltd at £2 per share. The option price was £15,000, and P acquired the shares at par on 31 March 1982. The option was to be exercised within 24 months of the date it was granted. In May 1993, T Ltd exercised the option. In July 1996, T Ltd sold the shares to another company for £280,000, their then market value.

Indexation factors	March 1982 to May 1993	0.770
	February 1992 to July 1996 (assumed)	0.100
	May 1993 to July 1996 (assumed)	0.063

P

		£
(*a*)	*Disposal of option*	
	Disposal consideration	15,000
	(No allowable cost)	—
	Chargeable gain (1991/92)	£15,000
(*b*)	*Disposal of shares*	
	Earlier assessment is vacated	
	Aggregate disposal proceeds	
	(£15,000 + £200,000)	215,000
	Allowable cost	100,000
	Unindexed gain	115,000
	Indexation allowance £100,000 × 0.770	77,000
	Chargeable gain (1993/94)	£38,000

T Ltd	£	£	£
Disposal of shares			
Disposal consideration			280,000
Allowable cost			
Shares		200,000	
Option	15,000		
Wasted $\dfrac{15}{24} \times$ £15,000	9,375	5,625	205,625
Unindexed gain			74,375
Indexation allowance			
Shares £200,000 × 0.063		12,600	
Option £5,625 × 0.100		563	
			13,163
Chargeable gain (1996/97)			£61,212

207   Enterprise Investment Scheme

[TCGA 1992, s 150A(1)(2A)(3); FA 1994, 15 Sch 28–30; FA 1995, s 67, 13 Sch]

207.1 DISPOSAL OF EIS SHARES MORE THAN FIVE YEARS AFTER ACQUISITION

On 8 November 1996 P subscribes £450,000 for 300,000 shares in the EIS company S Ltd, and obtains an EIS income deduction of £20,000 (£100,000 × 20%) in 1996/97. On 3 April 2008 he sells the entire holding for £900,000.

The chargeable gain arising is calculated as follows:

	£	£
Disposal proceeds		900,000
Cost	450,000	
Indexation *Note: Indexation of £112,500 has been assumed.*	112,500	562,500
It is not available to increase a loss.		
Gain		337,500
Less TCGA 1992, s 150A(3) restriction		
$£337,500 \times \dfrac{20,000}{90,000}$		75,000
Chargeable gain		£262,500
A = £100,000 × 20% =		£20,000
B = £450,000 × 20% =		£90,000

Notes

(*a*)   Gains arising on the sale of eligible shares within five years after issue are not chargeable gains unless the EIS relief is withdrawn before disposal.

(*b*)   Where the income tax relief is not given on the full EIS subscription, capital gains tax relief is given on a proportion of the gain on the disposal or part disposal.

The qualifying gain is reduced by the multiple A/B where

A = the actual income tax reduction and
B = the tax at the lower rate for that year on the amount subscribed for the issue.
[TCGA 1992, s 150A(3); FA 1994, 15 Sch 30].

207.2 LOSS ON DISPOSAL OF EIS SHARES MORE THAN FIVE YEARS AFTER ACQUISITION

Assuming the facts remain the same as 207.1 above but that the shares are sold for £300,000 on 3 April 2008.

The chargeable gain arising is calculated as follows:

	£	£
Disposal proceeds		300,000
Less Cost	450,000	
Less TCGA 1992, s 150A(3)		
Income tax relief not withdrawn	20,000	430,000
Allowable loss		£130,000

Note

(a)   Any loss arising is reduced by deducting the amount of the EIS relief granted from the purchase cost.

(b)   This point is also illustrated at 5.2(B).

207.3 LOSS ON DISPOSAL OF EIS SHARES WITHIN FIVE YEARS OF ACQUISITION

Assuming the facts remain the same as in 207.1 above but that shares are sold on 3 April 1998 for £30,000, income tax relief of $£30,000 \times 20\% \times \frac{20,000}{90,000} = £1,333$ would be withdrawn. The balance of £18,667 is not withdrawn and is attributable to the shares sold.

	£	£
Disposal proceeds		30,000
Less Cost	450,000	
Less TCGA 1992, s 150A attributable to the shares sold	18,667	431,333
Allowable loss		£401,333

Notes

(a)   There is no CGT exemption for shares disposed of within five years of acquisition and any EIS relief given will be withdrawn.

(b)   In calculating the EIS withdrawal, as not all the subscriber shares qualified for EIS income tax relief, the consideration must be reduced by applying the formula A/B, to the amount of the consideration received. For this purpose A is the actual income tax reduction and B is the tax at the lower rate for that year on the amount subscribed for the issue, ie £30,000 × 20,000/90,000 = £6,667. [*TA 1988 s 299(4)*]. The EIS relief withdrawn is then calculated on this result ie. £6,667 × 20% = £1,333.

(c)   However, if the sale results in a loss, loss relief will still be available. [*TCGA 1992, s 150A(1)(2A); FA 1994, 15 Sch 30*].

208 Exemptions and Reliefs

Cross-references. See also 219 PRIVATE RESIDENCES, 220 QUALIFYING CORPORATE BONDS and 227 WASTING ASSETS.

208.1 CHATTELS

(A) Marginal relief [*TCGA 1992, s 262(2)*]

On 1 April 1983, Y acquired by inheritance a painting valued for probate at £800. He sold it for £7,200 on 30 October 1996, incurring costs of £150. The indexation factor for the period April 1983 to October 1996 is assumed to be 0.789.

	£	£
Disposal proceeds	7,200	
Incidental costs	150	7,050
Acquisition cost		800
Unindexed gain		6,250
Indexation allowance £800 × 0.789		631
Chargeable gain		£5,619
Marginal relief		
Chargeable gain limited to $\frac{5}{3}$ × (£7,200 – £6,000)		£2,000

(B) Loss relief [*TCGA 1992, s 262(3)*]

Z bought a piece of antique jewellery for £7,000 in February 1985. In January 1997, he is forced to sell it, but at auction it realises only £1,500 and Z incurs costs of £100.

	£	£
Deemed disposal consideration		6,000
Cost of disposal	100	
Cost of acquisition	7,000	7,100
Allowable loss		£1,100

Note

(a)   For disposals on or after 30 November 1993 (subject to transitional provisions for disposals before 6 April 1995), an indexation allowance cannot increase a loss. [*TCGA 1992, s 53; FA 1994, s 93(1)–(3)*].

(C) Partial disposal of assets forming sets [*TCGA 1992, s 262(4)*]

AB purchased a set of six 18th century dining chairs in 1977 for £1,800. After incurring restoration costs of £600 in 1981, he sold two of them in May 1989 to an unconnected person for £2,900. In October 1996, he sold the other four to the same buyer for £4,900. The value of the complete set at 31 March 1982 was £2,600.

Indexation factors	March 1982 to May 1989 (actual)	0.448
	March 1982 to October 1996 (assumed)	0.898

The two disposals are treated as one for the purposes of the chattel exemption and marginal relief, the consideration for which is £7,800. Marginal relief on this basis would give a total chargeable gain of £3,000 ([£7,800 – £6,000] × $\frac{5}{3}$) which is to be compared with the following:

May 1989	£	£	£
Disposal proceeds		2,900	2,900
Acquisition cost	1,800		
Enhancement cost	600		
	2,400		
Cost of two chairs sold £2,400 × $\frac{2}{6}$		800	
Market value 31.3.82 £2,600 × $\frac{2}{6}$			867
Unindexed gain		2,100	2,033
Indexation allowance £867 × 0.448		388	388
Gain after indexation		£1,712	£1,645
Chargeable gain			£1,645

October 1996	£	£
Disposal proceeds	4,900	4,900
Allowable cost £2,400 × $\frac{4}{6}$	1,600	
Market value 31.3.82 £2,600 × $\frac{4}{6}$		1,733
Unindexed gain	3,300	3,167
Indexation allowance £1,733 × 0.898	1,556	1,556
Gain after indexation	£1,744	£1,611
Chargeable gain		£1,611
Total chargeable gains (£1,645 + £1,611)		£3,256

The total gain of £3,256 compares with a gain of £3,000 using marginal relief. Marginal relief is therefore effective and the total chargeable gain is £3,000.

The gain is apportioned to tax years as follows (note (*b*))

1989/90 £3,000 × $\dfrac{2,900}{7,800}$ =   £1,115

1996/97 £3,000 × $\dfrac{4,900}{7,800}$ =   £1,885

Notes

(*a*)   Prior to the second disposal, the first disposal would have been exempt, the proceeds being within the £6,000 chattel exemption.

(*b*)   The gain as reduced by marginal relief is apportioned between tax years in the same ratio as the proportion of total sale proceeds applicable to each year (Revenue Capital Gains manual, volume VII, para CG76637). In practice, it would seem that the Revenue cannot tax the earlier gain unless they are able to raise the assessment within normal time limits (as extended in cases of fraudulent or negligent conduct).

(*c*)   See also 202.4 ANTI-AVOIDANCE.

209   Hold-Over Reliefs

209.1 RELIEF FOR GIFTS [*TCGA 1992, s 260*]

(A)

B owns a house which he has not occupied as a private residence. He purchased the house for £2,200 inclusive of costs in 1973 and in January 1997 he gives it to a discretionary trust of which he is the settlor. The market value of the house is agreed to be £55,000 at the date of transfer, and B incurs transfer costs of £500. The indexation factor for the period March 1982 to January 1997 is assumed to be 0.908. The house had a value of £21,000 at 31 March 1982.

	£	£
Disposal consideration	55,000	55,000
Deduct Costs of disposal	500	500
	54,500	54,500
Cost	2,200	
Market value 31.3.82		21,000
Unindexed gain	52,300	33,500
Indexation allowance £21,000 × 0.908	19,068	19,068
Gain after indexation	£33,232	£14,432
Chargeable gain		£14,432

If B elects under *Sec 260*, his chargeable gain is reduced to nil, and the trustees' acquisition cost of the house is treated as £40,568 (£55,000 − £14,432).

Notes

(*a*)   Relief under *Sec 260* is restricted, generally, to transfers which are, or would but for annual exemptions be, chargeable lifetime transfers for inheritance tax purposes. It is not available for potentially exempt transfers. A more general relief for gifts, computed in an identical fashion, was available for transfers before 14 March 1989 [*FA 1980, s 79; FA 1981, s 78; FA 1982, s 82;* all repealed by *FA 1989, 17 Sch Pt VII*]. If, under this former relief, the house had been given to an individual, who had used it as his main residence, such that, in the event of his selling it, the private residence exemption would apply in full (see 219 PRIVATE RESIDENCES), the deferred gain would never become chargeable.

(*b*)   There are special rules where deferral took place after 31 March 1982 but before 6 April 1988, for which see 204.2 ASSETS HELD AT 31 MARCH 1982.

(B)

The facts are as in (A) above except that B sells the house to the trustees for £30,000.

	£	£
Chargeable gain (as above) note (*a*)		14,432
Deduct		
Actual consideration passing	30,000	
B's allowable costs note (*b*)	(21,000)	
		9,000
Held-over gain		£5,432
(i) B's chargeable gain is reduced to £14,432 − £5,432		£9,000
(ii) The trustees' allowable cost is reduced to £55,000 − £5,432		£49,568

Notes

(*a*)   The disposal consideration is taken as the open market value of the house at the date of disposal because B and the trustees are connected persons.

(*b*)   B's allowable costs are those allowable under *TCGA 1992, s 38*, which does not include indexation allowance.

(C)

The facts are as in (A) above. Before transferring the house, B had made substantial chargeable transfers. Inheritance tax of £11,000 is payable on the transfer. The trustees sell the house in December 1997 for £50,000. The indexation factor for the period January 1997 to December 1997 is assumed to be 0.034.

	£	£
Disposal proceeds		50,000
Acquisition cost	55,000	
Deduct held-over gain	14,432	
		40,568
Unindexed gain		9,432
Indexation allowance £40,568 × 0.034		1,379
		8,053
IHT attributable to earlier transfer (restricted)		8,053
Chargeable gain		Nil

Notes

(*a*)   The IHT deduction is not indexed as it is not relevant allowable expenditure under *TCGA 1992, s 53*.

(*b*)   The IHT deduction is limited to the amount of the gain and cannot create or increase a loss. [*TCGA 1992, s 260(7)*].

(*c*)   A similar inheritance tax relief operates where the original gain was held over under *FA 1980, s 79* (see note (*a*) to (A) above). [*TCGA 1992, s 67*].

209.2 RELIEF FOR GIFT OF BUSINESS ASSETS [*TCGA 1992, s 165, 7 Sch; FA 1993, 7 Sch 1; FA 1996, s 176*]

(A)

S has carried on his antique dealing business for 10 years. The assets of the business are valued as follows

	£
Freehold shop and office	285,000
Goodwill	90,000
Stocks	50,000
Debtors	9,500
Cash	4,500

Before the business began, S let the shop premises for one year. In October 1996, S transfers the business as a going concern to a company which he has formed with share capital of £1,000, held wholly by him. The transfer consideration is £1. At the time of the transfer S is 51. The gain arising in respect of the freehold is £250,000 and on goodwill it is £83,000 (both after deducting indexation allowance).

	£	£
Gains eligible for retirement relief		
(£250,000 + £83,000)		333,000
Relief £250,000 × 100%	250,000	
£83,000 × 50%	41,500	291,500
Chargeable gain		£41,500

If S and the company jointly claim relief under *TCGA 1992, s 165*, part of the chargeable gain may be rolled over, as follows

	Freehold £	Goodwill £	£
Total gain	250,000	83,000	
Reduction for non-trade use [*TCGA 1992, 7 Sch 5*] ($\frac{1}{11}$)	22,727		
	£227,273	£83,000	
Held-over gain before adjustment			310,273
Retirement relief [*TCGA 1992, 7 Sch 8*]			291,500
Held-over gain			£18,773

Notes

(a) The chargeable gain neither relieved nor held over is therefore £22,727 (£333,000 – £291,500 – £18,773).

(b) There is no statutory formula for apportioning retirement relief between different assets for the purpose of calculating hold-over relief under *Sec 165*. The following is one possible method of computing the revised base costs in the hands of the company.

Freehold

Gain held over $\dfrac{227,273}{310,273} \times £18,773$	£13,751
Revised base cost (£285,000 – £13,751)	£271,249

Goodwill

Gain held over $\dfrac{83,000}{310,273} \times £18,773$ £5,022

Revised base cost (£90,000 − £5,022) £84,978

(c)   If S had transferred the business to the company in consideration for the issue of shares, *TCGA 1992, s 162* (see 208.3 below) would have applied, but business assets relief under *Sec 165* would not. Retirement relief would still have applied in priority, so that the chargeable gain would have been £41,500. This gain would then have been rolled over against the base cost of the shares acquired by S.

(d)   See 204.2 ASSETS HELD AT 31 MARCH 1982 for the relief given under *TCGA 1992, 4 Sch* where gains were held over after 31 March 1982 and before 6 April 1988 and a disposal occurs after 5 April 1988. This relief applies, inter alia, to gains held over under the business gifts relief rules illustrated above.

(e)   For disposals after 28 November 1995 the age from which a person may qualify for retirement relief has been reduced from 55 to 50 unless the person is retiring on account of ill-health, subject to other conditions being satisfied.

(B)
K holds 10,000 shares in her personal trading company, LO Ltd, which she acquired by inheritance in January 1990 at a probate value of £200,000. In January 1997, she gifts 4,000 shares to her daughter. Their market value is £140,000 and the market value of K's remaining 6,000 shares is £210,000. K is 52 years of age at the time of the gift. K and her daughter jointly claim hold-over relief under *TCGA 1992, s 165*. At the date of disposal, the market values of the company's assets are as follows.

	Assets	Chargeable assets	
		Business	Non-business
	£	£	£
Business premises	200,000	200,000	
Goodwill	50,000	50,000	
Trading stock	30,000		
Debtors	10,000		
Cash	10,000		
Investments	50,000		50,000
Fixtures (all valued at less than £6,000)	20,000		
		£250,000	£50,000

The indexation factor for the period January 1990 to January 1997 is assumed to be 0.269.

The gain on the gift of shares is calculated as follows.

	£
Deemed consideration	140,000
Cost £200,000 $\times \dfrac{140,000}{140,000 + 210,000}$	80,000
Unindexed gain	60,000
Indexation allowance £80,000 × 0.269	21,520
Gain after indexation	£38,480

The gain eligible for retirement relief is as follows.

$$\frac{\text{Chargeable business assets}}{\text{Chargeable assets}} = \frac{250,000}{300,000} \times £38,480 \qquad\qquad £32,067$$

The maximum amount qualifying for retirement relief at 100% is calculated by reference to a six-year qualifying period and is thus £250,000 × 60% = £150,000. Thus, retirement relief of £32,067 is available at 100%, leaving a chargeable gain of £6,413 (£38,480 − £32,067).

The gain available for hold-over relief (disregarding retirement relief) is calculated as follows.

$$£38,480 \times \frac{250,000}{300,000} \quad [TCGA\ 1992,\ 7\ Sch\ 7] \qquad\qquad £32,067$$

However, the held-over gain is not to exceed the 'relevant proportion' of the chargeable gain disregarding hold-over relief under *Sec 165*. [*TCGA 1992, 7 Sch 8(3)*]. The maximum available for hold-over is thus

$$£6,413 \times \frac{250,000}{300,000} \qquad\qquad £5,344$$

The final position is thus as follows.

	£	£
Total gain after indexation		38,480
Eligible for retirement relief	32,067	
Eligible for hold-over relief	5,344	
		37,411
Chargeable gain 1996/97		£1,069

The base cost of the 4,000 shares in the hands of K's daughter is £134,656 (market value of £140,000 less held-over gain of £5,344).

Notes

(a) This example illustrates the provisions of *TCGA 1992, 7 Sch 7* (restriction of held-over gain under *Sec 165* on disposal of shares where some of the company's chargeable assets are not chargeable business assets) and those of *TCGA 1992, 7 Sch 8(3)* (interaction of hold-over relief and retirement relief).

(b) See also 222.2 RETIREMENT RELIEF for the calculation of gains qualifying for relief.

209.3 **TRANSFER OF BUSINESS TO A COMPANY** [*TCGA 1992, s 162*]

W carries on an antiquarian bookselling business. He decides to form an unquoted company, P Ltd, to carry on the business. He then transfers, in August 1996, the whole of the business undertaking, assets and liabilities to P Ltd, in consideration for the issue of shares, plus an amount left outstanding on interest-free loan. The business assets and liabilities transferred are valued as follows

	£	Value £	Chargeable gain (after indexation) £
Freehold shop premises		80,000	52,000
Goodwill		36,000	26,000
Fixtures and fittings		4,000	—
Trading stock		52,000	—
Debtors		28,000	—
		200,000	
Mortgage on shop	50,000		
Trade creditors	20,000	70,000	—
		£130,000	£78,000

The company issues 100,000 £1 ordinary shares, valued at par, to W in August 1996, and the amount left outstanding is £30,000. In December 1997, W sells 20,000 of his shares for £45,000 to X. W's remaining shareholding is then worth £155,000. The indexation factor from August 1996 to December 1997 is assumed to be 0.050.

(i) Amount of chargeable gain rolled over on transfer of the business

$$\frac{100,000}{130,000} \times £78,000 \qquad\qquad £60,000$$

Of the chargeable gain, £18,000 (£78,000 − £60,000) remains taxable.

The allowable cost of W's shares is £40,000 (£100,000 − £60,000).

(ii) On the sale of shares to X, W realises a chargeable gain

	£	£
Disposal consideration		45,000
Allowable cost £40,000 × $\dfrac{45,000}{45,000 + 155,000}$		9,000
Unindexed gain		36,000
Indexation allowance £9,000 × 0.050		450
Chargeable gain		£35,550

Notes

(*a*)   See 204.2 ASSETS HELD AT 31 MARCH 1982 for the relief given under *TCGA 1992, 4 Sch* where gains were held over after 31 March 1982 and before 6 April 1988 and a disposal occurs after 5 April 1988. This relief applies, inter alia, to gains held over under the rules illustrated above.

(*b*)   Relief under *Sec 162* is given automatically and without the need for a claim. W could defer up to the whole of the remaining £18,000 gain by claiming reinvestment relief under *TCGA 1992, s 164A* (see 221 REINVESTMENT RELIEF).

210   Indexation

210.1 **INDEXATION ALLOWANCE — GENERAL RULES** [*TCGA 1992, ss 53–56; FA 1994, s 93(1)–(5)(11)*]

(A) Calculation of indexation factor

M bought a freehold factory in December 1983 for £500,000. Further buildings are erected at a cost of £200,000 in May 1987. In November 1996 the factory is sold for £2m. The retail price index (RPI) was re-based in January 1987 from 394.5 to 100 and the relevant values are as follows

December 1983	342.8	
May 1987	101.9	
November 1996 (assumed)	150.9	

	£	£
Disposal consideration		2,000,000
Deduct Cost of factory and site	500,000	
Cost of additions	200,000	700,000
Unindexed gain		1,300,000
Indexation allowance		
(i) Factory and site		
Indexation factor		

$$\left(\frac{394.5 \times 150.9}{342.8}\right) - 100 = 73.7\%$$

Indexed rise		
£500,000 × 0.737	368,500	
(ii) Additions		
Indexation factor		

$$\frac{150.9 - 101.9}{101.9} = 0.481$$

Indexed rise		
£200,000 × 0.481	96,200	464,700
Chargeable gain		£835,300

Note

(*a*)   Alternatively the indexation factor on the pre-January 1987 expenditure can be calculated using the revised RPI figures so that

December 1983	=	86.89
November 1996 (assumed)	=	150.9

$$\text{Indexation from December 1983 to November 1996} = \frac{150.9 - 86.89}{86.89} = 0.737$$

(B) Disposal after 5 April 1988 of asset held on 31 March 1982

X acquired an antique for £6,000 in August 1979. He sold it for £16,000 in December 1996. The agreed market value of the clock at 31 March 1982 is £7,500. The indexation factor for March 1982 to December 1996 is assumed to be 0.904.

	£	£
Disposal consideration	16,000	16,000
Deduct Cost	6,000	
Market value 31.3.82		7,500
Unindexed gain	10,000	8,500
Indexation allowance £7,500 × 0.904	6,780	6,780
Gain after indexation	£3,220	£1,720
Chargeable gain		£1,720

Notes

(*a*)   In both the calculation using cost and that using 31 March 1982 value indexation is automatically based on 31 March 1982 value. If, however, a greater allowance would have been produced by basing indexation on cost, that would automatically have applied instead. If, however, an irrevocable election were to be made under *TCGA 1992, s 35(5)* for all assets to be treated as sold and re-acquired at 31 March 1982, indexation must then be based on 31 March 1982 value whether it is beneficial or not. [*TCGA 1992, s 55(1)(2)*].

(*b*)   See also 204.1 ASSETS HELD AT 31 MARCH 1982.

(C) Indexation allowance restriction and transitional relief [*FA 1994, s 93(11), 12 Sch*]

In August 1993, M disposes of an asset giving rise to a chargeable gain of £12,000. In June 1986, M had purchased two paintings, each for £25,000. In January 1994, he sells one of the paintings for £28,000.

In 1994/95, in addition to making further net chargeable gains of £18,000, M also sells the remaining painting, in January 1995, for £20,000.

He has allowable losses brought forward at 6 April 1993 of £2,500.

Indexation factors: June 1986 to January 1994 0.445
June 1986 to January 1995 0.493

M's taxable gains for 1993/94 and 1994/95 are calculated as follows

1993/94

	£
Sale of painting (January 1994)	
Proceeds	28,000
Cost	25,000
Unindexed gain	3,000
Indexation allowance:	
£25,000 × 0.445 = £11,125 but restricted to	3,000
Chargeable gain/allowable loss	Nil
Indexation loss (£11,125 − £3,000)	£8,125

CGT 210.1 Indexation

	£
Chargeable gains for the year	12,000
Annual exemption	5,800
	6,200
Indexation losses	6,200
Net chargeable gains	Nil

	£
Indexation losses	8,125
Less used in 1993/94 as above	6,200
Unused indexation losses c/f to 1994/95	£1,925

1994/95

	£
Sale of painting (January 1995)	
Proceeds	20,000
Cost	25,000
Allowable loss (no indexation allowance due)	£5,000

	£
Indexation loss £25,000 × 0.493	£12,325

		£
Net chargeable gains for the year (£18,000 − £5,000)		13,000
Annual exemption		5,800
		7,200
Indexation losses:		
B/f from 1993/94	1,925	
For 1994/95	12,325	
	£14,250	
But restricted to £10,000 − £6,200		3,800
		3,400
Allowable losses brought forward from 1992/93		2,500
Taxable gains		£900

Notes

(a) For disposals after 29 November 1993, an indexation allowance can only reduce or extinguish a gain. It cannot create or increase a loss. [*TCGA 1992, s 53(1)(2A); FA 1994, s 93(1)(3)*]. However, under transitional provisions in *FA 1994, 12 Sch,* indexation losses of up to £10,000 arising on disposals after 29 November 1993 and before 6 April 1995 may be set against gains in 1993/94 and 1994/95. Indexation losses are the amounts by which indexation allowances on disposals made in that period are reduced as a result of the restriction of the indexation allowance. [*12 Sch 2*]. Transitional relief is not available to companies or trustees of settlements created after 29 November 1993. [*12 Sch 1*].

(b) For the purposes of the transitional relief, gains are to be taken into account *after* deducting the annual exemption for the year but *before* any allowable losses brought forward, or carried back under *TCGA 1992, s 62* from the year of death. [*12 Sch 4*].

(*c*)   The balance of unused indexation losses in 1994/95 cannot be carried forward to 1995/96.

(D) Disposals on a no gain/no loss basis: inter-spouse transfers — asset acquired by first spouse before 1 April 1982 — no indexation allowance restriction on ultimate disposal [*TCGA 1992, ss 55(5)(6), 56(2), 58*]

Mr N inherited a country cottage in 1976 at a probate value of £12,000. Its market value at 31 March 1982 was £30,000. In July 1986, Mr N incurred enhancement expenditure of £5,000 on the cottage. In May 1988, he gave the cottage to his wife. In November 1996, Mrs N sells it for £75,000. At no time was the cottage the main residence of either spouse. The relevant indexation factors are as follows:

March 1982 to May 1988	0.337
July 1986 to May 1988	0.089
March 1982 to November 1996 (assumed)	0.900
July 1986 to November 1996 (assumed)	0.547

(i) Disposal in May 1988
Consideration deemed to be such that neither gain nor loss arises.

	£	£
Cost of cottage to Mr N		12,000
Enhancement expenditure		5,000
		17,000
Indexation allowance:		
£30,000 × 0.337	10,110	
£5,000 × 0.089	445	10,555
Cost of cottage to Mrs N		£27,555

(ii) Disposal in November 1996

	£	£	£
Sale proceeds		75,000	75,000
Cost	27,555		
Deduct indexation allowance previously given	10,555		
	17,000		
Deduct enhancement expenditure	5,000	(12,000)	
Market value 31.3.82			(30,000)
Enhancement expenditure (July 1986)		(5,000)	(5,000)
Unindexed gain		58,000	40,000
Indexation allowance:			
£30,000 × 0.900		(27,000)	(27,000)
£5,000 × 0.547		(2,735)	(2,735)
Gain after indexation		£28,265	£10,265
Chargeable gain			£10,265

Notes

(a)   Having acquired the asset by means of a no gain/no loss disposal, under *CGTA 1979, s 44* (now *TCGA 1992, s 58*), from her husband, who held it at 31 March 1982, Mrs N is deemed to have held the asset at 31 March 1982 for the purpose of the re-basing provisions, and also the provisions under which indexation allowance is computed using value at 31 March 1982. [*TCGA 1992, s 55(5)(6), 3 Sch 1*].

(b)   Where for re-basing/indexation purposes a person is deemed to have held an asset at 31 March 1982, that person can also be treated as having incurred enhancement expenditure which was in fact incurred after that date by a previous holder of the asset. (Revenue Tax Bulletin August 1992 p 32).

(c)   Re-basing does not apply to the no gain/no loss disposal. [*TCGA 1992, s 35(3)(d)(i)*].

(d)   See also (E)–(G) below and 215 MARRIED PERSONS.

(E) Disposals on a no gain/no loss basis: inter-spouse transfers — asset acquired by first spouse after 31 March 1982 — gain on ultimate disposal [*TCGA 1992, s 56(2)*]
The facts are as in (D) above except that Mr N inherited the cottage in April 1982 at a probate value of £30,000. The relevant indexation factors are:

April 1982 to May 1988	0.310
July 1986 to May 1988	0.089
May 1988 to November 1996 (assumed)	0.421

(i) Disposal in May 1988
Consideration deemed to be such that neither gain nor loss arises.

	£	£
Cost of cottage to Mr N		30,000
Enhancement expenditure		5,000
		35,000
Indexation allowance:		
£30,000 × 0.310	9,300	
£5,000 × 0.089	445	9,745
Cost of cottage to Mrs N		£44,745

(ii) Disposal in November 1996

	£
Sale proceeds	75,000
Cost (as above)	44,745
Unindexed gain	30,255
Indexation allowance £44,745 × 0.421	18,838
Chargeable gain	£11,417

Note

(a)   For further examples on inter-spouse transfers, see (D) above and 215 MARRIED PERSONS. The principles in (F) and (G) below also apply to inter-spouse transfers.

(F) Disposals on a no gain/no loss basis: intra-group transfers — asset acquired by group before 1 April 1982 — indexation allowance restricted on ultimate disposal [*TCGA 1992, ss 55(5)–(9), 56(2), 171; FA 1994, s 93(4)*]

J Ltd and K Ltd are 75% subsidiaries of H Ltd. J Ltd acquired a property in 1980 for £20,000. Its market value at 31 March 1982 was £25,000. In May 1988, J Ltd transferred the property to K Ltd. In November 1996, K Ltd sells the property outside the group. The sale proceeds are (1) £15,000 or (2) £26,000. The relevant indexation factors are as follows:

March 1982 to May 1988 (actual)	0.337
March 1982 to November 1996 (assumed)	0.900

(i) Disposal in May 1988
Consideration deemed to be such that neither gain nor loss arises.

	£
Cost of asset to J Ltd	20,000
Indexation allowance £25,000 × 0.337	8,425
Cost of asset to K Ltd	£28,425

(ii) Disposal in November 1996

(1) Proceeds £15,000

	£	£	£
Proceeds		15,000	15,000
Cost	28,425		
Deduct Indexation allowance previously given	8,425		
		(20,000)	
Market value 31.3.82			(25,000)
		(5,000)	(10,000)
Add Rolled-up indexation		(8,425)	(8,425)
Loss after rolled-up indexation		£(13,425)	£(18,425)
Allowable loss		£13,425	

(2) Proceeds £26,000

	£	£	£
Proceeds		26,000	26,000
Cost	28,425		
Deduct Indexation allowance previously given	8,425		
		(20,000)	
Market value 31.3.82			(25,000)
Unindexed gain		6,000	1,000
Indexation allowance:			
£25,000 × 0.900 = £22,500 but restricted to		(6,000)	(1,000)
		Nil	Nil
Excess of rolled-up indexation (£8,425) over indexation allowance given above		(2,425)	(7,425)
Loss after rolled-up indexation		£(2,425)	£(7,425)
Allowable loss		£2,425	

CGT 210.1 Indexation

Notes

(a) The calculation first follows that in (D) above. [*TCGA 1992, s 55(5)(6)*]. As the ultimate disposal is after 29 November 1993 and indexation allowance is either unavailable as in (1) above or restricted as in (2) above, special provisions enable the person making the disposal to obtain the benefit of any indexation allowance already accrued on no gain/no loss transfers made *before* 30 November 1993 (called 'rolled-up indexation'). [*TCGA 1992, s 55(7)–(9); FA 1994, s 93(4)*].

(b) The principles illustrated in this example apply equally to inter-spouse transfers.

(G) Disposals on a no gain/no loss basis: intra-group transfers — asset acquired by group after 31 March 1982 — loss on ultimate disposal [*TCGA 1992, ss 56(2)–(4), 171; FA 1994, s 93(5)*]

L Ltd, M Ltd and N Ltd are members of a 75% group of companies. L Ltd acquired a property in June 1990 for £50,000 and transferred it to M Ltd in June 1993. M Ltd transferred the property to N Ltd in June 1994, and N Ltd sold it outside the group in June 1996 for £55,000. The relevant indexation factors are as follows:

June 1990 to June 1993	0.113
June 1993 to June 1994	0.026

(i) Disposal in June 1993
Consideration deemed to be such that neither gain nor loss arises.

	£
Cost of asset to L Ltd	50,000
Indexation allowance £50,000 × 0.113	5,650
Cost of asset to M Ltd	£55,650

(ii) Disposal in June 1994

Cost of asset to M Ltd	55,650
Indexation allowance £55,650 × 0.026	1,447
Cost of asset to N Ltd	£57,097

(iii) Disposal in June 1996

Proceeds	55,000
Cost (as above)	57,097
Loss before adjustment under *Sec 56(3)*	2,097
Deduct Indexation on June 1994 disposal	1,447
Allowable loss	£650

Notes

(a) Where a loss accrues on the ultimate disposal, it is reduced by any indexation allowance included in the cost of the asset by virtue of a no gain/no loss disposal made *after* 29 November 1993. If this adjustment would otherwise convert a loss into a gain, the disposal is treated as giving rise to neither a gain nor a loss. [*TCGA 1992, s 56(3); FA 1994, s 93(5)*].

(b) The principles illustrated in this example apply equally to inter-spouse transfers.

210.2 **SHARE IDENTIFICATION RULES** [*TCGA 1992, ss 104, 105, 107–110; FA 1994, s 93(6)*]

(A) General

B has the following transactions in 25p ordinary shares of H plc, a quoted company.

		Cost/(proceeds) £
6.6.78	Purchased 500 at £0.85	425
3.11.81	Purchased 1,300 at £0.80	1,040
15.5.82	Purchased 1,000 at £1.02	1,020
8.9.82	Purchased 400 at £1.08	432
1.2.86	Purchased 1,200 at £1.14	1,368
29.7.87	Sold 2,000 at £1.30	(2,600)
8.6.90	Purchased 1,500 at £1.26	1,890
21.12.93	Received 1,000 from wife (cost £1,250, indexation to date £250)	1,500
10.5.96	Sold 3,900 at £1.90	(7,410)

The shares stood at £1.00 at 31.3.82.

Indexation factors	March 1982 to May 1995	0.883
	May 1982 to April 1985	0.161
	September 1982 to April 1985	0.158
	April 1985 to February 1986	0.019
	February 1986 to July 1987	0.054
	July 1987 to June 1990	0.245
	June 1990 to December 1993	0.120
	December 1993 to May 1996	0.078

Disposal on 10 May 1996

The 'new holding' pool immediately prior to the disposal should be as follows

	Shares	Qualifying expenditure £	Indexed pool £
15.5.82 acquisition	1,000	1,020	1,020
Indexation to April 1985			
£1,020 × 0.161			164
8.9.82 acquisition	400	432	432
Indexation to April 1985			
£432 × 0.158			68
Pool at 6.4.85	1,400	1,452	1,684
Indexed rise: Apr. 1985 — Feb. 1986			
£1,684 × 0.019			32
1.2.86 acquisition	1,200	1,368	1,368
	2,600	2,820	3,084
Indexed rise: Feb. 1986 — July 1987			
£3,084 × 0.054			167
	2,600	2,820	3,251
29.7.87 disposal	(2,000)	(2,169)	(2,501)
C/f	£600	£651	£750

	Shares	Qualifying expenditure £	Indexed pool £
B/f	600	651	750
Indexed rise: July 1987 — June 1990			
£750 × 0.245			184
8.6.90 acquisition	1,500	1,890	1,890
	2,100	2,541	2,824
Indexed rise: June 1990 — Dec. 1993			
£2,824 × 0.120			339
21.12.93 acquisition	1,000	1,250	1,500
	3,100	3,791	4,663
Indexed rise: Dec. 1993 — May 1996			
£4,663 × 0.078			364
	3,100	3,791	5,027

The 1982 holding is as follows

	Shares	Allowable expenditure £
6.6.78 acquisition	500	425
3.11.81 acquisition	1,300	1,040
	1,800	1,465

(ii) Identify 3,100 shares sold with new holding	£
Disposal consideration 3,100 × £1.90	5,890
Allowable cost	3,791
Unindexed gain	2,099
Indexation allowance £4,915 − £3,791	1,124
Chargeable gain	£975

(iii) Identify 800 shares sold with 1982 holding

	£	£
Disposal consideration 800 × £1.90	1,520	1,520
Cost $\dfrac{800}{1,800} \times £1,465$	651	
Market value 31.3.82 $\dfrac{800}{1,800} \times £1,800$		800
Unindexed gain	869	720
Indexation allowance £800 × 0.883	706	706
Gain after indexation	£163	£14
Chargeable gain		£14
Total chargeable gain (1996/97) (£975 + £14)		£989

Notes

(*a*)   Share disposals after 5.4.85 (31.3.85 for companies) are identified firstly with the 'new holding' and secondly with the 1982 holding, both of which are regarded as single assets.

(*b*)   On share disposals after 5.4.88 identified with shares held at 31.3.82, the re-basing provisions have effect and indexation is based on the higher of cost and 31.3.82 value. If an irrevocable election is made under *TCGA 1992, s 35(5)* for all assets to be treated as disposed of and re-acquired at their market value on 31.3.82, indexation must be based on the 31.3.82 value even if this is less than cost. [*TCGA 1992, s 55(1)(2)*].

(B) Special rules — 'same day' transactions and the 'ten day' rule [*TCGA 1992, ss 105, 107(3)–(6)*].

C has the following transactions in 25p ordinary shares of J plc.

		Cost/(proceeds)
		£
16.12.84	Purchased 20,000 at £1.92	38,400
5.8.87	Purchased 12,000 at £2.40	28,800
3.4.88	Sold 4,000 at £2.00	(8,000)
4.4.88	Purchased 4,000 at £2.02	8,080
14.9.91	Purchased 5,000 at £2.20	11,000
14.9.91	Sold 1,000 at £2.19	(2,190)
28.2.97	Purchased 2,000 at £2.45	4,900
3.3.97	Purchased 2,000 at £2.48	4,960
8.3.97	Sold 6,000 at £2.75	(16,500)

Holding at 5.4.97 – 34,000

Indexation factors	December 1984 to August 1987	0.124
	August 1987 to April 1988	0.036
	April 1988 to September 1991	0.271
	September 1991 to March 1997 (assumed)	0.133

CGT 210.2 Indexation

1987/88
Disposal on 3.4.88
Establish 'new holding' pool

	Shares	Qualifying expenditure £	Indexed pool £
16.12.84 acquisition	20,000	38,400	38,400
Indexed rise: December 1984 — August 1987 £38,400 × 0.124			4,762
5.8.87 acquisition	12,000	28,800	28,800
	32,000	67,200	71,962
Indexed rise: August 1987 — April 1988 £71,962 × 0.036			2,591
	32,000	67,200	74,553
3.4.88 disposal	(4,000)	(8,400)	(9,319)
4.4.88 acquisition	4,000	8,080	8,080
Pool carried forward	32,000	£66,880	£73,314

Disposal consideration		£8,000	
Cost $\dfrac{4,000}{32,000} \times £67,200$		8,400	
Unindexed loss		400	
Indexation allowance			

$$\frac{4,000}{32,000} \times £74,553 = £9,319$$

£9,319 − £8,400	919	
Allowable loss	£1,319	

1991/92
Disposal on 14.9.91
Match with acquisitions on the same day

Disposal consideration	£2,190
Cost $\dfrac{1,000}{5,000} \times £11,000$	2,200
Allowable loss	£10

Add balance of 14.9.91 acquisition to pool

	Shares	Qualifying expenditure £	Indexed pool £
Pool at 4.4.88	32,000	66,880	73,314
Indexed rise: April 1988 — September 1991 £73,314 × 0.271			19,868
Balance of 14.9.91 acquisition	4,000	8,800	8,800
Pool carried forward	36,000	£75,680	£101,982

1996/97
Disposal on 8.3.97
Match first with acquisition on 28.2.97

Disposal consideration 2,000 × £2.75	£5,500
Cost 28.2.97	4,900
Chargeable gain	£600

Match next with 3.3.97 acquisition

Disposal consideration 2,000 × £2.75	£5,500
Cost 3.3.97	4,960
Chargeable gain	£540

Match finally with 'new holding' pool

	Shares	Qualifying expenditure £	Indexed pool £
Pool at 14.9.91	36,000	75,680	101,982
Indexed rise: September 1991 — March 1996			
£101,982 × 0.133			13,564
	36,000	75,680	115,546
Balance of 8.3.97 disposal	(2,000)	(4,204)	(6,419)
Pool carried forward	34,000	£71,476	£109,127

Disposal consideration 2,000 × £2.75	£5,500
Cost $\dfrac{2,000}{36,000} \times$ £75,680	4,204
Unindexed gain	1,296
Indexation allowance	

$$\frac{2,000}{36,000} \times £115,546 = £6,419$$

£6,419 − £4,204 = £2,215 but restricted to	1,296
Chargeable gain	Nil

Total chargeable gain 1996/97 (£600 + £540)	£1,140

Notes

(a) Under *TCGA 1992, s 105*, a disposal of securities is matched as far as possible with an acquisition on the same day. It follows that no indexation can be available.

(b) Subject to the overriding rule described in (a) above, and for disposals after 5.4.85 (31.3.85 for companies), a disposal of securities is first matched with preceding acquisitions within a ten-day period on a first in/first out basis, and to the extent that they can be so matched, the securities are not pooled and no indexation allowance is due. [*TCGA 1992, s 107(3)–(6)*]. No special rules apply where an acquisition *follows* a disposal within the ten-day period; the above rules do not therefore affect a 'bed-and-breakfast' transaction.

211   Interest on Overpaid Tax

[TCGA 1992, s 283]

211.1 L realised net chargeable gains (after the annual exemption) of £20,000 in 1992/93. An assessment was raised on 15 January 1994, charging tax of £8,000. L paid the tax on 30 January 1994. In December 1994, L made a claim under *TCGA 1992, s 152* (rollover relief) and the 1992/93 assessment was reduced to £8,000, with tax payable of £3,200. A repayment of £4,800 was made by payable order issued on 15 April 1996.

Repayment supplement is		£
6.4.94 – 5.10.94	$£4,800 \times 5.5\% \times \frac{6}{12}$	132.00
6.10.94 – 5.3.95	$£4,800 \times 6.25\% \times \frac{5}{12}$	125.00
6.3.95 – 5.2.96	$£4,800 \times 7\% \times \frac{11}{12}$	308.00
6.2.96 – 5.5.96	$£4,800 \times 6.25\% \times \frac{3}{12}$	75.00
		£640.00

Note

(*a*)   The calculation may be made, or checked, using the interest factor tables published from time to time by the Revenue.

Factor for May 1996	3.2434
Factor for April 1994	3.1101
Difference	0.1333
£4,800 × 0.1333 =	£639.84

212   Interest on Unpaid Tax

[*TMA 1970, ss 69, 86–92; FA 1989, s 156(1)*]

212.1 **(A)**

P is assessed to CGT for 1994/95 by a notice of assessment dated 15 November 1995. The amount of tax charged is £45,000. P appeals on 20 November 1995 against the assessment, which is estimated, and applies to postpone payment of £20,000 of the tax charged. The Inspector agrees in writing to the postponement on 5 January 1996 and P makes a payment of £25,000 on 6 March 1996.

The appeal is determined by agreement on 10 May 1996, and a revised notice of assessment is issued on 15 May 1996, charging tax of £29,000. P pays the balance of £4,000 on 5 June 1996.

(i) Tax charged which is not postponed (£25,000)

Date tax would have been due and payable if no appeal	(D1)	15.12.95
Date tax actually becomes due and payable	(D2)	4.2.96
Table date	(D3)	1.6.96
Reckonable date Because D2 is not later than D3, D2		4.2.96

Interest runs from 4 February 1996 to 6 March 1996

$$£25,000 \times \frac{30}{365} \times 6.25\%$$

£128.42

(ii) Tax due which is postponed (£4,000)

Date tax would have been due and payable if no appeal	(D1)	15.12.95
Date tax actually becomes due and payable	(D2)	14.6.96
Table date	(D3)	1.6.96
Reckonable date Because D2 is later than D3, later of D1 and D3 (i.e. D3)		1.6.96

Interest runs from 1 June 1996 to 5 June 1996

$$£4,000 \times \frac{4}{365} \times 6.25\%$$

£2.74

Total interest payable   £131.16

(B)

V realised chargeable gains in 1994/95. On 6 September 1995, he informed the inspector of that fact and supplied him with details of the total sale proceeds. The amount of the gains could not be finalised as the total allowable expenditure was not yet quantifiable. On 15 October 1995, an estimated assessment was raised showing CGT payable of £8,000. V lodged an appeal but did not request any postponement of tax. He paid the £8,000 by the due date of 1 December 1995. The amount of the gains is later agreed at £12,600, the appeal is determined and a revised assessment raised on 15 March 1996. V pays the additional tax of £4,600 on 23 May 1996.

The £4,600 additional tax is treated as if it had been charged by the original assessment. [*TMA 1970, s 86(3)(3A); FA 1989, s 156(1)*].

Date tax would (notionally) have been due and payable if no appeal	(D1)	1.12.94
Date tax actually becomes due and payable	(D2)	14.4.95
Table date	(D3)	1.6.95
Reckonable date Because D2 is not later than D3, D2		14.4.95

Interest runs from 14.4.96 to 23.5.96 (39 days)

$$£4,600 \times \frac{39}{365} \times 6.25\% \qquad\qquad £30.72$$

Suppose that the revised assessment was not issued until 15 June 1996, with V paying the tax of £4,600 on 30 June 1996.

D1 and D3 remain the same as above; D2 becomes 15 July 1996.

Reckonable date Because D2 is later than D3, later of D1 and D3 (i.e. D3)	1.6.96

Interest runs from 1.6.96 to 30.6.96 (29 days)

$$£4,600 \times \frac{29}{365} \times 6.25\% \qquad\qquad £22.84$$

Note

(*a*)   If V had failed to inform the Revenue and supply them with sufficient details of his 1994/95 gains by 31 October 1995, interest could have been charged under *TMA 1970, s 88* from the normal due date of 1 December 1995 to the date of payment. (Revenue Statement of Practice SP 6/89 and Revenue Tax Bulletin August 1992 pages 25–28). No interest would then be charged under *Sec 86*.

212.2 SELF-ASSESSMENT

Mr Watson's 1998/99 capital gains liability as shown in his self-assessment amounts to £5,000. On 1 May 2000 Mr Watson pays £2,000 and on 1 August 2000 he pays the £3,000 balance.

Assuming the rate of interest on overdue tax is 7%, Mr Watson will be charged as follows:

Interest and Surcharge due

	£
Interest	
$£2,000 \times 7\% \times \frac{90}{366} =$	34.43
Interest	
$£3,000 \times 7\% \times \frac{182}{366} =$	104.43
	£138.86
Surcharge	
$£5,000 \times 5\%$	250
$£3,000 \times 5\%$	150
	£400

Notes

(*a*)   Under self-assessment capital gains tax is due on 31 January following the year of assessment together with the final income tax payment.

(*b*)   If any tax is paid more than 28 days late a 5% surcharge is levied in addition to interest. An additional surcharge is also levied if the tax is outstanding for more than 6 months. [*TMA 1970, s 59C(1)(2)(3); FA 1994, s 194, FA 1995, s 109(2)*].

213 Land

213.1 SMALL PART DISPOSALS [*TCGA 1992, s 242*]

C owns farmland which cost £134,000 in May 1983. In February 1991, a small plot of land is exchanged with an adjoining landowner for another piece of land. The value placed on the transaction is £18,000. The value of the remaining estate excluding the new piece of land is estimated at £250,000. In March 1997, C sells the whole estate for £300,000.

Indexation factors	May 1983 to February 1991	0.547
	February 1991 to March 1996 (assumed)	0.165
	May 1983 to March 1997 (assumed)	0.802

(i) No claim made under what is now *TCGA 1992, s 242(2)*

		£	£
(*a*)	*Disposal in February 1991*		
	Disposal proceeds		18,000
	Allowable cost $\dfrac{18,000}{18,000 + 250,000} \times £134,000$		9,000
	Unindexed gain		9,000
	Indexation allowance £9,000 × 0.547		4,923
	Chargeable gain 1990/91		£4,077
(*b*)	*Disposal in March 1996*		
	Disposal proceeds		300,000
	Allowable cost		
	Original land £(134,000 − 9,000)	125,000	
	Exchanged land	18,000	143,000
	Unindexed gain		157,000
	Indexation allowance		
	Original land £125,000 × 0.802	100,250	
	Exchanged land £18,000 × 0.165	2,970	103,220
	Chargeable gain 1995/96		£53,780

(ii) Claim made under what is now *TCGA 1992, s 242(2)*

		£
(*a*)	*No disposal in February 1991*	
	Allowable cost of original land	134,000
	Deduct disposal proceeds	18,000
	Adjusted allowable cost	£116,000
	Allowable cost of additional land	£18,000

	£	£
(b) *Disposal in March 1997*		
Disposal proceeds		300,000
Allowable cost		
Original land	116,000	
Additional land	18,000	134,000
Unindexed gain		166,000
Indexation allowance		
Original land £134,000 × 0.802	107,468	
Additional land £18,000 × 0.165	2,970	
	110,438	
Receipt set-off £18,000 × 0.165	2,970	107,468
Chargeable gain 1996/97		£58,532

Notes

(a)   A claim under *TCGA 1992, s 242* (previously *CGTA 1979, s 107*) may be made where the consideration for the part disposal does not exceed one-fifth of the value of the whole, up to a maximum of £20,000.

(b)   If the second disposal had also been made in 1990/91 no claim under *Sec 242(2)* could have been made on the part disposal as proceeds of all disposals of land in the year would have exceeded £20,000.

(c)   If the original land had been held at 31 March 1982 and the part disposal took place after that date, the disposal proceeds, on a claim under *Sec 242(2)*, would be deducted from the 31 March 1982 value for the purpose of the re-basing provisions.

213.2 COMPULSORY PURCHASE [*TCGA 1992, ss 243–248*]

(A) Rollover where new land acquired

(i) Rollover not claimed

D owns freehold land purchased for £75,000 in 1977. Part of the land is made the subject of a compulsory purchase order. The compensation of £70,000 is agreed on 10 April 1996. The market value of the remaining land is £140,000. The value of the total freehold land at 31 March 1982 was £99,000. The indexation factor for the period March 1982 to April 1996 is 0.921.

	£	£
Disposal consideration	70,000	70,000
Cost £75,000 × $\dfrac{70,000}{70,000 + 140,000}$	25,000	
Market value 31.3.82		
£99,000 × $\dfrac{70,000}{70,000 + 140,000}$		33,000
Unindexed gain	45,000	37,000
Indexation allowance £33,000 × 0.921	30,393	30,393
Gain after indexation	£14,607	£6,607
Chargeable gain		£6,607

(ii) Rollover claimed under *TCGA 1992, s 247*
If, in (i), D acquires new land costing, say, £80,000 in, say, December 1996, relief may be claimed as follows.

	£
Allowable cost of land compulsorily purchased	33,000
Indexation allowance	30,393
Deemed consideration for disposal	63,393
Actual consideration	70,000
Chargeable gain rolled over	£6,607
Allowable cost of new land (£80,000 − £6,607)	£73,393

(B) Small disposals

(i) No rollover relief claimed
T inherited land in June 1984 at a probate value of £290,000. Under a compulsory purchase order, a part of the land is acquired for highway improvements. Compensation of £32,000 and a further £10,000 for severance, neither sum including any amount in respect of loss of profits, is agreed on 15 April 1996. The value of the remaining land is £900,000. Prior to the compulsory purchase, the value of all the land had been £950,000. The indexation factor for the period June 1984 to April 1996 is 0.711.

	£
Total consideration for disposal (£32,000 + £10,000)	42,000
Deduct allowable cost $\dfrac{42,000}{42,000 + 900,000} \times £290,000$	12,930
Unindexed gain	29,070
Indexation allowance £12,930 × 0.711	9,193
Chargeable gain	£19,877

(ii) Rollover relief claimed under *TCGA 1992, s 243*
Total consideration for disposal is £42,000, less than 5% of the value of the estate before the disposal (£950,000). T may therefore claim that the consideration be deducted from the allowable cost of the estate.

Revised allowable cost (£290,000 − £42,000)	£248,000

Note
(a)   An indexation adjustment in respect of the amount deducted will be required on a subsequent disposal of the estate. [*TCGA 1992, ss 53(3), 57*]. For an example of the computation, see 206.4(E) DISPOSAL.

213.3 LEASES

(A) Short leases which are not initially wasting assets [*TCGA 1992, 8 Sch 1*]

On 31 August 1991, N purchased the remaining term of a lease of commercial premises for £55,000. The lease was subject to a 25-year sub-lease granted on 1 July 1969 at a fixed rental of £1,000 a year. The market rental was estimated at £15,000 a year. The term of the lease held by N is 60 years from 1 April 1967. The value of the lease in 1994, when the sub-lease expired, was estimated at 31 August 1991 as being £70,000. Immediately upon expiry of the sub-lease, N has refurbishment work done at a cost of £50,000 (payable on 30 July 1994), £40,000 of which qualifies as enhancement expenditure. On 31 March 1997, N sells the lease for £130,000.

Indexation factors (assumed)	August 1991 to March 1997	0.190
	July 1994 to March 1997	0.084

Term of lease at date of expiry of sub-lease	32 years 9 months
Relevant percentage $89.354 + \frac{9}{12} \times (90.280 - 89.354)$	90.049%
Term of lease at date of assignment	30 years
Relevant percentage	87.330%

	£	£
Disposal consideration		130,000
Deduct allowable cost	55,000	
enhancement costs	40,000	
	95,000	
Less Wasted		
$\dfrac{90.049 - 87.330}{90.049} \times 95,000$	2,868	
		92,132
Unindexed gain		37,868
Indexation allowance:		
Cost of lease		
$0.190 \times \dfrac{55,000}{95,000} \times £92,132$	10,135	
Enhancement costs		
$0.084 \times \dfrac{40,000}{95,000} \times £92,132$	3,259	13,394
Chargeable gain		£24,474

Note

(*a*)   The head-lease becomes a wasting asset on the expiry of the sub-lease. [*TCGA 1992, 8 Sch 1(2)*].

(B) Grant of long lease [*TCGA 1992, s 42, 8 Sch 2*]

In 1978, K acquired a long lease by assignment for £22,000. At the time he acquired it, the lease had an unexpired term of 82 years. On 10 April 1996, he granted a 55-year sub-lease for a premium of £100,000 and a peppercorn rent. The value of the reversion plus the capitalised value of the rents is £10,000. The value of the lease at 31 March 1982 was estimated at £55,000. The indexation factor for the period March 1982 to April 1995 is 0.921.

	£	£
Disposal consideration	100,000	100,000
Cost £22,000 × $\dfrac{100,000}{100,000 + 10,000}$		20,000
Market value 31.3.82		
£55,000 × $\dfrac{100,000}{100,000 + 10,000}$		50,000
Unindexed gain	80,000	50,000
Indexation allowance £50,000 × 0.921	46,050	46,050
Gain after indexation	£33,950	£3,950
Chargeable gain		£3,950

(C) Grant of short lease [*ICTA 1988, s 34; TCGA 1992, 8 Sch 2, 5*]
L is the owner of a freehold factory which he leases for a term of 25 years commencing in December 1996. The cost of the factory was £100,000 in April 1989. The lease is granted for a premium of £30,000 and an annual rent. The reversion to the lease plus the capitalised value of the rents amount to £120,000. The indexation factor for April 1989 to December 1996 is assumed to be 0.324.

	£	£
Amount chargeable to income tax		
Amount of premium		30,000
Deduct excluded $\dfrac{25 - 1}{50}$ × £30,000		14,400
Amount chargeable to income tax		£15,600
Chargeable gain		
Premium received	30,000	
Deduct charged to income tax	15,600	
		14,400
Allowable cost $\dfrac{14,400}{30,000 + 120,000}$ × £100,000		9,600
Unindexed gain		4,800
Indexation allowance £9,600 × 0.324		3,110
Chargeable gain		£1,690

Note
(*a*)   The amount chargeable to income tax is not deducted from the amount of premium appearing in the denominator of the apportionment fraction.

(D) Disposal by assignment of short lease: without enhancement expenditure [*TCGA 1992, 8 Sch 1*]

X buys a lease for £200,000 on 1 October 1992. The lease commenced on 1 June 1983 for a term of 60 years. X assigns the lease for £300,000 at the end of March 1997. The indexation factor for October 1992 to March 1997 is assumed to be 0.129.

Term of lease unexpired at date of acquisition		50 years 8 months
Relevant percentage		100%

Term of lease unexpired at date of assignment		46 years 2 months
Relevant percentage $98.490 + \frac{2}{12} \times (98.902 - 98.490)$		98.559%

	£	£
Disposal consideration		300,000
Allowable cost	200,000	
Deduct Wasted $\dfrac{100 - 98.559}{100} \times £200,000$	2,882	
		197,118
Unindexed gain		102,882
Indexation allowance £197,118 × 0.129		25,428
Chargeable gain		£77,454

(E) Disposal by assignment of short lease held at 31 March 1982 [*TCGA 1992, s 35, 8 Sch 1*]

A buys a lease for £100,000 on 1 March 1982. The lease commenced on 31 March 1972 for a term of 60 years. Its value at 31 March 1982 was estimated at £104,000. On 31 March 1997, A assigns the lease for £240,000. The indexation factor for the period March 1982 to March 1997 is assumed to be 0.920.

(i) The computation without re-basing to 1982 is as follows

Term of lease unexpired at date of acquisition (1.3.82)	50 years 1 month	
Relevant percentage	100%	

Term of lease unexpired at date of assignment	35 years 0 months	
Relevant percentage	91.981%	

	£	£
Disposal consideration		240,000
Cost	100,000	
Deduct Wasted $\dfrac{100 - 91.981}{100} \times £100,000$	8,019	91,981
Unindexed gain		148,019
Indexation allowance (see (ii) below)		88,310
Gain after indexation		£59,709

(ii) The computation with re-basing to 1982 is as follows

Term of lease unexpired at deemed date of acquisition (31.3.82)		
	49 years	
Relevant percentage	99.657%	
Term of lease unexpired at date of assignment	35 years	
Relevant percentage	91.981%	

	£	£
Disposal consideration		240,000
Market value 31.3.82	104,000	
Deduct Wasted $\dfrac{99.657 - 91.981}{99.657} \times £104,000$	8,011	95,989
Unindexed gain		144,011
Indexation allowance £95,989 × 0.920		88,310
Gain after indexation		£55,701
Chargeable gain		£55,701

Notes

(a) A is deemed, under *TCGA 1992, s 35*, to have disposed of and immediately re-acquired the lease on 31 March 1982 at its market value at that date.

(b) Both calculations produce a gain with the re-basing calculation producing the smaller gain. Therefore, re-basing applies. [*Sec 35(2)(3)(a)*].

(c) Indexation is based, in both calculations, on the assumption that the asset was sold and re-acquired at market value on 31 March 1982 since this gives a greater allowance than if based on original cost as reduced by the wasting asset provisions. [*TCGA 1992, s 55(1)(2)*].

(F) Disposal by assignment of short lease: with enhancement expenditure [*TCGA 1992, 8 Sch 1*]

D Ltd acquires the lease of office premises for £100,000 on 1 July 1988. On 1 January 1990, the company contracts for complete refurbishment of the premises at a total cost of £180,000, of which £120,000 can be regarded as capital enhancement expenditure. The work is done at the beginning of January 1990, and the money is payable in equal tranches in March 1990 and May 1990. The lease is for a term of 50 years commencing 1 April 1981. On 1 January 1997, the lease is assigned to a new lessee for £450,000.

Indexation factors (assumed)	July 1988 to January 1997	0.489
	March 1990 to January 1997	0.350
	May 1990 to January 1997	0.318

Term of lease unexpired at date of acquisition	42 years 9 months	
Relevant percentage 96.593 + $\frac{9}{12}$ × (97.107 − 96.593)	96.978%	

Term of lease unexpired at date of expenditure incurred (January 1989 — see note (*a*))	41 years 3 months	
Relevant percentage 96.041 + $\frac{3}{12}$ × (96.593 − 96.041)	96.179%	

Term of lease unexpired at date of assignment	34 years 3 months	
Relevant percentage 91.156 + $\frac{3}{12}$ × (91.981 − 91.156)	91.362%	

	£	£	£
Disposal consideration			450,000
Cost of acquisition	100,000		
Deduct Wasted			
$\dfrac{96.978 - 91.362}{96.978} \times 100,000$	5,791	94,209	
Enhancement expenditure	120,000		
Deduct Wasted			
$\dfrac{96.179 - 91.362}{96.179} \times 120,000$	6,010	113,990	208,199
Unindexed gain			241,801
Indexation allowance			
Cost of lease £94,209 × 0.489		46,068	
Enhancement costs			
March 1989 £56,995 × 0.350		19,948	
May 1989 £56,995 × 0.318		18,124	
			84,140
Chargeable gain			£157,661

Note

(*a*)   The wasting provisions apply to enhancement expenditure by reference to the time when it is first reflected in the nature of the lease. The indexation provisions apply by reference to the date the expenditure became due and payable. [*TCGA 1992, s 54(4)(b), 8 Sch 1(4)(b)*].

(G) Sub-lease granted out of short lease: premium not less than potential premium
[*TCGA 1992, 8 Sch 4, 5*]
On 1 November 1994, S purchased a lease of shop premises then having 50 years to run for a premium of £100,000 and an annual rental of £40,000. After occupying the premises for the purposes of his own business, S granted a sub-lease to N Ltd. The sub-lease was for a term of 21 years commencing on 1 August 1996, for a premium of £50,000 and an annual rental of £30,000. It is agreed that, had the rent under the sub-lease been £40,000, the premium obtainable would have been £20,000. The indexation factor for November 1994 to August 1996 is assumed to be 0.060.

Term of lease at date granted	50 years
Relevant percentage	100%
Term of lease at date sub-lease granted	48 years 3 months
Relevant percentage $99.289 + \frac{3}{12} \times (99.657 - 99.289)$	99.381%
Term of lease at date sub-lease expires	27 years 3 months
Relevant percentage $83.816 + \frac{3}{12} \times (85.053 - 83.816)$	84.125%

Premium chargeable on S under Schedule A £

Amount of premium	50,000
$Deduct \; \dfrac{21-1}{50} \times £50,000$	20,000
Amount chargeable under Schedule A	£30,000

Chargeable gain

Disposal consideration	50,000
Allowable expenditure	
$£100,000 \times \dfrac{99.381 - 84.125}{100}$	15,256
Unindexed gain	34,744
Indexation allowance £15,256 × 0.060	915
Chargeable gain	33,829
Deduct Amount chargeable under Schedule A	30,000
Net chargeable gain	£3,829

Note
(*a*) If the amount chargeable under Schedule A exceeded the chargeable gain, the net gain would be nil. The deduction cannot create or increase a loss. [*TCGA 1992, 8 Sch 5(2)*].

(H) Sub-lease granted out of short lease: premium less than potential premium
[*TCGA 1992, 8 Sch 4, 5*]
C bought a lease of a house on 1 May 1992, when the unexpired term was 49 years. The cost of the lease was £20,000, and the ground rent payable is £500 p.a. C then let the house on a monthly tenancy until 30 November 1996 when he granted a 10-year lease for a premium of £5,000 and an annual rent of £8,000. Had the rent under the sub-lease been £500 a year, the premium obtainable would have been £40,000. C does not at any time occupy the house as a private residence. The indexation factor for May 1992 to November 1996 is assumed to be 0.130.

Term of lease at date of acquisition	49 years
Relevant percentage	99.657%
Term of lease when sub-lease granted	44 years 5 months
Relevant percentage $97.595 + \frac{5}{12} \times (98.059 - 97.595)$	97.788%
Term of lease when sub-lease expires	34 years 5 months
Relevant percentage $91.156 + \frac{5}{12} \times (91.981 - 91.156)$	91.500%

Amount chargeable under Schedule A	£
Amount of premium	5,000
Deduct exclusion $\dfrac{10-1}{50} \times 5{,}000$	900
Chargeable under Schedule A	£4,100
Disposal consideration	5,000
Deduct allowable expenditure	
$£20{,}000 \times \dfrac{97.788 - 91.500}{99.657} \times \dfrac{5{,}000}{40{,}000}$	158
Unindexed gain	4,842
Indexation allowance £158 × 0.130	21
Chargeable gain	4,821
Deduct Amount chargeable under Schedule A	4,100
Net chargeable gain	£721

Note

(*a*)   If the amount chargeable under Schedule A exceeded the chargeable gain, the net gain would be nil. The deduction cannot create or increase a loss. [*TCGA 1992, 8 Sch 5(2)*].

214 Losses

Cross-reference. See 10.2 LOSSES for the set-off of trading losses against chargeable gains made by individuals.

214.1 GENERAL

On 30 April 1996 Q sells for £40,000 a part of the land which he owns. The market value of the remaining estate is £160,000. Q bought the land for £250,000 in March 1988.

	£
Disposal consideration	40,000
Allowable cost $\dfrac{40,000}{40,000 + 160,000} \times £250,000$	50,000
Allowable loss	£10,000

Note

(a)   For disposals after 29 November 1993, indexation allowance cannot increase or create a loss for CGT purposes. [*TCGA 1992, s 53; FA 1994, s 93(1)–(3)*]. This is subject to transitional relief under *FA 1994, 12 Sch* for indexation losses on disposals before 6 April 1995. See 210.1(C) INDEXATION.

214.2 INTERACTION WITH ANNUAL EXEMPT AMOUNT [*TCGA 1992, s 3(1)(5)*]

U has the following chargeable gains and allowable losses

	Gains	Losses	Net
	£	£	£
1993/94	8,000	12,300	(4,300)
1994/95	2,800	2,100	700
1995/96	6,200	—	6,200
1996/97	14,800	2,200	12,600

1993/94 £

Net chargeable gains	—
Losses carried forward	£4,300

1994/95

Net chargeable gains (covered by annual exemption)	£700
Losses brought forward and carried forward	£4,300

1995/96 £

Chargeable gains	6,000
Deduct losses brought forward (part)	200
Taxable amount (exempt)	£5,800
Losses carried forward (£4,300 – £200)	£4,100

1996/97	£
Net chargeable gains	12,600
Deduct losses brought forward	4,100
Taxable amount	8,500
Deduct exempt amount	6,300
Taxable gains	£2,200

Note

(*a*)   See 210.1(C) INDEXATION for the interaction of indexation losses in 1993/94 and 1994/95 with the annual exemption.

214.3 **LOANS TO TRADERS — QUALIFYING CORPORATE BONDS** [*TCGA 1992, ss 253–255*]

V subscribed on 15 July 1986 for £5,000 unsecured loan stock in W plc, a UK trading company which used the funds raised by the issue for the purposes of its retail trade. The security was issued at £95 per £100 nominal and is a qualifying corporate bond as defined by *TCGA 1992, s 117*. In 1995, the company went into liquidation, and on 30 June 1995, V makes a claim under *TCGA 1992, s 254* on the basis that the value of the security had become negligible. The Inspector agrees and V's allowable loss for 1995/96 is the lesser of

(*a*) the principal outstanding	£5,000

and

(*b*) V's acquisition cost	£4,750

Thus, V's allowable loss is	£4,750

On 1 May 1996, W plc makes a once and for all distribution of £15 per £100 of loan stock, V thus receiving £750.

V has a chargeable gain for 1996/97 of £750.

Notes

(*a*)   The provisions of *TCGA 1992, s 253* (relief in respect of loans to traders) are extended to include debts on security where the security is a qualifying corporate bond. [*TCGA 1992, ss 254, 255*].

(*b*)   No indexation allowance is due.

(*c*)   The amount recovered, restricted to the amount of loss claimed, is taxed in the year of recovery.

(*d*)   In the above example, a loss is claimed on the basis that the value of the security has become negligible. [*Sec 254(3)*]. There are two further conditions under which a loss can be claimed. [*Sec 254(4)(5)*].

(*e*)   See 220 QUALIFYING CORPORATE BONDS generally.

214.4 **LOSSES ON SHARES IN UNQUOTED TRADING COMPANIES** [*ICTA 1988, ss 574–576; FA 1994, s 210, 20 Sch 8*]

P subscribed for 3,000 £1 ordinary shares in W Ltd, a new unquoted trading company, at par in June 1989. In September 1990, P acquired a further 2,000 shares at £1.60 from another shareholder. In December 1996, P sold 3,800 shares at 90p.

Indexation factors   June 1989 to September 1990   0.120
                     June 1989 to December 1996 (assumed)   0.311
                     September 1990 to December 1996 (assumed)   0.170

(i)   Establish new holding pool

	Shares	Qualifying expenditure £	Indexed pool £
June 1989 subscription	3,000	3,000	3,000
Indexation to September 1990 £3,000 × 0.120			360
September 1990 acquisition	2,000	3,200	3,200
	5,000	6,200	6,560
Indexed rise: September 1990 to December 1996 £6,560 × 0.170			1,115
	5,000	6,200	7,675
December 1996 disposal	(3,800)	(4,712)	(5,833)
Pool carried forward	1,200	£1,488	£1,842

(ii)   The overall loss is calculated as follows   £

Disposal consideration 3,800 × £0.90   3,420

Allowable cost $\dfrac{3,800}{5,000}$ × £6,200   4,712

Allowable loss   £1,292

(iii)   The loss allowable against income is calculated as follows

Loss referable to 1,800 subscription shares $\dfrac{1,800}{3,800}$ × £1,292   £612

Loss restricted to actual loss on the subscription shares   £
Disposal consideration 1,800 × £0.90   1,620
Allowable cost 1,800 × £1.00   1,800

Allowable loss   £180

(iv)   The loss not relieved against income remains a capital loss

£1,292 – £180 =   £1,112

Notes

(*a*)   For capital gains tax purposes, the shares merge in a 'new holding' pool, but for the purposes of relief under *ICTA 1988, ss 574–576*, shares disposed of are identified with shares acquired later rather than with shares acquired earlier.

(*b*)   For disposals after 29 November 1993, indexation allowance cannot increase or create a loss for CGT purposes (and therefore for *ICTA 1988, s 574* purposes also). [*TCGA 1992, s 53; FA 1994, s 93(1)–(3)*]. This is subject to transitional relief under *FA 1994, 12 Sch* for indexation losses on disposals before 6 April 1995 (see 210.1(C) INDEXATION).

(*c*)   For further examples on this topic, see IT 10.5 LOSSES and CT 118.4 LOSSES.

215   Married Persons

215.1 INTER-SPOUSE TRANSFERS AND RATES OF TAX [*TCGA 1992, ss 4, 58*]

(A) No inter-spouse transfer

Paul and Heidi are a married couple with total income of £26,000 and £30,000 respectively for 1996/97. Of the total income, there is sufficient non-dividend income to fully utilise the lower rate band. On 4 April 1997, Heidi sells a painting which she had acquired in June 1992 at a cost of £5,000. Net sale proceeds amount to £17,300 and the indexation factor for the period June 1992 to April 1997 is assumed to be 0.110. Neither spouse disposed of any other chargeable assets during 1996/97.

Chargeable gain — Heidi

	£
Net proceeds	17,300
Cost	5,000
Unindexed gain	12,300
Indexation allowance £5,000 × 0.110	550
Chargeable gain	11,750
Annual exemption	6,300
Taxable gain	£5,450

	£
Total income	30,000
Personal allowance	3,765
Taxable income	£26,235

Basic rate limit = £25,500, so gain of £5,450 is all taxed at 40%.

Tax payable £5,450 × 40%	£2,180.00

(B) Inter-spouse transfer

The facts are as in (A) above except that in January 1997, Heidi gives the painting to Paul who then makes the sale on 4 April 1997.

Indexation factors (assumed)

June 1992 to January 1997   0.089
January 1997 to April 1997   0.020

Chargeable gain — Heidi

	£
Deemed consideration (January 1997)	5,445
Cost	5,000
Unindexed gain	445
Indexation allowance £5,000 × 0.089	445
Chargeable gain	Nil

Chargeable gain — Paul

	£
Net proceeds (4.4.97)	17,000
Cost (January 1997)	5,445
Unindexed gain	11,555
Indexation allowance £5,445 × 0.020	109
Chargeable gain	11,446
Annual exemption	6,300
Taxable gain	£5,146
Total income	26,000
Personal allowance	(3,765)
Taxable income	£22,235

Taxable income falls short of the basic rate limit (£25,500) by £3,265, so gain of £5,146 is taxed as follows.

	£
£3,265 at 24%	783.60
1,881 at 40%	752.40
Tax payable	£1,536.00
Tax saving compared with (A) above	£644.00

Notes

(a) The inter-spouse transfer is deemed to be for such consideration as to ensure that no gain or loss accrues. [*TCGA 1992, s 58*]. Effectively, the consideration is equal to cost plus indexation to date. See 210.1(D)(E) INDEXATION for further examples. The principles in 210.1(F)(G) INDEXATION also apply.

(b) The fact that transfers of assets between husband and wife are no gain/no loss transfers enables savings to be made by ensuring that disposals are made by a spouse with an unused annual exemption and/or lower tax rates.

(c) An inter-spouse transfer followed by a sale could be attacked by the Revenue as an anti-avoidance device. To minimise the risk, there should be a clear time interval between the two transactions and no arrangements made to effect the ultimate sale until after the transfer. The gift should be outright with no strings attached and with no 'arrangement' for eventual proceeds to be passed to the transferor.

215.2 **JOINTLY OWNED ASSETS**

Derek and Raquel are a married couple. Derek had for many years owned an investment property which he purchased for £70,000 in May 1984. On 5 January 1992, he transferred to Raquel a 10% share in the property which was thereafter held in their joint names under a joint tenancy. No declaration is made for income tax purposes under *ICTA 1988, s 282B*, with the result that the rental income from the property is treated, by virtue of *ICTA 1988, s 282A* as arising in equal shares. On 29 June 1996, the property is sold for £130,000.

Indexation factors May 1984 to January 1992	0.524
May 1984 to June 1996 (assumed)	0.683
January 1992 to June 1996 (assumed)	0.104

(i) Inter-spouse transfer

	£
Deemed consideration (January 1992)	10,668
Cost £70,000 × 10% (see note (*c*))	7,000
Unindexed gain	3,668
Indexation allowance £7,000 × 0.524	3,668
Chargeable gain	Nil

(ii) 1996/97 disposal

	Derek £	Raquel £
Disposal proceeds	117,000	13,000
Cost: Derek (£70,000 – £7,000)	63,000	
Raquel (see (i) above)		10,668
Unindexed gain	54,000	2,332
Indexation allowance: £63,000 × 0.683	43,029	
£10,668 × 0.104		1,109
Chargeable gains	£10,971	£1,223

Notes

(*a*) Where a joint declaration of unequal beneficial interests is made under *Sec 282B*, it is presumed that the same split applies for capital gains tax purposes. In the absence of a declaration, and regardless of the income tax treatment of income derived from the asset, a gain on an asset held in the joint names of husband and wife is apportioned in accordance with their respective beneficial interests at the time of disposal. (Revenue Press Release 21 November 1990).

(*b*) See note (*a*) to 215.1 above as to how the consideration for the inter-spouse transfer is arrived at.

(*c*) The allowable expenditure on the inter-spouse transfer should be apportioned in accordance with the part disposal rules in *TCGA 1992, s 42* (see *Sec 42(5)* and 206.2 DISPOSAL). In this case, as the property is to be held on a joint tenancy with neither spouse being free to dispose separately of his or her share, it is assumed that the value of a 10% share and a 90% share is, respectively, 10% and 90% of the value of the property as a whole.

216   Mineral Royalties

Cross-reference. See also 12.1 MINERAL ROYALTIES.

216.1 **GENERAL** [*ICTA 1988, s 122; TCGA 1992, ss 201–203*]

L Ltd, an investment company preparing accounts to 31 December, is the holder of a lease of land acquired in 1984 for £66,000, when the lease had an unexpired term of 65 years. In January 1991, L Ltd grants a 10-year licence to a mining company to search for and exploit minerals beneath the land. The licence is granted for £60,000 plus a mineral royalty calculated on the basis of the value of any minerals won by the licensee. The market value of the retained land (exclusive of the mineral rights) is then £10,000. L Ltd receives mineral royalties as follows

		£
Year ended	31 December 1991	12,000
	31 December 1992	19,000
	31 December 1993	29,000
	31 December 1994	38,000
	31 December 1995	17,000
	31 December 1996	10,000

On 2 January 1997, L Ltd relinquishes its rights under the lease and receives no consideration from the lessor.

(i) Chargeable gains 1991

		£
(*a*)	Disposal proceeds	60,000

$$\text{Allowable cost } \frac{60,000}{60,000 + 10,000} \times £66,000 \qquad 56,571$$

	£
Chargeable gain before indexation	£3,429

		£
(*b*)	$\frac{1}{2} \times £12,000$	£6,000

(ii) Chargeable gains 1992 to 1996

		£
1992	$\frac{1}{2} \times £19,000$	9,500
1993	$\frac{1}{2} \times £29,000$	14,500
1994	$\frac{1}{2} \times £38,000$	19,000
1995	$\frac{1}{2} \times £17,000$	8,500
1996	$\frac{1}{2} \times £10,000$	5,000

(iii) Loss 1997

		£
Proceeds of disposal of lease		Nil
Allowable cost £66,000 − £56,571	note (*a*)	9,429
Allowable loss		£9,429

(iv) The loss may be set off against the chargeable gains arising on the mineral royalties as follows

	£
1996 (whole)	5,000
1995 (part)	4,429
	£9,429

Note

(a) Under *ICTA 1988, s 122* and *TCGA 1992, s 201*, one half of mineral royalties is taxed as income and one half as a chargeable gain. The gain is deemed to accrue in the year of assessment or company accounting period for which the royalties are receivable and is not capable of being reduced by any expenditure or by indexation allowance.

217   Overseas Matters

217.1 OVERSEAS RESIDENT SETTLEMENTS

(A) Charge under TCGA 1992, s 87

M, resident and domiciled in the UK, is the sole beneficiary of a discretionary settlement administered in the Cayman Islands. The trustees are all individuals resident in the Cayman Islands. The settlement was created in 1987 by M's father, who is resident and domiciled in the UK. For 1987/88 to 1994/95 the trustees have chargeable gains and allowable losses, and make capital payments to M, as follows

	Chargeable gains £	Allowable losses £	Capital payments £
1987/88	50,000	60,000	20,000
1988/89	80,000	30,000	50,000
1989/90	95,000	—	—
1990/91	—	—	35,000
1991/92	32,000	7,000	20,000
1992/93	—	—	27,000
1993/94	—	—	—
1994/95	—	—	—
1995/96	—	—	—

See also (B) below.

1987/88	£
Trust gains (£50,000 – £60,000)	—
Capital payment	20,000
Balance of capital payment carried forward	£20,000
Trust losses carried forward	£10,000

1988/89		
Trust gains (£80,000 – £30,000 – £10,000)		£40,000
Capital payment	50,000	
Brought forward	20,000	£70,000
Chargeable gains assessable on M		£40,000
Capital payment carried forward (£70,000 – £40,000)		£30,000

1989/90	
Trust gains	£95,000
Capital payment brought forward	£30,000
Chargeable gains assessable on M	£30,000
Trust gains carried forward (£95,000 – £30,000)	£65,000

1990/91

Trust gains	—
Trust gains brought forward	£65,000
Capital payment	£35,000
Chargeable gains assessable on M	£35,000
Trust gains carried forward (£65,000 – £35,000)	£30,000

1991/92

	£
Trust gains (£32,000 – £7,000)	25,000
Trust gains brought forward	30,000
	£55,000
Capital payment	£20,000
Chargeable gains assessable on M	£20,000
Trust gains carried forward (£55,000 – £20,000)	£35,000

1992/93

	£
Trust gains	—
Trust gains brought forward	35,000
	£35,000
Capital payment	£27,000
Chargeable gains assessable on M	£27,000
Trust gains carried forward	£8,000

1993/94, 1994/95 and 1995/96

Trust gains b/f and c/f	£8,000

(B) Surcharge on CGT under TCGA 1992, s 87 [*TCGA 1992, ss 91–93, 97*]
The facts are as in (A) above. No further capital payments are made by the trustees until 1998/99 in which year a capital payment of £100,000 is made, the trustees having made gains in excess of that amount in the intervening years. For both 1992/93 and 1998/99, M is liable to CGT at the rate of 40% on chargeable gains attributed to him under *TCGA 1992, s 87,* and he has utilised his annual exemptions against personal gains.

(i) Determination of qualifying amounts [*Sec 92(1)(2)*]

Qualifying amount for 1990/91 (equivalent to trust gains carried forward at 5.4.91)	£30,000
Qualifying amount for 1991/92 (i.e. trust gains for that year only)	£25,000

(ii) Matching capital payments made after 5.4.91 [*Sec 92(3)–(6)*]

£20,000 paid in 1991/92 is matched (on first in, first out basis) with qualifying amount for 1990/91, leaving an unmatched qualifying amount of £10,000 for 1990/91.

£27,000 paid in 1992/93. £10,000 is matched with balance of qualifying amount for 1990/91 and £17,000 is matched with qualifying amount for 1991/92, leaving an unmatched qualifying amount of £8,000 for 1991/92.

£100,000 paid in 1998/99. £8,000 is matched with balance of qualifying amount for 1991/92 (leaving £92,000 to be matched with post-1991/92 qualifying amounts).

(iii) Surcharge payable by M [*Secs 91–93*]

1991/92

No surcharge is payable in respect of capital payments made before 6.4.92.

1992/93

As only part of the capital payment is matched with a qualifying amount for a year of assessment falling before that immediately preceding the year in which the payment is made, only that part (i.e. £10,000 — see (ii) above) is liable to surcharge, and the balance is ignored. [*Sec 93(3)*].

	£
CGT payable by M (subject to surcharge):	
£27,000 × 40%	10,800
Surcharge £10,000 × 40% = £4,000 × 10% × 2 years	
(1.12.91–30.11.93) [*Sec 91(3)(4)(5)(a)*]	800
Total tax payable	£11,600

1998/99	£
CGT payable by M (subject to surcharge):	
£100,000 × 40%	40,000
Surcharge on part of payment matched with	
1991/92 qualifying amount:	
£8,000 × 40% = £3,200 × 10% × 6 years (1.12.93–30.11.99)	
[*Sec 91(3)(4)(5)(b)*]	1,920
Surcharge on balance of payment (not illustrated)	X
Total tax payable	X

(C) Charge under TCGA 1992, s 87 — further example

T and M are the only beneficiaries under a Jersey settlement set up by their grandfather, who was then domiciled and resident in the UK. None of the trustees is resident in the UK.

T is resident in the UK but M is neither resident nor ordinarily resident in the UK. Both beneficiaries have a UK domicile. In 1994/95, the trustees sell shares realising a chargeable gain of £102,000. No disposals are made in 1995/96.

The trustees make capital payments of £60,000 to M in 1994/95. In 1995/96 they make capital payments of £60,000 to T and £10,000 to M.

1994/95	£
Trust gains	102,000
Capital payment	60,000
Trust gains carried forward	£42,000

M has chargeable gains of £60,000 but is not subject to CGT.

1995/96	£
Trust gains (brought forward)	42,000
Capital payments (£60,000 + £10,000)	70,000
Balance of capital payments carried forward	£28,000

The chargeable gains are apportioned as follows

	£
T $\dfrac{60,000}{70,000} \times £42,000$	36,000
M $\dfrac{10,000}{70,000} \times £42,000$ (not assessable)	6,000
	£42,000

The capital payments carried forward are apportioned as follows

	£
T £60,000 − £36,000	24,000
M £10,000 − £6,000	4,000
	£28,000

(D) Distributions of income and gains [*ICTA 1988, s 740(6); TCGA 1992, ss 87, 97*]
A Liechtenstein foundation was created in 1953 by a UK resident domiciled in Scotland. None of the trustees is resident in the UK and the trust administration is carried on in Switzerland. The foundation has the following income and chargeable gains for 1994/95 to 1996/97.

	Income	Chargeable gains
	£	£
1994/95	15,000	5,000
1995/96	24,000	12,000
1996/97	30,000	3,000

L, who is resident and domiciled in the UK, receives payments of £28,000 in 1994/95 and £50,000 in 1996/97.

	Total £	Income £	Chargeable gains £
1994/95			
Total income/gains	20,000	15,000	5,000
Payment	28,000	15,000	5,000
Balance	Nil	Nil	Nil
Balance of payment c/f	£8,000		
1995/96			
Total income/gains	36,000	24,000	12,000
Payment (balance b/f)	8,000	8,000	—
Balance c/f	£28,000	£16,000	£12,000
1996/97			
Total income/gains	33,000	30,000	3,000
Brought forward	28,000	16,000	12,000
	61,000	46,000	15,000
Payment	50,000	46,000	4,000
Balance c/f against future payments	£11,000	—	£11,000

Summary of assessments	Schedule D, Case VI £	Capital gains tax £
1994/95	15,000	5,000
1995/96	8,000	—
1996/97	46,000	4,000

217.2 COMPANY MIGRATION [*TCGA 1992, ss 185, 187*]

Z Ltd is a company incorporated in Ruritania, but regarded as resident in the UK by virtue of its being managed and controlled in the UK. It is the 75% subsidiary of Y plc, a UK resident company. On 1 October 1996, the management and control of Z Ltd is transferred to Ruritania and it thus ceases to be UK resident, although it continues to trade in the UK, on a much reduced basis, via a UK branch.

Details of the company's chargeable assets immediately before 1 October 1996 were as follows.

	Market value £	Capital gain after indexation where applicable if all assets sold £
Factory in UK	480,000	230,000
Warehouse in UK	300,000	180,000
Factory in Ruritania	350,000	200,000
Warehouse in Ruritania	190,000	100,000
UK quoted investments	110,000	80,000
Foreign trade investments	100,000	Loss (60,000)

CGT 217.2 Overseas Matters

The UK warehouse continues to be used in the UK trade. The UK factory does not, and is later sold. On 1 June 1997, the Ruritanian warehouse is sold for the equivalent of £210,000. On 1 October 1998, Y plc sells its shareholding in Z Ltd.

Prior to becoming non-UK resident, Z Ltd had unrelieved capital losses brought forward of £40,000.

The capital gains tax consequences assuming no election under *TCGA 1992, s 187* are as follows

Chargeable gain accruing to Z Ltd on 1.10.96

	£
Factory (UK)	230,000
Factory (Ruritania)	200,000
Warehouse (Ruritania)	100,000
UK quoted investments	80,000
Foreign trade investments	(60,000)
	550,000
Losses brought forward	40,000
Net gain chargeable to corporation tax	£510,000

The later sale of the UK factory does not attract CGT as the company is non-resident and the factory has not, since the deemed reacquisition immediately before 1.10.96, been used in a trade carried on in the UK through a branch or agency. Similarly, the sale of the overseas warehouse, and of any other overseas assets, is outside the scope of CGT. Any subsequent disposal of the UK warehouse *will* be within the charge to CGT, having been omitted from the deemed disposal on 1 October 1996, due to its being used in a trade carried on in the UK through a branch. On disposal, the gain will be computed by reference to original cost, or 31.3.82 value if appropriate, rather than to market value immediately before 1.10.96 — see also note (*d*).

Y plc will realise a capital gain (or loss) on the sale of its shareholding in Z Ltd on 1.10.97. There are no CGT consequences for Y plc on Z Ltd's becoming non-UK resident.

The capital gains tax consequences if an election is made under *TCGA 1992, s 187* are as follows

Chargeable gain accruing to Z Ltd on 1.10.96

	£
Factory (UK)	230,000
UK quoted investments	80,000
	310,000
Losses brought forward	40,000
Net gain liable to corporation tax	£270,000

Postponed gain on foreign assets

	£
Factory (Ruritania)	200,000
Warehouse (Ruritania)	100,000
	300,000
Foreign trade investments	(60,000)
	£240,000

On 1.6.97, a proportion of the postponed gain becomes chargeable as a result of the sale, within six years of Z Ltd's becoming non-resident, of one of the assets in respect of which the postponed gain accrued. The gain chargeable to corporation tax as at 1.6.97 on Y plc is

$$\frac{100{,}000 \ \text{(postponed gain on warehouse)}}{300{,}000 \ \text{(aggregate of postponed gains)}} \times £240{,}000 = £80{,}000$$

On 1 October 1998, in addition to any gain or loss arising on the sale of the shares, Y plc will be chargeable to corporation tax on the remainder of the postponed gain, i.e. on £160,000 (£240,000 – £80,000), by virtue of Z Ltd having ceased to be its 75% subsidiary as a result of the sale of shares.

The position as regards the UK warehouse is the same as if no election had been made.

Notes

(a)   The provisions of *TCGA 1992, s 185* apply where a company ceases to be resident in the UK. By virtue of *FA 1988, s 66, 7 Sch*, all companies incorporated in the UK are, subject to transitional provisions, regarded after 14 March 1988 as UK resident. As such a company cannot therefore cease to be resident, *Sec 185* can apply only to companies incorporated abroad which are UK resident. See also Revenue Statement of Practice SP 1/90 as regards company residence generally.

(b)   If, with an election, Z Ltd's allowable losses had exceeded its chargeable gains arising on 1.10.96, the excess could have been allowed against postponed gains at the time when they become chargeable on Y plc, subject to the two companies making a joint election to that effect under *TCGA 1992, s 187(5)*.

(c)   *FA 1988, ss 130–132* contain management provisions designed to secure payment of all outstanding tax liabilities on a company becoming non-UK resident. See also Revenue Statement of Practice SP 2/90.

(d)   If the UK warehouse ceases to be a chargeable asset by virtue of Z Ltd's ceasing to carry on a trade in the UK through a branch or agency, there will be a deemed disposal at market value at that time, under *TCGA 1992, s 25*. See 217.3 below.

217.3 **NON-RESIDENTS CARRYING ON TRADE, ETC. THROUGH UK BRANCH OR AGENCY** [*TCGA 1992, ss 10, 25*]

X, who is not resident and not ordinarily resident in the UK, practises abroad as a tax consultant and also practises in the UK through a London branch, preparing accounts to 5 April. The assets of the UK branch include premises bought in 1985 for £60,000 and a computer acquired in 1994 for £20,000. On 31 January 1997, the computer ceases to be used in the UK branch and is immediately shipped abroad, and on 28 February 1997, X closes down the UK branch. He sells the premises in June 1997 for £108,000. Capital allowances claimed on the computer up to and including 1995/96 were £8,000 and short-life asset treatment had been claimed.

Relevant market values of the assets are as follows

	£
Computer, at 31 January 1997	11,000
Premises, at 14 March 1989	70,000
at 28 February 1997	100,000
Indexation factor March 1989 to February 1997 (assumed)	0.354

The UK capital gains tax consequences are as follows

	£	£
Computer		
Market value 31.1.97		11,000
Deduct cost	20,000	
Less capital allowances claimed note (*f*)	9,000	11,000
Chargeable gain		Nil

	£
Premises	
Market value 28.2.97	100,000
Deduct market value 14.3.89	70,000
Unindexed gain	30,000
Indexation allowance £70,000 × 0.354	24,780
Chargeable gain	£5,220
Net chargeable gains 1996/97	£5,220

Notes

(a)   X is within the charge to UK capital gains tax for disposals after 13 March 1989 by virtue of his carrying on a profession in the UK through a branch or agency. Previously, the charge applied only to non-residents carrying on a *trade* in this manner. X is deemed to have disposed of (with no capital gains tax consequences) and reacquired immediately before 14 March 1989 all chargeable assets used in the UK branch at market value, so that any subsequent CGT charge will be by reference only to post-13 March 1989 gains. [*FA 1989, s 126(3)–(5); TCGA 1992, s 10(5)*].

(b)   There is a deemed disposal, at market value, of the computer on 31 January 1997 as a result of its ceasing to be a chargeable asset by virtue of its becoming situated outside the UK. [*TCGA 1992, s 25(1)*].

(c)   There is a deemed disposal, at market value, of the premises on 28 February 1997 as a result of the asset ceasing to be a chargeable asset by virtue of X's ceasing to carry on a trade, profession or vocation in the UK through a branch or agency. [*TCGA 1992, s 25(3)(8)*]. See also note (*g*) below.

(d)   There are no UK CGT consequences on the actual disposal of the premises in June 1997.

(e)   X is entitled to the £6,300 annual exemption against UK gains, regardless of his residence status.

(f)   Where a chargeable asset has qualified for capital allowances and a loss accrues on its disposal, the allowable expenditure is restricted, under *TCGA 1992, s 41*, by the net allowances given, which in this example amount to £9,000 (first-year allowance £8,000 plus balancing allowance £1,000 arising on the asset's ceasing to be used in the trade).

(g)   *TCGA 1992, s 25(3)* (see note (c) above) does not apply, on a claim under *TCGA 1992, s 172*, in relation to an asset where a non-UK resident company transfers its trade (carried on through a UK branch or agency) to a UK resident group company. The asset is deemed to be transferred at no gain/no loss.

217.4 TRANSFER OF ASSETS TO NON-RESIDENT COMPANY [*TCGA 1992, s 140*]

Q Ltd, a UK resident company, carries on business in a foreign country through a branch there. In September 1989, it is decreed that all enterprises in that country be carried on by locally resident companies. Q Ltd forms a wholly-owned non-UK resident subsidiary R and transfers all the assets of the branch to R wholly in consideration for the issue of shares. The assets transferred include the following

	Value	Chargeable gains
	£	£
Goodwill	100,000	95,000
Freehold land	200,000	120,000
Plant (items worth more than £3,000)	50,000	20,000
Other assets	150,000	—
	£500,000	£235,000

In March 1991, there is a compulsory acquisition of 50% of the share capital of R for £300,000 (market value). The value of the whole shareholding immediately before disposal is £750,000. The value of Q Ltd's remaining 50% holding is £300,000.

In June 1997, R is forced to sell its freehold land to the government.

Q Ltd's capital gains position is as follows

1989

The gain of £235,000 is deferred. The allowable cost of the shares in R is £500,000.

1991

	£
Consideration on disposal	300,000
Add Proportion of deferred gain £235,000 $\times \dfrac{300,000}{750,000}$	94,000
	394,000
Deduct Cost of shares sold £500,000 $\times \dfrac{300,000}{300,000 + 300,000}$	250,000
Unindexed gain	£144,000

1997

Proportion of deferred gain chargeable	£
Gain arising $\dfrac{120,000}{235,000} \times £235,000$	£120,000

Balance of gain still held over
(£235,000 – £94,000 – £120,000) £21,000

Notes

(a) The 1997 gain arises under *Sec 140(5)*. If the sale of freehold land had taken place more than six years after the original transfer of assets, no part of the deferred gain would have become chargeable as a result.

(b) The 1991 gain arises under *Sec 140(4)*. In this case, there is no time limit as in (a) above.

(c) The 1991 gain is subject to indexation allowance on £250,000 from September 1989 to March 1991.

218   Partnerships

218.1 **ASSETS** [*TCGA 1992, s 59*]

G, H and I trade in partnership. They share capital in the ratio 5:4:3. Land occupied by the firm is sold on 15 April 1996 for £84,000, having been acquired for £30,000 in 1981. The agreed market value of the land at 31 March 1982 is £27,000. G has elected under *TCGA 1992, s 35(5)* for his share of personal assets held on 31 March 1982 to be treated as disposed of and re-acquired at their market value on that date. G has personal gains in 1996/97 of £2,500, H has losses of £1,000 and I made no disposals of personal assets. None of the partners has any capital losses brought forward from earlier years. The indexation factor for the period March 1982 to April 1996 is 0.921.

The gains of G, H and I, without re-basing to 1982, are as follows

	G ($\frac{5}{12}$)	H ($\frac{4}{12}$)	I ($\frac{3}{12}$)
	£	£	£
Disposal consideration	35,000	28,000	21,000
Cost	12,500	10,000	7,500
Unindexed gain	22,500	18,000	13,500
Indexation allowance Cost × 0.921	11,513	9,210	6,908
Gain after indexation	£10,987	£8,790	£6,592

The gains of G, H and I, with re-basing to 1982, are as follows

	G ($\frac{5}{12}$)	H ($\frac{4}{12}$)	I ($\frac{3}{12}$)
	£	£	£
Disposal consideration	35,000	28,000	21,000
Market value 31.3.82	11,250	9,000	6,750
Unindexed gain	23,750	19,000	14,250
Indexation allowance (as above)	11,513	9,210	6,908
Gain after indexation	£12,237	£9,790	£7,342

Summary

Share of partnership gain	10,987	8,790	6,592
Personal gains/(losses)	2,500	(1,000)	—
Chargeable gain	13,487	7,790	6,592
Annual exemption	6,300	6,300	6,300
Taxable gain	£7,187	£1,490	£292

Note

(a)   An individual partner's election under *Sec 35(5)* in respect of his personal assets does not extend to his share of partnership assets and *vice versa*, this being by virtue of *Sec 35(7)*. (See Revenue Statement of Practice SP 4/92, para 10(i)).

218.2 CHANGES IN SHARING RATIOS

J and K have traded in partnership for several years, sharing capital and income equally. The acquisition costs and 31 March 1982 values of the chargeable assets of the firm are as follows

	Cost £	31.3.82 value £
Premises	60,000	150,000
Goodwill	10,000	50,000

The assets have not been revalued in the firm's balance sheet. On 1 June 1996, J and K admit L to the partnership, and the sharing ratio is J 35%, K 45% and L 20%. The indexation factor for March 1982 to June 1996 is assumed to be 0.885.

J and K are regarded as disposing of part of their interest in the firm's assets to L as follows

	£	£
J		
Premises		
Deemed consideration		
£60,000 × (50% − 35%)	9,000	
Add indexation allowance (see below)	19,913	
Total deemed consideration	28,913	
Allowable cost	9,000	
Unindexed gain	19,913	
Indexation allowance (50% − 35%) × £150,000 × 0.885	19,913	—
Goodwill		
Deemed consideration		
£10,000 × (50% − 35%)	1,500	
Add indexation allowance (see below)	6,638	
Total deemed consideration	8,138	
Allowable cost	1,500	
Unindexed gain	6,638	
Indexation allowance (50% − 35%) × £50,000 × 0.885	6,638	—
Chargeable gain/allowable loss		Nil
K		
Premises		
Deemed consideration		
£60,000 × (50% − 45%)	3,000	
Add indexation allowance (see below)	6,638	
Total deemed consideration	9,638	
Allowable cost	3,000	
Unindexed gain	6,638	
Indexation allowance (50% − 45%) × £150,000 × 0.885	6,638	—

Goodwill
Deemed consideration

£10,000 × (50% − 45%)	500
Add indexation allowance (see below)	2,213
Total deemed consideration	2,713
Allowable cost	500
Unindexed gain	2,213
Indexation allowance (50% − 45%) × £50,000 × 0.885	2,213

Chargeable gain/allowable loss	Nil

The allowable costs (inclusive, in L's case, of indexation allowance to June 1995) of the three partners are now

		Freehold land £	Goodwill £
J		21,000	3,500
K		27,000	4,500
L	note (*c*)	38,551	10,851

Notes

(*a*)   The treatment illustrated above is taken from Revenue Statement of Practice SP D12 (17.1.75), para 4 as extended by SP 1/89. Each partner's disposal consideration is equal to his share of current balance sheet value of the asset concerned plus, for disposals after 5 April 1988, indexation allowance, and each disposal treated as producing no gain and no loss.

(*b*)   As the deemed disposals are no gain/no loss disposals, re-basing to 1982 does not apply. The incoming partner, having acquired his share in the assets by means of a no gain/no loss disposal after 31 March 1982 is regarded as having held the asset at that date for the purposes of re-basing on a subsequent disposal. (Revenue Statement of Practice SP 1/89).

(*c*)   L's allowable costs comprise 20% of original cost, plus indexation allowance to June 1995 based on 20% of 31 March 1982 value.

218.3 ACCOUNTING ADJUSTMENTS

A, B and C trade in partnership. They share income and capital profits equally. The firm's only chargeable asset is its premises which cost £51,000 in 1985. C, who is 54, decides to retire. The remaining partners agree to share profits equally. Before C retires (in May 1997), the premises are written up to market value in the accounts, estimated at £81,000. C does not receive any payment directly from the other partners on his retirement.

The capital gains tax consequences are
On retiring, C is regarded as having disposed of his interest in the firm's premises for a consideration equal to his share of the then book value.

		£
Disposal consideration	$\frac{1}{3} \times$ £81,000	27,000
Acquisition cost	$\frac{1}{3} \times$ £51,000	17,000
Unindexed gain		£10,000

A and B will each be treated as acquiring a $\frac{1}{6}$ $(\frac{1}{2} \times \frac{1}{3})$ share in the premises, at a cost equal to one half of C's disposal consideration. Their acquisition costs are then

		A	B
		£	£
Cost of original share	$\frac{1}{3} \times$ £51,000	17,000	17,000
Cost of new share	$\frac{1}{2} \times$ £27,000	13,500	13,500
Total		£30,500	£30,500

Notes

(a)   If the asset had been held at 31.3.82, $\frac{1}{3}$ of its market value at that date would be substituted for $\frac{1}{3}$ of cost in C's capital gains tax computation, assuming that re-basing to 1982 applied. Indexation would be based on the higher of $\frac{1}{3}$ of cost and $\frac{1}{3}$ of 31.3.82 value.

(b)   If C retires for reasons of ill-health, he may be entitled to retirement relief. See 222 RETIREMENT RELIEF.

218.4 CONSIDERATION OUTSIDE ACCOUNTS

D, E and F are partners in a firm of accountants who share all profits in the ratio 7:7:6. G is admitted as a partner in May 1997 and pays the other partners £10,000 for goodwill. The new partnership shares are D $\frac{3}{10}$, E $\frac{3}{10}$, F $\frac{1}{4}$ and G $\frac{3}{20}$. The book value of goodwill is £18,000, its cost on acquisition of the practice from the predecessor in 1985.

The partners are treated as having disposed of shares in goodwill as follows

D	£	£
$\frac{7}{20} - \frac{3}{10} = \frac{1}{20}$		
Disposal consideration		
Notional $\frac{1}{20} \times$ £18,000	900	
Actual $\frac{7}{20} \times$ £10,000	3,500	
		4,400
Allowable cost $\frac{1}{20} \times$ £18,000		900
Unindexed gain		£3,500
E		
$\frac{7}{20} - \frac{3}{10} = \frac{1}{20}$		
Disposal consideration (as for D)		4,400
Allowable cost (as for D)		900
Unindexed gain		£3,500
F		
$\frac{6}{20} - \frac{1}{4} = \frac{1}{20}$		
Disposal consideration		
Notional $\frac{1}{20} \times$ £18,000	900	
Actual $\frac{6}{20} \times$ £10,000	3,000	
		3,900
Allowable cost		900
Unindexed gain		£3,000
G's allowable cost of his share of goodwill is therefore		
Actual consideration paid		10,000
Notional consideration paid $\frac{3}{20} \times$ £18,000		2,700
		£12,700

Note

(a)   In practice, the above calculations must be adjusted for indexation allowance which is added to the notional consideration and deducted from the unindexed gain—see 218.2 above and Revenue Statement of Practice SP 1/89.

218.5 SHARES ACQUIRED IN STAGES

Q is a partner in a medical practice. The partnership's only chargeable asset is a freehold house used as a surgery. The cost of the house to the partnership was £3,600 in 1961 and it was revalued in the partnership accounts to £50,000 in 1986. Q was admitted to the partnership in June 1964 with a share of $\frac{1}{6}$ of all profits. As a result of partnership changes, Q's profit share altered as follows

1969 $\frac{1}{5}$
1980 $\frac{1}{4}$
1997 $\frac{3}{10}$

For capital gains tax, Q's allowable cost of his share of the freehold house is calculated as follows

		£	
1964	$\frac{1}{6} \times £3,600$		£600
1969	$(\frac{1}{5} - \frac{1}{6}) \times £3,600$	120	
1980	$(\frac{1}{4} - \frac{1}{5}) \times £3,600$	180	
1997	$(\frac{3}{10} - \frac{1}{4}) \times £50,000$	2,500	£2,800

Notes

(*a*) The pre- and post-6.4.65 costs are not pooled.

(*b*) On Q's acquisition of an increased share of the property in 1995, any partner with a reduced share will be treated as having made a disposal and thus a chargeable gain. The re-basing rules of *TCGA 1992, s 35* will apply to the disposal (subject to the usual comparison with the gain or loss without re-basing).

218.6 PARTNERSHIP ASSETS DISTRIBUTED IN KIND

R, S and T are partners sharing all profits in the ratio 4:3:3. Farmland owned by the firm is transferred in 1997 to T for future use by him as a market gardening enterprise separate from the partnership business. No payment is made by T to the other partners but a reduction is made in T's future share of income profits. The book value of the farmland is £5,000, its cost in 1985, but the present market value is £15,000.

		£
R		
Deemed disposal consideration	$\frac{4}{10} \times £15,000$	6,000
Allowable cost	$\frac{4}{10} \times £5,000$	2,000
Unindexed gain		£4,000
S		
Deemed disposal consideration	$\frac{3}{10} \times £15,000$	4,500
Allowable cost	$\frac{3}{10} \times £5,000$	1,500
Unindexed gain		£3,000
T		
Partnership share	$\frac{3}{10} \times £5,000$	1,500
Market value of R's share		6,000
Market value of S's share		4,500
Allowable cost of land for future disposal		£12,000

219 Private Residences

219.1 PERIODS OF OWNERSHIP QUALIFYING FOR EXEMPTION AND LET PROPERTY EXEMPTION [*TCGA 1992, ss 222, 223*]

(A)

P sold a house on 1 July 1996 realising an otherwise chargeable gain of £53,000. The house was purchased on 1 February 1980 and was occupied as a residence until 30 June 1985 when P moved to another residence, letting the house as residential accommodation. He did not re-occupy the house prior to its sale.

	£
Gain on sale	53,000
Deduct Exempt amount under main residence rules	
$\dfrac{3\text{y }3\text{m} + 3\text{y}}{14\text{y }3\text{m}} \times £53{,}000$	23,246
	29,754
Deduct Let property exemption	23,246
Net chargeable gain	£6,508

Notes

(*a*) The final three years of ownership are always included in the exempt period of ownership. [*Sec 223(1)*].

(*b*) The period of ownership for the exemption calculation does not include any period before 31 March 1982. This applies regardless of whether the gain has been calculated by reference to cost or to 31 March 1982 value under the re-basing rules. [*Sec 223(7)*].

(*c*) The gain attributable to the letting (£29,754) is exempt to the extent that it does not exceed the lesser of £40,000 and the gain otherwise exempt (£23,246 in this example). [*Sec 223(4)*].

(B)

Q bought a house on 1 August 1980 for £40,000 and used it as his main residence. On 10 February 1982, he was sent by his employer to manage the Melbourne branch of the firm and continued to work in Australia until 4 August 1987, the whole of his duties being performed outside the UK. The house was let as residential accommodation during that period. Q took up residence in the house once again following his return to the UK, but on 30 November 1991 moved to Switzerland for health reasons, and again let the property. He returned to the UK in October 1994, but did not reside in the house at any time prior to its being sold on 30 November 1996 for £160,000. The house had a market value of £50,000 at 31 March 1982 and the indexation factor for the period March 1982 to November 1996 is assumed to be 0.900.

CGT 219.1   Private Residences

Computation of gain before applying exemptions

	£	£
Disposal consideration	160,000	160,000
Cost	40,000	
Market value 31.3.82		50,000
Unindexed gain	120,000	110,000
Indexation allowance £50,000 × 0.900	45,000	45,000
Gain after indexation	£75,000	£65,000
Gain before applying exemptions		£65,000

The gain is reduced by the main residence exemptions as follows

Period of ownership (excluding period before 31.3.82)		13y 8m
Exempt periods since 31.3.82:		
31.3.82 – 30.11.91	9y 8m	
1.12.93 – 30.11.96 (last three years)	3y 0m	12y 8m

	£
Gain as above	65,000
Deduct Exempt amount under main residence rules	

$$\frac{12\text{y }8\text{m}}{14\text{y }8\text{m}} \times £65,000 \qquad 56,136$$

	8,864
Deduct Let property exemption (maximum £40,000)	8,864
Net chargeable gain	Nil

Notes

(a) Periods of ownership before 31 March 1982 are excluded in applying the main residence exemptions. This is the case even if re-basing to 1982 does not apply. [*Sec 223(7)*].

(b) The period spent in Australia (regardless of its length but excluding that part of it before 31 March 1982) counts as a period of residence, as Q worked in an employment all the duties of which were performed outside the UK and used the house as his main residence at some time before and after this period of absence. [*Sec 223(3)(b)*].

(c) The period spent in Switzerland would have been exempt, having not exceeded three years, but the exemption is lost as Q did not occupy the property as a main residence at any time after this period. [*Sec 223(3)(a)*].

(d) The last three years of ownership are always exempt providing the property has been used as the owner's only or main residence at some time during the period of ownership, and for this purpose, 'period of ownership' is not restricted to the period after 30 March 1982. [*Secs 222, 223(1)*].

(e) The let property exemption is the lesser of the gain attributable to the period of letting (£8,864), the gain otherwise exempt (£56,136 in this example) and £40,000. It cannot create or increase a loss, and it is only available if the property is let as residential accommodation. [*Sec 223(4)*].

219.2 **ELECTION FOR MAIN RESIDENCE** [*TCGA 1992, s 222(5)*]

S purchased the long lease of a London flat on 1 June 1988. He occupied the flat as his sole residence until 31 July 1990 when he acquired a property in Shropshire. Both properties were thereafter occupied as residences by S until the lease of the London flat was sold on 28 February 1997, realising an otherwise chargeable gain of £75,000.

The possibilities open to S are

(i) Election for London flat to be treated as main residence throughout

Exempt gain   £75,000

(ii) Election for Shropshire property to be treated as main residence from 31.7.90 onwards

Exempt gain £75,000 $\times \dfrac{\text{2y 2m} + \text{3y}}{\text{8y 9m}}$ £44,286

(iii) Election for London flat to be treated as main residence up to 28 February 1994, with election for the Shropshire property to be so treated thereafter

Exempt gain £75,000 $\times \dfrac{\text{5y 9m} + \text{3y}}{\text{8y 9m}}$ £75,000

Note

(*a*)   The elections in (iii) are the most favourable, provided they could have been made by 31 July 1992 in respect of the London flat, and by 28 February 1996 in respect of the Shropshire property. Note that the last three years' ownership of the London flat is an exempt period in any case. The advantage of (iii) over (i) is that the period of ownership 1 March 1994 to 28 February 1997 of the Shropshire property will be treated as a period of residence as regards any future disposal of that property. Revenue practice is that the *initial* election (which can be varied) must be made within two years of acquisition of the second property, and this was upheld in *Griffin v Craig-Harvey ClD 1993*, [*1994*] *STC 54*.

220   Qualifying Corporate Bonds

[*TCGA 1992, ss 115–117*]

220.1 **DEFINITION** [*TCGA 1992, s 117; FA 1993, s 84(1)(3); FA 1995, s 50*]
B has the following transactions in 5% unsecured loan stock issued in 1983 by F Ltd.

		£
11.11.83	Purchase £2,000	1,800
10.7.85	Gift from wife £1,000 (original cost £900)	—
30.9.87	Purchase £2,000	1,700
5.6.96	Sale £4,000	(3,300)

Apart from the gift on 10.7.85, all acquisitions were arm's length purchases. B's wife acquired her £1,000 holding on 11.11.83. Indexation allowance of £89 arose on the transfer from wife to husband.

For the purposes of the accrued income scheme, the sale is without accrued interest and the rebate amount is £20. The stock is a corporate bond as defined by *TCGA 1992, s 117(1)* and a 'relevant security' as defined by *TCGA 1992, s 108(1)*.

Under the rules for matching relevant securities in *TCGA 1992, s 108* (see 210.3 INDEXATION), the stock disposed of is identified with acquisitions as follows.

(i) Identify £2,000 with purchase on 30.9.87 (LIFO)

	£
Disposal consideration £3,300 $\times \frac{2,000}{4,000}$	1,650
Add rebate amount £20 $\times \frac{2,000}{4,000}$	10
	1,660
Allowable cost	1,700
Loss	£40

The loss is *not* allowable as the £2,000 stock purchased on 30.9.87 is a qualifying corporate bond (note (*a*)). [*TCGA 1992, s 115*].

(ii) Identify £1,000 with acquisition on 10.7.85

	£
Disposal consideration £3,300 $\times \frac{1,000}{4,000}$	825
Add rebate amount £20 $\times \frac{1,000}{4,000}$	5
	830
Allowable cost (including indexation to 10.7.85)	989
Allowable loss	£159

The loss is allowable as the stock acquired on 10.7.85 is not a qualifying corporate bond (note (*b*)).

(iii) Identify £1,000 with purchase on 11.11.83

	£
Disposal consideration £3,300 $\times \frac{1,000}{4,000}$	825
Add rebate amount £20 $\times \frac{1,000}{4,000}$	5
	830
Allowable cost £1,800 $\times \frac{1,000}{2,000}$	900
Allowable loss	£70

The loss is allowable as the stock acquired on 11.11.83 is not a qualifying corporate bond (note (*c*)).

Notes

(*a*)   The acquisition on 30.9.87 is a qualifying corporate bond as it was acquired after 13 March 1984 otherwise than as a result of an excluded disposal. [*TCGA 1992, s 117(7)(b)*].

(*b*)   The acquisition on 10.7.85 was the result of an excluded disposal, being a no gain/no loss transfer between spouses where the first spouse had acquired the stock before 14 March 1984. It is therefore not a qualifying corporate bond. [*TCGA 1992, s 117(7)(b)(8)*].

(*c*)   Securities acquired before 14 March 1984 cannot be qualifying corporate bonds in the hands of the person who so acquired them.

(*d*)   See IT 22.1 SCHEDULE D, CASE VI for the income tax effects of the accrued income scheme.

(*e*)   See also CGT 214.3 LOSSES for allowable losses arising on qualifying corporate bonds in certain circumstances.

220.2 **REORGANISATION OF SHARE CAPITAL** [*TCGA 1992, s 116*]

D holds 5,000 £1 ordinary shares in H Ltd. He acquired the shares in April 1983 by subscription at par. On 1 August 1986, he accepted an offer for the shares from J plc. The terms of the offer were one 25p ordinary share of J plc and £10 J plc 10% unsecured loan stock (a qualifying corporate bond) for each H Ltd ordinary share. Both the shares and the loan stock are listed on the Stock Exchange. In December 1996, D sells £20,000 loan stock at its quoted price of £105 per cent.

The value of J plc ordinary shares at 1 August 1986 was £3.52 per share and the loan stock was £99.20 per cent. The indexation factor for April 1983 to August 1986 is 0.161.

The cost of the H Ltd shares must be apportioned between the J plc ordinary shares and loan stock.

	£
Value of J plc shares	
5,000 × £3.52	17,600
Value of J plc loan stock	
£50,000 × 99.2%	49,600
	£67,200

Allowable cost of J plc shares

$$\frac{17,600}{67,200} \times £5,000 \qquad £1,310$$

Allowable cost of J plc loan stock

$$\frac{49,600}{67,200} \times £5,000 \qquad £3,690$$

CGT 220.2   Qualifying Corporate Bonds

Chargeable gain on H Ltd shares attributable to J plc loan stock to date of exchange

	£
Deemed disposal consideration	49,600
Allowable cost	3,690
Unindexed gain	45,910
Indexation allowance £3,690 × 0.161	594
Deferred chargeable gain	£45,316

Deferred chargeable gain accruing on disposal of loan stock

Loan stock sold (nominal)	£20,000

Total holding of loan stock before disposal (nominal)	£50,000

Deferred chargeable gain accruing in 1996/97

$$\frac{20,000}{50,000} \times £45,316 \qquad £18,126$$

Notes

(a) The gain on the sale of J plc loan stock is exempt (as the stock is a qualifying corporate bond) except for that part which relates to the gain on the previous holding of H Ltd shares. [*TCGA 1992, ss 115, 116(10)*]. There will also be income tax consequences under the accrued income scheme (see IT 22.1 SCHEDULE D, CASE VI).

(b) The qualifying corporate bond is treated as acquired at the date of the reorganisation, so even if the original shares had been held at 31 March 1982, re-basing could *not* apply on the subsequent disposal, after 5 April 1988, of the loan stock. However, where the original shares were acquired before 31 March 1982, the reorganisation took place before 6 April 1988, and the qualifying corporate bonds are disposed of after 5 April 1988, the deferred chargeable gain is halved. [*TCGA 1992, 4 Sch 4*].

(c) The exchange of J plc ordinary shares for H Ltd shares is dealt with under *TCGA 1992, ss 127-130*, and no gain or loss will arise until the J plc shares are disposed of. See 225.1 SHARES AND SECURITIES.

221   Reinvestment Relief

[*TCGA 1992, ss 164A – 164N; FA 1993, s 87, 7 Sch Pt II; FA 1994, s 91, 11 Sch; FA 1995, ss 46, 47*]

221.1   NATURE AND EXTENT OF RELIEF

(A) General provisions

In April 1996 R sells a painting for £200,000 which he purchased in June 1986 for £65,000. In October 1995, R acquires 30,000 ordinary shares in A Ltd for £150,000. A Ltd is an unquoted company which exists wholly for the purpose of carrying on a manufacturing trade. R has no other chargeable gains in 1996/97. He wishes to make a claim under *TCGA 1992, s 164A* for reinvestment relief but so as to leave sufficient gains in charge to utilise £2,000 worth of capital losses brought forward and his annual exemption of £6,300. All transactions are at arm's length. The indexation factor for the period June 1986 to April 1996 is 0.562.

The chargeable gain on the disposal of the painting is calculated as follows

	£
Disposal consideration	200,000
Cost	65,000
Unindexed gain	135,000
Indexation allowance £65,000 × 0.562	36,530
Gain after indexation	£98,470

The disposal consideration received is treated as reduced by the smallest of

(i)	the chargeable gain		£98,470
(ii)	the amount reinvested		£150,000
(iii)	the amount specified in the claim for relief £[98,470 − (2,000 + 6,300)]		£90,170

[*Sec 164A(2)*].

The chargeable gain is recalculated as follows

	£
Disposal consideration	200,000
Less reduction under *Sec 164A* (see (iii) above)	90,170
	109,830
Cost	65,000
Unindexed gain	44,830
Indexation allowance as above	36,530
Gain after indexation	8,300
Less losses brought forward	2,000
Net gain (covered by annual exemption)	£6,300

The base cost of R's acquired shares in A Ltd is reduced by the same amount as above and thus becomes £59,830 (£150,000 − £90,170).

The cost of the painting in the hands of the purchaser is not affected by R's claim for reinvestment relief and is thus £200,000.

CGT 221.1   Reinvestment Relief

Notes

(a)   For disposals after 29 November 1993, relief is available where an individual makes a chargeable gain on the disposal of any asset (*Sec 164A(1)*) and acquires a qualifying investment at any time within the qualifying period of one year before or three years after the disposal (*Sec 164A(9)*). R's investment in A Ltd is a qualifying investment (*Sec 164A(8)*) comprising eligible shares (*Sec 164N(1)*) in a qualifying company (*Sec 164G*), i.e. broadly, any holding of ordinary shares in an unquoted trading company other than one substantially involved in dealing in land, finance, leasing, holding commodities as investments or legal and accountancy services.

(b)   For disposals after 15 March 1993 and before 30 November 1993, the provisions were restricted to chargeable gains made by a full-time working director or employee disposing of shares or securities in an unquoted trading company which was his personal trading company. The relief was further restricted to an acquisition of at least 5% of the eligible shares in the new qualifying company.

(B) Multiple claims and inter-spouse transfers [*TCGA 1992, ss 164FF, 164FG; FA 1995, s 47*]

T has the following transactions.

(1) On 1 October 1995, she disposes of a property (not her private residence) for £50,000, the indexed cost for CGT purposes being £35,000. T had already made sufficient gains in 1995/96 to utilise her £5,800 annual exemption.

(2) On 20 April 1996, she acquires from her husband 30,000 £1 shares in D Ltd, a qualifying company under *TCGA 1992, s 164G*. She pays her husband £30,000 for the shares, the market value of which at the time of the transfer was £40,000. Her husband had acquired the shares in February 1990 for £20,000. T's acquisition is a qualifying investment for reinvestment relief purposes. The indexation factor for the period February 1990 to April 1996 is 0.270.

(3) On 15 March 1997, she disposes of quoted shares for £31,000, their indexed pool cost for CGT purposes being £12,000. T makes no other diposals in 1996/97.

T claims the optimum reinvestment relief in respect of the investment in D Ltd, electing that the October 1995 disposal be taken into account first.

The chargeable gain on the October 1995 disposal is calculated as follows

	£
Disposal consideration	50,000
Indexed cost	35,000
Gain after indexation	£15,000

The disposal consideration is treated as reduced by the smallest of

(i)	the otherwise chargeable gain	£15,000
(ii)	the amount reinvested (actual consideration)	£30,000
(iii)	the market value of the qualifying investment (as acquisition not at arm's length)	£40,000

(iv) the claimant's acquisition cost (see below)
    (as investment acquired from spouse — *Sec 164FF*)   £25,400
(v) the amount specified in the claim   say £15,000

[*Sec 164A(2)*].

The amount in (iv) above is arrived at as follows

	£
Cost to husband of 30,000 D Ltd shares (February 1990)	20,000
Add Indexation to date of inter-spouse transfer	
£20,000 × 0.270	5,400
T's acquisition cost (April 1996)	£25,400

T's chargeable gain is recalculated as follows

	£
Disposal consideration	50,000
Less reduction under *Sec 164A* (see (i) and (v) above)	15,000
	35,000
Indexed cost	35,000
Chargeable gain	Nil

The base cost of T's acquired shares in D Ltd is reduced by the same amount as above and thus becomes £10,400 £(25,400 − 15,000).

The chargeable gain on the March 1997 disposal is calculated as follows

	£
Disposal consideration	31,000
Indexed cost	12,000
Gain after indexation	£19,000

The disposal consideration is treated as reduced by the smallest of

(i) the otherwise chargeable gain		£19,000
(ii) the amount reinvested (actual consideration)	30,000	
less reduction already made (*Sec 164FG*)	15,000	
		£15,000
(iii) the market value of the qualifying investment		
(as acquisition not at arm's length)	40,000	
less reduction already made (*Sec 164FG*)	15,000	
		£25,000
(iv) the claimant's acquisition cost (as investment)		
acquired from spouse — *Sec 164FF*)	25,400	
less reduction already made (*Sec 164FG*)	15,000	
		£10,400
(v) the amount specified in the claim		say £10,400

[*Sec 164A(2)*].

T's chargeable gain is recalculated as follows

	£
Disposal consideration	31,000
Less reduction under *Sec 164A* (see (iv) and (v) above)	10,400
	20,600
Indexed cost	12,000
Chargeable gain	8,600
Deduct Annual exemption	6,300
Taxable gains 1995/96	£2,300

The base cost of T's acquired shares in D Ltd is reduced by the same amount as above and thus becomes nil £(25,400 − 15,000 − 10,400).

221.2 **INTERACTION WITH RETIREMENT RELIEF**

S disposes of his shares in B Ltd for £550,000 in October 1996 when aged 51. He acquired the shares in April 1986 for £75,000 and has been a full-time working officer of the company throughout the intervening period. The disposal attracts retirement relief and B Ltd has no chargeable assets other than chargeable business assets at the date of disposal. In November 1996 S acquires 50,000 ordinary shares in C Ltd for £100,000. C Ltd is an unquoted trading company which exists wholly for the purpose of carrying on a qualifying trade within *TCGA 1992, s 164I*. S wishes to make a claim under *TCGA 1992, s 164A* for reinvestment relief so as to take maximum advantage of the reliefs available to him. S has another chargeable gain for 1996/97 of £300. The indexation factor for the period from April 1986 to October 1996 is assumed to be 0.591.

The gain after indexation is calculated as follows

	£
Disposal consideration	550,000
Cost	75,000
Unindexed gain	475,000
Indexation allowance £75,000 × 0.591	44,325
Gain after indexation	£430,675

Calculate reinvestment relief ignoring retirement relief

The disposal consideration received is treated as reduced by the smallest of

(i)	the chargeable gain	£430,675
(ii)	the amount reinvested	£100,000
(iii)	the amount specified in the claim under *Sec 164A* — see note (*b*)	£84,338

[*Sec 164A(2)*].

Calculate retirement relief ignoring reinvestment relief

		£
Gain subject to relief		430,675
Maximum available for 100% relief		
Qualifying period — 10 years		
$\frac{10}{10} \times £250,000$	250,000	
Maximum available for 50% relief		
£430,675 − £250,000 = £180,675		
£180,675 × 50%	90,337	
		(340,337)
Gain after retirement relief		£90,338

The chargeable gain for 1995/96 is as follows

	£
Consideration received	550,000
Less reduction under *Sec 164A*	84,338
	465,662
Indexed cost (£75,000 + £44,325)	119,325
Chargeable gain before retirement relief	346,337
Retirement relief given (as above)	340,337
	6,000
Add Gain B/F	300
	6,300
Annual exemption	6,300
Chargeable gain	Nil

Notes

(*a*)   Relief under *Sec 164A* is by way of reduction of the consideration received. However, where a disposal qualifies for both relief under *Sec 164A* and retirement relief, for the purposes of calculating retirement relief only, any such reduction is treated as a reduction of the unrelieved part of the chargeable gain after retirement relief. Retirement relief is therefore calculated using the unreduced level of consideration. [*Sec 164BA; FA 1994, 11 Sch 8*].

(*b*)   R maximises his reliefs by restricting his claim under *Sec 164A* to £84,338, i.e. the amount of the unrelieved gain after retirement relief (£90,338) less his unutilised annual exemption (£6,000). The balance reinvested of £15,662 (£100,000 − £84,338) is still available to reduce any other gains R may make before November 1997.

(*c*)   If R claimed reinvestment relief of more than £90,338, the excess would displace some of the retirement relief, as, subject to (*a*) above, reinvestment relief takes priority.

222   Retirement Relief

Cross-reference. See 221.2 REINVESTMENT RELIEF for the interaction between that relief and retirement relief.

[*TCGA 1992, ss 163, 164, 6 Sch; FA 1993, s 87, 7 Sch Pt I, 23 Sch Pt III(7); FA 1994, s 92; FA 1996, s 176*]

222.1   EXTENT OF RELIEF

(A) General provisions

N had been the proprietor of a retail business for more than ten years. In December 1996, when N was 51, he sold the whole of the business to a national group for £440,000. The consideration under the agreement is apportioned as follows

	£
Freehold shop	300,000
Flat over shop (occupied throughout by N as main residence)	60,000
Goodwill	60,000
Trading stock	12,000
Fixtures and fittings (one item over £6,000)	8,000
	£440,000

Chargeable gains after indexation are

	£
Freehold shop	222,160
Goodwill	45,540
Fixture	500
Aggregate	£268,200

Retirement relief is calculated as follows

Gain subject to relief	268,200
Maximum available for 100% relief	
Qualifying period — 10 years	

$$\frac{10}{10} \times £250,000 \qquad (250,000)$$

Maximum available for 50% relief
£268,200 − £250,000 = £18,200

£18,200 × $\frac{1}{2}$	(9,100)
Chargeable gain	£9,100

Notes

(a)   For disposals after 29 November 1993, the exemption is extended to one half of gains between £250,000 and £1 million, these limits being reduced by reference to qualifying periods of less than ten years. For disposals after 18 March 1991 and before 30 November 1993, the limits were £150,000 and £600,000 respectively.

(b)   For disposals after 28 November 1995 the age from which a person may qualify for retirement relief has been reduced from 55 to 50 unless the person is retiring on account of ill-health, subject to other conditions being satisfied.

(c)   The flat over the shop is exempt from capital gains tax as it has been N's main residence throughout the period of ownership.

(B) Retirement from business on ill-health grounds and relief restricted by reference to qualifying period [*TCGA 1992, s 163(1)–(3), 6 Sch 13; FA 1994, s 92*]
After giving up salaried employment in June 1990 at the age of 41, R purchased a small philately business. In June 1996, R finds he is unable to continue running the business because of ill-health and sells for the following amounts.

	Proceeds £	Chargeable gain (after indexation) £
Premises	180,000	136,000
Goodwill	30,000	22,800
Fixtures and fittings (none over £6,000)	8,000	—
Stock	25,000	—
		£158,800

Retirement relief is given as follows

	£
Gains eligible for relief	158,800

Maximum available for 100% relief
Qualifying period — 6 years

$$\frac{6}{10} \times £250,000 \qquad\qquad\qquad (150,000)$$

Maximum available for 50% relief

$$\frac{6}{10} \times £1 \text{ million} = £600,000$$

£158,800 (being less than £600,000) − £150,000 = £8,800	
£8,800 × ½	(4,400)
Chargeable gain	£4,400

Note
(a)   Relief is given where an individual has retired below the age of 50 on ill-health grounds provided the Board are satisfied that he has ceased work and is likely to remain permanently incapable of that kind of work. Claims for relief on the grounds of ill-health must be made to the Board within two years after the end of the year of assessment of the relevant disposal. [*TCGA 1992, 6 Sch 3, 5(2)(4)*].

(C) Operative date — ceasing to be a full-time working officer or employee [*TCGA 1992, s 163(5)(7), 6 Sch 1; FA 1993, s 87, 7 Sch Pt I*]
Q gave up full-time work at the age of 51 in June 1996 when she had been a director of Q Ltd, her personal company, for five years. She continued as a director, working three mornings per week until January 1997 when she sold her 40% shareholding in Q Ltd realising a chargeable gain of £540,000.

CGT 222.1 Retirement Relief

Retirement relief is given as follows

	£
Gain eligible for relief	540,000
Maximum available for 100% relief	
Qualifying period — 5 years	

$$\frac{5}{10} \times £250,000 \qquad (125,000)$$

Maximum available for 50% relief

$$\frac{5}{10} \times £1 \text{ million} = £500,000$$

£500,000 − £125,000 = £375,000
£375,000 × $\frac{1}{2}$ (187,500)

Chargeable gain   £227,500

Note

(a) If an individual ceases to be a full-time working officer or employee (director for disposals before 16 March 1993) of a company but remains an officer or employee (director for disposals before 16 March 1993) and works an average of ten hours per week in a technical or managerial capacity until the date of disposal, the operative date is deemed to be the date of ceasing to be a full-time working officer or employee (director for disposals before 16 March 1993). This enables retirement relief to be given, but by reference to the qualifying period ended on that earlier date rather than the date of disposal.

(D) Share for share exchange — relief available [*TCGA 1992, 6 Sch 2*]
In November 1996, D, aged 67, accepts an offer to exchange his 60% holding of 1,200 shares in C Ltd for shares in M plc on the basis of 10 for 1. He has been a full-time working officer of C Ltd for 15 years. He receives 12,000 shares in M plc valued at £180,000. The holding in C Ltd cost £5,000 in 1976. D elects not to treat the new shares and the holding disposed of as the same asset under *TCGA 1992, s 127*.

The market value of the C Ltd shares on 31 March 1982 is agreed at £50,000. The indexation factor from March 1982 to November 1996 is assumed to be 0.900.

C Ltd had no non-business assets.

The chargeable gain is calculated as follows

	£	£
Disposal consideration	180,000	180,000
Cost	5,000	
Market value 31.3.82		50,000
Unindexed gain	175,000	130,000
Indexation allowance £50,000 × 0.900	45,000	45,000
Gain after indexation	£130,000	£85,000
Gain subject to retirement relief		85,000
Retirement relief available (maximum £250,000 at 100% and £750,000 at 50%)		85,000
Chargeable gain		Nil

Note

(a)   The base cost for the new shares is £180,000.

222.2 GAINS QUALIFYING FOR RELIEF

(A) Non-business chargeable assets [*TCGA 1992, 6 Sch 6, 7, 12; FA 1993, s 87, 7 Sch Pt I*]

P Ltd carries on a trade of printing and bookbinding. Its directors include C who owns 10% of the issued share capital and of the voting rights. In December 1996, on reaching the age of 63, C gives his shares to his sister. At the date of transfer, the company's assets are valued as follows

	£	£	Market value £	Cost £
Leasehold printing works			190,000	50,000
Goodwill			60,000	—
Stocks of materials			80,000	75,000
Plant				
Printing presses No 1	8,000			3,000
No 2	8,500			3,500
No 3	6,500	23,000		2,000
Typesetter		10,500		15,000
Binding machine		16,500		12,000
Small tools, type etc.		7,000		10,000
Motor cars		20,000		30,000
Office fixtures and fittings (items under £6,000)		9,000	86,000	15,000
Shares in associated publishing company			60,000	40,000
Cash at bank and in hand			7,500	—
Debtors			11,500	—

The chargeable gain arising on the shares given to C's sister is £75,000.

The value of the company's chargeable assets is as follows

	Business £	Non-business £
Leasehold	190,000	—
Goodwill	60,000	—
Plant (£23,000 + £10,500 + £16,500)	50,000	—
Shares	—	60,000
	£300,000	£60,000

Gain eligible for retirement relief is therefore

$$£75,000 \times \frac{300,000}{300,000 + 60,000} \qquad £62,500$$

Note

(a)   Chargeable assets are all assets other than those on which any gain accruing on a disposal immediately before the end of the qualifying period would not be a chargeable gain.

CGT 222.2 Retirement Relief

(B) Shares in holding company — group holding non-business assets. [*TCGA 1992, 6 Sch 6, 8, 12; FA 1993, s 87, 7 Sch Pt I*]

D, aged 60, gives 20% of his shares in his personal company, N Ltd, to his son. The business of manufacturing and distributing double glazing units is carried on through two subsidiaries, X Ltd and Y Ltd. At the date of disposal in November 1996, the market value of the assets of the group are as follows.

	Assets	Chargeable assets Business	Non-business
	£	£	£
N Ltd			
Leasehold of factory	150,000	150,000	
Investment in subsidiaries			
X (100%)	60,000		
Y (60%)	40,000		
Quoted shares	10,000		10,000
X Ltd (100% owned)			
Plant	32,000	32,000	
Stock, debtors and cash	18,000		
		£182,000	£10,000
Y Ltd (60% owned)			
Freehold shop (half let)	50,000	25,000	25,000
Plant and machinery	15,000	15,000	
Stock, debtors and cash	9,000		
		£40,000	£25,000
60% thereof		£24,000	£15,000
Total		£206,000	£25,000

The chargeable gain on the gift of shares is £57,750.

The gain eligible for retirement relief is therefore

$$£57,750 \times \frac{206,000}{206,000 + 25,000} = £51,500$$

Notes

(a) A shareholding in another member of the trading group is not counted as a chargeable asset.

(b) Chargeable business and non-business assets of a part-owned subsidiary are reduced in proportion to the share capital owned.

(c) It is assumed that none of the items of plant and machinery are covered by the £6,000 chattel exemption.

(C) Associated disposal by trustees [*TCGA 1992, s 164(3)–(5), 6 Sch 13; FA 1993, s 87, 7 Sch Pt I*]

B has carried on a business for more than ten years in premises held by a family trust in which he has a life interest of 40%.

In May 1995 B, who is then 64, sells the business, realising a chargeable gain of £223,000. The trustees sell the property in April 1996, at a chargeable gain of £89,000.

Disposal by B

	£
Chargeable gain	223,000
Retirement relief (100%)	(223,000)
Chargeable gain	Nil

Disposal by trustees

	£
Chargeable gain	89,000
Gain subject to retirement relief: 40% × £89,000 = £35,600	
Relief available at 100% £(250,000 − 223,000)	(27,000)
Relief available at 50% £(35,600 − 27,000)	(4,300)
Chargeable gain	£57,700

Notes

(*a*)   For the purposes of calculating the maximum available retirement relief, a trustees' disposal is regarded as a qualifying disposal by the beneficiary. If disposals by trustees and a beneficiary are made on the same day, relief is given first to the gain by the beneficiary.

(*b*)   The qualifying period of full-time working must end not more than one year before the trustees' disposal. If the trustees' sale were deferred to, say, June 1996, no relief would be available except at the Board's discretion.

(D) Associated disposal — restriction for non-business use, qualifying period and rent [*TCGA 1992, 6 Sch 10*]

In May 1996, X, who had been a full-time working officer for 10 years and was aged 53, sold his qualifying holding of shares in W Ltd realising a chargeable gain of £90,000. The company had, since 1985, used a warehouse acquired by X personally in 1981. It was agreed that the company would vacate the property (for which it paid a rent of 75% market rate) after six months. X then sold the warehouse realising a chargeable gain of £31,500.

Disposal of shares

	£
Chargeable gain	90,000
Retirement relief (100%)	(90,000)
	Nil

Disposal of warehouse

	£
Chargeable gain	31,500

Gain subject to retirement relief
  (i)   Proportion of business use

$$\frac{10 \text{ years}}{15 \text{ years}} \times £31,500 = £21,000$$

  (ii) Qualifying period of ownership

$$\frac{10}{10\frac{1}{2}} \times £21,000 = £20,000 \qquad \text{note } (b)$$

  (iii) Proportion rent-free
        $25\% \times £20,000 = £5,000$

Balance of relief available (at 100%) £(250,000 − 90,000) = £160,000	
Retirement relief (restricted to £5,000 × 100%)	5,000
Chargeable gain	£26,500

Notes

(a)   Restricted retirement relief is available where the asset has not been used for business purposes throughout the period of ownership or where the individual was not concerned in carrying on the trade during part of the period of use in the business or where rent has been paid for the use of the asset. The part qualifying for relief is that which appears 'just and reasonable' to the Board. The above computation shows one way in which the Board might interpret 'just and reasonable'.

(b)   For the final six months of use of the warehouse in the business, W Ltd was not X's personal company.

(E) Partnerships [*TCGA 1992, s 163(8), 6 Sch 10*]

U, V and W trade in partnership. They have shared income and capital in the ratio 5:3:2 since 1972. On 30 April 1996, V retires aged 63 after 30 years as a partner and receives a lump sum of £50,000 from the other partners. Of the £50,000, £35,000 is expressed to relate to V's interest in the freehold depot, £10,000 to goodwill and £5,000 to non-chargeable assets. V also transfers to the firm, for £120,000, office premises which the firm has occupied for business purposes, paying an annual rent to V of £3,000. The open market rent for the property is £5,000 per annum. V's chargeable gain on the property is £82,000. The book values of the firm's chargeable assets are as follows.

Freehold depot   £40,000 (cost on 1.5.84)
Goodwill   £10,000 (valuation on 31.3.82)

Indexation factors May 1984 to April 1995	0.715
March 1982 to April 1995	0.921

Chargeable gains eligible for retirement relief are

		£	£	£
Freehold depot:	Consideration	35,000		
	Allowable cost $\frac{3}{10} \times$ £40,000	12,000		
Unindexed gain			23,000	
Indexation allowance £12,000 × 0.715			8,580	
				14,420
Goodwill:	Consideration	10,000		
	Allowable cost $\frac{3}{10} \times$ £10,000	3,000		
Unindexed gain			7,000	
Indexation allowance £3,000 × 0.921			2,763	
				4,237
Office premises				
Chargeable gain		£82,000		
Fraction eligible				

$$\frac{3}{10} + \left(\frac{7}{10} \times \frac{5,000 - 3,000}{5,000}\right) = \frac{29}{50} \times £82,000 \qquad\qquad 47,560$$

£66,217

Notes

(a)   The whole of the £66,217 attracts 100% retirement relief. V is therefore chargeable only on the non-eligible part of the gain on the office premises of £34,440 (£82,000 – £47,560).

(b)   Where rent, but at less than market rent, is paid by the partnership, *TCGA 1992, 6 Sch 10* gives relief for a 'just and reasonable' amount of the gain. The formula shown above is used by the Revenue (Revenue Capital Gains manual, volume VI, paras CG63836, CG63838).

(c)   See (D) above for restriction of relief where an asset has not been used for business purposes throughout the period of ownership.

(F) Capital distribution [*TCGA 1992, s 163(1)(2)(4), 6 Sch 11, 12(5)(6); FA 1993, s 87, 7 Sch Pt I*].

At 61, M decides to put his personal trading company into voluntary liquidation. He holds all the share capital and has been a working officer for 20 years. In November 1995, the company sold off machinery for £7,000. The company ceases to trade in February 1996, and in November 1996 the liquidator pays M a cash distribution of £12,000 and transfers to him the lease of its premises, then worth £24,000.

M's chargeable gain on disposal of his shares is £27,000.

At cessation, the company's assets (at market value) were

	Assets	Chargeable Business	Chargeable Non-business
	£	£	£
Lease of premises	25,000	25,000	
Flat over premises (let)	5,000		5,000
Plant, fixtures	13,000	13,000	
Motor cars	8,000		
Stock, debtors, cash	19,000		

M elects under *TCGA 1992, 6 Sch 12(5)* to substitute the machinery sold in November 1995 for the proceeds of its sale held at cessation in order to increase the proportion of chargeable business assets.

The chargeable gain is calculated as follows

	£
Gain on disposal	27,000

Restricted to cash portion of distribution   note (*b*)

$$\frac{12,000}{12,000 + 24,000} \times £27,000 = \underline{£9,000}$$

Allowable for retirement relief

$$\frac{25,000 + 13,000 + 7,000}{25,000 + 13,000 + 7,000 + 5,000} \times £9,000 \qquad 8,100$$

Chargeable gain	£18,900

Notes

(*a*)   The liquidator's distribution must be within one year of the date of cessation of business or such longer period as the Board allows.

(*b*)   No retirement relief is available on that part of the gain attributable to the proportion of the capital distribution represented by chargeable business assets. [*TCGA 1992, 6 Sch 11*].

(*c*)   It is assumed that no item of the plant and fixtures is covered by the £6,000 chattel exemption.

222.3 AMOUNT OF RELIEF

(A) Aggregation of earlier business periods [*TCGA 1992, 6 Sch 14*]

A sold the hotel he had owned and run for ten years in July 1988. In January 1989 he reinvested £65,000 in a similar business, rolling over the earlier chargeable gain of £50,000. When he was 51, in January 1997, the hotel was severely damaged by fire and A decided to retire. He received £250,000 from the insurance company and £60,000 for the sale of the land. The indexation factor for the period January 1989 to January 1997 is assumed to be 0.468.

	£	£
Disposal proceeds — sale of land	60,000	
— insurance monies	250,000	
		310,000
Cost	65,000	
Less deferred gain $\times \frac{1}{2}$ note (*b*)	25,000	
		40,000
		270,000
Indexation allowance £40,000 × 0.468		18,720
		251,280

Maximum retirement relief available at 100% £250,000
Restricted by qualifying period

$$\frac{8 + 1\frac{1}{2}}{10} \times £250,000 \times 100\%\qquad \text{note } (a)\qquad\qquad 237,500$$

	13,780

Maximum retirement relief available at 50%:

$$£1 \text{ million} \times \frac{9\frac{1}{2}}{10} = £950,000 - £237,500 = £712,500$$

£251,280 − £237,500 = £13,780 × 50%   6,890

Chargeable gain	£6,890

Notes

(*a*) The two business periods falling within the ten-year qualifying period are aggregated but the qualifying period is restricted by the gap between the ownership of the two businesses.

(*b*) See 204.2 ASSETS HELD ON 31 MARCH 1982 for relief in respect of gains deferred after 31 March 1982 and before 6 April 1988 and attributable, wholly or partly, to assets held on 31 March 1982.

(B) Earlier disposal [*TCGA 1992, 6 Sch 15*]
Y gave shares in his family trading company to his children on his 61st birthday in
September 1991 realising a chargeable gain of £120,000. He had been a full-time working
director for 8 years. The gain was eligible for retirement relief.

Retirement relief was given as follows

	£
Gain eligible for relief	130,000
Maximum available for 100% relief	
$\dfrac{8}{10} \times £150,000 \times 100\%$	(120,000)
Maximum available for 50% relief	
$\dfrac{8}{10} \times £600,000 = £480,000 - £120,000 = £360,000$	
£130,000 − £120,000 = £10,000 × 50%	(5,000)
Chargeable gain	£5,000

In September 1996 (when he had been a full-time working director for 13 years), Y gives
his remaining 30% holding to his children. The gain on the gift is £170,000.

Retirement relief is given as follows

		£
Gain eligible for relief		170,000
Maximum available for 100% relief		
$\dfrac{10}{10} \times £250,000 =$	£250,000	
Deduct Relief already given at 100%	120,000	(130,000)
Maximum available for 50% relief		
$\dfrac{10}{10} \times £1$ million = £1 million − £250,000 =	750,000	
Deduct (Relief already given £5,000) × 2 =	10,000	
	£740,000	
Restricted to (£170,000 − £130,000) £40,000 × 50%		(20,000)
Chargeable gain		£20,000

(C) Married persons — aggregation of spouses' qualifying periods — transfer on death [*TCGA 1992, 6 Sch 16*]

R acquired her late husband's 30% shareholding in X Ltd on his death in June 1988. She took over the office he had held for many years as a full-time working officer until, at the age of 63, she sold her shares in June 1996 incurring an otherwise chargeable gain of £264,000.

The chargeable gain is calculated as follows

	£
Gain eligible for relief	264,000
Maximum available for 100% relief	

$$\frac{8+2}{10} \times £250,000 \times 100\% \qquad (250,000)$$

Maximum available for 50% relief

$$\frac{8+2}{10} \times £1 \text{ million} = £1 \text{ million} - £250,000 = £750,000$$

£264,000 − £250,000 = £14,000 × 50%	(7,000)
Chargeable gain	£7,000

Note

(*a*)   Written election must be made, within two years after the end of the year of assessment in which the disposal occurs, for the qualifying period to be extended by the spouse's qualifying period.

(D) Married persons — aggregation of spouses' qualifying periods — lifetime transfer [*TCGA 1992, 6 Sch 16*]

In May 1989, J, who was 65 that month, gave 40% of the shares in Y Ltd, a trading company, to his son realising an otherwise chargeable gain of £20,000. He had been a full-time working director for 12 years. His wife G, aged 54, already held 20% of the share capital and both she and the son became full-time directors. Later that year, J's health failed and he transferred his remaining 40% holding to G who continued as a director until November 1996 when she gave her shares to her son realising an otherwise chargeable gain of £240,000. All the company's chargeable assets are chargeable business assets.

	£
Gift by J to son	
Gain eligible for relief	20,000
Retirement relief available (£20,000 × 100%)	20,000
Chargeable gain	Nil

Disposal by G

No election to aggregate qualifying periods

Gain eligible for relief	240,000
Maximum available for 100% relief	

$$\frac{7\frac{1}{2}}{10} \times £250,000 \qquad\qquad (187,500)$$

Maximum available for 50% relief

$$\frac{7\frac{1}{2}}{10} \times £1 \text{ million} = £750,000 - £187,500 = £562,500$$

£240,000 − £187,500 = £52,500 × 50%	(26,250)
Chargeable gain (see note (*a*))	£26,250

	£
Election made to aggregate qualifying periods	
Gain eligible for relief	240,000
Maximum available for 100% relief	

$$\frac{10}{10} \times £250,000 = \qquad\qquad 250,000$$

Deduct Relief at 100% previously given	20,000	(230,000)

Maximum available for 50% relief

$$\frac{10}{10} \times £1 \text{ million} = £1 \text{ million} - £250,000 = £750,000$$

£240,000 − £230,000 = £10,000 × 50%	(5,000)
Chargeable gain (see note (*a*))	£5,000

The election is beneficial.

Note

(*a*)   G and her son could make a joint claim for the gain on her gift to be held-over under *TCGA 1992, s 165*. The held-over gain would be the full gain accruing on the gift, less the retirement relief. [*TCGA 1992, 7 Sch 8(3)*]. See also 209.2 HOLD-OVER RELIEFS.

223   Rollover Relief — Replacement of Business Assets

Cross-reference. See also 204.2 ASSETS HELD ON 31 MARCH 1982 for relief under *TCGA 1992, s 36, 4 Sch* for certain gains accruing before 31 March 1982.

[TCGA 1992, ss 152–158]

223.1 NATURE OF RELIEF *[TCGA 1992, s 152]*

(A)

N Ltd carries on a manufacturing business. It makes the following disposals and acquisitions of assets during the company's accounting periods ended 31 December 1994, 31 December 1995 and 31 December 1996.

	Asset	Bought/ (sold) £	Chargeable gains £
1.10.94	Freehold depot	18,000	—
12.12.94	Leasehold warehouse	(50,000)	28,000
19.6.95	Business formerly carried on by another company:		
	Goodwill	20,000	—
	Freehold factory unit	90,000	—
1.2.96	Land adjacent to main factory, now surplus to requirements	(40,000)	19,000
8.9.96	Industrial mincer (fixed plant)	(30,000)	5,000
1.11.96	Extension to new factory	35,000	—

(i) The gain on the leasehold warehouse may be rolled over against the following

	Cost £		Gain £
Freehold depot	18,000	$\dfrac{18,000}{50,000} \times £28,000$	10,080
Goodwill	20,000	$\dfrac{20,000}{50,000} \times £28,000$	11,200
Freehold factory (part)	12,000	$\dfrac{12,000}{50,000} \times £28,000$	6,720
	£50,000		£28,000

See note (*b*)

(ii) The gain on the surplus land may be rolled over as follows

Freehold factory (part)	£40,000	Gain rolled over	£19,000

(iii) The gain on the industrial mincer may be rolled over as follows

Extension to new factory (part)	£30,000	Gain rolled over	£5,000

The position at 31 December 1996 is then as follows

	£
Freehold depot	
Cost	18,000
Deduct gains rolled over	10,080
Allowable cost	£7,920
Goodwill	
Cost	20,000
Deduct gains rolled over	11,200
Allowable cost	£8,800
Freehold factory	
Cost	90,000
Deduct gains rolled over (£6,720 + £19,000)	25,720
Allowable cost	£64,280
Extension to new factory	
Cost	35,000
Deduct gains rolled over	5,000
Allowable cost	£30,000

Notes

(a)   The expenditure still available to match against disposal proceeds is

Extension to factory (£35,000 − £30,000)   **£5,000**

The expenditure is available only against disposals up to 31 October 1997.

(b)   There is no statutory rule prescribing the way in which the gain on an asset must be rolled over against a number of different assets. The taxpayer's allocation of the rolled over gain against the cost of the new assets should be accepted by the Revenue, providing specified amounts of consideration are positively earmarked and set against the cost of specified new assets (Revenue Capital Gains manual, volume VI, para CG60775). In (i) the chargeable gain has been rolled over rateably to the costs of the items, but bringing in only part (i.e. the balance of proceeds) of the cost of the freehold factory.

(B)

L Ltd carries on a vehicle repair business. In December 1996 it sells a workshop for £90,000 net of costs. The workshop had cost £45,000 inclusive in April 1990. A new workshop is purchased for £144,000 (including incidental costs of acquisition) in January 1997 and sold for £168,000 in January 1999.

Indexation factors (assumed)	April 1990 to December 1996	0.324
	January 1997 to January 1999	0.080

L Ltd claims rollover of the chargeable gain.

	£
Allowable cost of original workshop	45,000
Indexation allowance £45,000 × 0.324	14,580
	59,580
Actual disposal consideration	90,000
Chargeable gain rolled over	£30,420
Cost of new workshop	144,000
Deduct amount rolled over	30,420
Deemed allowable cost	£113,580
Disposal consideration, replacement workshop	168,000
Allowable cost	113,580
Unindexed gain	54,420
Indexation allowance £113,580 × 0.080	9,086
Chargeable gain	£45,334

223.2 PARTIAL RELIEF

(A) Assets only partly replaced [*TCGA 1992, s 153*]

G carries on an accountancy practice. In March 1996, he agrees to acquire the practice of another sole practitioner, who is about to retire. As part of the acquisition, G pays £20,000 for goodwill. In January 1997, G moves to new premises, acquiring the remaining 70 years of a 99-year lease for £50,000. The sale of his former office in February 1997 realises £80,000, and a chargeable gain of £59,000 arises.

	£	£
Amount of proceeds of disposal of old office		80,000
Costs against which gains can be rolled over		
Goodwill	20,000	
Lease	50,000	
		70,000
Chargeable gain not rolled over		£10,000
Chargeable gain rolled over (£59,000 − £10,000)		£49,000
Allowable cost of assets (see note (*a*)):		
Goodwill	20,000	
Gain rolled over $\dfrac{20,000}{70,000} \times £49,000$	14,000	
		£6,000
Lease	50,000	
Gain rolled over $\dfrac{50,000}{70,000} \times £49,000$	35,000	
		£15,000

Notes

(*a*)   There is no statutory rule prescribing the way in which a gain is to be rolled over against more than one acquisition. See note (*b*) to 222.1(A).

(*b*)   It would not have been possible to roll over the gain only against the acquisition of the goodwill. The consideration not reinvested (£60,000) would be more than the gain (£59,000).

(B) Partial business use [*TCGA 1992, s 152(7)*]

N carries on a consultancy business from commercial premises formerly used as a shop. N has owned the property since 1 July 1976, but it was let until 1 September 1990 when N moved in, following the expiry of the lease held by the former tenant. The property cost £8,000. On 1 February 1997, N sells the property for £100,000, moving to a new office with a long lease which he acquires for £60,000 and which is wholly used for his business. The value at 31 March 1982 of the property sold was £43,000 and N has made the global re-basing election under *TCGA 1992, s 35(5)*. The indexation factor for March 1982 to February 1997 is assumed to be 0.913.

For rollover relief purposes, N is treated as having disposed of two separate assets, one representing his occupation and professional use of the property, the other his ownership of it as an investment. In practice, the proceeds and chargeable gain may be allocated by a simple time apportionment.

Business use

$$\text{Proceeds } £100,000 \times \frac{6\text{y } 5\text{m}}{13\text{y } 10\text{m}} \quad \text{note } (c) \qquad\qquad £46,389$$

Chargeable gain attributable to business use

$$[£100,000 - £43,000 - (£43,000 \times 0.913)] = £17,741 \times \frac{6\text{y } 5\text{m}}{13\text{y } 10\text{m}} \qquad £8,230$$

Notes

(*a*)   The proceeds attributable to business use are less than the cost of the new office, so that the whole of the chargeable gain attributable to business use can be rolled over. The allowable cost of the new office is then £51,770 (£60,000 – £8,230).

(*b*)   The balance of the chargeable gain, £9,511 (£17,741 – £8,230) is not eligible for rollover.

(*c*)   The time apportionment takes into account only the period of ownership after 30 March 1982. [*TCGA 1992, s 152(9)*].

223.3 **WASTING ASSETS** [*TCGA 1992, s 154*]

(A)
H Ltd carries on a motor agency trade. On 30 October 1996 it sells one of its branches to another company as a going concern. The purchaser pays H Ltd £20,000 for the unexpired term of the showroom lease and £18,000 for goodwill. Chargeable gains of £6,000 arise on disposal of the lease, and £15,000 on goodwill. H Ltd opens a new branch in June 1997, having purchased for £30,000 the remaining term of a lease which expires on 31 December 2011.

The most beneficial method of computing the hold over is

	Proceeds £	Chargeable gain held over £
Goodwill (whole)	18,000	15,000
Lease (part)	12,000	nil
Cost of new lease	£30,000	£15,000

Notes
(*a*)   The gain on the old lease remains chargeable because it is less than the amount of the proceeds not reinvested (£20,000 – £12,000 = £8,000).

(*b*)   There is no statutory formula for deciding which gains are to be held over where more than one asset has been disposed of. It is usually beneficial to consider first the asset on which the chargeable gain is higher in proportion to the disposal proceeds (the goodwill in the above example).

(B)
C Ltd, a manufacturing company, sells an item of fixed plant for £30,000 in February 1992. A chargeable gain of £7,200 arises. In 1994, the company buys storage facilities on a 20-year lease for £40,000. In 1996, an extension to the company's freehold factory is completed at a cost of £25,000.

The position is as follows
(i) The company may claim holdover of the £7,200 chargeable gain in 1992, against the cost of the lease.

(ii) In 1996, part of the chargeable gain can be rolled over against the cost of the factory extension, as follows

	£
Expenditure available for rollover	25,000
Maximum capable of rollover	
£7,200 – (£30,000 – £25,000)	2,200
Adjusted base cost of extension	£22,800

Notes
(*a*)   The balance of the chargeable gain, £5,000 (£7,200 – £2,200) may continue to be held over against the cost of the lease, either until it crystallises or until further rollover is possible.

(*b*)   Had the company not claimed holdover against the cost of the lease, a claim against the cost of the extension in 1996 would not have been possible, as the expenditure was incurred outside the normal time limit.

224   Settlements

Cross-reference. See 217.1 OVERSEAS MATTERS as regards capital gains of non-resident settlements.

224.1 **ANNUAL EXEMPTIONS AND RATES OF TAX** [*TCGA 1992, ss 3, 4(1), 1 Sch 2*]
The trustees of the E settlement, created in 1970, realise net chargeable gains and allowable losses as follows

	Chargeable gain/ (allowable loss) £
1992/93	(2,300)
1993/94	800
1994/95	4,200
1995/96	2,800
1996/97	10,000

The trust is not an accumulation or discretionary settlement, nor does the settlor have an interest therein (see notes (*a*) and (*b*)).

The trustees' capital gains tax liability is computed as follows

	£
1992/93	
Taxable amount	Nil
Losses carried forward	£2,300
1993/94	
Net chargeable gains	800
Losses brought forward	—
Taxable amount (covered by annual exemption)	£800
CGT	Nil
Losses carried forward	£2,300
1994/95	
Net chargeable gains	4,200
Losses brought forward	1,300
Taxable amount (covered by annual exemption)	£2,900
CGT	Nil
Losses carried forward (£2,300 − £1,300)	£1,000
1995/96	
Net chargeable gains	2,800
Losses brought forward	—
Taxable amount (covered by annual exemption)	£2,800
CGT	Nil
Losses carried forward	£1,000

	£
1996/97	
Net chargeable gains	10,000
Losses brought forward	1,000
Taxable amount	£9,000
CGT at 24% on £(9,000 − 3,150)	£1,404.00
Losses carried forward	Nil

Notes

(a)   If the trust had been an accumulation or discretionary settlement (within the meaning of *TCGA 1992, s 5(2)*), the rate of tax applicable to the net gain of £5,850 for 1996/97 would have been 34%, giving a liability of £1,989.00. [*TCGA 1992, s 5(1); FA 1993, 6 Sch 23, 25(1)*].

(b)   If the settlor had an interest in the settlement (as defined by *TCGA 1992, s 77(2)–(5)*) at any time during 1996/97, the gain of £9,000 (after deducting losses but before deducting the annual exemption) would be chargeable on the settlor and not on the trustees. His own annual exemption of £6,300 could be set against the gain, if not used against his own gains. Any tax payable could be recovered from the trustees. See also 224.2 below. [*TCGA 1992, ss 77–79; FA 1995, s 74, 17 Sch 27–29*].

(c)   See *TCGA 1992, 1 Sch 2(4)–(6)* for the annual exemption available to two or more settlements made by the same settlor after 6 June 1978.

224.2 **SETTLEMENT IN WHICH SETTLOR HAS AN INTEREST** [*TCGA 1992, ss 77–79; FA 1995, s 74, 17 Sch 27–29*]

In May 1995, Henry, a UK resident, settled £25,000 on trust to his wife for her life with the remainder to his adult daughter absolutely. The trustees are resident in the UK. For 1995/96, the trustees make disposals on which they incur losses of £200. For 1996/97, they realise gains of £3,100 and losses of £700. Henry has personal gains of £4,800 for 1996/97 with no losses brought forward. Henry's taxable income for 1996/97 is £50,000 and he is liable to tax at 40% on capital gains.

Henry's capital gains tax liability for 1996/97 is calculated as follows

	£	£
Personal gains		4,800
Settlement gains	3,100	
Deduct Losses	700	
	2,400	
Deduct Losses b/f	200	2,200
		7,000
Deduct Annual exemption		6,300
Gain liable to CGT		£700
CGT payable at 40%		£280.00
CGT recoverable from trustees	note (a)	£280.00

Notes

(a) The settlement gains are regarded as forming the highest part of the total amount on which Henry is liable to CGT. His personal gains are therefore fully covered by the annual exemption and the whole of the liability relates to the settlement gains; it is thus fully recoverable from the trustees. [*TCGA 1992, s 78*].

(b) If either Henry or his wife died during 1996/97, or if they ceased to be married during that year, *Secs 77–79* would not apply and the settlement gain of £2,400 (before deducting losses brought forward) would be covered by the trustees' annual exemption of £3,150, with losses of £200 carried forward to 1996/97. [*TCGA 1992, s 77(6); FA 1995, 17 Sch 27*].

224.3 **CREATION OF A SETTLEMENT** [*TCGA 1992, s 70*]

(A)

In December 1996, C transfers to trustees of a settlement for the benefit of his children 10,000 shares in W plc, a quoted company. The value of the gift is £80,000. C bought the shares in 1980 for £20,000 and their value at 31 March 1982 was £35,000. The indexation factor for March 1982 to December 1996 is assumed to be 0.904.

	£	£
Deemed disposal consideration	80,000	80,000
Cost	20,000	
Market value 31.3.82		35,000
Unindexed gain	60,000	45,000
Indexation allowance £35,000 × 0.904	31,640	31,640
Gain after indexation	£28,360	£13,360
Chargeable gain		£13,360
Trustees' allowable cost		£80,000

Note

(a) If the transfer is a chargeable lifetime transfer for inheritance tax purposes, or would be one but for the annual inheritance tax exemption, C could elect under *TCGA 1992, s 260* to roll the gain over against the trustees' base cost of the shares. The trustees do not join in any such election. This would normally cover only a transfer to a discretionary settlement.

(B)

In March 1997 H settles farmland on trust for himself for life, with interests in reversion to his children. The land cost £20,000 in 1970 and its agreed values are £60,000 at 31 March 1982 and £120,000 at the date of settlement. H's interest in possession in the settled property is valued at £90,000. The indexation factor from March 1982 to March 1997 is assumed to be 0.920.

The chargeable gain is computed as follows

	£	£
Deemed disposal proceeds	120,000	120,000
Cost	20,000	
Market value 31.3.82		60,000
Unindexed gain	100,000	60,000
Indexation allowance £60,000 × 0.920	55,200	55,200
Gain after indexation	£44,800	£4,800
Chargeable gain		£4,800

Notes

(a)   The value of H's interest in the settled property is ignored and the transfer is not treated as a part disposal.

(b)   For as long as H has an interest in the settlement the provisions of *TCGA 1992, ss 77–79* will apply to any settlement gains, with the effect that they will be chargeable on the settlor and not on the trustees. See 224.2 above.

224.4 PERSON BECOMING ABSOLUTELY ENTITLED TO SETTLED PROPERTY
[*TCGA 1992, s 71*]

(A)
M is a beneficiary entitled to an interest in possession in settled property, under a settlement made by her mother. The trustees exercise a power of appointment to advance capital to M, and, in 1996, transfer to her a house valued at £80,000. The house was acquired by the trustees by gift from the settlor in 1992, when its value was £45,000.

The trustees realise an unindexed gain of £35,000 (£80,000 – £45,000) on the advancement of capital to M.

Notes

(a)   An indexation allowance is available to the trustees and will be based on their deemed acquisition cost of £45,000.

(b)   If, while it was settled property, the house had been occupied by M as her private residence with the permission of the trustees, then all or part of the gain would be exempt under *TCGA 1992, s 225.*

(B)
F, who is a beneficiary under a discretionary settlement, realises chargeable gains of £40,000 on share transactions in May 1996. In June 1996, the trustees exercise a discretion to advance capital to F and do so by transferring to him ordinary shares purchased for £50,000. The shares have a value of £30,000 at the date of transfer. The trustees have no chargeable gains for 1996/97.

The consequences are

(i)   The shares cease to be settled property, and the trustees realise an allowable loss of £20,000 (£50,000 – £30,000).

(ii)   The loss is then available to F to set off against his chargeable gain of £40,000 in 1996/97.

224.5 **TERMINATION OF LIFE INTEREST ON DEATH** [*TCGA 1992, s 72*]

(A)

K is entitled to an interest in possession under a settlement. The settled property consists of shares and cash. On K's death, L takes a life interest in succession to K. K dies on 1 December 1996, when the shares are valued at £200,000. The trustees' allowable cost in respect of the shares is £40,000.

On K's death, the trustees are deemed to have disposed of and immediately reacquired the shares for £200,000, thus uplifting the CGT base cost, but no chargeable gain then arises.

(B)

In 1971, E created a settlement for the benefit of his children M and N and his grandchildren, transferring an investment property valued at £10,000 to the trustees. The terms of the settlement were that M and N each have a life interest in half of the trust income, with the remainder passing to E's grandchildren. In 1985, N assigned his interest to P, an unrelated party, for £35,000, its then market value. In 1996, N dies. The value of a half share of the trust property is then £65,000.

On N's death, his life interest terminates. There is no effect on the trustees as N was no longer the person entitled to the life interest within the meaning of *TCGA 1992, s 72*.

Notes

(*a*) No chargeable gain arises on the disposal by N of his interest. [*TCGA 1992, s 76*].

(*b*) P may claim an allowable loss on extinction of the interest. For an example of the computation if the interest is a wasting asset, see 227.3 WASTING ASSETS.

225 Shares and Securities

Cross-references. See also 203 ASSETS HELD ON 6 APRIL 1965, 204 ASSETS HELD ON 31 MARCH 1982, 210 INDEXATION and 220 QUALIFYING CORPORATE BONDS.

225.1 REORGANISATION OF SHARE CAPITAL — VALUATION OF DIFFERENT CLASSES OF SHARE ON SUBSEQUENT DISPOSAL [*TCGA 1992, ss 126–131*]

(A) Unquoted shares

V acquired 10,000 ordinary shares in X Ltd, an unquoted trading company, in April 1994 at a cost of £15,000. In April 1996, as part of a reorganisation of share capital, V was allotted 3,000 new 9% preference shares in X Ltd for which he paid £3,900. In June 1995, V sold his ordinary shareholding, in an arm's length transaction, for £20,000, but retained his preference shares, then valued at £4,000.

Indexation factors April 1994 to June 1996 (assumed)	0.065
April 1996 to June 1996 (assumed)	0.005

The chargeable gain on the disposal of the ordinary shares is calculated as follows

	£	£
Disposal consideration		20,000
Cost (£15,000 + £3,900) $\times \dfrac{20,000}{20,000 + 4,000}$		15,750
Unindexed gain		4,250
Indexation allowance $\dfrac{15,000}{18,900} \times £15,750 \times 0.065$	813	
$\dfrac{3,900}{18,900} \times £15,750 \times 0.005$	16	
		829
Chargeable gain		£3,421
Allowable cost of 3,000 preference shares (£15,000 + £3,900 − £15,750)		£3,150

Notes

(a) The ordinary shares and preference shares held after the reorganisation (the 'new holding') constitute a single asset. [*TCGA 1992, s 127*]. A disposal of part of the new holding is thus a part disposal. If neither class of shares comprising the new holding is quoted on a recognised stock exchange at any time not later than three months after the reorganisation, acquisition cost on a part disposal is apportioned by reference to market values at the date of disposal. [*TCGA 1992, s 129*].

(b) See (C) below for reorganisations taking place on or before 31 March 1982 and (D) below for reorganisations taking place after that date where the original holding was acquired on or before that date. See (B), (E) and (F) below as regards quoted shares. See 220.2 QUALIFYING CORPORATE BONDS as regards reorganisations involving qualifying corporate bonds.

(B) Quoted shares

Assume the facts to be as in (A) above except that both the ordinary and preference shares are quoted on a recognised stock exchange. On the first day of dealing after the reorganisation took effect, the ordinary shares were quoted at £1.90 and the preference shares at £1.25. V's holdings were therefore valued at £19,000 and £3,750 respectively.

The chargeable gain on the disposal of the ordinary shares is calculated as follows

	£	£
Disposal consideration		20,000
Cost (£15,000 + £3,900) $\times \dfrac{19,000}{19,000 + 3,750}$		15,785
Unindexed gain		4,215
Indexation allowance $\dfrac{15,000}{18,900} \times £15,785 \times 0.065$	814	
$\dfrac{3,900}{18,900} \times £15,785 \times 0.005$	16	
	—	830
Chargeable gain		£3,385
Allowable cost of 3,000 preference shares (£15,000 + £3,900 − £15,785)		£3,115

Notes

(a) Where one or more of the classes of shares or debentures comprising the new holding is quoted on a recognised stock exchange at any time not later than three months after the reorganisation, acquisition cost on a part disposal is apportioned by reference to market values on the first day of dealing on which the prices quoted reflect the reorganisation. [*TCGA 1992, s 130*].

(b) See (E) below for reorganisations taking place on or before 31 March 1982 and (F) below for reorganisations taking place after that date where the original holding was acquired on or before that date. See (A) above and (C) and (D) below as regards unquoted shares. See 220.2 QUALIFYING CORPORATE BONDS as regards reorganisations involving qualifying corporate bonds.

(C) Unquoted shares — reorganisation on or before 31 March 1982

W has since 1978 owned shares in L Ltd, an unquoted trading company. W subscribed for 5,000 £1 ordinary shares at par, and has not made any disposals. In November 1980, L Ltd offered ordinary shareholders two 7% preference shares per each five ordinary shares held. The full price payable was £1 for each preference share, on allotment. W took up his entitlement of 2,000 preference shares. In June 1995, W sells his preference shares at £1.30 each (total £2,600) to another shareholder. The sale price is the full market value. The value of W's ordinary shares at that time is £4.68 (total £23,400).

The total values of W's ordinary and preference shares at 31 March 1982 were £10,000 and £2,100 respectively. The indexation factor from March 1982 to June 1996 is assumed to be 0.885.

The calculation, without re-basing to 1982, is

	£
Disposal consideration	2,600
Cost (£5,000 + £2,000) × $\dfrac{2,600}{2,600 + 23,400}$	700
Unindexed gain	1,900
Indexation allowance £2,100 × 0.885	1,859
Gain after indexation	£41

The calculation, with re-basing to 1982, is

	£
Disposal consideration	2,600
Market value 31.3.82 note (b)	2,100
Unindexed gain	500
Indexation allowance (as above) but restricted to	500
Gain after indexation	Nil
Chargeable gain	Nil

Notes

(a)   On a subsequent disposal of the ordinary shares, the allowable cost would be £6,300 (£5,000 + £2,000 − £700) or, if re-basing applied, £10,000. In either case, indexation would be based on £10,000.

(b)   As there is a deemed disposal and reacquisition on 31 March 1982 for re-basing purposes, the assets deemed to have been reacquired are separate assets and no longer have to be treated as a single asset. There is therefore no need for any apportionment.

(c)   For disposals after 29 November 1993 (subject to transitional rules for disposals before 6 April 1995), indexation allowance cannot exceed an unindexed gain. [*TCGA 1992, s 53; FA 1994, s 93(1)–(3)*].

(D) Unquoted shares — reorganisation after 31 March 1982, original holding acquired on or before that date

Assume the facts to be as in (C) above except that the reorganisation took place in November 1986 rather than in 1980. The indexation factor from November 1986 to June 1996 is assumed to be 0.508.

The calculation, without re-basing to 1982, is

	£
Disposal consideration	2,600
Cost (£5,000 + £2,000) × $\dfrac{2,600}{2,600 + 23,400}$	700
Unindexed gain	1,900
Indexation allowance (see below)	1,152
Gain after indexation	£748

The calculation, with re-basing to 1982, is

	£
Disposal consideration	2,600
(31.3.82 value £10,000 + cost £2,000) × $\dfrac{2,600}{2,600 + 23,400}$	1,200
Unindexed gain	1,400

Indexation allowance $\dfrac{10,000}{12,000} \times £1,400 \times 0.885 = £1,033$

$$\dfrac{2,000}{12,000} \times £1,400 \times 0.508 = \underline{\quad 119}$$

	£
	1,152
Gain after indexation	£248
Chargeable gain	£248

Note

(a) On a subsequent disposal of the ordinary shares, their cost would be £6,300 (£5,000 + £2,000 − £700) or, if re-basing applied, £10,800 (£10,000 + £2,000 − £1,200). In either case, indexation would be based on £10,800.

CGT 225.1 Shares and Securities

(E) Quoted shares — reorganisation on or before 31 March 1982
Assume the shares held by W in (C) above were quoted shares. On the first day of dealing after the reorganisation the ordinary shares were quoted at £1.50 (total £7,500) and the preference shares at £1.02 (total £2,040). The calculation on the disposal of the preference shares is as follows

The calculation, without re-basing to 1982, is

	£
Disposal consideration	2,600
Cost (£5,000 + £2,000) × $\frac{2,040}{2,040 + 7,500}$	1,497
Unindexed gain	1,103
Indexation allowance £2,100 × 0.885 = £1,859 but restricted to	1,103
Gain after indexation	Nil

The calculation, with re-basing to 1982, is

	£
Disposal consideration	2,600
Market value 31.3.82	2,100
Unindexed gain	500
Indexation allowance (as above) but restricted to	500
Gain after indexation	Nil
Chargeable gain	Nil

Re-basing does not apply (in the absence of an election under *TCGA 1992, s 35(5)*) as neither a gain nor a loss accrues using cost. [*TCGA 1992, s 35(3)(c)*].

Notes
(a) On a subsequent disposal of the ordinary shares, the allowable cost would be £5,503 (£5,000 + £2,000 − £1,497) or, if re-basing applied, £10,000. In either case, indexation would be based on £10,000.

(b) See note (b) to (C) above which also applies to the re-basing calculation in this example.

(c) For disposals after 29 November 1993 (subject to transitional rules for disposals before 6 April 1995), indexation allowance cannot exceed an unindexed gain. [*TCGA 1992, s 53; FA 1994, s 93(1)–(3)*].

(F) Quoted shares — reorganisation after 31 March 1982, original holding acquired on or before that date

If the facts were as in (E) above, except that the reorganisation took place after 31 March 1982, the calculation would proceed along the same lines as (D) above, but substituting the fraction used in (E) for that used in (D).

(G) Shares held at 6 April 1965: effect of election for pooling at 1965 value

W purchased 1,000 £1 ordinary shares in N plc, a quoted company, in 1962. The cost was £3,000. The shares had a market value on 6 April 1965 of £3.20 per share. In 1966, he purchased a further 2,000 ordinary shares in N plc for £2.50 per share, and in 1968 he bought 2,000 3% convertible preference shares in the company for 98p per share. In 1977, N plc made a rights issue of 3% convertible preference shares to ordinary shareholders, on the basis of 1 preference share per two ordinary shares, at a price of £1.01. On the first dealing day after the reorganisation, N plc ordinary shares were quoted at £5.50 and preference shares at £1.03. In September 1996, W sold 1,500 preference shares for £1,400. He had already made an election under *TCGA 1992, 2 Sch 4* to pool pre-7.4.65 fixed interest securities. The indexation factor for March 1982 to September 1996 is assumed to be 0.895. The ordinary shares and preference shares were quoted at £6.50 and 96p respectively on 31 March 1982.

The calculation, without re-basing to 1982, is

(i)   The 1,000 ordinary shares purchased in 1962 are linked with 500 preference shares acquired on the rights issue. The allowable cost (6 April 1965 value) of these 500 preference shares is therefore computed as follows

$$[(1,000 \times £3.20) + (500 \times £1.01)] \times \frac{500 \times 1.03}{(500 \times 1.03) + (1,000 \times 5.50)} \qquad \underline{£317}$$

(ii)   The 2,000 ordinary shares purchased in 1966 are linked with 1,000 preference shares acquired on the rights issue. The allowable cost of these 1,000 preference shares is computed as follows

$$[(2,000 \times £2.50) + (1,000 \times 1.01)] \times \frac{1,000 \times 1.03}{(1,000 \times 1.03) + (2,000 \times 5.50)} \qquad \underline{£515}$$

(iii)   The 2,000 preference shares purchased in 1968 have an allowable
cost of   £1,960

The chargeable gain on the disposal of preference shares is calculated as follows

	£
Disposal consideration	1,400
Allowable cost £(317 + 515 + 1,960) $\times \dfrac{1,500}{3,500}$	1,197
Unindexed gain	203
Indexation allowance	
£(1,500 × 0.96) × 0.895 = £1,289 but restricted to	203
Gain after indexation	Nil

The calculation, with re-basing to 1982, is

The chargeable gain on the disposal of preference shares is calculated as follows

	£
Disposal consideration	1,400
Market value 31.3.82 £(3,500 × 0.96) × $\dfrac{1,500}{3,500}$	1,440
Unindexed loss	40
Indexation allowance note (c)	Nil
Loss	£40

Re-basing does not apply (in the absence of an election under *TCGA 1992, s 35(5)*) as neither a gain nor a loss accrues otherwise. [*TCGA 1992, s 35(3)(c)*].

Notes

(a)   The preference shares are pooled as a result of the election even though the original ordinary shares are not so pooled. [*TCGA 1992, 2 Sch 6*].

(b)   As regards the re-basing calculation, see also note (b) to (C) above.

(c)   For disposals after 29 November 1993 (subject to transitional rules for disposals before 6 April 1995), indexation allowance cannot exceed an unindexed gain. [*TCGA 1992, s 53; FA 1994, s 93(1)–(3)*].

225.2 **BONUS ISSUES** [*TCGA 1992, ss 126–128, 130*]

(A) Bonus of same class

In October 1988, Y plc made a scrip issue of one ordinary share for every 10 held. L held 5,000 ordinary shares, which he acquired in May 1984 for £6,000, and therefore received 500 shares in the bonus issue. In October 1996, L sells 3,000 of his shares for £6,500.

| Indexation factors | May 1984 to April 1985 (actual) | 0.065 |
| | April 1985 to October 1996 (assumed) | 0.591 |

New holding	Shares	Qualifying expenditure £	Indexed pool £
May 1984 acquisition	5,000	6,000	6,000
Indexed rise: May 1984 – April 1985			
£6,000 × 0.065			390
Pool at 6.4.85	5,000	6,000	6,390
October 1988 bonus issue	500		
Indexed rise: April 1985 – October 1996			
£6,390 × 0.591			3,776
	5,500	6,000	10,166
October 1996 disposal	(3,000)	(3,273)	(5,545)
Pool carried forward	2,500	£2,727	£4,621

Calculation of chargeable gain	£
Disposal consideration	6,500
Allowable cost $\dfrac{3,000}{5,500} \times £6,000$	3,273
Unindexed gain	3,227
Indexation allowance	
$\dfrac{3,000}{5,500} \times £10,166 = £5,545$	
£5,545 – £3,273	2,272
Chargeable gain	£955

(B) Bonus of different class

At various dates after 5 April 1982 and before 6 April 1985, R bought a total of 2,000 'A' shares in T plc for £3,800. The value of the indexed pool immediately before 6 April 1985 was £4,460. In June 1986, R bought a further 500 'A' shares for £800. In October 1986 T plc made a bonus issue of 2 'B' shares for each 5 'A' shares held, and R received 1,000 'B' shares, valued at £1.20 each (total value £1,200) on the first dealing day after the issue. On the same day, the 'A' shares were quoted at £2 each (total value £5,000). In December 1996 R sells his 1,000 'B' shares for £2,000.

Indexation factors	April 1985 to June 1986 (actual)	0.032
	June 1986 to October 1986 (actual)	0.007
	October 1986 to December 1996 (assumed)	0.537

New holding – 'A' shares

	Shares	Qualifying expenditure £	Indexed pool £
Pool at 6.4.85	2,000	3,800	4,460
Indexed rise: April 1985 to June 1986			
£4,460 × 0.032			143
June 1986 acquisition	500	800	800
	2,500	4,600	5,403
Indexed rise: June 1986 to October 1986			
£5,403 × 0.007			38
	2,500	4,600	5,441
October 1986 bonus issue of 'B' shares: transfer proportion of expenditure and indexed pool to 'B' shares (see note (a))		(890)	(1,053)
Pool of 'A' shares carried forward	2,500	£3,710	£4,388

New holding – 'B' shares

	Shares	Qualifying expenditure £	Indexed pool £
October 1986 bonus issue: proportion of pools transferred from 'A' shares holding	1,000	890	1,053
Indexed rise: October 1986 to December 1996			
£1,053 × 0.537			565
	1,000	890	1,618
December 1996 disposal	1,000	890	1,618
	—	—	—

Calculation of chargeable gain on disposal of 'B' shares

	£
Disposal consideration	2,000
Allowable cost (as allocated)	890
Unindexed gain	1,110
Indexation allowance £1,618 – £890	728
Chargeable gain	£382

Notes

(a)   The cost of the 'A' shares is apportioned between 'A' and 'B' shares by reference to market values on the first day of dealing after the reorganisation. The indexed pool is apportioned in the same way.

$$\text{Proportion of qualifying expenditure } £4,600 \times \frac{1,200}{1,200 + 5,000} \qquad £890$$

$$\text{Proportion of indexed pool } £5,441 \times \frac{1,200}{1,200 + 5,000} \qquad £1,053$$

(Revenue Capital Gains manual, volume IV, paras CG51954 and CG51965 to CG51981).

(b)   A different basis of apportionment applies to unquoted shares (see Revenue Capital Gains manual, volume IV, paras CG51919 to CG51953).

225.3 **RIGHTS ISSUES** [*TCGA 1992, ss 42, 123(1), 128(4)*]

Cross-reference. See 224.7(B) below as regards sale of rights.

(A) Rights issue of same class
W plc is a quoted company which in June 1989 made a rights issue of one £1 ordinary share for every eight £1 ordinary shares held, at £1.35 payable on allotment. V, who held 16,000 £1 ordinary shares purchased in May 1983 for £15,000, took up his entitlement in full, and was allotted 2,000 shares. In December 1995, he sells 6,000 of his shares for £12,000.

Indexation factors		
May 1983 to April 1985 (actual)		0.120
April 1985 to June 1989 (actual)		0.218
June 1989 to December 1996 (assumed)		0.311

New holding	Shares	Qualifying expenditure £	Indexed pool £
May 1983 acquisition	16,000	15,000	15,000
Indexed rise: May 1983 – April 1985 £15,000 × 0.120			1,800
Pool at 6.4.85	16,000	15,000	16,800
Indexed rise: April 1985 – June 1989 £16,800 × 0.218			3,662
June 1989 rights issue	2,000	2,700	2,700
	18,000	17,700	23,162
Indexed rise: June 1989 – December 1996 £23,162 × 0.311			7,203
			30,365
December 1996 disposal	(6,000)	(5,900)	(10,122)
Pool carried forward	12,000	£11,800	£20,243

Calculation of chargeable gain	£
Disposal consideration	12,000
Allowable cost $\dfrac{6,000}{18,000} \times £17,700$	5,900
Unindexed gain	6,100
Indexation allowance	

$$\frac{6,000}{18,000} \times £30,365 = £10,122$$

£10,122 − £5,900	4,222
Chargeable gain	£1,878

(B) Rights issue of different class
At 6 April 1985, A's 'new holding' of 6,000 quoted £1 ordinary shares in S plc has a pool of expenditure of £7,800 and an indexed pool of £9,200. In October 1990, S plc made a rights issue of one 50p 'B' share for every five £1 ordinary shares held, at 60p payable in full on application. A took up his entitlement in full, acquiring 1,200 'B' shares. On the first dealing day after issue, the 'B' shares were quoted at 65p and the £1 ordinary shares at £1.50. A sells his 'B' shares in March 1997 for £1,500.

| Indexation factors | April 1985 to October 1990 (actual) | 0.375 |
| | October 1990 to March 1997 (assumed) | 0.170 |

New holding — ordinary shares	Shares	Qualifying expenditure £	Indexed pool £
Pool at 6.4.85	6,000	7,800	9,200
Indexed rise: April 1985 to October 1990			
£9,200 × 0.375			3,450
October 1990 rights issue of 'B' shares	—	720	720
	6,000	8,520	13,370
Transfer proportion of expenditure and indexed pool to 'B' shares note (a)		(680)	(1,066)
Pool of ordinary shares carried forward	6,000	£7,840	£12,304

New holding—'B' shares	Shares	Qualifying expenditure £	Indexed pool £
October 1990 rights issue: proportion of pools transferred from ordinary shares holding	1,200	680	1,066
Indexed rise: October 1990 to March 1997			
£1,066 × 0.170			181
	1,200	680	1,247
March 1997 disposal	(1,200)	(680)	(1,247)
	—	—	—

Calculation of chargeable gain on disposal of 'B' shares	£
Disposal consideration	1,500
Allowable cost (as allocated)	680
Unindexed gain	820
Indexation allowance £1,247 – £680	567
Chargeable gain	£253

Notes

(a) The cost of the original shares is apportioned between the original shares and the 'B' shares by reference to market values on the first day of dealing after the reorganisation. The indexed pool is apportioned in the same way.

Proportion of qualifying expenditure

$$£8,520 \times \frac{1,200 \times 0.65}{(1,200 \times 0.65) + (6,000 \times 1.50)} \qquad £680$$

Proportion of indexed pool

$$£13,370 \times \frac{1,200 \times 0.65}{(1,200 \times 0.65) + (6,000 \times 1.50)} \qquad \underline{£1,066}$$

(Revenue Capital Gains manual, volume IV, paras CG51954 and CG51965 to CG51981).

(b) A different basis of apportionment applies to unquoted shares (see Revenue Capital Gains manual, volume IV, paras CG51919 to CG51953).

(C) Rights issue of same class: disposal out of new holding and 1982 holding
G holds 75,000 25p ordinary shares in C plc, acquired as follows

Date	Number of shares acquired	Cost
		£
22.5.80	20,000	0.80
5.11.83	15,000	1.10
14.9.84	40,000	1.00

In May 1991, C made a rights issue of one ordinary share for every five held, at £1.50 payable in full on application. G took up his rights in full (15,000 ordinary shares). He sells 80,000 shares in August 1996 for £2.40 per share. The shares were quoted at 90p on 31 March 1982.

Indexation factors	March 1982 to August 1996 (assumed)	0.890
	November 1983 to April 1985 (actual)	0.094
	September 1984 to April 1985 (actual)	0.052
	April 1985 to May 1991 (actual)	0.409
	May 1991 to August 1996 (assumed)	0.124

New holding

	Shares	Qualifying expenditure £	Indexed pool £
5.11.83 acquisition	15,000	16,500	16,500
Indexed rise: November 1983 to April 1985 £16,500 × 0.094			1,551
14.9.84 acquisition	40,000	40,000	40,000
Indexed rise: September 1984 to April 1985 £40,000 × 0.052			2,080
Pool at 6.4.85	55,000	56,500	60,131
Indexed rise: April 1985 to May 1991 £60,131 × 0.409			24,594
May 1991 rights issue	11,000	16,500	16,500
	66,000	73,000	101,225
Indexed rise: May 1991 to August 1996 £101,225 × 0.124			12,552
	66,000	73,000	113,777
August 1996 disposal	(66,000)	(73,000)	(113,777)
	—	—	—

1982 holding

	Shares	Cost £	Market value 31.3.82 £
22.5.80 acquisition	20,000	16,000	18,000
May 1991 rights issue note (a)	4,000	6,000	6,000
	24,000	22,000	24,000
August 1996 disposal	(14,000)	(12,833)	(14,000)
Pool carried forward	10,000	£9,167	£10,000

Calculation of chargeable gain	£
(i) Identify 66,000 shares sold with new holding	
Disposal consideration 66,000 × £2.40	158,400
Allowable cost	73,000
Unindexed gain	85,400
Indexation allowance £113,777 − £73,000	40,777
Chargeable gain	£44,623

(ii) Identify 14,000 shares with 1982 holding

Without re-basing to 1982

	£
Disposal consideration 14,000 × £2.40	33,600
Cost $\dfrac{14,000}{24,000} \times £22,000$	12,833
Unindexed gain	20,767
Indexation allowance (see below)	9,779
Gain after indexation	£10,988

With re-basing to 1982

	£
Disposal consideration	33,600
Allowable expenditure $\dfrac{14,000}{24,000} \times £24,000$	14,000
Unindexed gain	19,600
Indexation allowance	

$£14,000 \times \dfrac{18,000}{24,000} \times 0.890$	£9,345	
$£14,000 \times \dfrac{6,000}{24,000} \times 0.124$	434	
		9,779
Gain after indexation		£9,821
Chargeable gain		£9,821
Total chargeable gain £44,623 + £9,821		£54,444

Note

(a)   The 1982 holding cannot be increased by an 'acquisition', but can be increased by a rights issue as this is not treated as involving an acquisition. [*TCGA 1992, ss 109(2), 128*].

225.4 COMPANY AMALGAMATIONS [*TCGA 1992, ss 135, 137, 138*]

(A) Takeover by quoted company

S was a shareholder in N Ltd, an unquoted company. He subscribed for his 10,000 50p ordinary shares at 60p per share in 1976 and the shares were valued at £3 each at 31 March 1982. In July 1986, the shareholders accepted an offer by a public company, M plc, for their shares. Each ordinary shareholder received one £1 ordinary M plc share plus 45p cash for every two N Ltd shares held. S acquired 5,000 M plc shares and received cash of £2,250. The M plc shares were valued at £7.50 each at the time of the acquisition. In March 1997, S sells 2,000 of the M shares for £27,000.

Indexation factors   March 1982 to July 1986 (actual)   0.228
                      March 1982 to March 1997 (assumed)   0.920

(i) On the merger in 1986/87, S makes a disposal only to the extent that he receives cash

	£
Disposal consideration	2,250
Allowable cost $\dfrac{2,250}{2,250 + (5,000 \times £7.50 = £37,500)} \times £6,000$	340
Gross gain	1,910
Indexation allowance £340 × 0.228	78
Chargeable gain	£1,832

Note

(*a*)   The fraction applied to allowable cost corresponds to 5.66%. If the percentage had not exceeded 5% the cash distribution of £2,250 could have been deducted from allowable cost. [*TCGA 1992, s 122*]. No gain would then have arisen in 1986/87, but the allowable cost and indexed pool would each be reduced by £2,250. See also 224.7(B)(i) below.

(ii) The chargeable gain on disposal in 1996/97 is

Without re-basing to 1982

	£
Consideration for disposal of M plc shares	27,000
Allowable cost $(6,000 - 340) \times \dfrac{2,000}{5,000}$	2,264
Unindexed gain	24,736
Indexation allowance (see below)	10,415
Gain after indexation	£14,321

With re-basing to 1982

	£
Disposal consideration (as above)	27,000
Market value 31.3.82	
$£(10,000 \times £3) \times \dfrac{37,500}{37,500 + 2,250} \times \dfrac{2,000}{5,000}$ note (*b*)	11,321
Unindexed gain	15,679
Indexation allowance £11,321 × 0.920	10,415
Gain after indexation	£5,264

Chargeable gain £5,264

Notes

(a) The M plc shares are regarded as the same asset as the original N Ltd shares. [*TCGA 1992, ss 127, 135*]. Re-basing to 31 March 1982 can thus apply, as the original shares were held on that date.

(b) Where there has been a part disposal after 31 March 1982 and before 6 April 1988 of an asset held on the earlier of those dates, and this is followed by a disposal after 5 April 1988 to which re-basing applies, the re-basing rules are deemed to have applied to the part disposal. [*TCGA 1992, 3 Sch 4(1)*].

(B) Takeover by unquoted company

Y Ltd, a small unquoted company, is taken over in June 1992 by another unquoted company, C Ltd. The terms of the acquisition are that holders of £1 ordinary shares in Y Ltd receive two £1 ordinary shares and one £1 deferred share in C Ltd in exchange for every two ordinary shares held.

B acquired his holding of 500 Y Ltd shares on the death of his wife in May 1988, at probate value of £10,000. In January 1997, B sells his 250 C Ltd deferred shares for £4,500. The value of his 500 C Ltd ordinary shares is then £25,000. The indexation factor for May 1988 to January 1997 is assumed to be 0.427.

There is no CGT disposal in 1992/93. The chargeable gain on the 1996/97 disposal is calculated as follows

	£
Disposal consideration	4,500
Allowable cost $\dfrac{4,500}{4,500 + 25,000} \times £10,000$	1,525
Unindexed gain	2,975
Indexation allowance £1,525 × 0.427	651
Chargeable gain	2,324

The allowable cost of the 500 C Ltd ordinary shares is (£10,000 − £1,525) £8,475

(C) Takeover before 1 April 1982

S was the sole shareholder in R Ltd. He subscribed for 5,000 £1 ordinary shares at par in 1968. In July 1981, he accepted an offer for his shares from N plc, a substantial quoted public group. The terms accepted by S were that he would receive one ordinary and five 10% preference shares in N plc for each of his shares in R Ltd. On the first day after the takeover on which the shares are dealt in, N plc ordinary shares have a market value of £8.50 and the value of the preference shares is £1.02, a value maintained at 31 March 1982. In September 1996, S sold 10,000 of his 25,000 preference shares for 140p a share. The indexation allowance for March 1982 to September 1996 is assumed to be 0.895.

(i) Allowable cost of N plc ordinary shares (assuming no re-basing to 1982)

$$£5,000 \times \frac{5,000 \times £8.50}{(5,000 \times £8.50) + (25,000 \times £1.02)} \qquad\qquad £3,125$$

(ii) Allowable cost of N plc preference shares (assuming no re-basing to 1982)

£5,000 − £3,125 £1,875

(iii) Calculation without re-basing to 1982

	£
Disposal consideration	14,000
Allowable cost $\dfrac{10,000}{25,000} \times £1,875$	750
Unindexed gain	13,250
Indexation allowance $10,000 \times £1.02 \times 0.895$	9,129
Gain after indexation	£4,121

(iv) Calculation with re-basing to 1982

	£
Disposal consideration	14,000
Market value 31.3.82 $\dfrac{10,000}{25,000} \times (25,000 \times £1.02)$	10,200
Unindexed gain	3,800
Indexation allowance £10,200 × 0.895 = £9,129 but restricted to	3,800
Gain after indexation	Nil

(v) Outcome

Chargeable gain Nil

Notes

(a)   See also 225.1(C) (note (b)) above.

(b)   For disposals after 29 November 1993 (subject to transitional rules for disposals before 6 April 1995), indexation allowance cannot exceed the unindexed gain. [*TCGA 1992, s 53; FA 1994, s 93(1)–(3)*].

(D) Takeover involving issue of qualifying corporate bond
See 220.2 QUALIFYING CORPORATE BONDS for an example.

(E) Earn-outs

K owns 10,000 ordinary shares in M Ltd, which he acquired for £12,000 in December 1989. In July 1996, the whole of the issued share capital of M Ltd was acquired by P plc. Under the terms of the takeover, K receives £2 per share plus the right to further consideration up to a maximum of £1.50 per share depending on future profit performance. The initial consideration is receivable in cash, but the deferred consideration is to be satisfied by the issue of shares in P plc. In December 1997, K duly receives 2,000 ordinary shares valued at £6 per share in full settlement of his entitlement. The right to future consideration is valued at £1.40 per share in July 1996. The indexation factor for the period December 1989 to July 1996 is assumed to be 0.263.

Without a claim by K under Inland Revenue extra-statutory concession D27 the position would be

1996/97

	£	£
Disposal proceeds 10,000 × £2	20,000	
Value of rights 10,000 × £1.40	14,000	34,000
Cost	12,000	
Indexation allowance £12,000 × 0.263	3,156	15,156
Chargeable gain		£18,844

1997/98

	£
Disposal of rights to deferred consideration:	
Proceeds — 2,000 P plc shares @ £6	12,000
Deemed cost of acquiring rights	14,000
Allowable loss	£2,000
Cost for CGT purposes of 2,000 P plc shares	£12,000

On a claim under extra-statutory concession D27, the position would be

1996/97

	£
Proceeds (cash) (as above)	20,000
Cost £12,000 × $\dfrac{20,000}{20,000 + 14,000}$	7,059
Unindexed gain	12,941
Indexation allowance £7,059 × 0.263	1,857
Chargeable gain	£11,084
Cost of rights for CGT purposes (£12,000 − £7,059)	£4,941

1997/98

The shares in P plc stand in the place of the right to deferred consideration and will be regarded as having been acquired in July 1996 for £4,941. No further gain or loss arises until a disposal of the shares takes place.

Notes

(a) Under Inland Revenue extra-statutory concession D27, on a claim by the vendor, the right to deferred consideration is treated as a security within the meaning of *TCGA 1992, s 132(3)(b)*. The gain on the original shares (to the extent that it does not derive from cash consideration) can then be held over against the value of the new shares.

(b) Various conditions must be satisfied for a claim to be admitted. In particular, the deferred consideration must be wholly in the form of shares or debentures, although the immediate consideration may be in cash, and as a consequence of the right being treated as a security, the conditions of *TCGA 1992, s 135* must be satisfied as regards the disposal of the original shares.

(c) See 206.3(B)(C) DISPOSAL above for deferred consideration generally.

225.5 **SCHEMES OF RECONSTRUCTION OR AMALGAMATION** [*TCGA 1992, s 136*]
N Ltd carries on a manufacturing and wholesaling business. In 1989, it was decided that the wholesaling business should be carried on by a separate company. Revenue clearance under what is now *TCGA 1992, s 138* was obtained, and a company, R Ltd, was formed which, in consideration for the transfer to it by N Ltd of the latter's wholesaling undertaking, issued shares to the shareholders of N Ltd. Each holder of ordinary shares in N Ltd received one ordinary share in R Ltd per each N Ltd share he held. W, who purchased his 2,500 N shares for £10,000 in December 1986, received 2,500 R shares. None of the shares involved is quoted. In August 1996, W sells 1,500 of his N shares for £6 each, a total of £9,000, agreed to be their market value. The value of W's remaining N shares is also £6 per share, and the value of his R shares is £4.50 per share. The indexation factor for the period December 1986 to August 1996 is assumed to be 0.507.

	£
Disposal consideration	9,000
Allowable cost £10,000 $\times \dfrac{9,000}{9,000 + (1,000 \times £6) + (2,500 \times £4.50)}$	3,429
Unindexed gain	5,571
Indexation allowance £3,429 × 0.507	1,738
Chargeable gain	£3,833

225.6 **CONVERSION OF SECURITIES** [*TCGA 1992, s 132*]
N bought £10,000 8% convertible loan stock in S plc, a quoted company, in June 1986. The cost was £9,800. In August 1990, N exercised his right to convert the loan stock into 'B' ordinary shares of the company, on the basis of 50 shares for £100 loan stock, and acquired 5,000 shares. In June 1996, N sells 3,000 of the shares for £2.50 each. The indexation factor for June 1986 to June 1996 is 0.532.

	£
Disposal consideration	7,500
Cost $\dfrac{3,000}{5,000} \times £9,800$	5,880
Unindexed gain	1,620
Indexation allowance £5,880 × 0.532 = £3,128	
but restricted to	1,620
Chargeable gain	Nil

Notes

(a) The shares acquired on the conversion in 1990 stand in the shoes of the original loan stock. [*TCGA 1992, s 132*].

(b) The loan stock cannot be a corporate bond (and thus cannot be a qualifying corporate bond) as it is convertible into securities other than corporate bonds, i.e. into ordinary shares. [*ICTA 1988, 18 Sch 1(5); TCGA 1992, s 117(1)*].

(c) For disposals after 29 November 1993 (subject to transitional rules for disposals before 6 April 1995), indexation allowance cannot exceed the unindexed gain. [*TCGA 1992, s 53; FA 1994, s 93(1)–(3)*].

225.7 CAPITAL DISTRIBUTIONS

(A) [*TCGA 1992, s 122*]

T holds 10,000 ordinary shares in a foreign company M SA. The shares were bought in April 1993 for £80,000. In February 1997, M SA has a capital reconstruction involving the cancellation of one-fifth of the existing ordinary shares in consideration of the repayment of £10 to each shareholder per share cancelled. T's holding is reduced to 8,000 shares, valued at £96,000. The indexation factor for the period April 1993 to February 1997 is assumed to be 0.081.

	£
Disposal consideration (2,000 × £10)	20,000
Allowable cost $\dfrac{20,000}{20,000 + 96,000} \times £80,000$	13,793
Unindexed gain	6,207
Indexation allowance £13,793 × 0.081	1,117
Chargeable gain	£5,090
The allowable cost of the remaining shares is £80,000 − £13,793	£66,207

(B) Sale of rights [*TCGA 1992, ss 122, 123*]

X is a shareholder in K Ltd, owning 2,500 £1 ordinary shares which were purchased for £9,000 in September 1992. K Ltd makes a rights issue, but X sells his rights for £700 in May 1996 without taking them up. The ex-rights value of X's 2,500 shares at the date of sale was £14,500. The indexation factor for the period September 1992 to May 1996 is 0.073.

New holding of K £1 ordinary shares	Shares	Qualifying expenditure £	Indexed pool £
September 1992 acquisition	2,500	9,000	9,000
Indexed rise: September 1992 to May 1996 £9,000 × 0.073			657
	2,500	£9,000	£9,657

(i) If the Inspector so directs, the capital distribution will not be treated as a disposal, as the £700 received for the rights does not exceed 5% of (£700 + £14,500). [*TCGA*

1992, s 122(2)]. The £700 is then deducted from the allowable cost of the shares and from the indexed pool, leaving balances of £8,300 (cost) and £8,957 (indexed pool). In practice, the Inspector will not make such a direction if the taxpayer prefers to have the capital distribution treated as a disposal, for example if the resulting gain would be covered by his annual exemption. (Revenue Tax Bulletin November 1992 p 46).

(ii)   If the rights are sold for £1,000 so that no direction is made, X is treated as having made a part disposal

	£
Disposal proceeds	1,000
Allowable cost $\dfrac{1,000}{1,000 + 14,500} \times £9,000$	581
Unindexed gain	419
Indexation allowance: $£9,657 \times \dfrac{1,000}{1,000 + 14,500} = £623$	
£623 − £581	42
Chargeable gain	£377

The allowable cost of the shares is then reduced to £8,419 (£9,000 − £581) and the balance on the indexed pool to £9,034 (£9,657 − £623).

(C) Distributions in a liquidation — unquoted shares held at 6 April 1965
The shareholders of N Ltd, an unquoted company, resolve that the company be put into liquidation, and a liquidator is appointed on 1 July 1994. An interim distribution of 60p per share is made on 1 April 1995, and a final distribution of 3p per share is made on 1 April 1997. The liquidator's estimates of the share value are

1.4.94   2p
1.4.97   Nil

S subscribed for 10,000 £1 ordinary shares at par on 30 June 1962. He does not elect for 6.4.65 value to be used instead of time apportionment. The shares were valued at £4,000 at 31.3.82.

Indexation factors	March 1982 to April 1995	0.876
	March 1982 to April 1997 (assumed)	0.921

His allowable losses are as follows

1994/95

(i) Without re-basing to 1982

	£
Disposal consideration 10,000 × £0.60	6,000
Cost £10,000 $\times \dfrac{6,000}{6,000 + 200}$	9,677
Loss before time apportionment	£3,677
Time apportionment $£3,677 \times \dfrac{23\text{y }0\text{m}}{32\text{y }9\text{m}}$	£3,368

Loss after time apportionment	£3,368

(ii) With re-basing to 1982

	£
Disposal consideration	6,000
Market value 31.3.82 £4,000 × $\dfrac{6,000}{6,000 + 200}$	3,871
Unindexed gain	2,129
Indexation allowance £9,677 × 0.876 = £8,477	
but restricted to	2,129
Gain after indexation	Nil

(iii) Outcome

Chargeable gain/(allowable loss)	Nil

1996/97

(i) Without re-basing to 1982

	£
Disposal consideration £10,000 × £0.03	300
Cost £10,000 − £9,677	323
Loss before time apportionment	£23
Time apportionment £23 × $\dfrac{30\text{y }0\text{m}}{32\text{y }9\text{m}}$	21
Loss after time apportionment	£21

(ii) With re-basing to 1982

	£
Disposal consideration	300
Market value 31.3.82 £4,000 − £3,871	129
Unindexed gain	171
Indexation allowance £323 × 0.921 = £297	
but restricted to	171
Gain after indexation	Nil

(iii) Outcome

Chargeable gain/(allowable loss)	Nil

Notes

(a) The time apportionment fraction is calculated at the time of the first distribution. See Revenue Statement of Practice D3.

(b) For disposals after 29 November 1993, indexation allowance cannot increase a loss. [*TCGA 1992, s 53; FA 1994, s 93(1)–(3)*]. Transitional relief may be available for 1993/94 under *FA 1994, 12 Sch* on the indexation loss of £5,758 (£7,887 − £2,129). See 210.1(C) INDEXATION.

226   Underwriters

226.1 **PREMIUMS TRUST FUND GAINS AND LOSSES** [*TCGA 1992, s 206*]

(A)

S is a member of the R syndicate and for the 1993 Account he is allocated £6,800 of the total capital gain on the premiums trust fund (syndicate gains). His only other chargeable gains/(losses) for 1993/94 arose from his Lloyd's personal reserves and deposits and comprised a net gain of £1,000. He had no losses brought forward from earlier years. His taxable income for 1993/94 is £50,000.

His capital gains tax position for 1993/94 is as follows

Initially, no assessment will be made as net gains of £1,000 are covered by the £5,800 annual exemption.

Following agreement of the syndicate gains position, S will be assessed as follows

	£
Syndicate gains	6,800
Other gains	1,000
	7,800
Annual exemption	5,800
Taxable gains	£2,000
CGT payable £2,000 at 40%	800
Deduct CGT paid by syndicate £6,800 at 25%	1,700
Repayment due	£900

Notes

(*a*)   S is entitled to a refund of part of the CGT paid by the syndicate on his share of syndicate gains, which would have been charged at a rate of 25%.

(*b*)   With effect for the underwriting year 1994 and subsequent years, premiums trust fund gains and losses are to be removed from the CGT regime and will instead be taken into account in computing underwriting profits and losses for income tax purposes. [*FA 1993, s 174, 23 Sch Pt III(12)*].

(*c*)   There is no change to the treatment of gains on the disposal of assets in Lloyd's personal funds (ancillary funds) and these gains will continue to be assessed to CGT but under the Riesco formula capital appreciation will be allocated for the year to 31 December 1994 to accounts 1992, 1993 and 1994.

(B)

Q is a member of the P syndicate and for the 1993 Account he is allocated £2,000 of the total capital loss on the premiums trust fund (syndicate losses). His other chargeable gains and allowable losses for 1993/94 are

	Gain/(loss) £
Personal investments	12,000
Special reserve fund	(3,000)
Lloyd's deposits	1,500

His taxable income is £100,000.

Q's capital gains tax position for 1993/94 is as follows

Original assessment	£
Gains on personal investments	12,000
Net losses on Lloyds non-syndicate investments (i.e. £3,000 loss – £1,500 gain)	1,500
	10,500
Annual exemption	5,800
Taxable amount	£4,700
CGT payable £4,700 at 40%	£1,880

The revised position following agreement of syndicate losses is

		£
Chargeable gains	(£12,000 + £1,500)	13,500
Allowable losses	(£3,000 + £2,000)	5,000
		8,500
Annual exemption		5,800
Taxable amount		£2,700
CGT payable £2,700 at 40%		£1,080
Repayment due (£1,880 – £1,080)		£800

Note

(a)   See note (b) to (A) above.

227   Wasting Assets

Cross-reference. See also 213.3 LAND.

227.1 GENERAL [*TCGA 1992, ss 44–47*]

(A)

V bought an aircraft on 31 May 1992 at a cost of £90,000 for use in his air charter business. It has been agreed that V's non-business use of the aircraft amounts to one-tenth, on a flying hours basis, and capital allowances and running costs have accordingly been restricted for income tax purposes. On 1 February 1997, V sells the aircraft for £185,000. The aircraft is agreed as having a useful life of 20 years at the date it was acquired. The indexation factor for May 1991 to February 1997 is assumed to be 0.139.

		£
Amount qualifying for capital allowances		
Relevant portion of disposal consideration $\frac{9}{10} \times$ £185,000		166,500
Relevant portion of acquisition cost $\frac{9}{10} \times$ £90,000		81,000
Unindexed gain		85,500
Indexation allowance £81,000 × 0.139		11,259
Chargeable gain		£74,241
Amount not qualifying for capital allowances		
Relevant portion of disposal consideration $\frac{1}{10} \times$ £185,000		18,500
Relevant portion of acquisition cost		
$\frac{1}{10} \times$ £90,000	9,000	
Deduct Wasted £9,000 $\times \dfrac{4\text{y } 8\text{m}}{20\text{y}}$	2,100	6,900
Gain		£11,600

The whole of the £11,600 is exempt.

The total chargeable gain is therefore		£74,241

Note

(a) Gains on tangible moveable property which are wasting assets not qualifying for capital allowances are exempt (and any losses would not be allowable). [*TCGA 1992, s 45*].

(B)

The facts are as in (A) above except that the date of acquisition was 31 May 1981. The 31 March 1982 value of the aircraft was £92,000 and the indexation factor for the period March 1982 to February 1997 is assumed to be 0.913.

The gain on the part qualifying for capital allowances (the remainder being exempt as in (A) above) is as follows

	£	£
Relevant portion of disposal consideration	166,500	166,500
Relevant portion of acquisition cost	81,000	
Relevant portion of 31.3.82 value $\frac{9}{10}$ × £92,000		82,800
Unindexed gain	85,500	83,700
Indexation allowance £82,800 × 0.913	75,596	75,596
Gain after indexation	£9,904	£8,104
Chargeable gain		£8,104

Note

(a) Machinery and plant qualifying for capital allowances is excluded from any election under *TCGA 1992, s 35(5)* (election to treat all assets as disposed of and re-acquired at their market value at 31 March 1982). [*TCGA 1992, 3 Sch 7*]. However, the general re-basing provisions can apply.

227.2 OPTIONS [*TCGA 1992, ss 44, 46, 146*]

Cross-reference. See also 206.5 DISPOSAL.

(A) Unquoted shares

On 1 July 1994, R grants C an option to purchase unquoted shares held by R. The cost of the option is £600 to purchase 10,000 shares at £5 per share, the option to be exercised by 31 December 1996. On 1 September 1996 C assigns the option to W for £500. The indexation factor for July 1994 to September 1996 is assumed to be 0.070.

	£	£
Disposal consideration		500
Acquisition cost	600	
Deduct Wasted £600 × $\frac{26}{30}$	520	80
Unindexed gain		420
Indexation allowance £80 × 0.070		6
Chargeable gain		£414

(B) Traded options

On 1 December 1996, C purchases 6-month options on T plc shares for £1,000. Two weeks later, he sells the options, which are quoted on the Stock Exchange, for £1,200.

	£
Disposal consideration	1,200
Allowable cost	1,000
Chargeable gain	£200

Note

(*a*)   The wasting asset rules do not apply to traded options. [*TCGA 1992, s 146*].

227.3 **LIFE INTERESTS** [*TCGA 1992, s 44(1)(d)*]

(A)

N is a beneficiary under a settlement. On 30 June 1983, when her actuarially estimated life expectancy was 40 years, she sold her life interest to an unrelated individual, R, for £50,000. N dies on 31 December 1996, and the life interest is extinguished.

R will have an allowable loss for 1996/97 as follows

	£	£
Disposal consideration on death of N		Nil
Allowable cost	50,000	
Deduct wasted		
$\dfrac{13\text{y 6m}}{40\text{y}} \times £50,000$	16,875	
		33,125
Allowable loss		£33,125

Notes

(*a*)   The amount of the cost wasted is computed by reference to the predictable life, not the actual life, of the wasting asset.

(*b*)   No indexation allowance is available as, for disposals after 29 November 1993 (subject to transitional rules for disposals before 6 April 1995), such allowance cannot increase a loss. [*TCGA 1992, s 53; FA 1994, s 93(1)–(3)*].

(B)

Assume the facts to be as in (A) above except that the sale of the life interest was on 30 June 1981 and N's life expectancy at that date was 40 years. The value of the life interest was still £50,000 at 31 March 1982.

Calculation without re-basing

	£	£
Disposal consideration on death of N		Nil
Allowable cost	50,000	
Deduct wasted		
$\dfrac{15y\ 6m}{40} \times £50,000$	19,375	
	———	30,625
Loss		£30,625

Calculation with re-basing

	£	£
Disposal consideration		Nil
Market value 31.3.82	50,000	
Deduct wasted		
$£50,000 \times \dfrac{14y\ 9m}{39y\ 3m}\ \begin{array}{l}(31.3.82-31.12.96)\\ \text{(life expectancy at 31.3.82)}\end{array}$	18,790	
	———	31,210
Loss		£31,210
Allowable loss 1996/97		£30,625

Note

(a)   The second of the above calculations shows how the wasting assets provisions interact with the re-basing provisions of *TCGA 1992, s 35*. Where, by virtue of the re-basing rules, an asset is deemed to have been disposed of and re-acquired at its market value on 31 March 1982, that market value must be reduced in accordance with the period of ownership *after* that date and the predictable life of the wasting asset *at* that date.

Inheritance Tax

301   Accumulation and Maintenance Trusts

[IHTA 1984, s 71]

301.1 On 1 January 1981 G settled £50,000 on trust equally for his great nephews and nieces born before 1 January 1999. The beneficiaries were to take life interests at age 18, income being accumulated for minor beneficiaries. By 1999 G had three great nephews and nieces, A (his brother's grandson) born in 1976 and B and C (his sister's grandsons) born in 1991 and 1996 respectively. The settlement was valued at £150,000 on 1 January 2006.

On 1 January 2006 the settlement fails to qualify as an accumulation and maintenance settlement as more than 25 years have elapsed since the date of settlement and the beneficiaries do not have a common grandparent. A has an interest in possession in one-third as he is over 18, but the remaining two-thirds which is held equally for B and C is not subject to an interest in possession. There will be a charge to IHT on two-thirds of the value of the settlement on 1 January 2006.

The rate of tax is the aggregate of

0.25% for each of the first	40 quarters	10%
0.20% for each of the next	40 quarters	8%
0.15% for each of the next	20 quarters	3%
	100	21%

The IHT charge is $21\% \times \frac{2}{3} \times £150,000 = \underline{£21,000}$

Note

(a)   There was no charge to IHT on A becoming entitled to an interest in possession in one-third on his eighteenth birthday in 1994.

302   Agricultural Property

[*IHTA 1984, ss 115–124B; FA 1986, 19 Sch 22; F(No 2)A 1992, 14 Sch 4, 8; FA 1995, s 155*]

302.1   RELIEF FOR TRANSFERS AND OTHER EVENTS OCCURRING AFTER 9 MARCH 1981

(A) Relief given at 100% [*IHTA 1984, ss 116(1)(2)(7), 124A(1)(3); F(No 2)A 1992, 14 Sch 4, 8; FA 1995, s 155*]

X has owned since 1983 1,000 acres of land. In June 1990 he began to farm the land, utilising 800 acres for that purpose. The remaining 200 acres are not used for any business purposes. On 1 July 1996 X transfers all the land to his son, Y, at a time when its agricultural value was £1,000 per acre and its open market value £1,500 per acre. He had not used his annual exemptions for 1995/96 and 1996/97. X died on 6 September 1998. Y has continued to run the farm business since the date of the gift.

The value of the gift for inheritance tax purposes before relief is

	£	£
1,000 acres at £1,500 per acre		£1,500,000

The transfer subject to tax is

(i)   Agricultural value of land

	£	£
800 acres × £1,000	800,000	
Less agricultural property relief at 100%	(800,000)	—

(ii)   Non-agricultural value of land

	£	£
800 acres × £500		400,000

(iii)   Value of land not used in business

	£	£
200 acres at £1,500 per acre		300,000
		700,000
Deduct Annual exemptions (1995/96 and 1996/97)		6,000
Value transferred by PET becoming chargeable on death		£694,000

Notes

(*a*)   Relief is at 100% because

(i)   immediately before the transfer, X enjoyed the right to vacant possession;

(ii)   X had farmed the land for two years before the transfer;

(iii)   X had acquired the land more than seven years before the transfer and it had been farmed throughout those seven years (by X or any other person); and

(iv)   the land was farmed by Y between the date of gift and X's death.

Note that although conditions (ii) and (iii) were both satisfied in this case, it is only necessary to satisfy one of them to qualify for 100% relief.

(*b*)   Annual exemptions are deducted *after* deducting the agricultural property relief.

(*c*)   Business property relief may be available in respect of the £400,000 excess of the open market value over the agricultural value.

(*d*)   IHT will be charged at 80% of full rates as X died more than 3 but not more than 4 years after the gift.

(*e*)   The 100% relief applies in relation to transfers of value made, and other events occurring, after 9 March 1992, and replaced a 50% relief.

(B) Transfer after 14 March 1983 where land is held tenanted under an agricultural lease entered into before 1 September 1995. [*IHTA 1984, s 116(1)(2)(7); F(No 2)A 1992, 14 Sch 4, 8; FA 1995, s 155*]

A is the freehold owner of agricultural land which at current vacant possession value is estimated to be valued at £850,000. On 29 September 1989, he enters into an agricultural tenancy with a farming partnership comprising his two sons and his grandson for a full market rental of £25,000 p.a. The tenanted value is estimated at £500,000.

In July 1996 his grandson is killed in a farming accident and a new letting agreement is made between the two sons and A for a full market rent of £35,000 p.a. on 15 September 1996.

A dies on 1 October 1996 when the tenanted value of the land has risen to £600,000.

	£
Transfer at death (tenanted valuation)	600,000
Deduct Agricultural property relief	600,000
IHT payable on	NIL

Note

(*a*)   No IHT charge arises on the grant of the lease to the partnership on the basis that it is for full consideration. [*IHTA 1984, s 16*].

(*b*)   As A terminated the existing agricultural tenancy and entered into a new tenancy on or after 1 September 1995, agricultural property relief of 100% is available. Only 50% relief would have been available if the existing tenancy had continued, [*FA 1995, s 15; FA 1996, s 185*].

(C) Interaction with capital gains tax

A discretionary settlement has 400 acres of tenanted agricultural land. On 31 October 1995, the trustees appoint the agricultural land to a beneficiary who then becomes absolutely entitled to the land. 50% agricultural property relief is available. The value of the 400 acres as tenanted is £450,000. The trustees fail to pay the capital gains tax due of £60,000 by 1 December 1997 and the beneficiary is assessed and pays the liability.

	£
Value transferred	450,000
Agricultural property relief 50%	225,000
	225,000
Capital gains tax	60,000
Chargeable transfer (subject to grossing-up)	£165,000

Notes

(a)   An election may be made for the CGT to be held over. [*TCGA 1992, s 260(1)–(5)*].

(b)   If the trustees fail to pay all or part of the capital gains tax within twelve months of the due date, an assessment may be made on the beneficiary [*TCGA 1992, s 282*] and the amount of such tax borne by the donee is treated as reducing the value transferred. The beneficiary must become absolutely entitled to the property to obtain the relief. [*IHTA 1984, s 165*].

(c)   If it were possible for the trustees to arrange for a new tenancy to begin after 31 August 1995 but before the transfer, the transfer would have attracted 100% agricultural property relief. [*FA 1995, s 155*]. This could possibly be achieved by terminating the existing lease and entering into a new lease with the same tenants, subject to the terms of the existing lease, the tenants' agreement and general legal requirements.

(D) Transitional relief for property acquired before 10 March 1981 [*IHTA 1984, s 116(2)–(4); F(No 2)A 1992, 14 Sch 4, 8; FA 1995, s 155*]
Q owns 1,200 acres of tenanted agricultural land, acquired before 10 March 1981 and let to a partnership in which he is a partner. The land is valued at £833 per acre.

On a chargeable transfer in, say, December 1994, without transitional relief

	£
Value of 1,200 acres land (tenanted)	999,600
50% relief on 1,200 acres worth £999,600	499,800
Chargeable transfer (subject to grossing-up)	£499,800

On a chargeable transfer in, say, December 1994, with transitional relief

	£
Value of 1,200 acres land (tenanted)	999,600
Relief:	
100% on 1,000 acres worth £833,000	(833,000)
50% on 200 acres worth £166,600	(83,300)
Chargeable transfer (subject to grossing-up)	£83,300

Note

(a)   Under the transitional provisions, 100% relief applies up to a maximum of £250,000 or 1,000 acres whichever is the more favourable to the taxpayer.

302.2 **SHARES ETC. IN AGRICULTURAL COMPANIES** [*IHTA 1984, ss 122, 123*] AC Ltd is an unquoted agricultural company of which A owns 60% of the shares.

	£
The company owns	
4,000 acres of land — agricultural value	4M
Other trading assets (net)	2M
Total value of company	£6M
A's shareholding is valued at	£4.5M

All necessary conditions for relief are satisfied.

IHT 302.2 Agricultural Property

If A were to die in, say, November 1996 the position as regards his shareholding would be as follows

	Total Value £	Land £	Other Assets £
Value of assets of company	£6M	£4M	£2M
Value of shares, split in same proportions	4.5M	£3M	£1.5M
Agricultural property relief (100% of £3M)	(3.0M)		
Business property relief (100% of £1.5M)	(1.5M)		
Chargeable to IHT	Nil		

Notes

(a) Part of the value transferred is attributable to the agricultural value of agricultural property, so agricultural property relief is available. [*IHTA 1984, s 122*].

(b) The legislation appears to require that both agricultural property relief and business property relief be given, each against its appropriate part of the value. [*IHTA 1984, s 114*]. See also 304 BUSINESS PROPERTY. When some of the land owned by the company is tenanted (agreement in force before 1 September 1995), attracting only 50% agricultural property relief, the total relief given will be less than would be the case if business property relief at 100% were given on the whole value.

303 Anti-Avoidance

303.1 **ASSOCIATED OPERATIONS** [*IHTA 1984, s 268*]

(A)

H owns a set of four Chippendale chairs valued, as a set, at £6,000. Individually they would be valued at only £1,000, although a pair would be worth £2,500 and three £4,000.

He gives one chair to his son each year over four years, during which time all values increase at 10% p.a. (simple). In the fifth year A dies.

	£	£
Year 1		
Value of four chairs	6,000	
Deduct value of three	4,000	
Value transferred		2,000
Year 2		
Basic computation ignoring the associated operations rule		
Current value of three chairs	4,400	
Deduct value of two	2,750	
Value transferred	£1,650	
Revised to take account of associated operations rule		
Current value of four chairs	6,600	
Deduct value of two	2,750	
	3,850	
Deduct value transferred in Year 1	2,000	
		1,850
Year 3		
Current value of four chairs	7,200	
Deduct value of one	1,200	
	6,000	
Deduct value transferred in Years 1 and 2	3,850	
		2,150
Year 4		
Current value of four chairs	7,800	
Deduct value transferred in Years 1, 2 and 3	6,000	
Value transferred		1,800
Total values transferred		£7,800

Note

(*a*)   The normal rule would be that the transfer of value is the loss to the donor's estate, as in Year 1. However, if a series of transfers are treated as associated operations, the transfer is treated as if made at the time of the latest transfer, reduced by the value transferred by the earlier transfers.

(B)

If in (A) above H had wished to give away the chairs over two years instead of four, he might first have given two chairs to his wife, so that each could give the son one chair each year.

		£	£
Year 1			
(i)	Value transferred by husband to son		
	Value of two chairs (as half of a set of		
	four linked by the related property rule)	3,000	
	Deduct value of one chair (as half of a pair)	1,250	
			1,750
(ii)	Value transferred by wife		
	(similar calculation)		1,750
Year 2			
(i)	Value transferred by husband,		
	applying the associated operations rule		
	Current value of four chairs	6,600	
	Deduct value transferred in Year 1 by		
	H to son	1,750	
	Value transferred		4,850
Total values transferred			£8,350

Notes

(*a*)   In this case, the total of the values transferred can exceed the value of the assets, although it must be doubtful whether the Inland Revenue would seek to apply the full rigours of the section unless the transfer by the wife in Year 1 had fallen within her annual exemptions, or she had survived seven years so that the gift was exempt.

(*b*)   See *IHTA 1984, s 161* for the related property rule, and see also 325.2 VALUA-TION.

304   Business Property

[IHTA 1984, ss 103–114, 269; FA 1987, s 58, 8 Sch; F(No 2)A 1992, 14 Sch 1–3, 8, 9; FA 1996, s 184]

304.1 RELEVANT BUSINESS PROPERTY

(A) Shares or securities

A has owned for many years 60,000 shares in X Ltd, an unquoted company, whose issued share capital is 100,000 shares of £1 each. All shares carry full voting rights. A gifts to his son 20,000 shares in June 1994, a further 20,000 in June 1995 and the remaining 20,000 in June 1996. The son agrees to pay any IHT on all gifts. A dies in March 2000, at which time his son still owns the shares. A has made previous transfers of value since June 1989 amounting to £170,000. It is assumed that the IHT rate and the nil rate band remain at 40% and £154,000 up to and including 1998/99.

The value of holdings at all three dates of transfer were as follows

60% holding	£10 per share
40% holding	£4 per share
20% holding	£3 per share

First gift	£
Value of holding before transfer	600,000
Value of holding after transfer	160,000
Reduction in value of estate	440,000
Deduct business property relief (100%) note (*a*)	440,000
Value transferred	Nil

Second gift	
Value of holding before transfer	160,000
Value of holding after transfer	60,000
Reduction in value of estate	100,000
Deduct business property relief (100%) note (*a*)	100,000
Value transferred	Nil

Third gift	
Value of shares transferred	60,000
Deduct business property relief (100%) note (*a*)	60,000
	60,000
Value transferred	NIL

Notes

(*a*)   Pre-6 April 1996 rules apply to the first and second transfer. Business property relief on the first transfer is 100% as the gift was made from a controlling interest in an unquoted company. On the second transfer, 100% relief is due as the gift was from a holding yielding more than 25% of the voting rights. Post-6 April 1996 rules apply to the third transfer, whereupon all unquoted shares (not securities) in qualifying companies held for at least two years qualify for business property relief at 100% regardless of the size of holding or voting entitlement. The third transfer qualifies for relief at 50%.

(*b*)   The 100% and 50% rates apply in relation to transfers of value made, and other events occurring, after 9 March 1992, replacing 50% and 30% rates respectively. [*IHTA 1984, s 104; F(No 2)A 1992, 14 Sch 1, 8*]. See also 304.2 below.

(B) Shares in a holding company with a non-qualifying subsidiary [*IHTA 1984, s 111*]

A owns 85% of the share capital of H Ltd, an unquoted company which has two wholly-owned subsidiary companies S Ltd and P Ltd. H Ltd and S Ltd are trading companies and P Ltd is a property investment company. The issued share capital of H Ltd is 100,000 ordinary shares of £1 each valued at £8 per share. The values of the issued shares in S Ltd and P Ltd are £250,000 and £300,000 respectively.

A gives 10,000 shares in H Ltd to his son in August 1996. He has already made chargeable transfers using up his basic exemptions. His son agrees to pay any IHT. A dies in January 1999, at which time his son still owns the shares. It is agreed that the fall in value in A's estate (reduction of a 85% holding to a 75% holding), by which the value of the gift for IHT purposes is measured, is equivalent to the actual value of the shares transferred.

	£	£
Value of gift		80,000
Deduct business property relief 100% × £80,000	80,000	
Less $100\% \times 80,000 \times \dfrac{300,000}{800,000}$	30,000	
		50,000
PET becoming chargeable transfer on death		£30,000

(C) Land used by a business

M has for many years owned a factory used in the business of Q Ltd, of which he has control. In September 1996, M gives the factory to his son S when its value is £375,000. He has made no previous chargeable transfer, but made a gift of £3,000 in 1995/96. M dies in October 1997, when the factory is being used for business purposes by S's partnership. S agreed to pay any IHT on the gift.

	£
Value of gift	475,000
Deduct business property relief (50%)	237,500
	237,500
Deduct annual exemption	(3,000)
PET becoming chargeable transfer on death	£234,500
IHT payable at full rates (death within 3 years)	£13,800

Notes

(*a*)   If M wishes also to dispose of shares in Q Ltd by sale or gift after which he would no longer have control, he should give the factory to his son *before* disposing of the shares, or else the business property relief would not be available on the gift of the factory.

(*b*)   If the factory had been used by Q Ltd at the date of M's death, no business property relief would be available on the gift since the factory would not be relevant business property in S's hands at the date of death.

(D) Land and buildings owned by trustees

X died in 1976 leaving a life interest in factory premises to his son A, with remainder to his grandsons B and C. A occupies the premises for the purposes of his trade, rent-free. In September 1996 A gives up his life interest when the value of the premises is £460,000. B and C agree to pay any IHT. A has already made chargeable transfers using up his annual exemptions. A dies in November 1998, when the factory is still being used in the trade which was then being carried on by B and C in partnership.

	£
Value of gift	460,000
Deduct business property relief (50%)	(230,000)
PET becoming chargeable transfer on death	£230,000
IHT payable at full rates (death within 3 years)	£12,000

304.2 TRANSFERS BEFORE 10 MARCH 1992, DEATH ON OR AFTER THAT DATE

Y held 99,000 shares in an unquoted company, WX Ltd, with an issued share capital of 100,000 shares. On 1 August 1990, he settled 39,000 shares on a discretionary trust, paying the IHT himself. The transfer was valued at £350,000 before BPR. On 1 August 1991, he gave a further 5,000 shares to his daughter, Z. The transfer was valued at £25,000 before BPR and Z agreed to pay any IHT arising from the gift. Y died in August 1996 when his remaining 55,000 shares were worth £600,000 and the rest of his estate was valued at £500,000 for IHT purposes. The conditions for the granting of BPR on the two lifetime transfers are fulfilled at death. Y had made no other transfers of value except such as to fully utilise annual exemptions for all relevant years.

Gift 1 August 1990
The gift to a discretionary trust is a chargeable transfer (net) attracting BPR at the then 50% rate.

	£	£
Net chargeable transfer		350,000
Deduct BPR (50%)		175,000
		175,000
IHT on £175,000 net:		
0–128,000		—
128,001–175,000 at 25%	11,750	
	£11,750	11,750
Gross chargeable transfer		£186,750

Gift 1 August 1991
The transfer of £12,500 (as reduced by the then 50% BPR) is a PET and is not immediately chargeable.

Death August 1996

(i)
No additional tax becomes payable in respect of the transfer on 1 August 1990. As death occurs after 9 March 1992, the business property attracts relief at the 100% rate applicable after that date and the transfer is thus reduced to nil. However, this applies *only* for the purpose of calculating additional tax payable as a result of the death. The gross chargeable transfer retains its value of £186,750 for cumulation purposes. The IHT paid is not repayable.

(ii)
The PET on 1 August 1991 would normally become chargeable as a result of death within seven years. However, it is reduced to nil by the availability of 100% BPR. There is thus no tax effect resulting from the transfer, and the transfer *has no effect* for cumulation purposes.

(iii)
The estate attracts BPR at the 100% rate on £600,000. Part of £500,000 remains chargeable.

IHT payable	
£	
186,751–200,000	£NIL
200,001–686,750 at 40%	£194,700

Note
(a) The 1992 increases in the rates of BPR apply not only in relation to transfers of value made after 9 March 1992 but to other events occurring (in this example, a death) after that date. [*F(No 2)A 1992, 14 Sch 8*]. The effect on the lifetime transfers as outlined in (i) and (ii) above is based on correspondence between the publishers and the Inland Revenue.

305   Calculation of Tax

305.1   THE CUMULATION PRINCIPLE: POTENTIALLY EXEMPT TRANSFERS
[*IHTA 1984, ss 3, 3A, 7*]

On 1 May 1993 A gave £50,000 to his daughter, D, and on 1 May 1996 he gave £188,000 to his son, S. Both D and S agreed to pay any IHT due on the gifts.

On 7 March 2001 A died, leaving his estate, valued at £300,000, equally to D and S. The only other transfer made by A was an immediately chargeable transfer of £86,000 during 1991/92.

Gift on 1 May 1993
The gift is a PET, which becomes exempt since A does not die within seven years of the date of the gift. No IHT is payable.

Gift on 1 May 1996
This PET becomes chargeable since A dies between 4 and 5 years after the gift. IHT is payable by S following the death at 60% of full rates on the basis of the Table of rates in force in 2000/01 (which is assumed to be the same as that in force for transfers after 5 April 1995).

As this PET has become chargeable, it must be cumulated with other chargeable transfers made in the seven years before the date of the gift. The PET made on 1 May 1993 has become exempt and is excluded from the computation but the immediately chargeable transfer of £86,000 made during 1991/92 must be cumulated with the 1996 gift. Note that a transfer made more than seven years before the death of the transferor and which is not itself aggregated with the estate on death is thus brought into the computation of the IHT payable on the 1996 gift.

	£	£
Gift		188,000
Deduct annual exemptions 1996/97	3,000	
1995/96	3,000	
	6,000	
		£182,000

IHT on £182,000 charged in band £86,000 to £268,000

86,001–200,000 at nil%	—	
200,001–268,000 at 40%	27,200	
	£27,200	
IHT payable at 60% of full rates — £27,200 at 60%		£16,320

Death 7 March 2001

The chargeable transfers in the seven years prior to death comprise only the gift on 1 May 1996 of £182,000.

IHT on death on estate of £300,000 chargeable in band £82,000 to £382,000

	£
82,001–200,000 at nil%	
200,001–382,000 at 40%	72,800
IHT payable	£72,800

Notes

(a) If A directs in his will that, despite the earlier agreement, any IHT due on the gift to S is to be borne by his estate, this amounts to a pecuniary legacy to S of the amount of the tax. The reduction in A's estate by the transfer is unchanged at £188,000 as is the tax of £16,320. The legacy is paid out of the death estate of £300,000 with previous chargeable transfers of £82,000. Since the whole of the estate is liable on death, the IHT remains at £72,800.

(b) If S has not by 1 April 2002 paid the IHT of £16,320 due on the gift from A, the personal representatives of A become liable for the tax as it has not been paid by S within 12 months after the end of the month in which A died. The IHT due remains £16,320 since the gross chargeable transfer is £182,000. A had no liability for the tax at the time the transfer was made and the reduction in value to his estate was, therefore, the amount of the gift to S, £188,000. The personal representatives have a right under general law to reimbursement for the tax from S. To the extent that reimbursement is probable, the tax is not a deduction from the estate. Since the personal representatives can claim reimbursement from the half estate due to S, no deduction will be given. Tax on the estate remains, therefore, at £72,800. [*IHTA 1984, ss 199, 204; FA 1986, 19 Sch 28*]. If S had not benefited under A's will so that no assets were available to reimburse the personal representatives, the tax due of £16,320 might fall to be met from the estate.

305.2 THE CUMULATION PRINCIPLE: GROSSING UP A CHARGEABLE TRANSFER [*IHTA 1984, ss 3, 3A, 5, 7*]

(A)

On 13 July 1992 B gave £212,000 to his nephew N, who agreed to pay any IHT on the gift. On 24 December 1993 B settled £213,000 on discretionary trusts for his great-nephews and nieces, paying the IHT himself.

On 9 July 1999 B died with an estate worth £50,000, having made no other gifts.

Gift 13 July 1992

The gift is a PET but becomes chargeable since B dies between 6 and 7 years after the gift. The annual exemption for 1992/93, and that brought forward from 1991/92 are, however, available, reducing the chargeable transfer to £206,000.

IHT is charged on the transfer at 20% of full rates, using the Table of rates in force in 1999/2000 (which is assumed to be the same as that in force for transfers after 5 April 1996).

	£
IHT on gift	
1–200,000 at nil%	—
200,001–206,000 at 40%	2,400
	£2,400

IHT payable by N at 20% of full rates, i.e. 20% × £2,400	£480

Gift 24 December 1993

Initial liability

The gift to the discretionary trust is an immediately chargeable transfer on which the transferor, B, has agreed to pay the IHT. The annual exemption for 1993/94 is set against the chargeable transfer, reducing it to £164,000.

As B is paying the tax on the transfer, his estate is reduced by two amounts: the gross amount of the transfer itself (i.e. before deducting the annual exemptions) and by the tax due on the net transfer (i.e. after deducting the annual exemptions). The total tax will not merely comprise the tax due on the transfer, but the tax upon that tax, and so on. In order to determine the total tax due, where applicable the excess of the chargeable transfer above the nil rate band (or part thereof) is grossed up, using the following formula:

$$E \times \frac{100}{100 - T} \times T\% = G$$

E = excess over nil rate band
T = applicable rate of tax
G = tax due on gross chargeable transfer

In this example, as chargeable lifetime transfers are charged at 20%, being one half of the full death rates, T will be 20. The computation therefore proceeds as follows.

	£
Value of transfer	167,000
Deduct Annual exemption	(3,000)
	164,000
IHT payable on gift	
$£(164,000 - 150,000) \times \dfrac{100}{100 - 20} \times 20\%$	3,500
B's gross chargeable transfer	£167,500

Revision on death

B's death occurs between 5 and 6 years after the gift, so the tax on the chargeable transfer is revised to the IHT payable at 40% of full rates. The PET on 13 July 1992 becomes chargeable, so IHT is charged on the gross chargeable transfer of £167,500 in the bracket £206,001 to £373,500.

	£
206,001–373,500 at 40%	67,000
IHT at 40% of £67,000	26,800
Less paid on chargeable lifetime transfer	3,500
Additional IHT payable following death	£23,300

Death 9 July 1999

Chargeable transfers in the seven years prior to death amount to £373,500, so IHT is charged on the death estate of £50,000 in the bracket £373,501 to £427,500.

	£
IHT payable	
373,501–423,500 at 40%	£20,000

(B)
Facts are as in (A) above except that B died on 9 July 2000.

The PET on 13 July 1992 is exempt and thus not cumulated when reworking the IHT on the chargeable transfer on 24 December 1993 or on death.

Gift 24 December 1993
IHT on gift, as before   £3,500

Following B's death between 6 and 7 years after the gift, IHT is reworked at 20% of full rates. No additional IHT is payable as the cumulative transfers fall within the NIL rate band.

Death 9 July 2000
Chargeable transfers in the previous 7 years amount to £167,500 so IHT is charged on the death estate of £50,000 in the bracket £167,501 to £217,500.

IHT payable
200,000–217,500 at 40%   £7,000

Note
(*a*)   No IHT is repayable in respect of the chargeable transfer on 24 December 1993, even though the IHT on death is less than the IHT originally paid on the gift.

305.3 **PARTLY EXEMPT TRANSFERS** [*IHTA 1984, ss 36–42*]

(A) Where the only chargeable part of a transfer is specific gifts which do not bear their own tax
A, a widow, dies on 8 June 1996. Her estate is valued at £380,000 and her will provides for a tax-free legacy to her nephew of £270,000 and the residue of her estate to the National Trust. A had made no chargeable transfers during her lifetime.

Gross-up tax-free legacy at 'death' rates

	£
Tax-free legacy	270,000
Tax thereon	

$$(270,000 - 200,000) \times \frac{100}{100 - 40} \times 40\% \qquad 46,667$$

Gross chargeable transfer	£316,667

Calculation of net residuary estate   £

Value of estate	380,000
Deduct gross value of legacy	(316,667)
Residue	£63,333

Allocation of estate at death

Nephew	270,000
National Trust	63,333
Tax	46,667
	£380,000

(B) Where tax-free specific gifts are not the only chargeable gifts
A dies on 1 January 1997 leaving a widow, son and nephew. His estate is valued at £520,000 before deduction of business property relief of £40,000 and his will provides for a tax-free legacy to his son of £225,000, a legacy to the nephew of £13,000 bearing its own tax, a bequest to charity of £26,000, with the residue shared three-quarters by his widow and one-quarter by the son. A had made no previous chargeable transfers.

Allocation of business property relief [*IHTA 1984, s 39A; FA 1986, s 105*]
Since the will made no specific gifts of the business property, the business property relief is apportioned between each of the specific gifts and the residue, i.e. each is multiplied by

$$\frac{\text{Estate less business property relief}}{\text{Estate before business property relief}}$$

Son	£225,000	$\times$	$\dfrac{480,000}{520,000}$	=	£207,692
Nephew	£13,000	$\times$	$\dfrac{480,000}{520,000}$	=	£12,000
Charity	£26,000	$\times$	$\dfrac{480,000}{520,000}$	=	£24,000
Residue	£256,000	$\times$	$\dfrac{480,000}{520,000}$	=	£236,308
	£520,000				£480,000

Hypothetical chargeable estate	£	£	£
Tax-free legacy to son			207,692
Tax thereon			
$£(207,692 - 200,000) \times \dfrac{100}{100 - 40} \times 40\%$			5,128
			212,820
Legacy to nephew			12,000
			224,820
Chargeable residue:			
Gross estate		480,000	
Deduct gross legacies	224,820		
charity	24,000		
		(248,820)	
		£231,180	
Son's one-quarter share			57,795
Hypothetical chargeable estate			£282,615

IHT 305.3 Calculation of Tax

Hypothetical chargeable estate — calculation of assumed tax rate

Tax on £282,615   £33,046

Assumed rate $\dfrac{33,046}{282,615} \times 100 = 11.69294\%$

Re-gross tax-free legacy to son using assumed rate

£207,692 × $\dfrac{100}{100 - 11.69294}$ £235,193

Calculate chargeable estate and tax thereon	£	£	£
Grossed-up value of tax-free legacy			235,193
Legacy to nephew			12,000
			247,193
Chargeable residue			
Gross estate		480,000	
Deduct gross legacies	247,193		
charity	24,000		
		(271,193)	
		£208,807	
Son's one-quarter share			52,202
Chargeable estate			£299,395
Tax on estate			
0–200,000		—	
200,001–299,395 at 40%		39,758	
		£39,758	

Estate rate is $\dfrac{39,758}{299,395} \times 100 = 13.27945\%$

Calculation of residue	£	£
Gross estate		520,000
Specific legacies — son	225,000	
— nephew	13,000	
— charity	26,000	
	264,000	
Tax on son's legacy		
£235,193 at 13.27945%	31,232	
Legacies plus tax thereon		295,232
Residue		£224,768

Distribution of estate	£	£
Widow — three-quarters of residue		168,576
Son — specific legacy	225,000	
— one quarter share of residue	56,192	
	281,192	
Deduct tax on share of residue		
£52,202 × 13.27945%	6,932	
		274,260
Nephew — specific legacy	13,000	
Deduct tax thereon		
£12,000 × 13.27945%	1,594	
		11,406
Charity		26,000
Tax payable £(31,232 + 6,932 + 1,594)		39,758
		£520,000

(C) As (B) above but with settled property

The facts are as in (B) above except that in addition to his free estate valued at £520,000, A has a life interest, worth £100,000 at 1 January 1997, in his late father's estate, with remainder to his son.

The hypothetical chargeable estate is £282,615 as in (B) above and thus the assumed rate remains at 11.69294%. The settled property is ignored at this stage — see note (*a*).

Calculate chargeable estate and tax thereon	£
Chargeable free estate as in (B) above	299,395
Settled property	100,000
Chargeable estate	£399,395
Tax on estate	
0–200,000	—
200,001–399,395	79,758
	£79,758

Estate rate is $\dfrac{79,758}{399,395} \times 100 = 19.96970\%$

Calculation of residue	£	£
Gross estate		520,000
Specific legacies — son	225,000	
— nephew	13,000	
— charity	26,000	
	264,000	
Tax on son's legacy		
£235,193 at 19.96970%	46,967	
Legacies plus tax thereon		310,967
Residue		£209,033

IHT 305.3   Calculation of Tax

Distribution of estate

	£	£
Widow — three quarters of residue		156,775
Son — specific legacy	225,000	
— one quarter share of residue	52,258	
— settled property	100,000	
Deduct		
tax on share of residue		
£52,201 × 19.96970%	(10,424)	
tax on settled property		
£100,000 × 19.96970%	(19,970)	
		346,864
Nephew — specific legacy	13,000	
Deduct tax thereon		
£12,000 × 19.96970%	2,396	
		10,604
Charity		26,000
Tax payable (46,967 + 10,424 + 19.970 + 2,396)		79,757
		£620,000

Notes

(*a*)   Where gifts take effect separately out of the deceased's free estate and out of a settled fund the provisions of *IHTA 1984, ss 36–39A* (partly exempt transfers) apply separately to each fund. [*IHTA 1984, s 40*]. The Revenue take the view that the rate of tax to be used for grossing up, i.e. the 'assumed rate' in this example, should be found by looking at each fund separately and in isolation. Thus, the settled property is not taken into account above in the calculation of the assumed rate for gifts out of the free estate.

(*b*)   The IHT on the settled property, payable by the trustees, is found by applying the estate rate of 19.96970% to the value of that property.

306   Charities

[*IHTA 1984, s 70*]

306.1 PROPERTY LEAVING TEMPORARY CHARITABLE TRUSTS

(A) Gross payment to beneficiaries
On 1 January 1971 A settled £100,000 on temporary charitable trusts. The income and capital were to be applied for charitable purposes only for a period of 25 years from the date of settlement, and thereafter could be applied for charitable purposes or to or for the settlor's grandchildren. On 1 January 1997 the trustees paid £50,000 to charity and the balance of the settlement, valued at £75,000, to the three grandchildren.

The relevant period is the period from settlement of the funds or, if later, 13 March 1975 to 1 January 1997, i.e. 87 complete quarters, and the amount on which tax is charged is £75,000 gross.

The rate of tax is

	%
	%
0.25% for 40 quarters	10.00
0.20% for 40 quarters	8.00
0.15% for 7 quarters	1.05
	19.05%

IHT payable is 19.05% × £75,000 = £14,287

(B) Net payment to beneficiaries
Assume the same facts as in (A) above except that the trustees apply £75,000 net for the settlor's three grandchildren, and the balance to charity.

The rate of tax is, as before, 19.05%

IHT payable is $\dfrac{19.05}{100 - 19.05} \times £75,000 = £17,650$

The gross payment to the beneficiaries is £75,000 + £17,650 – £92,650.

307   Close Companies

[IHTA 1984, ss 94–98, 102]

307.1   VALUE TRANSFERRED

The ordinary shares of companies A and B are held as follows (in January 1997)

	A	B
Individuals X	80%	
Y	20%	
Z		10%
Company A		90%

Company B is non-resident and Z is domiciled in the UK. Company A sells a property valued at £220,000 to a mutual friend of X and Y for £20,000. The following month, company B sells a foreign property worth £100,000 to X for £90,000.

Company A

	£
The transfer of value is £220,000 − £20,000	200,000

Apportioned to X	80% × £200,000	160,000
Y	20% × £200,000	40,000
		£200,000

Company B

The transfer of value of £10,000 is apportioned

To X	80% × 90% × £10,000	7,200
	Deduct increase in X's estate	10,000
		—

To Y	20% × 90% × £10,000	1,800
To Z	10% × £10,000 note (*c*)	1,000
		£2,800

Notes

(*a*)   If the sale by company A were to X (or Y), there would be no apportionment because the undervalue would be treated as a net distribution, thus attracting income tax.

(*b*)   On the sale by company B, X would not be liable to income tax.

(*c*)   If Z were not domiciled in the UK, his share of the transfer of value would not be apportioned to him. *[IHTA 1984, s 94(2)(b)]*.

307.2 **CHARGE ON PARTICIPATORS**

Assume the values transferred by X, Y and Z in 307.1 above and that X and Y have each made previous chargeable transfers in excess of £154,000 since January 1989 and have used up their annual exemptions for 1995/96.

Company A

	X £	Y £	Z £
Value transferred	160,000	40,000	
Annual exemptions 1996/97	(3,000)	(3,000)	
	157,000	37,000	
Tax (25% of net)	39,250	9,250	
Gross transfer	£196,250	£46,250	
IHT	£39,250	£9,250	

Company B

	X	Y	Z
Value transferred	7,200	1,800	1,000
Deduct increase in X's estate	(10,000)	—	—
		1,800	1,000
Deduct annual exemption		—	1,000
		1,800	—
Tax (25% of net)		450	
Gross transfer		£2,250	
IHT		£450	

Note

(a) Although it is understood that the Inland Revenue would follow this method of calculation, there is an alternative view which follows the exact wording of *IHTA 1984, s 94(1)*. This view is that the grossing-up should take place before the increase in X's estate is deducted. In the above example, it makes no difference as the gross transfer would still be less than the increase in X's estate. But suppose that X held 90% of the ordinary shares in Company A. His value transferred would then be £8,100 (90% × 90% × £10,000) and this alternative method would proceed as follows.

	£
Value transferred	8,100
Tax (25% of net)	2,025
	10,125
Deduct increase in X's estate	(10,000)
	£125
IHT thereon at 20%	£25

307.3 ALTERATION OF SHARE CAPITAL

In January 1997 the share capital of company H, an investment company, is owned by P and Q as follows

P	600
Q	400

1,000 ordinary £1 shares

The shares are valued at £10 per share for P's majority holding and £4 per share for Q's minority holding.

The company issues 2,000 shares at par to Q and the shares are then worth £3.50 per share for Q's majority holding and £1.50 per share for P's minority holding. P has previously made chargeable transfers in excess of £154,000 since January 1989 and has utilised his 1995/96 and 1994/95 annual exemptions.

The transfer of value for P is

	£
Value of holding previously	6,000
Value of holding now	900
Decrease in value	5,100
Tax (25% of net)	1,275
Gross transfer	£6,375
IHT thereon at 20%	£1,275

Notes

(a)   P's transfer of value is *not* a potentially exempt transfer. [*IHTA 1984, s 98(3)*].

(b)   An alternative charge may arise under *IHTA 1984, s 3(3)* (omission to exercise a right) but the transfer would then be potentially exempt and only chargeable if P died within seven years.

308   Deeds Varying Dispositions on Death

[*IHTA 1984, ss 17, 142*]

308.1 A died in December 1996 leaving his estate of £200,000 to his wife absolutely. His wife, having an index-linked widow's pension, agreed with her sons, B and C, that they could benefit from the estate to the extent of £200,000 in equal shares, i.e. £100,000 each. A deed of variation is duly executed, and an election made under *IHTA 1984, s 142(2)*.

A had made no chargeable transfers before his death.

	£
Exempt transfer to widow	50,000
Transfer to B	100,000
Transfer to C	100,000
	£200,000
IHT payable	Nil

Note

(*a*) If A's widow died 5 years later when her estate was valued at, say, £204,000, IHT payable would be £1,600. If no deed of family arrangement had been made on A's death and his widow's estate was, as a result, £404,000, the IHT payable on her death would have been £81,600. The disclaimer has thus saved IHT of £80,000 (ignoring any increase in value in the funds originally intended for the children and assuming no changes in the rates of IHT).

309 Double Taxation Relief

[IHTA 1984, s 159]

309.1 UNILATERAL RELIEF

(A) Where property is situated in an overseas territory only

A, domiciled in the UK, owns a holiday home abroad valued at £264,000 which he gives to his son in July 1996. He is liable to local gifts tax of, say, £12,750. He has made no previous transfers and does not use the home again at any time before his death in February 2001.

	£	£
Market value of holiday home		264,000
Annual exemption 1996/97	(3,000)	
1995/96	(3,000)	
		(6,000)
Chargeable transfer		£258,000
IHT payable at 60% of full rates by son (death between 4 and 5 years after gift)		
£58,000 × 40% × 60%		13,920
Unilateral relief for foreign tax		(12,750)
IHT borne		£1,170

Note

(*a*)   If the overseas tax suffered exceeded the UK liability before relief, there would be no IHT payable but the excess would not be repayable.

(B) Where property is situated in both the UK and an overseas territory

M, domiciled in the UK, owns company shares which are regarded as situated both in the UK and country X under the rules of the respective countries. On M's death in June 1996 the shares pass to M's son S. The UK IHT amounts to £5,000 before unilateral relief. The equivalent tax liability arising in country X amounts to £2,000.

Applying the formula $\dfrac{A}{A + B} \times C$

where A = amount of IHT
   B = amount of overseas tax
   C = smaller of A and B

The unilateral relief available is

$$\frac{5,000}{5,000 + 2,000} \times £2,000 = £1,429$$

IHT payable = £5,000 − £1,429 = £3,571

(C) Where tax is imposed in two or more overseas territories on property situated in the UK and each of those territories

Assume the facts in (B) above except that a third country imposes a tax liability on the death as the shares are regarded as also situated in that country.

UK IHT before unilateral relief	£5,000
Tax in country X	£2,000
Tax in country Y	£400

Applying the formula $\dfrac{A}{A+B} \times C$

where A = amount of IHT

B = aggregate of overseas tax

C = aggregate of all, except the largest, of A and the overseas tax imposed in each overseas territory

The unilateral relief available is

$$\frac{5,000}{5,000 + 2,000 + 400} \times (2,000 + 400) = £1,622$$

IHT payable £5,000 − £1,622 = £3,378

(D) Where tax in one overseas territory is relieved against another overseas territory's tax

Assume the same facts as in (C) above except that country X allows a credit for tax paid in country Y.

Unilateral relief for IHT

$$\frac{5,000}{5,000 + (2,000 - 400) + 400} \times £((2,000 - 400) + 400) = £1,429$$

IHT payable £5,000 − £1,429 = £3,571

310   Exempt Transfers

310.1 ANNUAL EXEMPTION [*IHTA 1984, s 19*]

(A)
S, who has made no other transfers of value, made gifts to his sister of £5,000 on 1 June 1995 and £4,000 on 1 May 1996. S dies on 1 September 2000 with an estate valued at £200,000.

Annual exemptions are available as follows

1995/96	£	£
1 June 1995 Gift		5,000
Deduct 1995/96 annual exemption	3,000	
1994/95 annual exemption (part)	2,000	
		5,000
		Nil

1996/97	£
1 May 1996 Gift	4,000
Deduct 1996/97 annual exemption	3,000
PET becoming chargeable on death	£1,000

The PET, having become a chargeable transfer as a result of death within seven years, is covered by the nil rate band but is aggregated with the death estate in computing the IHT payable on death.

Note
(*a*)   Although the annual exemption, to the extent that it is not fully utilised in the year, can be carried forward to the following year, the current year's exemption is treated as utilised before any exemption brought forward. [*IHTA 1984, s 19(1)(2)*]. If S had gifted £6,000 in 1995/96 and £3,000 in 1996/97, the total gifts would have been the same but they would have been fully covered by annual exemptions.

(B)
T made a gift to his son of £2,000 on 1 June 1996. On 9 November 1996, he settled £20,000 on a discretionary trust for his children and grandchildren. T had made no other gifts since 6 April 1996, but had used his annual exemptions in each year up to and including 1995/96. T died on 13 February 2002.

The gift on 1 June 1996 is a potentially exempt transfer which becomes chargeable since T died within seven years of the gift. The gift on 9 November 1996 is a chargeable transfer.

There are now two conflicting approaches (see notes (*a*) and (*b*) below) to **allocation of the annual exemption** where a chargeable transfer is preceded by a PET in the same tax year.

Approach 1 (see note (*b*) below)

	£
1 June 1996 Gift to son — PET becoming chargeable	2,000
Deduct annual exemption 1996/97 (part)	2,000
	Nil
9 November 1996 Gift to trust	20,000
Deduct annual exemption 1996/97 (balance)	1,000
Chargeable transfer	£19,000

Approach 2 (see note (*a*) below)

	£
1 June 1996 Gift to son — PET becoming chargeable	2,000
9 November 1996 Gift to trust	20,000
Deduct annual exemption 1996/97	3,000
Chargeable transfer	£17,000

Notes

(*a*)   The second approach was, prior to 1991, widely understood to be the correct approach. It is based on *IHTA 1984, s 19(3A)* as inserted by *FA 1986, 19 Sch 5*. Although the annual exemption is generally allocated to transfers within the same tax year in the order in which they are made [*IHTA 1984, s 19(3)*], a PET is treated for this purpose as having been made later in the year than any transfer of value which is not a PET. The advantages are that the immediately chargeable transfer is reduced and the annual exemption is not wasted if the PET turns out to be exempt due to the donor's surviving for seven years.

(*b*)   The first of the two approaches illustrated above allocates the annual exemption to earlier rather than later transfers within the same tax year regardless of whether they are PETs or chargeable transfers. Although this approach seems to render *section 19(3A)* otiose, it is understood, based on reported correspondence and on the examples given in pamphlet IHT 1 (1991) that *this is the Inland Revenue's current interpretation*. The only way of securing the advantages in (*a*) above (i.e. Approach 2) would be to make the chargeable transfer earlier in the year than the PET.

310.2 NORMAL EXPENDITURE OUT OF INCOME [*IHTA 1984, s 21*]

A wife pays annual life assurance premiums on a policy in favour of her son. The income of her husband and herself for 1996/97 is

	£
Husband's salary	25,000
Wife's salary	6,295
	£31,295

Income levels are not expected to fluctuate wildly from year to year.

The wife's disposable income is

	£
Salary	6,295
Tax thereon (personal allowance £3,765)	506
Personal income	£5,789

Notes

(*a*)   Depending on her lifestyle, the wife is probably able to show that she has sufficient income to justify a 'normal expenditure' gift of, say, a £1,000 premium paid annually (and therefore habitual).

(*b*)   If the wife was also accustomed to pay personally for an annual holiday costing, say, £2,500, it might be difficult to show that the life assurance premium was paid out of income.

311   Gifts with Reservation

[FA 1986, s 81, 20 Sch; SI 1987 No 1130]

311.1 (A) Reservation released within 7 years before death

On 19 June 1990 D gave his house to his grandson G, but continued to live in it alone paying no rent. The house was valued at £130,000. On 5 May 1993 D remarried, and went to live with his new wife F. G immediately moved into the house, which was then valued at £230,000.

On 3 January 1998 D died, leaving his estate of £200,000 equally to his granddaughter H and his wife F.

Gift 19 June 1990

As the gift was made more than seven years before death, it is a PET which has become exempt.

5 May 1993 release of reservation

The release of D's reservation is a PET which becomes chargeable by reason of D's death between 4 and 5 years later. IHT is charged, at 60% of full rates on the basis of the Table of rates in force at the time of death, on the value of the house at the date of release of reservation.

	£	£
Gift		230,000
Deduct annual exemptions 1993/94	3,000	
1992/93	3,000	
		6,000
Chargeable transfer		£224,000
Tax thereon (assuming no change in rates)		
0–200,000 at nil%	—	
200,001–224,000 at 40%	9,600	
	£9,600	
IHT payable at 60% of full rates, 60% × £9,600 =		£5,760

Death 3 January 1998

IHT is charged at full rates on the chargeable estate of £100,000 (£100,000 passing to the wife is exempt) in the bracket £224,000 to £324,000.

Tax thereon

224,001–324,000 at 40%	£40,000

(B) Reservation not released before death

The facts are as in (A) above except that the gift was on 19 June 1992 when the house was valued at £206,000, that D remained in his house on remarriage, and that G did not move in until D's death. The house was valued at £228,000 at the date of D's death on 3 January 1998.

Gift 19 June 1992

This is a potentially exempt transfer which becomes chargeable by reason of D's death within seven years.

Death 3 January 1998

As the reservation had not been released at the date of D's death, D is treated as beneficially entitled to the house, which thus forms part of his chargeable estate on death.

A double charge would arise by virtue of the house being the subject of a PET and a part of the chargeable estate on death. *The Inheritance Tax (Double Charges Relief) Regulations 1987 [SI 1987 No 1130]* provide relief as follows.

First calculation under Reg 5(3)(a)

Charge the house in the death estate and ignore the PET.

	£
Chargeable estate	
Free estate passing to H	100,000
House	228,000
	£328,000

There are no chargeable transfers within the previous seven years.

	£
IHT payable	
First £200,000	—
£200,001 – 328,000 at 40%	51,200
	£51,200

Second calculation under Reg 5(3)(b)

Charge the PET and ignore the value of the house in the death estate.

	£	£
Gift 19 June 1992		206,000
Deduct annual exemptions 1992/93	3,000	
1991/92	3,000	
		6,000
Chargeable transfer		£200,000
Tax thereon		
0–200,000	Nil	

	£
Chargeable estate on death (excluding house)	100,000

IHT payable in the bracket £200,001 to £300,000

	£
£200,001–300,000 at 40%	£40,000
Total IHT payable	£40,000

The first calculation yields the higher amount of tax (£51,200), so tax is charged by reference to the value of the gift with reservation in the estate, ignoring the PET.

312   Interest on Tax

[IHTA 1984, s 233; FA 1989, s 178; SI 1989 No 1297]

312.1 B died on 10 February 1995. The executors made a payment on account of IHT of £90,000 on 30 June 1995 on delivery of the account. The final notice of determination was raised by the Capital Taxes Office on 19 June 1996 in the sum of £102,500. The rate of interest is assumed to be 5%.

Date of chargeable event (death)	10 February 1995
Date on which interest starts to accrue	1 September 1995

	£
IHT payable	102,500
Payment made on account 30 June 1995	90,000
Balance due	£12,500

Assessment raised by Capital Taxes Office 19 June 1996	
Interest payable (1.9.95 to 19.6.96)	
£12,500 at 5% for 292 days	£500

Note

(*a*)   Further interest may be charged if payment of the balance is not made promptly.

312.2 F gave his holiday home in Cornwall to his granddaughter G on 7 August 1995. On 23 May 1998 F died. He had made no use of the property at any time after 7 August 1995. G made a payment of £15,000, on account of the IHT due, on 1 January 1999. The liability was agreed at £17,000, and the balance paid, on 17 February 1999. The rate of interest is assumed to be 5%.

Date of PET	7 August 1995
Date on which PET becomes chargeable	23 May 1998
Date on which IHT is due	1 December 1998

	£
IHT payable	17,000
Payment made on account 1 January 1998	15,000
Balance due	£2,000

Interest payable

On £17,000 from 1.12.98 – 1.1.99	
£17,000 at 5% for 31 days	72
On £2,000 from 1.1.99 – 17.2.99	
£2,000 at 5% for 47 days	13
Total interest payable	£85

313   Liability for Tax

313.1 LIFETIME TRANSFERS [*IHTA 1984, ss 199(1), 204(2)(3)(5)(6)*]

(A) Transferor
A settled £78,000 on discretionary trusts in December 1996, having previously made chargeable transfers on 31 March 1996 totalling £235,000.

A's liability is as follows	£
Gift	78,000
Deduct 1995/96 annual exemption	3,000
	£75,000
Grossed at 20%	£93,750
IHT thereon at 20%	£18,750

(B) Transferee
In example (A) above A pays only £10,000 of IHT and defaults on the balance of £8,750, so that the trustees become liable as transferee.

The trustees' liability is not however £8,750 but is as follows	£
Original gross	93,750
Deduct IHT unpaid	8,750
Revised gross	£85,000
IHT thereon at 20%	17,000
Deduct Paid by A	10,000
Now due from trustees	£7,000

(C) Person in whom property is vested
In January 1997 C transferred to trustees of a discretionary trust shares in an unquoted property company worth, as a minority holding, £50,000. However the transfer deprives C of control of the company with the result that the value of his estate is reduced by £210,000. He has already used his nil rate band and annual exemptions.

C's liability is as follows	
Net loss to him	£210,000
Grossed at 20%	£262,500
IHT thereon at 20%	£52,500

C fails to pay so that the trustees become liable, as follows

	£
Original gross	262,500
Deduct unpaid IHT	52,500
	£210,000
IHT thereon at 20%	£42,000

Notes

(a)   The trustees' liability cannot exceed the value of the assets which they hold, namely the proceeds of sale of the shares, less any CGT and costs incurred since acquisition, plus any undistributed income in their hands.

(b)   If the trustees have already distributed net income of £2,000 to beneficiary D who is liable to pay higher rate income tax of £154 thereon, D can be made to pay IHT of £1,846, being the net benefit received by him.

313.2   **TRANSFERS ON DEATH** [*IHTA 1984, ss 200(1)(3), 204(1)–(3)(5), 211*]
Personal representatives of E, who died on 30 September 1999, received the following assets

	£
Free personal property	128,500
Land bequeathed to F (which, under the terms of the Will, bears its own IHT)	27,500
Private residence, bequeathed to spouse	50,000

A trust in which E had a life interest was valued at £110,000. Under the will of E, legacies of £15,000, each free of IHT, were given to F and G and the residue was left to H. E had made no chargeable transfers during his lifetime.

	Persons liable	£	IHT £
IHT is borne as to			
Chargeable transfer			
Free personal property	PRs	128,500	12,753
Land bequeathed to F	F	27,500	2,730
Private residence to spouse	—	Exempt	Nil
Trust fund	Trustees	110,000	10,917
		£220,000	£26,400

The residue left to H is as follows	£	£
Free personal property		128,500
Deduct IHT	12,753	
Legacies to F and G	30,000	42,753
		£85,747

Note

(a)   If the will had not directed that the IHT on the land bequeathed to F be borne by F, the IHT would be payable out of residue. [*IHTA 1984, s 211*].

313.3 **LIFETIME TRANSFER WITH ADDITIONAL LIABILITY ON DEATH** [*IHTA 1984, ss 131, 199(2), 201(2), 204(4)*]

(A)

On 31 December 1996, H, who had made no earlier chargeable transfers other than to utilise his annual exemptions for 1996/97 and earlier years, transferred £206,000 into a discretionary trust and, a month later, settled an asset worth £20,000 into the same trust. H paid the appropriate IHT. On 30 June 2000, H died.

The trustees become liable to further IHT as follows

	£	£
Original net gift	£206,000	£20,000
Grossed-up at half of full rates	£207,500	£25,000
IHT (paid by H)	£1,500	£5,000
IHT at 80% of death rates applicable in June 2000 on original gross (death between 3 and 4 years after gifts)	2,400	8,000
Deduct paid originally by H	1,500	5,000
Now due from trustees	£900	£3,000

Note

(*a*)   The additional IHT on death is calculated using the rates in force at the date of death. If the IHT at the new death rates, as tapered, was less than the IHT paid on the original chargeable transfer, there would be no repayment.

(B)

The second gift in (A) above had fallen in value to £18,000 by the time of H's death.

The trustees may claim to reduce the IHT payable as follows

	£
Original gross gift	25,000
Deduct drop in value (£20,000 − £18,000)	2,000
Revised gross	£23,000
IHT thereon at 80% of death rate applicable in June 2000	7,360
Deduct paid by H	5,000
	£2,360

Note

(*a*)   If the asset had fallen in value to £10,625 or less, so that the revised gross became £15,625 or less and the IHT at 80% of death rates £5,000 or less, the trustees would have no liability because H had already paid IHT of £5,000.

313.4 **POTENTIALLY EXEMPT TRANSFER BECOMING CHARGEABLE ON DEATH**
[*IHTA 1984, ss 199, 201, 204; FA 1986, 19 Sch 26–28*]
On 19 May 1996 M gave N £212,000. M died on 3 August 1998 having made no other gifts.

	£
Gift	212,000
Deduct annual exemptions 1995/96	(3,000)
1994/95	(3,000)
	£206,000

The IHT at 80% of full rates on the gift to N is payable by N on 1 March 1999.

	£
First £200,000 at nil	—
Next £6,000 at 40%	2,400
	£2,400

IHT payable by N 80% × £2,400 = £1,920

Notes

(*a*) If N has not paid the IHT due of £1,920 by 1 March 2000 the personal representatives of M are liable, although their liability cannot exceed the death estate of M. The amount is a deductible liability from the estate only to the extent that reimbursement from N cannot be obtained.

(*b*) See also 305.1 CALCULATION OF TAX for liability to tax on potentially exempt transfers.

314   Life Assurance Policies

[IHTA 1984, ss 21, 167]

314.1   A has paid premiums of £2,000 p.a for 6 years on a policy on his own life. He gives the policy to his son B. The market value of the policy at the date of gift is £11,000. A also pays annual premiums of £2,000 on a policy on his life written in favour of his son.

Assignment of policy
The gift is valued either at
 (i)   market value (£11,000), or
 (ii)   the accumulated gross premiums paid (£12,000) if greater.

Annual premiums
The payment of an annual premium is regarded as an annual gift, the amount of the transfer being the net premium after deduction of any tax relief at source or the gross premium where paid without deduction.

Notes
(*a*)   The gifts are PETs. The assignment of the policy will only become chargeable if A dies within seven years, and only the annual premiums paid within seven years of A's death will be chargeable.

(*b*)   Exemptions available for reduction of the chargeable transfer on assignment include the annual exemption and the marriage exemption.

(*c*)   The normal expenditure exemption may be available to A for premiums paid and the annual exemption may also be claimed to exempt the gift in whole or in part.

(*d*)   Normal expenditure relief is not available when a policy and annuity have been effected on a back-to-back basis (with certain exceptions).

315   Mutual Transfers

[FA 1986, s 104; SI 1987 No 1130]

315.1 POTENTIALLY EXEMPT TRANSFERS AND DEATH

A, who has made no previous transfers of value other than to use his annual exemptions for 1991/92 and 1992/93, makes a gift of £160,000 to B on 1 July 1992. On 15 July 1993 and 20 January 1994, he makes gifts of £117,000 and £66,000 respectively into a discretionary trust and the trustees pay the IHT due of £6,000 on the later transfer. On 2 January 1995, B dies and the 1992 gift is returned to A by virtue of B's Will. On 4 April 1996, A dies. His taxable estate on death is valued at £400,000 which includes the 1992 gift returned to him in 1995 which is still valued at £160,000.

First calculation under Reg 4(4)(a)

The gift in 1992 is a PET and would normally become a chargeable transfer by virtue of A's death within seven years of making the gift. However, for the purpose of this calculation, it is ignored and the returned gift is charged as part of A's death estate.

Additional tax due on chargeable lifetime transfers

	£
Gift on 15 July 1993	117,000
Deduct 1993/94 annual exemption	3,000
	114,000
Gift on 20 January 1994	66,000
	£180,000

	£
IHT at death rates on £180,000	10,400
IHT paid	6,000
Additional IHT payable by trustees	£4,400

Tax on death estate of £400,000 charged at 40%

IHT payable note (*a*)	£160,000

Total IHT payable as consequence of death (£4,400 + £160,000)	£164,400

Second calculation under Reg 4(4)(b)

The 1992 gift is charged as a PET but the returned gift is ignored in the death estate.

The tax due on PET of £160,000 at death rates

	£
0–154,000	Nil
154,001–160,000 at 40%	2,400
	£2,400

IHT payable at 80% of full rates (death between 3 and 4 years after gift)	£1,920

Tax due on chargeable lifetime transfers of £180,000 (after annual exemption) charged at 40%

	£
IHT payable	72,000
IHT paid	6,000
Additional IHT payable	£66,000

Tax on death estate of £240,000 charged at 40%

IHT payable	£96,000

Total IHT payable as consequence of death (£1,920 + £66,000 + £96,000)	£163,920

The first calculation gives the higher amount of tax, so the PET is ignored and the returned gift included in the death estate, the tax liabilities being as in the first calculation above.

Note

(a)   Quick succession relief under *IHTA 1984, s 141* (see 319.1 QUICK SUCCESSION RELIEF below) might be due in respect of the returned PET by reference to any tax charged on that PET in connection with B's death. If, as a result of such relief, the first calculation produces a lower tax charge than the second, then the second calculation will prevail, i.e. the PET will be charged and the returned gift ignored in the death estate.

315.2 CHARGEABLE TRANSFERS AND DEATH

C, who had made no other transfer of value, gifted £156,000 on 31 May 1986 into discretionary trust, on which IHT of £13,750 was paid. On 5 October 1986, he gave D a life interest in shares worth £85,000; IHT of £19,500 was paid. On 3 January 1992, C makes a PET of £30,000 to E. On 31 December 1992, D dies and the settled shares return to C, the settlor (no tax charge arises on D's death). On 10 August 1993, C dies; his death estate is valued at £260,000 which includes the shares returned from D, now worth £60,000.

First calculation under Reg 7(4)(a)
The gift in October 1986 is ignored and the returned shares included as part of the taxable estate on death.

No additional tax arises on the May 1986 lifetime transfer of £150,000 (after annual exemptions) as it was made more than seven years before death.
Tax due on PET of £30,000 made in January 1992 charged in band £150,001–180,000.

£30,000 at 40% = £12,000.

Tax on death estate of £260,000 charged in band £30,001–290,000 (the gift to the discretionary trust having fallen out of cumulation)

	£	£
30,001–150,000	Nil	
150,001–290,000 at 40%	56,000	56,000

Total IHT payable as consequence of death
(£12,000 + £56,000) (but see note (*a*) below) £68,000

Second calculation under Reg 7(4)(b)
The October 1986 gift is charged and the returned shares are excluded from the taxable estate on death.
Additional tax due on October 1986 transfer as a result of death — charged in band £150,001 to £235,000.

150,001–235,000 at 40%	£34,000

IHT payable at 20% of full rates	
(death between 6 and 7 years after gift)	6,800
IHT paid £19,500, but credit restricted to	6,800
Additional IHT	Nil

Tax due on PET of £30,000 charged in band £235,001–265,000.

£30,000 at 40%	£12,000

Tax on death estate of £200,000 charged in band £115,001–315,000.

115,001–150,000	Nil	
150,001–315,000 at 40%	66,000	£66,000

Total IHT payable as consequence of death (£12,000 + £66,000) £78,000

The second calculation gives the higher amount of tax so the returned gift is excluded from the death estate, the tax liabilities being as in the second calculation above.

Note
(*a*)   If the first calculation had given the higher amount, a credit for IHT would have been due, restricted to the lower of

   (i)   the IHT paid on the lifetime transfer (i.e. £19,500); and
   (ii)   the IHT attributable to the returned shares on death, calculated as follows:

$$\text{Estate rate } \frac{56,000}{260,000} = 21.53846\%$$

£60,000 × 21.53846% = £12,923

The IHT actually payable as a consequence of death would have been £55,077 (£68,000 − £12,923).

316   National Heritage

[*IHTA 1984, ss 30–35, 57A, 77–79, 207, 2 Sch 5, 6, 4 Sch, 5 Sch; FA 1987, s 59, 9 Sch*]

316.1 **CONDITIONALLY EXEMPT TRANSFERS AFTER 6 APRIL 1976**

(A) Chargeable event during lifetime of relevant person

C, who has made previous chargeable transfers during 1992 of £230,000, makes a conditionally exempt gift of property in February 1993. In October 1996, the property is sold for £500,000 and capital gains tax of £100,000 is payable.

		£
Cumulative total of previous chargeable transfers of relevant person		230,000
Net sale proceeds of conditionally exempt property	500,000	
Deduct Capital gains tax payable	(100,000)	
Chargeable transfer		400,000
Revised cumulative total for relevant person		£630,000

Inheritance tax payable (by reference to lifetime rates in October 1995)

£400,000 at 20% =   £80,000

(B) Chargeable event after relevant person is dead

D died in April 1990 leaving a taxable estate of £350,000 together with conditionally exempt property valued at £600,000 at the breach in October 1996.

	£
Value of relevant person's estate at death	350,000
Value of conditionally exempt property at date of breach	600,000
	£950,000

Inheritance tax payable (by reference to full rates applicable in October 1995).

£600,000 at 40% =   £240,000

Note

(*a*)   As the chargeable event occurs after tax is reduced by the substitution of a new Table of rates, the new rates are used.

(C) Multiple conditionally exempt transfers

D died in December 1983 leaving a conditionally exempt property to his son E. D's taxable estate at death was £230,000. In 1990 E gave the property to his daughter F. F gave the necessary undertakings so this transfer was also conditionally exempt. In December 1996 F sold the property for its market value of £500,000 and paid capital gains tax of £80,000. During 1989 E had made chargeable transfers of £20,000 and he has made no other transfers.

	£	£
Value of relevant person's estate at death		230,000
Net sale proceeds of conditionally exempt property	500,000	
Deduct capital gains tax	80,000	
Chargeable transfer		420,000
		£650,000

Inheritance tax payable by F

£420,000 at 40% =	£168,000
Previous cumulative total of E	20,000
Add chargeable transfer	420,000
E's revised cumulative total	£440,000

Notes

(*a*)   There have been two conditionally exempt transfers within the period of 30 years ending with the chargeable event in December 1996. The Inland Revenue may select either D or E as the 'relevant person' for the purpose of calculating the tax due. The IHT liability will be higher if D is selected. [*IHTA 1984, ss 33(5), 78(3)*].

(*b*)   As F receives the proceeds of sale, she is the person liable to pay the IHT. [*IHTA 1984, s 207(1)*].

(*c*)   Although the IHT is calculated by reference to D's cumulative total, it is E whose cumulative total is adjusted as he made the last conditionally exempt transfer of the property. [*IHTA 1984, s 34(1)*].

(*d*)   As the chargeable event occurs after a reduction in the rates of tax, the new rates are used to calculate the tax payable. [*IHTA 1984, 2 Sch 5*].

316.2 **CONDITIONALLY EXEMPT TRANSFERS ON DEATH BEFORE 7 APRIL 1976**

Chargeable event more than 3 years after death

B died on 31 December 1975 leaving a taxable estate of £100,000 together with a conditionally exempt painting valued at £50,000. In June 1995 the painting was sold for £110,000.

		£
Value of deceased's taxable estate		100,000
Value of exempt property at date of chargeable event	note (*a*)	110,000
		£210,000
Recalculated IHT liability	note (*b*)	£90,750

IHT payable on conditionally exempt property

$$£90,750 \times \frac{110,000}{210,000} \qquad £47,536$$

No further liability accrues to the estate of the deceased.

Notes

(*a*)   The value of the exempt property will be reduced by any capital gains tax chargeable in respect of the sale. [*TCGA 1992, s 258(8)*].

(*b*)   The IHT liability is calculated using rates in force at the date of death.

316.3 **CHARGE TO TAX**

Tax credit [*IHTA 1984, s 33(7)*]
Property inherited in 1984 from A's estate by B, who gave the necessary undertakings so that the property is conditionally exempt, is given in December 1996 by B to C. C agrees to pay any inheritance tax arising from the transfer but does not wish to give the necessary undertakings, so a chargeable event arises. B dies in March 1997.

	£
A's estate at date of death in 1984	180,000
B's cumulative chargeable transfers at date of chargeable event in December 1996 (all in 1995/96)	58,000
Value of property at date of chargeable event	250,000

Inheritance tax on chargeable event (subject to tax credit)

	£
Value of A's estate at date of death	180,000
Value of property at date of chargeable event	250,000
	£430,000
Inheritance tax payable	
£230,000 at 40% =	£92,000

Inheritance tax on B's gift

Cumulative total of previous transfers		58,000
Value of property gifted	250,000	
Deduct Annual exemption 1996/97	3,000	247,000
		£305,000
Inheritance tax arising on gift of £247,000		£42,000

Tax credit

IHT on B's gift		42,000
IHT on chargeable event	92,000	
Deduct tax credit	(42,000)	
		50,000
Total inheritance tax borne		£92,000

316.4 SETTLEMENTS — EVENTS AFTER 8 MARCH 1982

(A) Chargeable events following conditionally exempt occasions

A, who is still alive, settled property and investments on discretionary trusts in September 1983, conditional exemption being granted in respect of designated property. In April 1996, the designated property was appointed absolutely to beneficiary C who gave the necessary undertakings for exemption to continue. However, in February 1997, C sold the property for £139,000 net of costs, suffering a capital gains tax liability of £20,000. At the time of C's sale, A had cumulative chargeable transfers of £40,000.

		£
Cumulative total of previous chargeable transfers of relevant person		40,000
Net sale proceeds of conditionally exempt property		115,000
		£155,000

Inheritance tax payable by C

£110,000 at nil	—	
£5,000 at 20%	1,000	
£115,000	£1,000	£1,000

Notes

(*a*)   A is the relevant person in relation to the chargeable event as he is the person to effect the only conditionally exempt transfer *and* the person who is settlor in relation to the settlement in respect of which the only conditionally exempt occasion arose. [*IHTA 1984, ss 33(5), 78(3)*].

(*b*)   The Inland Revenue have discretion to select either the conditionally exempt transfer (by A to the trustees) in 1983 or the conditionally exempt occasion (from the trustees to C) in 1996 as the 'last transaction' for the purposes of determining who is the relevant person. A is the relevant person regardless of which is selected but the Revenue are more likely to choose the earlier transfer as this will result in a greater amount of tax being collected. [*IHTA 1984, ss 33(5), 78(3)(4)*].

(*c*)   The chargeable amount of £115,000 does not increase either A's cumulative total or that of the trustees for the purpose of calculating the IHT liability on any subsequent transfers. As the last conditionally exempt transaction before the chargeable event was a conditionally exempt occasion rather than a conditionally exempt transfer, the provisions of *IHTA 1984, s 34* (which allow for an increase in the cumulative total) do not apply. [*IHTA 1984, s 78(6)*].

(B) Exemption from the ten-year anniversary charge [*IHTA 1984, s 79*]
Trustees own National Heritage property for which the necessary undertakings have been given and the property has been designated by the Treasury. The property was settled in July 1974 and is the sole asset of the trust. No appointments or advances of capital have been made. On 30 October 1996, there is a breach of the undertakings. At this date the property is valued at £150,000.

Ten-year anniversary charge
There is no liability in 1984 or 1994.

Breach in October 1996

Value of property at time of event   £150,000

The relevant period is the period from the date of settlement or, if later, 13 March 1975 to 29 October 1996, i.e. 82 complete quarters.

The rate of tax is

	%
0.25% for 40 quarters	10.00
0.20% for 40 quarters	8.00
0.15% for 6 quarters	0.90
	18.90%

IHT payable is 18.9% × £150,000 = £28,350

316.5 **MAINTENANCE FUNDS FOR HISTORIC BUILDINGS** [*IHTA 1984, 2 Sch 6, 4 Sch 8, 12–14*]

On 1 January 1989 P settled £500,000 in an approved maintenance fund for his historic mansion during the lives of himself and his wife, W. P died in February 1994, his taxable estate and lifetime transfers chargeable on death amounting to £140,000. On 1 January 2004, the date of death of W, the fund, which has been depleted by extensive repairs to the mansion, is valued at £300,000. £80,000 is transferred to the National Trust, which also accepts the gift of the mansion, and the balance is paid to P's grandson G.

No IHT is payable on the £80,000 paid to the National Trust, but the balance passing to G is liable to IHT at the higher of a tapered scale rate (the 'first rate') and an effective rate calculated by reference to P's estate (the 'second rate'). [*IHTA 1984, 4 Sch 12–14*].

First rate

The property was comprised in the maintenance fund for 15 years, i.e. 60 quarters.

The scale rate is

	%
0.25% for each of the first 40 quarters	10
0.20% for each of the next 20 quarters	4
	14%

Second rate

The effective rate is calculated, using half Table rates applying on 1 January 2004, as if the chargeable amount transferred (£220,000) had been added to the value transferred by P on his death (£140,000) and had formed the highest part of the total. Half Table rates are used because the fund was set up in P's lifetime. (It is assumed that Table rates do not change.)

	£
£60,000 at nil	—
£160,000 at 20%	32,000
£220,000	£32,000

The effective rate is $\dfrac{32,000}{220,000} \times 100\% =$ 14.55%

As the second rate (14.55%) is higher than the first rate (14%) the second rate is used.

IHT payable is £220,000 at 14.55% = £32,010

317   Payment of Tax

[*IHTA 1984, ss 227, 228, 234; FA 1986, 19 Sch 31; F(No 2)A 1992, 14 Sch 5, 6*]

317.1 PAYMENT BY INSTALMENTS ON TRANSFER OR DEATH

(A)

F died on 17 December 1996 leaving a free estate of £354,000, including £75,000 (after business property relief at 50%) in respect of plant and machinery in a partnership. An election is made to pay inheritance tax on the plant and machinery by 10 equal yearly instalments.

Inheritance tax on free estate	£
On first £200,000	Nil
On next £154,000 at 40%	61,600
£354,000	£61,600

IHT applicable to unquoted shares

$$\frac{75,000}{354,000} \times £61,600 \qquad\qquad £13,050$$

1st instalment due 1.7.97	£1,305
2nd instalment due 1.7.98	£1,305

and so on.

Notes

(*a*)   Even though the shares did not give F control of the company, the tax due can be paid by instalments as they attract not less than 20% of the tax payable on death. No such restriction applies where shares (whether quoted or unquoted) give control of the company.

(*b*)   Instalments continue to be due at yearly intervals for 10 years or until the shares are sold, at which time all unpaid IHT becomes payable.

(*c*)   Interest is payable on each instalment from the day it falls due. If payments are made on time, no interest is payable.

(B)

On 1 December 1996 G gave his land in a partnership of which G was a partner to his son S who agreed to pay any IHT on the transfer. The shareholding was valued at £200,000. G had made prior chargeable transfers of £140,000, had already used his 1995/96 and 1996/97 annual exemptions, and he died on 31 December 2000.

S elected to pay the IHT by 10 yearly instalments and paid the first on 1 August 2001, and the second on 1 September 2002. On 1 December 2002 he sold the shareholding, and paid the balance of the IHT outstanding on 1 February 2003. It is assumed that the rate of interest on unpaid inheritance tax is 5% throughout.

Inheritance tax on gift

	£
Value of shareholding	200,000
Deduct business property relief at 50%	100,000
PET becoming chargeable on death	£100,000

IHT payable in the band £140,001–£240,000

	£
£140,001–200,000	Nil
£200,001–240,000 at 40%	16,000
	£16,000

		£
Total IHT payable at 60% of full rates (death between 4 and 5 years after gift)		£9,600
1st instalment due 1.7.2001	960	
Interest at 5% from 1.7.2000 to 1.8.2000		
$\frac{31}{365}\times$ £960 × 5%	4	
		964
2nd instalment due 1.7.2002	960	
Interest at 5% from 1.7.2002 to 1.9.2002		
$\frac{62}{365}\times$ £960 × 5%	8	
		968
Balance due on sale on 1.12.2002	7,680	
Interest at 5% from 1.12.2002 to 1.2.2003		
$\frac{62}{365}\times$ £7,680 × 5%	65	
		7,745
Total IHT and interest		£9,677

318   Protective Trusts

318.1   FORFEITURE BEFORE 12 APRIL 1978 [*IHTA 1984, s 73*]

In 1951 X left his estate on protective trusts for his son Z. On 1 January 1978 Z attempted to assign his interest and the protective trusts were accordingly determined. On 1 May 1983 the trustees advanced £25,000 to Z to enable him to purchase a flat. At the same time, they also advanced £10,000 (net) to his granddaughter D. On 1 March 1997 Z died and the trust fund, valued at £200,000, passed equally to his grandchildren absolutely.

1 May 1983

There is no charge to IHT on the payment to Z, but a charge arises on the payment to D. The relevant period is the period from the determination of the protective trusts (1 January 1978) to 1 May 1983 i.e. 21 complete quarters.

The rate of tax is 0.25% for each of 21 quarters   <u>5.25%</u>

IHT payable is $\dfrac{5.25}{100 - 5.25} \times £10,000 = \underline{£554}$

The gross payment is <u>£10,554</u>

1 March 1997

There is a charge to IHT when the trust vests on the death of Z. 72 complete quarters have elapsed since the protective trusts determined.

The rate of tax is

	%
0.25% for each of the first 40 quarters	10.0
0.20% for each of the next 36 quarters	7.2
	<u>17.2%</u>

IHT payable is 17.2% × £200,000 = <u>£34,400</u>

318.2   FORFEITURE AFTER 11 APRIL 1978 [*IHTA 1984, s 88*]

Assume the same facts as in 318.1 above but that Z attempted to assign his interest on 1 January 1980.

1 May 1983

There is no charge to IHT on the payment to Z who is treated as beneficially entitled to an interest in possession under the trust. The payment to D is a chargeable transfer. Tax is charged at Z's personal cumulative rate of tax so that if he had made no previous transfers, the payment would be covered by his nil rate tax band. If the payment had been made after 16 March 1987, it would have been a potentially exempt transfer.

1 March 1997

There is a charge to IHT when the trust vests on the death of Z, calculated by aggregating £200,000 with all other chargeable property passing on his death and applying the normal death rates.

319   Quick Succession Relief

[IHTA 1984, s 141]

319.1 **TRANSFERS AFTER 9 MARCH 1981**

On 1 January 1997 A died with a net estate valued at £365,000. In December 1992 he had received a gift from B of £20,000. B died in November 1994 and A paid the IHT (amounting to £8,000) due as a result of B's potentially exempt transfer becoming chargeable.

A was also entitled to an interest in possession in the whole of his father's estate. His father had died in February 1994 with a net estate of £160,000 on which the IHT paid was £4,000. On A's death, the property passed to A's sister and was valued at £145,000. A had made no previous transfers and left his estate to his brother.

	£
Free estate	365,000
Settled property	145,000
Taxable estate	£510,000

IHT on an estate of £510,000 = £124,000

Quick succession relief

The gift from B was made more than four but not more than five years before A's death so quick succession relief at 20% is available.

$$QSR = 20\% \times £8,000 \times \frac{12,000}{20,000} \qquad £960$$

Interest in possession in father's will trust	£
Net estate before tax	160,000
Tax	4,000
Net estate after tax	£156,000

A's death was more than two but not more than three years after his father's so relief is given at 60%.

$$QSR = 60\% \times £4,000 \times \frac{156,000}{160,000} \qquad £2,340$$

Tax payable on death of A	£	£
IHT on an estate of £510,000		124,000
Deduct QSR		
On gift from B	960	
On father's estate	2,340	
		3,300
IHT payable		£120,700

On free estate $\dfrac{365,000}{510,000} \times £120,700$ £86,383

On settled property $\dfrac{145,000}{510,000} \times £120,700$ £34,317

Note

(*a*)   The relief is given only by reference to the tax charged on the part of the value received by the donee. Therefore, the tax paid must be apportioned by applying the fraction 'net transfer received divided by gross transfer made'.

320   Settlements with Interests in Possession

[IHTA 1984, ss 49(1), 51(1), 52(1), 54A, 54B, 57; F(No 2)A 1987, s 96, 7 Sch]

320.1 TERMINATION OF AN INTEREST IN POSSESSION

A had an interest in possession in a settlement valued at £100,000 with remainder to his son S. On 1 July 1996, A released his life interest to S in consideration of S's marriage on 2 July 1995. A had made no gifts since 5 April 1996 but had used his annual exemptions prior to that date. His cumulative total of chargeable transfers at 5 April 1996 was £68,000, and these had all been made since 1 July 1989. A died on 30 June 1997.

The release of A's life interest is a potentially exempt transfer which becomes chargeable by reason of A's death within seven years. The charge is at full rates with no tapering relief as the transfer took place within three years before death.

	£	£
Value of property		200,000
Exemptions		
Annual	3,000	
In consideration of marriage	5,000	
		8,000
Chargeable transfer		£192,000

	Gross	Tax	Net
	£	£	£
Cumulative total b/f	68,000	—	68,000
Chargeable transfer	192,000	24,000	168,000
	£260,000	£24,000	£236,000

Tax payable by trustees as a consequence of A's death	£24,000

Notes

(a) The annual gifts exemption and the exemption of gifts in consideration of marriage apply if notice is given to the trustees by the donor within 6 months of the gift. This requirement seems to apply even though the gift is potentially exempt when made.

(b) The tax payable is computed by reference to the transferor's cumulative total of chargeable transfers within the previous seven years, and the chargeable transfer forms part of his cumulative total carried forward.

320.2 POTENTIALLY EXEMPT TRANSFER TO INTEREST IN POSSESSION TRUST — ANTI-AVOIDANCE PROVISIONS *[IHTA 1984, ss 54A, 54B; F(No 2)A 1987, 7 Sch]*

B transferred £100,000 on 1 October 1994 into an interest in possession trust of which his brother C is the life tenant. On 31 August 1997, C released his life interest, then valued at £116,000, to a discretionary settlement in favour of his children. At 1 October 1994, B's cumulative chargeable transfers in the last seven years amounted to £230,000. B was still alive on 31 August 1997, at which date C's cumulative chargeable transfers in the last seven years amounted to £80,000 and he (C) had not used his annual exemptions for

1996/97 and 1997/98. It is assumed that there is no change in IHT rates from 6 April 1996.

The transfer by B on 1 October 1994 is a potentially exempt transfer which will not become chargeable unless B dies before 1 October 2001.

The transfer by C is a chargeable lifetime transfer which is charged at lifetime rates, i.e. one half of death rates, taking into account cumulative transfers of £80,000. If, however, a higher tax liability would be produced by substituting B's cumulative transfers at the time of his PET for those of C at the time of his transfer, this takes precedence over the normal calculation.

Normal calculation

	£	£
Value transferred by C on 31 August 1997		116,000
Deduct annual exemptions 1997/98	3,000	
1996/97	3,000	6,000
		£110,000

IHT on £110,000 is charged in the band £130,001 to £240,000.

	£
130,001–200,000	Nil
200,001–240,000 at 20%	8,000
	£8,000

Calculation under Section 54A

Value transferred by C on 31 August 1997, after exemptions as above	£110,000

IHT on £110,000 is charged in the band £230,001 to £340,000.

230,001–340,000 at 20%	£22,000

IHT payable is therefore £22,000.

Notes

(a)   C's cumulative chargeable transfers following the gift in August 1997 will be £240,000 (*not* £340,000).

(b)   If B dies after 31 August 1997 and before 1 October 2001, the IHT liability of £22,000 may increase. For example, B's cumulative chargeable transfers at 1 October 1994 may increase due to his having made other PETs prior to that date but within seven years of death. If the IHT liability had been determined under normal rules because this produced a liability greater than that produced by a calculation under *IHTA 1984, s 54A*, such liability could not be affected by the death of B. [*IHTA 1984, s 54B(1)*].

321 Settlements without Interests in Possession

Note
In all examples in this chapter, where the value of trust property is given, it is assumed that this does not include any undistributed and unaccumulated income. Such income is not treated as a taxable trust asset. (Revenue Statement of Practice SP 8/86).

321.1 RATE OF TEN-YEAR ANNIVERSARY CHARGE

(A) Post-26 March 1974 settlements [*IHTA 1984, ss 64, 66*]

On 1 May 1984 S settled £150,000 net, £100,000 to be held on discretionary trusts and £50,000 in trust for his brother B for life. At the date of the transfer S had a cumulative total of chargeable transfers of £48,000. £20,000 (gross) was advanced from the discretionary trusts to C on 1 March 1992.

The property held on discretionary trusts was valued at £177,000 on 1 May 1994.

On 1 January 1999 B died, when the property subject to his interest in possession was valued at £95,000. The whole trust property was valued at £322,000 on 1 May 2004 of which £105,000 derived from B's fund. The trustees had made no advances other than that to C.

It is assumed that rates of tax remain at the level for transfers after 5 April 1996.

1 May 1994 Ten-year anniversary charge

Assumed chargeable transfer	£
(i) value of relevant property immediately before the ten-year anniversary	177,000
(ii) value, at date of settlement, of property which was not, and has not become, relevant property	50,000
(iii) value, at date of settlement, of property in related settlement	—
	£227,000

Assumed transferor's cumulative total	
(i) value of chargeable transfers made by settlor in seven-year period ending on date of settlement	48,000
(ii) amounts on which proportionate charges have been levied in ten years before the anniversary	20,000
	£68,000

	Gross £	Tax £
Assumed cumulative total	68,000	—
Assumed transfer	227,000	29,000
	£295,000	£29,000

Effective rate of tax $\dfrac{29,000}{227,000} \times 100 = \underline{12.775\%}$

Ten-year anniversary charge

The IHT payable is at 30% of the effective rate on the relevant property

IHT payable = 30% × 12.775% × £177,000 = £6,783

1 May 2004 Ten-year anniversary charge

Assumed chargeable transfer	£
(i) value of relevant property immediately prior to the ten-year anniversary	322,000
(ii) value at date of settlement of property which was not and has not become relevant property	—
(iii) value at date of settlement of property in related settlement	—
	£322,000

Assumed transferor's cumulative total	
(i) value of chargeable transfers made by settlor in seven-year period ending on date of settlement	48,000
(ii) amounts on which proportionate charges have been levied in ten years before the anniversary	—
	£48,000

	Gross £	Tax £
Assumed cumulative total	48,000	—
Assumed transfer	322,000	34,000
	£370,000	£34,000

Effective rate of tax $\dfrac{34,000}{322,000} \times 100 = \underline{10.559\%}$

Ten-year anniversary charge

Of the relevant property, £105,000 had not been relevant property for the period 1 May 1994–1 January 1999, i.e. 18 complete quarters.

IHT payable

			£
At 30% × 10.559%	= 3.17%	on £217,000	6,879
At 30% × 10.559%	= 3.17%		
Less 18/40 × 30% × 10.559%	= 1.43%		
	1.74%	on £105,000	1,827
Total IHT payable			£8,706

IHT 321.1   Settlements without Interests in Possession

(B) Pre-27 March 1974 settlements [*IHTA 1984, ss 64, 66*]
On 1 June 1971 T settled property on discretionary trusts. The trustees made the following advances (gross) to beneficiaries

1.1.74	H	£10,000
1.1.77	B	£20,000
1.1.82	C	£60,000
1.1.88	D	£40,000
1.1.94	E	£80,000

On 1 June 1991 the settled property was valued at £175,000 and on 1 June 2001 £180,000.

1 June 1991 Ten-year anniversary charge

Assumed chargeable transfer			
Value of relevant property			£175,000

			£	
Assumed transferor's cumulative total				
(i)	Aggregate of distribution payments made between 1 June 1981 and 8 March 1982		60,000	
(ii)	Aggregate of amounts on which proportionate charge arises between 9 March 1982 and 1 June 1991		40,000	£100,000

	Gross £	Tax £
Assumed cumulative total	100,000	—
Assumed chargeable transfer	175,000	27,000
	£275,000	£27,000

$$\text{Effective rate of tax} = \frac{27,000}{175,000} \times 100 = \underline{15.429\%}$$

Ten-year anniversary charge

The IHT payable is at 30% of the effective rate on the relevant property.
IHT payable = 30% × 15.429% × £175,000 = £8,100

1 June 2001 Ten-year anniversary charge

It is assumed that rates of tax remain at the level for transfers after 5 April 1996.

Assumed chargeable transfer		
Value of relevant property		£180,000

Assumed transferor's cumulative total	
Aggregate of amount on which proportionate charge arises between 1 June 1991 and 1 June 2001	£80,000

	Gross £	Tax £
Assumed cumulative total	80,000	—
Assumed chargeable transfer	180,000	12,000
	£260,000	£12,000

$$\text{Effective rate of tax} = \frac{12,000}{180,000} \times 100 = \underline{6.6666\%}$$

Ten-year anniversary charge

The IHT payable is at 30% of the effective rate on the relevant property.
IHT payable = 30% × 6.6666% × £180,000 = £3,600

321.2 RATE OF PROPORTIONATE CHARGE BEFORE THE FIRST TEN-YEAR ANNIVERSARY

(A) Post-26 March 1974 settlements [*IHTA 1984, ss 65, 68*]
On 1 April 1987 M settled £60,000 (net) on discretionary trusts. His cumulative total of chargeable transfers (gross) prior to the settlement was £125,000. On 3 December 1995 he added £20,000 (net), having made no chargeable transfers since 1 April 1987.

On 11 October 1995 the trustees had advanced £40,000 to N, and on 1 March 1996 the trustees distributed the whole of the remaining funds equally to P and Q. The remaining funds were valued at £110,000, of which £88,000 derived from the original settlement, and £22,000 from the addition.

11 October 1995 proportionate charge

Assumed chargeable transfer
(i)	Value of property in the settlement at date of settlement	60,000
(ii)	Value at date of settlement of property in related settlement	—
(iii)	Value at date of addition of property added	—
		£60,000

Assumed transferor's cumulative total
Value of chargeable transfers made by settlor in seven-year period ending on date of settlement   £125,000

	Gross £	Tax £
Assumed cumulative total	125,000	—
Assumed transfer	60,000	6,200
	£185,000	£6,200

$$\text{Effective rate of tax} = \frac{6,200}{60,000} \times 100 = \underline{10.33\%}$$

Appropriate fraction
The number of complete quarters that have elapsed between the date of settlement, 1 April 1987, and the advance on 11 October 1995 is 34.

IHT 321.2   Settlements without Interests in Possession

IHT is charged at the appropriate fraction of the effective rate on the property advanced.

$$\text{IHT payable} = 30\% \times \frac{34}{40} \times 10.33\% \times £40,000$$

$$= 2.634\% \times £40,000$$
$$= £1,053$$

Had the advance of £40,000 been net, the IHT payable would be

$$\frac{2.634}{100 - 2.634} \times £40,000 = £1,082$$

and the gross advance would be £41,082

1 March 1996 proportionate charge

As property has been added to the settlement, the effective rate of tax is recalculated.

		£
Assumed chargeable transfer		
(i)	Value of property in settlement at date of settlement	60,000
(ii)	Value at date of settlement of property in related settlement	—
(iii)	Value at date of addition of property added	20,000
		£80,000

	£
Assumed transferor's cumulative total	
Value of chargeable transfers made by settlor in seven-year period ending on date of settlement	£125,000

	Gross £	Tax £
Assumed cumulative total	125,000	—
Assumed transfer	80,000	10,200
	£205,000	£10,200

$$\text{Effective rate of tax} = \frac{10,200}{80,000} \times 100 = 12.75\%$$

Appropriate fraction

The number of complete quarters that have elapsed between the date of settlement, 1 April 1987, and the advance on 1 March 1996 is 35.

The number of complete quarters that elapsed between the date of settlement, 1 April 1987, and 3 December 1995, the date on which property was added, was 34.

The IHT is charged at the appropriate fraction of the effective rate on the property advanced

£

$$30\% \times \frac{35}{40} \times 12.75\% \qquad\qquad \text{on} \quad £88,000 \;=\; \qquad\qquad 2,945$$

$$30\% \times \frac{(35-34)}{40} \times 12.75\% \qquad\quad \text{on} \quad \underline{£22,000} \;=\; \qquad\qquad\quad 21$$
$$£110,000$$

IHT payable on advance of £110,000 $\qquad\qquad\qquad\qquad\qquad\qquad$ £2,966

(B) Settlor dies within 7 years of settlement — post-26 March 1974 settlement
On 1 July 1993 T settled £170,000 net on discretionary trusts. His only other transfer had been a gift of £50,000 to his brother B on 1 June 1992. On 7 March 1995 the trustees advanced £70,000 to B, who agreed to pay any IHT due.
On 30 August 1997 T died.

It is assumed that rates do not change subsequent to the change made on 6 April 1995.

Proportionate charge 7 March 1995
At the time of the advance, T had made no chargeable transfers in the seven years prior to the settlement (the gift to B being a PET).

Assumed chargeable transfer
  Value of property in the settlement
  at the date of settlement $\qquad\qquad\qquad\qquad\qquad\qquad\qquad$ £170,000

Assumed transferor's cumulative total $\qquad\qquad\qquad\qquad\qquad\qquad$ Nil

Tax on an assumed transfer of £170,000 = $\qquad\qquad\qquad\qquad$ £4,000

$$\text{Effective rate of tax} = \frac{4,000}{170,000} \times 100 = 2.35\%$$

Appropriate fraction
The number of complete quarters that have elapsed between the date of the settlement, 1 July 1993, and the advance on 7 March 1995 is 6.
IHT is charged at the appropriate fraction of the effective rate on the property advanced.

$$\text{IHT} = 30\% \times \frac{6}{40} \times 2.35\% \times £70,000$$

$$= 0.1057\% \times £70,000$$
$$= £74$$

On the settlor's death within seven years, the PET on 1 June 1992 becomes a chargeable transfer. There will be additional IHT payable by the trustees on the creation of the settlement, and additional IHT payable by B on the advance to him from the settlement.

IHT 321.2 Settlements without Interests in Possession

The gross gift to the settlement, after deducting the 1993/94 annual exemption, was

	Gross	Tax	Net
	£	£	£
	150,000	—	150,000
	21,250	4,250	17,000
	£171,250	£4,250	£167,000

Additional IHT is payable to increase the charge to 60% of full rates at the time of death (death between 4 and 5 years after gift), with a previous chargeable transfer to B of £47,000 (after deducting the 1992/93 annual exemption).

	Gross	Tax	Net
	£	£	£
Prior transfer	47,000	—	47,000
	171,250	25,700	145,550
	£218,250	£25,700	£192,550

	£
IHT at 60% of full rates 60% × £25,700	15,420
Deduct paid on lifetime chargeable transfer	4,250
Additional IHT payable	£11,170

The additional IHT is payable by the trustees, reducing the value of property settled to £170,000 − £11,170 = £158,830

The IHT on the advance to B is recalculated
Assumed chargeable transfer   £158,830

Assumed transferor's cumulative total
  Chargeable transfers made by the settlor in 7 years prior to the
  settlement (gift 1 June 1992)   £47,000

	Gross	Tax
	£	£
Assumed cumulative total	47,000	—
Assumed transfer	158,830	11,166
	£205,830	£11,166

Effective rate of tax $= \dfrac{11,166}{158,830} \times 100 = 7.030\%$

The appropriate fraction is $\frac{6}{40}$ (unchanged).

IHT borne $= 30\% \times \dfrac{6}{40} \times 7.030\% \times £70,000$

$\quad\quad = 0.3164\% \times £70,000$
$\quad\quad = £221$

	£
IHT due	221
Deduct already paid	74
IHT payable	£147

(C) Pre-27 March 1974 settlements [*IHTA 1984, ss 65, 68*]

A discretionary trust was set up on 1 June 1972.

The following advances (gross) have been made by the trustees

	£
1 January 1982 to V	50,000
1 June 1985 to W	92,000
1 November 1991 to X	40,000

1 November 1991 proportionate charge on advance to X

	£	£
Assumed chargeable transfer		
Property advanced		£40,000

Assumed transferor's cumulative total

	£	£
(i) distribution payments in period 1 November 1981 to 8 March 1982	50,000	
(ii) amounts on which proportionate charge is payable in period 9 March 1982–1 November 1991	92,000	£142,000

	Gross £	Tax £
Assumed cumulative total	142,000	400
Assumed transfer	40,000	8,000
	£182,000	£8,400

$$\text{Effective rate of tax} = \frac{8,000}{40,000} \times 100 = \underline{20\%}$$

IHT payable on advance to X is calculated at 30% of the effective rate.

IHT payable = 30% × 20% × £40,000 = $\underline{£2,400}$

321.3 RATE OF PROPORTIONATE CHARGE BETWEEN TEN-YEAR ANNIVERSARIES [*IHTA 1984, ss 65, 69, 2 Sch 3*]

On 1 January 1982 G settled £50,000 (net) on discretionary trusts. His cumulative total of chargeable transfers at that date was £70,000. On 1 January 1992 the funds were valued at £110,000, no advances having been made. On 1 February 1994 the trustees advanced £30,000 (gross) to H. On 1 January 1995 G added £60,000 to the settlement, having made cumulative chargeable transfers in the previous seven years of £30,000. On 1 February 1997 the trustees advanced £40,000 to F from the funds originally settled.

IHT 321.3 Settlements without Interests in Possession

It is assumed that rates of tax remain unchanged following the change of rates on 6 April 1995.

1 February 1994 advance to H

8 complete quarters have elapsed since the ten-year anniversary charge so the appropriate fraction is 8/40ths. The rate of tax is therefore 8/40ths of the rate at which IHT would have been charged on the last ten-year anniversary if the Table of Rates in force at 1 February 1994 had been in force at the date of the ten-year anniversary, 1 January 1992.

Tax would have been charged at the last ten-year anniversary as follows

	£
Assumed chargeable transfer	
(i) value of relevant property immediately before the ten-year anniversary	110,000
(ii) value, at date of settlement, of property which was not, and has not become, relevant property	—
(iii) value at date of settlement of property in related settlement	—
	£110,000

	£
Assumed transferor's cumulative total	
(i) value of chargeable transfers made by settlor in seven-year period ending on date of settlement	70,000
(ii) amounts on which proportionate charges have been levied in ten years before the anniversary	—
(iii) amounts of distribution payments in period 1 January 1982 to 8 March 1982	—
	£70,000

	Gross £	Tax £
Assumed cumulative total	70,000	—
Assumed transfer	110,000	6,000
	£180,000	£6,000

$$\text{Effective rate} = \frac{6,000}{110,000} \times 100 = \underline{5.455\%}$$

Rate of tax at ten-year anniversary = 30% × 5.455% = $\underline{1.6365\%}$

Therefore rate of tax on advance to H
$$= 8/40 \times 1.6365\%$$
IHT payable = 8/40 × 1.6365% × £30,000 = $\underline{£98}$

1 February 1996 advance to F

Since property has been added to the settlement, a hypothetical rate of tax at the previous ten-year anniversary must be recalculated as if the added property had been added prior to the anniversary.

	£	Gross £	Tax £
Assumed cumulative total		70,000	—
Assumed transfer			
property at anniversary	110,000		
added property	60,000	170,000	8,000
		£240,000	£8,000

$$\text{Effective rate} = \frac{8,000}{170,000} \times 100 = \underline{4.7059\%}$$

Rate of tax that would have been charged at the ten-year anniversary
$$= 30\% \times 4.7059\%$$
$$= 1.412\%$$

The advance to F took place 20 complete quarters after the ten-year anniversary. The rate of tax is $20/40 \times 1.412\% = \underline{0.706\%}$

If the advance to F was £40,000 gross

IHT payable $= £40,000 \times 0.706\% = £\underline{282}$

If the advance to F was £40,000 net

$$\text{IHT payable} \quad = \frac{0.706}{100 - 0.706} \times £40,000 = £\underline{284.41}$$

The gross distribution would then be £40,284.

322 Transfers on Death

322.1 POTENTIALLY EXEMPT TRANSFER FOLLOWED BY LOAN FROM DONEE TO DONOR [FA 1986, ss 103, 104; SI 1987 No 1130, Reg 6]

X gives cash of £201,000 to Y on 1 November 1994. On 20 December 1994, Y makes a loan of £155,000 to X. On 31 May 1995, X makes a gift of £20,000 into a discretionary trust. X dies on 15 April 2000, his death estate is worth £258,000 before deducting the liability of £201,000 to Y which remains outstanding. X has made no lifetime transfers other than those specified, except that he has used his annual exemptions for all relevant years. It is assumed that rates of tax remain unchanged following the change made on 6 April 1996.

First calculation under Reg 6(3)(a)

The transfer of £155,000 in November 1994 is a PET which becomes chargeable by virtue of X's death within seven years. However, for the purpose of this calculation the PET is ignored but no deduction is allowed against the death estate for the outstanding loan.

No IHT is due in respect of the chargeable transfer in May 1995 as it is covered by the Nil rate band.

The estate of £258,000 is charged in the band £20,001 to £278,000.

	£
20,001–200,000	Nil
200,001–278,000 at 40%	31,200
IHT due	£31,200

Second calculation under Reg 6(3)(b)

The PET in November 1994 is charged on death in the normal way and the loan is deducted from the death estate.

The PET is charged in the band £0 to £201,000.

	£
0–200,000	Nil
200,001–201,000 at 40%	400
	£400

IHT at 40% of full rates (death between 5 and 6 years after transfer)	£160

Additional tax is due on the chargeable transfer in May 1995, £20,000 is charged in the band £201,001 to £221,000.

20,000 at 40%	£8,000

IHT at 60% of full rates (death between 4 and 5 years after transfer)	£4,800

Tax is charged on the death estate of £57,000 (£258,000–201,000) in the band £221,001 to £278,000.

221,001–278,000 at 40%	£22,800
Total IHT due £(160 + 4,800 + 22,800)	£27,760

The first calculation gives the higher amount of tax, so the PET is ignored and no deduction is allowed against the death estate.

Notes

(*a*)   If the PET had exceeded the loan, the excess would not be ignored for the purpose of the first calculation above.

(*b*)   If X had made more than one PET to Y and the total PETs exceeded the amount of the loan, only PETs up to the amount of the loan are ignored for the purpose of the first calculation above, later PETs being disregarded in preference to earlier ones.

323   Trusts for Disabled Persons

[*IHTA 1984, ss 74, 89*]

323.1 PROPERTY SETTLED BEFORE 10 MARCH 1981

In 1972 Q settled £50,000 in trust mainly for his disabled son P, but with power to apply property to his daughter S. On 1 January 1997 the trustees advanced £5,000 gross to S on her marriage.

There will be a charge to IHT on the payment to S.

The relevant period is the period from settlement of the funds or, if later, 13 March 1975, to 1 January 1997, i.e. 87 complete quarters.

The rate of IHT is the aggregate of

0.25% for each of the first 40 quarters	10.00%
0.20% for each of the next 40 quarters	8.00%
0.15% for each of the next 7 quarters	1.05%
87	19.05%

IHT payable is £5,000 × 19.05% = £952

323.2 PROPERTY SETTLED AFTER 9 MARCH 1981

Assume the facts in 323.1 above except that the settlement was made on 1 July 1982.

If the trust secures that not less than half the settled property which is applied during P's life is applied for his benefit, then P is treated as beneficially entitled to an interest in possession in the settled property. The transfer to S is a potentially exempt transfer which may become chargeable in the event of P's death within seven years of the transfer. The gift in consideration of marriage exemption applies (£1,000 on a gift from brother to sister) subject to the required notice.

Otherwise, the trust is discretionary and the IHT liability, if any, would be calculated under the rules applying to SETTLEMENTS WITHOUT INTERESTS IN POSSESSION (321).

324   Trusts for Employees

[*IHTA 1984, s 72*]

324.1 POSITION OF THE TRUST

A qualifying trust for employees of a close company was created on 1 July 1983. On 4 May 1993, £15,000 is paid to a beneficiary who is a participator in the close company and holds not less than 5% of the issued ordinary shares. On 4 August 1996, the whole of the remaining fund of £200,000 ceases to be held on qualifying trusts.

4 May 1993

There is a charge to IHT. The relevant period is the period from 1 July 1983 to 4 May 1993 i.e. 39 complete quarters.

The rate of tax is

0.25% for 39 quarters = 9.75%

IHT payable is $\dfrac{9.75}{100 - 9.75} \times £15,000 = \underline{£1,620}$

1 July 1993

There is no liability at the ten-year anniversary.

4 August 1996

There is a charge to IHT. The relevant period is the period from 1 July 1983 to 4 August 1996, i.e. 52 complete quarters.

The rate of tax is

0.25% for 40 quarters =	10.00
0.20% for 12 quarters =	2.40
	12.40%

IHT payable is £200,000 × 12.40% = $\underline{£24,800}$

325   Valuation

325.1 LAND SOLD WITHIN FOUR YEARS OF DEATH
[*IHTA 1984, ss 190–198; FA 1993, s 199*]

(A)

A (a bachelor) died on 1 May 1992 owning four areas of land, as follows.
   (i)   10 acres valued at death £20,000
   (ii)   15 acres valued at death £30,000
   (iii) 20 acres valued at death £30,000
   (iv)   30 acres valued at death £40,000

He also owned a freehold house valued at death at £50,000.

In the four years following A's death, his executors made the following sales.
(A)   Freehold house sold 15.11.93, proceeds £53,000, expenses £2,000.
(B)   Land area (iii) sold 1.6.95, proceeds £29,500, expenses £1,500.
(C)   Land area (ii) sold 8.8.96, proceeds £27,000, expenses £1,000.
(D)   Land area (iv) sold 19.9.96, proceeds £42,000, expenses £3,000.

The following revisions must be calculated on a claim under IHTA 1984, Pt VI, Chapter IV

	£	
Gross sale proceeds of house	53,000	
Deduct probate value	50,000	£3,000
Gross sale proceeds of land area (ii)	27,000	
Deduct probate value	30,000	£(3,000)
Gross sale proceeds of land area (iii)	29,500	
Deduct probate value	30,000	£(500)

Notes

(*a*)   The sale of area (iii) is disregarded as the loss on sale (before allowing for expenses) is less than 5% of £30,000 (£1,500) and is also lower than £1,000. [*IHTA 1984, s 191*].

(*b*)   The overall allowable reduction on all sales is therefore nil even though there is a loss after expenses.

(*c*)   For deaths after 15 March 1990, a sale *for less than the value at death* which is made in the fourth year after death is treated as having been made in the three years after death. [*IHTA 1984, s 197A; FA 1993, s 199*].

(B) Further purchases of land

A died on 30 June 1995 owning a house and a seaside flat.
At death the valuations were

	£
House	50,000
Flat	30,000
	£80,000
Sales by the executors realised (gross)	
House proceeds 1.7.97	42,000
Flat proceeds 1.12.97	33,000
	£75,000

On 1.5.97, the executors bought a town house for the daughter for £40,000 (excluding costs).

Initially relief is due of £(80,000 − 75,000)   £5,000

Recomputation of relief

$$\text{Appropriate fraction} = \frac{\text{Purchase price}}{\text{Selling price}} = \frac{40,000}{75,000} = \frac{8}{15}$$

	£	House £	£	Seaside Flat £
Value on death		50,000		30,000
Sale price	42,000			
Add (£50,000 − £42,000) × 8/15	4,267			
Revised value for IHT		46,267		
Sale price			33,000	
Deduct (£33,000 − £30,000) × 8/15			1,600	
Revised value for IHT				31,400
Revised relief		£3,733		£(1,400)
Total			£2,333	

Note

(a)   The purchase is taken into account because it is made within the period 30 June 1996 (date of death) and 1 April 1998 (four months after the last of the sales affected by the claim). [*IHTA 1984, s 192(1)*]. If a sale made in the fourth year after death was affected by the claim (under *IHTA 1984, s 197A*), it would *not* be taken into account in determining the above-mentioned period. [*IHTA 1984, s 197A(3); FA 1993, s 199*].

325.2 RELATED PROPERTY

(A) General [*IHTA 1984, s 161*]

On the death of a husband on 31 October 1996, the share capital of a private company was held as follows

	Shares	
Issued capital	10,000	
Husband	4,000	40%
Wife	4,000	40%
Others (employees)	2,000	20%
	10,000	100%

The value of an 80% holding is £80,000, while the value of a 40% holding is £24,000. In his will, the husband left his 4,000 shares to his daughter.

The related property rules apply to aggregate the shares of

Husband	4,000
Wife	4,000
Related property	8,000 shares

Chargeable transfer on legacy to daughter

IHT value of 8,000 shares (80%)	£80,000
IHT value attributed to legacy of husband's shares (4,000)	£40,000

(Subject to 100% business property relief if conditions satisfied)

325.3 SHARES AND SECURITIES

Quoted shares sold within twelve months after death [*IHTA 1984, ss 178–189; FA 1993, s 198*]

An individual died on 30 June 1996 and included in his estate was a portfolio of quoted investments. The executors sold certain investments within twelve months of death. The realisations were as follows

	Probate Value £	Gross Sales £
Share A	7,700	7,200
Share B	400	600
Share C	2,800	2,900
Share D	13,600	11,600
Share E	2,300	2,300
Share F	5,700	5,100
Share G	19,400	17,450
Share H	8,500	8,600
	£60,400	55,750
Incidental costs of sale		2,750
Net proceeds of sale		£53,000

On 1 September 1996, share J, having a probate value of £200 and still held by the executors was cancelled.

On 1 December 1996, share K, having a probate value of £1,000 has its stock exchange quotation suspended. On 30 June 1996, the investment is still held by the executors, its estimated value is £49 and the quotation remains suspended.

On 30 April 1997, the executors purchased a new holding for £1,750.

The executors would initially be able to claim a reduction of (£60,400 − £55,750) + (£200 − £1) + (£1,000 − £49) =	£5,800

After the purchase, the reduction is restricted as follows

$$\text{Relevant proportion} = \frac{\text{Reinvestment}}{\text{Total sales}} = \frac{1,750}{£55,750 + £1 + £49} = \frac{1,750}{55,800}$$

Original relief restricted by

$$\frac{1,750}{55,800} \times £5,800 = £182$$

Total relief £5,800 less £182	£5,618

Notes

(*a*) No costs of selling investments may be deducted from the sale proceeds.

(*b*) The cancelled shares are treated as sold for £1 immediately before cancellation. The suspended shares are treated as sold on the first anniversary of death at their value at that time (provided that value is less than their value on death). [*IHTA 1984, ss 186A, 186B; FA 1993, s 198*].

(c) The purchase is taken into account as it is made during the period beginning on date of death and ending two months after the end of the last sale taken into account (including deemed sales as in (b) above).

(d) The probate value of each of the investments sold will be adjusted, both for CGT and IHT purposes, to the gross sale proceeds plus the relevant proportion of the fall in value. Thus the probate value of share A will be revised from £7,700 to

$$£7,200 + \left(\frac{1,750}{55,800} \times (7,700 - 7,200) \right) = £7,216$$

(e) Although excluded from computation of the loss on sale for inheritance tax purposes, incidental costs of sale are deductible from proceeds in calculating CGT.

326   Woodlands

[*IHTA 1984, ss 114(2), 125–130, 208, 226(4), 2 Sch 4*]

326.1 TAX CHARGE

(A)

A died owning woodlands valued at £275,000 being land valued at £200,000 and trees growing on the land valued at £75,000. The woodlands passed to his son D. The marginal IHT rate applicable was 50% but the executors elected to exclude the value of the trees from the taxable estate on A's death. D died six years later leaving the woodlands to trustees for his grandchildren. They were then valued at £400,000 being land at £250,000 and trees at £150,000. The rate of tax which would have applied to the value of trees on D's death was 40%, but once again the executors elected to exclude the value of the trees from his estate.

The trustees sold the woodlands for £500,000, including trees valued at £180,000, four years later.

The IHT on the trees is payable when the trees are sold. The trustees of the settlement pay IHT at what would have been the marginal rate on D's death had the tax scale at the time of the sale applied on D's death, e.g. 40% on £180,000 (the proceeds of sale) = £72,000.

Note

(*a*)   If D had gifted the land (with the trees) just before his death, the IHT would have become payable on the trees at what would have been the marginal rate on A's death had the scale at the time of the gift applied on A's death, on the value of the trees at the date of the gift. IHT would also have been payable on D's lifetime transfer (this being a PET but becoming chargeable by virtue of D's death shortly afterwards) but the value transferred by this transfer would have been reduced by the deferred IHT charge. See (B) below.

(B)

B died in 1984 leaving woodlands, including growing timber valued at £100,000, to his daughter C. The executors elected to exclude the value of the timber from the taxable estate on B's death. B had made prior transfers of £50,000 and his taxable estate (excluding the growing timber) was valued at £210,000.

On 1 February 1994 C gave the woodlands to her nephew N, when the land was valued at £330,000 and the growing timber at £125,000. N agreed to pay any IHT on the gift. C died in January 1998, and had made no prior transfers other than to use her annual exemptions each year. It is assumed that IHT rates remain at their current level.

IHT on B's death

No IHT is payable on the growing timber until C's disposal when tax is charged on the net value at that time. The rates are those which would have applied (using the death scale applying on 1 February 1994) if that value had formed the highest part of B's estate on death. The tax is payable on 1 September 1994.

Deferred IHT payable £125,000 at 40% =   £50,000

IHT 326.1 Woodlands

IHT on C's lifetime transfer

IHT is payable on C's gift to N as C died within 7 years of the gift. The deferred IHT is deduct[ed] from the value transferred.

	£
Value of land and timber	455,000
Deduct deferred IHT	50,000
Chargeable transfer	£405,000

IHT at death rates	
On first £200,000	—
On next £205,000 at 40%	82,000
£405,000	£82,000

IHT payable at 80% of full rates (death between 3 and 4 years after gift)	£65,600

Total IHT payable

Deferred IHT	50,000
Lifetime transfer	65,600
	£115,600

Note

(*a*) In the above calculations it has been assumed that the woodlands were not run as a business either at the time of B's death or at the time of C's gift. If B had been running the woodlands as a business, such that business property relief would have been available on his death, the amount chargeable on C's disposal would have been reduced by 50%, i.e. to £62,500, on which IHT payable would have been £25,000. [*IHTA 1984, s 127(2)*]. If C ran the woodlands as a business (whether or not B had done so), business property relief would be available on her gift to N provided N also ran the woodlands as a business, but would be given after the credit for the deferred IHT. (With business property relief now usually at 100%, the order of set-off is not so relevant.)

		£
Value of land and timber		455,000
Deduct deferred IHT	say	25,000
		430,000
Deduct business property relief at, say, 100%		430,000
Chargeable transfer		Nil

Value Added Tax

401 Bad Debt Relief

[VATA 1994, s 36; SI 1995 No 2518, Regs 156–172; C & E Leaflet 700/18/91]

401.1 PART PAYMENTS AND MUTUAL SUPPLIES

W Ltd has supplied goods to A Ltd. The sales ledger reveals the following amounts due

	Gross	Net	VAT
Invoice	£	£	£
16159 dated 31.7.95	497.99	423.82	74.17
15874 dated 12.7.95	364.19	364.19	—
14218 dated 12.6.95	238.04	238.04	—
14104 dated 10.6.95	262.17	223.12	39.05
	1,362.39	£1,249.17	£113.22
Less paid on account on 14104	100.00		
Amount due from A Ltd	£1,262.39		

A Ltd was, however, used by W Ltd for delivery work and there is one unpaid invoice for £143.75.

The bad debt relief claimable is as follows

	£
Amount due from A Ltd	1,262.39
Less amount due to A Ltd	143.75
Debt due from A Ltd	£1,118.64

The debt is attributed to

	Gross	VAT
	£	£
Invoice 16159	497.99	74.17
Invoice 15874	364.19	—
Invoice 14218	238.04	—
Invoice 14104 (part)	18.42	2.74*
	£1,118.64	76.91

The amount of bad debt relief claimable is £76.91

$$* \frac{18.42}{262.17} \times £39.05 = £2.74$$

Notes

(a) For supplies made after 31 March 1992, relief can be claimed six months after the date of supply, provided the debt has been written off as a bad debt in the supplier's accounts.

(b) Where payments on account are specifically allocated by the customer, this allocation must be followed. General payments on account must be allocated to earliest supplies first, supplies on the same day being aggregated. Where the claimant owes money to the purchaser which can be set off, the amount of the debt for bad debt relief purposes must be reduced by the amount so owed.

(c)   For supplies made after 31 March 1989 and before 1 April 1992, relief could be claimed one year after the date of supply. Otherwise similar rules applied as in (a) and (b) above.

(d)   For supplies made before 1 April 1989, A Ltd must be formally insolvent for a bad debt relief claim to be made. The set-off of mutual supplies must be made for VAT purposes whether or not the debt can be so set off under insolvency law.

402   Capital Goods

402.1 **THE CAPITAL GOODS SCHEME** [*SI 1995 No 2518, Regs 112–116; C & E Leaflet 706/2/90*]

On 1 July 1990, A Ltd, a partly exempt business, acquired the freehold of a five storey office block for £750,000 plus VAT of £112,500. The premises are used as the head office administration block for the whole company. Due to cash flow problems, the company subleases one floor for one year with effect from 1 January 1994 without exercising the option to tax. The building is sold on 1 October 1997 for £1.5 million to a company which only makes exempt supplies. Again the option to tax is not exercised.

A Ltd's partial exemption year runs to 31 March. Its claimable percentage of non-attributable input tax is as follows.

Year ended
31 March 1991	80%	31 March 1995	75%
31 March 1992	90%	31 March 1996	85%
31 March 1993	75%	31 March 1997	90%
31 March 1994	60%	31 March 1998	95%

The input tax position is as follows

Year ended 31 March 1991 (Interval 1)
Initial input tax claim £112,500 × 80% =   £90,000

Year ended 31 March 1992 (Interval 2)
Additional input tax claimed from C & E

$$\frac{112,500}{10} \times (90 - 80)\% = $$ £1,125

Year ended 31 March 1993 (Interval 3)
Input tax repayable to C & E

$$\frac{112,500}{10} \times (80-75)\% = $$ (£562.50)

Year ended 31 March 1994 (Interval 4)
Adjustment percentage for the year

$$\frac{(275 \times 60\%) + (90 \times 80\% \times 60\%) + (90 \times 20\% \times 0\%)}{365} = \quad 57.04\%$$

Input tax repayable to C & E

$$\frac{112,500}{10} \times (80 - 57.04)\% = $$ (£2,583)

Year ended 31 March 1995 (Interval 5)
Adjustment percentage for the year

$$\frac{(275 \times 80\% \times 75\%) + (275 \times 20\% \times 0\%) + (90 \times 75\%)}{365} = \quad 63.70\%$$

Input tax repayable to C & E

$$\frac{112,500}{10} \times (80 - 63.70)\% = $$ (£1,833.75)

Year ended 31 March 1996 (Interval 6)
Additional input tax claimed from C & E

$$\frac{112,500}{10} \times (85 - 80)\% =$$

£562.50

Year ended 31 March 1997 (Interval 7)
Additional input tax claimed from C & E

$$\frac{112,500}{10} \times (90 - 80)\% =$$

£1,125.00

Year ended 31 March 1998 (Interval 8)
Additional tax claimed from C & E

$$\frac{112,500}{10} \times (95 - 80)\% =$$

£1,687.50

Adjustment in respect of Intervals 9 and 10
Input tax repayable to C & E

$$2 \times \frac{112,500}{10} \times (80 - 0)\% =$$

£18,000.00

(£16,312.50)

Notes

(*a*)   The adjustment period for buildings is normally ten years.

(*b*)   During the period of the sublease, as the option to tax has not been exercised, one floor of the building (20%) is used for the purposes of making exempt supplies. The claimable percentage of non-attributable input tax must be restricted on a day-to-day basis to allow for this.

(*c*)   For the interval in which the building is sold, the adjustment is calculated in the normal way as if it had been used for the whole of the interval. This applies whether it was sold on the first or last day of the interval. For the remaining intervals, the recovery percentage is nil as the option to tax has not been exercised and the supply of the building is therefore exempt.

(*d*)   If the option to tax is exercised on the sale of the building, then in Interval 8, instead of input tax of £18,000 being repayable to C & E in respect of Intervals 9 and 10, further input tax is claimable of

$$2 \times \frac{112,500}{10} \times (100 - 80)\% = £4,500$$

On the other hand, VAT of £262,500 is chargeable on the sale which is not recoverable by the exempt company, increasing the effective price to £1,762,500 which might not be acceptable to the purchaser.

Note also that if the option to tax is exercised in respect of the sublease, not only is the adjustment percentage in Intervals 4 and 5 increased (to allow for 100% recovery in respect of that floor) but VAT has to be charged on the subsequent sale as, after an initial three-month period, the option is irrevocable for 20 years from the date it has effect.

(*e*)   See 2.4 CAPITAL ALLOWANCES for the interaction between the VAT Capital Goods Scheme and capital allowances on assets within the scheme.

403 Catering

403.1 **SPECIAL METHOD FOR CATERERS** [*SI 1995 No 2518, Reg 73; C & E Leaflet 709/2/91*]

A fish bar sells both fried fish and chips and wet fish and seafoods. It also has a small restaurant. It is impractical for the owner to keep a record of each sale. He can, however, note his zero-rated supplies over a limited period and for a representative month the results are

	£
Receipts from wet fish rounds	724
Shops sales of wet fish and seafoods	285
Sundries (cold leftovers)	28
	£1,037
Overall gross takings	£7,580

At the end of a given quarterly tax period, gross takings total £24,016.28.

Standard-rated percentage is

$$\frac{(7,580 - 1,037)}{7,580} \times 100 = 86\%$$

Standard-rated sales for the tax period are

£24,016.28 × 86%	20,654.00
Add cost of standard-rated goods taken for own consumption (say)	54.50
	£20,708.50
Output tax = £20,708.50 × $\frac{7}{47}$	£3,084.24

Notes

(*a*) It is essential that the local VAT office is advised of any change in the percentage used and that the figure is reviewed at least once a year, over a different period. The figure must be reviewed immediately if the pattern of trade changes.

(*b*) There is no legislation governing the way in which any estimate of standard-rated sales should be made.

404   Hotels and Holiday Accommodation

404.1 LONG STAY ARRANGEMENTS IN HOTELS ETC. [*VATA 1994, 6 Sch 9; C & E Leaflet 709/3/93*]

S stays for five weeks at a hotel, arriving on Monday evenings and leaving on Friday mornings. The hotel normally prints all bills in tax-inclusive form: it does not offer reduced rates to long stay guests. A typical charge is £40 per night, including breakfast, broken down as

	£	Gross £		£	VAT £
Breakfast		3.45	@ $\frac{7}{47}$		0.51
Facilities	7.31		@ $\frac{7}{47}$	1.09	
Accommodation	29.24		@ $\frac{7}{47}$	4.35	
		36.55	@ $\frac{7}{47}$		5.44
		£40.00			£5.95

For 'long stay' guests, no VAT is due on accommodation and the charge is broken down as

	£	Gross £		£	VAT £
Breakfast		3.45	@ $\frac{7}{47}$		0.51
Facilities	8.29		@ $\frac{7}{47}$	1.23	
Accommodation	28.26		Nil	—	
		36.55	@ $\frac{7}{207}$		1.23
		£40.00			£1.74

The charge for S is therefore made up as follows

	Gross £	VAT £	Net £
20 Breakfasts	69.00	10.20	58.80
16 Facilities	116.96	17.44	99.52
4 Facilities (long stay)	33.16	4.92	28.24
16 Accommodation	467.84	69.60	398.24
4 Accommodation (long stay)	113.04	—	113.04
	£800.00	£102.16	£697.84

Notes

(*a*)   The VAT-exclusive charge for facilities is shown at the 20% minimum, hence the fraction

$$\frac{17.5 \times \text{facilities element}\%}{100 + (17.5 \times \text{facilities element}\%)} = \frac{17.5 \times 20\%}{100 + (17.5 \times 20\%)} = \frac{7}{207}$$

At a specialist hotel, such as a health farm, the charge for facilities could be as high as 40% and the VAT fraction would then be correspondingly higher.

(*b*)   The taxable turnover of a hotel with many long stay guests is very different from its gross takings. It may not therefore need to apply for registration.

405 Input Tax

405.1 **NON-BUSINESS ACTIVITIES** [*VATA 1994, s 24(5); C & E Notice 700, para 39, Appendix J*]

A cathedral receives income not only by way of grants and donations, but also through the sale of books, cards and light refreshments in its bookcentre and coffee shop. For the first quarter its total income is £34,671.49 of which £11,246.22 is grants and donations. VAT on purchases directly attributable to religious activities is £217.95, VAT on purchases related to the bookcentre and coffee shop is £738.95, VAT on general repairs, maintenance and overheads is £2,185.27.

Input tax is calculated as follows	£
VAT on purchases related to business activities	738.95
Add proportion of VAT on general repairs etc.	

$$\frac{(34{,}671.49 - 11{,}246.22)}{34{,}671.49} \times £2{,}185.27$$

	1,476.44
	£2,215.39

Notes

(*a*)   VAT on purchases directly attributable to religious activities (non-business) is not input tax and cannot be recovered.

(*b*)   The calculation continues in the same way, quarter by quarter, until the VAT year end when an annual adjustment is made by applying the same calculation to the total figures for the year.

(*c*)   There is no UK legislation covering the apportionment of VAT to arrive at input tax. If computations based on times, attendance, floor areas, etc. produce a fairer result, they can be used. Prior approval of Customs and Excise is, however, required.

(*d*)   If some element of business income arises from exempt supplies, input tax may have to be further apportioned to arrive at deductible input tax. See 408 PARTIAL EXEMPTION.

406   Land and Buildings

406.1 **DEVELOPERS' SELF-SUPPLY** [*VATA 1994, 10 Sch 5, 6; SI 1995 No 279*]

D plc carries on a partially exempt business. It decides to build new offices on a plot of land which it acquired some years ago for £20,000. Construction commenced in July 1994 and the building was completed and the offices ready for occupation on 1 February 1995. Standard-rated supplies made to D plc in connection with the construction amounted to £800,000 (excluding VAT). The company can deduct 10% of its input tax for the quarter to 31 March 1995 under the partial exemption rules (see 408 PARTIAL EXEMPTION).

D plc can recover VAT charged on the construction costs of £140,000 (£800,000 at 17.5%) as it is incurred (subject to the normal rules).

D plc is deemed to make a taxable supply to itself on 31 March 1995 of an amount equal to the cost of the land plus the standard-rated supplies made to it in connection with the construction. The effect of the self-supply on the company's VAT position for the quarter to 31 March 1995 is as follows

Output tax		£
£20,000 × 17.5%		3,500
£800,000 × 17.5%		140,000
£820,000	Output tax	£143,500

Deductible input tax	
On self-supply:	
£820,000 × 17.5% × 10%	£14,350

Notes

(*a*)   There is no restriction on deductibility of the actual input tax suffered as it is attributable to a taxable supply, i.e. the self-supply.

(*b*)   The input tax on the self-supply is not regarded as attributable to the self-supply and must therefore be restricted under the partial exemption rules. [*SI 1995 No 2518, Reg 104*].

(*c*)   The self-supply rules illustrated in this example apply to construction commencing after 31 July 1989 of non-residential and non-charitable buildings. After 31 December 1991, they are extended to certain reconstructions, enlargements and extensions of existing buildings. In all cases, no supply is treated as having been made where the value of the supply would be less than £100,000.

(*d*)   The charge has been abolished for all developments commencing on or after 1 March 1995. Where developments commenced before 1 March 1995, a self-supply charge is deemed to arise on 1 March 1997 if such a charge has not already been triggered under the provisions before that date. There are transitional provisions for developments in progress at 1 March 1995.

407   Motor Cars

[C & E Notice 700, Appendix C]

407.1 VAT ON SCALE CHARGE FOR PRIVATE FUEL
[VATA 1994, ss 56, 57; FA 1995, s 30; SI 1995 No 3040]
L Ltd provides its employees with cars and pays all day-to-day running expenses, including the cost of any petrol used for private motoring. Each employee submits a monthly return showing opening and closing mileage, together with fuel and servicing receipts for the period.

T, the sales director, has a 2,000cc car and puts in a monthly claim for July 1996 which includes petrol used for private motoring. He supports this with petrol bills totalling £97.80 and a service invoice for £94.00 (£80.00 plus VAT £14.00). The company prepares monthly VAT returns.

The company will code the expenses claim as follows

Debit		£
Servicing		80.00
Fuel £97.80 $\times \frac{40}{47}$	83.23	
Scale charge note (*a*)	11.02	
		94.25
Input VAT — on service	14.00	
— on petrol £97.80 $\times \frac{7}{47}$	14.57	
		28.57
		£202.82

Credit		
Expenses reimbursed to T		
£97.80 + £94.00		191.80
Output VAT		11.02
		£202.82

Notes

(*a*)   A fuel benefit scale is used to assess a VAT charge where any petrol or other motor fuel is provided by registered traders for private journeys made by employees, directors, partners or proprietors. The monthly scale charge for prescribed accounting periods beginning after 5 April 1996 for a 2,000cc car which does not have a diesel engine is £74. The VAT charge is therefore £74 $\times \frac{7}{47}$ = £11.02

(*b*)   For return periods beginning before 6 April 1993, the scale charge would have been reduced by 50% where T travelled 1,500 business miles or more in the month.

408   Partial Exemption

408.1 STANDARD METHOD [*SI 1995 No 2518, Regs 99–109; C & E Notice 706*]
In its tax year beginning on 1 April 1996, X Ltd makes the following supplies

	Total supplies (excl VAT) £	Standard rated supplies (excl VAT) £	Exempt supplies £
First quarter	442,004	392,286	49,718
Second quarter	310,929	266,712	44,217
Third quarter	505,867	493,614	12,253
Fourth quarter	897,135	876,387	20,748
	£2,155,935	£2,028,999	£126,936

Input tax for the year is analysed as follows

	Attributable to taxable supplies £	Attributable to exempt supplies £	Remaining input tax £	Total input tax £
First quarter	36,409	4,847	11,751	53,007
Second quarter	20,245	311	5,212	25,768
Third quarter	34,698	1,195	10,963	46,856
Fourth quarter	69,707	5,975	9,357	85,039
	£161,059	£12,328	£37,283	£210,670

The proportion of remaining input tax attributable to taxable supplies is calculated using the ratio of

Value of taxable supplies
Value of all supplies

expressed as a percentage and, if not a whole number, rounded *up* to the next whole number.

First quarter

	£	£
Input tax attributable to taxable supplies	36,409	

Proportion of remaining input tax deductible

$$\frac{392,286}{442,004} = 88.75\%$$

£11,751 × 89% =   10,458

c/f 46,867

VAT 408.1 Partial Exemption

	£	£
		b/f 46,867

Second quarter
Input tax attributable to taxable supplies   20,245

Proportion of remaining input tax deductible

$$\frac{266,712}{310,929} = 85.78\%$$

£5,212 × 86% =   4,482

                                                 £24,727

The value of exempt input tax is
£1,041 (311 + [5,212 − 4,482]). As this is not more than
£625 per month on average and is less than 50% of all
input tax in the quarter, all input tax in the quarter is
recoverable.

Deductible input tax   25,768

Third quarter
Input tax attributable to taxable supplies   34,698

Proportion of remaining input tax deductible

$$\frac{493,614}{505,867} = 97.58\%$$

£10,963 × 98% =   10,744

                                                 £45,442

The value of exempt income tax is
£1,414 (1,195 + [10,963 − 10,744]). As this is not
more than £625 per month on average and is less than 50% of all input tax in the quarter,
all input tax in the quarter is recoverable.

Deductible input tax   46,856

Fourth quarter
Input tax attributable to taxable supplies   69,707

Proportion of remaining input tax deductible

$$\frac{876,387}{897,135} = 97.69\%$$

£9,357 × 98% =   9,170

                                                                                 78,877

                                                                                £198,368

Annual adjustment

At the end of the tax year the company carries out an annual adjustment.

Input tax attributable to taxable supplies	161,059

Proportion of remaining input tax deductible

$$\frac{2,028,999}{2,155,935} = 94.11\%$$

£37,283 × 95% =	35,419
Deductible input tax for year	196,478
Deducted over the four quarters	198,368
Under declaration to be paid to Customs & Excise	£1,890

408.2 **SPECIAL METHOD** [*SI 1995 No 2518, Regs 99–109; C & E Notice 706*]

The facts are the same as in 408.1 above except that C & E allow X Ltd to use a special method and calculate the proportion of remaining input tax attributable to taxable supplies by the formula

$$\text{Remaining input tax} \times \frac{\text{Input tax attributable to taxable supplies}}{\text{Total input tax}}$$

	£	£
First quarter		
Input tax attributable to taxable supplies	36,409	

Proportion of remaining input tax deductible

	£	£
$£11,751 \times \dfrac{36,409}{53,007} =$	8,071	
		44,480
Second quarter		
Input tax attributable to taxable supplies	20,245	

Proportion of remaining input tax deductible

	£	£
$£5,212 \times \dfrac{20,245}{25,768} =$	4,095	
	£24,340	

The value of exempt input tax is £1,428 (311 + [5,212 − 4,095]). As this is not more than £625 per month on average and is less than 50% of all input tax in the quarter, all input tax in the quarter is recoverable.

Deductible input tax	25,768
	c/f 70,248

VAT 408.2   Partial Exemption

	£	£
		b/f 70,248
Third quarter		
Input tax attributable to taxable supplies	34,698	
Proportion of remaining input tax deductible		
$£10,963 \times \dfrac{34,698}{46,856} =$	8,118	
		42,816
Fourth quarter		
Input tax attributable to taxable supplies	69,707	
Proportion of remaining input tax deductible		
$£9,357 \times \dfrac{69,707}{85,039} =$	7,670	
		77,377
		£190,441

Annual adjustment

At the end of the tax year the company
carries out an annual adjustment.

	£
Input tax attributable to taxable supplies	161,059
Proportion of remaining input tax deductible	
$£37,283 \times \dfrac{161,059}{210,670} =$	28,503
Deductible input tax for year	189,562
Deducted over the four quarters	190,441
Under declaration to be paid to Customs & Excise	£879

Note

(*a*)   In fact, this special method leaves X Ltd worse off than in 408.1 above, but is
included here for illustration purposes.

409   Records

409.1 ADJUSTMENTS OF ERRORS ON INVOICES [C & E Notice 700, para 72]

F sells a vast range of foodstuffs. Due to a programming error some wholesale packs of citric acid are incorrectly invoiced as zero-rated 'lemon flavouring'. The company decides not to raise supplementary invoices.

The following adjustment is required

	£
Citric acid sales	1,725.00
VAT charged	64.70
	£1,789.70
£1,789.70 × $\frac{7}{47}$ =	266.55
Less VAT charged	(64.70)
Additional VAT payable	£201.85

Note

(*a*)   With many computer systems it is difficult to raise invoices or credit notes for VAT only. It is essential to ensure that any VAT amount will appear in the correct position on the documentation and will be posted by the system to the VAT account.

410   Retail Schemes

[VATA 1994, 11 Sch 2(6); SI 1995 No 2518, Regs 66–73; C & E Notice 727]

410.1 **RETAIL SCHEME A** *[C & E Leaflet 727/7/93]*

K has a small shop selling standard-rated sweets and cigarettes only. At the end of his tax period, the gross takings are £14,285.21.

Output tax is calculated as follows

£14,285.21 × $\frac{7}{47}$ =   £2,127.58

Note

(*a*)   The method of calculation is the same for all VAT periods.

410.2 **RETAIL SCHEME B** *[C & E Leaflet 727/8/93]*

K expands his confectionery and tobacco business by the acquisition of a newsround. At the end of his VAT period the gross takings are £18,714.55 and the expected selling prices of newspapers and magazines purchased total £8,154.27.

Standard-rated sales are calculated as follows

	£
Gross takings	18,714.55
Less expected selling prices of zero-rated items	(8,154.27)
	£10,560.28

Output tax = £10,560.28 × $\frac{7}{47}$ £1,572.81

Notes

(*a*)   The method of calculation is the same for all VAT periods.

(*b*)   Scheme B can only be used if zero-rated sales do not exceed 50% of gross takings in a year.

(*c*)   If K were to charge for delivery and show the charge separately on his newspaper bills, the charge would be standard-rated. Any standard-rated charge is simply included in gross takings.

(*d*)   Scheme B cannot be used for supplies of catering.

410.3 **RETAIL SCHEME B1** [*C & E Leaflet 727/8A/93*]

K is eligible to use Scheme B1. When he starts to use the scheme, his opening stock of zero-rated goods, valued at expected selling price, is £2,250.00. For his first four quarters, the relevant details are

Gross takings	Expected selling price of zero-rated goods purchased	Output tax
£	£	£
18,714.55	8,154.27	1,572.81
20,726.40	11,667.67	1,349.17
20,855.88	10,124.75	1,598.25
22,649.04	11,008.62	1,733.68
£82,945.87	£40,955.31	£6,253.91

Output tax for each quarter is calculated using the principle illustrated in 410.2 above. Stock of zero-rated goods at the end of the fourth period, valued at expected selling price, is £3,440.80.

The annual adjustment is as follows

	£	£
Gross takings		82,945.87
Less opening zero-rated stock	2,250.00	
expected selling prices of zero-rated items received	40,955.31	
	43,205.31	
Less closing zero-rated stock	3,440.80	39,764.51
		£43,181.36
Output tax = £43,181.36 × $\frac{7}{47}$		£6,431.27
Output tax previously calculated		6,253.91
Additional VAT payable with return for fourth quarter		£177.36

Notes

(*a*)   The closing stock figure is used as the opening stock figure for the next year.

(*b*)   The restriction in 410.2 (note (*b*)) above does not apply to Scheme B1.

VAT 410.4 Retail Schemes

410.4 RETAIL SCHEME B2 [*C & E Leaflet 727/8B/93*]

K further expands his business to include the sale of paperback novels. At the end of his VAT period the gross takings are £25,668.52. The costs of purchases for resale are: newspapers and magazines £8,245.44 and books £1,418.50.

Standard-rated sales are calculated as follows

	£	£
Gross takings		25,668.52
Less cost of newspapers/magazines	8,245.44	
Add fixed mark-up 33%	2,721.00	(10,966.44)
cost of books	1,418.50	
Add fixed mark-up 40%	567.40	(1,985.90)
		£12,716.18

Output tax = £12,716.18 × $\frac{7}{47}$ £1,893.90

Notes

(*a*)   The method of calculation is the same for all VAT periods.

(*b*)   The fixed mark-ups for various types of goods are listed in *C & E Leaflet 727/8B/93*.

(*c*)   For a retailer to be eligible to use Scheme B2, his taxable turnover (standard- and zero-rated and inclusive of VAT) must not exceed £750,000 per year. Once accepted into the scheme, it may still be used where turnover grows because of inflation or expansion provided turnover does not exceed £937,500.

410.5 RETAIL SCHEME C [*C & E Leaflet 727/9/93*]

K, whose annual taxable turnover will not exceed £125,000, is eligible to use the Scheme C fixed mark-up of $15\frac{1}{2}$% applicable to his trade classification 8214. At the end of his VAT period the total cost, including VAT, of sweets and cigarettes bought for retailing is £9,524.06.

Standard-rated sales are calculated as follows

	£
Cost of standard-rated goods for resale	9,524.06
Add fixed mark-up of $15\frac{1}{2}$%	1,476.23
	£11,000.29

Output tax = £11,000.29 × $\frac{7}{47}$ £1,638.34

Notes

(*a*)   The method of calculation is the same for all VAT periods.

(*b*)   If K was to charge for standard-rated services (e.g. window advertising), sell standard-rated goods he had produced himself (e.g. home-made toffee and fudge) or make supplies of catering, these would have to be dealt with outside the scheme. Taxable turnover outside the scheme counts towards the £125,000 per annum turnover limit for this scheme. Once accepted into the scheme, it may still be used where turnover grows because of inflation or expansion provided turnover does not exceed £156,250.

410.6 **RETAIL SCHEME D** [*C & E Leaflet 727/10/93*]

K is eligible to use Scheme D. His figures for the four quarterly periods in a VAT year are

	Cost of standard-rated goods for resale (incl VAT)	Total cost of goods for resale (incl VAT)	Gross takings
	£	£	£
First quarter	9,429	15,701	18,714.55
Second quarter	10,418	17,840	21,316.51
Third quarter	9,972	15,919	18,899.29
Fourth quarter	7,076	11,293	13,149.61
	£36,895	£60,753	£72,079.96

First quarter

Standard-rated sales are

$\dfrac{9,429}{15,701} \times £18,714.55 =$ £11,238.74

Output tax = £11,238.74 $\times \frac{7}{47}$ = 1,673.85

By similar calculations output tax in the remaining quarters is

Second quarter	1,853.98
Third quarter	1,763.24
Fourth quarter	1,227.13
	£6,518.20

Annual adjustment

To allow for seasonal variations, K must now look at his year as a whole. Standard-rated sales are

$\dfrac{36,895}{60,753} \times £72,079.96 =$ £43,773.81

Output tax = £43,773.81 $\times \frac{7}{47}$ = £6,519.50

As he has computed VAT of only £6,518.20 for his quarterly returns, he must therefore add £1.30 to the amount of VAT payable for his fourth quarter, which then becomes £1,228.43 (£1,227.13 + £1.30).

Notes

(*a*)   If K was to charge for any services (e.g. newspaper deliveries) he would have to account for these services outside the scheme. Similarly, if he was to supplement his income by the sale of any goods he had produced himself (e.g. home-grown vegetables) he would, even where the goods are zero-rated, have to deal with them outside the scheme. Supplies of catering must also be dealt with outside the scheme.

(*b*)   The annual taxable turnover limit for this scheme is £1 million although once accepted into the scheme, it may still be used where turnover grows because of inflation or expansion provided turnover does not exceed £1,250,000.

(c)   The annual adjustment must be made on a specified date in each year; the first such adjustment may cover less than a full year.

410.7 **RETAIL SCHEME E** [*C & E Leaflet 727/11/93*]

M owns a shop through which she sells a wide range of herbs and spices (zero-rated). She also does a small trade in ancillary items such as salt pots, pepper mills etc. (standard-rated). She decides to use Scheme E and the value of her standard-rated opening stock, based on VAT-inclusive retail prices, is £465.78.

The expected selling prices of standard-rated items purchased are

First period   £184.45
Second period   £108.75

First period

Standard-rated sales are

	£
Opening stock of standard-rated items	465.78
Additional standard-rated purchases	184.45
	£650.23
Output tax = £650.23 × $\frac{7}{47}$	£96.84

Second period

Output tax = £108.75 × $\frac{7}{47}$	£16.20

Notes

(a)   After the first period, opening stock is ignored.

(b)   On ceasing to use Scheme E, credit may be taken for any VAT paid on standard-rated goods in stock at that time.

(c)   Supplies of services or catering must be dealt with outside the scheme.

410.8 **RETAIL SCHEME E1** [*C & E Leaflet 727/11A/93*]

M, in 410.7 above, is eligible to use Scheme E1. She sells pepper mills at £2.99 each. At the beginning of her VAT period, she has 150 mills in stock. She buys 144 during the VAT period and has a stock of 174 at the end of the period.

Her standard-rated sales of pepper mills are

Opening stock	150
Add purchases	144
	294
Less closing stock	174
Sales	120
Takings 120 × £2.99	£358.80
Output tax £358.80 × $\frac{7}{47}$	£53.44

This calculation must be repeated for each line of standard-rated goods supplied to arrive at the total output tax for the VAT period. A line is taken to be any goods supplied that have the same unit selling price including VAT.

410.9 **RETAIL SCHEME F** [*C & E Leaflet 727/12/93*]

N Ltd is a market garden selling flowers, vegetables and fruit. It also sells gardening books and magazines. Due to the product mix and the fact that much of the sales volume is from own-produced goods, the company splits takings at the time of sale using multi-button tills. At the end of its VAT period the *standard-rated* gross takings are totalled at £26,094.74.

Output tax = £26,094.74 × $\frac{7}{47}$ £3,886.45

Note

(*a*)   The method of calculation is the same for all VAT periods.

410.10 **RETAIL SCHEME G** [*C & E Leaflet 727/13/93*]

P has a supermarket selling a broad mix of standard-rated and zero-rated goods. He elects to use Scheme G despite its 'uplift'. He values opening stock of all goods (at cost, including VAT) at £51,742. The value of the standard-rated lines (at cost, including VAT) is £30,458.

His trading figures are

	Standard-rated goods received for resale (incl VAT)	Total goods received for resale (incl VAT)	Gross takings
	£	£	£
First quarter	66,002	109,909	131,002.45
Second quarter	72,926	124,879	149,216.24
Third quarter	69,807	111,431	132,295.74
Fourth quarter	79,186	127,719	152,047.24

VAT 410.10   Retail Schemes

	Standard-rated (incl VAT) £	Total (incl VAT) £
First quarter		
Opening stock	30,458	51,742
First quarter goods	66,002	109,909
Standard-rated sales are	£96,460	£161,651

$$\frac{96,460}{161,651} \times £131,002.45 \qquad \qquad £78,171.47$$

Output tax = £78,171.47 $\times \frac{7}{47} \times \frac{9}{8}$ £13,097.88

	Standard-rated (incl VAT) £	Total (incl VAT) £
Second quarter		
Opening stock	30,458	51,742
First quarter goods	66,002	109,909
Second quarter goods	72,926	124,879
Standard-rated sales are	£169,386	£286,530

$$\frac{169,386}{286,530} \times £149,216.24 \qquad \qquad £88,211.15$$

Output tax = £88,211.15 $\times \frac{7}{47} \times \frac{9}{8}$ £14,780.06

	Standard-rated (incl VAT) £	Total (incl VAT) £
Third quarter		
Opening stock	30,458	51,742
First quarter goods	66,002	109,909
Second quarter goods	72,926	124,879
Third quarter goods	69,807	111,431
Standard-rated sales are	£239,193	£397,961

$$\frac{239,193}{397,961} \times £132,295.74 \qquad \qquad £79,515.87$$

Output tax = £79,515.87 $\times \frac{7}{47} \times \frac{9}{8}$ £13,323.14

	Standard-rated (incl VAT) £	Total (incl VAT) £
Fourth quarter		
First quarter goods	66,002	109,909
Second quarter goods	72,926	124,879
Third quarter goods	69,807	111,431
Fourth quarter goods	79,186	127,719
Standard-rated sales are	£287,921	£473,938

$$\frac{287,921}{473,938} \times £152,047.24 \qquad \qquad £92,369.87$$

Output tax = £92,369.87 $\times \frac{7}{47} \times \frac{9}{8}$ £15,476.87

Notes

(a)   For the fifth quarter, the method of calculation continues as for the fourth quarter above, the first period goods being dropped and the fifth period added to produce a rolling average across the year.

(b)   If P was to supply any services (e.g. shoe repairs), sell goods he had produced himself (e.g. fresh bread) or make supplies of catering, he would, even if they were zero-rated, have to deal with them outside the scheme.

(c)   If it had proved impossible to take stock when the scheme started, P could have used instead the values of goods purchased in the previous three months.

(d)   Where standard-rated purchases represent a very significant proportion of the total, it is vital to check that the scheme calculations do not yield an output tax figure greater than gross takings times $\frac{7}{47}$.

410.11 **RETAIL SCHEME H** [*C & E Leaflet 727/14/93*]

Z Ltd has a number of superstores spread across the country and can analyse all purchases of stock for resale. Having decided to use Scheme H, the accountant calculates that the expected selling price (ESP), including VAT, of all goods received, made and grown for resale in the previous quarter was £42,648,510. Of this, £17,184,289 represented standard-rated lines. (Alternatively, a complete stocktake could have been made and the VAT-inclusive selling prices of goods in stock for resale used instead of the previous quarter's figures.)

Trading figures are

	ESP of standard-rated goods received etc. for resale (incl VAT) £	Total ESP of goods received etc. for resale (incl VAT) £	Gross takings £
First quarter	12,891,658	36,905,859	41,584,617
Second quarter	18,703,932	41,641,326	38,718,265
Third quarter	20,609,199	52,818,703	43,740,861
Fourth quarter	18,463,685	46,235,087	55,619,817

	Standard-rated (incl VAT) £	Total (incl VAT) £
First quarter		
Previous quarter	17,184,289	42,648,510
First quarter	12,891,658	36,905,859
Standard-rated sales are	£30,075,947	£79,554,369

$$\frac{30,075,947}{79,554,369} \times £41,584,617 \qquad\qquad £15,721,283$$

Output tax = £15,721,283 × $\frac{7}{47}$ £2,341,467.68

	£	£
Second quarter		
Previous quarter	17,184,289	42,648,510
First quarter	12,891,658	36,905,859
Second quarter	18,703,932	41,641,326
	£48,779,879	£121,195,695

Standard-rated sales are

$$\frac{48,779,879}{121,195,695} \times £38,718,265 \qquad\qquad £15,583,658$$

Output tax = £15,583,658 × $\frac{7}{47}$ £2,320,970.34

	£	£
Third quarter		
Previous quarter	17,184,289	42,648,510
First quarter	12,891,658	36,905,859
Second quarter	18,703,932	41,641,326
Third quarter	20,609,199	52,818,703
	£69,389,078	£174,014,398

Standard-rated sales are

$$\frac{69,389,078}{174,014,398} \times £43,740,861 \qquad\qquad £17,441,879$$

Output tax = £17,441,879 × $\frac{7}{47}$ £2,597,726.66

	£	£
Fourth quarter		
First quarter	12,891,658	36,905,859
Second quarter	18,703,932	41,641,326
Third quarter	20,609,199	52,818,703
Fourth quarter	18,463,685	46,235,087
	£70,668,474	£177,600,975

Standard-rated sales are

$$\frac{70,668,474}{177,600,975} \times £55,619,817 \qquad\qquad £22,131,453$$

Output tax = £22,131,453 × $\frac{7}{47}$ £3,296,173.85

Notes

(a) For the fifth quarter, the method of calculation continues as in the fourth period above, the first quarter's figures being dropped and the fifth quarter's added to produce a rolling average across the last year.

(b) All supplies of services or catering must be dealt with outside the scheme.

410.12 **RETAIL SCHEME J** [*C & E Leaflet 727/15/93*]

The S Co-operative Society deals in foodstuffs and dry goods. It also offers funeral services. The Society decides to use Scheme J and the accountant calculates the opening stock figures for all lines at expected resale prices, including VAT. This amounts to £1,357,508, including standard-rated lines totalling £859,340. Figures do not include any lines within the funeral service department.

Trading figures are

	ESP of standard-rated goods received etc. for resale (incl VAT) £	Total ESP of goods received etc. for resale (incl VAT) £	Gross takings excluding services £
First quarter	1,256,659	2,895,779	3,627,690
Second quarter	1,474,486	3,071,845	2,421,526
Third quarter	1,061,542	2,464,812	2,615,816
Fourth quarter	1,233,948	3,150,680	3,014,216
			£11,679,248

At the end of the fourth quarter the stock figures are again calculated for all lines at expected resale prices, including VAT. This amounts to £1,246,219, including standard-rated lines totalling £772,656. Figures do not include any items within the funeral services department.

	Standard-rated (incl VAT) £	Total (incl VAT) £	£
First quarter			
Opening stock	859,340	1,357,508	
Purchases	1,256,659	2,895,779	
	£2,115,999	£4,253,287	

Standard-rated sales are

$$\frac{2,115,999}{4,253,287} \times £3,627,690 \qquad £1,804,766$$

Output tax = £1,804,766 × $\frac{7}{47}$ 268,794.94

Second quarter			
Opening stock	859,340	1,357,508	
First quarter	1,256,659	2,895,779	
Second quarter	1,474,486	3,071,845	
	£3,590,485	£7,325,132	

Standard-rated sales are

$$\frac{3,590,485}{7,325,132} \times £2,421,526 \qquad £1,186,934$$

Output tax = £1,186,934 × $\frac{7}{47}$ 176,777.40

c/f £445,572.34

	£	£	£
			b/f 445,572.34
Third quarter			
Opening stock	859,340	1,357,508	
First quarter	1,256,659	2,895,779	
Second quarter	1,474,486	3,071,845	
Third quarter	1,061,542	2,464,812	
	£4,652,027	£9,789,944	

Standard-rated sales are

$$\frac{4,652,027}{9,789,944} \times £2,615,816 \qquad £1,242,994$$

Output tax = £1,242,994 × $\frac{7}{47}$ 185,126.77

Fourth quarter			
Opening stock	859,340	1,357,508	
First quarter	1,256,659	2,895,779	
Second quarter	1,474,486	3,071,845	
Third quarter	1,061,542	2,464,812	
Fourth quarter	1,233,948	3,150,680	
	£5,885,975	£12,940,624	

Standard-rated sales are

$$\frac{5,885,975}{12,940,624} \times £3,014,216 \qquad £1,371,000$$

Output tax = £1,371,000 × $\frac{7}{47}$ 204,191.49

         £834,890.60

Annual adjustment			
Opening stock	859,340	1,357,508	
First quarter	1,256,659	2,895,779	
Second quarter	1,474,486	3,071,845	
Third quarter	1,061,542	2,464,812	
Fourth quarter	1,233,948	3,150,680	
Closing stock	(772,656)	(1,246,219)	
	£5,113,319	£11,694,405	

Standard-rated sales are

$$\frac{5,113,319}{11,694,405} \times £11,679,248 \qquad £5,106,692$$

Output tax = £5,106,692 × $\frac{7}{47}$ £760,571.15

Over the year, the Society has shown output tax of £834,890.60 on its quarterly returns. It must therefore deduct £74,319.45 from the output tax for the fourth quarter, which thus becomes £129,872.04 (£204,191.49 – £74,319.45).

Notes

(*a*)   For the fifth quarter the calculations begin again using the closing stock figures as opening stock for the new year.

(*b*)   This scheme is potentially very accurate but the product mix in stocks can be very different from the mix in day-to-day purchases, resulting in large over-declaration adjustments at the year end. There are two accepted adaptations, one where the stock adjustment is carried out period by period (so that no annual adjustment is required), the other where opening stocks are ignored until the final period of the year.

(*c*)   All supplies of services and catering must be dealt with outside the scheme.

411   Self-Supply

Cross reference. See also 406.1 LAND AND BUILDINGS.

411.1 **STATIONERY** [*SI 1995 No 2518, Regs 101, 104; C & E Leaflet 706/1/92*]

R Ltd acquires a small printing business and decides to produce its own office stationery. In the quarter to 31 December 1995 it incurs £1,584.61 input tax on printing paper, inks, press repairs etc. and values its self-supplies as

	Net £	VAT £
Standard-rated	7,845.21	1,372.91
Zero-rated	428.79	—
	£8,274.00	£1,372.91

For partial exemption purposes the company uses the standard method (see 408.1 PARTIAL EXEMPTION). In the quarter it receives £2,035,352 from exempt supplies and £379,412 (net) from taxable supplies. It breaks down the related input tax as follows

Attributable to exempt supplies	£1,014.27
Attributable to taxable supplies	£10,428.55
Non-attributable (office overheads)	£88.61

The deductible percentage is

$$\frac{379,412}{2,035,352 + 379,412} \times 100 = 15.7\% \text{ which is rounded up to 16\%}$$

Deductible input tax is

	£
VAT on goods and services for use in manufacture of stationery	1,584.61
VAT on taxable supplies	10,428.55
VAT on self-supplies £1,372.91 × 16%	219.67
VAT on overheads £88.61 × 16%	14.18
	£12,247.01

Against this figure of £12,247.01 the company must show output tax of £1,372.91, as well as the output tax due on taxable supplies of £379,412.

Notes

(a)   For simplicity, all tax on self-supplies has been shown as non-attributable and apportioned accordingly. The company should, however, attribute its self-supplies as far as possible to either exempt or taxable outputs. VAT on a self-supply cannot, however, be attributed to the self-supply itself.

(b)   The value of self-supplies must be excluded from the computation of the deductible percentage.

412   Valuation

412.1 **SETTLEMENT DISCOUNTS** [*VATA 1994, 6 Sch 4*]
T offers settlement discounts of $3\frac{3}{4}\%$ for seven days and $2\frac{1}{2}\%$ for thirty days. He wishes to raise an invoice for 250 jigsaw puzzles at £4.50 exclusive of VAT.

VAT is calculated as follows	£
250 Jigsaw puzzles at £4.50	1,125.00
Less $3\frac{3}{4}\%$ discount	(42.19)
	£1,082.81
VAT at 17.5%	£189.49

The invoice reads

250 jigsaws @ £4.50	1,125.00
VAT	189.49
	£1,314.49

Notes

(*a*)   VAT is calculated using the highest rate of discount offered whether or not the discount is actually taken by the customer.

(*b*)   Discount terms must be clearly stated. The invoice should state 'VAT strictly net' or 'Amount payable in seven days £1,272.30 [£1,314.49 – £42.19], amount payable in thirty days £1,286.37 [£1,314.49 – $(2\frac{1}{2}\% \times$ £1,125.00)]'.

Table of Statutes

Table of Statutes

Table of Statutes

Table of Statutes

Table of Statutes

Table of Statutes

Table of Statutes

Table of Statutes

Index

This index is referenced to chapter and paragraph number within the five main sections of the book. The entries in bold capitals are chapter headings in the text.

Index

Index

Index

Index

Index

Index

Tolley's Taxwise 1996-97

Arnold Homer FCA ATII and Rita Burrows MBA ACIS ATII
and Peter Gravestock FCA FTII ATT

Published in two volumes for ease of reference, *Tolley's Taxwise I & II* provide expert guidance on how to approach current tax regulations in the context of real-life situations.

Almost 200 worked examples covering a broad range of circumstances from the everyday to the more unusual, provide detailed step-by-step computations with references to relevant legislation, case law and other official material.

● Written by tax experts renowned not only for their technical skills but also for their ability to explain tax simply and effectively
● Illustrates by example how legislation works in practice

● An invaluable study aid for all students in professional tax examinations, with examples taken from past papers
● Includes a summary of the relevant provisions of the 1996 Finance Act

Tolley's Taxwise I 1996-97
● Income Tax ● National Insurance
● Corporation Tax ● Capital Gains Tax
Order Code TW196
730 pages approx   1 86012 301-5
July 1996   **£27.95**

Tolley's Taxwise II 1996-97
● Value Added Tax ● Inheritance Tax
● Taxation of Trusts ● Tax Planning
Order Code TW296
560 pages approx   1 86012 302-3
August 1996   **£26.95**

For further information please contact our Customer Services Department on: 0181-686 9141

Tolley Publishing Company Ltd. FREEPOST, Tolley House, 2 Addiscombe Road, Croydon, Surrey, CR9 5WZ.
Telephone: 0181-686 9141   Fax: 0181-686 3155

Tolley's TAX GUIDE 96-97

The new look, independent tax guide from the UK's leading tax publisher

"...a must for anyone who wants to reduce his tax liabilities."
SUNDAY TELEGRAPH

With the tax system in a state of flux, *Tolley's Tax Guide 96-97* provides a much needed source of clear, independent guidance on how to manage tax and minimise liabilities under the current rules.

The new look 1996/97 guide explains the impact of all the latest changes, including:

● The latest provisions on self-assessment, the current year basis of assessment, and the transitional rules

● The provisions of the Finance Act 1996, and 1996/97 tax rates and allowances

● New lower rate of tax on savings income

● New rules for interest payable to and by companies

● Tax exemption on certain insurance policy proceeds

● Changes to share option schemes, capital gains tax and VAT

Tolley's Tax Guide 96-97 is the most wide-ranging and detailed guide of its kind. Divided into 45 separate chapters, with a comprehensive contents list and index, full tables of rates and allowances, worked examples and tax hints, it enables you to find the answers you need quickly and easily.

In addition, *Tolley's Tax Guide 96-97*:

● Offers valuable advice on dealing with the Inland Revenue and completing tax returns

● Provides 150 practical worked examples and over 300 'tax points'

● Looks in detail at how the various taxes interact in some 40 different personal and commercial situations

● Is a haven of clear, objective guidance on all aspects of taxation.

May 1996	672 pages	1 86012 284 1
Hardback	Order Code TG96	£25.95

To order, please contact Tolley's Customer Services Dept.

By Post
To: Tolley Publishing Co. Ltd.,
Tolley House, 2 Addiscombe Road,
Croydon, Surrey CR9 5AF, UK

By Telephone
Tel: 0181-686 9141

By Fax
Fax: 0181-686 3155

Registered No. 729731 England   VAT Registered No.243 3583 67

Tolley
A United News & Media company

TAXATION PUBLICATIONS

Tax Reference Annuals –

Tolley's Income Tax 1996-97 £37.95

Tolley's Corporation Tax 1996-97 £34.95

Tolley's Capital Gains Tax 1996-97 £34.95

Tolley's Inheritance Tax 1996-97 £29.95

Tolley's Value Added Tax 1996-97 £33.95

Tolley's National Insurance Contributions 1996-97 £39.95

Looseleafs

Manual of Accounting £95.00 approx

Accountancy Litigation Support £120.00 approx

Form and Content of Financial Statements £45.00

Charities Manual £99.50

Tax on Transactions £95.00 approx

VAT on Construction Land and Property £45.00

Tax Periodicals

Audit Briefing £79 p.a.

Tolley's Practical Tax £123 p.a.

Taxation £112 p.a.

Tolley's National Insurance Brief £135 p.a.

Tax Sources

Tolley's Tax Tables 1997-98 £13.95 approx

Tolley's Tax Data 1996-97 £17.95

Tolley's Tax Cases 1995 £35.95

Tolley's Tax Office Directory 1997 £11.95 approx

Tax Planning

Tolley's Tax Planning 1996-97 £74.50 (2 volumes)

Tolley's Estate Planning 1996-97 £39.95

Tolley's Tax Planning for Family Companies £34.95

General Tax Guides

Financial Management Handbook £49.95 approx

Share Valuation £44.95 approx

Professional Partnership Handbook £35.95

Tolley's Guide to Self-Assessment for the Self-Employed £18.95

Tolley's Guide to Self-Assessment for Employers and Employees £18.95

Tolley's Accounting Principles for Tax Purposes £42.95 approx

Tolley's Self-Assessment £39.95

Tolley's Tax Guide 1996-97 £24.95 (pre-pub offer)

Specialist Tax Guides

Tolley's Taxation of Lloyds Underwriters £59.95 approx

Treasury Management Handbook £85.00 approx

Tax Indemnities and Warranties £75.00 approx

Fund Raising for Charity £35.95

Taxation of Securities and Financial Instruments £49.95

Double Taxation Relief £39.95 approx

Tolley's Taxation in Corporate Insolvency £39.95

Tolley's Taxation of Foreign Exchange Gains and Losses £49.95 (pre-pub offer)

Tolley's Property Taxes 1996-97 £39.95 approx

Tolley's Stamp Duties and Stamp Duty Reserve Tax £33.95

Tolley's Purchase and Sale of a Private Company's Shares £39.95 approx

Tolley's UK Taxation of Trusts £41.95 approx

Business Tax

Tolley's Tax on Business Profits (Formerly Taxation of Trades and Professions) £49.95 approx

Tolley's Capital Allowances 1996-97 £33.95

Tolley's Roll-over, Hold-over and Retirement Reliefs £42.95

Tolley's Partnership Taxation £36.95

Employee Taxation

Tolley's Taxation of Employments £34.95

Value Added Tax

Tolley's VAT Planning 1996-97 £39.95

Tolley's Practical VAT (Newsletter) £113 p.a.

Tolley's VAT Cases 1996 £64.50

Tolley's VAT and Duties Appeals £29.95

Tax Computations

Tolley's Tax Computations 1996-97 £38.95

Tolley's Taxwise I 1996-97 £27.95

Tolley's Taxwise II 1996-97 £26.95

Overseas Tax

Tolley's International Tax Planning (2 volumes) £99.50

Tolley's Tax Havens £54.50

Tolley's Taxation of Offshore Trusts and Funds £65.00 approx

Tolley's Taxation in the Republic of Ireland 1996-97 £32.95

Tolley's Taxation in the Channel Islands and Isle of Man 1996-97 £32.95

Client and Adviser Guides

Client and Adviser Guide: Hotels £34.95

Client and Adviser Guide: Housing Associations £34.95

Client and Adviser Guide: Charities £34.95

Tax Planning

Tolley's Tax Planning 1996-97

Pinpoints clear, practical taxation strategies across a whole range of financial decisions required of individuals, partnerships and corporate bodies.

Tolley's Tax Planning 1996-97 provides an invaluable source of ideas on keeping tax payments to a minimum. With new chapters on Venture Capital Trusts and Manufactured Dividends.

Order Code TP97
(For a set of 2 volumes)
2,000 pages approx in total
1 86012 305-8   August 1996   £74.50

Tolley's VAT Planning 1996-97

Provides practical advice on achieving the optimum tax position, preventing unnecessary VAT liabilities, and avoiding the many pitfalls of this complicated tax.

- Incorporates changes introduced by recent UK and EC legislation
- Discusses the procedures which a taxpayer might take in contentious situations

Order Code VATP97   850 pages approx
1 86012 297-3   August 1996   £39.95

Tolley's Estate Planning 1996-97

Price Waterhouse

Detailed guidance on how to formulate a plan for the provision, holding and transfer of personal and family resources at the lowest tax cost. Covers all aspects of estate planning from making life-time gifts and wills to post-death planning and international aspects. New chapter on planning for a change of government.

Order Code EP97   570 pages approx
1 86012 289-2   August 1996   £39.95

Tolley's International Tax Planning

Third Edition
Malcolm J Finney BSc MSc(Bus Admin) AFIMA MBIM (Nabarro Nathanson) and John C Dixon LLB ATII (Grant Thornton)

Written by an unrivalled team of more than forty experts from around the world, this extensive work deals with all the major issues in international tax planning.

New to this edition:
- Money laundering, tax evasion and professional liability
- The International Headquarters Company
- Investing in India

Order Code ITP3   2 volumes
1,300 pages approx
1 86012 331-7   August 1996   £120.00

For further information please contact our Customer Services Department on: 0181-686 9141

Tolley Publishing Company Ltd. FREEPOST, Tolley House, 2 Addiscombe Road, Croydon, Surrey, CR9 5WZ.
Telephone: 0181-686 9141   Fax: 0181-686 3155